FEMALE SEXUALITY

FEMALE SEXUALITY

CONTEMPORARY ENGAGEMENTS

edited by
Donna Bassin, Ph.D.

JASON ARONSON INC.
Northvale, New Jersey
London

Production Editor: Elaine Lindenblatt

This book was set in 10 pt. Galliard and printed and bound by Book-mart Press, Inc. of North Bergen, NJ.

Library of Congress Cataloging-in-Publication Data

Female sexuality : contemporary engagements / edited by Donna Bassin.
     p. cm.
  Includes bibliographical references and index.
  ISBN 0-7657-0081-6 (alk. paper)
    1. Women and psychoanalysis. 2. Women—Psychology.
3. Femininity. I. Bassin, Donna.
BF175.F425 1998
155.3'33—DC21   97–34280

Printed in the United States of America on acid-free paper. For information and catalog write to Jason Aronson Inc., 230 Livingston Street, Northvale, NJ 07647-1726, or visit our website: www.aronson.com

In loving memory of my foremothers,
Doris Bernstein, Betsy Distler, Zenia Fleigel,
and Mae Maskit Lord,
who have given the language into my hands

Contents

Preface   xi

Acknowledgments   xv

About the Editor   xvi

Contributors   xvii

EDITOR'S INTRODUCTION

1   **Donna Bassin on Walter Benjamin**   3

Working Through Our Predecessors' and
Our Own Readings   5
Donna Bassin

Unpacking My Library:
A Talk about Book Collecting (1931)   21
Walter Benjamin

CLASSICS

2   **Lora Heims Tessman on Sigmund Freud**   31

A Cry of Fire, an Old Flame, the Matter of Fireplace   33
Lora Heims Tessman

Observations on Transference-Love (Further
Recommendations on the Technique of
Psycho-Analysis III) (1915)   49
Sigmund Freud

3 **Kerry Kelly Novick and Jack Novick
   on Anna Freud**   **61**

   Creativity and Compliance   63
   Kerry Kelly Novick and Jack Novick

   The Relation of Beating-Phantasies to a
   Day-Dream (1923)   71
   Anna Freud

4 **Jessica Benjamin on Karen Horney**   **85**

   Women's Oedipal Conflicts and Boys'
   Oedipal Ideology   87
   Jessica Benjamin

   The Flight from Womanhood: The
   Masculinity-Complex in Women, as Viewed
   by Men and by Women (1926)   97
   Karen Horney

5 **Adria E. Schwartz on Joan Riviere**   **113**

   Postmodern Masquerade   115
   Adria E. Schwartz

   Womanliness as a Masquerade (1929)   127
   Joan Riviere

6 **Leon Hoffman on Ernest Jones**   **139**

   Focusing on Active Sexuality in Women   141
   Leon Hoffman

   The Phallic Phase (1933)   153
   Ernest Jones

7 **Adrienne Applegarth on Karen Horney**   **185**

   Ahead of Her Time   187
   Adrienne Applegarth

The Denial of the Vagina: A Contribution
to the Problem of the Genital Anxieties
Specific to Women (1933)   193
  Karen Horney

8 Elsa First on Joan Riviere   207

   Getting Worse for Their Sake   209
     Elsa First

   A Contribution to the Analysis of the
   Negative Therapeutic Reaction (1936)   221
     Joan Riviere

9 Nancy J. Chodorow on Melanie Klein   239

   From Subjectivity in General to Subjective
   Gender in Particular   241
     Nancy J. Chodorow

   Mourning and Its Relation to
   Manic-Depressive States (1940)   251
     Melanie Klein

10 Dana Birksted-Breen on Melanie Klein   279

   Holding the Tension   281
     Dana Birksted-Breen

   The Effects of Early Anxiety-Situations on
   the Sexual Development of the Girl (1952)   287
     Melanie Klein

CONTEMPORARY CLASSICS

11 Gerald I. Fogel on William I. Grossman
   and Walter A. Stewart   337

   A Postmodern Turn for Classical
   Metapsychology   339
     Gerald I. Fogel

   Penis Envy: From Childhood Wish to
   Developmental Metaphor (1976)   347
     William I. Grossman and Walter A. Stewart

12 Owen Renik on Elizabeth Lloyd Mayer   363

Empiricism and Clinically Relevant
Theory Building   365
   Owen Renik

"Everybody Must Be Just Like Me":
Observations on Female Castration Anxiety (1985)   377
   Elizabeth Lloyd Mayer

13 Muriel Dimen on Margo Rivera   405

From Breakdown to Breakthrough   407
   Muriel Dimen

Linking the Psychological and the
Social: Feminism, Poststructuralism,
and Multiple Personality (1989)   421
   Margo Rivera

14 Adam Phillips on Christiane Olivier   439

Having It Both Ways   441
   Adam Phillips

Oedipal Difference: Where the Trouble
Starts (1989)   445
   Christiane Olivier

15 Betsy Distler on Doris Bernstein   465

A Bold Return to the Body   467
   Betsy Distler

Female Genital Anxieties, Conflicts,
and Typical Mastery Modes (1990)   475
   Doris Bernstein

Credits   501
Index   503

Preface

Alas! A woman that attempts the pen
Such an intruder on the rights of men
Such a presumptuous creature is esteem'd
The fault can by no virtue be redeem'd.
                                    —Anne Finch
                        Countess of Winchilsea, 1903

This volume will satisfy more than the obvious need to provide easy access
to some of the most generative texts to date on women in psychoanalytic
thought. *Female Sexuality: Contemporary Engagements* is the collaborative
project of fifteen contemporary psychoanalysts who were asked to select
a classic paper, or soon-to-be classic paper, that had been generative in
their clinical practice with women or that had served as a theoretical
forebear of their own work and writings. Besides selecting an "originating"
paper, each contributing analyst, serving as a temporary curator of her or
his intellectual property, has written a commentary in this volume. Each
commentary, a substantive essay in its own right, introduces the classic
selected, reexamines it from a contemporary zeitgeist, and maps out the
contributor's specific stepping-stones, from transmission of the inherited
work to her or his now-generative reading. I owe a debt to the spirit of
dialogue in Jean Strouse's very successful edited collection, *Women and*

Analysis: Dialogues on Psychoanalytic Views of Femininity (1974). Her collection includes ten classic papers paired with ten response essays by contemporary writers of various disciplines. Each commissioned paper, in Strouse's words, was "to appear in dialogue with its subject" (p. 20) for the purpose of examining the classic paper from a fresh point of view. In this volume as well, the latent interaction with another person, part and parcel of all writing, becomes manifest.

The original spirit of this collection and the underlying subtext (which sets this collection apart from the many other edited volumes on women in psychoanalysis) has to do with the role of the heir, with ideas as "possessions" in route to transmissibility, and with the notions of legacies and the inheritance of thoughts and idea. All the commentators, in their own styles, have traced their lineage from the paper selected to their own current work. They have all entered into an imaginative play space between author, text, and audience, resulting in a subjectively created collaboration, or continuing dialogue, with their authors' texts. Tracing their origins as they "unpacked" their texts from the perspective of their clinical and theoretical work, they have brought forth a legacy for the next generation of theorists and clinicians. They have located our origins and left us with possible directions for the future. The contributors have all made a significant impact on our current literature and on the clinical practice of psychoanalysis for women. Many have already written the classics of the future. As the editor of this collection, I have the responsibility and pleasure of providing a context for the contributions of all the authors. I have borrowed the image of collecting and unpacking a library from Walter Benjamin's essay "Unpacking My Library" as a fanciful thematic connection and as a literal activity in the genesis of this book. To begin, I looked around at my own "library" and the extended community of scholars and clinicians I have read, worked with, or spoken with—all the important members of my particular interpretive community. I asked them, these expert "collectors" in their own right, for their "personal favorites," recommendations for texts to be included in this collection, as one might ask a respected food critic or gourmet chef what their most memorable meal was. Listening to them reflect on the texts they chose, I understood that not only had they taken possession of a text, they had already begun to unpack it, or remove some of the contents from its container and rupture the encasements in order to imagine new and fresh material. Walter Benjamin's work, which I discuss in my commentary, followed the quest of the critic-commentator in seeking to contribute to the task of revealing the fuller meaning of a selected text. That is, he believed that all readings of a text contribute to the original work itself, and, as Alice Walker has suggested, "Each writer writes the missing parts to the other writer's story" (as noted in Gates 1990, p. 11). As exemplified by the commentaries, the selected classics (or generative texts) in this collection are valuable because they endure and thus can be reused. They are not destroyed, exhausted, or used up by any one reading of them. For example, each volume of the series *Contemporary Freud: Turning Points and Critical Issues* (1991–1997) is dedicated to the many individual readings of a seminal paper by Freud. The series, founded by Ethel Person and Joseph Sandler based on an idea of Robert Wallerstein's, demonstrates the generative power of classics, which are living histories and remain dynamic as long as readers become writers from them. Each succeeding generation can view them critically and "temporarily" complete the text. Classics need to be rewritten so that each subsequent generation can view them in its own time and select relevant aspects from a contemporary point of view. Our dialogue on women and psychoanalysis is a collective and connective community effort. Even Thoreau, who seemed the epitome of isolated individualism, created from and through community. He brought and dismantled an old cabin in the woods of a neighbor so that he would have timber for his own home. Thinking about the use of his neighbor's ax to cut down tall white pines to build his house, he offered that "it is difficult to begin without borrowing, but perhaps it is the most generous course thus to permit your fellow-men to have an interest in your enterprise" (1980, p. 32). The ax that Thoreau borrowed was his neighbor's prized possession. Thoreau notes that he returned this ax sharper than he received it. As significant links in the chain, the contributors to this volume have had enlivened "conversations" with their influential predecessors, which required taking possession of their selected texts and borrowing aspects from them. Like Thoreau, they have returned what they borrowed with sharpened relevance for the contemporary reader.

Although in these progressive readings of a classic text one has a sense of the commentators' pleasure with their "authors," each author has found a balance between immersion and distance, conservation and revolt. The commentaries begin with an appreciation of theoretical ancestors, yet they clearly move beyond the original texts themselves and capture the generative power of reading.

In spite of our wish that the conceptualizations of developmental narratives will enable us to understand our patients' here-and-now experience, we find that we cannot explain the present based solely on what preceded it, nor can we "explain the flower by the fertilizer" (Bachelard 1969, p. xxvi). Similarly, the exchange within these dialogues is as "mysterious as love" (Missac 1995, p. 47). The exchange requires a co-mingling where the edges unravel and reweave, like the embroidery of Penelope.

Coen (1994) contends that successful creative contributors to psychoanalysis "are able to assimilate what is most valuable within their tradition while daring to transform or transcend it" (p. 84). Although reading is the beginning of writing, the commentaries in this volume reflect the imaginative act of constructing something new out of a tradition, out of a reading. Harrison (1996) refers to the banyan tree, one she recalls having covered three acres, to describe this relationship. In this truly unique tree, each branch emerges from its trunk, its origin, a part of the tree's beginning, but then it sets roots on its own to establish its own integrity.

Although not explicit in each commentary, this volume as a whole provides a window into creativity within psychoanalytic thought. It reflects the task of working through our history. Each dialogue between inherited text and heir contributes toward the tracing of the development of our history of theory and theorizing for and about women. It is my hope that it will also provide insight into how we can continue to go forward from where we start to the future, and that we can continue to build our library with context, continuity, and creativity in dialogue with our predecessors and contemporaries.

—*Donna Bassin*

REFERENCES

Bachelard, G. (1969). *The Poetics of Space,* trans. M. Jolas. Boston: Beacon.

Coen, S. (1994). *Between Author and Reader.* New York: Columbia University Press.

Contemporary Freud: Turning Points and Critical Issues (1991–1997). Four-volume series founded by R. Wallerstein. New Haven, CT: Yale University Press.

Gates, H. L. Jr., ed. (1990). *Reading Black, Reading Feminist.* New York: Meridian.

Grizzuti, H. B. (1996). *An Accidental Autobiography.* New York: Houghton Mifflin.

Miller, N. (1990). *Subject to Change.* New York: Columbia University Press.

Missac, P. (1995). *Walter Benjamin's Passages,* trans. W. Nicholsen. Cambridge, MA: MIT Press.

Strouse, S., ed. (1974). *Women and Analysis: Dialogues on Psychoanalytic Views of Femininity.* New York: Dell.

Thoreau, H. (1980). *Walden.* New York: New American Library.

Acknowledgments

I want to thank all the contributors for their deep understanding of this project and the wonderfully written and delightfully engaging products. Many thanks go to publisher Michael Moskowitz of Jason Aronson Inc. for his invitation and his willingness to keep the faith. My deepest appreciation to my psychoanalytic soul mates and colleagues, Jessica Benjamin, Daisy Franco, Stanley Grand, Carol Kaye, Kathy Krauthamer, Marilyn LaMonica, Judith Luongo, Arthur Robbins, and Adria Schwartz. They have each in their own way mentored and comforted me and, moreover, encouraged me to hold on to the pen.

In recognition and appreciation of the mutuality of influence, I must acknowledge all the partners whose contributions consisted of probing questions regarding the design limits and purpose of this project—as well as all those unnamed influences whose work has made an impact without leaving a direct remembrance of its source. I also wish to express, in print, my gratitude to my husband, Daniel Hill, who has provided love and respect, personally and professionally, in addition to careful and critical readings of my work, for the last twenty years. My parents, Norman and Estelle Bassin, deserve more love and appreciation than I have often remembered to show or tell. They have always lent their hands and hearts—no questions asked. And finally, big hugs to my sons, Ari and Ezra Bassin-Hill, who have shown me the pleasures of generativity and the necessity of bearing one's date in time.

About the Editor

Donna Bassin, Ph.D., is an art therapist, clinical psychologist, and a certified psychoanalyst with a private practice in Manhattan. She is a member of the Institute for Psychoanalytic Training and Research in New York, where she serves as Director of the Women's Center at the IPTAR Clinical Center. As a founding member of the Doris Bernstein Memorial Section on Gender Issues in Psychoanalysis at IPTAR, she has encouraged contemporary investigations into the role and meaning of gender in psychoanalytic theory and practice. Dr. Bassin is Associate Professor of Psychology at Pratt Institute, New York; Supervising Analyst at the Contemporary Center for Advanced Psychoanalytic Studies, New Jersey; and a member of the International Psychoanalytic Association. She has co-edited *Representations of Motherhood* (1994). Her papers and reviews have appeared in the *International Journal of Psycho-Analysis*, *Journal of the American Psychoanalytic Association*, and *Psychoanalytic Psychology*.

Contributors

Adrienne Applegarth, M.D., is currently Clinical Professor of Psychiatry at the University of California School of Medicine, San Francisco, California. She is Training and Supervising Analyst at the San Francisco Psychoanalytic Institute, and the author of a number of psychoanalytic papers.

Jessica Benjamin, Ph.D., a psychoanalyst in New York City, is the author of *The Bonds of Love: Psychoanalysis, Feminism and the Problem of Domination*. She is on the faculty of the New York University Postdoctoral Program in Psychotherapy and Psychoanalysis and the New School for Social Research program in Psychoanalytic Studies. Her essays on intersubjectivity and gender in psychoanalysis were collected in *Like Subjects and Love Objects: On Recognition and Sexual Differences*. A new volume continuing these themes, *The Shadow of the Other: Intersubjectivity and Gender in Psychoanalysis*, was published in 1997. She is an associate editor of *Gender and Psychoanalysis* and on the editorial board of *Psychoanalytic Dialogues*.

Dana Birksted-Breen is Training Psychoanalyst of the British Institute of Psychoanalysis. She is the author of *The Birth of a First Child: Towards an Understanding of Femininity* (1975) and *Talking with Mothers* (1989). She has also edited *The Gender Conundrum, Contemporary Psychoanalytic Perspectives on Femininity and Masculinity* (1993). The author of many psychoanalytic papers, she maintains a full time private practice in London.

Nancy J. Chodorow, Ph.D., is Professor of Sociology at the University of California, Berkeley, a faculty member of the San Francisco Psychoanalytic Institute, and a psychoanalyst in private practice. She is the author of numerous papers and the following books: *The Reproduction of Mothering* (1978), *Feminism and Psychoanalytic Theory* (1979), and *Femininities, Masculinities, Sexualities: Freud and Beyond* (1994). She is working on a book currently titled *The Power of Feelings: Personal Meaning in Psychoanalysis, Gender and Culture*.

Muriel Dimen, Ph.D., is Clinical Professor of Psychology and training analyst at the New York University Postdoctoral Program in Psychotherapy and Psychoanalysis, and the Derner Institute in Psychotherapy and Psychoanalysis at Adelphi University. She is the author of *Surviving Sexual Contradictions* (1986) and *The Anthropological Imagination* (1977). Her co-edited books include *Storms in Her Head: New Clinical and Theoretical Perspectives on Breuer and Freud's "Studies on Hysteria"* (in press, Jason Aronson) and *Gender in Psychoanalytic Space* (forthcoming). She is an associate editor of *Gender and Psychoanalysis* and Book Review Editor of *Psychoanalytic Dialogues*. At work on a book about psychoanalytic theories of sexuality, she maintains a private practice in Manhattan.

Betsy Distler, M.P.S., was Training and Supervising Analyst at the Institute for Psychoanalytic Training and Research, where she served as President until October 1997. She was also Training and Supervising Analyst of the International Psychoanalytic Association and a supervisor in the City College Clinical Psychology Doctoral Program. A founding member of the Doris Bernstein Memorial Section on Gender Issues in Psychoanalysis, she co-edited the volume of Doris Bernstein's major papers. She wrote on the impact of the father on the woman's creative process. Betsy Distler died October 17, 1997 after a long fight with breast cancer.

Elsa First is Associate Clinical Professor at New York University's Postdoctoral Program in Psychotherapy and Psychoanalysis. A member of the International Psychoanalytic Association, she is a Training and Supervising Analyst at the New York Freudian Society, and teaches and supervises widely. Her published articles have included studies of mother–child interactions, and of the psychoanalytic process from a two-person viewpoint. She maintains a private practice in psychoanalysis and psychotherapy with adults and with children in New York City.

Gerald I. Fogel, M.D., is Training and Supervising Analyst at the San Francisco Psychoanalytic Institute and the Oregon Psychoanalytic New Training facility. He has written many papers on psychoanalysis and gender and has edited *The Psychology of Men: New Psychoanalytic Perspectives* (1986), *Perversions and Near Perversions in Clinical Practice: New Psychoanalytic Perspectives* (1991), and *The Work of Hans Loewald: An Introduction and Commentary* (Jason Aronson, 1991). He is currently on the editorial board of the *Journal of the American Psychoanalytic Association* and has been an editor for the *Bulletin of the Association for Psychoanalytic Medicine*, the *Newsletter of the American Psychoanalytic Association*, the *International Journal of Psycho-Analysis,* and the *International Review of Psycho-Analysis.*

Leon Hoffman, M.D., is Training and Supervising Analyst in Child, Adolescent, and Adult Psychoanalysis at the New York Psychoanalytic Institute. He is certified by the American Board of Psychiatry and Neurology, Psychiatry, and Child Psychiatry. He is the Director of the Parent Child Center at the New York Psychoanalytic Society, and the editor of *The Evaluation and Care of Severely Disturbed Children and their Families* (1981). Currently he is writing and publishing in the area of female psychology.

Jack Novick, Ph.D., is Training and Supervising Analyst at the New York Freudian Society, Supervisor at the Michigan Psychoanalytic Institute, former Supervisor at the Anna Freud Centre, and former faculty member of the British Psycho-Analytic Society. He is a currently co-director of research at Allen Creek Therapeutic Preschool, and Clinical Associate Professor of Psychiatry at the University of Michigan and Wayne State University Medical Schools. The author of numerous psychoanalytic articles, he has recently written a book with Kerry Kelly Novick, *Fearful Symmetry: The Development and Treatment of Sadomasochism* (Jason Aronson, 1996).

Kerry Kelly Novick is on the faculty of the Michigan Psychoanalytic Institute and is Clinical Director of Allen Creek Therapeutic Preschool. Formerly on the staff of the Anna Freud Centre and the Centre for the Study of Adolescence, and a Lecturer in Psychoanalysis at the University of Michigan Medical School, she has published many psychoanalytic articles. She is co-author with Jack Novick of *Fearful Symmetry: The Development and Treatment of Sadomasochism* (Jason Aronson, 1996).

Adam Phillips, Ph.D., was formerly Principal Child Psychotherapist at Charing Cross Hospital and is the author of several books on psychoanalysis, most recently *Monogamy* (1997) and *The Beast in the Nursery* (1998).

Owen Renik, M.D., is a Training and Supervising Analyst and member of the faculty of the San Francisco Psychoanalytic Institute. He is currently the Chair of the Program Committee of the American Psychoanalytic Association. He is has published numerous psychoanalytic papers. He has been the Editor-in-Chief of the *Psychoanalytic Quarterly* since 1992.

Adria E. Schwartz, Ph.D., is Supervisory and Training Analyst at the New York University Postdoctoral Program in Psychotherapy and Psychoanalysis. She is also on the faculties of the Institute for Contemporary Psychotherapy, Psychoanalytic Psychotherapy Study Center, and Institute for Expressive Analysis, and Adjunct to the Ferkauf Graduate Program in Psychology and the Mt. Sinai Medical Center Department in Psychiatry. The author of numerous articles on issues of gender and sexuality, she maintains a private practice in Manhattan. Her book *Multiple Subjects: Lesbians, Gender and Psychoanalysis* was published in 1998.

Lora Heims Tessman, Ph.D., is Supervising Psychoanalyst and a faculty member of the Massachusetts Institute for Psychoanalysis; as well as on the faculty of the Program in Psychoanalytic Studies, Boston Psychoanalytic Institute and Society, and of Harvard Medical School. She is the author of the book *Children of Parting Parents* (1978, reissued as *Helping Children Cope with Parting Parents*, Jason Aronson, 1996). She is in private practice in Newton, Massachusetts, while also currently Principal Investigator in a research project on changes over time in how the psychoanalyst's own analyst is experienced in his or her post-analytic psychic life.

EDITOR'S INTRODUCTION

1

DONNA BASSIN
ON WALTER BENJAMIN

Working Through Our Predecessors' and Our Own Readings

Donna Bassin

I.

"I am unpacking my library. Yes, I am." So begins Walter Benjamin's essay (1931). Benjamin, sitting in the midst of his unpacked library, books not yet shelved or categorized, a philosopher, literary critic, and passionate book collector, contemplates his disordered collection of literature. As he attempts to capture the state of mind best suited to the creative reading and commentary necessary for the process of transmission of inherited knowledge and its transformation into new thought, he uses the image of the book collector surrounded by, moving within, and inhabiting his private library. Book collecting, a true preoccupation of Benjamin's, for him went beyond the material activity of accumulation. The object of Benjamin's attention is not books as objects in themselves (although he clearly communicates his love of books), but rather the true reader's passionate task of possession. Collecting is not merely about the acquiring of keepsakes from the past, but, like the act of possession, it is about making someone else's thought one's own. According to Missac (1995), many analogies have been made between the act of reading and collecting books, since a book is the locus of an exchange, a site where ideas are confronted. "Taking possession," or "occupying" a text—the works and workings of his predecessors—was for Benjamin a necessary condition for the subjective and creative use of knowledge. The word *library* has a material meaning, but it also suggests a relationship, an interaction, between reader and author. Coen (1994, p. 21) cites Holland (1975) as suggesting that the "reader regards the text as well as its author as a 'gratifying other,' " and Fraiberg (1968), according to Holland (1975, p. 127), observes that "the book itself has taken over as a partner and is invested with some of the qualities of a human relationship." Reading is the beginning of writing, and Benjamin was a voracious reader. However, as Missac (1995) has speculated, Benjamin used abundant reading to put off the moment of his own writing. That moment, of separating oneself from the gratifying other, is both wished for and feared. Although we depend on a text as an initial container and structure and allow our thoughts to mingle with another in a co-union, writing requires a leave-taking. Green (1978) describes writing as "communication with the absent" (p. 282). The writer Joyce Carol Oates (1993) argues that "most writing is engendered out of a feeling of loss and nostalgia, a desire to memorialize what we have experienced and where we have lived" (p. 16).

Much of "Unpacking My Library," which is only an excerpt from Walter Benjamin's abundant writings, is committed to understanding the transformative alchemy of the reader–writer experience and can be unpacked further by reference to Benjamin's other writings. In his major though unfinished work *The Arcades Project*, Benjamin concretizes his interest in "living within," as manifested in the activity of the *flaneur*, a nineteenth-century stroller wandering through the streets of Paris. The concept of the flaneur embodies the internal state of being that is necessary for the historical process of transformation through interpretation. The image of aimless wandering is a graphic one of movement through time as well as of the structures of living history, and augments Benjamin's story of the creative interpretive process of the true reader-writer. He has often implied in his writings that it takes practice to lose one's way in a city. Benjamin's unpacking "suggests" browsing, or strolling, which requires that one remain somewhat alert, lest one miss one's intention or miss the fruit of the special effort to let go. This frame of mind, of evenly suspended attention, or, to use Bollas's (1995) version of the process, "evenly hovering attentiveness," is the very activity that leads to the free association we strive for on both sides of the couch. The activity of Benjamin's flaneur is perhaps what Bion (1965) referred to when he suggested the necessity of letting go of memory and desire in order to intuitively pursue emotional truth in an analytic session.

Rabinbach (1979) has argued that Benjamin's absorption in history was not submissive, but rather relied on an appropriate disrespect "toward knowledge that claims the authority of tradition" (p. 9). Benjamin's push for creative commentary, according to his friend and contemporary Gershom Shalom, did away with the dogmatic character of tradition and used tradition in a revolutionary way to meld new creations. Tradition is seen as a way of knowing, albeit still pending a messianic redemption. Walter Benjamin's preference for allegory, simile, and metaphor suggests his commitment to the breakdown of the authority of thought: in allegory, the vision of the reader is larger than the vision of the text; the locus of action is not in the text, but in the transformation of the reader. In contrast to the rigid and limited meanings of abstract thought, imagery allows for individual possession, subjectivity, and personal interpretation.

In his essay, "Goethe's Elective Affinities" (1919–1922),[1] Benjamin compared the task of creative commentary to the concerns of the alchemist, an analogy that captured his thoughts about the nature of the historical process that brings about transformation, rather than the continuity and renewal of truths of the fathers by the sons. He suggested that a critique is concerned with the truth-content of a work of art, while the commentary is concerned with its subject or effective contents. Through this simile Benjamin found a way of avoiding a fixed authoritarian abstraction. He suggested that the critic is like an alchemist, the commentator a chemist. The commentator, as a chemist, looks at and brings to light the effective contents—the wood and ash in a funeral pyre. On the other hand, the critic, beginning with the effective contents (the wood and ash), inquiries about the context of the reading, that is, the enigma of the flame itself. Both these steps are necessary.

Benjamin's greatest, although unfinished, project was to create a work composed entirely of quotes. He filled many little black notebooks with quotes selected from his daily readings. This miniaturized and condensed private library of thought fragments constituted what Arendt (1970) viewed as Benjamin's ultimate legacy, that is, a way of understanding the value of the past for the purpose of present renewal. Arendt saw Benjamin's daily catches of pearls and coral—netted and aggressively severed from their origins, torn out of context and out of their time—as breaking the authority of the original. While the past is gathered and collected it is not seen

---

[1]See Rabinbach (1979) for a fuller explication of Benjamin's analogy.

as received wisdom. Quotes are not invoked to support or prove anything. Eagleton (1981), following up on this, suggested that collecting is a "kind of creative digression from a classical narrative, a 'textualizing' of history that reclaims repressed and unmapped areas" (p. 61). As a collector one protects the past, but the preservation is also a destruction, for it requires separating the books from the historical strata of which they are part and "purging them of the accreted cultural ménages with which they are encrusted" (p. 61).

Benjamin's understanding of the relation between critic and commentator and his critique of the relation between tradition and authority (described in the romantic, mystical language of his own time and discipline) find contemporary psychoanalytic embodiment in the likes of Feldman, Gallop, Irigarary, and Whitford. Writing with the benefit of Lacan and the French critique of ego psychology, they have all challenged the very notion of a position of mastery. More specifically, Gallop (1982) suggests that Lacan's message that we are all castrated recognizes our gain, for to realize that we are all inadequate encourages us all in letting us know that we have the right to speak or, in this case, the right to write.

II.

Although one can be swept away by Benjamin's almost mystical respect for the transmission of knowledge and the bequeathing of libraries, those concerned with the development of a female psychology have questioned the what and how of transmissibility and transformation. As women, we have inherited a literature that has been seen by many contemporary theorists as taking male development as the normative subject. Gilbert and Gubar (1979) suggest that for the female writer the battle "is not against her (male) precursor's reading of the world but against [their] reading of her" (p. 49).

Beginning with the debates of the 1940s (see Fliegel 1973) and pushed to central attention by the efforts of feminists in psychoanalysis and literary criticism, those of us seeking to increase our understanding of female development have refused to be left out of the legacy. This refusal to be left out of the chain has resulted in a new history, one with extensive contributions to our psychoanalytic history, as we have created and collected our own libraries to draw upon and work through. Far beyond the initial critique of a deficit psychology, we have begun to examine the very stance of reading, the categories of how we read and of how we have been read.

Although women have contributed to psychoanalytic theory from the beginning, much of their work can now be seen as operating from a female masquerade. Even the early female theorists, such as Anna Freud and Helene Deutsch, were seen as the dutiful daughters of Freud.[2] Only Horney, who was relegated to a marginal position, was able to challenge Freud's view regarding the "entirely masculine grammar of the psyche" (Heilbrun 1991, p. 37).

Further understanding of the authority of authorship, both concrete and metaphoric, remains a task for us. As psychoanalysts we have just begun to turn our attention to a deeper understanding of the dynamics of creative theoretical and clinical work in our own field. Coen (1994) and Phillips (1993) have both noted gaps in our psychoanalytic theory that are relevant to an understanding of the development of a theory about revisions. Coen (1994) has noted that "psychoanalysts have written surprisingly little about the psychology of writing and reading" (p. 8)—the interrelations between author, text, and audience. Phillips (1993) writes that "though uniquely suited to the task, psychoanalysis has yet to produce a theory of admiration that does not involve submission (or that most furtive form of submission called gratitude)—a theory that would include a nonsadomasochistic description of relationships to theoretical precursors" (p. xiv).[3]

Literary figures have long been preoccupied with the question of literary history as writers "continue" one other. Bloom (1973), writing about the development of influence and tradition in the literary world, has pointed out that poetic influence is a relationship of sonship, "a battle between strong equals, father and son as mighty opposites, Laius and Oedipus at the crossroads" (as cited by Gubar and Gilbert 1979, p. 6). Gubar and Gilbert (1979) have suggested that we see the author of a text as a father, an aesthetic patriarch "whose pen is an instrument of generative power like his penis." Bloom's model, keeping within the monolithic phallocentrism of western philosophical thought, allowed only a male metaphor for the transmission of inheritance and influence.

Historically, as Showalter (1987) has argued, models of male literary transmission were restrictive and inhibiting for women writers, leaving them

---

[2]Heilbrun (1991) writes in her essay, "Freud's Daughters," that Anna Freud, along with Freud's other "daughters"—Lou Andreas-Salomé, Marie Bonaparte, Helene Deutsch, and Melanie Klein—never escaped his fatal gender bifurcation.

[3]See *Bonds of Love* by Jessica Benjamin (1988), who would argue otherwise.

with the impossible choice between the fulfillment of intellectual ambitions and maternal wishes. In *King Lear* Shakespeare observed that the son needs to take over, and in doing so he symbolically destroys the father. But then, what is the task of the daughters, like Cordelia, who are asked to maintain and not take over? Miller (1990) recognized that historically women "dream not of making art, but of being in love with Paris" (p. 278) and so must make the move from being art to making it. Rich (1980) speaks of the woman artist who must struggle to break away from traditional and internalized ideas "for the dutiful daughter of the father can only be a hack" (p. 201).[4] The dilemma of the dutiful daughter is a central problem for the further development of a theory of female development, for without a model, what do female authors-theorists have to rely on?

In their concern with the tradition of female influence, Gilbert and Gubar (1979) have suggested that Bloom's metaphor of literary paternity and the metaphor of the anxiety of influence are not useful for women. Instead, they suggest what they have called the anxiety of authorship, an anxiety that the woman cannot create (and can never become a precursor) for fear of isolation or personal destruction. Coen (1994) underlines the difficulty of the arrogance of creative thought, and of the competitiveness with and destructiveness to one's forebears and contemporaries felt in daring to be original, better, or different. This necessary process of revision, of entering an old text from a new critical direction (which Rich [1975] has described as an act of survival), calls for "an acceptance and respect for aggression and hubris" (p. 90) Conflicts over useful aggression, which are necessary according to Meissner (1997) for overcoming obstacles and achieving objectives, while not ubiquitous for women, may have gender-specific conflicts and resolutions. Applegarth (1977) turned her attention to an understanding of the dynamics of work inhibitions in women and attempted to delineate gender-specific obstacles for women and work, citing conflicts over aggression, fears of being alone, and wishes to be dependent. Certainly, assuming the authority of authorship requires that we further understand gender-specific obstacles for women in matters of agency, aggression, competitiveness, and arrogance. In fact, when aggression is turned inward, rather than used for overcoming obstacles, one may feel defective or that something is missing (Meissner 1997).

------

[4]In her book *Of Woman Born*, Rich (1976) describes breaking away from the intellectual influence of her father.

III.

They are not mine,
they are my mother's,
her mother's before,
handed down like an heirloom . . .
—Anne Sexton,
"The Red Shoes," 1972

One initial response to the dilemma of the dutiful daughter was the work of the French *écriture feminine* (writing of the feminine). This work attempted to deconstruct male-generated images of women and to construct images that more closely approximated something inherent and essential within the female herself. The attempt to illuminate symbolic possibilities for the female, based on a uniquely female body–ego schema, provided a specific mode of activity, self-knowledge, organization, and subjectivity as counterpoints to having to look to phallus and castration metaphors for bodily and mental organization (Bassin 1982). Now, however, it can be seen as a new version of the essentialism that Freud strove to deconstruct. A bodily based imaginary, like other new norms of female behavior—for example, "women's ways of knowing" or "self in connection"—may pose as great a threat to psychoanalytic work as did those of the fin-de-siècle (see also Grossman and Kaplan 1988). Along similar lines, Showalter (1987) expressed this dilemma in her discussions about the use of the female tradition of quilting, piecework, and patching as truly female models of aesthetics for the organization of a text in which no hierarchical structure exists. The quilt, made from a collection of past treasures and odds and ends and passed on, reflected a process of continuity and apprenticeship for the female. However, while the assembly of these fragments led to ingenious and intricate designs, Showalter asks, "To what degree are these traditions burdens rather than treasures?" (p. 228).[5] Thus, although the search for our own ways of knowing and creating the world and the recovery of our lost foremothers have been necessary in our attempt to find our own authority and authorship,[6] recent history has seen them as merely other stepping-stones.

---

[5]Freud related women's contribution to civilization, weaving, as symbolically connected to covering up their "genital deficiency," or hiding what is missing.
[6]When I asked my software's spell-checker for this text, the program suggested forefathers as the "spelling" of foremothers!

Through the efforts of feminist psychoanalysts, psychoanalytic clinical theory has illuminated a phallocentric logic that affects the way we perceive gender, mature object relations, and sexuality. Being informed by a postmodernist view that contributed to the breakdown of the either-or has propelled new ways of reading, and new stances in regard to clinical material and theoretical authority. The word *phallic* and its erroneously literal tie to the male genital distract us from articulating the limitations of the phallic order for both sexes. Unduly privileging male gender, the phallocentric logic excludes the complex variability within each sex, and by polarization and repression provides a fixed, normative, and rigid gender identity. Normative models of female behavior and fantasy, as we understand them, only negate the underlying multiplicity of sexual organization and create a female version of a phallocentric theory. A normative model of female behavior and fantasies that excludes the presence of masculine wishes and strivings may represent just another fantasy of gender consistency to normalize characteristics of interiority, relatedness, and connectedness at the psychic expense of competition, assertion, and aggression (Harris 1987).

McDougall (1995) has long argued that the acceptance of deep bisexual longings and the conflicts they produce is a necessary requirement for creative activity. In fact, for McDougall, the creative moment is a symbolic solution to the wish to be both mother and father and to reproduce. This emergent model of organization for the female, which emphasizes the possibility and value of her cross-sex identification with paternal figures as well as her same-sex synthesis with maternal figures, has been used by feminist literary critics. Showalter (1987) talks of Edith Wharton's successful assertion of herself and the integration of the male and female sides of her lineage. In *The House of Mirth*, Wharton killed Lily, her infantile self, the dutiful daughter who repressed her imaginative impulses, her anger, and her sexual desire. Gilbert and Gubar (1979) have also understood this valuable integration in Margaret Fuller. Fuller, being a special example of a nineteenth-century female writer, was able to integrate the female and male aspects of her lineage. Gilbert and Gubar suggest her success was a function of her use both of her father's library, a place of patriarchal intellect, and her mother's garden, a warm and nurturing nest.

Recent and varied formulations of a postoedipal position in the female psyche (Bassin 1996, J. Benjamin 1996, Elise 1996, Stimmel 1996) suggest a potential for the recuperation of early bisexuality, gender overinclusiveness, masculine strivings, body–ego representations, and cross-gender identifications in the context of a differentiated self that allows for a transcending of normative, polarized sexual positions and gender conformity without recourse to a disturbed gender identity. This capacity of the female mind to assimilate cross-sex or paternal representations along with same-sex or maternal representations simply for their value in internal and external mastery, rather than for their with-or-without-penis status (Bassin 1996), facilitates further understanding of the anxiety of authorship for women, both concrete and metaphoric. In addition, although our phallocentric logic has made us blind to the transformational aspect of the maternal object, more contemporary readings have allowed us a fuller appreciation of the mother as a subject in her own right (see J. Benjamin 1988, Bassin et al. 1994). The discovery of the maternal subject, the active, independent maker, is possible after a mourning for the loss of the maternal object. The maternal function, emancipated as an object, can become an aspect of the self (Bassin 1994). Our nostalgic relationship to mother, searching for the old object, enables us to avoid loss, but the mourning of the object and our subsequent identification with the subjectivity of the mother together allow for a generative stance.

A paper by Arden (1987) begins by lamenting the lack of explicit recognition of the work of Sylvia Payne and Margaret Brierley. Writing more than sixty-five years ago, Payne (1935) and Brierley (1932) highlighted the possibility of the integration and coordination of conflicting male and female elements in the personality without the destruction or inhibition of biological sex. They began to sketch the differences between primary masculine elements in women's psyche and the masculinity complex, or reactive identifications with the father, in a fight from femininity. In fact, Payne (1935) picked up from Brierley the idea that a "psychological definition of femininity might have to be made in terms of integration and co-ordination of conflicting male and female elements in the personality" (p. 25). This body of work emphasized the importance of symbolization in sexual development and argued that much of what was considered normal femininity was actually a pathology, perhaps a failure to obtain symbolic representation of concrete infantile experience. Arden (1987) underlined that symbolization, as opposed to concrete thinking, enables a useful separation of female and male thinking separate from male and female bodies and furthermore that female organization must include a phallic symbol that is not necessarily pathological. Arden (1987) suggested that when Brierley published *Trends in Psychoanalysis* in 1951, she left out her two papers on female sexuality because of their failure to achieve a synthesis with Freud's work. These important stepping-stones have gone unrecognized except for Arden's attempt, itself published in the *International Review of Psycho-Analysis* (now combined with, and perhaps always a historic stepchild of the *International Journal of Psycho-Analysis*).

Whitford (1991), citing Feldman's (1977) important paper in the *Yale French Studies* on the relation of transference to mastery and authority, playfully describes a male and female reading of any text. The male reading assumes a belief in mastery over the text, while the female reading, evoking a knowledge of transference, allows us to see interpretation as provisional and useful insofar as it enables other readings. Whitford (1991) prefers, of course, the creative, symbolic possibilities of fertile intercourse or the embodiment of "the symbolic possibilities of sexual difference" (p. 25).

IV.

and through my lips come the voices
of the ghosts of our ancestors
living and moving among us.
                    —Audrey Lorde, 1982

A deeper understanding of the relation between writer and reader—and an alternative to the sadomasochistic model of faithful, dutiful submission or destruction—can be found in the work of Loewald. One of the many undeveloped contributions of Loewald (1979) was his deep understanding of succession and of children succeeding parents. In fact, Lear (1996) in particular asks us to consider Loewald's own exegesis of Freud's work, a "unique blend of creativity and faithfulness," as part of the oedipal task. Lear submits that Loewald's relation to Freud's work was a profound demonstration of something Loewald attempted to describe in his understanding of the oedipal dilemma, that is, both gratitude and succession. Lear suggests that Loewald "displays real filial piety in the very creative act by which he goes beyond anything Freud thought" (p. 675). Connecting these threads, Lear further suggests an understanding of legacy as a task, part of the unfinished business a child needs to complete in order to manifest love, atone for ambivalence, and succeed the parent. He writes: "A corollary of the Oedipus complex is that creativity requires that one has to come to grips with legacies of one's intellectual parents" (p. 675). This honoring of the past can occur simultaneously, as Loewald argues, without total submission. According to Loewald, the move toward self-assertion, self-articulation, and self-responsibility requires owning and mastering the guilt of the criminal activity of parricide (the murder or serious betrayal of a parent or one who symbolizes parental authority). This, he proposes, is accomplished by internalizing atonement. Rather than there being a sadomasochistic–masochistic outcome, what should be left after the severance of oedipal ties is mutual trust, respect, and tenderness, all signs of equality. Loewald offers a psychoanalytic understanding of what Walter Benjamin argued: that it is through criticism that the work moves toward fulfillment or completion.

This mastering of owning, and the mastering of the guilt of parricide, beginning even in the earliest preoedipal phases, was deeply understood by Melanie Klein. She begins her paper "Envy and Gratitude" (1957) by thanking and acknowledging Karl Abraham, noting the satisfaction of being able to contribute to the growing recognition of the full significance of Abraham's discovery, yet also acknowledging throughout her paper the value of envy and aggression. Acknowledgment, perhaps like other symbolic activities of ritual, wards off fears of retaliation and allows for the use of aggression in the service of the ego and in the community. Turner (1985) has written extensively on the reconciliation aspect of ritual that enables the community to continue by remembering ancestors, restoring the past, and purifying relationships of envy, jealousy, and hate.

Most of our theoretical writing about overcoming the oedipal phase has been looked at from the perspective of the child—the killing of the parents—as has our writing about the mother as an object of the child. Yet we also need to continue to elaborate on the role of the parents, the forebears, and the parents' willingness to be replaced. Specifically for the creative revisioner in any field, as Robbe-Gillet has suggested, we need "to bear [our] date, knowing that there are no masterpieces in eternity, only works" (cited in Miller 1990, p. 1). Winnicott suggested that to grow, to reach a two-person encounter, requires that the other be destroyed and still survive the destruction. Jessica Benjamin (1988) has written extensively about the way the child comes to recognize how separateness (object loss) is the other side of connectedness with the other, stressing the necessity that the mother be a subject (which cannot be destroyed) for this to occur.

Erickson (1950) wrote about what might be the most difficult conflict of human life: that between the nurturance and generativity of the next generation, and the preservation of one's own power, strength, and creativity. Although Erickson illuminated this relatively unexplored area—of human development in middle age—he lacked a consolidated definition that, as he was quick to point out, had only existential terms, as opposed to strictly psychoanalytic ones, to define it. Erickson's use of the word *conflict* might better be changed to *dilemma*, with the later implying insolubility. Freud (1914) discussed this dilemma in "On Narcissism." The individual actually does carry on a twofold existence: one to serve his or her own purposes, and the other as a link in a chain. As far as the link in the chain is concerned, Freud suggested, the individual serves against his or her will, or at least serves involuntarily, "like the inheritor of an entailed property who is only the temporary holder of an estate which serves him" (p. 78). The process of inheritance captured Walter Benjamin (1931) when he wrote about his own collecting: "Actually, inheritance is the soundest way of acquiring a collection. For a collector's attitude towards his possession stems from an owner's feeling of responsibility towards his property. This is, in the highest sense, the attitude of an heir, and the most distinguished trait of a collection will always be its transmissibility" (p. 66).

Whereas Freud (1914) discussed ego instincts and sexual instincts as two separate trajectories, Kernberg's (1980) discussion of normal narcissism in middle age suggests, paradoxically, a consolidation. An outcome of mourning the past and a renewed overcoming of the Oedipus complex during middle age is the development of a strong internal reality, of a world of the past. Keeping alive the world of our parents, possible after the working through of ambivalence, provides a security that diminishes the envy of the young and the fear of aggression in competitiveness with them, as well as a new source of creativity. Freud (1938, p. 207) quoted Goethe's *Faust*, "What thou hast inherited from thy fathers, acquire it to make it thine" (Part 1, Scene 1). I can only wish, however, that "fathers" be extended to "mothers" as well.

V.

Benjamin wrote nothing about female development, and his essay is clearly outside our psychoanalytic literature. Nonetheless, his attention to and reverence for the relationship of predecessors and heirs and his attention to tradition, legacy, and inheritance—and to generativity and the transformation of thought in our psychoanalytic writings and theoretical development—underlie the spirit of this volume. Moreover, the essay addresses a crucial obstacle for those pursuing the task of editing a volume such as this one—itself a form of collecting a library. Benjamin's image of a library, with all its disparate texts, also supports using a private library of nonpsychoanalytic writers who have augmented their own clinical and theoretical understandings, and giving oneself the freedom, as Edith Wharton describes, of having the full rein of books in the library.

When Michael Moskowitz, my editor at Jason Aronson, asked me to assemble a collection of useful papers on women and psychoanalysis, I initially declined. Underneath my conscious concerns that a project like this would offer little in the way of learning (little did I know at the time how much I would learn) was an uncomfortable awareness of my anxiety at taking on the authority of editorship. This awareness caused me to face the problem with all the stimulation of a challenge and a search for a creative solution. The challenge of finding my own improvisation for what initially seemed a pedantic task melded with a wish and a fear to explore the gender-specific issue of authorship, authority, and influence.

I had been struggling with this particular issue since I began my psychoanalytic training. During my analysis with Doris Bernstein and after the publication of my first psychoanalytic paper and her presentation of her seminal paper on the genital anxieties of women, I had a dream that alerted me to my own anxiety over influence and succession. In the dream I was being attacked by one of the lion statues in front of the New York Public Library. The lion was yellow-haired, as was my very blond analyst. By way of useful enactment—and a few helpful interpretations regarding my anxiety of destroying and being destroyed—I began to interview major psychoanalytic thinkers about the impact of their mentors-supervisors and analysts on their own work, with the grandiose wish that I might contribute to the creation of a history of the development of psychoanalytic ideas.[7] I interviewed Donald Kaplan regarding the impact of one of his psychoanalytic supervisors, Theodore Reik, on his work and thinking. Although the details of the interview are now lost, the spirit of Kaplan's loving respect for his brilliant but difficult forefather, as well as his seeming utter ease with his disagreements with Reik, has stayed with me. (One of the pleasures of being an analyst is the privilege of turning our master narratives and a caring psychoanalytic eye and ear toward our own activities, and one of the pains is just that responsibility.) We have used psycho-

---

[7]See Nancy J. Chodorow (1989), "Seventies Questions for Thirties Women," where she reports on her interviews with early women psychoanalysts—women trained in the 1920s, 1930s, and 1940s.

analytic concepts to understand the motivations and obstacles of artists and writers, but for the most part we have neglected to turn this ear toward an understanding of creativity and scientific developments in our field. The dread of exposing conflict transforms into the excitement of having new materials to work with. For myself, as with many other women, writing and theorizing—becoming active creators (aside from reproduction), taking on the mantle and climbing atop the body of knowledge—remains problematic and conflicted. We need to examine gender-specific obstacles to women, who are not equally represented in our current published material, and offer the necessary support to the next generation.

> So I have erected one of his dwellings, with books as the building stones, before you, and now he is going to disappear inside, as is only fitting.
>
> —Walter Benjamin

So ends Walter Benjamin's "Unpacking My Library"—at least for now.

REFERENCES

Applegarth, A. (1977). Some observations on work inhibitions in women. In *Female Psychology*, ed. H. Blum, pp. 251–268. New York: International Universities Press.

Arden, M. (1987). A concept of "femininity": Sylvia Payne's 1935 paper reassessed. *International Review of Psycho-Analysis* 14:237–244.

Arendt, H. (1970). Introduction. In Benjamin, W., *Illuminations*, ed. H. Arendt, trans. H. Zohn, pp. 1–58. New York: Schocken.

Bassin, D. (1982). Women's images of inner space: data towards expanded interpretative categories. *International Review of Psycho-Analysis* 9(2):191–203.

——— (1994). Maternal subjectivity in the culture of nostalgia: mourning and memory. In *Representations of Motherhood*, ed. D. Bassin, M. Honey, and M. Kaplan, pp. 162–173. New Haven, CT: Yale University Press.

——— (1996). Beyond the he and she: toward the reconciliation of masculinity and femininity in the postoedipal female mind. *Journal of the American Psychoanalytic Association* 44(suppl.):157–190.

Bassin, D., Honey, M., and Kaplan, M., eds. (1994). *Representations of Motherhood*. New Haven, CT: Yale University Press.

Benjamin, J. (1988). *The Bonds of Love*. New York: Pantheon.

——— (1996). In defense of gender ambiguity. *Gender and Psychoanalysis* 1:27–44.

Benjamin, W. (1931). Unpacking my library. In *Illuminations*, ed. H. Arendt, trans. H. Zohn. New York: Schocken, 1970.

——— (1919–1922). Goethe's elective affinities. In *Walter Benjamin: Selected Writings*. Volume 1: 1913–1926, ed. C. M. Bullock and M. W. Jennings.

Cambridge, MA: Belknap Press of Harvard University. Originally published 1924–1925 in *Gesammelte Schriften*, vol. 1, pp. 125–126.

Bion, W. R. (1965). *Transformations*. New York: Jason Aronson.

Bloom, H. (1973). *The Anxiety of Influence: A Theory of Poetry*. New York: Oxford University Press.

Bollas, C. (1995). *Cracking Up: The Work of Unconscious Experience*. New York: Hill and Wang.

Brierley, M. (1932). Some problems of integration in women. *International Journal of Psycho-Analysis* 13:433–448.

——— (1951). *Trends in Psychoanalysis*. London: Hogarth.

Coen, S. (1994) *Between Author and Reader*. New York: Columbia University Press.

Chodorow, N. J. (1978). *The Reproduction of Mothering*. Berkeley, CA: University of California Press.

——— (1989). Seventies questions for thirties women: gender and generation in a study of early women psychoanalysts. In *Feminism and Psychoanalytic Theory*, pp. 199–219. New Haven, CT: Yale University Press.

Eagleton, T. (1981). *Walter Benjamin or Towards a Revolutionary Criticism*. London and New York: Verson.

Elise, D. (1996). *Primary femininity, bisexulity, and the female ego ideal*. Paper delivered at a meeting of Division 39, American Psychological Association, New York, April.

Erikson, E. (1950). *Childhood and Society*. New York: Norton.

Feldman, S. (1977). To open the question. *Yale French Studies* 55:5–10.

Fliegel, Z. (1973). Feminine psychosexual development in Freudian theory: a historical reconstruction. *Psychoanalytic Quarterly* 42(3):385–407.

Fraiberg, S. (1968). Parallel and divergent patterns in blind and sighted infants. *Psychoanalytic Study of the Child* 24:9–21. New York: International Universities Press.

Freud, S. (1914). On narcissism: an introduction. *Standard Edition* 14:73–104.

——— (1938). An Outline of Psychoanalysis. *Standard Edition* 23:141–208.

Gallop, J. (1982). *The Daughter's Seduction: Feminism and Psychoanalysis*. Ithaca, NY: Cornell University Press.

Gilbert, S. M., and Gubar, S. (1979). *The Madwoman in the Attic: The Woman Writer and the Nineteenth-Century Literary Imagination*. New Haven, CT: Yale University Press.

Green, A. (1978). The double and the absent. In *Psychoanalysis, Creativity and Literature: A French-American Inquiry*, ed. A. Roland, pp. 271–292. New York: Columbia University Press.

Grossman W. I., and Kaplan, D. (1988). Three commentaries on gender in Freud's thoughts: a prologue to the psychoanalytic theory of sexuality. In *Fantasy, Myth, and Reality*, ed. H. P. Blum, Y. Kramer, A. K. Richards, and A. D. Richards, pp. 339–370. New York: International Universities Press.

Harris, A. (1987). Women in relation to power and words. *Issues in Ego Psychology* 10:29–38.

Heilbrun, C. (1991). *Hamlet's Mother and Other Women*. New York: Valentine.

Holland, N. (1975). *Five Readers Reading*. New Haven, CT: Yale University Press.

Kernberg, O. (1980). Normal narcissism in middle age. In *Internal World and External Reality*, pp. 121–137. Northvale, NJ: Jason Aronson.

Klein, M. (1957). Envy and gratitude. In *Envy and Gratitude and Other Works 1946–1963*. New York: Dell, 1975.

Lear, J. (1996). The introduction of eros. *Journal of the American Psychoanalytic Association* 44(3):673–698.

Loewald, H. (1979). The waning of the Oedipus complex. In *Papers on Psychoanalysis*, pp. 384–404. New Haven, CT: Yale University Press.

McDougall, J. (1995). *The Many Faces of Eros*. New York: Norton.

Meissner, W. W. (1997). The self and the principle of work. In *Work and Its Inhibitions*, ed. C. Socarides and S. Kramer, pp. 35–60. Madison, CT: International Universities Press.

Miller, N. (1990). *Subject to Change*. New York: Columbia University Press.

Missac, P. (1995). *Walter Benjamin's Passages*, trans. S. W. Nicholsen. Cambridge, MS: MIT Press.

Oates, J. C. (1993). Sidebar. *New York Times Book Review* August 15, p. 16.

Payne, S. (1935). A concept of femininity. *British Journal of Medical Psychology* 15:18–33.

Phillips, A. (1993). Introduction. In Eigen, M., *The Electrified Tightrope*, ed. A. Phillips, pp. xiii–xvi. Northvale, NJ: Jason Aronson.

Rabinbach, A. (1979). Critique and commentary/alchemy and chemistry: some remarks on Walter Benjamin and this special issue. *New German Critique* 17:3–14.

Rich, A. (1975). When we dead awaken; writing as re-Vision. In *Adrienne Rich's Poetry*, ed. B. C. Gelpi and A. Gelpi, p. 90. New York: Norton.

——— (1995). *On Lies, Secrets, and Silence: Selected Prose 1966–1978*. New York: Norton.

Sexton, A. (1972). The red shoes. In *The Book of Folly*, pp. 28–29. Boston: Houghton Mifflin.

Showalter, E. (1987). Piecing and writing. In *The Poetics of Gender*, ed. N. Miller, pp. 222–247. New York: Columbia University Press.

——— (1994). *Sister's Choice*. New York: Oxford University Press.

Stimmel, B. (1996). Bisexuality and metaphors of the mind. *Journal of the American Psychoanalytic Association* 44(Supp.):191–214.

Turner, V. (1985). Images of anti-temporality: an essay in the anthropology of experience. In *On the Edge of the Bush*, ed. E. Turner, pp. 227–246. Tucson, AZ: University of Arizona Press.

Whitford, M. (1986). *Of Woman Born: Motherland as Experience and Institution*. New York: Norton.

——— (1991). *Luce Irigary: Philosophy in the Feminine*. London and New York: Routledge.

Unpacking My Library: A Talk about Book Collecting

WALTER BENJAMIN

I am unpacking my library. Yes, I am. The books are not yet on the shelves, not yet touched by the mild boredom of order. I cannot march up and down their ranks to pass them in review before a friendly audience. You need not fear any of that. Instead, I must ask you to join me in the disorder of crates that have been wrenched open, the air saturated with the dust of wood, the floor covered with torn paper, to join me among piles of volumes that are seeing daylight again after two years of darkness, so that you may be ready to share with me a bit of the mood—it is certainly not an elegiac mood but, rather, one of anticipation—which these books arouse in a genuine collector. For such a man is speaking to you, and on closer scrutiny he proves to be speaking only about himself. Would it not be presumptuous of me if, in order to appear convincingly objective and down-to-earth, I enumerated for you the main sections or prize pieces of a library, if I presented you with their history or even their usefulness to a writer? I, for one, have in mind something less obscure, something more palpable than that; what I am really concerned with is giving you some insight into the relationship of a book collector to his possessions, into collecting rather than a collection. If I do this by elaborating on the various ways of acquiring books, this is something entirely arbitrary. This or any other procedure is merely a dam against the spring tide of memories which surges toward any collector as he contemplates his possessions. Every passion borders on the chaotic, but the collector's passion borders on the chaos of memories. More than that: the chance, the fate, that suffuse the past before my eyes are conspicuously present in the accustomed confusion of these books. For what else is this collection but a disorder to which habit has accommodated itself to such an extent that it can appear as order? You have all heard of people whom the loss of their books has turned into invalids, or of those who in order to acquire them became criminals. These are the very areas in which any order is a balancing act of extreme precariousness. "The only exact knowledge there is," said Anatole France, "is the knowledge of the date of publication and the format of books." And indeed, if there is a counterpart to the confusion of a library, it is the order of its catalogue.

Thus there is in the life of a collector a dialectical tension between the poles of disorder and order. Naturally, his existence is tied to many other things as well: to a very mysterious relationship to ownership, something about which we shall have more to say later; also, to a relationship to objects which does not emphasize their functional, utilitarian value—that is, their usefulness—but studies and loves them as the scene, the stage, of their fate. The most profound enchantment for the collector is the locking of individual items within a magic circle in which they are fixed as the final thrill, the thrill of acquisition, passes over them. Everything remembered and thought, everything conscious, becomes the pedestal, the frame, the base, the lock of his property. The period, the region, the craftsmanship, the former ownership—for a true collector the whole background of an item adds up to a magic encyclopedia whose quintessence is the fate of his object. In this circumscribed area, then, it may be surmised how the great physiognomists—and collectors are the physiognomists of the world of objects—turn into interpreters of fate. One has only to watch a collector handle the objects in his glass case. As he holds them in his hands, he seems to be seeing through them into their distant past as though inspired. So much for the magical side of the collector—his old-age image, I might call it.

Habent sua fata libelli: these words may have been intended as a general statement about books. So books like *The Divine Comedy*, Spinoza's *Ethics*, and *The Origin of Species* have their fates. A collector, however, interprets this Latin saying differently. For him, not only books but also copies of books have their fates. And in this sense, the most important fate of a copy is its encounter with him, with this own collection. I am not exaggerating when I say that to a true collector the acquisition of an old book is its rebirth. This is the childlike element which in a collector mingles with the element of old age. For children can accomplish the renewal of existence in a hundred unfailing ways. Among children, collecting is only one process of renewal; other processes are the painting of objects, the cutting out of figures, the application of decals—the whole range of childlike modes of acquisition, from touching things to giving them names. To renew the old world—that is the collector's deepest desire when he is driven to acquire new things, and that is why a collector of older books is closer to the well-springs of collecting than the acquirer of luxury editions. How do books cross the threshold of a collection and become the property of a collector? The history of their acquisition is the subject of the following remarks.

Of all the ways of acquiring books, writing them oneself is regarded as the most praiseworthy method. At this point many of you will remember with pleasure the large library which Jean Paul's poor little schoolmaster Wutz gradually acquired by writing, himself, all the works whose titles interested him in bookfair catalogues; after all, he could not afford to buy them. Writers are really people who write books not because they are poor, but because they are dissatisfied with the books which they could buy but do not like. You, ladies and gentlemen, may regard this as a whimsical definition of a writer. But everything said from the angle of a real collector is whimsical. Of the customary modes of acquisition, the one most appropriate to a collector would be the borrowing of a book with its attendant non-returning. The book borrower of real stature whom we envisage here proves himself to be an inveterate collector of books not so much by the fervor with which he guards his borrowed treasures and by the deaf ear which he turns to all reminders from the everyday world of legality as by his failure to read these books. If my experience may serve as evidence, a man is more likely to return a borrowed book upon occasion than to read it. And the non-reading of books, you will object, should be characteristic of collectors? This is news to me, you may say. It is not news at all. Experts will bear me out when I say that it is the oldest thing in the world. Suffice it to quote the answer which Anatole France gave to a philistine who admired his library and then finished with the standard question, "And you have read all these books, Monsieur France?" "Not one-tenth of them. I don't suppose you use your Sèvres china every day?"

Incidentally, I have put the right to such an attitude to the test. For years, for at least the first third of its existence, my library consisted of no more than two or three shelves which increased only by inches each year. This was its militant age, when no book was allowed to enter it without the certification that I had not read it. Thus I might never have acquired a library extensive enough to be worthy of the name if there had not been an inflation. Suddenly the emphasis shifted; books acquired real value, or, at any rate, were difficult to obtain. At least this is how it seemed in Switzerland. At the eleventh hour I sent my first major book orders from there and in this way was able to secure such irreplaceable items as *Der blaue Reiter* and Bachofen's *Sage von Tanaquil*, which could still be obtained from the publishers at that time.

Well—so you may say—after exploring all these byways we should finally reach the wide highway of book acquisition, namely, the purchasing of books. This is indeed a wide highway, but not a comfortable one. The purchasing done by a book collector has very little in common with that done in a bookshop by a student getting a textbook, a man of the world buying a present for his lady, or a businessman intending to while away his next train journey. I have made my most memorable purchases on trips, as a transient. Property and possession belong to the tactical sphere. Collectors are people with a tactical instinct; their experience teaches them that when they capture a strange city, the smallest antique shop can be a fortress, the most remote stationery store a key position. How many cities have revealed themselves to me in the marches I undertook in the pursuit of books!

By no means all of the most important purchases are made on the premises of a dealer. Catalogues play a far greater part. And even though the purchaser may be thoroughly acquainted with the book ordered from a catalogue, the individual copy always remains a surprise and the order always a bit of a gamble. There are grievous disappointments, but also happy finds. I remember, for instance, that I once ordered a book with colored illustrations for my old collection of children's books only because it contained fairy tales by Albert Ludwig Grimm and was published at Grimma, Thuringia. Grimma was also the place of publication of a book of fables edited by the same Albert Ludwig Grimm. With its sixteen illustrations my copy of this book of fables was the only extant example of the early work of the great German book illustrator Lyser, who lived in Hamburg around the middle of the last century. Well, my reaction to the consonance of the names had been correct. In this case too I discovered the work of Lyser, namely *Linas Märchenbuch*, a work which has remained unknown to his bibliographers and which deserves a more detailed reference than this first one I am introducing here.

The acquisition of books is by no means a matter of money or expert

knowledge alone. Not even both factors together suffice for the establishment of a real library, which is always somewhat impenetrable and at the
same time uniquely itself. Anyone who buys from catalogues must have
flair in addition to the qualities I have mentioned. Dates, place names,
formats, previous owners, bindings, and the like: all these details must tell
him something—not as dry, isolated facts, but as a harmonious whole; from
the quality and intensity of this harmony he must be able to recognize
whether a book is for him or not. An auction requires yet another set of
qualities in a collector. To the reader of a catalogue the book itself must
speak, or possibly its previous ownership if the provenance of the copy
has been established. A man who wishes to participate at an auction must
pay equal attention to the book and to his competitors, in addition to
keeping a cool enough head to avoid being carried away in the competition. It is a frequent occurrence that someone gets stuck with a high pur-
chase price because he kept raising his bid—more to assert himself than to
acquire the book. On the other hand, one of the finest memories of a
collector is the moment when he rescued a book to which he might never
have given a thought, much less a wishful look, because he found it lonely
and abandoned on the market place and bought it to give it its freedom—
the way the prince bought a beautiful slave girl in *The Arabian Nights*. To
a book collector, you see, the true freedom of all books is somewhere on
his shelves.

To this day, Balzac's *Peau de chagrin* stands out from long rows of
French volumes in my library as a memento of my most exciting experience at an auction. This happened in 1915 at the Rümann auction put up
by Emil Hirsch, one of the greatest of book experts and most distinguished
of dealers. The edition in question appeared in 1838 in Paris, Place de la
Bourse. As I pick up my copy, I see not only its number in the Rümann
collection, but even the label of the shop in which the first owner bought
the book over ninety years ago for one-eightieth of today's price. "Papeterie
I. Flanneau," it says. A fine age in which it was still possible to buy such
a de luxe edition at a stationery dealer's! The steel engravings of this book
were designed by the foremost French graphic artist and executed by the
foremost engravers. But I was going to tell you how I acquired this book.
I had gone to Emil Hirsch's for an advance inspection and had handled
forty or fifty volumes; that particular volume had inspired in me the ardent desire to hold on to it forever. The day of the auction came. As chance
would have it, in the sequence of the auction this copy of *La Peau de chagrin* was preceded by a complete set of its illustrations printed separately

on India paper. The bidders sat at a long table; diagonally across from me sat the man who was the focus of all eyes at the first bid, the famous Munich collector Baron von Simolin. He was greatly interested in this set, but he had rival bidders; in short, there was a spirited contest which resulted in the highest bid of the entire auction—far in excess of three thousand marks. No one seemed to have expected such a high figure, and all those present were quite excited. Emil Hirsch remained unconcerned, and whether he wanted to save time or was guided by some other consideration, he proceeded to the next item, with no one really paying attention. He called out the price, and with my heart pounding and with the full realization that I was unable to compete with any of those big collectors I bid a somewhat higher amount. Without arousing the bidder's attention, the auctioneer went through the usual routine—"Do I hear more?" and three bangs of his gavel, with an eternity seeming to separate each from the next—and proceeded to add the auctioneer's charge. For a student like me the sum was still considerable. The following morning at the pawnshop is no longer part of this story, and I prefer to speak about another incident which I should like to call the negative of an auction. It happened last year at a Berlin auction. The collection of books that was offered was a miscellany in quality and subject matter, and only a number of rare works on occultism and natural philosophy were worthy of note. I bid for a number of them, but each time I noticed a gentleman in the front row who seemed only to have waited for my bid to counter with his own, evidently prepared to top any offer. After this had been repeated several times, I gave up all hope of acquiring the book which I was most interested in that day. It was the rare *Fragmente aus dem Nachlass eines jungen Physikers* [Posthumous Fragments of a Young Physicist] which Johann Wilhelm Ritter published in two volumes at Heidelberg in 1810. This work has never been reprinted, but I have always considered its preface, in which the author-editor tells the story of his life in the guise of an obituary for his supposedly deceased unnamed friend—with whom he is really identical—as the most important sample of personal prose of German Romanticism. Just as the item came up I had a brain wave. It was simple enough: since my bid was bound to give the item to the other man, I must not bid at all. I controlled myself and remained silent. What I had hoped for came about: no interest, no bid, and the book was put aside. I deemed it wise to let several days go by, and when I appeared on the premises after a week, I found the book in the secondhand department and benefited by the lack of interest when I acquired it.

Once you have approached the mountains of cases in order to mine the books from them and bring them to the light of day—or, rather, of night—what memories crowd in upon you! Nothing highlights the fascination of unpacking more clearly than the difficulty of stopping this activity. I had started at noon, and it was midnight before I had worked my way to the last cases. Now I put my hands on two volumes bound in faded boards which, strictly speaking, do not belong in a bookcase at all: two albums with stick-in pictures which my mother pasted in as a child and which I inherited. They are the seeds of a collection of children's books which is growing steadily even today, though no longer in my garden. There is no living library that does not harbor a number of booklike creations from fringe areas. They need not be stick-in albums or family albums, autograph books or portfolios containing pamphlets or religious tracts; some people become attached to leaflets and prospectuses, others to handwriting facsimiles or typewritten copies of unobtainable books; and certainly periodicals can form the prismatic fringes of a library. But to get back to those albums: Actually, inheritance is the soundest way of acquiring a collection. For a collector's attitude toward his possessions stems from an owner's feeling of responsibility toward his property. Thus it is, in the highest sense, the attitude of an heir, and the most distinguished trait of a collection will always be its transmissibility. You should know that in saying this I fully realize that my discussion of the mental climate of collecting will confirm many of you in your conviction that this passion is behind the times, in your distrust of the collector type. Nothing is further from my mind than to shake either your conviction or your distrust. But one thing should be noted: the phenomenon of collecting loses its meaning as it loses its personal owner. Even though public collections may be less objectionable socially and more useful academically than private collections, the objects get their due only in the latter. I do know that time is running out for the type that I am discussing here and have been representing before you a bit *ex officio*. But, as Hegel put it, only when it is dark does the owl of Minerva begin its flight. Only in extinction is the collector comprehended.

Now I am on the last half-emptied case and it is way past midnight. Other thoughts fill me than the ones I am talking about—not thoughts but images, memories. Memories of the cities in which I found so many things: Riga, Naples, Munich, Danzig, Moscow, Florence, Basel, Paris; memories of Rosenthal's sumptuous rooms in Munich, of the Danzig Stockturm where the late Hans Rhaue was domiciled, of Süssengut's musty book cellar in North Berlin; memories of the rooms where these books had been housed, of my student's den in Munich, of my room in Bern, of the solitude of Iseltwald on the Lake of Brienz, and finally of my boyhood room, the former location of only four or five of the several thousand volumes that are piled up around me. O bliss of the collector, bliss of the man of leisure! Of no one has less been expected, and no one has had a greater sense of well-being than the man who has been able to carry on his disreputable existence in the mask of Spitzweg's "Bookworm." For inside him there are spirits, or at least little genii, which have seen to it that for a collector—and I mean a real collector, a collector as he ought to be—ownership is the most intimate relationship that one can have to objects. Not that they come alive in him; it is he who lives in them. So I have erected one of his dwellings, with books as the building stones, before you, and now he is going to disappear inside, as is only fitting.

CLASSICS

2

LORA HEIMS TESSMAN ON SIGMUND FREUD

A Cry of Fire, an Old Flame, the Matter of Fireplace

LORA HEIMS TESSMAN

"There is a complete change of scene," Freud tells us in "Observations on Transference-Love," the last of his series of six papers on technique, published between 1911 and 1915. "It is as though some piece of make-believe had been stopped by the sudden irruption of reality—as when a cry of fire is raised during a theatrical performance. No doctor who experiences this for the first time will find it easy to retain his grasp on the analytic situation and keep clear of the illusion that treatment is really at an end" (p. 162). The irruption of reality, the cry of fire, to which Freud refers consists of "the case in which a woman patient shows by unmistakable indications, or openly declares, that she has fallen in love, as any other mortal woman might, with the doctor who is analyzing her" (p. 159). By locating the fuel for psychoanalysis in the patient's feeling toward the analyst, Freud had arrived at what we still view as centrally mutative today. And in speaking of the "make-believe . . . stopped by the . . . irruption of reality" which threatens the treatment, he declares that the "illusion" of love belonging to transference has abruptly become real.

The irresistible charm of "Observations on Transference-Love" lies in the directness with which Freud invites the reader to partake of the human dilemmas embodied in his paradoxical view of the powers and perils of erotic love in the transference. Like the psychoanalytic process itself, the struggle takes us from meanings to further, concurrent but opposite meanings. Thus we are drawn into the dialectic between Freud's appreciation of passion and the forces of reason, between the real and the illusionary, and between an intrapsychic and fleetingly interpersonal portrayal of what determines the fate of the transference.

Freud forecasts that unless attention is given to making potentially mutative interventions at the time of affectively heated moments, access to the neurosis, and even to the patient who has the neurosis, may be lost. With further conceptual groundbreaking about what is needed so that the treatment might survive the affective heat, he proposes felicitous functions of abstinence and neutrality, concepts which became important underpinnings of the framework for psychoanalytic technique.

With "Observations" Freud launched a number of controversies in psychoanalysis which are still alive and well in contemporary times, and thus seems to restore his vivid companionship to us among the living. Although Freud conceptualized the transference as a "refinding," essentially a repetition, the paper itself was not a repetition, but surprising and fresh. Yet, while I was always attracted to "Observations" as proof that Freud was a person who could fathom the consummate power of love, I nevertheless recall that one effect of my initial reading of the paper, over thirty-five years ago, was that his pronouncements about what constituted higher and lower forms of love gave rise to the secret dread that my own analyst might view me as totally unreasonable, "repelled" by whatever erotic wishes toward him had escaped their disguise and continued to kindle my "illusionary" love. Still, the heartening consolation at the time was to witness Freud's dedication to truthfulness, another fuel of psychoanalysis, which prodded him to transcend the boundaries between illusion and the real and to posit that because the cry of fire was heir to an old flame, namely a real infantile attachment, it also infused the "normal" love of mortals, in addition to the transference.

With more hindsight today, I would want to debate with him about a number of his assumptions: I would ask about the ways that the polarities of passion and reason in his view of women might have skewed his judgment; I would express doubt about whether transference love is truly confined to being an old flame; and I would question his belief in the technical advantages of convincing the woman to relinquish her love, rather than attempting to value its containment for generative possibilities within the analytic dyad. My comments will focus mostly on these three realms.

It is likely that Freud's admonitions to analysts about their conduct in relation to women patients who declared they had fallen in love was a timely reference to a number of boundary transgressions between analytic dyads who had turned to him for some resolution or treatment (e.g., Jung with Sabine Spielrein, Ferenczi with Elma Palos, etc.). These problematic mutual embroilments were coming to light to trouble the psychoanalytic movement and its public interface, as they still do now, and the need to formulate a frame of boundaries between patient and analyst was urgent. There was no precedent yet, in actual practice, for insulating the analytic situation from a personal or potentially erotic relationship. Freud's formulations may further have reflected his afterthoughts about how transference interpretations might have prevented Dora's sudden ending of treatment, or been useful in understanding the abrupt defection of Breuer from the treatment of Anna O. However, in addition to these factors, a confluence of Freud's overvaluation of rationality, and misgivings about the sexuality of women, attitudes which were culturally prevalent but also characterologically congenial to Freud, may have colored his assumptions in particular ways. Although he advocates that the analyst pursue a delicate pathway of neither gratifying nor scorning transference love, he sees the task of the analyst as progressively persuading his patient that her love is illusion and should be renounced. He opines that this goal can be accomplished because the analyst has joined the force of his authority to reason, ironic in view of Freud's ready acknowledgment that: "As we know, the passions are little affected by sublime speeches" (p. 164)!

The ways that Freud chose to gender his view of transference love serve to amplify his rationalistic predilections. It seems to me that while in the throes of having to grapple with women's erotic wishes, Freud felt pressed to fortify himself not just against "unreasonable" women, but also against aspects of his own psychic life; in particular, he seemed to lose access to his own newly constructed notions about the creative uses of analytic space, that is, "the transference as a playground" (1914). I would like to conjecture about how Freud's views of the female with an erotic transference may have prevented his ability to envision dyadic containment for the "cry of fire," the matter of a safely generative fireplace.

Freud notes "This phenomenon [transference love] . . . may be evaluated from two points of view, that of the doctor who is carrying out the analysis and that of the patient who is in need of it" (p. 160). As the papers on technique are written for analysts rather than patients, inevitably Freud becomes spokesperson for both "points of view," making an initial and partial foray into a two-person psychology within the analytic process.

However, in spite of these intentions, for Freud the incendiary transference becomes clearly located within the patient alone (when evoked by the nature of the psychoanalytic situation), resulting for her in only "two alternatives: either she must relinquish psychoanalytic treatment or she must accept falling in love with her doctor as an inescapable fate" (p. 161). Let us assume that there are "two points of view," the analyst's and the woman's perspective, to explore what each might bring to the transference love conundrums he describes.

Freud portrays women as the carriers of transference passions, which progressively get out of hand in the following way: "One will have noticed in the patient the signs of an affectionate transference, and one will have been able to feel certain that her docility, her acceptance of the analytic explanations, her remarkable comprehension, and the high degree of intelligence she showed were to be attributed to this attitude toward her doctor." But all this is swept away when "resistance is beginning to make use of her love" (p. 162), at which point her manipulative aim includes "to destroy the doctor's authority by bringing him down to the level of a lover and to gain all the other promised advantages incidental to the satisfaction of love" (p. 163). Elsewhere he points out "It is not a patient's crudely sensual desires which constitute the temptation. These are more likely to repel, and it will call for all the doctor's tolerance if he is to regard them as a natural phenomenon. It is rather, perhaps, a woman's subtler and aim-inhibited wishes which bring with them the danger of making a man forget his technique and his medical task for the sake of a fine experience" (p. 170). The pejorative attitude evident toward repellent sensual desires, that is, the physical love which might bring one "down to the level of a lover" is not questioned, but is contrasted to sublimated wishes evocative of "a fine experience."

Carrying the deprecatory imagery further, Freud identifies "one class" of women diagnostically as having such an "intractable need for love" that psychoanalysis is doomed to failure. This group of patients would now be diagnosed as having borderline personality, and indeed, as we have all had to learn, require special care in negotiations around inevitable border incidents with either male or female analysts. Freud elaborates: "These are woven of elemental passionateness who tolerate no surrogates. They are children of nature who refuse to accept the psychical in place of the material, who, in the poet's words, are accessible only to 'the logic of soup, with dumplings for arguments.' . . . One has to withdraw, unsuccessful . . ." (p. 167).

In contrast "other women, who are less violent in their love, can be gradually made to adopt the analytic attitude." Freud advocates stressing the "unmistakable element of resistance in the 'love' . . . to treat it as something unreal" (p. 166). "Genuine love, we say, would make her docile and intensify her readiness to solve the problems of her case, simply because the man she was in love with expected it of her. . . . She would choose the road to completion of the treatment in order to acquire value in the doctor's eyes. . . . Instead of this . . . we point out she is showing a stubborn and rebellious spirit" (p. 167)!

Thus for Freud the woman's docility to the authority of the physician is the indication of being a good patient, with hope of "acquiring value in the doctor's eyes" (rather than already having value) while her declarations of love signify unacceptable rebellion. As suggested by Jessica Benjamin (1995), this brings into collision Freud's "two conceptions of psychoanalysis: as submission to the physician's rational authority and as a project of liberation" (p. 149). The aim of detaching from the old love object according to Freud is for the patient "to gain free command over a function which is of such inestimable importance to her" (p. 150). Ironically, submission to authority may in itself inflame erotic experience, creating the very conditions Freud needed to subdue. "Freud tells us, 'She has to learn from him to overcome the pleasure principle . . . to achieve this overcoming of herself [learn self control] to acquire that extra piece of mental freedom. . . .'" (p. 170, cited in Benjamin 1995, p. 153). In essence his contradictory message to the female patient would be "submit to be free"! Thus the resolution of the erotic transference consists in the patient's identification, in a state of docility, with the self-mastering analyst. Rather than loving him as an object she must move from love to identification with him.

This notion, of being able to renounce an object tie through identification, has had far-reaching influence as a pillar of psychoanalytic thinking. Both the resolution of the Oedipus complex and the capacity to detach libido from a lost object have relied conceptually on identification as fulcrum. My own clinical experience with children in treatment who have lost a parent through death or divorce has taught me (Tessman 1978) that the libidinal investment in the object tie persists, that identifications cohabit with an inner mental representation of the lost object, albeit often unconscious, which continues to fuel a quest symbolic of re-engagement with the wanted absent person in the external world. In long-held psychoanalytic paradigms for the resolution of the transference at termination, internalization of the analytic attitude is attained through identification with the analyst, becoming the basis for the development of the valuable self-analytic function. I would contend that if one assumes that the desired fate of transference love, when renounced, is limited to identification, one must ignore the generative possibilities of the remembered, though ever-changing love for the analyst, internalized in mental representations of dyadic attunement, and mediated by a sense of knowing and being deeply known as oneself, hypothetically a different route to the self-analytic function. Analysts' individual preferences in stressing either the self-generated or the relational sources of mutative internalizations accompanying conflict amelioration are on a continuum, but a solid body of theory rests on the premise that the quality of the relationship with the analyst, as with others, is intrapsychically active in influential ways. Strachey in 1934 already introduced the analyst as a new and kinder superego figure. Balint (1968) viewed constructive regression in analysis as dependent on "an interaction between the particular patient and the particular analyst, that is, a phenomenon belonging to the field of two-person psychology" (p. 156). He believed that a "crucial influence on the treatment" may stem from "whether the analyst interprets any particular phenomenon as a demand for gratification or as a need for a particular form of object relationship," and located the technical problems of differentially diagnosing this as belonging "to the borderland between one-person and two-person psychologies" (p. 162). Modell (1984) highlighted the complementarity of one-person and two-person psychologies in psychoanalysis, as both systems of thought are essential to each other (p. 21).

This brings us to the topic of old and new flames. In arguing against the "genuineness of this [transference] love" Freud (1915) contends that "it exhibits not a single new feature arising from the present situation, but is entirely composed of repetitions and copies of earlier reactions, including infantile ones" (p. 167). In contemporary times, the analyst is more often conceptualized as both an old and a new object and it is taken for granted that a complicated (though nonsymmetrical) engagement of both members of the analytic dyad is required for an analysis to deepen productively. Gill (1984) ventured that "the notion of an 'uncontaminated' transference is a myth because the expression of the transference is always influenced by the here-and-now interaction between the analyst and patient" (p. 164). Contained countertransference experience (as broadly rather than narrowly defined), may be looked to as the inner register for the analyst's self-analytic inquiry, to be honed for whatever spontaneous responsiveness to the patient is deemed to be optimal (Jacobs 1991, Renik 1993). We now more often think of the yield of the psychoanalytic process as a profound reordering of the inner experience of self and others than as a progressive lifting of repression. Such reordering of inner experience is generated in the affective oscillations between the repetition of the unconscious organization of the past which has formed anticipations of the present, and the novel, surprising interchange with the analyst (Loewald 1975) who becomes a new rather than old flame. As distorted, transference-based perceptions stemming from the past diminish in the framework of encountering a new object (the analyst), one may experience new love. In this context, the aim of abstinence can be viewed as not in the service of lifting repression, but rather to aid the clear transference emergence of the old object, with whom the psychic relationship becomes retransfigured as novel interactionist possibilities are experienced with the analyst. There are lively differences of opinion regarding the relative contribution to inner change attributed to insight derived from interpretation versus the experiential aspects of the transference.

In a contemporary perspective, one would of course also question the place of authority and compliance within the analytic dyad in lieu of more collaborative paradigms. We attempt to guard against the patient's acceptance of an interpretive intervention out of compliance rather than inner conviction.

Yet in spite of those autocratic leanings in Freud which infused his advice about technique, his observations that women are particularly prone to experiencing transference love seem to have stood the test of time. From the vantage of the "point of view" of the woman patient to which Freud alluded, what might account for her proneness to experiencing transference love?

Person (1985) noted that, empirically, "women patients, more than men, have a greater propensity to exhibit overt and sustained expressions of the erotic transference toward the analyst, whether male or female, and to experience the erotic transference as such" (p. 166). Person posits that "the erotic transference utilized as resistance is more common among women, while resistance to the awareness of the erotic transference is more common among male patients" (p. 160). She traces the difference to a confluence of social and developmental determinants: "In women, the preoccupation with pair-bonding, both establishing and preserving it, has social determinants that are self-evident" (pp. 174–175), and "the female preoccupation with pair-bonding may be best understood in the context of the female oedipal constellation," involving the father as primary libidinal object, while her erotic rival, the mother, is also a source of dependent gratification, leading "the girl to experience dread of loss of love, a fear that is displaced from mother onto all subsequent love objects." In this context, she views erotic longing as "compensatory against the fear of loss of love" (p. 175).

I fully concur with Person about the centrality of pair-bonding as well as the clinically greater prevalence of manifest transference love in women in analysis (with both male and female analysts), but I want to extend the developmental reach of gender further, to infancy. Certain female propensities which make themselves known from earliest infancy on may favor the development of particular libidinal and defensive configurations. Observed infant gender differences have to do with the average degree of openness to, rather than self-protectiveness from, affect contagion in a context of attending to relational interests. For example, beginning at one to three days, infant girls appear to be more intensely involved in the "gazing dialogue" with their caretakers than boy, while boys exceed in use of "gaze aversion" when looked at by the caretaker (Hittleman and Dickes 1979). Gender differences in seeking and maintaining eye contact versus gaze aversion continue through the first weeks of life, through childhood to adulthood (Haviland and Maletesta 1981). One need not, indeed cannot conclude that such differences occur on a "genetic" basis, for the less mature state of myelination, on average, for boys at birth may require greater initial protection from arousal. Newborn girls (mean ages 66 to 72 hours old) are more apt to cry in response to another infant's cry than newborn boys, the "mean cry duration" is longer, and the autonomic level of arousal is correlated with the likelihood of crying (Sagi and Hoffman 1976, Simner 1971). Other studies, for example with regard to early interest in social stimulation, affect matching, and so on, not cited here, suggest similar differences. The responsiveness-to-affect contagion has physiologic correlates, affecting the earliest schemata of attunement in body experience. Silverman (1987) has suggested that "the female infant has more awareness of her mother's inner need states than does the male. Thus her mother's various feeling states may be dimly experienced by the female infant, setting into motion her reactivity." Other data (Weinberg 1992) have led me to speculate that an internalized representation of the affectively connected dyad may, on the average, happen earlier with girls than boys, and become key to generating the girl's initial orientation to others. This interpretation of early differences has different implications than attributing the girl's well-known interest in relatedness either to socialization (which may cement the pattern) or to incomplete differentiation from the mother, reactive to the mother's clinging to a symbiotic tie. The point I make is that very early proclivities in seeking out an affectively responsive dialogue with another are demonstrated by little girls, for example by choosing to maximize the gazing dialogue. The implication is that this urge is propelled by the affects belonging to libidinal connection, a value with high priority, rather than denoting deficiencies in differentiation. I do not mean that boys are less libidinally impelled, only that the pathways to experiencing may configure differently.

The girl's cathexis of these affects in turn may favor early internalization, or presymbolic mental representation (Beebe and Lachmann 1988) of the dyadic interaction. Later aspects of female experience, such as heterosexual desire, may become assimilated to the libidinal framework of these early gender propensities. In the analytic situation, as well, these predilections may make the female more prone to relate to the analyst through the sustained experience of erotic transference, which in turn may be more familiar to the female patient than to the male analyst. Cherishing the intrapsychic life of the analyst as person may be an intrinsic component. But as Gabbard (1994) notes, "For many analysts the experience of being loved intensely may be far more disconcerting than being lusted after sexually" (p. 402). The question remains as to what can make the affective intensity bearable enough to both patient and analyst to allow for its elaboration in ways that are most useful to the analysis.

Freud already conceived of a playful transitional space in analysis, a concept later deepened and elaborated by Winnicott and others. He speaks of the transference as creating "an intermediate region between illness and real life through which the transition from the one to the other is made" (1914, p. 154). It is portrayed as "a region for play, a locale for transforming acting out into memory . . . The main instrument, however, for curbing the patient's compulsion to repeat and for turning it into a motive for remembering lies in the handling of the transference. We render the compulsion harmless, and indeed useful, by giving it the right to assert itself in a definite field. We admit it into the transference as a playground in which it is allowed to expand in almost complete freedom and in which it is expected to display to us everything in the way of pathogenic instincts that is hidden in the patient's mind" (p. 154). The analyst's role is depicted as consequential, but only in the service of bringing the pathology to light.

The analytic transitional space is now more often acknowledged as having value to both analyst and patient in their interaction. Loewald (1975), who spoke of "patient and analyst as co-authors of the play," notes that the impact of the play "depends on its being experienced both as actuality and as a fantasy creation. This Janus-face quality is an important ingredient of the analyst's experience in the analytic situation and becomes, if things go well, an important element in the patient's experience" (p. 355). The patient is enabled to experience the transference as fantasy when it is ameliorated by the actuality of the relationship with the analyst. Transference reenactments acquire the character of fantasy play when the present actuality becomes clearly distinguishable from the past actuality. If the analyst reacts to the patient's expressed longing as though it were an actual demand there will be a collapse of analytic space for both. Wilkinson and Gabbard (1995) offer the concept of "romantic space" for "understanding enduring love." Analogous to Winnicott's "transitional space,"

> romantic space is mapped out in the intermediate area between the lover and the beloved, unchallenged with respect to its belonging to inner or external (shared) reality. It is both an intrapsychic and interpersonal experience evolving between the lover and the beloved that involves the paradoxical coexistence of depressive and paranoid-schizoid modes of relatedness within each partner. . . . The interplay between these two modes of experience allows the lover and the beloved to offer each other a relatedness that is reassuringly familiar as well as abruptly fresh. Inflexibility in either partner leads to pathology of romantic space characterized by rigid adherence to the mode of relatedness. [p. 201]

Although, as Freud realized, it is crucial for the analyst to know and convey that transference love cannot be either reciprocal, romantic, or enduring, rigid adherence to particular modes of relatedness can constrict the analytic experience when the subtle power of affective interplay between the two characters is not considered. The relationship to the analyst is simultaneously a refinding and a new object relationship, and the complexities of the "new" must not be dismissed as belonging to paternal transference.

Formulations about the source and fates of the transference have changed considerably over the past few decades. Pfeffer (1959, 1961, 1963, 1991) has reported in follow-up studies after the termination of analysis, that "satisfactorily analyzed patients experienced brief, transient, but vivid recurrences of the analytic transference neurosis, including the symptoms for which analysis was first sought" (1963). He observed the persistence of a double psychic representation of the analyst: a memory of the analyst around whom is organized the transference neurosis and, in addition, a memory of the analyst around whom remains organized the resolution of that transference neurosis (1991). "In new or difficult life situations, a low intensity of the transference neurosis as well as its resolution are displaced from the analyst onto the current actual situation leading to better adaptation" (1993, pp. 335–336). The criterion of resolution of the transference as a sign for successful or completed analysis has given way over time to an acknowledgment that wishes in the transference do not get "resolved," but transformed in a variety of ways, usually with an amelioration of earlier idealizations and transference love.

Renik (1995) speaks of "the idealization of the analyst in which the patient is encouraged to participate" when there is reluctance to acknowledge the analyst's interpretive fallibility, and emphasizes the ways in which the analyst's attempts to avoid self-disclosure contribute to a myth of ideal anonymity. Freud encouraged patriarchal idealization of the analyst, but in practice he was not averse to self-disclosures which conveyed his preferred and expected paradigms for transference to his patients. The poet H. D., who was profoundly helped by her psychoanalysis with Freud (1933), reported in her journal:

> I did not know what enraged him suddenly. [p. 14] The Professor . . . is beating with his hand, his fist, on the head piece of the old fashioned horsehair sofa. . . . Consciously I was not aware of having said anything that might account for the Professor's outburst. And even as I veered around, facing him, my mind was detached enough to wonder if this was some idea of his for speeding up the analytic content or redirecting the flow of associated images. The Professor said, "The trouble is— I am an old man—and you do not think it worth your while to love me."! [pp. 15–16]

Freud chose to represent himself to H. D. as abhorring maternal aspects of the analyst's role. She recalls:

> He had said "And—I must tell you (you were frank with me and I will be frank with you), I do not like to be the mother in transference—it always surprises and shocks me a little. I feel so very masculine." I asked him if others had what he called this mother-transference on him. He said ironically and I thought a little wistfully "Oh, very many." [p. xxxvii]

Freud does advise us that "to urge the patient to suppress, renounce or sublimate her instincts . . . would be not an analytic way of dealing with them, but a senseless one. It would be just as though, after summoning up a spirit from the underworld by cunning spells, one were to send him down again without having asked him a single question" (1915, p. 164). Surely then, it is fitting that when we summon up the spirit of Freud as participant-observer in the profound insights that led to the discovery of transference, that we have raised questions. Freud aspired that "where id was, there ego shall be" (1933, p. 80). We might respond that where fires flame, there fireplace might contain.

And what might develop in the analytic fire-space? For some time I have contended (Tessman 1978, 1982, 1989a,b) that the goal of transformation of libidinal impulse into sublimated aim (where id was there ego shall be) is misguided, as sublimation is predicated on the underlying drive connection becoming unconscious, and the energy "neutralized." For women, such a goal favors a detachment from bodily desires, associated with a loss of pleasure in bodily sensations of both interiority and prowess, and with self-devaluation in regard to loving freely in womanly ways. In recent Western cultural contexts we have seen a diminution of such detachment on the one hand, as women attempt to transcend earlier stereotypes of femininity, such as women developing pleasure in their use of their bodies in athletic skills without having to view their prowess as "male." On the other hand, the alarming prevalence of eating disorders, with their associated loathing of the body as it is, signifies considerable conflict.

It seems to me now that the problem with the ideal of sublimation is this: within the analytic dyad, the compulsion to transform erotic into "aim inhibited wishes" (as Freud advises) stems from a particular confusion. Psychic representations of male and female genitals and their much fantasized interplay are developmentally early, though ever-changing organizers in how the child makes sense of relating her sensual and affective experience to the people to whom she is emotionally attached. Such organizers become unconscious not only because of those forces of socialization which are invoked to tame the intensity of taboo sexual wishes, but also because the burgeoning complexity of affective interchange with meaningful intimates makes these early representations inadequate to the task. If erotic desires and their symbolizations toward the analyst in the analysis are "sublimated" into "higher forms," that is, if passion is replaced by "reason," the passions have been both overvalued and undervalued. Overvalued, or over-feared as though the cry of fire were the actual endangering conflagration, and undervalued as a potential crucible for the re-ordering of the inner experience of self and others that occurs in productive analyses. As Loewald (1988) has noted, the symbol and the symbolized mutually enrich and reciprocally transform each other. He points out that the snake cannot be reduced to simply mean the penis, for once so symbolized both are transformed forever in psychic life.

In past work (Tessman 1989a) I have alluded to some developmental functions of the particular dialogue of affects between fathers and daughters. When the daughter's erotic desires and their associated affects are not disquieting to the father in ways that might lead him to control or trivialize them, and are also not overstimulated by him, then a tender engagement between them fosters her motivation for conceiving ideas. I considered the role of heightened affects in generating symbol formation which imbues memorability with shape; and the place of shared symbolization, in turn, as transitional phenomena which lead to new vistas of experience, a view of horizons beyond the substantive land (and body) of the transitional object. In moving from the need for the transitional object as body, and toward symbolic richness imbued with affect, the father can have a catalytic role because he is simultaneously object of desire and model in the transformation of erotic excitement. In the transference, the resurgence of intense erotic wishes toward the analyst opens the possibility for reworking of bodily metaphors insofar as they have remained a source of pathologic self-organizing assumptions, transcending whatever early fixed associations between gender and function, object and aim may be constricting current experience. In such reworking, the difficult task of the analyst is to light the passage from old flame to new, but not to carry a torch.

In the analytic space, the function of the analysand's free affective interchange in play with her analyst is not just to tolerate her fantasies in lieu of action (that is, "I wish to make love with my analyst even though I know we will never do that"), but also to broaden the range of a generative affective and ideational interchange which is possible in a strong and flexibly boundaried emotional closeness. "That extra piece of mental freedom" (Freud 1915, p. 170), so rightly prized by Freud, may spring from the richness of emotional interplay that is not yet possible for the child when first the genitals become such important and conflicted symbols of man and woman. This may require that the analyst also acquire "that extra piece of mental freedom" in order to create and protect the kind of analytic space—a matter of fireplace—in which sexual desire may continue to fuel as unfettered an exploration of humanness in the analytic experience a possible. If Freud could have had the good fortune of experiencing transference love toward an analyst capable of engaging his infinite curiosity, with its finely textured and courageous proclivity for self-observation, and then could wrestle with his own penchant for first passionately idealizing and then renouncing (and denouncing) his mentors, confronting the affective interchange which such wrestling would evoke, might he have wanted to recognize "the dark continent" as his symbolic attribution to women of what he tended to disavow in himself, such as his feminine identifications and irrational passions? We know not.

Freud (1933) acknowledged his limited exploration of "femininity" and added, "It is certainly incomplete . . . and does not always sound friendly. But do not forget that I have only been describing women in so far as their nature is determined by their sexual function. It is true that that influence extends very far; but we do not overlook the fact that an individual woman may be a human being in other respects as well. If you want to know more about femininity, . . . inquire from your own experience of life . . . or turn to the poets . . ." (p. 135). Freud's "turn to the poets" reveals another access in him, to that "extra piece of mental freedom"—perhaps the hopeful reach beyond rationality which moves poetry critic Helen Vendler to say (1995): "Poetry, by its concision and free play, can represent better than most prose the fluid access of a daring and unhampered mind to its own several regions."

REFERENCES

Balint, M. (1968). *The Basic Fault: Therapeutic Aspects of Regression*. London: Tavistock.

Beebe, B., and Lachmann, F. (1988). The contribution of mother–infant mutual influence to the origins of self- and object representations. *Psychoanalytic Psychology* 5(4):305–337.

Benjamin, J. (1995). *Like Subjects, Love Objects: Essays on Recognition and Sexual Difference*. New Haven, CT: Yale University Press.

Freud, S. (1914). Remembering, repeating and working through. *Standard Edition* 12:147–156.

——— (1915). Observations on transference-love. *Standard Edition* 12:159–171.

——— (1931). Female sexuality. *Standard Edition* 21:223–243.

——— (1933). Femininity. In New introductory lectures on psychoanalysis. *Standard Edition* 22:112–135.

Gabbard, G. O. (1994). On love and lust in erotic transference. *Journal of the American Psychoanalytic Association* 42:385–405.

Gill, M. (1984). Psychoanalysis and psychotherapy: a revision. *International Review of Psycho-Analysis* 11:161–179.

Haviland, J. M., and Malatesta, C. Z. (1981). The development of sex differences in nonverbal signals: fallacies, facts and fantasies. In *Gender and Non-Verbal Behavior*, ed. C. Mayo and N. Henly, pp. 183–208. Heidelberg, Germany; New York: Springer-Verlag.

Hittelman, J. H., and Dickes, R. (1979). Sex differences in neonatal eye contact time. *Palmer Quarterly* 25:171–184.

H. D. [Hilda Doolittle] (1933). *Tribute to Freud: Writing on the Wall*. Boston: Godine, 1956.

Jacobs, T. (1991). *The Use of the Self: Countertransference and Communication in the Analytic Situation*. Madison, CT: International Universities Press.

Loewald, H. W. (1975). Psychoanalysis as an art and the fantasy character of the psychoanalytic situation. In *Papers on Psychoanalysis*, pp. 352–371. New Haven, CT: Yale University Press, 1980.

——— (1988). *Sublimation*. New Haven, CT: Yale University Press.

Modell, A. H. (1984). *Psychoanalysis in a New Context*. New York: International Universities Press.

Person, E. S. (1985). The erotic transference in women and in men: differences and consequences. *Journal of the American Academy for Psychoanalysis* 13:159–180.

Pfeffer, A. Z. (1959). A procedure for evaluating the results of psychoanalysis: a preliminary report. *Journal of the American Psychoanalytic Association* 7:418–444.

——— (1961). Follow-up study of a satisfactory analysis. *Journal of the American Psychoanalytic Association* 9:698–718.

——— (1963). The meaning of the analyst after analysis. *Journal of the American Psychoanalytic Association* 11:229–244.

——— (1991). *After the analysis, analyst as both old and new object*. Paper presented at the meeting of the American Psychoanalytic Association, New Orleans, LA, May.

Renik, O. (1993). Analytic interaction: conceptualizing technique in light of the analyst's irreducible subjectivity. *Psychoanalytic Quarterly* 62:553–571.

——— (1995). The ideal of the anonymous analyst and the problem of self-disclosure. *Psychoanalytic Quarterly* 64:466–495.

Sagi, A., and Hoffman, M. L. (1976). Empathic distress in the newborn. *Developmental Psychology* 12:175–176.

Silverman, D. (1987). Female bonding: some supportive findings for Melanie Klein's views. *Psychoanalytic Review* 74(2):201–215.

Simner, M. L. (1971). Newborn's response to the cry of another infant. *Developmental Psychology* 5:136–150.

Strachey, J. (1934). The nature of the therapeutic action of psychoanalysis. *International Journal of Psycho-Analysis* 15:127–159.

Tessman, L. H. (1978). *Children of Parting Parents*. New York: Jason Aronson.

——— (1982). A note on the father's contribution to the daughter's ways of loving and working. In *Father and Child: Developmental and Clinical Perspectives*, ed. S. Cath, A. Gurwitt, and J. M. Ross, pp. 197–223. Boston: Little, Brown.

——— (1989a). *Conceptions and contraceptions in a dialogue of affects between father and daughter*. Paper presented at the meeting of the American Psychoanalytic Association, San Francisco, May.

——— (1989b). Fathers and daughters: early tones, later echoes. In *Fathers and Their Families*, ed. S. Cath, A. Gurwitt, and L. Gunsberg, pp. 219–238. Hillsdale, NJ: Analytic Press.

Vendler, H. (1995). *Soul Says: On Recent Poetry*. Cambridge, MA: Belknap Press/ Harvard University Press.

Weinberg, K. (1992). Boys and Girls: Sex Differences in Emotional Expressivity and Self-Regulation during Early Infancy. Paper presented at the symposium on Early Emotional Self-Regulation: New Approaches to Understanding Developmental Change and Individual Differences, International Conference on Infant Studies, Miami, May.

Wilkinson, S. M., and Gabbard, G. (1995). On romantic space. *Psychoanalytic Psychology* 12:201–219.

Observations on Transference-Love: (Further Recommendations on the Technique of Psycho-Analysis III) *

SIGMUND FREUD

Every beginner in Psycho-Analysis probably feels alarmed at first at the difficulties in store for him when he comes to interpret the patient's associations and to deal with the reproduction of the repressed. When the time comes, however, he soon learns to look upon these difficulties as insignificant, and instead becomes convinced that the only really serious difficulties he has to meet lie in the management of the transference.

Among the situations which arise in this connection I shall select one which is very sharply circumscribed; and I shall select it, partly because it occurs so often and is so important in its real aspects and partly because of its theoretical interest. What I have in mind is the case in which a woman patient shows by unmistakable indications, or openly declares, that she has fallen in love, as any other mortal woman might, with the doctor who is analysing her. This situation has its distressing and comical aspects, as well as its serious ones. It is also determined by so many and such complicated factors, it is so unavoidable and so difficult to clear up, that a discussion of it to meet a vital need of analytic technique has long been overdue. But since we who laugh at other people's failings are not always free from them

---

*The present translation, with a changed title, is a modified version of the one published in 1924.

ourselves, we have not so far been precisely in a hurry to fulfill this task. We are constantly coming up against the obligation to professional discretion—a discretion which cannot be dispensed with in real life, but which is of no service in our science. In so far as Psycho-Analytic publications are a part of real life, too, we have here an insoluble contradiction. I have recently disregarded this matter of discretion at one point,[1] and shown how this same transference situation held back the development of Psycho-Analytic therapy during its first decade.

To a well-educated layman (for that is what the ideal civilized person is in regard to Psycho-Analysis) things that have to do with love are incommensurable with everything else; they are, as it were, written on a special page on which no other writing is tolerated. If a woman patient has fallen in love with her doctor it seems to such a layman that only two outcomes are possible. One, which happens comparatively rarely, is that all the circumstances allow of a permanent legal union between them; the other, which is more frequent, is that the doctor and the patient part and give up the work they have begun which was to have led to her recovery, as though it had been interrupted by some elemental phenomenon. There is, to be sure, a third conceivable outcome, which even seems compatible with a continuation of the treatment. This is that they should enter into a love-relationship which is illicit and which is not intended to last for ever. But such a course is made impossible by conventional morality and professional standards. Nevertheless, our layman will beg the analyst to reassure him as unambiguously as possible that this third alternative is excluded.

It is clear that a Psycho-Analyst must look at things from a different point of view.

Let us take the case of the second outcome of the situation we are considering. After the patient has fallen in love with her doctor, they part; the treatment is given up. But soon the patient's condition necessitates her making a second attempt at analysis, with another doctor. The next thing that happens is that she feels she has fallen in love with this second doctor too; and if she breaks off with him and begins yet again, the same thing will happen with the third doctor, and so on. This phenomenon, which occurs without fail and which is, as we know, one of the foundations of

---

[1] In the first section of my contribution to the history of the psychoanalytic movement (1914). [This refers to Breuer's difficulties over the transference in the case of Anna O. (*Standard Edition* 14:12).]

the Psycho-Analytic theory, may be evaluated from two points of view, that of the doctor who is carrying out the analysis and that of the patient who is in need of it.

For the doctor the phenomenon signifies a valuable piece of enlightenment and a useful warning against any tendency to a counter-transference which may be present in his own mind.[2] He must recognize that the patient's falling in love is induced by the analytic situation and is not to be attributed to the charms of his own person; so that he has no grounds whatever for being proud of such a "conquest," as it would be called outside analysis. And it is always well to be reminded of this. For the patient, however, there are two alternatives: either she must relinquish Psycho-Analytic treatment or she must accept falling in love with her doctor as an inescapable fate.[3]

I have no doubt that the patient's relatives and friends will decide as emphatically for the first of these two alternatives as the analyst will for the second. But I think that here is a case in which the decision cannot be left to the tender—or rather, the egoistic and jealous—concern of her relatives. The welfare of the patient alone should be the touchstone; her relatives' love cannot cure her neurosis. The analyst need not push himself forward, but he may insist that he is indispensable for the achievement of certain ends. Any relative who adopts Tolstoy's attitude to this problem can remain in undisturbed possession of his wife or daughter; but he will have to try to put up with the fact that she, for her part, retains her neurosis and the interference with her capacity for love which it involves. The situation, after all, is similar to that in a gynaecological treatment. Moreover, the jealous father or husband is greatly mistaken if he thinks that the patient will escape falling in love with her doctor if he hands her over to some kind of treatment other than analysis for combating her neurosis. The difference, on the contrary, will only be that a love of this kind, which is bound to remain unexpressed and unanalysed, can never make the contribution to the patient's recovery which analysis would have extracted from it.

---

[2] [The question of the "countertransference" had already been raised by Freud in his Nuremberg Congress paper (1910), *Standard Edition* 11:144–145. He returns to it below. Apart from these passages, it is hard to find any other explicit discussions of the subject in Freud's published works.]

[3] We know that the transference can manifest itself in other, less tender feelings, but I do not propose to go into that side of the matter here. [See the paper on "The Dynamics of Transference" (1912).]

It has come to my knowledge that some doctors who practise analysis frequently[4] prepare their patients for the emergence of the erotic transference or even urge them to "go ahead and fall in love with the doctor so that the treatment may make progress." I can hardly imagine a more senseless proceeding. In doing so, an analyst robs the phenomenon of the element of spontaneity which is so convincing and lays up obstacles for himself in the future which are hard to overcome.[5]

At a first glance it certainly does not look as if the patient's falling in love in the transference could result in any advantage to the treatment. No matter how amenable she has been up till then, she suddenly loses all understanding of the treatment and all interest in it, and will not speak or hear about anything but her love, which she demands to have returned. She gives up her symptoms or pays no attention to them; indeed, she declares that she is well. There is a complete change of scene; it is as though some piece of make-believe had been stopped by the sudden irruption of reality—as when, for instance, a cry of fire is raised during a theatrical performance. No doctor who experiences this for the first time will find it easy to retain his grasp on the analytic situation and to keep clear of the illusion that the treatment is really at an end.

A little reflection enables one to find one's bearings. First and foremost, one keeps in mind the suspicion that anything that interferes with the continuation of the treatment may be an expression of resistance.[6] There can be no doubt that the outbreak of a passionate demand for love is largely the work of resistance. One will have long since noticed in the patient the signs of an affectionate transference, and one will have been able to feel certain that her docility, her acceptance of the analytic explanations, her remarkable comprehension and the high degree of intelligence she showed were to be attributed to this attitude towards her doctor. Now all this is swept away. She has become quite without insight and seems to be swallowed up in her love. Moreover, this change quite regularly occurs precisely at a point of time when one is having to try to bring her to admit or remember some particularly distressing and heavily repressed piece of her

---

[4] ["*Häufig.*" In the first edition only, the word here is "*frühzeitig*" ("early").]
[5] [In the first edition only, this paragraph (which is in the nature of a parenthesis) was printed in small type.]
[6] [Freud had already stated this still more categorically in the first edition of "The Interpretation of Dreams" (1900), *Standard Edition* 5:517. But in 1925 he added a long footnote to the passage, explaining its sense and qualifying the terms in which he had expressed himself.]

life-history. She has been in love, therefore, for a long time; but now the resistance is beginning to make use of her love in order to hinder the continuation of the treatment, to deflect all her interest from the work and to put the analyst in an awkward position.

If one looks into the situation more closely one recognizes the influence of motives which further complicate things—of which some are connected with being in love and others are particular expressions of resistance. Of the first kind are the patient's endeavour to assure herself of her irresistibility, to destroy the doctor's authority by bringing him down to the level of a lover and to gain all the other promised advantages incidental to the satisfaction of love. As regards the resistance, we may suspect that on occasion it makes use of a declaration of love on the patient's part as a means of putting her analyst's severity to the test, so that, if he should show signs of compliance, he may expect to be taken to task for it. But above all, one gets an impression that the resistance is acting as an *agent provocateur*; it heightens the patient's state of being in love and exaggerates her readiness for sexual surrender in order to justify the workings of repression all the more emphatically, by pointing to the dangers of such licentiousness. All these accessory motives, which in simpler cases may not be present, have, as we know, been regarded by Adler as the essential part of the whole process.

But how is the analyst to behave in order not to come to grief over this situation, supposing he is convinced that the treatment should be carried on in spite of this erotic transference and should take it in its stride?

It would be easy for me to lay stress on the universally accepted standards of morality and to insist that the analyst must never under any circumstances accept or return the tender feelings that are offered him: that, instead, he must consider that the time has come for him to put before the woman who is in love with him the demands of social morality and the necessity for renunciation, and to succeed in making her give up her desires, and, having surmounted the animal side of herself, go on with the work of analysis.

I shall not, however, fulfil these expectations—neither the first nor the second of them. Not the first, because I am writing not for patients but for doctors who have serious difficulties to contend with, and also because in this instance I am able to trace the moral prescription back to its source, namely to expediency. I am on this occasion in the happy position of being able to replace the moral embargo by considerations of analytic technique, without any alteration in the outcome.

Even more decidedly, however, do I decline to fulfill the second of the expectations I have mentioned. To urge the patient to suppress, renounce, or sublimate her instincts the moment she has admitted her erotic transference would be, not an analytic way of dealing with them, but a senseless one. It would be just as though, after summoning up a spirit from the underworld by cunning spells, one were to send him down again without having asked him a single question. One would have brought the repressed into consciousness, only to repress it once more in a fright. Nor should we deceive ourselves about the success of any such proceeding. As we know, the passions are little affected by sublime speeches. The patient will feel only the humiliation, and she will not fail to take her revenge for it.

Just as little can I advocate a middle course, which would recommend itself to some people as being specially ingenious. This would consist in declaring that one returns the patient's fond feelings but at the same time in avoiding any physical implementation of this fondness until one is able to guide the relationship into calmer channels and raise it to a higher level. My objection to this expedient is that Psycho-Analytic treatment is founded on truthfulness. In this fact lies a great part of its educative effect and its ethical value. It is dangerous to depart from this foundation. Anyone who has become saturated in the analytic technique will no longer be able to make use of the lies and pretences which a doctor normally finds unavoidable; and if, with the best intentions, he does attempt to do so, he is very likely to betray himself. Since we demand strict truthfulness from our patients, we jeopardize our whole authority if we let ourselves be caught out by them in a departure from the truth. Besides, the experiment of letting oneself go a little way in tender feelings for the patient is not altogether without danger. Our control over ourselves is not so complete that we may not suddenly one day go further than we had intended. In my opinion, therefore, we ought not to give up the neutrality towards the patient, which we have acquired through keeping the counter-transference in check.

I have already let it be understood that analytic technique requires of the physician that he should deny to the patient who is craving for love the satisfaction she demands. The treatment must be carried out in abstinence. By this I do not mean physical abstinence alone, nor yet the deprivation of everything that the patient desires, for perhaps no sick person could tolerate this. Instead, I shall state it as a fundamental principle that the patient's need and longing should be allowed to persist in her, in order that they may serve as forces impelling her to do work and to make changes, and that we must beware of appeasing those forces by means of surrogates. And what we could offer would never be anything else than a surrogate, for the patient's condition is such that, until her repressions are removed, she is incapable of getting real satisfaction.

Let us admit that this fundamental principle of the treatment being carried out in abstinence extends far beyond the single case we are considering here, and that it needs to be thoroughly discussed in order that we may define the limits of its possible application.[7] We will not enter into this now, however, but will keep as close as possible to the situation from which we started out. What would happen if the doctor were to behave differently and, supposing both parties were free, if he were to avail himself of that freedom in order to return the patient's love and to still her need for affection?

If he has been guided by the calculation that this compliance on his part will ensure his domination over his patient and thus enable him to influence her to perform the tasks required by the treatment, and in this way to liberate herself permanently from her neurosis—then experience would inevitably show him that his calculation was wrong. The patient would achieve *her* aim, but he would never achieve *his*. What would happen to the doctor and the patient would only be what happened, according to the amusing anecdote, to the pastor and the insurance agent. The insurance agent, a free-thinker, lay at the point of death and his relatives insisted on bringing in a man of God to convert him before he died. The interview lasted so long that those who were waiting outside began to have hopes. At last the door of the sick-chamber opened. The free-thinker had not been converted; but the pastor went away insured.

If the patient's advances were returned it would be a great triumph for her, but a complete defeat for the treatment. She would have succeeded in what all patients strive for in analysis—she would have succeeded in acting out, in repeating in real life what she ought only to have remembered, to have reproduced as psychical material, and to have kept within the sphere of psychical events. In the further course of the love-relationship she would bring out all the inhibitions and pathological reactions of her erotic life, without there being any possibility of correcting them; and the distressing episode would end in remorse and a great strengthening of

---

[7][Freud took this subject up again in his Budapest Congress paper (1919), *Standard Edition* 17:162–163.]

her propensity to repression. The love-relationship in fact destroys the patient's susceptibility to influence from analytic treatment. A combination of the two would be an impossibility.

It is, therefore, just as disastrous for the analysis if the patient's craving for love is gratified as if it is suppressed. The course the analyst must pursue is neither of these; it is one for which there is no model in real life. He must take care not to steer away from the transference-love, or to repulse it or to make it distasteful to the patient; but he must just as resolutely withhold any response to it. He must keep firm hold of the transference-love, but treat it as something unreal, as a situation which has to be gone through in the treatment and traced back to its unconscious origins and which must assist in bringing all that is most deeply hidden in the patient's erotic life into her consciousness and therefore under her control. The more plainly the analyst lets it be seen that he is proof against every temptation, the more readily will he be able to extract from the situation its analytic content. The patient, whose sexual repression is of course not yet removed but merely pushed into the background, will then feel safe enough to allow all her preconditions for loving, all the phantasies springing from her sexual desires, all the detailed characteristics of her state of being in love, to come to light; and from these she will herself open the way to the infantile roots of her love.

There is, it is true, one class of women with whom this attempt to preserve the erotic transference for the purposes of analytic work without satisfying it will not succeed. These are women of elemental passionateness who tolerate no surrogates. They are children of nature who refuse to accept the psychical in place of the material, who, in the poet's words, are accessible only to "the logic of soup, with dumplings for arguments." With such people one has the choice between returning their love or else bringing down upon oneself the full enmity of a woman scorned. In neither case can one safeguard the interests of the treatment. One has to withdraw, unsuccessful; and all one can do is to turn the problem over in one's mind of how it is that a capacity for neurosis is joined with such an intractable need for love.

Many analysts will no doubt be agreed on the method by which other women, who are less violent in their love, can be gradually made to adopt the analytic attitude. What we do, above all, is to stress to the patient the unmistakable element of resistance in this "love." Genuine love, we say, would make her docile and intensify her readiness to solve the problems of her case, simply because the man she was in love with expected it of her. In such a case she would gladly choose the road to completion of the treatment, in order to acquire value in the doctor's eyes and to prepare herself for real life, where this feeling of love could find a proper place. Instead of this, we point out, she is showing a stubborn and rebellious spirit, she has thrown up all interest in her treatment, and clearly feels no respect for the doctor's well-founded convictions. She is thus bringing out a resistance under the guise of being in love with him; and in addition to this she has no compunction in placing him in a cleft stick. For if he refuses her love, as his duty and his understanding compel him to do, she can play the part of a woman scorned, and then withdraw from his therapeutic efforts out of revenge and resentment, exactly as she is now doing out of her ostensible love.

As a second argument against the genuineness of this love we advance the fact that it exhibits not a single new feature arising from the present situation, but is entirely composed of repetitions and copies of earlier reactions, including infantile ones. We undertake to prove this by a detailed analysis of the patient's behavior in love.

If the necessary amount of patience is added to these arguments, it is usually possible to overcome the difficult situation and to continue the work with a love which has been moderated or transformed; the work then aims at uncovering the patient's infantile object-choice and the phantasies woven round it.

I should now like, however, to examine these arguments with a critical eye and to raise the question whether, in putting them forward to the patient, we are really telling the truth, or whether we are not resorting in our desperation to concealments and misrepresentations. In other words: Can we truly say that the state of being in love which becomes manifest in analytic treatment is not a real one?

I think we have told the patient the truth, but not the whole truth regardless of the consequences. Of our two arguments the first is the stronger. The part played by resistance in transference-love is unquestionable and very considerable. Nevertheless the resistance did not, after all, *create* this love; it finds it ready to hand, makes use of it and aggravates its manifestations. Nor is the genuineness of the phenomenon disproved by the resistance. The second argument is far weaker. It is true that the love consists of new editions of old traits and that it repeats infantile reactions. But this is the essential character of every state of being in love. There is no such state which does not reproduce infantile prototypes. It is precisely from this infantile determination that it receives its compulsive character,

verging as it does on the pathological. Transference-love has perhaps a
degree less of freedom than the love which appears in ordinary life and is
called normal; it displays its dependence on the infantile pattern more clearly
and is less adaptable and capable of modification; but that is all, and not
what is essential.

By what other signs can the genuineness of a love be recognized? By
its efficacy, its serviceability in achieving the aim of love? In this respect
transference-love seems to be second to none; one has the impression that
one could obtain anything from it.

Let us sum up, therefore. We have no right to dispute that the state
of being in love which makes its appearance in the course of analytic treatment has the character of a "genuine" love. If it seems so lacking in normality, this is sufficiently explained by the fact that being in love in ordinary life, outside analysis, is also more similar to abnormal than to normal
mental phenomena. Nevertheless, transference-love is characterized by certain features which ensure it a special position. In the first place, it is provoked by the analytic situation; secondly, it is greatly intensified by the
resistance, which dominates the situation; and thirdly, it is lacking to a
high degree in a regard for reality, is less sensible, less concerned about
consequences and more blind in its valuation of the loved person than we
are prepared to admit in the case of normal love. We should not forget,
however, that these departures from the norm constitute precisely what is
essential about being in love.

As regards the analyst's line of action, it is the first of these three
features of transference-love which is the decisive factor. He has evoked
this love by instituting analytic treatment in order to cure the neurosis.
For him, it is an unavoidable consequence of a medical situation, like the
exposure of a patient's body or the imparting of a vital secret. It is therefore plain to him that he must not derive any personal advantage from it.
The patient's willingness makes no difference; it merely throws the whole
responsibility on the analyst himself. Indeed, as he must know, the patient
had been prepared for no other mechanism of cure. After all the difficulties have been successfully overcome, she will often confess to having had
an anticipatory phantasy at the time when she entered the treatment, to
the effect that if she behaved well she would be rewarded at the end by
the doctor's affection.

For the doctor, ethical motives unite with the technical ones, to re-
strain him from giving the patient his love. The aim he has to keep in view
is that this woman, whose capacity for love is impaired by infantile fixa-

tions, should gain free command over a function which is of such inestimable importance to her; that she should not, however, dissipate it in the
treatment, but keep it ready for the time when, after her treatment, the
demands of real life make themselves felt. He must not stage the scene of
a dog-race in which the prize was to be a garland of sausages but which
some humorist spoilt by throwing a single sausage on to the track. The
result was, of course, that the dogs threw themselves upon it and forgot all
about the race and about the garland that was luring them to victory in the
far distance. I do not mean to say that it is always easy for the doctor to
keep within the limits prescribed by ethics and technique. Those who are
still youngish and not yet bound by strong ties may in particular find it a
hard task. Sexual love is undoubtedly one of the chief things in life, and the
union of mental and bodily satisfaction in the enjoyment of love is one of
its culminating peaks. Apart from a few queer fanatics, all the world knows
this and conducts its life accordingly; science alone is too delicate to admit
it. Again, when a woman sues for love, to reject and refuse is a distressing
part for a man to play; and, in spite of neurosis and resistance, there is an
incomparable fascination in a woman of high principles who confesses her
passion. It is not a patient's crudely sensual desires which constitute the temptation. These are more likely to repel, and it will call for all the doctor's
tolerance if he is to regard them as a natural phenomenon. It is rather, perhaps, a woman's subtler and aim-inhibited wishes which bring with them
the danger of making a man forget his technique and his medical task for
the sake of a fine experience.

And yet it is quite out of the question for the analyst to give way.
However highly he may prize love he must prize even more highly the
opportunity for helping his patient over a decisive stage in her life. She
has to learn from him to overcome the pleasure principle, to give up a
satisfaction which lies at hand but is socially not acceptable, in favor of a
more distant one, which is perhaps altogether uncertain, but which is both
psychologically and socially unimpeachable. To achieve this overcoming, she
has to be led through the primal period of her mental development and on
that path she has to acquire the extra piece of mental freedom which distinguishes conscious mental activity—in the systematic sense—from unconscious.

The analytic psychotherapist thus has a threefold battle to wage—in his
own mind against the forces which seek to drag him down from the
analytic level; outside the analysis, against opponents who dispute the importance he attaches to the sexual instinctual forces and hinder him from

making use of them in his scientific technique; and inside the analysis, against his patients, who at first behave like opponents but later on reveal the overvaluation of sexual life which dominates them, and who try to make him captive to their socially untamed passion.

The lay public, about whose attitude to psychoanalysis I spoke at the outset, will doubtless seize upon this discussion of transference-love as another opportunity for directing the attention of the world to the serious danger of this therapeutic method. The psychoanalyst knows that he is working with highly explosive forces and that he needs to proceed with as much caution and conscientiousness as a chemist. But when have chemists ever been forbidden, because of the danger, from handling explosive substances, which are indispensable, on account of their effects? It is remarkable that Psycho-Analysis has to win for itself afresh all the liberties which have long since been accorded to other medical activities. I am certainly not in favour of giving up the harmless methods of treatment. For many cases they are sufficient, and, when all is said, human society has no more use for the *furor sanandi*[8] than for any other fanaticism. But to believe that the psychoneuroses are to be conquered by operating with harmless little remedies is grossly to under-estimate those disorders both as to their origin and their practical importance. No; in medical practice there will always be room for the *"ferrum"* and the *"ignis"* side by side with the *"medicina"*;[9] and in the same way we shall never be able to do without a strictly regular, undiluted Psycho-Analysis which is not afraid to handle the most dangerous mental impulses and to obtain mastery over them for the benefit of the patient.

---

[8] ["Passion for curing people."]
[9] [An allusion to a saying attributed to Hippocrates: "Those diseases which medicines do not cure, iron (the knife?) cures; those which iron cannot cure, fire cures; and those which fire cannot cure are to be reckoned wholly incurable." *Aphorisms* 7:87 (trans. 1849).]

3

KERRY KELLY NOVICK AND JACK NOVICK ON ANNA FREUD

Creativity and Compliance

KERRY KELLY NOVICK
AND JACK NOVICK

It is creative apperception more than anything else that makes the individual feel that life is worth living. Contrasted with this is a relationship to external reality which is one of compliance . . . .
—Winnicott 1971, p. 65

The International Psycho-Analytic Congress of 1971 was held in Vienna. It was the first time since World War II that Anna Freud and other pioneer luminaries of psychoanalysis had returned. Emotions were varied, but all intense. The topic was "Aggression," and Anna Freud was to give the plenary address. The great political issue of the Congress concerned the place of child analysis—lobbying and politicking were nonstop and feelings ran very high. A tragic note was sounded when Lothar Rubinstein, an analyst who had been a kindergarten pupil of Anna Freud's, suffered a sudden heart attack and died in the corridors of the Hofburg.

As a footnote to these great events of the psychoanalytic world, we were at the Congress to present the results of our study on beating fantasies in children. Anna Freud had cautioned us against presenting the paper, saying that the analysts would be "very negative" and it would be very hard for us. Only years later did we connect this with the fact that Anna Freud, at almost the same age as Kerry Novick was then, had presented her very first paper, in Vienna, on beating fantasies. She had been anxious in 1922 that she would be attacked and humiliated in response to "The Relation of Beating-Phantasies to a Day-Dream"; when she was sharply criticized by one person in the discussion, she was "shocked into silence" (Young-Bruehl 1988, p. 108) and then rescued by her father's intervention. The coincidence of topic, age, and setting turned our attention not only to the content of Anna Freud's paper, but also to its context.

A psychoanalytic paper invites us to read and think at many levels. This paper contains even more than usual, as we consider the manifest content, which traces the evolution of a beating fantasy, the role of the paper in Anna Freud's professional and personal development, the impact on contemporary thinking, its place in current understanding, and our interaction with our teacher Anna Freud, her work, and our own work in the difficult and problematic arena of sadomasochism.

We had become interested in beating fantasies because we found them to be integral to the pathology of our most difficult clinical cases at the Hampstead Clinic (cf, for example, Novick and Novick 1970). This led to our searching all the child and adolescent analytic cases (111 at the time) described in the Hampstead Psychoanalytic Index for material relating to beating wishes, beating fantasies, and sadomasochism. These formed the basis of the two-year study reported in the 1971 Congress paper (Novick and Novick 1972). Since then we have continued to explore the sadomasochistic elements in pathology, with the beating fantasy as an organizing framework, the delusion of omnipotence as a core element, and externalization as a major mechanism in the development and functioning of sadomasochism (J. Novick and K. K. Novick 1991, 1996a,b, 1997, K. K. Novick and J. Novick 1987, 1994).

In all this work, we built upon the descriptions in Freud's classic 1919 paper, "A Child Is Being Beaten." Anna Freud's 1922 paper follows on Freud's work; they should be read together, as they constitute to some degree a theoretical and clinical whole. Both papers have been rather neglected, as they were superceded and contradicted by "The Economic Problem of Masochism" (S. Freud 1924). This has tended to obscure some important points that are relevant to current ideas about sadomasochism. In relation to "A Child Is Being Beaten" we have noted (J. Novick and K. K. Novick 1997) that Freud described the narcissistic components of sadomasochism, provided a model for the object-related aspects, pointed to the character effects of the beating fantasy, and clearly emphasized the oedipal sexualization of impulses that earlier were aggressive in nature. He delineated the pervasiveness of sadomasochism and described the beating fantasy as the "essence of masochism," indicating its central role as an organizer of pathology. All these ideas can also be found in Anna Freud's paper.

Freud's 1919 paper was the only one he wrote in which women were the model for development. In Anna Freud's paper, this is doubly emphasized—the evolution of a beating fantasy in a young woman is described by a young woman. The discussion of masturbation is central to her paper. We must note that she was writing at a time when the universally held professional opinion among physicians, psychiatrists, and even psychoanalysts was that masturbation was highly injurious. As late as 1918, Ernest Jones asserted the connection between masturbation in young men and the development of neurasthenia (Comfort 1970). Sigmund Freud had described female masturbation in childhood development, but Anna Freud elaborated and discussed it as taken for granted in the sexual life of women. The concept of autonomous female sexual desire is still conspicuous by its relative absence in the psychoanalytic literature.

Anna Freud billed her paper as an illustration of Freud's remarks about two women who had created an elaborate superstructure of daydreams over the masochistic beating fantasy. She traces the evolution of the beating fantasy in the mental and sexual life of a girl from its first appearance at the age of 5 or 6, through distinct developmental changes at 8 or 9, around 15, and in late adolescence. Here we may see in both Sigmund Freud and Anna Freud the assumption that mental contents are transformed through development, and an emphasis, gradually elided by later writers, on the importance of postoedipal development (K. K. Novick and J. Novick 1994).

The focus on daydreams links to Freud's 1908 paper on "Creative Writers and Day-Dreaming," and Anna Freud first implies that the young patient's *creation* of the "nice stories" is an artistic sublimation of the beating fantasy. But when she talks about the late adolescent *writing* of the story, she describes it quite differently. She goes beyond her father's explanation of instinctual motivation and reaches, through the ideas of a different man, Siegfried Bernfeld, for an alternative or additional wellspring for the motive. In terms of our modern theory of sadomasochistic functioning, we could see here the germ of our description of two potential systems of conflict resolution—a pathological, closed system, dominated by sadomasochistic functioning, ordered by omnipotent fantasies based on the structure of the beating fantasy, and a healthy, open system, powered by pleasure and satisfaction gained from competent interactions with reality.

Both Sigmund Freud and Anna Freud describe beating as the punishment for incestuous wishes. In Anna Freud's story, the youth is given the opportunity to leave his tormentor but chooses nevertheless to stay. In our research, guilt appeared in relation to wishes for separation and autonomy at all levels, including having one's own sexuality and desire. The beating fantasy serves as a punishment for these wishes, but also keeps the child tied to the primary objects through incestuous sexual pleasure. Anna Freud's personal history may be relevant to understanding this aspect of her paper, wherein she alludes to, but does not follow, the connection between the sadomasochistic relationship and separation. When Anna Freud was 17, she suffered a breakdown and was sent to Merano to recuperate and regain her strength and spirits. That same summer of 1913, her father was very depressed, particularly by the prospect of his beloved daughter Sophie's impending marriage, and the defections of Jung and Adler. He described Anna as suffering from "psychasthenia"; she described herself as "stupid" whenever she struggled with intense impulses to masturbate. In 1914, just before the outbreak of war, Anna Freud journeyed to England to visit relatives. Freud was anxious and controlling about the trip, struggling with the separation and worried that Jones might offer attentions to his daughter. Both father and daughter suffered over issues of separation; the decision was repeatedly that Anna Freud stay at home, with ever-increasing involvement in her father's work.

The role of separation highlights a continuing controversy as to whether the main determinants of sadomasochistic pathology are oedipal or preoedipal. We have said that the beating fantasy and sadomasochism have roots at every level of development. Painful experiences in infancy are transformed into a mode of attachment, then into an embraced marker of specialness and unlimited destructive power, then into a conviction of equality with oedipal parents, and, finally, into a conviction of an omnipotent capacity to gratify infantile wishes through the coercion of others. By latency, there is a closed system of magical omnipotent thinking that undermines alternate means of competent interactions with reality. Self-destructive behavior in adolescence and adulthood represents an attempt to deny, distort, or avoid reality. In our research (J. Novick and K. K. Novick 1972, K. K. Novick and J. Novick 1987) we found that the beating fantasy of both boys and girls surfaced at times of separation. The very act of masturbation was experienced in many cases as a hostile move toward independence: as all the subjects felt their mothers owned their bodies, giving themselves pleasure was an aggressive attack on her functions. The beating fantasy was then used as a means to deny intentionality and responsibility, as well as a punishment not only for the incestuous wishes, but also for the aggression attributed to autonomous functioning. The content of many beating fantasies mandated that pleasure, even incestuous pleasure, was at the hands of others. This was literally true in many cases, where both girls and boys found methods of masturbating that avoided using their hands (Laufer 1984, J. Novick and K. K. Novick 1996c).

In the fall of 1918, Anna Freud entered analysis with Freud. Both were aware of the intrinsic difficulties, and both hoped to relieve her of her troubling symptoms and equip her for doing clinical analytic work without blind spots. By April 1922 she wished to join an analytic society. "The Relation of Beating-Phantasies to a Day-Dream" was Anna Freud's membership paper for the Vienna Psycho-Analytic Society. But Anna Freud had seen no patients at the time she presented this material. Thus began the puzzle about the source of her material. For many years there were intimations, but no definitive solution, that she was describing her own analysis. With his grave illness and multiple surgeries in the two years after her paper was given, Freud became dependent on Anna Freud as his nurse and helper. She became the inheritor of his mantle.

At the IPA Congress in 1971, our paper was actually very well received by the discussant Renata Gaddini and the audience, who engaged in lively debate about the information and formulations we presented. But we continued to be puzzled and intrigued by Anna Freud's uncharacteristically discouraging attitude. Her reaction was too extreme to be only anxiety over our reception and it was so different from her prior and subsequent warm support of our research, teaching, and clinical work. Only in relation to the beating fantasy paper did she insist on going over our data with us, and then she still objected to publicizing two of our conclusions, even while concurring that they were demonstrated by the material. The first concerned the link between the beating fantasy and the nature of the relationship with the preoedipal mother. Neither Freud in his 1919 paper, nor Anna Freud in 1922 mentions the role of the mother in this pathology.

The second was our finding that there are two kinds of beating fantasy: there is a *transitory* fantasy present in some girls postoedipally. When it did occur, it clearly represented both oedipal strivings in regressed form and punishment for them, as Freud described, but it did not appear in the vague third-person form he found in adult patients. The beaten victim of these fantasies consciously personified the child herself, as for the little girl who imagined herself to be a slave beaten every four hours by an emperor, whose first slave had been beaten to death and replaced by the patient. Gradually sexual excitement and masturbation were divorced from the fantasy and the wishes appeared in increasingly distanced forms, the content elaborated with material borrowed from reading and schoolwork. Cinderella, Snow White, and the Sleeping Beauty were favorite sources of inspiration, and they demonstrate the link between beating fantasies and the "typical" latency fantasies of the family romance and of rescue. The adult derivatives appear in pleasure in romance stories.

We also described a *fixed* fantasy, found in both sexes, that is associated with serious pathology. The determinants of the fixed fantasy go back to a disturbed mother–infant pleasure economy. The fixed fantasy is part of a severe sadomasochistic disorder and is highly resistant to change, even in psychoanalytic treatment. The case Anna Freud describes seems at first to be struggling toward transformation of the transitory fantasy, but this development collapses repeatedly and, in our view, she is describing the persistence of an underlying fixed beating fantasy. When a woman patient brings a beating fantasy, it is important to determine whether it involves a regressive revival or a persistence. The presence or absence of a beating fantasy is not in itself diagnostic; rather it is the transformation that differentiates normal development from sadomasochistic pathology.

Only when we read Young-Bruehl's 1988 biography did the pieces of the puzzle fall into place. Young-Bruehl confirmed that Anna Freud was indeed the patient described in the 1922 paper, and described her lifelong struggle with a fixed beating fantasy. We realized too that we had never referred to this paper in all our writings on beating fantasies and sadomasochism, and Anna Freud had never suggested its inclusion in our work. It seems now that the paper was like a family secret—there were mysterious references to it, odd tones and uncharacteristic related responses, but we, the children, were not supposed to know the whole story. And we complied! Recent rereading of Freud's 1919 paper and this paper of Anna Freud's has opened up levels of richness and complexity in the material that we had not earlier appreciated, and clarified difficulties in theoretical formulations and historical issues.

A long-standing reproach to Freud and psychoanalysis in general is his equation of feminity, passivity, and masochism. Our studies indicate that, to the extent a woman opts for sadomasochistic solutions to conflicts, so will her development be limited. Anna Freud had a specific limitation in her inability or unwillingness to integrate early mother–infant interactions into her theoretical views. Perhaps more serious was a general quality of sometimes drawing back at the last minute, as if she did not truly trust or believe in the power of her own thinking or in her political standing within psychoanalysis. It was as if she continually compromised between the beating fantasy and gratification through real effectance. After 1965, her theoretical views were moving in a powerfully radical direction toward including the implications of ego psychology and child analysis for psychoanalysis as a whole. But she continued to insist that these were only about child work.

Under pressure from influential American psychoanalysts at the 1971 Congress, Anna Freud retreated from her support for the Dutch proposal, which was to put child psychoanalysis on a par with adult. The passage of that proposal would have made child analysis the inclusive model for theory and technique. It is conceivable that mainstream analysis could then more easily have encompassed self-psychology, object relations theories, interactive and intersubjective points of view, and so forth, as all of these have comfortable places in child theory and technique.

Anna Freud achieved great things despite her continuing struggle with beating fantasies. This paper represents the limitations of her pathology; it also contains the seeds of the themes she was to explicate brilliantly for the rest of her career. We may see in this work an emphasis on development, as assertion of particularities of female development, the importance of postoedipal transformations, an understanding of the role of the ego and conscious life, and the impact of environment and education, to name but a few. It marked the beginning of Anna Freud's monumental roles in psychoanalysis, child psychoanalysis, and the continuing intellectual contribution of women to our field. For us this paper holds intrinsic interest, as well as a place in our ongoing personal and professional understanding and exploration of how ideas evolve and how we all integrate our pasts, presents, and futures.

REFERENCES

Comfort, A. (1970). *The Anxiety Makers: Some Curious Preoccupations of the Medical Profession*. New York: Dell.

Freud, A. (1922). The Relation of Beating-Phantasies to a Day-Dream. *The Writings of Anna Freud, Vol. 1*, pp. 137–157. New York: International Universities Press, 1974.

Freud, S. (1908). Creative writers and day-dreaming. *Standard Edition* 9:141–154.

———— (1919). A child is being beaten. *Standard Edition* 17:175–204.

———— (1924). The economic problem of masochism. *Standard Edition* 19:157–170.

Laufer, M. (1984). *Adolescence and Development Breakdown: A Psychoanalytic View*. New Haven: Yale University Press.

Novick, J., and Novick, K. K. (1970). Projection and externalization. In *Psychoanalytic Study of the Child* 25:69–95. New York: International Universities Press.

——— (1972). Beating fantasies in children. *International Journal of Psycho-Analysis* 53:237–242.

——— (1991). Some comments on masochism and the delusion of omnipotence from a developmental perspective. *Journal of the American Psychoanalytic Association* 39:307–328.

——— (1994). Externalization as a pathological form of relating: the dynamic underpinnings of abuse. In *Victims of Abuse: The Emotional Impact of Child and Adult Traumas*, ed. A. Sugarman, pp. 45–68. Madison, CT: International Universities Press.

——— (1996a). A development perspective on omnipotence. *Journal of Clinical Psychoanalysis* 5:129–173.

——— (1996b). *Fearful Symmetry: The Development and Treatment of Sadomasochism*. Northvale, NJ: Jason Aronson.

——— (1996c). *"I Won't Dance": A psychoanalytic perspective on interferences with performance*. Unpublished manuscript.

——— (1997). Not for barbarians: an appreciation of Freud's "A Child Is Being Beaten." In *On Freud's "A Child is Being Beaten,"* ed. E. Person, P. Fonagy, and S. A. Figueira. New Haven, CT: Yale University Press.

Novick, K. K., and Novick, J. (1987). The essence of masochism. *Psychoanalytic Study of the Child* 42:353–384. New Haven, CT: Yale University Press.

——— (1994). Postoedipal transformations: latency, adolescence, and pathogenesis. *Journal of the American Psychoanalytic Association* 42:143-170.

Winnicott, D. W. (1971). *Playing and Reality*. London: Tavistock.

Young-Breuhl, E. (1988). *Anna Freud: A Biography*. New York: Summit.

The Relation of Beating-Phantasies to a Day-Dream[1]

ANNA FREUD

In his paper "A Child Is Being Beaten" Freud deals with a phantasy which, according to him, is met with in a surprising number of the people who come in search of analytic treatment on account of an hysteria or of an obsessional neurosis. He thinks it very probable that it occurs even more often in other people who have not been obliged by a manifest illness to come to this decision. This "beating-phantasy" is invariably charged with a high degree of pleasure and has its issue in an act of pleasurable auto-erotic gratification. I shall take for granted that the content of Freud's paper—the description of the phantasy, the reconstruction of the phases which preceded it, and its derivation from the Oedipus complex—is known to the reader. In the course of my paper I shall return to and dwell on it at some length.

In one paragraph of his paper Freud says: "In two of my four female cases an artistic superstructure of day-dreams, which was of great significance for the life of the person concerned, had grown up over the masochistic phantasy of beating. The function of this superstructure was to make

[1]The following paper was written on the basis of several discussions which I had with Frau Lou Andreas-Salomé.—A. F.

possible the feeling of gratified excitement, even though the onanistic act was abstained from." Now I have been able from a variety of day-dreams to select one which seemed especially well calculated to illustrate this short remark. This day-dream was formed by a girl of 15, whose phantasy-life, in spite of its abundance, had never come into conflict with reality; the origin, evolution and termination of the day-dream could be established with certainty; and its derivation from and dependence on a beating-phantasy of long standing was proved in analysis.

I.

I shall now trace the course of development of the phantasy-life of this day-dreamer. When in her fifth or sixth year—before school, certainly— she began to entertain a beating-phantasy of the type described by Freud. In the beginning its content remained monotonous: "A boy is being beaten by a grown-up person." Later on it was changed to: "Many boys are being beaten by many grown-up persons." The boys, however, as well as the grown-ups remained indeterminate and so did the misdeed for which the castigation was administered. It is to be supposed that when enacted before the imagination of the girl the various scenes were very vivid; the record, however, given of them during analysis was anything but circumstantial or illuminating. Whenever the phantasy was called up it was accompanied by strong sexual excitement and terminated in an onanistic act.

The sense of guilt which attaches itself to the phantasy in his cases, as with this child also, is explained by Freud in the following way. He says that the form of beating-phantasy just described is not the initial one, but is the substitute in consciousness for an earlier unconscious phase. In this unconscious phase the persons who afterwards became unrecognizable and indifferent were very well-known and important—the boy who was being punished was the child who produced the phantasy, the adult who dealt out the punishment was the dreamer's own father. Further, according to Freud's paper even this phase is not the primary one, but is only a transformation of a preceding first phase, which belongs to the period of the greatest activity of the parental complex. This first phase had in common with the second that the person beating was the dreamer's father; the child that was being beaten, however, was not the one who produced the phantasy but some other one, a brother or sister, i.e., a rival in the struggle for the father's affection. The content and meaning of the phantasy of beating was, in its first phase, therefore: that the child claimed the whole of its father's love for itself and left the others to his anger and wrath. Later on a process of repression took place, a sense of guilt appeared and, to reverse the former triumph, the punishment was turned back upon the child itself. At the same time, however, in consequence of a regression took from the genital to the pregenital anal-sadistic organization, the phantasy of being beaten still stood to the child for a phantasy of being loved. Thus the second phase was formed; but it remained unconscious because of its all-too-significant content, and was substituted in consciousness by a third phase, better calculated to meet the demands of the censorship. To this third phase, however, was attached the libidinal excitement and the sense of guilt, since the secret meaning hidden under its strange form still ran: "My father loves only me."

With the child mentioned this sense of guilt attached itself less to the content of the phantasy itself—though the latter too was disapproved of from the beginning—than to the auto-erotic gratification which regularly occurred at its climax. The little girl therefore for a number of years made ever-renewed but ever-failing attempts to separate the one from the other, i.e., to retain the phantasy as a source of pleasure and, at the same time, to break herself of the auto-erotic habit, which was felt to be irreconcilable with the moral standard demanded by her ego. The content of the phantasy at that period went through the most complicated alterations and elaborations. In the attempt to enjoy the legitimate pleasure as long as possible, and to put off its tabooed climax indefinitely, she added on descriptions of a wealth of details indifferent in themselves. She constructed whole institutions, schools and reformatories in which the scenes of beating were imagined to take place, and established definite rules which determined the construction of the various scenes. The persons beating were at that time invariably teachers; only later and in exceptional cases the fathers of the boys were added—as spectators mostly. But even in this elaborate embroidering of the phantasy the daydreamer left the figures indeterminate and denied them all characteristic traits, as for instance, individual faces and names, or personal histories.

I certainly do not want to imply that postponing the pleasurable situation in this way by prolonging and amplifying the whole phantasy is in all cases the manifestation of a sense of guilt, i.e., the consequence of an attempt to separate the phantasy from an onanistic act. The same technical device may be met with in phantasies which have never given rise to a sense of guilt. With these it simply serves to reinforce the excitation and thus to heighten the final pleasure gained by the dreamer.

In the case of this girl the phantasies of beating after a time entered upon a new phase of development. As years went on the ego-tendencies in which the moral demands set up by her environment were incorporated slowly gained strength. Consequently she resisted more and more the temptation to indulge in the phantasy in which her libidinal tendencies had become concentrated. She gave up as a failure all her attempts to separate the phantasy of beating from the onanistic act, and consequently the content of the phantasy fell under the same taboo as the sexual gratification. Every re-activation of the phantasy meant a serious struggle with strong opposing forces and was followed by self-reproaches, pangs of conscience and a short period of depression. The pleasure derived from the phantasy was more and more confined to the climax itself, which was preceded as well as followed by "pain." Since in the course of time the phantasies of beating came to serve less and less as a source of pleasure, they were largely restricted in their activity.

II.

At about the same time—apparently between her eighth and tenth year—the girl began to entertain a new kind of phantasies, which she herself distinguished by the name of "nice stories," to separate them from the unpleasant phantasies of beating. These "nice stories" seemed, at first sight at least, to contain a wealth of pleasurable, agreeable situations describing instances of kind, considerate and affectionate behaviour. The figures in these nice stories were distinguished by individual names, their looks and personal appearance were described in detail and their life-histories given, the latter sometimes reaching far back into their imaginary past. The circumstances of the various persons, their acquaintance and relationship with one another, were laid down and the details of their daily life moulded after the pattern of reality. Alterations in the surroundings of the day-dreamer were followed by alternations in the imaginary scenes, and the effects to reading could also be easily traced in the latter. The climax of each situation was invariably accompanied by a strong feeling of pleasure; no sense of guilt appeared and no auto-erotic gratification took place in connection with it. The girl consequently felt no resistance against indulging largely in this kind of day-dreaming referred to in Freud's paper. How far one is justified in assuming that it had grown up over the masochistic phantasies of beating I hope to show in the further course of this analysis.

The day-dreamer herself knew nothing about any connection which her pleasant stories might have with the phantasies of beating. If a possibility of this kind had been pointed out to her at that time she would certainly have rejected the idea energetically. The phantasies of beating were to her the personification of everything she considered ugly, prohibited and depraved, whereas the "nice stories" stood to her for beauty and pleasure. She was firmly convinced of the mutual independence of the two kinds of phantasies, the more so since no figure out of a "nice story" ever penetrated into the sphere of the beating-phantasies. The two were kept apart very carefully—even in regard to time: for every re-activation of the phantasies of beating had to be followed by a temporary renunciation of the "nice stories."

Even during analysis, as was mentioned before, the girl never gave any detailed account of any individual scene of beating. Owing to her shame and resistance all she could ever be induced to give were short and covert allusions which left to the analyst the task of completing and reconstructing a picture of the original situation. She behaved quite differently in regard to the "nice stories." As soon as her first resistance to free talking had been overcome, she volunteered vivid and circumstantial descriptions of her various day-dreams. Her eagerness in doing so was such that she even gave the impression of experiencing while she was talking a similar or even greater pleasure than while actually day-dreaming. In these circumstances it was comparatively easy to get a general survey of the wealth of figures and situations produced by her fantasy. It turned out that the girl had formed not one but a whole series of so-called "continued stories," each having a different plot and describing a different set of figures. One of these "continued stories" may be considered the cardinal and most important one; it contained the largest number of figures, existed for years, and underwent various transformations; moreover, other stories branched off from it, which—just as in legends or mythology—acquired in the course of time complete independence. Alongside this main story the girl maintained various smaller and less important ones which she employed in turn. All these day-dreams invariably belonged to the type termed "continued stories." To gain insight into their organization we will now turn our attention to one particular "nice story" which, because of its brevity and clearness, is best suited to serve the purposes of this paper.

In her fourteenth or fifteenth year, after having formed a number of continued stories which she maintained side by side, the girl accidentally came upon a boy's story-book; it contained among others a short story of which the action was laid in the Middle Ages. She went through it once or twice with great interest; when she had finished, she returned the book to its owner and did not see it again. Her imagination, however, had already taken possession of the various figures and a number of the details described in the book. She immediately took up the thread of the story, continued to spin out the action and, retaining it henceforward as one of her "nice stories," she behaved exactly as if she were dealing with a spontaneous product of her own imagination.

In spite of various attempts made during analysis it remained impossible to establish with certainty what had been included in the original story. Its content had been dismembered and devoured by her active imagination, and new phantasies had overlaid it until every attempt at distinction between spontaneous and borrowed details was bound to fail. There remained nothing, therefore, but to leave aside the question of origin and to deal with the content of the imaginary scenes without regard to the sources it had sprung from.

The subject of the story was a follows: A mediaeval Knight has for years been at feud with a number of nobles who have leagued together against him. In the course of a battle a noble youth of 15 (the age of the day-dreamer) is captured by the Knight's henchmen. He is taken to the Knight's castle and there kept prisoner some time, until at last he gains his freedom again.

Instead of spinning out and continuing the tale (as in a novel published by installments), the girl made use of the plot as a sort of outer frame for her daydream. Into this frame she inserted a wealth of scenes, every single one of which was organized like an independent story, containing an introduction, development of the plot and climax. Thus there was no logical sequence in the working out of the whole tale. She was free at any moment to choose between the different parts of the tale according to her mood; and she could always interpose a new situation between two others which had been finished and previously joined up with each other.

In this comparatively simple day-dream there are only two really important figures; all the others may be disregarded, as of episodical importance merely. One of these main figures is the young prisoner, who is endowed in the day-dream with various noble and pleasing character-traits; the other is the Knight who is described as harsh and brutal. Several incidents relating to their past and their family-histories were worked out and added to the plot to deepen the hostility between them. This furnished a basis of an apparently irreconcilable antagonism between one character who is strong and mighty and another who is weak and in the power of the former.

Their first meeting was described in a great introductory scene during which the Knight threatens to put the prisoner on the rack, so as to force him to betray important secrets. The youth thus becomes aware of his utter helplessness and begins to dread his enemy. On these two factors—fear and helplessness—all the subsequent situations were based; e.g., in pursuance of his plan, the Knight nearly goes as far as to torture the prisoner, but at the last moment he desists. He nearly kills him through imprisonment in the dungeon of his castle, but has him nursed back to life again before it is too late for recovery. As soon as the prisoner has recovered the Knight returns to his original plan, but a second time he gives way before the prisoner's fortitude. And while he is apparently bent upon doing harm to the youth, he actually grants him one favour after the other. Similar situations form the later part of the tale, e.g., the prisoner accidentally goes beyond the boundaries of the castle; the Knight meets him there, but does *not* punish him by renewed imprisonment, as he would have expected. Another time the Knight discovers a similar transgression on the part of the prisoner, but he himself saves him from the humiliating consequences of the deed. Several times the prisoner is subjected to great hardships. These experiences then serve to heighten his enjoyment of some luxuries granted to him by the Knight. All these dramatic scenes were enacted very vividly before the imagination of the girl. In every single one she shared the prisoner's feelings of fear and fortitude in a state of great excitement. At the climax of each situation, i.e., when the anger and rage of the torturer were transformed into kindness and pity, this excitement resolved itself into a feeling of pleasure.

Going through the scenes mentioned and forming some new similar situations usually took the girl from a few days up to one or two weeks. At the beginning of each of these periods of day-dreaming the elaboration and development of every single scene was methodically carried out. When forming one particular scene in her imagination, she was able to disregard the existence of all the other adventures which had happened before or after it; consequently at the moment she honestly believed in the prisoner's dangerous position and in the actual possibility of a final catastrophe; so that the prisoner's dread and anxiety, i.e., the anticipation of the climax, were dwelt on at great length. After several days of day-dreaming, however, a disturbing remembrance of the happy issue of scenes already imagined seemed to penetrate into the day-dream; dread and anxiety were described with less conviction, the tone of gentleness and clemency which at the beginning had marked the climax spread farther and farther over it and finally absorbed all the interest formerly taken up by the introduction and development of the plot. The final result of this transformation was that the whole story was rendered unfit for further use, and had to be replaced—at least for a period of some weeks—by another story, which after a certain length of time met the same fate. It was only the main day-dream which lasted so immeasurably longer than the other less important continued stories; the reason probably lay in the great wealth of figures contained in it, as well as in its manifold ramifications. On the other hand, it is not unlikely that this broader elaboration was carried through for the very purpose of ensuring it a longer life every time it was re-activated.

A general survey of the various single scenes of the Knight and Prisoner day-dream revealed a surprising monotony in their construction. The day-dreamer herself—though on the whole intelligent and critical of what she read—had never noticed this fact, not even when relating the story during analysis. But on examination of each scene it was only necessary to detach from the plot itself the manifold minor details which at a first glance gave it its appearance of individuality; in every instance the structure then laid bare was as follows: antagonism between a strong and a weak person; a misdeed—mostly unintentional—on the part of the weak one which puts him at the other's mercy; the latter's menacing attitude giving rise to the gravest apprehensions; a slow and sometimes very elaborate intensification almost to the limit of endurance of the dread and anxiety; and finally, as a pleasurable climax, the solution of the conflict, i.e., pardon for the sinner, reconciliation and, for a moment, complete harmony between the former antagonists. With a few variations the same structure held good also for every single scene out of the other "nice stories" invented by the girl.

It is this underlying structure which constitutes the important analogy between the nice stories and the phantasies of beating—an analogy quite unsuspected by the dreamer herself. In the beating-phantasies too, the figures were divided into strong and weak person, i.e., adults and children respectively; there also it was a matter of a misdeed, though it remained as indefinite as the persons themselves; in the same manner they too contained a period of dread and anxiety. The only decisive disparity between the two kinds of phantasies lies in the difference between their respective solutions, which in the one case consisted of the beating-scene, in the other of the reconciliation-scene.

In the course of analysis the girl became acquainted with these striking points of resemblance in the construction of the two apparently distinct products of her imagination. The suspicion of a connection between them slowly dawned on her; once the possibility of their relationship had been accepted she quickly began to perceive a whole series of connections between them.

Even so the content at least of the beating-phantasies appeared to have nothing in common with that of the nice stories; but this too was disproved by further analysis. Closer observation showed that the theme of the beating-phantasies had in more than one place succeeded in penetrating into the nice stories. As an example we may take the Knight and Prisoner day-dream which has already been discussed. There the Knight threatened to apply torture to the prisoner. This menace always remained unfulfilled; but nevertheless a great number of scenes was built up on it, to which it supplied an unmistakable colouring of anxiety. In the light of previous considerations this menace may easily be recognized as the echo of the earlier scenes of beating: but no description of them was permissible in the nice story. There were other ways in which the theme of beating encroached into the day-dream, not in the Knight and Prisoner day-dream itself, but in the other continued stories produced by the girl.

The following observations are taken from the main story, as far as it was revealed during analysis: In the main story the passive, weak character (corresponding to the youth in the Knight and Prisoner day-dream) was occasionally represented by two figures. After committing identical misdeeds, one of these two had to undergo punishment, while the other was pardoned. Here the scene of punishment was in itself neither pleasurably nor "painfully" accentuated; it simply served to bring the reconciliation into relief and to heighten by contrast the pleasure derived from the latter. In other places the passive person in the day-dream had to live through in memory a past scene of beating while he was actually being treated affectionately. Here again the contrast served to heighten the pleasure. Or, as a third possibility, the active, strong person, dominated by the gentle mood necessary for the climax, remembered a past scene of beating in which, after committing the same misdeed, he had been the punished one.

Besides penetrating into the day-dream in this manner the beating-theme sometimes formed the actual content of a nice story, on the condition that one characteristic indispensable in the beating-phantasy was left out. This characteristic was the humiliation connected with being beaten. In a few impressive scenes in the main day-dream, for example, the climax consisted of a blow or punishment; when it was a blow, however, it was described as unintentional, when a punishment, it took the form of a self-punishment.

These instances of an irruption of the beating-theme into the nice stories all constituted as many arguments proving the relationship already suggested between the two phantasies. In the further course of analysis the girl furnished another convincing proof of this intimate connection. She one day admitted that on a few rare occasions a sudden reversal from nice stories into beating-phantasies had taken place. In hard times, when things were difficult, for instance, a nice story had sometimes failed to fulfill its function and had been replaced at the climax by a beating-scene; so that the sexual gratification connected with the latter had obtained full discharge for the dammed-up excitation. She had afterwards, however, energetically excluded these occurrences from her memory.

Investigation into the relationship between beating-phantasies and nice stories has so far yielded the following results: (1) a striking analogy in the construction of the single scenes; (2) a certain parallelism in the content; (3) the possibility of a sudden change over from the one to the other. The essential difference between the two lies in the fact that in the nice stories affectionate treatment takes the place of the chastisement contained in the phantasies of beating.

Now these considerations lead back to Freud's paper, in which the previous history of the beating-phantasies is reconstructed. As already mentioned, Freud says that the form of beating-phantasy here described is not the initial one, but is a substitute for an incestuous love-scene. The combined influence of repression and of regression to the anal-sadistic phase of libido-organization has transformed the latter into a beating-scene. From this point of view the apparent advance from the beating-phantasies to the nice stories might be explained as a return to a former phase. The nice stories seem to relinquish the original theme of the phantasies of beating; but they simultaneously bring out their original meaning, i.e., the phantasy of love that was hidden in them.

This attempt at explanation is, however, so far deficient in one important point. We have seen that the climax of the beating-phantasies was invariably connected with a compulsive onanistic act, as well as with a subsequent sense of guilt. The climax of the nice stories on the other hand is free from both. At a first glance this seems inexplicable; for the onanistic act as well as the sense of guilt are both derived from the repressed love phantasy, and the latter, though it is disguised in the phantasies of beating, is represented in the nice stories.

A solution of the problem is furnished by the fact that the nice stories do not take up the whole of the incestuous wish-phantasy belonging to early childhood. At that time all the sexual instincts were being concentrated on a first object, the father. Afterwards repression of the Oedipus complex forced the child to renounce most of these infantile sexual ties. The "sensual" object-ties were banned to the unconscious, so that their re-emergence in the phantasies of beating signifies a partial failure of this attempt at repression.

While the phantasies of beating thus represent a return of the repressed, i.e., of the incestuous wish-phantasy, the nice stories on the other hand represent a sublimation of it. The beating-phantasies constitute a gratification for the directly sexual tendencies, the nice stories for those which Freud describes as "inhibited in their aim." Just as in the development of a child's love for its parents, the originally complete sexual current is divided into sensual tendencies which undergo repression (here represented by the beating-phantasies) and into a sublimated and purely tender emotional tie (represented by the nice stories).

The tasks which the two phantasies were each required to fulfill may now be sketched as follows: the beating-phantasies always represent the same sensual love-scene which, expressed in terms of the anal-sadistic phase of libido-organization, comes to be disguised as a beating-scene. The nice stories, on the other hand, contain a variety of tender emotional object-ties. Their theme, however, is also monotonous; it invariably consists of a friendship formed between two characters opposed in strength, in age, or in social position.

The sublimation of sensual love into tender friendship was naturally favoured by the fact that already in the early stages of the beating-phantasy the girl had abandoned the difference of sex and was invariably represented as a boy.

III.

It was the object of this paper to examine a special case in which beating-phantasies and day-dreams co-existed side by side. The relationship between them and their dependence on each other has been ascertained. Apart from this, analysis of this particular day-dreamer also provided an opportunity for observing the further development of a continued story.

Some years after the first emergence of the Knight and Prisoner day-dream the girl suddenly made an attempt to write down its content. As a result she produced a sort of short story describing the youth's life during his imprisonment. It began with a description of the torture he underwent and ended with the prisoner's refusal to try to escape from the castle. His readiness to remain in the Knight's power suggested the beginning of their friendship. In contrast to the day-dream all the events were laid in the past and appeared in the form of a conversation between the prisoner's father and the Knight.

Thus, while retaining the theme of the day-dream, the written story completely changed the elaboration of the content. In the day-dream the friendship between the strong and the weak character developed anew in every single scene; in the written story, on the other hand, the friendship developed slowly and its formation took up the whole length of the action. In the new elaboration the single scenes of the day-dream were abandoned; part of the material contained in them was used for the story, their various single climaxes, however, were not replaced by a main climax terminating the latter. The end, i.e., a harmony between the former antagonists, was anticipated but not described in the story. Consequently here the interest, which in the daydream concentrated on particular points, was more equally diffused over the whole course of the action.

These modifications in the structure corresponded also to modifications in the gratification obtained. In the day-dream every new formation or repetition of a single scene provided another opportunity for pleasurable instinctual gratification. This direct way of obtaining pleasure was abandoned in the written story. The girl indeed did the actual writing in a state of pleasurable excitement, similar to her mental state when day-dreaming; the finished story, however, did not call forth this excitement. Reading the story had no more effect on the girl than reading a story with a similar content produced by a stranger.

This brings the surmise very near that the two essential changes from the day-dream to the written story, i.e., abandoning the single scenes and renouncing the pleasure derived from the various single climaxes, were intimately connected. It seems obvious that the written story had other motives and served another purpose than the day-dream. If this were not so then the development of the Knight's Story out of the day-dream would signify a transformation of something useful into something utterly useless.

When asked the reasons which had induced her to write the story the girl could give only a single conscious one. She said the story had originated at a period when the day-dream had been unusually vivid. Writing it was a defence against over-indulgence in it. The characters were so real to her and took up so much of her time and interest that she formed the purpose of creating a sort of independent existence for them. As a matter of fact, after it was written down the Knight and Prisoner day-dream actually faded away. This explanation, however, does not altogether clear the matter up. If it were the vividness of the scenes which induced her to write the story it remains inexplicable why, in writing it, she abandoned those particular scenes and dwelt on others which were not included in the day-dream (e.g. the torture-scene). The same reasoning holds good for the character; for in the story some of the characters that were fully developed in the day-dream are lacking and are replaced by others unknown in the former (as, for instance, the prisoner's father).

Another motivation for the written story is shown by following out a remark of Dr. Bernfeld's, relating to literary attempts by adolescents. Bernfeld says that in these cases the motive for writing out a day-dream may be extrinsic, not intrinsic. According to him it is most often prompted by certain ambitious ego-tendencies, as, for example, the wish to be regarded as a poet and to win in that capacity the love and esteem of others. In applying this theory to the case under discussion the development from the day-dream to the written story may be represented as follows:

The private phantasy was transformed under the pressure of the ambitious tendencies mentioned above into a communication for others. During the transformation all regard for the dreamer's personal needs was replaced by consideration of the future readers of the story. It was no longer necessary for the girl to gain pleasure directly from the content, since the written story as such gratified her ambition, and was thus indirectly pleasurable. After having renounced the direct way of attaining pleasure, there was then no reason left for retaining the various single climaxes which had been the source of pleasure before. Similarly she was now free to disregard the restrictions which had forbidden her to describe situations derived from the phantasies of beating. The torture, for example, could be introduced. When writing the story she regarded the whole content of the day-dream from the point of view of its suitability for representation and made her choice between the different parts accordingly. The better she succeeded in rounding off the action, the greater would be the impression she created and, simultaneously, the pleasure she indirectly derived from the story. By renouncing her private pleasure in favour of the impression she could create in others she turned from an autistic to a social activity, and thus found her way back from the life of imagination to life in reality.

4

JESSICA BENJAMIN ON KAREN HORNEY

Women's Oedipal Conflicts and Boys' Oedipal Ideology

JESSICA BENJAMIN

It is not easy to choose among the historically important papers that have contributed to our understanding of what used to be called feminine or female psychology, and yet for me Karen Horney's (1926) "Flight from Womanhood" was an easy choice. For this essay represents a decisive moment in psychoanalytic history, and so a marker by which we may help locate ourselves in that history. Horney's work, situated in the debates on women's sexuality in the twenties, offers a perspective in many ways similar to ours, yet marked by the more precarious position of feminism in the early psychoanalytic movement. While it appears that she was cast out by the psychoanalytic movement only for her later revisions of psychoanalytic metapsychology and technique, these early challenges to Freud had already made her a controversial figure. At the time, both Jones (1927) and Klein (1928), in different ways, also challenged Freud's view, lining up against Deutsch (1944) and Lampl-de-Groot (1928) who assumed the role of loyal daughters (see Fliegel 1986). Yet Horney's was the most frontal challenge to Freud's doctrine of femininity, for it named the as yet unspoken and unspeakable problem: the masculine or patriarchal underpinnings of Freud's thought.

In addition, this was no mere doctrinal dispute. The matter on which Horney went toe to toe (do I mean toe?) with Freud was one that would affect all women seeking analytic help for the next fifty years: penis envy. I shall try to briefly suggest both the psychoanalytic acumen and the feminist (im)pertinence embodied in her work, as well as the ways in which her arguments, as Fliegel (1986) put it in her landmark history of the debates, were "more Freudian than Freud." At the same time, Horney already delineated the major issues that would be taken up time and again by those opposing Freud's view of femininity. Her other essays, especially on the denial of the vagina, female masochism, the feminine overvaluation of love, and the dread of the mother are all of sufficient contemporary interest to make me regret I must confine my discussion to this one piece.

In particular, the statement in this essay cannot be fully understood without reference to Horney's earlier formulations, in "On the Genesis of the Castration Complex in Women" (1924), first delivered in 1922. I would have selected that essay to present, were it not that "Flight from Womanhood" makes a far bolder statement, offering a piece of psychoanalytic criticism the likes of which were not to be repeated until the Second Wave of feminism in the seventies. It will be useful to recapitulate briefly Horney's argument in the "Genesis of the Castration Complex." In her first statements about the castration complex Horney is actually not far removed from Freud's ideas about the masculinity complex articulated in the 1919 essay "A Child Is Being Beaten." These ideas present female sexuality in a way more consistent or parallel with Freud's ideas about the Oedipus complex—which is to say, the boy's version. The girl reaches the complex by way of her libidinal strivings toward the father rather than through the narcissistic injury of not having a penis.

The narcissistic preoccupation with having the exhibitionistic satisfaction of a visible urethral organ, Horney affirms, can be found in any girl who is not intimidated. But she relegates it to what we now call the preoedipal, and does not consider it to be the primary motive for oedipal strivings. Here Horney seems to be intuiting the position later developed by Fast (1984), in which preoedipal children inspired by a developmentally appropriate narcissism wish to have everything that the other sex has as well. This concrete interest in the penis is distinguished from the dynamically inspired regression toward penis envy. That regression occurs in the face of unmanageable oedipal guilt and anxiety, fear of rejection, and of rivalry with mother; it leads to the flight from what Horney insists is a "wholly womanly love" for the father. The kind of fantasies Horney finds in her woman patients—the fear that sexual penetration or appropriation by the father has led to the punishment of castration so that "being a woman is in itself culpable"—reflect the vicissitudes of desire, rejection, humiliation, identification, guilt, and envy in relation to mother and father. They are no simple response to anatomical awareness, no mere result of fixation on an organ.

Horney makes of anatomy not a set of concrete facts to be discovered but material to be shaped by a symbolic world of feelings, fantasies, and identifications. They reveal the concreteness, the fetishism involved in the idea of anatomical destiny. That is why her perspective is more compatible with a contemporary object-relations view, a precursor to women psychoanalysts like Chasseguet-Smirgel (1970) and Bernstein (1983) who developed a Freudian revisionism in the 1970s and 1980s.

Above all, Horney secures for women a version of the conflicts around sexuality and aggression analogous to those that so deeply mark male subjectivity in Freud's account, and so gives women their full due as subjects. Fliegel (1986) has argued that Freud's rejection of Horney's statement, which followed so closely on his own papers up to that point, was inspired by his inability to accept the idea of a female sexuality inspired by pleasure. The libidinal motives Horney offered would, Fliegel thought, conflict with his view of the libido as masculine; such a view could not form a basis for taking up a specifically feminine position, it could not set up the feminine as the impossibility of being masculine. Indeed, this idea of the feminine as impossible, an "empty set," the negative of the masculine has been valorized by feminists like Rose (1985) as showing the inherent instability of Freud's idea of sexuality. But this view is inconsistent insofar as it never reverses the terms and reveals masculinity in its unstable, reactive aspect. As we shall see, Horney does just that.

In "The Flight from Womanhood" Horney made her decisive response to that definition of the feminine position, by rejoining that only for men— in fact for little boys—was the impossibility of being masculine so horror-inspiring. Women had plenty to be satisfied with. But still, she reflected, many had accepted Freud's viewpoint, which was the dominant one in psychoanalysis. How explain that acceptance, culturally and psychoanalytically? Horney becomes the first (we might say, the first in a long line of feminists) to deconstruct a psychoanalytic theory by revealing its meaning as fantasy; to subject Freud's thought to analysis. This is a bold move, and if Horney's cultural theory of masculine bias leans on the work of a well-known social theorist, Georg Simmel (no one to sneeze at), her willingness to expose the mind of the little oedipal boy hidden in the assumptions about female sexuality puts her out on a limb by herself. Thus Horney traces the basics of Freud's ideas about femininity to a projection of the little boy's belief that the girl must be mutilated, that this represents a punishment, and that she can never get over her loss or envy. If women accept this position, Horney's argument from "Genesis" suggests, it is out of guilt and anxiety, not its truth value.

We should note the way in which this catalogue of beliefs prefigures Chasseguet-Smirgel's (1976) striking arguments in "Freud and Female Sexuality: The Consideration of Some Blind Spots in the Exploration of the 'Dark Continent'" made at the historically important juncture of the mid-1970s (a paper which surely represents another crucial moment). In it Chasseguet-Smirgel shows how psychoanalytic theory, specifically the theory of phallic sexual monism, postulates female sexuality as a series of "lacks" designed to reverse the unconscious belief in the mother's overwhelming potency and so undo the child's narcissistic injury of being helpless and dependent on mother. Indeed, Chasseguet-Smirgel (1970) believes that women feel deep guilt about their identification with the mother's power to engulf, castrate, and overpower the father, and so flee into idealization of the paternal, which they make inaccessible to themselves.

For her part, Horney argues that the male perspective, which has been imposed because of "man's position of advantage," also undoes a psychically painful condition, namely, the male envy of female reproduction. By emphasizing the genital difference, Horney says, men counter what is surely a far greater disparity—that between the father's role in reproduction and the mother's fecundity and creativity. Whereas in fact women's part in sexual pleasure is no less than men's, the latter's part in reproduction is objectively smaller. Interestingly, Horney does not quite state that the unconscious depreciation springs from a defense against envy, but she places the ideas in a suggestive contiguity. Indeed, Horney stresses that male envy of motherhood is so intense that men require much more sublimation than women to get over it. In other words, Horney traces the masculine perspective on femininity to the fear of being in the position of the negative, the "empty set," of being not-mother. We can see how this way of thinking prefigures the radical critiques of both Chodorow (1978) and Dinnerstein (1976).

While these ideas were radical for their time, they would hardly surprise us today. But I often find that my students are stimulated to rethink certain notions about femininity when reading Horney, and I should like therefore to suggest some of the interesting questions that arise from a careful reading of this essay. First, we should note some important ideas that later gained currency through Klein (1928, 1945), such as the fear of damage to the female genital—known through "the unerring accuracy of the unconscious" as Horney puts it—about which the girl cannot visibly reassure herself; and especially the envy of and rivalry with the mother. This form of oedipal rivalry was, of course, oddly neglected in Freud's own account (the girl resents her mother for not giving her a penis rather than envying mother's relation to father and his babies—the latter, again, a view Freud himself held when he wrote about his female homosexual case). But particularly interesting is the idea that women or girls might prefer the position of envying the man, prefer the feeling of inferiority to the feeling of guilt. Buying their freedom from punishment or affliction through the sacrifice of their womanly sexuality, they wrap themselves in the innocence of humiliation. Thus, a woman patient prefers to perseverate on her feeling of awkwardness with her male colleagues than focus on her triumph over a female rival. This analysis of guilt has gotten a bit sidelined in more recent object-relational thinking (with the exception of Chasseguet-Smirgel [1970]), yet Horney gives it a major place in woman's psychology. It is this guilt that inspires woman's flight from womanhood, and makes her acquiesce in the man's scornful version of femininity.

This flight from the heterosexual position as father's lover further dovetails with the fears of injury that Horney explored earlier in "Genesis"— the transformation of gratification into punishment because the father is understood to be too big, too overwhelming for the little girl. It has struck me that Horney's thinking points the way to an important insight about the oedipal dilemma, in which guilt functions as the flip side of humiliation: if the girl were to succeed in unseating her mother she would be guilty, but if she failed, she would be excluded, humiliated, left with nothing. Such is the case of the woman in "Genesis" who spoke of the time "after the disappointment." Ultimately, it is this oedipal humiliation against which the humiliation of not being male protects her (this idea was developed at length by Kaplan [1991]). Another way to think of this would be, that it is still more acceptable to fail at becoming the father than mother, to fail at embodying the cross-sex ideal than the ideal of one's own sex. The latter represents, perhaps, a deeper cut in the sense of self.

Finally, in this essay Horney suggests that there is a positive gain to identifying with the father. Horney not only suggests that identification can serve as an escape route for the girl who finds the feminine position of envying and rivaling her mother too threatening. She also recognizes the deep significance of Freud's (1917) exploration of identificatory processes in "Mourning and Melancholia," proposing that identification with the opposite sex "looms large" and forms the fundament for the castration complex. What particularly captured my attention was Horney's recognition of the important role played by identification with father in the wish to possess the penis. I found in her thinking further support for my idea (Benjamin 1988, 1991) that the symbolic function of the organ would be disproportionate precisely when that identification can not be fulfilled. A thwarted relationship of identificatory love and mutual recognition with the preoedipal father, who represents the position "subject of desire," would lead to a focus on the "missing penis," a stand-in for the missing father. The phallus would thus be taken as the unattainable object that signifies one's own desire, which might otherwise be represented through a sense of likeness with the father. As I conceived it, this early relationship of identificatory love with father represents strivings different than the oedipal, yet it can be transformed into the oedipal: I wish to be like father, and in that way in which I cannot be him I shall strive to have him.

Horney seems to be working her way toward another argument that appeals not to the natural but to psychic reality. She implies that the girl's heterosexual love of the father is prepared not so much by disappointment in having no penis but in another way: "admiring envy" often paves the way to love. In other words, identification and envy are closely related, and if the relationship is not too frustrating or demeaning, the girl can transform her envious wish to have what father has, to be him, into a wish to have him as an object.

We can see Horney working toward articulating this idea when she says that narcissistic and object currents are so interwoven as to be hardly distinguishable, as the words "desire for it" (in German: wanting to have) imply. Identification and envy, narcissistic and object love are indeed so closely interwoven in this important part of the text that it seems Horney is very close to a notion closer to our contemporary one, in which we see the positions of *being* and *having* oscillating rather than remaining absolutely fixed in the psyche. In other words, we can see how identificatory love and object love actually come together in many relationships, rather than being polar opposites as in Freud's simpler formulations of the Oedipus complex (Benjamin 1995a, 1996). Only in the oedipal phase do gender and object choice appear in this mutually exclusive way, so that if one loves X one has to be Y, if one loves Y one has to be X (and conversely, if one is Y one has to love X, if one is X one has to love Y). This principle of heterosexuality is not supported by the more overinclusive (Fast 1984) identifications that children form with parents of both genders (Aron 1995, Bassin 1996).

However, Horney's views also seemed to require taking heterosexuality for granted. Perhaps the most frequently criticized aspect of Horney's thought was her culturalist assumptions. Yet, critical feminists in our time, especially Mitchell (1974), focus on her biological essentialism, showing how problematic it is that Horney assumes the girl's heterosexuality when she says that Freud may be making matters more complicated than necessary by trying to explain, rather than simply assuming, "so elementary a principle as that of the mutual attraction of the sexes." From Mitchell's point of view this, the girl's turn to the father, is the very thing that ought to be explained. Mitchell's critique was intended to show that if one does not make the issue of castration primary, one ends with a naturalizing assumption of heterosexuality, in which women are born, not made. There is merit to this contention. But I think Horney's arguments show the problem in reverse, the one which followed from Freud's position, manifest in the work of Mitchell and other feminist Lacanians: that if one tries to make the explanation of heterosexuality the main thing (why does the girl switch to her father?), one ends up naturalizing the power of the phallus as an elemental principle. In other words, both positions have to locate a primary lever in some element outside psychic reality.

The naturalization of the phallus, ironically, detracts in Freud's theory from woman's position as an oedipal subject: desiring her father as an object, seeking sexual pleasure, being rivalrous and aggressive with her mother. It takes at face value her defense against guilt and humiliation. In a sense, both positions force us to neglect certain issues, naturalize certain phenomena.

Can we say that this deadlock still determines many debates today, for example, those between Lacanian and object-relations feminists? Perhaps this grasping for a causal lever is a problem that emerges in any construction seeking one primary explanation for the gendered condition, indeed any striving for a centered theory. That striving is common to the thinking of both Freud and Horney. Despite the equally problematic "blind spot" in constructing both theoretical positions, in my view it is clear which theory is clinically more experience-near. Horney's account, with its immersion in psychic rather than anatomical destiny, its richer range of fantasies and desires, seems to me the clear winner. That this account was nonetheless easily occluded by Freud's for over half a century may be a fact already explained quite well by Horney herself, traced back to what she mildly called "man's position of advantage." As we have succeeded in challenging that position far more forcefully, and as feminist theorizing about that social reality has become more complex, it is now possible to put to good use Horney's ideas about psychic reality and her insights into the position of women. This we can do without taking uncritically her lapses into naturalism or culturalism, and with appreciation for what she was able to achieve under conditions of far greater adversity than we know today.

REFERENCES

Aron, L. (1995). The internalized primal scene. *Psychoanalytic Dialogues* 5(2):195–237.

Bassin, D. (1996). Beyond the he and she: toward the reconciliation of masculinity and femininity in the postoedipal female mind. *Journal of the American Psychoanalytic Association* 44(suppl.):157–190.

Benjamin, J. (1988). *The Bonds of Love: Psychoanalysis, Feminism and the Problem of Domination*. New York: Pantheon.

——— (1991). Father and daughter: Identification with difference—a contribution to gender heterodoxy. *Psychoanalytic Dialogues* 1(3):277–299.

——— (1995a). Sameness and difference: an "overinclusive" view of gender constitution. In *Like Subjects, Love Objects: Essays on Recognition and Sexual Difference*, pp. 49–80. New Haven, CT: Yale University Press.

——— (1995b). The omnipotent mother: A psychoanalytic study of fantasy and reality. In *Like Subjects, Love Objects: Essays on Recognition and Sexual Difference*, pp. 81–114. New Haven, CT: Yale University Press.

——— (1996). In defense of gender ambiguity. *Gender and Psychoanalysis* I(1):27–44.

Bernstein, D. (1983). The female superego: a different perspective. *International Journal of Psycho-Analysis* 64:187–202.

Chasseguet-Smirgel, J. (1970). Feminine guilt and the Oedipus complex. In *Female Sexuality: New Psychoanalytic Views*, ed. J. Chasseguet-Smirgel, pp. 94–134. Ann Arbor, MI: University of Michigan Press.

——— (1976). Freud and female sexuality: the consideration of some blind spots in the exploration of the "Dark Continent." *International Journal of Psycho-Analysis* 57:275–286.

Chodorow, N. (1978). *The Reproduction of Mothering*. Berkeley: University of California Press.

Deutsch, H. (1944). *The Psychology of Women*. New York: Grune & Stratton.

Dinnerstein, D. (1976). *The Mermaid and the Minotaur*. New York: Harper & Row.

Fast, I. (1984). *Gender Identity: A Differentiation Model*. Hillsdale, NJ: Analytic Press.

Fliegel, Z. (1986). Women's development in analytic theory: six decades of controversy. In *Psychoanalysis and Women: Contemporary Reappraisals*, ed. J. Alpert, pp. 1–31. Hillsdale, NJ: Analytic Press.

Freud, S. (1917). Mourning and melancholia. *Standard Edition* 14:237–260.

——— (1919). A child is being beaten. *Standard Edition* 17:179–204.

Horney, K. (1924). On the genesis of the castration complex in women. *International Journal of Psycho-Analysis* 5:50–65.

——— (1926). The flight from womanhood: the masculity-complex in women, as viewed by men and by women. In *Feminine Psychology*, pp. 54–70. New York: Norton, 1967.

Jones, E. (1927). Early development of female sexuality. In *Papers on Psychoanalysis*, pp. 438–451. Boston: Beacon, 1961.

Kaplan, L. (1991). *Female Perversions*. New York: Doubleday.

Klien, M. (1928). Early stages of the Oedipus complex. In *Contributions to Psychoanalysis 1921–1945*, pp. 202–214. London: Hogarth, 1948.

——— (1945). The Oedipus complex in light of early anxieties. In *Contributions to Psycho-Analysis 1921–1945*, pp. 339–390. London: Hogarth, 1948.

Lampl-de-Groot, J. (1928) The evolution of the Oedipal Complex in women. *International Journal of Psycho-Analysis* 9:332–345.

Mitchell, J. (1974). *Psychoanalysis and Feminism*. New York: Pantheon.

Rose, J. (1985). Dora: fragment of an analysis. In *In Dora's Case: Frued–Hysteria–Feminism*, ed. C. Bernheimer and C. Kahane, pp. 128–148. New York: Columbia University Press.

The Flight from Womanhood: The Masculinity-Complex in Women, as Viewed by Men and by Women

KAREN HORNEY

In some of his latest works Freud has drawn attention with increasing urgency to a certain one-sidedness in our analytical researches. I refer to the fact that till quite recently the mind of boys and men only was taken as the object of investigation.

The reason of this is obvious. Psycho-analysis is the creation of a male genius, and almost all those who have developed his ideas have been men. It is only right and reasonable that they should evolve more easily a masculine psychology and understand more of the development of men than of women.

A momentous step towards the understanding of the specifically feminine was made by Freud himself in discovering the existence of penis-envy, and soon after the work of van Ophuijsen and Abraham showed how large a part this factor plays in the development of women and in the formation of their neuroses. The significance of penis-envy has been extended quite recently by the hypotheses of the "phallic phase." By this we mean that in the infantile genital organization in both sexes only one genital organ, namely the male, plays any part, and that is just this which distinguishes the infantile organization from the final genital organization of the adult.[1]

---

[1]Freud: "The Infantile Genital Organization of the Libido." *Collected Papers*, vol. 2, no. 20.

According to this theory, the clitoris is conceived of as a phallus, and we assume that little girls as well as boys attach to the clitoris in the first instance exactly the same value as to the penis.[2]

The effect of this phase is partly to inhibit and partly to promote the subsequent development. Helene Deutsch has demonstrated principally the inhibiting effects. She is of opinion that, at the beginning of every new sexual function (e.g. at the beginning of puberty, of sexual intercourse, of pregnancy and child-birth), this phase is re-animated and has to be overcome every time before a feminine attitude can be attained. Freud has elaborated her exposition on the positive side, for he believes that it is only penis-envy and the overcoming of it which gives rise to the desire for a child and thus forms the love-bond to the father.[3]

The question now arises whether these hypotheses have helped to make our insight into feminine development (insight which Freud himself has stated to be unsatisfactory and incomplete) more satisfactory and clearer.

Science has often found it fruitful to look at long-familiar facts from a fresh point of view. Otherwise there is a danger that we shall involuntarily continue to classify all new observations amongst the same clearly defined groups of ideas.

The new point of view of which I wish to speak came to me by way of philosophy, in some essays by Georg Simmel.[4] The point which Simmel makes there and which has been in many ways elaborated since, especially from the feminine side,[5] is this: our whole civilization is a masculine civilization. The state, the laws, morality, religion, and the sciences are the creation of men. Simmel by no means deduces from these facts, as is commonly done by other writers, an inferiority in women, but he first of all gives considerable breadth and depth to this conception of a masculine civilization:

> The requirements of art, patriotism, morality in general and social ideas in particular, correctness in practical judgement and objectivity in theoretical knowledge, the energy and the profundity of life—all these are categories which belong as it were in their form and their claims to humanity in general, but in their actual historical configuration they are

---

[2]H. Deutsch: *Psychoanalyse der weiblichen Sexualfunktionen*, 1925.
[3]Freud: "Einige psychische Folgen der anatomischen Geschlechtsunterschiede." *Internationale Zeitschrift für Psychoanaluse*, bd. 11, 1925.
[4]Georg Simmel: *Philosophische Kultur*.
[5]Cf. in particular Vaerting: *Männliche Eigenart im Frauenstaat und Weibliche Eigenart im Männerstaat*.

masculine throughout. Supposing that we describe these things, viewed as absolute ideas, by the single word "objective," we then find that in the history of our race the equation objective = masculine is a valid one.

Now Simmel thinks that the reason why it is so difficult to recognize these historical facts is that the very standards by which mankind has estimated the values of male and female nature are "not neutral, arising out of the difference of the sexes, but in themselves essentially masculine."

> We do not believe in a purely "human" civilization, into which the question of sex does not enter, for the very reason that prevents any such civilization from in fact existing, namely, the (so to speak) naïve identification of the concept "human being" [6] and the concept "man," [7] which in many languages even causes the same word to be used for the two concepts. For the moment I will leave it undetermined whether this masculine character of the fundamentals of our civilization has its origin in the essential nature of the sexes or only in a certain preponderance of force in men, which is not really bound up with the question of civilization. In any case this is the reason why in the most varying fields inadequate achievements are contemptuously called "feminine," while distinguished achievements on the part of women are called "masculine," as an expression of praise.

Like all sciences and all valuations, the psychology of women has hitherto been considered only from the point of view of men. It is inevitable that the man's position of advantage should cause objective validity to be attributed to his subjective, affective relations to the woman, and according to Delius[8] the psychology of women hitherto does actually represent a deposit of the desires and disappointments of men.

An additional and very important factor in the situation is that women have adapted themselves to the wishes of men and felt as if their adaptation were their true nature. That is, they see or saw themselves in the way that their men's wishes demanded of them; unconsciously they yielded to the suggestion of masculine thought.

If we are clear about the extent to which all our being, thinking, and doing conform to these masculine standards, we can see how difficult it is for the individual man and also for the individual woman really to shake off this mode of thought.

---

[6]German *Mensch*.
[7]German *Mann*.
[8]Delius: *Vom Erwachen der Frau*.

The question then is how far analytical psychology also, when its researches have women for their object, is under the spell of this way of thinking, in so far as it has not yet wholly left behind the stage in which frankly and as a matter of course masculine development only was considered. In other words, how far has the evolution of women, as depicted to us to-day by analysis, been measured by masculine standards and how far therefore does this picture not fail to present quite accurately the real nature of women?

If we look at the matter from this point of view our first impression is a surprising one. The present analytical picture of feminine development (whether that picture be correct or not) differs in no case by a hair's breadth from the typical ideas which the boy has of the girl.

We are familiar with the ideas which the boy entertains. I will therefore only sketch them in a few succinct phrases, and for the sake of comparison will place in a parallel column our ideas of the development of women.

The Boy's Ideas:	*Our Ideas of Feminine Development:*
Naïve assumption that girls as well as boys possess a penis.	For both sexes it is only the male genital which plays any part.
Realization of the absence of the penis.	Sad discovery of the absence of the penis.
Idea that the girl is a castrated, mutilated boy.	Belief of the girl that she once possessed a penis and lost it by castration.
Belief that the girl has suffered punishment which also threatens him.	Castration is conceived of as the infliction of punishment.
The girl is regarded as inferior.	The girl regards herself as inferior. Penis-envy.
The boy is unable to imagine how the girl can ever get over this loss or envy.	The girl never gets over the sense of deficiency and inferiority and has constantly to master afresh her desire to be a man.
The boy dreads her envy.	The girl desires throughout life to avenge herself on the man for possessing something which she lacks.

The existence of this over-exact agreement is certainly no criterion of its objective correctness. It is quite possible that the infantile genital organization of the little girl might bear as striking a resemblance to that of the boy as has up till now been assumed.

But it is surely calculated to make us think and take other possibilities into consideration. For instance, we might follow Georg Simmel's train of thought and reflect whether it is likely that female adaptation to the male structure should take place at so early a period and in so high a degree that the specific nature of a little girl is overwhelmed by it. Later I will return for a moment to the point that it does actually seem to me probable that this infection with a masculine point of view occurs in childhood. But it does not seem to me clear off-hand how everything bestowed by nature could be thus absorbed into it and leave no trace. And so we must return to the question I have already raised: whether the remarkable parallelism which I have indicated may not perhaps be the expression of a one-sidedness in our observations, due to their being made from the man's point of view.

Such a suggestion immediately encounters an inner protest, for we remind ourselves of the sure ground of experience upon which analytical research has always been founded. But at the same time our theoretical scientific knowledge tells us that the ground is not altogether trustworthy, but that all experience by its very nature contains a subjective factor. Thus, even our analytical experience is derived from direct observation of the material which our patients bring to analysis in free associations, dreams, and symptoms and from the interpretations which we make or the conclusions which we draw from this material. Therefore, even when the technique is correctly applied, there is in theory the possibility of variations in this experience.

Now, if we try to free our minds from this masculine mode of thought, nearly all the problems of feminine psychology take on a different appearance.

The first thing that strikes us is that it is always, or principally, the genital difference between the sexes which has been made the cardinal point in the analytical conception and that we have left out of consideration the other great biological difference, namely, the different parts played by men and by women in the function of reproduction.

The influence of the man's point of view in the conception of motherhood is most clearly revealed in Ferenczi's extremely brilliant genital theory.[9] His view is that the real incitement to coitus, its true, ultimate

---

[9]Ferenczi, *Versuch einer Genitaltheorie*, 1924.

meaning for both sexes, is to be sought in the desire to return to the mother's womb. During a period of contest man acquired the privilege of really penetrating once more, by means of his genital organ, into a uterus. The woman, who was formerly in the subordinate position, was obliged to adapt her organizations to this organic situation and was provided with certain compensations. She had to "content herself" with substitutes of the nature of fantasy and above all with harbouring the child, whose bliss she shares. At the most, it is only in the act of birth that she perhaps has potentialities of pleasure which are denied to the man.[10]

According to this view the psychic situation of a woman would certainly not be a very pleasurable one. She lacks any real primal impulse to coitus, or at least she is debarred from all direct—even if only partial—fulfilment. If this is so, the impulse toward coitus and pleasure in it must undoubtedly be less for her than for the man. For it is only indirectly, by circuitous ways, that she attains to a certain fulfillment of the primal longing—i.e., partly by the roundabout way of masochistic conversion and partly by identification with the child which she may conceive. These, however, are merely "compensatory devices." The only thing in which she ultimately has the advantage over the man is the, surely very questionable, pleasure in the act of birth.

At this point I, as a woman, ask in amazement, and what about motherhood? And the blissful consciousness of bearing a new life within oneself? And the ineffable happiness of the increasing expectation of the appearance of this new being? And the joy when it finally makes its appearance and one holds it for the first time in one's arms? And the deep pleasurable feeling of satisfaction in suckling it and the happiness of the whole period when the infant needs her care?

Ferenczi has expressed the opinion in conversation that in that primal period of conflict which ended so grievously for the female, the male as victor imposed upon her the burden of motherhood and all that it involves.

Certainly, regarded from the standpoint of the social struggle, motherhood *may* be a handicap. It is certainly so at the present time, but it is much less certain that it was so in times when human beings were closer to nature.

---

[10]Cf. also Helene Deutsch, *Psychoanalyse der Weiblichen Sexual-funktionem*; and Groddeck, *Das Buch vom Es.*

Moreover, we explain penis-envy itself by its biological relations and not by social factors; on the contrary, we are accustomed without more ado to construe the woman's sense of being at a disadvantage socially as the rationalization of her penis-envy.

But from the biological point of view woman has in motherhood, or in the capacity for motherhood, a quite indisputable and by no means negligible physiological superiority. This is most clearly reflected in the unconscious of the male psyche in the boy's intense envy of motherhood. We are familiar with this envy as such, but it has hardly received due consideration as a dynamic factor. When one begins, as I did, to analyse men only after a fairly long experience of analysing women, one receives a most surprising impression of the intensity of this envy of pregnancy, childbirth, and motherhood, as well as of the breasts and of the act of suckling.

In the light of this impression derived from analysis one must naturally enquire whether an unconscious masculine tendency to depreciation is not expressing itself intellectually in the above-mentioned view of motherhood? This depreciation would run as follows: In reality women do simply desire the penis; when all is said and done motherhood is only a burden which makes the struggle for existence harder, and men may be glad that they have not to bear it.

When Helene Deutsch writes that the masculinity-complex in women plays a much greater part than the femininity-complex in man, she would seem to overlook the fact that the masculine envy is clearly capable of more successful sublimation than the penis-envy of the girl, and that it certainly serves as one, if not as the essential, driving force in the setting-up of cultural values.

Language itself points to this origin of cultural productivity. In the historic times which are known to us this productivity has undoubtedly been incomparably greater in men than in women. Is not the tremendous strength in men of the impulse to creative work in every field precisely due to their feeling of playing a relatively small part in the creation of living beings, which constantly impels them to an overcompensation in achievement?

If we are right in making this connection we are confronted with the problem why no corresponding impulse to compensate herself for her penis-envy is found in woman? There are two possibilities; either the envy of the woman is absolutely less than that of the man or it is less successfully worked off in some other way. We could bring forward facts in support of either supposition.

In favour of the greater intensity of the man's envy we might point out that an actual anatomical disadvantage on the side of the woman exists only from the point of view of the pregenital levels of organization.[11] From that of the genital organization of adult women there is no disadvantage, for obviously the capacity of women for coitus is not less but simply other than that of men. On the other hand, the part of the man in reproduction is ultimately less than that of the woman.

Further, we observe that men are evidently under a greater necessity to depreciate women than conversely. The realization that the dogma of the inferiority of women had its origin in an unconscious male tendency could only dawn upon us after a doubt had arisen whether in fact this view were justified in reality. But if there actually are in men tendencies to depreciate women behind this conviction of feminine inferiority, we must infer that this unconscious impulse to depreciation is a very powerful one.

Further, there is much to be said in favour of the view that women work off their penis-envy less successfully than men from a cultural point of view. We know that in the most favourable case this envy is transmuted into the desire for a husband and child, and probably by this very transmutation it forfeits the greater part of its power as an incentive to sublimation. In unfavourable cases, however, as I shall presently show in greater detail, it is burdened with a sense of guilt instead of being able to be employed fruitfully, while the man's incapacity for motherhood is probably felt simply as an inferiority and can develop its full driving power without inhibition.

In this discussion I have already touched on a problem which Freud has recently brought into the foreground of interest:[12] namely, the question of the origin and operation of the desire for a child. In the course of the last decade our attitude toward this problem has changed. I may therefore be permitted to describe briefly the beginning and the end of this historical evolution.

The original hypothesis[13] was that penis-envy gave a libidinal reinforcement both to the wish for a child and the wish for the man, but that the latter wish arose independently of the former. Subsequently the accent

---

[11]S. Horney, "On the genesis of the castration-complex in women," *International Journal of Psycho-Analysis*, vol. 5, 1924.
[12]Freud: "Über einige psychische Folgen der anatomischen Geschlechtsunterschiede."
[13]Freud: "On the Transformation of Instincts with Special Reference to Anal Erotism." *Collected Papers*, vol. II, no. 16.

became more and more displaced on to the penis-envy, till in his most recent work on this problem Freud expressed the conjecture that the wish for the child arose only through penis-envy and the disappointment over the lack of the penis in general, and that the tender attachment to the father came into existence only by this circuitous route—by way of the desire for the penis and the desire for the child.

This latter hypothesis obviously originated in the need to explain psychologically the biological principle of heterosexual attraction. This corresponds to the problem formulated by Groddeck, who says that it is natural that the boy should retain the mother as a love-object, "but how is it that the little girl becomes attached to the opposite sex?"[14]

In order to approach this problem we must first of all realize that our empirical material with regard to the masculinity-complex in women is derived from two sources of very different importance. The first is the direct observation of children, in which the subjective factor plays a relatively insignificant part. Every little girl who has not been intimidated displays penis-envy frankly and without embarrassment. We see that the presence of this envy is typical and understand quite well why this is so; we understand how the narcissistic mortification of possessing less than the boy is reinforced by a series of disadvantages arising out of the different pregenital cathexes: the manifest privileges of the boy in connection with urethral erotism, the scoptophilic instinct, and onanism.[15]

I should like to suggest that we should apply the term *primary* to the little girl's penis-envy which is obviously based simply on the anatomical difference.

The second source upon which our experience draws is to be found in the analytical material produced by adult women. Naturally it is more difficult to form a judgement on this, and there is therefore more scope for the subjective element. We see here in the first instance that penis-envy operates as a factor of enormous dynamic power. We see patients rejecting their female functions, their unconscious motive in so doing being the desire to be male. We meet with phantasies of which the content is: "I once had a penis; I am a man who has been castrated and mutilated," from which proceed feelings of inferiority and which have for after-effect all

---

[14]Groddeck: *Das Buch vom Es.*
[15]I have dealt with this subject in greater detail in my paper "On the Genesis of the Castration-complex in women."

manner of obstinate hypochondriacal ideas. We see a marked attitude of hostility toward men, sometimes taking the form of depreciation and sometimes of a desire to castrate or maim them, and we see how the whole destinies of certain women are determined by this factor.

It was natural to conclude—and especially natural because of the male orientation of our thinking—that we could link these impressions on to the primary penis-envy and to reason *a posteriori* that this envy must possess an enormous intensity, an enormous dynamic power, seeing that it evidently gave rise to such effects. Here we overlooked the fact, more in our general estimation of the situation than in details, that this desire to be a man, so familiar to us from the analyses of adult women, had only very little to do with that early, infantile, primary penis-envy, but that it is a secondary formation embodying all that has miscarried in the development toward womanhood.

From beginning to end my experience has proved to me with unchanging clearness that the Oedipus complex in women leads (not only in extreme cases where the subject has come to grief, but *regularly*) to a regression to penis-envy, naturally in every possible degree and shade. The difference between the outcome of the male and the female Oedipus complexes seems to me in average cases to be as follows. In boys the mother as a sexual object is renounced owing to the fear of castration, but the male role itself is not only affirmed in further development but is actually overemphasized in the reaction to the fear of castration. We see this clearly in the latency and prepubertal period in boys and generally in later life as well. Girls, on the other hand, not only renounce the father as a sexual object but simultaneously recoil from the feminine role altogether.

In order to understand this flight from womanhood we must consider the facts relating to early infantile onanism, which is the physical expression of the excitations due to the Oedipus complex.

Here again the situation is much clearer in boys, or perhaps we simply know more about it. Are these facts so mysterious to us in girls only because we have always looked at them through the eyes of men? It seems rather like it when we do not even concede to little girls a specific form of onanism but without more ado describe their autoerotic activities as male; and when we conceive of the difference, which surely must exist, as being that of a negative to a positive, i.e. in the case of anxiety about onanism, that the difference is that between a castration threatened and castration that has actually taken place! My analytical experience makes it most decidedly possible that little girls have a specific feminine form of onanism (which incidentally differs in technique from that of boys), even if we assume that the little girl practises exclusively clitoral masturbation, an assumption which seems to me by no means certain. And I do not see why, in spite of its past evolution, it should not be conceded that the clitoris legitimately belongs to and forms an integral part of the female genital apparatus.

Whether in the early phase of the girl's genital development she has organic vaginal sensations is a matter remarkably difficult to determine from the analytical material produced by adult women. In a whole series of cases I have been inclined to conclude that this is so and later I shall quote the material upon which I base this conclusion. That such sensations should occur seems to me theoretically very probable for the following reasons. Undoubtedly the familiar phantasies that an excessively large penis is effecting forcible penetration, producing pain and hemorrhage and threatening to destroy something, go to show that the little girl bases her Oedipus phantasies most realistically (in accordance with the plastic concrete thinking of childhood) on the disproportion in size between father and child. I think too that both the Oedipus phantasies and also the logically ensuing dread of an internal, i.e. vaginal injury go to show that the vagina as well as the clitoris must be assumed to play a part in the early infantile genital organization of women.[16] One might even infer from the later phenomena of frigidity that the vaginal zone has actually a stronger cathexis (arising out of anxiety and attempts at defense) than the clitoris, and this because the incestuous wishes are referred to the vagina with the unerring accuracy of the unconscious. From this point of view frigidity must be regarded as an attempt to ward off the phantasies so full of danger to the ego. And this would also throw a new light on the unconscious pleasurable feelings which, as various authors have maintained, occur at parturition or, alternatively, on the dread of childbirth. For (just because of the disproportion between the vagina and the baby and because of the pain to which this gives rise) parturition would be calculated to a far greater extent than subsequent sexual intercourse to stand to the unconscious for a realization of those early incest-phantasies, a realization to which no guilt is attached. The female genital anxiety, like the castration-dread of boys, invariably bears the impress of feelings of guilt and it is to them that it owes its lasting influence.

---

[16]Since the possibility of such a connection occurred to me I have learnt to construe in this sense, i.e. as representing the dread of vaginal injury, many phenomena which I was previously content to interpret as castration-phantasies in the male sense.

A further factor in the situation, and one which works in the same direction, is a certain consequence of the anatomical difference between the sexes. I mean that the boy can inspect his genital to see whether the dreaded consequences of onanism are taking place; the girl, on the other hand, is literally in the dark on this point and remains in complete uncertainty. Naturally this possibility of a reality-test does not weigh with boys in cases where the castration-anxiety is acute, but in the slighter cases of fear, which are practically more important because they are more frequent, I think that this difference is very important. At any rate the analytical material which has come to light in women whom I have analysed has led me to conclude that this factor plays a considerable part in feminine mental life and that it contributes to the peculiar inner uncertainty so often met with in women.

Under the pressure of this anxiety the girl now takes refuge in a fictitious male role.

What is the economic gain of this flight? Here I would refer to an experience which probably all analysts have had: they find that the desire to be a man is generally admitted comparatively willingly and that, when once it is accepted, it is clung to tenaciously, the reason being the desire to avoid the realization of libidinal wishes and phantasies in connection with the father. Thus the wish to be a man subserves the repression of these feminine wishes or the resistance against their being brought to light. This constantly recurring, typical experience compels us, if we are true to analytical principles, to conclude that the phantasies of being a man were at an earlier period devised for the very purpose of securing the subject against libidinal wishes in connection with the father. The fiction of maleness enabled the girl to escape from the female role now burdened with guilt and anxiety. It is true that this attempt to deviate from her own line to that of the male inevitably brings about a sense of inferiority, for the girl begins to measure herself by pretensions and values which are foreign to her specific biological nature and confronted with which she cannot but feel herself inadequate.

Although this sense of inferiority is very tormenting, analytical experience emphatically shews us that the ego can tolerate it more easily than the sense of guilt associated with the feminine attitude, and hence it is undoubtedly a gain for the ego when the girl flees from the Scylla of the sense of guilt to the Charybdis of the sense of inferiority.

For the sake of completeness I will add a reference to the other gain which, as we know, accrues to women from the process of identification with the father which takes place at the same time. I know of nothing with reference to the importance of this process itself to add to what I have already said in my earlier work.

We know that this very process of identification with the father is one answer to the question why the flight from feminine wishes in regard to the father always leads to the adoption of a masculine attitude. Some reflections connected with what has already been said reveal another point of view which throws some light on this question.

We know that, whenever the libido encounters a barrier in its development, an earlier phase of organization is regressively activated. Now according to Frued's latest work penis-envy forms the preliminary stage to the true object-love for the father. And so this train of thought suggested by Freud helps us to some comprehension of the inner necessity by which the libido flows back precisely to this preliminary stage whenever and in so far as it is driven back by the incest-barrier.

I agree in principle with Freud's notion that the girl develops toward object-love by way of penis-envy, but I think that the nature of this evolution might also be pictured differently.

For when we see how large a part of its strength accrues to primary penis-envy only by retrogression from the Oedipus complex, we must resist the temptation to interpret in the light of penis-envy the manifestations of so elementary a principle of nature as that of the mutual attraction of the sexes.

Whereupon, being confronted with the question how we should conceive psychologically of this primal, biological principle, we should again have to confess ignorance. Indeed, in this respect the conjecture forces itself more and more strongly upon me that perhaps the causal connection may be the exact converse and that it is just the attraction to the opposite sex, operating from a very early period, which draws the libidinal interest of the little girl to the penis. This interest, in accordance with the level of development reached, acts at first in an autoerotic and narcissistic manner, as I have described before. If we view these relations thus, fresh problems would logically present themselves with regard to the origin of the male Oedipus complex, but I wish to postpone these for a later paper. But, if penis-envy were the first expression of that mysterious attraction of the sexes, there would be nothing to wonder at either when analysis discloses its existence in a yet deeper layer than that in which the desire for a child and the tender attachment to the father occur. The way to this tender attitude toward the father would be prepared not simply by disappointment in regard to the penis but in another way as well. We should then instead have to conceive of the libidinal interest in the penis as a kind of "partial love," to use Abraham's term.[17] Such love, he says, always forms a preliminary stage to true object-love. We might explain the process too by an analogy from later life: I refer to the fact that admiring envy is specially calculated to lead to an attitude of love.

With regard to the extraordinary ease with which this regression takes place I must mention the analytical discovery[18] that in the associations of female patients the narcissistic desire to possess the penis and the object-libidinal longing for it are often so interwoven that one hesitates as to the sense in which the words "desire for it"[19] are meant.

One word more about the castration-phantasies proper, which have given their name to the whole complex because they are the most striking part of it. According to my theory of feminine development I am obliged to regard these phantasies also as a secondary formation. I picture their origin as follows: when the woman takes refuge in the fictitious male role her feminine genital anxiety is to some extent translated into male terms—the fear of vaginal injury becomes a phantasy of castration. The girl gains by this conversion, for she exchanges the uncertainty of her expectation of punishment (an uncertainty conditioned by her anatomical formation) for a concrete idea. Moreover, the castration-phantasy too is under the shadow of the old sense of guilt—and the penis is desired as a proof of guiltlessness.

Now these typical motives for flight into the male role—motives whose origin is the Oedipus complex—are reinforced and supported by the actual disadvantage under which women labour in social life. Of course we must recognize that the desire to be a man, when it springs from this last source, is a peculiarly suitable form of rationalization of those unconscious motives. But we must not forget that this disadvantage is actually a piece of reality and that it is immensely greater than most women are aware of.

Georg Simmel says in this connection that "the greater importance attaching to the male sociologically is probably due to his position of superior strength," and that historically the relation of the sexes may be crudely described as that of master and slave. Here, as always, it is "one of the

---

[17]Abraham: *Versuch einer Entwicklungsgeschichte der Libido*; 1924.
[18]Freud referred to this in *The Taboo of Virginity*.
[19]German: *Haben-Wollen*.

privileges of the master that he has not constantly to think that he is master, whilst the position of the slave is such that he can never forget it."

Here we probably have the explanation also of the under-estimation of this factor in analytical literature. In actual fact a girl is exposed from birth onwards to the suggestion—inevitable, whether conveyed brutally or delicately—of her inferiority, an experience which must constantly stimulate her masculinity complex.

There is no further consideration. Owing to the hitherto purely masculine character of our civilization it has been much harder for women to achieve any sublimation which should really satisfy their nature, for all the ordinary professions have been filled by men. This again must have exercised an influence upon women's feelings of inferiority, for naturally they could not accomplish the same as men in these masculine professions and so it appeared that there was a basis in fact for their inferiority. It seems to me impossible to judge to how great a degree the unconscious motives for the flight from womanhood are reinforced by the actual social subordination of women. One might conceive of the connection as an interaction of psychic and social factors. But I can only indicate these problems here, for they are so grave and so important that they require a separate investigation.

The same factors must have quite a different effect on the man's development. On the one hand they lead to a much stronger repression of his feminine wishes, in that these bear the stigma of inferiority; on the other hand it is far easier for him successfully to sublimate them.

In the foregoing discussion I have put a construction upon certain problems of feminine psychology which in many points differs from the views hitherto current. It is possible and even probable that the picture I have drawn is one-sided from the opposite point of view. But my primary intention in this paper was to indicate a possible source of error arising out of the sex of the observer, and by so doing to make a step forward toward the goal which we are all striving to reach: to get beyond the subjectivity of the masculine or the feminine standpoint and to obtain a picture of the mental development of woman which shall be truer to the facts of her nature—with its specific qualities and its differences from that of man—than any we have hitherto achieved.

5

ADRIA E. SCHWARTZ
ON JOAN RIVIERE

Postmodern Masquerade

ADRIA E. SCHWARTZ

> The reader may now ask how I define womanliness or where I draw the
> line between genuine womanliness and the 'masquerade'. My suggestion
> is not however, that there is any such difference; whether radical or su-
> perficial, they are the same thing.
>
> Joan Riviere 1929, p. 306.

"Womanliness as a Masquerade" persists to my mind as a catalytic paper
because it continues to resonate so profoundly both with my clinical experience in the consulting room and with an evolving theoretical discourse within
psychoanalysis informed by gender studies and queer theory (Domenici and
Lesser 1995, Schwartz 1998).

A postmodern reading of Riviere's paper reveals her prescience in cir-
cumnavigating current themes in gender theory: the obsolescence of the
gender binary (Goldner 1991, Harris 1991); gender as performance (Butler 1990); the importance for young girls of paternal recognition and
identificatory love (Benjamin 1988, 1992); the worry voiced by some lesbians and their assertively ambitious heterosexual sisters, that they are not "real
girls" (Schwartz 1986, 1996).

Riviere seems to be on the cusp of acknowledging the insufficiency
of psychoanalytic categories of masculinity and femininity for the "modern"
woman, but she was unable to make the necessary leap required to transcend
the particular locatedness of her theory. Psychoanalysis, Victorian born but

mother itself to the modern era, was, in the late 1920s when this paper was
written, in the midst of a burgeoning feminist crisis.[1] Followers of Freud
(Horney 1924, 1926, Jones 1927, 1935, Klein 1928, Riviere 1929) found
psychoanalytic theory inadequate to the task of explaining the complex psychosexual development of women. Freud's (1905, 1925) insistence that libido was masculine in nature, whether it occurs in women or men, that the
notion of a "feminine libido" was an oxymoron, that penis envy was of biological rather than psychic determination were in question. At issue were
the existence of an innate femininity undergoing its own maturational processes (Jones 1927, 1935), and an inherently pleasurable female sexuality
(Horney 1924). Riviere's paper appears amidst these "great debates" over
the nature of feminine psychology, as she aligns herself with Jones (1927)
and Klein (1928).

For Freud (1925), a girl's feminine attitudes developed secondarily
to her phallic jealousy and resignation to the fact of her "castration." In the
process, she gives up the masculine attitude, her clitoral cathexes, and active
libidinal posture.[2] One might say, she renounces her sexual subjectivity.

Freud's (1937) concept of bisexuality is an attempt to deal with the
actual multiplicity of character and disposition that Freud so accurately
observed in his clinical work, though the how and why of their vagaries
remains elusive, as Riviere notes with seeming bewilderment:

> Of all the women encountered in professional work today, it would be
> hard to say where the greater number are more feminine than
> masculine. . . . women who seem to fulfill every criterion of complete
> feminine development. . . . At the same time they fulfill the duties of
> their profession at least as well as the average man. *It is really a puzzle
> to know how to classify this type psychologically.* [p. 304, italics added]

Riviere is puzzled, as well she should be, but it would be another sixty-
plus years before the categories, as unitary discrete entities in themselves,

---

[1] Although the objections to Freud's theories, within the psychoanalytic dominion, were not
presented with a feminist cast, Freud seemed to perceive them that way. In his classic paper
entitled "Some Psychical Consequences of the Anatomical Distinction Between the Sexes," he
states, "We must not be deflected . . . by the denials of the feminists, who are anxious to force
us to regard the two sexes as completely equal in position and worth" (1925, p. 258). For an
interesting and detailed account of the development of the controversies, see Fliegel (1986).
[2] "For distinguishing between male and female in mental life we make use of what is obviously
an inadequate empirical and conventional equation: we call everything that is strong and active male, and everything that is weak and passive female" (Freud 1940, p. 188).

were questioned within the psychoanalytic frame (Butler 1990, Goldner 1991, Harris 1991).

The brilliance of Riviere's paper is that she grasps the paradox intrinsic to feminine identity as we know it in Western culture, the conflicts and tensions that women bear—as that culture of femininity is inscribed upon them, as they attempt to embody it. This paper is remarkable for its "collapsing of genuine womanliness and the masquerade together" (Heath 1986, p. 50).

Riviere presents the case of a successful American woman lecturer who would follow each acclaimed public appearance by compulsive coquetry and approval seeking from the older men in attendance. This was understood by Riviere as an unconscious attempt at reassurance that this obviously bright and assertive woman who had laid claim to the public arena was in fact a *woman* desired and desirable (she had no phallus), and furthermore, served as a denial of her wishes to castrate the phallically privileged father-figures in her midst.

According to Riviere, her patient, though married and professing no strongly averred conscious lesbian desires, corresponded to that group of women who Jones (1927) categorized as homosexual: women who wish for " 'recognition' of their masculinity from men and claim to be the equals of men, or in other words, to be men themselves" (Riviere 1929, p. 305).

Jones (1927) maintained that there are two groups of homosexual women. The first, to which Riviere's patient did *not* belong, manifest little or no interest in men. Their libido centers on women, and he postulates that they use these women as a way of enjoying their femininity. These women have allegedly given up the male (paternal) object, replacing him with themselves through identification. Women are wooed partly as a means of covertly having their femininity, which has been renounced in the service of a defense against incestuous wishes.

The second group, in which Riviere enrolls her patient, retain their interest in men but set their hearts on being accepted by men as one of themselves. To this group we ascribe the feminists, or in Jones's (1927) words "the familiar type of women who ceaselessly complain of the unfairness of women's lot and their unjust ill-treatment by men" (p. 467). The aim in this group is to obtain recognition of their identification.

Jones's analysis, embedded as it is in the modern, suffers from a constricted binary thinking. To my mind, Riviere intuitively grasps this but is unable to articulate it. It is an "unthought known" (Bollas 1987).

According to Jones, a child confronting the oedipal taboo (under the

threat of castration which Jones had reconceived of as *aphanisis*, the annihilation of sexual pleasure) is forced to either *have* the object or *be* it. Sexual
orientation becomes conflated with gender identity, each fixed in their
unipolar modalities. Femininity for women is collapsed within heterosexuality.

Female homosexuality then, becomes a flight from the oedipal by way
of male identification. For women, the search for recognition or valida-
tion by men for one's equality becomes a sign of male identification, a.k.a.
homosexuality.

Riviere's patient, too, "had quite conscious feelings of rivalry and
claims to superiority over many of the 'father figures' whose favor she would
then woo after her performances! She bitterly resented any assumption that
she was not equal to them, and (in private) would reject the idea of being
subject to their judgment or criticism" (p. 305).

This American lecturer seemed to fulfill every requirement for complete feminine development deemed germane at that time. She was an
excellent wife and mother, accomplished in the domestic arts, and full
participant and orgasmic partner in lovemaking with her husband. Riviere
noted the intense homosexual passion she also evinced in some dreams as
they arose in the analysis, and the fact that she had orchestrated her own
defloration. But these were correlative rather than constitutive of her argument. Although Riviere was surprised that her patient had not had homosexual liaisons this was not the basis of her cover-up. Benjamin's (1988)
conception of the preoedipal girl's normative search for identificatory love
from available male caretakers, and her yearning for recognition of her subjectivity was unavailable to Riviere. Had it been, Riviere might have been
helped out of the constraints by which she found herself so encumbered.

What then was the masquerade? According to Riviere, this masquerade of womanliness was essentially a reaction formation against the aggression, evident in dreams and fantasies, toward both women and men.
In this successful woman, it took the form of a periodic obsequiousness
and servile coquetry assumed in order to avert the anxiety and the retribution she feared from both men and women because of her covetousness of
and fictive identification with the phallus. Her intellectual and speaking
life represented a partial identification with her father, himself a literary
man who later took to the political life. Her aforementioned identification
with her mother's gender role was clear as well. This woman evidenced a
strong rivalry with both mother for father and father for mother. She sought
to be both the subject and object of desire.

In sharp contradistinction to Freud (1937), who despaired at the seeming intransigence of woman's desire to transcend her culturally prescribed feminine/object status, Jacqueline Rose (1986) has placed the "resistance to identity" at the heart of psychic life. In her dreams and fantasies, Riviere's patient was bisexual. In our postmodern world we might see that bisexuality as an unconscious refusal to be limited to one position of desire or one form of loving.

Daumer (1992), in an essay on bisexuality, elaborates on the point. "Because bisexuality occupies an ambiguous position between identities, it is able to shed light on the gaps and contradictions of all identity, on what we might call the differences within identity" (p. 98). Bisexuality allows us to problematize heterosexuality in ways that distinguish compulsory heterosexuality and efforts to resist heterosexualism within and without heterosexual relationships. Riviere's patient allows us to do that as well.

However, Riviere and her patient lived in the modern world, and as such her "resistance to identity" rendered her vulnerable; she feared retaliation from within and without, and sought to "propitiate the avenger" (Riviere 1929, p. 306) by offering herself sexually.

This brings to mind a lesbian patient, a talented composer and performer who worked in the world of ethnic music. Early in the analysis, when playing in clubs marked by a particularly patriarchal culture, she was aware of being alternatively passive and obsequious in relation to the club owners, or flamboyantly seductive, flaunting her "heterosexuality." Her power, she sought to assure them, was in her sexual allure rather than her professional achievement. She was not aspiring to compete with the men; they need not be threatened by her. Later on in the analysis, when pretenses to active heterosexuality were no longer at issue, she began to be troubled by her observation that the quality and feeling of her performances seemed to vary according to what she was wearing.

During concerts she primarily performed in pants, she generally felt wonderful, free to interact with the audience and savor their appreciation. She was conscious of her intense rivalry with one of the senior men in her music consort, a rivalry that both plagued and intimidated her, but this took place largely offstage as they competed for leadership and recognition. When she performed at weddings, she always dressed "femme" . . . heels and sleek black dress. She felt inhibited, constricted both in her playing and repartee with the audience . . . "not really there," not herself. Part of this constriction was a result of a reaction formation against her aggression, her envious retaliation at the heterosexual privilege that marriage confers. But of greater valence in the situation, was her attempt to convince them/herself that she too was a "real girl"; that her sexual orientation did not define her gender.

A femininity which assumes passivity, which collapses a lack of subjectivity with heterosexuality, and equates activity with masculinity leads to an impossibly constricted and false sense of gender coherence. Elsewhere (Schwartz 1986, 1996, 1998) I have described my work with women who experience that sense of inauthenticity and constriction. They are often confused and struggling to find the language to represent that which they cannot be. When speaking about their sense of gendered self, they tend to describe themselves in the *not* voice rather than in a positive declarative form, "*not* a regular girl," "*not* at all like my mother or sister," "*not* a real girl." They are what they are *not* rather than what they *are*; for refusing to accept what is perceived to be their femininity, they have foreclosed an affirmative sense of gender.

Riviere's patient struggles with this de-identification with mother-as-female (Schwartz 1986, 1998). Her pseudocompliant interactions with significant male others mask paternal identifications and an assertive subjectivity which she (and her analyst) confuse with masculinity.

Riviere commented upon how common she found this women's masquerade outside of the consulting room, among her friends and colleagues. She makes reference to a personal friend, a housewife, who hid her technical knowledge and expertise of more "masculine" matters in front of workmen and merchants. Assuming an air of deference, she hoped to get her way by acting the part of an uneducated, foolish, and bewildered woman. Riviere follows with an anecdote about another university lecturer, always joking and being flip, so as to reassure male colleagues that she need not be taken seriously. In common vernacular today, we might call these performances "dumbing down." In the annals of a girl's education, as I know personally from coming of age in the 1950s, and hearing from female patients growing up in the sixties and seventies, the maternal admonition is to "take care of a man's ego . . . it's a fragile thing . . ."

Hence taking on the mantle of femininity, performing the masquerade of womanliness, has as one of its functions the bolstering of masculinity through the reification of difference. "Womanliness therefore could be assumed and worn as a mask, both to hide the possession of masculinity and to avert the reprisals expected if she were found to possess it" (Riviere 1929, p. 306).

In this essay, Riviere scoops Butler by recognizing gender as performance. "The reader may now ask how I define womanliness or where I draw the line between genuine womanliness and the 'masquerade.' My suggestion is not, however, that there is any such difference; whether radical or superficial, they are the same thing" (Riviere 1929, p. 306).

Sixty years later, Butler (1990) radically suggests all gender is performative—that acts, gestures, and desires produce "the effect of an internal core or substance, but produce this on the surface of the body," that the gendered body "is performative in the sense that the essence of the identity that they purport to express becomes a *fabrication* . . . manufactured and sustained through corporeal signs and other discursive means" (p. 336, italics added). For Butler, the gendered body has no ontological status apart from these performative acts. Butler seeks to resist the force of gender fixities, including an interior gender identity as a coherent intrapsychic entity with a certain normative history which would foreclose complexities or disruptions as they occur.

Within the psychoanalytic world there has been a slow but steady revolution brewing in the ways in which we analyze and conceptualize gender (Bassin 1996, Dimen 1991, Goldner 1991, Harris 1991). Informed by postmodern critiques (Butler 1990, Foucault 1978, 1980) we ask whether we really need to keep on "doing sex and gender" as we have in the past—that is, do sex and gender necessarily have a mimetic relation to each other?

More disruptive questions come to mind. Informed by the postmodern, we ask: Is a fixed, discrete, or coherent *gendered* sense of self intrinsic to our experience of actualized well-being? Does that gendered sense self have to correspond to some "objective reality" about the *sexed* body? Are there constitutive constraints that are relative here? Is there a "real" body onto which we superimpose meaning or does the meaning construct the body itself?

Riviere's analysis manifests her confusion of the concrete penis with the symbolic phallus. Riviere's patient identified with those characterological aspects of her father which fostered his assumption of a place in the public arena and his search for recognition there. Lacking a concept of identificatory love (Benjamin 1988), Riviere is constrained by a rigid sex/gender binary in which women are forced to "castrate" men in order to assume their phallic powers.

Butler (1990) suggests that gendered subjectivity may be understood as a history of identifications in which gender identities emerge and sexual desires shift and vary so that different identifications come into play depending upon given interpersonal contexts and cultural opportunities.

As it becomes possible to understand gendered subjectivity as the culmination of a history of internalized interactions which do not of necessity imply an unbending internal coherence, it becomes possible to understand cross-gender identifications as normative rather than pathognomonic. Freud's (1937) formulation of bisexuality as male/activity, female/passivity assumes an internal coherence of gender which belies the multifaceted identifications which so intrigue Riviere both in and outside the consulting room.

Current theory recognizes that children identify with caretakers of both sexes as a function of the internalization of multiple aspects of repetitive interactions (Schwartz 1993, Stern 1989). Thus, the child begins to symbolize genital meanings and unconsciously assimilate the gestures, behavior, and vocabulary supplied by the culture to express masculinity and femininity. Psychoanalytic theorists (Aron 1995, Bassin 1996, Benjamin 1995) have begun to see the ability to represent and symbolize the role of the other, consequent to the conscious or preconscious access to cross-gender identifications, as contributory to creativity and hence leading to personal expansion rather than necessarily to the pain and suffering experienced by Riviere's patient, friends, and, one might infer, Riviere herself.[3]

Bassin (1996) has written extensively about this and defines the more mature female mind as overinclusive, by which she means identifications with the opposite-sex parent based on early body–ego experiences. "The physical impossibility of cross-sex behavior does not prevent the mind from playing with reality, symbolizing, creating imaginative and empathic identifications. Symbols serve as intrapsychic bridges over rigid gender polarities, and help the self reconcile the dilemma of bisexuality . . . without recourse to repression or perversion" (p. 24–25).

In Bassin's schema there is a body–ego experience that is both differentiated *and* overinclusive. She locates two strands of development, one that moves toward a firm gender identity based on identification with the same-sexed parent, and the other, that simultaneously allows the psyche to move away from the containing limitations of gender based on an early overinclusive body–ego experience with early nongenitaled parents and form identifications with parents of the "opposite" sex.[4]

---

[3] Riviere was, as Heath (1986) points out, such a woman herself—an intellectual woman who Jones himself described as having a "masculine cast" (Jones 1957).

[4] Bassin's theory assumes heterosexual dual parenting and heterosexual orientation.

What Bassin suggests as mature female genital development, that is, the optimal transcendence of sexual polarities and rigid gender identities, is very much like what women do—and often—worry about: that is, their use of overinclusive body–ego symbolizations, often phallic in their sexual fantasies and gender performance. The use of such symbolizations does not necessarily reflect a femaleness gone askew but rather a "flexible female organization [that] facilitates the mourning of lost omnipotence by identification and imaginative elaboration through symbolization. . . . The mastery and symbolic use of cross-sex identifications contributes to the ability to play beyond the gender-normative structures, as in the musician's ability to improvise after mastering basic musical techniques" (Bassin 1996, p. 187).

Riviere was caught between the Scylla and Charybdis of a culturally constructed femininity and one which has been written upon the body. The very conception of womanliness as a "masquerade" illustrates the ongoing tensions within psychoanalysis around the conception of a coherent, discrete, gendered identity, and whether gender is to be viewed as a construction reflecting a certain sociocultural locatedness, or a biological journey upon which certain psychic detours are visited.

Riviere, like Jones, was locked into a gender system constructed atop a foundation of normative heterosexuality. She struggled with this gender system, recognizing that it flew in the face of her clinical and everyday reality. Feminine/heterosexual identity in Riviere's time required the acceptance of "castration"—or, in today's discourse, the renunciation of an agentic subjectivity. Riviere recognized that that the cultural dictates of womanliness entailed the repression of any assertion of prowess or aggression that might be misconstrued as phallic. The masquerade became a performance designed to forestall retaliation for any such transgression, and to convince oneself and others of one's being a "real girl."

REFERENCES:

Aron, L. (1995). The internalized primal scene. *Psychoanalytic Dialogues* 5:195–237.

Bassin, D. (1996). Beyond the he and she: toward the reconciliation of masculinity and femininity in the postoedipal female mind. *Journal of the American Psychoanalytic Association* 44(suppl.):157–190.

Benjamin, J. (1988). *The Bonds of Love: Psychoanalytic Feminism and the Problem of Domination*. New York: Pantheon.

——— (1992). Recognition and destruction: an outline of intersubjectivity. In *Relational Perspectives in Psychoanalysis*, ed. N. Skolnick and S. Warshaw, pp. 35–66. Hillsdale, NJ: Analytic Press.

———— (1995). Sameness and difference: an "overinclusive" view of gender constitution. *Psychoanalytic Inquiry* 15:125–142.

Bollas, C. (1987). *The Shadow of the Object: Psychoanalysis of the Unthought Known*. London: Free Association Books.

Butler, J. (1990). *Gender Trouble and the Subversion of Identity*. New York and London: Routledge.

Daumer, E. (1992). Queer ethics, or the challenge of bisexuality to lesbian ethics. *Hypatia* 7:91–106.

Dimen, M. (1991). Deconstructing difference: gender, splitting, and transitional space. *Psychoanalytic Dialogues* 1(3):335–352.

Domenici, T., and Lesser, R., eds. (1995). *Disorienting Sexuality*. New York and London: Routledge.

Fliegel, Z. (1986). Women's development in analytic theory: six decades of controversy. In *Psychoanalysis and Women: Contemporary Reappraisals*, ed. J. Alpert, pp. 3–31. Hillsdale, NJ: Analytic Press.

Foucault, M. (1978). *History of Sexuality: Vol. 1, An Introduction*, trans. R. Hurley. New York: Random House.

———— (1980). *Herculine Barbin: Being the Recently Discovered Memoirs of the Nineteenth Century French Hermaphrodite*, trans. R. McDougal. New York: Pantheon.

Freud, S. (1905). Three essays on the theory of sexuality. *Standard Edition* 7:135–243.

———— (1925). Some psychological consequences of the anatomical distinctions between the sexes. *Standard Edition* 19:248–258.

———— (1937). Analysis terminable and interminable. *Standard Edition* 23:209–245. London: Hogarth, 1966.

———— (1940). An outline of psychoanalysis. *Standard Edition* 23:144–207.

Goldner, V. (1991). Towards a critical relational theory of gender. *Psychoanalytic Dialogues* 1:249–272.

Harris, A. (1991). Gender as contradiction. *Psychoanalytic Dialogues* 1:197–224.

Heath, S. (1986). Joan Riviere and the masquerade. In *Formations of Fantasy*, ed. V. Burgin, J. Donald, and C. Kaplan, pp. 45–61. London and New York: Methuen.

Horney, K. (1924). On the genesis of the castration complex in women. *International Journal of Psycho-Analysis* 5:50–65.

———— (1926). The flight from womanhood. *International Journal of Psycho-Analysis* 7:324–339.

Jones, E. (1927). The early development of female sexuality. *International Journal of Psycho-Analysis* 8:457–472.

———— (1935). Early female sexuality. In *Papers on Psychoanalysis*, pp. 485–495. Boston: Beacon, 1961.

———— (1957). *The Life and Work of Sigmund Freud*. New York: Basic Books.

Klein, M. (1928). Early stages of the Oedipus complex. *International Journal of Psycho-Analysis* 9:167–180.

Riviere, J. (1929). Womanliness as a masquerade. *International Journal of Psycho-Analysis* 10:303–313.

Rose, J. (1986). *Sexuality in the Field of Vision*. London: Verso.

Schwartz, A. (1986). Some notes on the development of female gender role identity. In *Psychoanalysis and Women: Contemporary Reappraisals*, ed. J. Alpert, pp. 57–79. Hillsdale, NJ: Analytic Press.

—— (1993). Thoughts on the construction of maternal representations. *Psychoanalytic Psychology* 10:331–344.

—— (1996). *Coming out/being heard*. Paper presented at the annual spring meeting of the American Psychological Association, Division of Psychoanalysis, New York, April.

—— (1998). *Sexual Subjects: Lesbians, Gender and Psychoanalysis*. New York and London: Routledge.

Stern, D. (1989). The representation of relational patterns: developmental considerations. In *Relationship Disturbances in Early Childhood*, ed. A. Sameroff and R. N. Emde, pp. 52–69. New York: Basic Books.

Womanliness as a Masquerade

Joan Riviere

Every direction in which psycho-analytic research has pointed seems in its turn to have attracted the interest of Ernest Jones, and now that of recent years investigation has slowly spread to the development of the sexual life of women, we find as a matter of course one by him among the most important contributions to the subject. As always, he throws great light on his material, with his peculiar gift both clarifying the knowledge we had already and also adding to it fresh observations of his own.

In his paper on "The Early Development of Female Sexuality"[1] he sketches out a rough scheme of types of female development, which he first divides into heterosexual and homosexual, subsequently subdividing the latter homosexual group into two types. He acknowledges the roughly schematic nature of his classification and postulates a number of intermediate types. It is with one of these intermediate types that I am today concerned. In daily life types of men and women are constantly met with who, while mainly heterosexual in their development, plainly display strong features of the other sex. This has been judged to be an expression of the bisexuality inherent in us all; and analysis has shown that what appear as

---

[1]*International Journal of Psycho-Analysis*, vol. 8, 1927.

homosexual or heterosexual character-traits, or sexual manifestations, are the end-result of the interplay of conflicts and not necessarily evidence of a radical or fundamental tendency. The difference between homosexual and heterosexual development results from differences in the degree of anxiety, with the corresponding effect this has on development. Ferenczi pointed out a similar reaction in behavior,[2] namely, that homosexual men exaggerate their heterosexuality as a "defense" against their homosexuality. I shall attempt to show that women who wish for masculinity may put on a mask of womanliness to avert anxiety and the retribution feared from men.

It is with a particular type of intellectual woman that I have to deal. Not long ago intellectual pursuits for women were associated almost exclusively with an overtly masculine type of woman, who in pronounced cases made no secret of her wish or claim to be a man. This has now changed. Of all the women engaged in professional work today, it would be hard to say whether the greater number are more feminine than masculine in their mode of life and character. In university life, in scientific professions and in business, one constantly meets women who seem to fulfill every criterion of complete feminine development. They are excellent wives and mothers, capable housewives; they maintain social life and assist culture; they have no lack of feminine interests, e.g. in their personal appearance, and when called upon they can still find time to play the part of devoted and disinterested mother-substitutes among a wide circle of relatives and friends. At the same time they fulfil the duties of their profession at least as well as the average man. It is really a puzzle to know how to classify this type psychologically.

Some time ago, in the course of an analysis of a woman of this kind, I came upon some interesting discoveries. She conformed in almost every particular to the description just given; her excellent relations with her husband included a very intimate affectionate attachment between them and full and frequent sexual enjoyment; she prided herself on her proficiency as a housewife. She had followed her profession with marked success all her life. She had a high degree of adaptation to reality, and managed to sustain good and appropriate relations with almost everyone with whom she came in contact.

Certain reactions in her life showed, however, that her stability was not as flawless as it appeared; one of these will illustrate my theme. She

---

[2] "The Nosology of Male Homosexuality," *Contributions to Psycho-Analysis* (1916).

was an American woman engaged in work of a propagandist nature, which consisted principally in speaking and writing. All her life a certain degree of anxiety, sometimes very severe, was experienced after every public performance, such as speaking to an audience. In spite of her unquestionable success and ability, both intellectual and practical, and her capacity for managing an audience and dealing with discussions, etc., she would be excited and apprehensive all night after, with misgivings whether she had done anything inappropriate, and obsessed by a need for reassurance. This need for reassurance led her compulsively on any such occasion to seek some attention or complimentary notice from a man or men at the close of the proceedings in which she had taken part or been the principal figure; and it soon became evident that the men chosen for the purpose were always unmistakable father-figures, although often not persons whose judgement on her performance would in reality carry much weight. There were clearly two types of reassurance sought from these father-figures: first, direct reassurance of the nature of compliments about her performance; secondly, and more important, indirect reassurance of the nature of sexual attentions from these men. To speak broadly, analysis of her behaviour after her performance showed that she was attempting to obtain sexual advances from the particular type of men by means of flirting and coquetting with them in a more or less veiled manner. The extraordinary incongruity of this attitude with her highly impersonal and objective attitude during her intellectual performance, which it succeeded so rapidly in time, was a problem.

Analysis showed that the Oedipus situation of rivalry with the mother was extremely acute and had never been satisfactorily solved. I shall come back to this later. But beside the conflict in regard to the mother, the rivalry with the father was also very great. Her intellectual work, which took the form of speaking and writing, was based on an evident identification with her father, who had first been a literary man and later had taken to political life; her adolescence had been characterized by conscious revolt against him, with rivalry and contempt of him. Dreams and phantasies of this nature, castrating the husband, were frequently uncovered by analysis. She had quite conscious feelings of rivalry and claims to superiority over many of the "father-figures" whose favor she would then woo after her own performances! She bitterly resented any assumption that she was not equal to them, and (in private) would reject the idea of being subject to their judgement of criticism. In this she corresponded clearly to one type Ernest Jones has sketched: his first group of homosexual women who, while taking no interest in other women, wish for "recognition" of their masculinity from men and claim to be the equals of men, or in other words, to be men themselves. Her resentment, however, was not openly expressed; publicly she acknowledged her condition of womanhood.

Analysis then revealed that the explanation of her compulsive ogling and coquetting—which actually she was herself hardly aware of till analysis made it manifest—was as follows: it was an unconscious attempt to ward off the anxiety which would ensue on account of the reprisals she anticipated from the father-figures after her intellectual performance. The exhibition in public of her intellectual proficiency, which was in itself carried through successfully, signified an exhibition of herself in possession of the father's penis, having castrated him. The display once over, she was seized by horrible dread of the retribution the father would then exact. Obviously it was a step towards propitiating the avenger to endeavour to offer herself to him sexually. This phantasy, it then appeared, had been very common in her childhood and youth, which had been spent in the southern states of America: if a Negro came to attack her, she planned to defend herself by making him kiss her and make love to her (ultimately so that she could then deliver him over to justice). But there was a further determinant of the obsessive behaviour. In a dream which had a rather similar content to this childhood phantasy, she was in terror alone in the house; then a negro came in and found her washing clothes, with her sleeves rolled up and arms exposed. She resisted him, with the secret intention of attracting him sexually, and he began to admire her arms and to caress them and her breasts. The meaning was that she had killed father and mother and obtained everything for herself (alone in the house), became terrified of their retribution (expected shots through the window), and defended herself by taking on a menial role (washing clothes) and by *washing off* dirt and sweat, guilt and blood, everything she had obtained by the deed, and "disguising herself" as merely a castrated woman. In that guise the man found no stolen property on her which he need attack her to recover and, further, found her attractive as an object of love. Thus the aim of the compulsion was not merely to secure reassurance by evoking friendly feelings toward her in the man; it was chiefly to make sure of safety by masquerading as guiltless and innocent. It was a compulsive reversal of her intellectual performance; and the two together formed the "double-action" of an obsessive act, just as her life as a whole consisted alternately of masculine and feminine activities.

Before this dream she had had dreams of people putting masks on their faces in order to avert disaster. One of these dreams was of a high tower on a hill being pushed over and falling down on the inhabitants of a village below, but the people put on masks and escaped injury!

Womanliness therefore could be assumed and worn as a mask, both to hide the possession of masculinity and to avert the reprisals expected if she was found to possess it—much as a thief will turn out his pockets and ask to be searched to prove that he has not the stolen goods. The reader may now ask how I define womanliness or where I draw the line between genuine womanliness and the "masquerade." My suggestion is not, however, that there is any such difference; whether radical or superficial, they are the same thing. The capacity for womanliness was there in this woman—and one might even say it exists in the most completely homosexual woman—but owing to her conflicts it did not represent her main development, and was used far more as a device for avoiding anxiety than as a primary mode of sexual enjoyment.

I will give some brief particulars to illustrate this. She had married late, at 29; she had had great anxiety about defloration, and had had the hymen stretched or slit before the wedding by a woman doctor. Her attitude to sexual intercourse before marriage was a set determination to obtain and experience the enjoyment and pleasure which she knew some women have in it, and the orgasm. She was afraid of impotence in exactly the same way as a man. This was partly a determination to surpass certain mother-figures who were frigid, but on deeper levels it was a determination not to be beaten by the man.[3] In effect, sexual enjoyment was full and frequent, with complete orgasm; but the fact emerged that the gratification it brought was of the nature of a reassurance and restitution of something lost, and not ultimately pure enjoyment. The man's love gave her back her self-esteem. During analysis, while the hostile castrating impulses toward the husband were in process of coming to light, the desire for intercourse very much abated, and she became for periods relatively frigid. The mask of womanliness was being peeled away, and she was revealed either as castrated (lifeless, incapable of pleasure), or as wishing to castrate (therefore afraid to receive the penis or welcome it by gratification). Once, while for a period her husband had had a love-affair with another woman, she had detected a very intense identification with him in regard

---

[3] I have found this attitude in several women analysands and the self-ordained defloration in nearly all of them (five cases). In the light of Freud's "Taboo of Virginity," this latter symptomatic act is instructive.

to the rival woman. It is striking that she had had no homosexual experiences (since before puberty with a younger sister); but it appeared during analysis that this lack was compensated for by frequent homosexual dreams with intense orgasm.

In every-day life one may observe the mask of femininity taking curious forms. One capable housewife of my acquaintance is a woman of great ability, and can herself attend to typically masculine matters. But when, e.g. any builder or upholsterer is called in, she has a compulsion to hide all her technical knowledge from him and show deference to the workman, making her suggestions in an innocent and artless manner, as if they were "lucky guesses." She has confessed to me that even with the butcher and baker, whom she rules in reality with a rod of iron, she cannot openly take up a firm straightforward stand; she feels herself as it were "acting a part," she puts on the semblance of a rather uneducated, foolish, and bewildered woman, yet in the end always making her point. In all other relations in life this woman is a gracious, cultured lady, competent and well-informed, and can manage her affairs by sensible rational behaviour without any subterfuges. This woman is now aged 50, but she tells me that as a young woman she had great anxiety in dealings with men such as porters, waiters, cabmen, tradesmen, or any other potentially hostile father-figures, such as doctors, builders, and lawyers; moreover, she often quarrelled with such men and had altercations with them, accusing them of defrauding her and so forth.

Another case from every-day observation is that of a clever woman, wife and mother, a university lecturer in an abstruse subject which seldom attracts women. When lecturing, not to students but to colleagues, she chooses particularly feminine clothes. Her behaviour on these occasions is also marked by an inappropriate feature: she becomes flippant and joking, so much so that it has caused comment and rebuke. She has to treat the situation of displaying her masculinity to men as a "game," as something *not real*, as a "joke." She cannot treat herself and her subject seriously, cannot seriously contemplate herself as on equal terms with men; moreover, the flippant attitude enables some of her sadism to escape, hence the offence it causes.

Many other instances could be quoted, and I have met with a similar mechanism in the analysis of manifest homosexual men. In one such man with severe inhibition and anxiety, homosexual activities really took second place, the source of greatest sexual gratification being actually masturbation under special conditions, namely, while looking at himself in a mirror dressed in a particular way. The excitation was produced by the sight of himself with hair parted in the center, wearing a bow tie. These extraordinary "fetishes" turned out to represent a *disguise of himself* as his sister; the hair and bow were taken from her. His conscious attitude was a desire to *be* a woman, but his manifest relations with men had never been stable. Unconsciously the homosexual relation proved to be entirely sadistic and based on masculine rivalry phantasies of sadism and *"possession of a penis"* could be indulged only while reassurance against anxiety was being obtained from the mirror that he was safely "disguised as a woman."

To return to the case I first described. Underneath her apparently satisfactory heterosexuality it is clear that this woman displayed well-known manifestations of the castration complex. Horney was the first among others to point out the sources of that complex in the Oedipus situation; my belief is that the fact that womanliness may be assumed as a mask may contribute further in this direction to the analysis of female development. With that in view I will now sketch the early libido-development in this case.

But before this I must give some account of her relations with women. She was conscious of rivalry of almost any woman who had either good looks or intellectual pretensions. She was conscious of flashes of hatred against almost any woman with whom she had much to do, but where permanent or close relations with women were concerned she was none the less able to establish a very satisfactory footing. Unconsciously she did this almost entirely by means of feeling herself superior in some way to them (her relations with her inferiors were uniformly excellent). Her proficiency as a housewife largely had its root in this. By it she surpassed her mother, won her approval and proved her superiority among rival "feminine" women. Her intellectual attainments undoubtedly had in part the same object. They too proved her superiority to her mother; it seemed probable that since she reached womanhood her rivalry with women had been more acute in regard to intellectual things than in regard to beauty, since she could usually take refuge in her superior brains where beauty was concerned.

The analysis showed that the origin of all these reactions, both to men and to women, lay in the reaction to the parents during the oral-biting sadistic phase. These reactions took the form of the phantasies sketched by Melanie Klein[4] in her Congress paper, 1927. In consequence of disappointment or frustration during sucking or weaning, coupled with experi-

---

[4] "Early Stages of the Oedipus Conflict," *International Journal of Psycho-Analysis*, vol. 9, 1928.

ences during the primal scene, which is interpreted in oral terms, extremely intense sadism develops toward both parents.[5] The desire to bite off the nipple shifts, and desires to destroy, penetrate, and disembowel the mother and devour her and the contents of her body succeed it. These contents include the father's penis, her feces, and her children—all her possessions and love-objects, imagined as within her body.[6] The desire to bite off the nipple is also shifted, as we know, on to the desire to castrate the father by biting off his penis. Both parents are rivals in this stage, both possess desired objects; the sadism is directed against both and the revenge of both is feared. But, as always with girls, the mother is the more hated, and consequently the more feared. She will execute the punishment that fits the crime—destroy the girl's body, her beauty, her children, her capacity for having children, mutilate her, devour her, torture her, and kill her. In this appalling predicament the girl's only safety lies in placating the mother and atoning for her crime. She must retire from rivalry with the mother, and if she can, endeavour to restore to her what she has stolen. As we know, she identifies herself with the father; and then she uses the masculinity she thus obtains by *putting it at the service of the mother*. She becomes the father, and takes his place; so she can "restore" him to the mother. This position was very clear in many typical situations in my patient's life. She delighted in using her great practical ability to aid or assist weaker and more helpless women, and could maintain this attitude successfully so long as rivalry did not emerge too strongly. But this restitution could be made on one condition only: it must procure her a lavish return in the form of gratitude and "recognition." The recognition desired was supposed by her to be owing for her self-sacrifices; more unconsciously what she claimed was recognition of her *supremacy* in *having* the penis to give back. If her supremacy were not acknowledged, then rivalry became at once acute; if gratitude and recognition were withheld, her sadism broke out in full force and she would be subject (in private) to paroxysms of oral-sadistic fury, exactly like a raging infant.

In regard to the father, resentment against him arose in two ways: (1) during the primal scene he took from the mother the milk, etc., which the child missed; (2) at the same time he gave to the mother the penis or

---

[5]Ernest Jones, op cit., p. 469, regards an intensification of the oral-sadistic stage as the central feature of homosexual development in women.

[6]As it was not essential to my argument, I have omitted all reference to the further development of the relation to children.

children instead of to her. Therefore all that he had or took should be taken from him by her; he was castrated and reduced to nothingness, like the mother. Fear of him, though never so acute as of the mother, remained; partly, too, because his vengeance for the death and destruction of the mother was expected. So he too must be placated and appeased. This was done by masquerading in a feminine guise for him, thus showing him her "love" and guiltlessness toward him. It is significant that this woman's mask, though transparent to other women, was successful with men, and served its purpose very well. Many men were attracted in this way, and gave her reassurance by showing her favour. Closer examination showed that these men were of the type who themselves fear the ultra-womanly woman. They prefer a woman who herself has male attributes, for to them her claims on them are less.

At the primal scene the talisman which both parents possess and which she lacks is the father's penis; hence her rage, also her dread and helplessness.[7] By depriving the father of it and possessing it herself she obtains the talisman—the invincible sword, the "organ of sadism"; he becomes powerless and helpless (her gentle husband), but she still guards herself from attack by wearing toward him the mask of womanly subservience, and under that screen, performing many of his masculine functions herself—"for him"—(her practical ability and management). Likewise with the mother: having robbed her of the penis, destroyed her and reduced her to pitiful inferiority, she triumphs over her, but again secretly; outwardly she acknowledges and admires the virtues of "feminine" women. But the task of guarding herself against the woman's retribution is harder than with the man; her efforts to placate and make reparation by restoring and using the penis in the mother's service were never enough; this device was worked to death, and sometimes it almost worked her to death.

It appeared, therefore, that this woman had saved herself from the intolerable anxiety resulting from her sadistic fury against both parents by creating in phantasy a situation in which she became supreme and no harm could be done to her. The essence of the phantasy was her *supremacy* over the parent-objects; by it her sadism was gratified, she triumphed over them. By this same supremacy she also succeeded in averting their revenges; the means she adopted for this were reaction-formations and concealment of her hostility. Thus she could gratify her id-impulses, her narcissistic ego,

---

[7]Cf. M. N. Searl, "Danger Situations of the Immature Ego," Oxford Congress, 1929.

and her super-ego at one and the same time. The phantasy was the mainspring of her whole life and character, and she came within a narrow margin of carrying it through to complete perfection. But its weak point was the megalomanic character, under all the disguises, of the necessity for supremacy. When this supremacy was seriously disturbed during analysis, she fell into an abyss of anxiety, rage, and abject depression; before the analysis, into illness.

I should like to say a word about Ernest Jones's type of homosexual woman whose aim is to obtain "recognition" of her masculinity from men. The question arises whether the need for recognition in this type is connected with the mechanism of the same need, operating differently (recognition for services performed), in the case I have described. In my case direct recognition of the possession of the penis was not claimed openly; it was claimed for the reaction-formations, though only the possession of the penis made them possible. Indirectly, therefore, recognition was nonetheless claimed for the penis. This indirectness was due to apprehension lest her possession of a penis *should be* "recognized," in other words "found out." One can see that with less anxiety my patient too would have openly claimed recognition from men for her possession of a penis, and in private she did in fact, like Ernest Jones's cases, bitterly resent any lack of this direct recognition. It is clear that in his cases the primary sadism obtains more gratification; the father has been castrated, and shall even acknowledge his defeat. But how then is the anxiety averted by these women? In regard to the mother, this is done of course by denying her existence. To judge from indications in analyses I have carried out, I conclude that, first, as Jones implies, this claim is simply a displacement of the original sadistic claim that the desired object, nipple, milk, penis, should be instantly surrendered; secondarily, the need for recognition is largely a need for absolution. Now the mother has been relegated to limbo; no relations with her are possible. Her existence appears to be denied, though in truth it is only too much feared. So the guilt of having triumphed over both can only be absolved by the father; if he sanctions her possession of the penis by acknowledging it, she is safe. By *giving* her recognition, he *gives* her the penis and to her instead of to the mother; then she has it, and she may have it, and all is well. "Recognition" is always in part reassurance, sanction, love; further, it renders her supreme again. Little as he may know it, to her the man has admitted his defeat. Thus in its content such a woman's phantasy-relation to the father is similar to the normal Oedipus one; the difference is that it rests on a basis of sadism. The mother she has indeed killed, but she is thereby excluded from enjoying much that the mother had, and what she does obtain from the father she has still in great measure to extort and extract.

These conclusions compel one once more to face the question: What is the essential nature of fully developed femininity? What is *das ewig Weibliche*? The conception of womanliness as a mask, behind which man suspects some hidden danger, throws a little light on the enigma. Fully developed heterosexual womanhood is founded, as Helene Deutsch and Ernest Jones have stated, on the oral-sucking stage. The sole gratification of a primary order in it is that of receiving the (nipple, milk) penis, semen, child from the father. For the rest it depends upon reaction-formations. The acceptance of "castration," the humility, the admiration of men, come partly from the over-estimation of the object on the oral-sucking plane; but chiefly from the renunciation (lesser intensity) of sadistic castration-wishes deriving from the later oral-biting level. "I must not take, I must not even ask; it must be *given* me." The capacity for self-sacrifice, devotion, self-abnegation expresses efforts to restore and make good, whether to mother or to father figures, what has been taken from them. It is also what [Sandor] Rado has called a "narcissistic insurance" of the highest value.

It becomes clear how the attainment of full heterosexuality coincides with that of genitality. And once more we see, as Abraham first stated, that genitality implies attainment of a *post-ambivalent* state. Both the "normal" woman and the homosexual desire the father's penis and rebel against frustration (or castration); but one of the differences between them lies in the difference in the degree of sadism and of the power of dealing both with it and with the anxiety it gives rise to in the two types of women.

6

LEON HOFFMAN
ON ERNEST JONES

Focusing on Active Sexuality in Women

LEON HOFFMAN

INTRODUCTION

The psychoanalytic debate during the 1920s and 1930s regarding the nature of feminine sexuality retains contemporary significance because of the ongoing dialogue regarding the nature of feminine desire and sexuality and, more recently, the nature of masculine sexuality (for example, see Hoffman 1996b, 1997, Young-Bruehl 1996). Freud considered masculinity to be primary in both boys and girls, and eventually contended that femininity was a secondary construction in development (1925, 1931, 1933). On the other hand, Horney (1924, 1926, 1933) and Jones (1927, 1933, 1935) presumed that masculinity and femininity developed along more or less parallel lines. Their disagreements with Freud's hypotheses about women's development were "forgotten"—or rather repressed—by the mainstream psychoanalytic community until recent years. A review of this early history makes it abundantly clear that modern revisions of classical theory should be considered to be "the outcome of seeds germinated in earlier epoch" (Levinson 1991).

Why were Horney's and Jones's ideas repressed for so long? Can one hypothesize a connection between this repression and the oft-held contention that feminine sexuality is an unknown continent? Kulish (1993) has proposed that feminine sexuality is considered to be an unknown continent because neither men nor women wish to recognize the intensity of feminine passion. Fliegel (1973) contends that perhaps Freud found Horney's theories unacceptable because Horney's ideas imply that there is *"an intrinsic pleasure-oriented feminine sexuality"* (p. 388). Fliegel maintains that despite Freud's stress on the importance of sexuality, the notion of an intrinsic pleasure-oriented feminine sexuality was alien to him. I argue that the construct of feminine sexual pleasure, and by extension feminine subjectivity, was difficult for Freud and others to posit because of the implicit association of several mental phenomena (subject, activity, and libido) with masculinity. Therefore, by implication, the *absence* of an independent actively desirous state is considered to be a feminine attribute (Hoffman 1996b).

A greater awareness of Jones's work can remind analysts of the central importance of a little girl's lust and passion, including aggression, and the coexisting conflicts which lead to their defensive dampening. Jones (1927) stressed the importance of a girl's desire and the problems consequent to its privation. An appreciation of this idea, of *aphanisis* or the threat of total and permanent extinction of the capacity for sexual enjoyment, can help current analysts understand and explore clinically the many defenses employed both by men and women in order to avoid the expression or even the awareness of a woman's potential sexual excitement. Furthermore, "aphanisis as a clinical concept is a welcome contribution because Jones links fears of loss of sexual excitement to separation anxiety and, thus, underscores the importance of the preoedipal tie to the mother, especially in females" (Levinson 1991). Jones (1933) came to hypothesize that the phallic phase in both boys and girls was not a simple progressive developmental process but instead represented a secondary solution to psychic conflict, namely a defensive compromise formation between libido and anxiety that is a compromise between the libidinal impulses and the wish to avoid mutilation.

Certainly a contributing factor leading to the neglect of Jones's work all these years was Freud's (1931) curt public dismissal of Jones's 1927 article, "The Early Development of Female Sexuality." Jones then wrote to Freud:

> As you could imagine, it was a surprise to find my work and experience in them could be dismissed in a couple of sentences . . . it was, however, gratifying to find you laying stress on the prolonged mother attachment in women with a strong father-fixation . . . and on the early

aggressivity to the mother . . . But we do not find that this stage is entirely a matter between the girl and the mother *alone*, the phantasy of the father (especially of his penis in her womb) playing also a part of some importance. I remember years ago you remarked about Jung's long paper in 1913: "Previously . . . he forgot the mother, and now he has forgotten the father." Hitherto you have laid such stress on the father and male side (owing to the obscurity of the female) that *I hope some passages in your essay discounting the father and the triple Oedipus situation in the young girl will not influence some analysts to proceed to a similarly one-sided view as you then indicated.* [Paskauskas 1993, p. 689, italics added]

Freud replied:

That I am supposed to have forgotten the father is generally not like me. I state that the father does not yet play a role, or only a negligible one, in a certain developmental phase . . . in your circles this chronological order is neglected, and too many disparate elements are thrown onto the same plane, probably under the influence of Kleinian interpretations . . . . [Paskauskas 1993, p. 690]

In retrospect, I believe that Jones's warning to Freud was prescient when he said, and I repeat, *"I hope some passages in your essay discounting the father and the triple Oedipus situation in the young girl will not influence some analysts to proceed to a similarly one-sided view as you then indicated."*

As Jones predicted, analysts did come to concentrate more and more on the girl's conflicts with the preoedipal mother. The active oedipal situation in girls and women and the inevitable role of aggression in the triangular situation came to be underemphasized. In recent years, the stress on the theoretical importance of *both* boys' and girls' preoedipal struggles with mother has contributed to a diminished appreciation in some analysts of the cardinal importance of the conflicted, passionate, active oedipal struggles to the development of compromise formations in both boys and girls. Freud's difficulty in recognizing women's active sexuality and aggression has inadvertently contributed to the many attempts to abandon the central role in mental life of infantile sexuality and the Oedipus complex (Hoffman 1996b, 1997).

As I previously discussed (Hoffman 1996b), Freud rejected Jung's (1913) attempts to conceive of a parallel between the boy's and girl's triangular jealous conflict and dismissed Jung's term "Electra complex" (which connotes Electra's passionate desire to take vengeance on her mother

Clytemnestra for murdering Agamemnon, Electra's father). Freud (1913) felt that only in the boy does one observe the "fateful combination of love for the one parent and simultaneous hatred for the other as rival" (p. 229). He maintained that a girl's hostile feelings toward her mother are not a result of an oedipal rivalry but a result of her feeling that the mother did not provide her with a penis (1931, 1933). Therefore the little girl escapes *to* the Oedipus complex for an indeterminate length of time, "as though into a haven of refuge," in order to escape *from* her extreme preoedipal hostility toward the mother (1931, p. 230, 1933, p. 129).

To the contrary, Klein (1945) maintained that the oedipal struggles of both girls and boys contain intense passions, both love and hate. Freud (1930) may have overlooked the importance of these ideas because he and Anna Freud disputed Melanie Klein's overall theoretical formulations of an oedipal construction in the first year of life. Although he acknowledged Klein's influence in his understanding that suppressed retaliatory aggression toward a frustrating object plays an important role in the formation of the superego, he continued to view the intense hostility of the oedipal period as characteristic only of boys. Although Klein's oedipal constructions of the first year of life seem mythical, her theory includes a crucial focus on the importance of analyzing aggression in triangular situations. Chasseguet-Smirgel (1964) has argued against Freud's notion that the oedipal situation is a haven of safety for the girl. She affirms that the oedipal situation is as threatening to the girl as it is to the boy. She maintains that a girl's prolonged relationship to her father is in actuality a childlike relationship, so that the girl avoids the dangers of becoming a woman and taking the mother's place.

However, Freud *was* acutely aware of the many defenses employed by both men and women in order to avoid awareness of a woman's potential sexual excitement because of the accompanied fantasied aggression. In "The Taboo of Virginity" (1918), for example, he demonstrates his awareness that a man may project his own aggression onto a woman and then consider her to be the source of danger, especially at the first act of intercourse. Freud clearly delineates how a woman responds to her aggressive feelings by inhibiting her passions and a man avoids the woman because she is potentially destructive. In other words, *both men and women* have fantasies that women's passions can be terrifying (compare Chasseguet-Smirgel 1964, p. 127).

Yet, throughout that paper Freud stresses that a man has *good reason* to avoid a woman's aggression, as if the woman *really* were dangerous. His difficulties accepting and analyzing the expression of aggression in women may have contributed to his idea that the development of normal femininity includes the dampening of *all* desire, including the renunciation of the woman's sense of herself as an active desirous individual. In essence Freud came to theorize that women's aggression, with its inevitable role in subjectivity, has to be denied and avoided, both by the man who might doubt a woman's capacity to sublimate and control her aggression and by the woman *herself* who is frightened of retribution if she comes to be an active or aggressive subject (Hoffman 1996b).

Riviere (1929, 1932, 1934, 1936) carefully spells out the clinical and theoretical importance of these problematic reactions to aggression by women. She convincingly demonstrates that the masking of desire in women includes a *defense against frightening aggression*. Her concept of womanliness as a masquerade, which Lacan appropriated, underscores the defensive nature of a woman's renunciation of her aggressive wishes in favor of fantasies in which those wishes are denied *by the woman herself*. This denial might take the form of ideas such as, "*I must not take, I must not even ask; it must be given to me*" (1929, p. 101). In a similar vein, McDougall (1991) has discussed the common belief among some women that they have no right to any erotic or narcissistic pleasure that is independent of the mother's will and pleasure. In essence women masquerade as guiltless, innocent, and "castrated" in order to avoid punishment for active sexual or aggressive desires (Riviere 1929).

JONES'S (1933): "THE PHALLIC PHASE"

In "The Phallic Phase," published in 1933, Jones extends the argument begun in 1927 by considering the nature of the phallic phase in *both* boys and girls. He examines the works of Freud, Horney, and Melanie Klein (compare Klein 1945) and comes to demonstrate that the phallic phase is not a normal developmental phase but a neurotic compromise formation in both sexes. His use of Kleinian construction contributes to a difficulty appreciating this paper outside a Kleinian framework. If one were to focus on a critique of the Kleinian conjectures, one could overlook Jones's many astute clinical observations and generalizations. These clinical insights need to be borne in mind by current clinicians and theoreticians when trying to help men and women having conflicts with the expression and gratification of their passionate desires.

Jones frames his argument with a consideration of two interrelated clinical phenomena: fear of castration and dread of the vulva by boys, and a desire to own a penis and hate of the mother by girls. The essential nature of the conflict in both sexes is common: avoidance of penetration and fear of injury from the parent of the same sex. The boy fears castration at the hands of the father if he were to penetrate the vagina and the girl fears mutilation at the hands of the mother if she allowed herself to have a penetrable vagina. The hostility toward the rival parent of the same sex is defended against by the projection of the aggression onto the parent of the opposite sex. In this way, Jones conceptualizes the phallic phase to be, not a progressive libidinal development, but rather a neurotic compromise between libido and anxiety, that is, a compromise between the libidinal impulses and the wish to avoid mutilation (1933, p. 32).

Because Jones believes, like Horney and Klein, that heterosexual desire is innate, he maintains that heterosexual allo-erotism is transmuted into a substitutive homosexual autoerotism during the phallic phase in both sexes. Despite this arguable assumption of a biological essentialism, Jones provides us with an exquisite clinical description of the little girl's quandary vis-à-vis her mother and father. His description can help contemporary clinicians and theoreticians who continue to expand and refine the theory of both masculine and feminine sexuality, particularly with a greater understanding of feminine passion (Hoffman 1997). Jones writes:

> Now if the mother gets all this—just what the girl longs for—from the father, then a situation of normal Oedipus rivalry must surely exist, and in exact proportion to the girl's own dissatisfaction. The accompanying hostility is in direct line with that felt previously towards the mother in the suckling period, being of the same order; and it reinforces it. The mother has got something the girl wants and will not give it to her. In this something the idea of the father's penis soon comes to crystallize more and more definitely, and the mother has obtained it from the father in successful competition with the girl, as well as the baby she can make from it. This is in disagreement with Freud's formidable statement that the concept of the Oedipus complex is strictly applicable only in male children and "it is in male children that there occurs the fateful conjunction of love for the one parent and hatred of the other as rival" (Freud 1931, p. 229). We seemed compelled here to be *plus royalist que le roi*. [p. 23]

"The Phallic Phase" was Jones's penultimate public attempt to continue to engage Freud in this debate. His final attempt came two years later (Jones 1935), when he failed to bridge the gap between the London school and the Vienna school, that is, between Melanie Klein and Freud and Anna Freud. In 1935, Jones reiterated his argument that "there was more femininity in the young girl than analysts generally admit, and that the masculine phase through which she may pass is more complex in its motivation than is commonly thought" (p. 264). The theoretical dispute between Freud and Anna Freud with Melanie Klein clearly affected Freud's judgment about Jones's contribution. Jones (1935) summarized the dispute stating that the issue centered on the presence or absence of an early Oedipus complex—Klein (the English school) maintaining that an early Oedipus follows an oral dissatisfaction, while Freud and Anna Freud (the Vienna school) maintaining that the Oedipus occurs later. Although Freud (1930) acknowledged Klein's influence in understanding that suppressed retaliatory aggression toward a frustrating object plays an important role in the formation of the superego, he continued to consider that the intense hostility of the oedipal period was characteristic only of boys. In contrast, throughout "The Phallic Phase" Jones stresses the importance of retaliatory aggression for oral privations for *both* boys and girls. For example, he states that the little girl envies the penis because of its sadistic value as exemplified by its power in directing destructive urine.

ORAL, OEDIPAL, PHALLIC—INEXTRICABLE LINKAGE

All analysts, especially child analysts, have observed clinical material in which there is an interweaving of early privation and separation themes with phallic themes. One needs to evaluate the unfolding of the analytic material in order to determine the plausibility of Jones's hypothesis concerning the impact of retaliatory aggression for oral privations on phallic phase development. When a little girl's fantasy life comes to be dominated by intense phallic concerns, for example, the analyst needs to bear in mind that intense penis envy may signify a turn toward the penis as a compromise formation. In such situations the intensification of phallic preoccupation may be a symptom as a result of a traumatic deprivation, so that the phallus comes to serve as a substitute for an unavailable preoedipal object. In other words, the deprivations inherent to oedipal frustrations become very much intensified by the earlier frustrations.

I believe that Jones's idea that the Phallic phase is a compromise formation is very useful clinically for both boys and girls. One often observes little boys who are labelled as "phallic little boys." They constantly play at killing, shooting, and so on. Analytic observation makes it abundantly clear that they are defending themselves against various calamities, including castration. If such little boys come to have intense conflicts with their libidinal and aggressive wishes they may become extremely phobic or more overtly aggressive, appearing "more phallic," as a counterphobic defense. In fact, at times one can conceptualize that the key signal affect in such situations is depressive affect rather than anxiety because the child may have the conviction in fantasy that the calamity (castration) has already occurred rather than have a worry that the castration may occur in the future (Hoffman 1992). In like fashion, little girls who experience intense conflicts with their desires can manifest intense penis envy as a result of similar mental mechanisms.

With little girls who express manifest envy of people who have penises, it is important that the analyst not offer a simplistic formulation of penis envy, to the effect that girls automatically have to accept a sense of deficiency as the bedrock of their sexual being. Rather, as Grossman and Stewart (1976) have described, the analyst needs to understand that a girl's expression of penis envy is a compromise formation that needs to be analyzed and understood. For example, children who have experienced early deprivations may reexperience the deprivation in the transference, especially at times when they discover evidence of the presence of other patients. If such a little girl has intense penis envy, she may focus her aggression at the analyst's penis, wishing to hurt it. If the analyst can understand and analyze the connection between the little girl's aggression towards the rival patients and the analyst's penis and the particular roots in the family situation, such as the birth of a baby brother, the analyst may uncover evidence of the child's fear that she might be or has been abandoned. In such situations the intense phallic preoccupation can be conceptualized as a compromise formation as a result of the threat of object loss. Such a child may have the fantasy that the possession of a penis would ward off the major calamity of abandonment (Hoffman 1995, 1997). In other words, attachment and separation feelings in a caring, nurturing relationship are intricately interwoven with intense oedipal wished and phallic preoccupations.

CLITORIS

Another of Jones's important clinical insights, far ahead of his time, involved his ideas about the clitoris. He said, "We should not take it too much for granted that the use of the clitoris is altogether the same thing psychologically as the use of the penis simply because they are physio-genetically homologous. Sheer accessibility may also play its part. The clitoris is after all a part of the female genitals. Clinically the correspondence between clitoris masturbation and a male attitude is very far from being invariable" (p. 19).

Many current psychoanalytic clinicians (Richards 1996, Shaw 1994) have rightly pointed out that stimulations and sensations in the vulva, vagina, perineum, and anal area play an important role in the development of a little girl's fantasies about herself. Although the clitoris is the one organ in either sex whose only function is the provision of pleasure, most authors do not particularly highlight the role of the clitoris in women's sexual excitement (Kulish 1993). For example, it is significant to note that in a collection of Doris Bernstein's papers (Freedman and Distler 1993), the word clitoris is absent from the index. Lerner (1976) wrote that parents' failure to explicitly acknowledge by name the vulva and *especially* the clitoris contributes to a woman's sense that she doesn't have "permission" to develop into a sexually responsive complete woman. Masters and Johnson (1966) wrote that "most women prefer to avoid the overwhelming intensity of sensual focus that may develop from direct clitoral contract" (p. 64). Kulish maintains that "it is more difficult to attain mastery over impulses with the ill-defined representation of the clitoris" (p. 518), and Bernstein (Panel, 1976) has argued that the girl's fear of overwhelming orgiastic excitement leads to suppression of early masturbation and vaginal sensations. Kulish suggests that this fear leads to suppression of awareness of the clitoris, the trigger of such sensations. The paucity of current psychoanalytic writing about the clitoris may reflect conflicts in both patients and analysts about its role and function in the mental life of both men and women. Do women psychoanalytic patients and their analysts defensively avoid or temper a woman's intensity of clitoral excitement (Hoffman 1996a, Kulish 1993)?

Psychoanalysts always have had a difficult time integrating the importance of girls' and women's passion and the coexisting conflicts which result in their dampening. In recent years modern conflict theorists have begun to deepen their understanding of the conflicts both men and women have coping with women's passions, and relational analysts have begun to address more directly sexuality, aggression, and the body (Dimen 1995, Hoffman 1997, Mitchell 1993, 1996). In any psychoanalytic theory of feminine psychology there has to be an awareness of the central importance of the little girl's lust and passion and the coexisting conflicts which may lead to their defensive dampening. Jones's work reminds us of the central importances of the little girls' lust and passion, the coexisting conflicts, and the resultant compromise formations.

REFERENCES

Chasseguet-Smirgel, J. (1964). Feminine guilt and the Oedipus complex. In *Essential Papers on the Psychology of Women,* ed. C. Zanardi, pp. 83–131. New York: New York University Press, 1990.

Dimen, M. (1995). Introduction to symposium on sexuality/sexualities. *Psychoanalytic Dialogues* 5(2):157–163.

Fliegel, Z. O. (1973). Feminine psychosexual development in Freudian theory. *Psychoanalytic Quarterly* 42:385-409.

Freedman, N., and Distler, B., eds. (1993). *Female Identity Conflict in Clinical Practice by Doris Bernstein* (Introduction by C. Bollas). IPTAR Monograph 2. Northvale, NJ: Jason Aronson.

Freud, S. (1918). The taboo of virginity. *Standard Edition* 11:191–208.

—— (1925). Some psychical consequences of the anatomical distinction between the sexes. *Standard Edition* 19:243–258.

—— (1930). Civilization and its discontents. *Standard Edition* 21:59–145.

—— (1931). Female sexuality. *Standard Edition* 21:223–245.

—— (1933). New introductory lectures on psychoanalysis. *Standard Edition* 22:3–182.

Grossman, W. I., and Stewart, W. (1976). Penis envy: from childhood wish to developmental metaphor. *Journal of the American Psychoanalytic Association* 24(suppl.):193–212.

Hoffman, L. (1992). On the clinical utility of the concept of depressive affect as signal affect. *Journal of the American Psychoanalytic Association* 40:413–431.

—— (1995). *Analysis of an overstimulated girl in the phallic phase: reconsideration of Jones's (1933) "The Phallic Phase."* Presented at The Association for Child Analysis, Toronto.

—— (1996a). *Discussion of "Primary femininity and female genital anxiety" by A. K. Richards.* Presented at the New York Psychoanalytic Institute, May.

—— (1996b). Freud and feminine subjectivity. *Journal of the American Psychoanalytic Association* 44(suppl.):23–44.

—— (1997). *Passions in girls and women: toward a bridge between critical relational theory of gender and modern conflict theory.* Paper presented at the Baltimore–Washington Psychoanalytic Society and the New York Psychoanalytic Society, February.

Horney, K. (1924). On the genesis of the castration complex in women. In *Feminine Psychology*, ed. H. Kelman, pp. 37–53. New York: Norton, 1967.

—— (1926). The flight from womanhood: the masculinity complex in women as viewed by men and by women. In *Feminine Psychology*, ed. H. Kelman, pp. 54–70. New York: Norton, 1967.

—— (1933). The denial of the vagina: a contribution to the problem of the genital anxieties specific of women. In *Feminine Psychology,* ed. H. Kelman, pp. 147–161. New York: Norton, 1967.

Jones, E. (1927). The early development of female sexuality. *International Journal of Psycho-Analysis* 8(4):459–472.

——— (1933). The phallic phase. *International Journal of Psycho-Analysis* 14(1):1–33.

——— (1935). Early female sexuality. *International Journal of Psycho-Analysis* 16(3):263–273.

Jung, C. G. (1913). The Oedipus complex. *In C. G. Jung: The Collected Works,* vol. 4, *Freud and Psychoanalysis,* pp. 151–156. London: Routledge & Kegan Paul, 1961.

Klein, M. (1945). The Oedipus complex in the light of early anxieties. In *Essential Papers on the Psychology of Women,* ed. C. Zanardi, pp. 65–87. New York: New York University Press, 1990.

Kulish, N. (1993). The mental representation of the clitoris. *Psychoanalytic Inquiry* 11:511–536.

Lerner, H. (1976). Parental mislabeling of female genitals as a determinant of penis envy and learning inhibitions in women. *Journal of the American Psychoanalytic Association* 24(suppl.):269–283.

Levinson, N. (1991). *Ernest Jones, female sexuality, and modern views of female psychology.* Unpublished.

Masters, W. H., and Johnson, V. E. (1966). *Human Sexual Response.* Boston: Little, Brown.

McDougall, J. (1991). Sexual identity, trauma, and creativity. *Psychoanalytic Inquiry* 11(4):559–581.

Mitchell, S. A. (1993). *Hope and Dread in Psychoanalysis.* New York: Basic Books.

——— (1996). Gender and sexual orientation in the age of postmodernism: the plight of the perplexed clinician. *Gender and Psychoanalysis* 1(1):45–73.

Olesker, W. (1990). Sex differences during the early separation-individuation process: implications for gender identity formation. *Journal of the American Psychoanalytic Association* 38(2):325–346.

Paskauskas, R. A., ed. (1993). *The Complete Correspondence of Sigmund Freud and Ernest Jones: 1908–1939* (Introduction by R. Steiner). Cambridge, MA: Belknap Press, Harvard University Press.

Richards, A. K. (1996). Primary femininity and female genital anxiety. *Journal of the American Psychoanalytic Association* 44(suppl.):261–281.

Riviere, J. (1929). Womanliness as a masquerade. In *The Inner World and Joan Riviere,* ed. A. Hughes, pp. 89–101. London: Karnac, 1991.

——— (1932). Jealousy as a mechanism of defense. In *The Inner World and Joan Riviere,* ed. A. Hughes, pp. 103–115. London: Karnac, 1991.

——— (1934). Review of Sigmund Freud, *New Introductory Lectures on Psycho-Analysis.* In *The Inner World and Joan Riviere,* ed. A. Hughes, pp. 117–131. London: Karnac, 1991.

——— (1936). A contribution to the analysis of the negative therapeutic reaction. In *The Inner World and Joan Riviere,* ed. A. Hughes, pp. 133–153. London: Karnac, 1991.

Shaw, R. (1994). Female genital anxieties. *Journal of Clinical Psychoanalysis* 4(3):269–276.

Young-Bruehl, E. (1996). Gender and psychoanalysis: an introductory essay. *Gender and Psychoanalysis* 1(1):7–18.

Panel (1976). Psychology of women. *Journal of the American Psychoanalytic Association* 24:141–160.

The Phallic Phase [1]

ERNEST JONES

If one studies closely the many important contributions made in the past ten years, particularly by women analysts, to the admittedly obscure problems relating to the early development of female sexuality one perceives an unmistakable disharmony among the various writers, and this is beginning to show also in the field of male sexuality. Most of these writers have been laudably concerned to lay stress on the points of agreement with their colleagues, so that the tendency to divergence of opinion has not always come to full expression. It is my purpose here to investigate it unreservedly in the hope of crystallizing it. If there is confusion it is desirable to clear it up; if there is a divergence of opinion we should, by defining it, be able to set ourselves interesting questions for further research.

For this purpose I will select the theme of the phallic phase. It is fairly circumscribed, but we shall see that it ramifies into most of the deeper and unsolved problems. In a paper read before the Innsbruck Congress in 1927,[2] I put forward the suggestion that the phallic phase in the develop-

---

[1] Read in brief before the Twelfth International Psycho-Analytical Congress, Wiesbaden, September 4, 1932, and in full before the British Psycho-Analytical Society, October 19 and November 2, 1932.
[2] "The Early Development of Female Sexuality," *International Journal of Psycho-Analysis*, 1927, vol. 8, pp. 468-469.

ment of female sexuality represented a secondary solution of psychical conflict, of a defensive nature, rather than a simple and direct developmental
process; last year Professor Freud[3] declared this suggestion to be quite
untenable. Already at that time I had in mind similar doubts about the
phallic phase in the male also, but did not discuss them since my paper
was concerned purely with female sexuality; recently Dr. Horney[4] has voiced
scepticism about the validity of the concept of the male phallic phase, and
I will take this opportunity to comment on the arguments she has advanced.

I will first remind you that in Freud's[5] description of the phallic phase
the essential feature common to both sexes was the belief that only one
kind of genital organ exists in the world—a male one. According to Freud,
the reason for this belief is simply that the female organ has at this age
not yet been discovered by either sex. Human beings are thus divided, not
into those possessing a male organ and those possessing a female organ,
but into those who possess a penis and those who do not: there is the penis-
possessing class and the castrated class. A boy begins by believing that
everyone belongs to the former class, and only as his fears get aroused does
he begin to suspect the existence of the latter class. A girl takes the same
view, save that here one should at first use the corresponding phrase, "cli-
toris-possessing class"; and only after comparing her own with the male
genital does she form a conception of a mutilated class, to which she belongs. Both sexes strive against accepting the belief in the second class, and
both for the same reason, namely—from a wish to disbelieve in the supposed reality of castration. This picture as sketched by Freud is familiar to
you all, and the readily available facts of observation from which it is drawn
have been confirmed over and again. The interpretation of the facts, however, is of course another matter and is not so easy.

I would now call your attention to a consideration which is implied
in Freud's account, but which needs further emphasis for the sake of clarity. It is that there would appear to be two distinct stages in the phallic
phase. Freud would, I know, apply the same term, "phallic phase," to both,
and so has not explicitly subdivided them. The first of the two—let us call
it the *proto-phallic phase*—would be marked by innocence or ignorance—at

---

[3]Freud: "Female Sexuality," *International Journal of Psycho-Analysis*, 1932, vol. 13, p. 297.
[4]Karen Horney: "The Dread of Women," *International Journal of Psycho-Analysis*, 1932, vol.
13, p. 353.
[5]Freud: "The Infantile Genital Organisation of the Libido," *Collected Papers* (International
Psycho-Analytical Library, 1924), vol. 2, p. 245.

least in consciousness—where there is no conflict over the matter in question, it being confidently assumed by the child that the rest of the world is built like itself and has a satisfactory male organ—penis or clitoris, as the case may be. In the second or *deutero-phallic phase* there is a dawning suspicion that the world is divided into two classes: not male and female in the proper sense, but penis-possessing and castrated (though actually the two classifications overlap pretty closely). The deutero-phallic phase would appear to be more neurotic than the proto-phallic—at least in this particular context. For it is associated with anxiety, conflict, striving against accepting what is felt to be reality, i.e. castration, and overcompensatory emphasis on the narcissistic value of the penis on the boy's side with a mingled hope and despair on the girl's.

It is plain that the difference between the two phases is marked by the idea of castration, which according to Freud is bound up in both sexes with actual observation of the anatomical sex differences. As is well known, he[6] is of opinion that the fear or thought of being castrated has a weakening effect on the masculine impulses with both sexes. He considers that with the boy it drives him away from the mother and strengthens the phallic and homosexual attitude, i.e. that the boy surrenders some of his incestuous heterosexuality to save his penis; whereas with the girl it has the more fortunate opposite effect of impelling her into a feminine, heterosexual attitude. According to this view, therefore, the castration complex weakens the boy's Oedipus relationship and strengthens the girl's; it drives the boy *into* the deutero-phallic phase, while—after a temporary protest on that level—it drives the girl *out of* the deutero-phallic phase.

As the development of the boy is supposed to be better understood, and is perhaps the simpler of the two, I will begin with it. We are all familiar with the narcissistic quality of the phallic phase here, which Freud says reaches its maximum about the age of 4, though it is certainly manifest long before this;[7] I am speaking particularly of the deutero-phallic phase. There are two outstanding differences between it and the earlier stages: (1) it is less sadistic, the main relic of this being a tendency to omnipo-

---

[6]Freud: "Some Psychological Consequences of the Anatomical Distinction between the Sexes," *International Journal of Psycho-Analysis*, 1927, vol. 8, pp. 133, 141.
[7]When this paper was read before the British Psycho-Analytical Society three child analysts (Melanie Klein, Melitta Schmideberg, and Nina Searl) gave it as their experience that traces of the *deutero*-phallic phase can be detected before the end of the first year.

tence phantasies; and (2) it is more self-centred, the chief allo-erotic attribute still remaining being its exhibitionistic aspect. It is thus less aggressive and less related to other people, notably to women. How has this change been brought about? It would seem to be a change in the direction of phantasy and away from the real world of contact with other human beings. If so, this would in itself justify a suspicion that there is a flight element present, and that we have not to do simply with a natural evolution toward greater reality and a more developed adjustment.

This suspicion is very evidently borne out in one set of circumstances, namely—when the phallic phase persists into adult life. In applying the psycho-analytic microscope to investigate a difficult problem we may make use of the familiar magnification afforded by neurosis and perversion. Elucidation of the operative factors there gives us pointers to direct our attention in examining the so-called normal; as will be remembered, this was the path Freud followed to reach in general the infantile sexuality of the normal. Now with these adult cases it is quite easy to ascertain the presence of secondary factors in the sexual life, factors particularly of fear and guilt. The type I have especially in mind is that of the man, frequently hypochondriacal, who is concerned with the size and quality of his penis (or its symbolic substitutes) and who shows only feeble impulses toward women, with in particular a notably weak, or even non-existent, impulse toward penetration; narcissism, exhibitionism (or undue modesty), masturbation and a varying degree of homosexuality are common accompanying features. In analysis it is easily seen that all these inhibitions are repressions or defences motivated by deep anxiety; the nature of the anxiety I shall discuss presently.

Having our eyes sharpened by such experiences to the secondary nature of narcissistic phallicism, we may now turn to similar attitudes in boyhood—I am again referring to the deutero-phallic phase and in pronounced examples—and I maintain that we find there ample evidence to come to a similar conclusion. To begin with, the picture is essentially the same. There is the narcissistic concentration on the penis, with doubts or uncertainties about its size and quality. Under the heading of "secondary reinforcement of penis-pride," Melanie Klein[8] has in her recent book discussed at length the value of the penis to the boy in mastering deep anxieties from various

---

[8]Melanie Klein: *The Psycho-Analysis of Children* (International Psycho-Analytical Library, 1932), p. 341.

sources, and she maintains that the narcissistic exaggeration of phallicism—
i.e. the phallic phase, although she does not use that term in this connection—is due to the need of coping with specially large amounts of anxiety.

It is noteworthy how much of the boy's sexual curiosity of this period, to which Freud[9] called special attention in his original paper on the
subject, is taken up, not with interest in females, but with comparisons
between himself and other males. This is in accord with the striking absence of the impulse toward penetration, an impulse which would logically
lead to curiosity and search for its complement. Karen Horney[10] has rightly
called special attention to this feature of inhibited penetration, and as the
impulse to penetrate is without doubt the main characteristic of penis functioning it is surely remarkable that just where the idea of the penis dominates the picture its most salient characteristic should be absent. I do not
for a moment believe that this is because the characteristic in question has
not yet been developed, a retardation due perhaps to simple ignorance of a
vaginal counterpart. On the contrary, in earlier stages—as child analysts in
particular have shown—there is ample evidence of sadistic penetrating tendencies in the phantasies, games, and other activities of the male infant. And
I quite agree with Karen Horney[11] in her conclusion that "the undiscovered
vagina is a denied vagina." I cannot resist comparing this supposed ignorance of the vagina with the current ethnological myth that savages are ignorant of the connection between coitus and fertilization. In both cases they
know, but do not know that they know. In other words, there is knowledge, but it is *unconscious knowledge*—revealed in countless symbolic ways.
The conscious ignorance is like the "innocence" of young women—which
still persists even in these enlightened days; it is merely unsanctioned or
dreaded knowledge, and it therefore remains unconscious.

Actual analysis in adult life of the memories of the phallic stage yields
results that coincide with the state of affairs where the phallic stage has
persisted into adult life, as mentioned above, and also with the results
obtained from child analysis[12] during the phallic stage itself. They are, as
Freud first pointed out, that the narcissistic concentration on the penis goes
hand in hand with dread of the female genital. It is also generally agreed
that the former is secondary to the latter, or at all events to the fear of

---

[9]Freud: "The Infantile, etc.," op. cit., p. 246.
[10]Karen Horney: "The Dread, etc.," op. cit., pp. 353, 354.
[11]Karen Horney: "The Dread, etc.," op. cit., p. 358.
[12]See in particular Melanie Klein: *The Psycho-Analysis of Children*.

castration. It is not hard to see, further, that these two fears—of the female genital and of castration—stand in a specially close relationship to each other, and that no solution of the present group of problems can be satisfactory which does not throw equal light on both.

Freud himself does not use the word "anxiety" in regard to the female genital, but speaks of "horror" *(Abscheu)* of it. The word "horror" is descriptive, but it implies an earlier dread of castration and therefore demands an explanation of this in its turn. Some passages of Freud's read as if the horror of the female were a simple phobia protecting the boy from the thought of castrated beings, as it would from the sight of a one-legged man, but I feel sure he would admit a more specific relationship than this between the idea of castration and the particular castrated organ of the female; the two ideas must be innately connected. I think he implies that this horror is an associative reminder of what awful things, i.e. castration, happen to people (like women) who have feminine wishes or who get treated as women. It is certainly plain, as we have long known, that the boy here equates copulation with castration of one partner; and he evidently fears lest he might be that unfortunate partner. In this connection we may remember that to the neurotic phallic boy the idea of the female being castrated involves not simply a cutting off, but an opening being made into a hole, the well-known "wound theory" of the vulva. Now in our everyday practice we should find it hard to understand such a fear except in terms of a repressed wish to play the feminine part in copulation, evidently with the father. Otherwise castration and copulation would not be equated. A fear of this wish being put into effect would certainly explain the fear of being castrated, for by definition it is identical with this, and also the "horror" of the female genital, i.e. a place where such wishes had been gratified. But that the boy equates copulation with castration seems to imply a previous knowledge of penetration. And it is not easy on this hypothesis to give adequate weight to the well-known connection between the castration fear and rivalry with the father over possession of the mother, i.e. to the Oedipus complex. But we can at least see that the feminine wish must be a nodal point in the whole problem.

There would seem to be two views on the significance of the phallic phase, and I shall now attempt to ascertain in what respect they are opposed to each other and how far they may be brought into harmony. We may call them the simple and the complex view respectively. On the one hand, the boy, in a state of sex ignorance, may be supposed to have always assumed that the mother has a natural penis of her own until actual experience of the female genital, together with ideas of his own concerning castration (particularly his equating of copulation with castration), makes him reluctantly suspect that she has been castrated. This would accord with his known wish to believe that the mother has a penis. This simple view rather skims over the evidently prior questions of where the boy gets his ideas of copulation and castration from, but it does not follow that these could not be answered on this basis; that is a matter to be held in suspension for the moment. On the other hand, the boy may be supposed to have had from very early times an unconscious knowledge that the mother has an opening—and not only the mouth and anus—into which he could penetrate. The thought of doing so, however, for reasons we shall discuss in a moment, brings the fear of castration, and it is as a defense against this that he obliterates his impulse to penetrate, together with all idea of a vagina, replacing these respectively by phallic narcissism and insistence on his mother's similar possession of a penis. The second of these views implies a less simple—and avowedly a more remote—explanation of the boy's insistence on the mother's having a penis. It is, in effect, that he dreads her having a female organ more than he does her having a male one, the reason being that the former brings the thought and danger of penetrating into it. If there were only male organs in the world there would be no jealous conflict and no fear of castration; the idea of the vulva must precede that of castration. If there were no dangerous cavity to penetrate into there would be no fear of castration. This is, of course, on the assumption that the conflict and danger arise from his having the same wishes as his father, to penetrate into the same cavity; and this I believe—in conjunction with Melanie Klein and other child analysts—to be true of the earliest period, and not simply after the conscious discovery of the cavity in question.

We come now to the vexed question of the source of castration fears. Various authors hold different views on this question. Some of them are perhaps differences in accent only; others point to opposing conceptions. Karen Horney,[13] who has recently discussed the matter in relation to the boy's dread of the female genital, has very definite views on the matter. Speaking of the dread of the vulva she says: "Freud's account fails to explain this anxiety. A boy's castration-anxiety in relation to his father is not an adequate reason for his dread of a being whom this punishment has

---

[13]Karen Horney: "The Dread, etc.," op. cit., p. 351.

already overtaken. Besides the dread of the father there must be a further dread, the object of which is the woman or the female genital." She even maintains the exceptional opinion that this dread of the vulva is not only earlier than that of the father's penis—whether external or concealed in the vagina—but deeper and more important that it; in fact much of the dread of the father's penis is artificially put forward to hide the intense dread of the vulva.[14] This is certainly a very debateable conclusion, although we must admit the technical difficulty of quantitatively estimating the amount of anxiety derived from different sources. We listen with curiosity to her explanation of this intense anxiety in regard to the mother. She mentions Melanie Klein's view of the boy's talion dread born in relation to his sadistic impulses toward the mother's body, but the most important source of his dread of the vulva she would derive from the boy's fear of his self-esteem being wounded by knowing that his penis is not large enough to satisfy the mother, the mother's denial of his wishes being interpreted in this sense; the talion dread of castration by the mother is later and less important than the fear of ridicule.[15] One often gets, it is true, a vivid clinical picture of how strong this motive can be, but I doubt whether Dr. Horney has carried the analysis of it far enough. In my experience the deep shame in question, which can certainly express itself as impotence, is not simply due to the fear of ridicule as an ultimate fact; both the shame and the fear of ridicule proceed from a deeper complex—the adoption of a feminine attitude toward the father's penis that is incorporated in the mother's body. Karen Horney also calls attention to this feminine attitude, and even ascribes to it the main source of castration fear, but for her it is a secondary consequence of the dread of ridicule. We are here again brought back to the question of femininity and perceive that to answer it satisfactorily is probably to resolve the whole problem.

I will now try to reconstruct and comment on Karen Horney's argument about the connection between the dread of the vulva and the fear of castration. At the start the boy's masculinity and femininity are relatively free. Karen Horney quotes Freud's well-known views on primal bisexuality in support of her belief that the feminine wishes are primary. There probably are such primary feminine wishes, but I am convinced that conflict arises only when they are developed or exploited as a means of deal-

---

[14]Karen Horney: "The Dread, etc.," op. cit., pp. 352, 356.
[15]Karen Horney: "The Dread, etc.," op. cit., p. 357.

ing with a dreaded father's penis. However, Karen Horney thinks that before this happens the boy has reacted to his mother's denial of his wishes and, as described above, feels shame and a deep sense of inadequacy in consequence. As a result of this he can no longer express his feminine wishes freely. There is a gap in the argument here. In the first place we are to assume that the boy at once equates his phallic inadequacy with femaleness, but it is not explained how the equation is brought about. At all events, he is now ashamed of his earlier feminine wishes and dreads these being gratified because it would signify castration at the hands of the father; in fact, this is the essential cause of these castration fears. Surely there is another big gap in the argument here. How does the father suddenly appear on the scene? The essential point in the argument, and one on which I would join issue with Dr. Horney, would appear to be that the boy's sense of failure due to his mother's refusal leads him to fall back from his masculine wishes to feminine ones, which he then applies to the father but dreads to have gratified because of the admission they imply of his masculine inferiority (as well as the equivalence of castration). This is rather reminiscent of Adler's early views on the masculine protest. My experience leads me, on the contrary, to see the crucial turning-point in the Oedipus complex itself, in the dreaded rivalry with the father. It is to cope with this situation that the boy falls back on a feminine attitude with its risk of castration. Whereas Dr. Horney regards the feminine attitude as a primary one which the boy comes to repress because of the fear of ridicule of his masculine inferiority, this fear being the active dynamic agent, I should consider that the sense of inferiority itself, and the accompanying shame, are both secondary to the feminine attitude *and to the motive for this*. This whole group of ideas is strongest in men with a "small penis" complex, often accompanied by importance, and it is with them that one gets the clearest insight into the genesis. What such a man is really ashamed of is not that his penis is "small," but the reason *why* it is "small."

On the other hand I fully agree with Karen Horney and other workers, notably Melanie Klein,[16] in the view that the boy's reaction to the crucial situation of the Oedipus complex is greatly influenced by his earlier relationship with his mother. But this is a much more complicated matter than wounded vanity: far grimmer factors are at work. Melanie Klein lays

---

[16] Melanie Klein: "Early Stages of Oedipus Conflict," *International Journal of Psycho-Analysis*, vol. 9, 1928, p. 167.

stress on the fear of the mother's retaliation for the boy's sadistic impulses against her body; and this independently of any thought of the father or his penis, though she would agree that the latter heightens the boy's sadism and thus complicates the picture. As she has pointed out in detail, however, these sadistic impulses have themselves an elaborate history. We have to begin with the alimentary level to appreciate the nature of the forces at work. Privations on this level—especially perhaps oral privations—are undoubtedly of the greatest importance in rendering harder the later task of coping with the parents on the genital level, but we want to know exactly why this should be so. I could relate cases of a number of male patients whose failure to achieve manhood—in relation to either men or women—was strictly to be correlated with their attitude of needing first to acquire something from women, something which of course they never actually could acquire. Why should imperfect access to the nipple give a boy the sense of imperfect possession of his own penis? I am quite convinced that the two things are intimately related, although the logical connection between them is certainly not obvious.

I do not know to what extent a boy in the first year of life feels sure his mother has a genital organ like his own, on grounds of natural identification, but my impression is that any such idea has no serious interest for him until it gets involved in other associations. The first of these would appear to be the symbolic equivalency of nipple and penis. Here the mother's penis is mainly a more satisfying and nourishing nipple, its size alone being an evident advantage in this respect. Now how precisely does a bilateral organ, the breast, get changed into a medial one, the penis? When this happens does it mean that the boy, perhaps from his experiences or phantasies of the primal scene, has already come across the idea of the father's penis, or is it possible that even before this his early masturbatory experiences—so often associated with oral ones—together with the commonly expressed oral attitude toward his own penis, alone suffice for the identification? I am inclined to the latter opinion, but it is hard to get unequivocal data on the matter. Whichever of these alternatives is true, however, the attitude toward the mythical material penis must from the very first be ambivalent. On the one side there is the conception of a visible, and therefore accessible, friendly and nourishing organ which can be received and sucked. But on the other side the sadism stimulated by oral frustration—the very factor that first created the conception—must by projection create the idea of a sinister, hostile, and dangerous organ which has to be destroyed by swallowing before the boy can feel safe. This ambivalence, beginning in regard to the mother's nipple (and nipple-penis), is greatly intensified when the father's penis becomes involved in the associations. And it does so, I feel convinced, very early in life—certainly by the second year. This may be quite irrespective of actual experiences, even of the father's very existence, and is generated mainly by the boy's own libidinal sensations in his penis with their inevitable accompaniment of penetrative impulses. The ambivalent attitude is intensified on both sides. On the one hand the tendency to imitate the father gets related to the idea of acquiring strength from him, first of all orally, and on the other hand we get the well-known Oedipus rivalry and hostility, which also is first dealt with in terms of oral annihilation.

These considerations relating to the oral level begin to throw light to the riddle I propounded earlier, namely, why so many men feel unable to put something into a woman unless they have first got something out of her; why they cannot penetrate; or—put more broadly—why they need to pass through a satisfactory feminine stage before they can feel at home in a masculine one. I pointed out earlier on that in the feminine wishes of the boy must lie the secret of the whole problem. The first clue is that this feminine stage is an alimentary one, primarily oral. Satisfaction of wishes in this stage has to precede masculine development; failure in this respect results in fixation on the woman at an oral or anal level, a fixation which although originating in anxiety may become intensely eroticised in perverse forms.

I shall now try to proceed further in the answering of our riddle, and for the sake of simplicity shall consider separately the boy's difficulties with the mother and father respectively. But I must preface this by laying stress on its artificiality. When we consider the parents as two distinct beings, to be viewed separately one from the other, we are doing something that the infant is not yet capable of and something that does not greatly concern the infant in his (or her) most secret phantasies. We are artificially dissecting the elements of a concept (the "combined parent concept," as Melanie Klein well terms it) which to the infant are still closely interwoven. The findings of child analysis lead us to ascribe ever-increasing importance to the phantasies and emotions attaching to this concept, and I am very inclined to think that the expression "pre-Oedipal phase" used recently by Freud and other writers must correspond extensively with the phase of life dominated by the "combined parent" concept.

At all events let us consider first the relation to the mother alone. Leaving the father's penis quite out of account, we are concerned with the riddle of how the boy's acquiring something from the mother is related to his secure possession of the use of his own penis? I believe this connection between the oral and the phallic lies in the sadism common to both. The oral frustration evokes sadism and the penetrating penis is used in phantasy as a sadistic weapon to reach the oral aims desired, to open a way to the milk, feces, nipple, babies, and so on, all of which the infant wants to swallow. The patients I alluded to earlier as having a perverse oral fixation on women were all highly sadistic. The equation tooth = penis is familiar enough, and it must begin in this sadistic pregenital stage of development. The sadistic penis has also important anal connections, e.g. the common phantasy of fetching a baby out of the bowel by the penis. The penis itself thus comes to be associated with the acquiring attitude, and thwarting of the latter to be identified with thwarting of the former; i.e. not being able to get milk, etc., is equivalent to not being able to use the penis. The thwarting leads further to retaliation fears of the mother damaging the weapons themselves. This I have even found on occasion equated with the earliest frustration. The mother's withholding of the nipple gave her the character of a nipple or penis hoarder who would surely keep permanently any penis brought near her, and the boy's sadism can in such cases manifest itself—as a sort of double bluff—by a sadistic policy of withholding from the woman whatever she may desire, e.g. by being impotent.

Though this conflict with the mother no doubt lays the basis for later difficulties, my experience seems to teach me that greater importance is to be attached in the genesis of castration fear to the conflict with the father. But I have at once to add a very important proviso. In the boy's imagination the mother's genital is for so long inseparable from the idea of the father's penis dwelling there that one would get a very false perspective if one confined one's attention to his relationship to his actual "external" father; this is perhaps the real difference between Freud's pre-Oedipal stage and [the] Oedipus complex proper. It is the hidden indwelling penis that accounts for a very great part of the trouble, the penis that has entered the mother's body or been swallowed by her—the dragon or dragons that haunt cloacal regions. Some boys attempt to deal with it on directly phallic lines, to use their penis in their phantasy for penetrating the vagina and crushing the father's penis there, or even—as I have many times found—by pursuing this phantasy to the length of penetrating into the father's body itself, i.e. sodomy. One sees again, by the way, how this illustrates the close interchangeability of the father and mother *imagines;* the boy can suck either or penetrate into either. What we are more concerned with here, however, is the important tendency to deal with the father's penis on feminine lines. It would be better to say "on apparently feminine lines," for true feminine lines would be far more positive. Essentially I mean "on oral- and anal-sadistic lines," and I believe it is the annihilation attitude derived from this level that affords the clue to the various apparently feminine attitudes: the annihilation is performed by the mouth and anus, by teeth, feces and—on the phallic level—urine. Over and again I have found this hostile and destructive tendency to lie behind not merely the obviously ambivalent attitude in all femininity in men, but behind the affectionate desire to please. After all, apparently complacent yielding is the best imaginable mask for hostile intentions. The ultimate aim of most of this femininity is to get possession of, and destroy, the dreaded object. Until this is done the boy is not safe; he cannot really attend to women let alone penetrate into them. He also projects his oral and anal destructive attitude, which relates to the father's penis, on to the cavity that is supposed to contain it. This projection is facilitated by association with the earlier sadistic impulses, oral and phallic, against the mother's body, with their talion consequences. Destruction of the father's penis further means robbing the penis-loving mother of her possession. To penetrate into this cavity would therefore be as destructive to his own penis as he knows penetration of his father's penis into his mouth would be to it. We thus obtain a simple formula for the Oedipus complex: my (so-called feminine, i.e. oral destructive) wishes against my father's penis are so strong that if I penetrate into the mother's vagina with them still in my heart the same fate will happen to me, i.e. if I have intercourse with my mother my father will castrate me. Penetration is equated with destruction, or—to recur to the more familiar phrase used earlier—copulation is equated with castration. But—and this is the vital point—what is at stake is not castration of the mother, but of the boy or else his father.

After having considered the various sources of castration anxiety, and the problem of femininity in the male, I now return to the original question of why the boy in the phallic phase needs to imagine that his mother really has a penis, and I will couple with it the further question—not often raised—of whose penis it really is. The answer is given in preceding considerations, and to avoid repetition I will simply express it as a statement. *The presence of a visible penis in the mother would signify at once a reassurance in respect of the early oral needs, with a denial of any need for dangerous sadism to deal with privation, and above all a reassurance that no castration has taken place, that neither his father nor himself is in danger of it.* This conclusion also answers the question of whose penis it is the mother must have.[17] It is her own only in very small part, the part derived from the boy's earliest oral needs. To a much greater extent it is the father's penis; though it may also in a sense be said to be the boy's own, inasmuch as his fate is bound up with it through the mutual castration danger to both his father and himself.

The reason why actual sight of the female genital organ signalizes the passage from the proto- to the deutero-phallic phase has also to be given. Like the experiences of puberty, it makes manifest what had previously belonged solely to the life of phantasy. It gives an actuality to the fear of castration. It does this, however, not by conveying the idea that the father has castrated the mother—this is only a mask of rationalization in consciousness—but by arousing the possibility that a dangerous repressed wish may be gratified in reality, namely, the wish to have intercourse with the mother and to destroy the father's penis. In spite of various suggestions to the contrary, the Oedipus complex provides the key to the problem of the phallic phase, as it has done to so many others.

We have travelled far from the conception that the boy, previously ignorant of the sex difference, is horrified to find that a man has violently created one by castrating his mate and turning her into a woman, a castrated creature. Even apart from actual analysis of the early childhood years, the proposition that the boy has no intuition of the sex difference is on logical grounds alone hard to hold. We have seen that the (deutero-) phallic phase depends on the fear of castration and that this in its turn implies the danger of penetration; it would appear to follow from this alone that intuition of a penetrable cavity is an early underlying assumption in the whole complex reaction. When Freud says that the boy renounces his incest wishes toward his mother in order to save his penis, this implies that the penis was the offending carrier of those wishes (in the proto-phallic phase). Now what could these penis wishes that endanger its existence have been if not to perform the natural function of the penis—penetration? And this inference is amply substantiated by actual research.

I may now summarize the conclusions reached. The main one is that *the typical phallic stage in the boy is a neurotic compromise rather than a natural evolution in sexual development.* It varies, of course, in intensity, probably with the intensity of the castration fears, but it can be called inevi-

---

[17]Melanie Klein, "The Psycho-Analysis of Children," p. 333, answers this question categorically: "The woman with a penis" always means, I should say, the woman with the father's penis."

table only in so far as castration fears, i.e. infantile neuroses, are inevitable; and how far these are inevitable we shall know only when we have further experience of early child analysis. At all events the mere need to renounce incest wishes does not make it inevitable; it is not the external situation that engenders the phallic phase, but—probably avoidable—complications in the boy's inner development.

To avoid the imagined and self-created dangers of the Oedipus situation the boy in the phallic phase abandons the masculine attitude of penetration, which all interest in the inside of the mother's body, and comes to insist on the assured existence of his own and his "mother's" external penis. This is tantamount to Freud's "passing of the Oedipus complex," the renunciation of the mother to save the penis, but it is not a direct stage in evolution; on the contrary, the boy has later to retrace his steps in order to evolve, he has to claim again what he had renounced—his masculine impulses to reach the vagina; he has to revert from the temporary neurotic deutero-phallic phase to the original and normal proto-phallic phase. Thus the typical phallic phase, that is, the deutero-phallic phase, in my opinion, represents a neurotic obstacle to development rather than a natural stage in the course of it.[18]

Turning now to the corresponding problem in girls we may begin by noting that the distinction mentioned earlier between the proto- and the

---

[18]It may be of interest to note the respects in which the conclusions here put forward agree with or differ from those of the two authors, Freud and Karen Horney, with whose views there has been most occasion to debate. In agreement with Freud is the fundamental view that the passage from the proto- to the deutero-phallic phase is due to fear of castration at the hands of the father, and that this essentially arises in the Oedipus situation. Freud would, I think, also hold that the feminine wishes behind so much of the castration fear are generated as a means of dealing with the loved and dreaded father: he would possibly lay more stress on the idea of libidinally placating him, whereas I have directed more attention to the hostile and destructive impulses behind the feminine attitude. On the other hand I cannot subscribe to the view of sex ignorance on which Freud repeatedly insists—though in one passage on primal scenes and primal phantasies (*Ges. Sch.*, bd. XI, s. 11) he appears to keep the question open—and I regard the idea of the castrated mother as essentially a mother whose man has been castrated. Nor do I consider the deutero-phallic phase as a natural stage in development.

With Karen Horney there is agreement in her scepticism about sex ignorance, in her doubts about the normality of the (deutero-) phallic phase, and in her opinion that the boy's reaction to the Oedipus situation is greatly influenced by his previous relation to his mother. But I think she is mistaken in her account of the connection between these two last matters, and consider that the boy's fear of his feminine wishes—which we all appear to hold behind the castration fear—arise not in shame at his literal masculine inferiority in his relation to his mother, but in the dangers of his alimentary sadism when this operates in the Oedipus situation.

deutero-phallic phase is if anything more prominent with girls than with boys. So much so that when I made the suggestion that the phallic phase in girls represents a secondary solution of conflict I was under the impression that by the phallic phase was meant what I now see to be only the second half of it, a misapprehension Professor Freud corrected in a recent correspondence; incidentally, his condemnation of my suggestion[19] was partly based on the same misunderstanding, since on his part he naturally thought I was referring to the whole phase. In extenuation I may remark that in his original paper Freud gave no account of the phallic phase in girls, on the score of its extreme obscurity, and that his definition—a phase in which it is believed that the sex difference is between penis-possessing and castrated beings—strictly applies only to the deutero-phallic phase, the penis being supposed to be unknown in the first one.

The difference between the two halves of the phase in Freud's conception is similar to that pointed out earlier with boys. According to him, a clitoris supremacy sets in at a certain age when the girl is ignorant of the difference between the clitoris and the penis and so is in a state of contented bliss in the matter; this I am calling for the moment the proto-phallic phase of girls, which corresponds with that of boys when they are similarly supposed to be ignorant of the sex difference. In the deutero-phallic phase, the one I had suggested was a secondary defensive reaction, the girl is aware of the difference and, like the boy, either admits it reluctantly—and in this case resentfully—or tries to deny it. In the denial, however, unlike the state of affairs alleged to exist with boys, there is implied some real knowledge of the difference, for the girl does not maintain the previous belief—that both sexes have a satisfactory clitoris—but wishes that she now had a different organ from before, viz. a real penis. This wish goes on to imaginary fulfilment with homosexual women, who reveal implicitly in their behaviour and explicitly in their dreams the belief that they really have a penis; but even with the more normal girl during her deutero-phallic phase the same belief that she has a penis alternates with the wish to have one.

As with boys, the two halves of the phase are divided by the castration idea, by the idea that women are nothing but castrated beings—there being no such thing as a true female organ. The boy's wish in the deutero-phallic stage is to restore the security of the proto-phallic one which has been disturbed by the supposed discovery of castration; to revert to the original identity of the sexes. The girl's wish in the deutero-phallic stage is

---

[19]Freud: "Female Sexuality," op. cit., p. 297.

similarly to restore the undisturbed proto-phallic one, and even to intensify its phallic character; thus to revert to the original identity of the sexes. This I take to be a more explicit statement of Freud's conception.

Two distinct views appear to be held in respect of female sexual development, and to bring out the contrast between them I will exaggerate them in the following over-simple statement. According to one, the girl's sexuality is essentially male to start with (at least as soon as she is weaned), and she is driven into femaleness by failure of the male attitude (disappointment in the clitoris). According to the other, it is essentially female to start with, and she is—more or less temporarily—driven onto a phallic maleness by failure of the female attitude.

This is avowedly an imperfect statement, which does not do justice to either view, but it may serve to point a discussion. I will call the two A and B respectively and add a few obvious modifications which will make them more exact and also diminish the grossness of the difference between them. The supporters of A would, of course, admit an early bisexuality, though they maintain that the male (clitoris) attitude predominates; they would also agree to the so-called regressive (anxiety) factors in the deutero-phallic phase, though they hold these to be less important than the libidinal impulse to maintain the original maleness. On the other side the supporters of B would also admit an early bisexuality, an early clitoris maleness in addition to the more pronounced femaleness: or—to put it more cautiously without begging any question—the coexistence of active and passive aims which tend to get associated with particular genital areas. They would also admit that there is often little apparent love for the father, who is regarded mainly as a rival, in the early stage of mother fixation; and in the deutero-phallic phase they would agree that direct auto-erotic, and therefore libidinal, penis envy plays an important part together with the anxiety factors in driving the girl from femaleness into the phallic maleness. Again, there is general agreement that the experience of seeing a penis powerfully influences the transition from the proto- to the deutero-phallic phase, though not about the reasons why it does so. Further, both views agree that in the deutero-phallic phase the girl desires a penis,[20] and blames

---

[20]Incidentally, I may comment here on the ambiguity of such phrases as "to desire a penis," "the wish for a penis." In fact three meanings of such phrases are to be discerned in connection with infantile female sexuality: (1) The wish to acquire a penis, usually by swallowing, and to retain it within the body, often converting it there into a baby; (2) the wish to possess a penis in the clitoritic region: for this purpose it may be acquired in more than one way; (3) The adult wish to enjoy a penis in coitus. I shall try to make it clear in each case which meaning is intended.

the mother for her lack of it, though whose penis she desires and why she desires it are questions not so readily answered.

Nevertheless, in spite of these modifications, there remain differences of opinion, in regard to both halves of the phase, and by no means in respect of accent only. In investigating the corresponding obscurity of male sexual development it proved useful to lay stress on the correlation between the problems of castration fear and dread of the vulva. Here I would similarly bring into prominence a correlation between the problems of the girl's desire to own a penis and her hate of her mother, since I feel sure that to explain either of these is to explain the other. And I will anticipate my conclusions to the extent of remarking that it may prove possible to combine in a single formula the male equation of problems with the female one.

In attempting to elucidate the contrasting views described above I will avail myself of two clues, both provided by Freud. The first of them is contained in his remark[21] that the girl's earliest attachment to her mother "has in analysis seemed to me so elusive, lost in a past so dim and shadowy, so hard to resuscitate that it seemed as if it had undergone some specially inexorable repression." We must all agree when he points out that the ultimate solution of all these problems lies in a finer analysis of the girl's very earliest period of attachment to the mother, and it is highly probable that the differences of opinion in respect of the later stage of development are mainly, and perhaps altogether, due to different assumptions concerning the earlier stage.

To give an example of this: Freud,[22] in criticizing Karen Horney, describes her view as being that the girl, from fear of advancing to femininity, *regresses* in the deutero-phallic stage. So sure is he that the earlier (clitoris) stage can only be a phallic one. But this is just one of the questions at issue; to anyone taking the opposite view the process just mentioned would not be a regression, but a neurotic new-formation. And it is a question to be discussed. We should not take it too much for granted that the use of the clitoris is altogether the same thing psychologically as the use of the penis simply because they are physio-genetically homologous. Sheer accessibility may also play its part. The clitoris is after all a part of the female genitals. Clinically the correspondence between clitoris masturbation and a male attitude is very far indeed from being invariable. I have known, on the one hand,

---

[21]Freud: "Female Sexuality," op. cit., p. 282.
[22]Freud: "Female Sexuality," op. cit., p. 296.

a case where the clitoris could not function because of a congenital malformation, but where the vulval masturbation was distinctly male in type (prone posture, etc.). On the other hand, cases where clitoris masturbation in the adult accompanies the most pronouncedly feminine heterosexual phantasies are an everyday experience, and Melanie Klein[23] states that this combination is characteristic of the earliest infancy. In my Innsbruck paper I expressed the opinion that vaginal excitation played a more important part in the earliest childhood than was recognised—in contradistinction from Freud's[24] opinion that it begins only at puberty—a view that had been previously expressed by several women analysts, Melanie Klein (1924),[25] Josine Müller (1925),[26] and Karen Horney (1926).[27] This opinion I had reached first from the same class of material as Josine Müller quotes: namely, women who show strong masculine propensities in conjunction with vaginal anesthesia. What is important about this early vaginal functioning, so deeply repressed, is the extraordinary amount of anxiety that goes with it (far more than with clitoric functioning), a matter to which we shall have to recur. Actual vaginal masturbation is often considered by physicians to be commoner than clitoris masturbation in the first four or five years of life, whereas it certainly is not so during the latency period—a fact in itself suggesting a change from feminine to more masculine attitudes. Apart, however, from actual vaginal functioning there is extensive evidence of feminine phantasies and wishes in early childhood to be obtained from both adult and early analyses: phantasies relating to the mouth, vulva, womb, anus, and the receptive attitude of the body in general. For all these reasons I feel that the question of the alleged clitoritic and therefore masculine primacy of the female infant may well be kept in suspense until we know more about the sexuality of this very early stage.

A cognate example of misunderstanding due to differing primary assumptions arises in connection with the problem of the intensity and of the direction (aim) characteristic of the deutero-phallic phase. Freud, who

---

[23]Melanie Klein: *The Psycho-Analysis of Children*, op. cit., p. 288.
[24]Freud: "Female Sexuality," op. cit., p. 283.
[25]Melanie Klein: "From the Analysis of an Obsessional Neurosis in a Six-year-old Child," First German Psycho-Analytical Assembly, Würzburg, October 11, 1924.
[26]Josine Müller: "A Contribution to the Problem of Libidinal Development of the Genital Phase in Girls," *International Journal of Psycho-Analysis*, 1932, vol. 13, p. 361.
[27]Karen Horney: "The Flight from Womanhood," *International Journal of Psycho-Analysis*, 1926, vol. 7, p. 334. She has comprehensively sustained this opinion in a paper published in the present number of *International Journal of Psycho-Analysis*, see vol. 7, p. 57.

holds that both intensity and direction are to be explained in terms of the proto-phallic masculine phase, and that the trauma of seeing the penis only reinforces this, criticizes Karen Horney for believing that the direction alone is given by the proto-phallic phase, the intensity being derived from later (anxiety) factors.[28] In so far, however, as Karen Horney is a supporter of view B—and I cannot of course say just how far this is so—she would maintain the exact converse of the view Freud ascribes to her; she would agree with him that the intensity of the deutero-phallic phase is derived from the earlier one (though with displacement) and differ from him only in holding that its direction is not so derived, being in the main determined by secondary factors. All this again depends on whether the earlier phase is regarded predominantly masculine and autoerotic or predominantly feminine and allo-erotic.

Freud[29] would appear to hold that the question is settled by the very fact that many young girls have a long and exclusive mother attachment. He calls this a pre-Oedipal stage of development, one where the father plays very little part and that a negative one (rivalry). These facts of observation are not to be doubted—I can myself quote an extreme case where the exclusive mother attachment was prolonged till near puberty, at which age an equally exclusive transference to father took place. But they do not in themselves exclude a positive Oedipus complex in girl's unconscious imagination: they prove only that, if this does exist, it has not yet learned to express itself in relation to the actual father. In my experience of typical cases of this kind, however, and in that of child analysts, particularly of Melanie Klein, Melitta Schmideberg, and Nina Searl, analysis shows that the girls had from very early times definite impulses toward an imaginary penis, one incorporated into the mother but derived from the father, together with elaborate phantasies on the subject of parental coitus. I would again remind you at this point of the stress laid in the earlier part of the paper on the "combined parent concept," the picture of parents fused in coitus.

We are here led to consider the second of the clues to which I referred just now. It concerns the young girl's theories of coitus, which play a highly important part in her sexual development. They should be helpful in the present connection, since—as Freud has long ago shown—the sexual

---

[28]Freud: "Female Sexuality," op. cit., p, 296.
[29]Freud: "Female Sexuality," op. cit., p. 296.

theories of a child are a mirror of its particular sexual constitution. A few years ago Professor Freud wrote to me that of the two points of which he felt most sure in the obscurity of female sexual development one was that of the young girl's first idea of coitus was an oral one, i.e. fellatic.[30] Here, as usual, he put his finger on a central point. But it is probable that the matter is more complex: at all events, this central consideration has several corollaries that are worth pursuing. In the first place, it is hardly likely that a purely oral conception would develop if the first thought of coitus occurred years after the infant's own oral experiences; and detailed analysis of this early period, especially by child analysts, confirms what one might expect:— namely, that the experiences and the conception are closely related not only genetically, but also chronologically. Melanie Klein[31] attributes great importance to the stimulus given to the child's desires by the inevitable imperfections and dissatisfactions of the suckling period, and would connect the weaning time both with the deepest sources of hostility to the mother and with a dawning idea of a penis-like object as a more satisfying kind of nipple. That nipple wishes are transferred to the idea of the penis, and that the two objects are extensively identified in the imagination, is fairly familiar ground, but it is hard to say when this transference begins to be applied to the father in person. It is, I think, certain that for a relatively long time they apply more to the mother than to the father, i.e. that the girl seeks for a penis in her mother. By the second year of life this vague aspiration is getting more definite and is getting connected with the idea of the mother's penis having been derived from the father in the supposed act of fellatio between the parents.

In the next place, the fellatic idea can hardly be confined to the notion of purposeless sucking. The child well knows that one sucks for a purpose—to get something. Milk (or semen) and (nipple-) penis are thus things to swallow, and by the familiar symbolic equations, as well partly from the child's own alimentary experiences, we reach also the ideas of excrement and baby—equally obtained from this primordial sucking act. According to Freud,[32] the child's love and sexuality are essentially devoid of aim (ziellos), and for this very reason are doomed to disappointment. The con-

---

[30]I may also quote the other point, since any pronouncement from such a source must command interest. It was that the girl gives up masturbation because of her dissatisfaction with the clitoris (in comparison with the penis).
[31]Melanie Klein: *The Psycho-Analysis of Children,* op. cit., p. 326.
[32]Freud: "Female Sexuality," op. cit., p. 286.

trary view is that in the unconscious there are very definite aims, and the disappointment is due to their not being reached.

I wish to make clear at this point that the wishes here referred to are in my opinion essentially allo-erotic. The girl infant has not yet had the occasion to develop auto-erotic envy at the sight of a boy's penis; the desire to possess one herself, for the reasons so clearly stated by Karen Horney,[33] comes later. At the earlier stage the wish to take the penis into the body, through the mouth, and make a (fecal) baby out of it is, though still on an alimentary level, nevertheless akin to the allo-erotism of the adult woman. Freud[34] holds that when the girl's wish to own a penis is disappointed it is replaced by a substitute—the wish to have a child. I would, however, agree rather with Melanie Klein's[35] view that the penis–child equation is more innate, and that the girl's wish to have a child—like the normal woman's wish—is a direct continuance of her allo-erotic desire for the penis; she wants to enjoy taking the penis into the body and to make a child from it, rather than to have a child because she cannot have a penis of her own.

The purely libidinal nature of the wishes manifests itself in many ways, of which I will mention only one. The insertion of the nipple into the mouth is followed by the anal-erotic pleasure at the passage of feces, and the cleansing process associated with this is often felt by the girl to be a sexual experience with the mother (or nurse). The point of this observation is that the mother's hand or finger is equated to a penis and is often the seduction that leads to masturbation.

Now if the mother gets all this—just what the girl longs for—from the father, then a situation of normal Oedipus rivalry must surely exist, and in exact proportion to the girl's own dissatisfaction. The accompanying hostility is in direct line with that felt previously toward the mother in the suckling period, being of the same order; and it reinforces it. The mother has got something the girl wants and will not give it to her. In this something the idea of the father's penis soon comes to crystallize more and more definitely, and the mother has obtained it from the father in successful competition with girl, as well as the baby she can make from it.

---

[33]Karen Horney: "On the Genesis of the Castration Complex in Women," *International Journal of Psycho-Analysis*, 1924, vol. 5, pp. 52–54.
[34]Freud: "Some Psychological Consequences, etc.," op. cit., p. 140.
[35]Melanie Klein: *The Psycho-Analysis of Children*, op. cit., p. 309.

This is in disagreement with Freud's[36] formidable statement that the concept of the Oedipus complex is strictly applicable only to male children and "it is only in male children that there occurs the fateful conjunction of love for the one parent and hatred of the other as rival." We seem compelled here to be *plus royalist que le roi*.

Freud's fellatio account of coitus, however, from which we started, yields no explanation for the important observation on which he insists,[37] that the girl infant feels rivalry for her father. The fellatio conception of coitus, in fact, would seem to be only one half of the story. One finds also the complementary idea that the father not only gives to the mother, but receives from her; that in short she suckles him. And it is here that the direct rivalry with the father is so strong, for the mother is giving him just what the girl wants (nipple and milk); other sources of rivalry, hate, and resentment in respect of the father I shall mention presently. When this "mammalingus" conception, as it may be called, gets sadistically cathected, then we have the familiar feminist idea of the man who "uses" the woman, exhausts her, drains her, exploits her, and so on.

The girl infant doubtless identifies herself with both sides in these conceptions, but in the nature of the case her wanting, receiving desires must be more prominent than the giving ones; there is so much that she wants and so little that she has to give at that age.

What then of the phallic activity against the mother recorded by Helene Deutsch, Jeanne Lampl-De-Groot, Melanie Klein, and other women analysts? We must not forget how early the child apprehends the penis not simply as an instrument of love, but also as a weapon of destruction. In the girl's sadistic furor against the mother's body, due largely to her inability to suffer thwarting, she clutches at all weapons, mouth, hands, feet; and in this connection the sadistic value of the penis, and the power it gives of directing destructive urine, is perhaps not the least of its uses which she envies the boy. We know that thwarting stimulates sadism, and, to judge from their phantasies as well as actual conduct, it would seem very difficult to overestimate the quantity of sadism present in infants. On talion grounds this leads to corresponding fear, and again it seems difficult to overestimate the depth and intensity of fear in infants. We must regard the sexual development of both boys and girls as influenced at all points

---

[36]Freud: "Female Sexuality," op. cit., p. 284.
[37]Freud: "Female Sexuality," op. cit., p. 282.

by the need to cope with fear, and I must agree with Melanie Klein's[38] scepticism about the success of Freud's[39] avowed endeavour to depict sexual development without reference to the super-ego, i.e. to the factors of guilt and fear.

At this point I am constrained to express the doubt whether Freud does not attach too much significance to the girl's concern about her external organs (clitoris-penis) at the expense of her terrible fears about the inside of her body. I feel sure that to her the inside is a much stronger source of anxiety and that she often parades concern about the outside as a defensive attitude, a conclusion the truth of which Melanie Klein[40] has demonstrated in great detail in her penetrating investigations of the earliest years of female development. Josine Müller[41] has happily remarked that the anatomical fact of the girl's having two genital organs—the internal vagina (and womb) and the external clitoris—enables her to displace erotogenicity from the internal to the external when the former is threatened. After all, the central dread of the guilty girl—even in consciousness—is that she will never be able to bear children, i.e. that her internal organs have been damaged. We are reminded of Helene Deutsch's[42] triad of equivalent female fears; castration, defloration, and parturition—though the first of these needs careful definition—and of the characteristic adult fears of "internal diseases," prominent among which is cancer of the womb.

The early dread of the mother, just as the hate of her, is transferred to the father, and both dread and hate are often curiously concentrated on the idea of the penis itself. Just as the boy projects his sadism on to the female organs, and then exploits these dangerous organs as a means of destroying his father homosexually, so does the girl project her sadism on to the male organ, and very largely with a similar outcome. It is one of the oddest experiences to find a woman who has devoted herself to a penis-acquiring career (homosexually) having at the same time fear, disgust, and hatred of any real penis. In such cases one gets a vista of the dread and horror that get developed in regard to the penis, the most destructive

---

[38]Melanie Klein: *The Psycho-Analysis of Children*, op. cit., p. 323.
[39]Freud: "Female Sexuality," op. cit., p. 294.
[40]Melanie Klein: *The Psycho-Analysis of Children*, op. cit., pp. 269 et seq.
[41]Josine Müller, op. cit., p. 363.
[42]Helene Deutsch: "The Significance of Masochism in the Mental Life of Women," *International Journal of Psycho-Analysis*, 1930, vol. 11, p. 48.

of all lethal weapons, and how terrifying can be the idea of its penetrating into the inside of the body.[43] This particular projection is so important that one must ask how much of the girl's fear is the result of her sadistic wishes to bite away (and swallow) the penis, tearing it from the mother, or later the father, with the consequent dread lest the dangerous—because sadistically conceived—penis penetrate her; it is hard to say, but this may possibly be the very centre of the matter.

As the girl grows she often transfers her resentment from the mother to the father when she more clearly understands that it is he who really owns (and withholds) the penis. Freud[44] quotes this curious transference of hostility, resentment, and dissatisfaction from the mother to the father as a proof that it cannot arise from rivalry with the mother, but we have just seen that another explanation is at least possible. It is fully intelligible that there should be resentment at the thwarting of the allo-erotic penis desire, which the father's presence stimulates, and that this applies first to the mother and then to the father. An additional tributary flows into the resentment against the father for his thwarting the libidinal desire; namely, that this thwarting has also the effect of exposing the girl to her dread of the mother. For where there is a dread of punishment for a wish then gratification of this wish may be the strongest safeguard against the anxiety, or at least is commonly believed by the unconscious to be so; and anyone, therefore, who denies this gratification commits a double crime—he refuses at the same time both libidinal pleasure and security.

We have to bear in mind all this background, which is doubtless only an extract of the true complexity, when we attempt to reconstruct the development of the deutero-phallic phase. At this point the girl becomes *consciously* aware of a real penis attached to male beings, and she characteristically reacts to it by wishing to possess one herself. Why exactly does she have this wish? What does she want the penis for? That is a crucial question, and the answer to it must also provide the answer to the equally crucial question of the source of the girl's hostility to her mother. Here we get a fairly clear-cut issue between views A and B, one which should prove stimulating to further research.

---

[43]Hence, amongst other things, the frequency of beating phantasies where penetration is obviated.

[44]Freud: "Female Sexuality," op. cit., pp. 281, 286.

The answer to both questions given by view A undoubtedly has the merit of being simpler than that given by view B. According to it the girl wishes to possess the penis she sees because that is the sort of thing she has always prized, because she sees in it her wildest dreams of an efficient clitoris being realised in the nth degree. There is no serious internal conflict in the matter, only resentment, particularly against her mother whom she holds responsible for the disappointment that inevitably ensues. Envy of the penis is the principal reason for turning from the mother. The actual value of the clitoris-penis would appear to be essentially auto-erotic, the best exposition of which was given years ago by Karen Horney.[45] The wish is almost entirely libidinal, and is in the same direction as the girl's earlier tendencies. When this wish is disappointed, the girl falls back on a feminine incestuous allo-erotic attitude, but as a second best. Any so-called defence there may be against femininity, or rather objection to it, is dictated not so much by any deep fear of it in itself, but by the desire to retain the masculine clitoris–penis position, which it imperils; in other words, by the same objection boys would have were they offered the alternative, namely, because it is tantamount to castration. This view, which in a word explains both the hate of the mother and the strength of the deutero-phallic phase by one main factor—the auto-erotic desire to possess a clitoris-penis—is both simple and consistent. The question is, however, whether it is also comprehensive, i.e. whether its underlying assumptions in the proto-phallic phase take into due account all the ascertainable factors.

The answer given by view B is that the girl originally desired the penis allo-erotically, but is driven into an auto-erotic position (in the deutero-phallic phase) in the same way that boys are—from fear of the supposed dangers attaching to the allo-erotic desires. I may here cite a few authors who illustrate sharply the contrasting views. On the one hand Helene Deutsch,[46] in accord with Freud, writes: "My view is that the Oedipus complex in girls is inaugurated by the castration-complex." On the other hand Karen Horney[47] speaks of "these typical motives for flight into the male role—motives whose origin is the Oedipus complex," and Melanie Klein[48] asserts "in my view the girl's defence against her feminine attitude springs less from her masculine tendencies than from her fear of her mother."

---

[45]Karen Horney: "On the Genesis, etc.," loc. cit.
[46]Helene Deutsch: "The Significance, etc.," op. cit., p. 53.
[47]Karen Horney: "The Flight, etc.," op. cit., p. 337.
[48]Melanie Klein: *The Psycho-Analysis of Children*, op. cit., p. 324.

The masculine from of auto-erotism is thus here the second best; it is adopted because femininity—the real thing desired—brings danger and intolerable anxiety. The deepest source of resentment against the mother is the imperfect oral satisfaction, which leads the girl to seek a more potent nipple—a penis—in an allo-erotic and later in a hetero-erotic, direction; the libidinal attitude toward the nipple here expresses itself as feminine phantasies associated with vulval—either vaginal or clitoritic—masturbation, alone or with the nurse in cleansing operations. She is homosexually attached to the mother at this stage, because it is only from her that she can hope to obtain the desired penis satisfaction, by guile or force. This is all the easier because after all the mother is still at this early age the main source of (allo-erotic) libidinal gratification. And she is dependent on her mother not only for affection and gratification, but also for the satisfying of all her vital needs. Life would be impossible without the mother and the mother's love. There are therefore the strongest possible motives for the girl's intense attachment to her mother.

Nevertheless in the unconscious there is another side to the picture, and a much grimmer one. The sadistic impulse to assault and rob the mother leads to intense dread of retaliation, which often develops—as was explained earlier—into dread of the penetrating penis; and this is revived when she comes across a real penis attached, not to the mother, but to the father or brother. Here she is actually no worse off than before—she still has a clitoris, and the mother has taken nothing away from her. She blames her, however, for not having given her more—a penis—but behind this reproach that the mother has insufficiently attended to her auto-erotic desires lies the deeper and stronger one that she has thwarted the true, feminine needs of her receptive and acquisitive nature and has threatened to destroy her body if she persists in them. View B would therefore appear to give more adequate reasons for hostility to the mother than does view A. Both agree about the pregenital thwarting at the mother's hands, but they differ in their estimate of the thwarting on the genital level. There, according to the one view, A, the mother deprives the girl of nothing, but there is resentment at not being given more; according to other view, B, the mother both thwarts the feminine aims (toward the penis) and also threatens to mutilate the body—i.e. to destroy the real feminine penis-receiving and child-bearing organs—unless the girl renounces those aims. Small wonder that she does renounce them, always to some extent and often altogether.

The deutero-phallic phase is her reaction to this situation, her defence against the dangers of the Oedipus complex.[49] Her desire in it to possess a penis of her own saves her threatened libido by deflecting it into the safer auto-erotic direction, just as it is saved when deflected into a perversion. This shifting on to the auto-erotic (and therefore more ego-syntonic), with its consequent neurotic intensification, meets in its turn with disappointment. There are very few girls who do not deceive themselves—to some extent throughout life—about the source of their inferiority feelings. The real source, as always with inferiority feelings, is internal forbiddenness because of guilt and fear, and this applies to the allo-erotic wishes far more than to the auto-erotic ones.

But there are additional advantages in this phallic position, hence its great strength. It is a complete refutation of the feared mother's attack on her femininity, because it denies its very existence and therefore all reason for any such attack. And there are also still more irrational unconscious phantasies. The ambivalence toward the mother can be dealt with. On the one hand the girl is now armed with the most powerful weapon of attack, and therefore of protection; Joan Riviere[50] has called special attention to this motive. On the other hand, by the important mechanism of restitution, one to which Melanie Klein has devoted important studies in this connection, she can compensate for her dangerous wishes to rob the mother of a penis: she now has a penis to restore to the deprived mother, a process which plays an extensive part in female homosexuality. Further, she no longer runs any risk of being sadistically assaulted by the man's dangerous penis. Freud[51] asks whence, if there were any flight from femininity, could it derive its source except from masculine strivings. We have seen that there may be much deeper sources of emotional energy in the girl than masculine strivings, though these can often prove a well-disguised outlet for them.

There will, I think, be general agreement on one point at least—namely, that the girl's desire for a penis is bound up with her hate of the mother. The two problems are inherently related, but it is over the nature

---

[49]This view, maintained in my Innsbruck Congress paper, was, I think, first put forward by Karen Horney ("On the Genesis, etc.," op. cit., p. 50), and has been elaborately developed by Melanie Klein: *The Psycho-Analysis of Children*, op. cit., pp. 271, etc.

[50]Joan Riviere: "Womanliness as a Masquerade," *International Journal of Psycho-Analysis*, 1929, vol. 10, p. 303.

[51]Freud: "Female Sexuality," op. cit., p. 297.

of this relationship that there is the sharpest division of opinion. Whereas Freud holds that the hate is a resentment at the girl's not being granted a penis of her own, the view presented here, one which has been well sustained by Melanie Klein,[52] is that the hate is essentially a rivalry over the father's penis. In the one view the deutero-phallic phase is a natural reaction to an unfortunate anatomical fact, and when it leads to disappointment the girl falls back on hetero-erotic incest. In the other view the girl develops at a very early age hetero-erotic incest, with Oedipus hate of the mother, and the deutero-phallic phase is an escape from the intolerable dangers of that situation; it thus has exactly the same significance as the corresponding phenomenon with the boy.

I should like now in summing up to institute a general comparison between these problems in boys and girls respectively. With both the idea of functioning in the hetero-erotic direction appropriate to their nature (penetrating with boys, receiving penetration with girls) is absent—? renounced—in the deutero-phallic phase. And with both there is an equally strong denial—? repudiation—of the vagina: every effort is made toward the fiction that both sexes have a penis. There must surely be a common explanation for this central feature of the deutero-phallic phase in both sexes, and both the views here discussed provide one. According to the first, it is the discovery of the sex difference—with its unwelcome implication; according to the second it is a deep dread of the vagina, derived from anxiety about the ideas of parental coitus associated with it, a dread which is often re-activated by seeing the genital organ of the opposite sex.

Probably the central difference between the two views, the one from which other differences emanate and where therefore our research must be specially directed, is over the varying importance attached by different analysts to the early unconscious phantasy of the father's penis incorporated in the mother. That the phantasy in question occurs has been well known to analysts for more than twenty years, but—as a result especially of Melanie Klein's notable researches—we may have to recognise it as a never-failing feature of infantile life and to learn that the sadism and anxiety surrounding it play a dominating part in the sexual development of both boys and girls. This generalization could profitably be extended to all the phantasies described by Melanie Klein and other child analysts in connec-

---

[52]Melanie Klein: *The Psycho-Analysis of Children*, op. cit., p. 270.

tion with what she has called the "combined parent" concept, one which I suggested earlier is closely associated with Freud's pre-Oedipal stage of development.

Not only is the main characteristic of the deutero-phallic phase—the suppression of hetero-erotic functioning—essentially the same with boys and girls, but so also is the motive for it. The renunciation is effected in both cases for the sake of bodily integrity, to save the sexual organs (external with the boy, internal with the girl). The girl will not risk having her vagina or womb damaged any more than the boy will his penis. Both sexes have the strongest motives for denying all ideas of coitus, i.e. of penetration, and they therefore keep their minds set on the outside of the body.[53]

In the two sections of this paper I used as a starting-point a pair of related problems: with boys the fear of castration and the dread of the vulva, with girls the desire to own a penis and the hate of the mother. It is now possible to show that the essential nature of these two apparently unlike pairs is common to both sexes. The common features are the avoidance of penetration and fear of injury from the parent of the same sex. The boy fears castration at the hands of his father if he penetrates into the vagina; the girl fears mutilation at the hands of the mother if she allows herself to have a penetrable vagina. That the danger is often associated, by projection, with the parent of the opposite sex, in the manner I have described above, is a secondary manifestation; its real source is hostility toward the rival parent of the same sex. We have in fact the typical Oedipus formula: incestuous coitus brings with it fear of mutilation by the rival parent. And this is as true of the girl as of the boy, in spite of the more extensive homo-sexual disguise she is compelled to adopt.

To return to the concept of the phallic phase. If the view here advanced is valid, then the term proto-phallic I suggested earlier applies to the boy only. It is unnecessary, since it really means simply genital; it can even be misleading, since it predisposes one to think of the boy's early genital functions in a purely phallic, i.e. auto-erotic, sense to the exclusion of the allo-erotism that exists from the earliest times—in the first year or life itself. For girls the term will be still more misleading in the eyes of

---

[53] I am not suggesting that this is the only motive force at work. As Joan Riviere pointed out in the discussion when this paper was read before the British Society, it falls into line with the general tendency toward exteriorization in the growing child's search to establish contact with the outer world.

those who hold that the earliest stage of their development is essentially feminine. As to the sex ignorance said to characterise the proto-phallic phase this is no doubt true of consciousness, but there is extensive evidence to show that it is not true of the unconscious; and the unconscious is an important part of the personality.

I come now to what I call the deutero-phallic phase, the one generally meant when one uses simply the term "phallic phase." View A we have discussed above tends to regard the deutero-phallic phase as a natural development, in both sexes, out of a proto-phallic phase, its direction being much the same in the two. View B lays more stress on the extent to which the deutero-phallic phase is a deflection from the earlier one, comprising in important respects even a reversal of the direction of the latter. This may perhaps be most sharply expressed by saying that *the previous heterosexual allo-erotism of the early phase is in the deutero-phallic one—in both sexes—largely transmuted into a substitutive homosexual auto-erotism. This later phase would thus—in both sexes—be not so much a pure libidinal development as a neurotic compromise between libido and anxiety*, between the natural libidinal impulses and the wish to avoid mutilation. Strictly speaking, it is not a neurosis proper, inasmuch as the libidinal gratification still open is a conscious one, not unconscious as it is in neurosis. It is rather a sexual aberration and might well be given the name of the *phallic perversion*. It is closely akin to sexual inversion, manifestly so with girls. This connection is so close that—although it is not strictly germane to the purpose of my paper—I will venture to apply to the problem of inversion some considerations that arise from the present theme. It would seem as if inversion is in essence hostility to the rival parent that has been libidinised by the special technique of appropriating the dangerous organs of the opposite sex, organs that have been made dangerous by sadistic projection. We saw earlier to what an extent the genital sadism was derived from the earlier oral sadism, so it may well be that the oral sadism I suggested on an earlier occasion[54] was the specific root of female homosexuality is that of male homosexuality also.[55]

To avoid any possible misunderstanding I would remind you that the phallic phase, or phallic perversion, is not to be regarded as a definitely fixed entity. We should think of it, as of all similar processes, in dynamic

---

[54]E. Jones, 1927, op. cit.
[55]Melanie Klein (op. cit., p. 326) would trace this to an "oral-sucking fixation."

and economic terms. It shows, in other words, every possible variation. It varies in different individuals from slight indications to the most pronounced perversion. And in the same individual it varies in intensity from one period to another according to the current changes in stimulation of the underlying agencies.

Nor do I commit myself to the view that the phallic phase is necessarily pathological, though it obviously may become so through exaggeration or fixation. It is a deviation from the direct path of development, and it is a response to anxiety, but nevertheless, for all we know, research may show that the earliest infantile anxiety is inevitable and that the phallic defence is the only one possible at that age. Nothing but further experience in analysis at early ages can answer such questions. Further, the conclusions here come to do not deny the biological, psychological, and social value of the homosexual constituent in human nature; there we come back to our one and only gauge—the degree of free and harmonious functioning in the mental economy.

I will allow myself now to single out the *conclusions* which seem to me to be the most significant.

The first is that the typical (deutero-) phallic phase is a perversion subserving, as do all perversions, the function of salvaging some possibility of libidinal gratification until the time comes—if it ever comes—when fear of mutilation can be dealt with the temporarily renounced hetero-erotic development be once more resumed. The inversion that acts as a defence against the fear depends on the sadism that gave rise to the fear.

Then we would seem to have warrant for recognising more than ever the value of what perhaps has been Freud's greatest discovery—the Oedipus complex. I can find no reason to doubt that for girls, no less than for boys, the Oedipus situation, in its reality and phantasy, is the most fateful psychical event in life.

Lastly I think we should do well to remind ourselves of a piece of wisdom whose source is more ancient than Plato: In the beginning . . . male and female created He them.

7

ADRIENNE APPLEGARTH ON KAREN HORNEY

Ahead of Her Time

ADRIENNE APPLEGARTH

One of the most impressive and alluring features of Freud's writing for me has always been his reliance on observable data in constructing his theories, especially the clinical theory. He drew on data not only from actual psychoanalytic treatments that he and others conducted, but also from child observation, literature, and myth. To this reader, exhilarated by such clear use of good science in Freud's thinking, it was startling to encounter what has always seemed to me to be a significant departure from these principles as he developed his ideas about female sexual function and development. A number of his formulations did not seem to fit either the experiences of my patients or my own, although this observation made more sense when considered in the light of his admission that he found the details of female psychology and development rather mysterious and difficult for him to access directly. Some of the features of his theories of female sexuality seemed then and continue to seem cramped and constrained by his choice to base them on his ideas and observations of male development.

Certain aspects of his theories provoked controversy very early and in more recent years have been extensively examined and debated. These aspects include the view of libido as basically male, and of the girl as being a "little man" in her earliest development. Thus the boy and girl supposedly have the same psychosexual development until the onset of penis envy in the girl forces divergence; then, out of disappointment at not having a penis, she gives up her negative oedipal attachment to her mother and takes her father as her sexual object. Moreover, the wish for a child was regarded as reactive and compensatory for the lack of the penis. Finally, superego development was regarded as less firm and complete in the girl because the principal stimulus for its formation, that is, castration anxiety, was absent in girls.

With all of these points Horney took issue in a series of papers, mainly in the *International Journal of Psycho-Analysis*, published between 1924 and 1933. These were entitled: "On the Genesis of the Castration Complex in Women" (1924), "The Flight From Womanhood" (1926), "The Dread of Women" (1932), "The Problem of Feminine Masochism" (1935), and "The Denial of the Vagina" (1933), which I want to mention particularly here.

What I found especially impressive, coming to psychoanalysis from physiology, was Horney's clear reliance on observation, both from children's and from adult analyses, in her challenge to Freud's ideas. On this basis she followed Freud's example and principles most closely and was therefore able to give the clearest challenge to his ideas. In this she was supported at the time by several of the pioneers, notably Jones and Fenichel. It is interesting that she was not supported by other female analysts, although they were said to be better able to study female sexuality in their women patients. A full summary of these debates is given by Fliegel (1973).

One can only conjecture what the climate of these debates might have been at that time, since the published material is fairly decorous and circumspect. Hints appear, for example, in Freud's terse rejection, in his paper of 1931, of both Horney's and Jones's contributions. In that paper, Freud not only appeared to bring his authority to bear rather than to compare his evidence with that offered by others, but he also accepted as supporting evidence material from Lampl-de-Groot (1927) that under other circumstances he would have surely regarded with a skeptical eye. I refer to Lamp-de-Groot's assertion that material indicating a strong maternal attachment appearing late in the analysis (1) was negative-oedipal, that is, triangular, in nature, and that, (2) because it came out after the other material in the analysis, it must have occurred earlier developmentally. These deviations from scientific discourse must indicate strong underlying emotional complications in the discussion.

It must thus have required a great deal of courage for Horney to move out of the ranks of the other analysts and to step into whatever "battle of the sexes" would inevitably have been swept into these debates. In the realm of relations between the sexes and ideas about what is native to men and women, many vested interests, emotional and otherwise, become involved. For such reasons, and probably because Horney later followed a somewhat divergent path, the debate on female sexuality more or less disappeared until more favorable circumstances allowed its resumption in the late 1960s. One of these favorable circumstances was the appearance of new evidence in the work of Masters and Johnson (1966), which I will describe more fully below. In addition, their work was highlighted by Mary Jane Sherfey (1966), whose work, in turn, touched off new and more extensive discussions of these issues in the Volume 16, Number 3, 1968, and Volume 24, Number 5, 1976, issues of the *Journal of the American Psychoanalytic Association*. The social climate of the times also undoubtedly contributed heavily to a renewed determination to study female development more fully. In any case, the topic has remained very much on the table since then.

I would like to turn now in more detail to "The Denial of the Vagina" (Horney 1933). In this paper, Horney summarizes some material from her earlier work, and then emphasizes certain points where observations seem to contradict several of Freud's ideas.

First of all, concerning the idea of the girl being initially a little man, she calls attention to what anyone could see of little girls, namely, that they are typically feminine in important ways very early in life, between the ages of 2 and 5 behaving coquettishly toward men, for example. She also notes that evidences of penis envy can be present without any suggestion of masculinity, and finds that breast and childbearing envy can be present in boys without their being feminine. She suggests that innate bisexuality leads to uncertain sexual role designation for a time, this only being settled as feelings of object love develop. In her earlier papers, she developed at length her ideas about the genesis of penis envy and the role that she suggests it plays in female development.

In the paper under discussion here, and as part of her argument in favor of innate feminine drives, she cites evidence of various kinds, often from children, showing that awareness of the vagina exists early and that it plays an important role in masturbation. This point is made in response to Freud's contention that, since the clitoris is basically an undeveloped penis embryologically and anatomically and therefore must be functionally male, it must consequently be the main masturbatory organ during the pregenital, masculine development of the girl; the vagina, as an aspect of being female, only comes into its own after male masturbation is renounced under the pressure of the female castration complex arising out of penis envy. (This line of reasoning is an excellent example of a "genetic fallacy," as Hartmann [1955] has called it.) Horney points out the difficulty of investigating this in adult female patients who have various sexual problems, and whose fantasies about the function of their sexual organs may not correspond to the actual functions during development or adulthood.

Horney then develops the theme of the vaginal anxieties which girls have, including the girl's ideas of rape and injury by the large penis of the father, were her positive oedipal wishes to be fulfilled. In addition, girls develop fears that they have injured themselves by masturbation, fears fueled by observation of menstrual blood and childbirth. She regards these anxieties as a more dynamic explanation for the suppression of masturbation in girls than Freud's idea that girls give up clitoral masturbation because of an inadequate organ. She also suggests a further source of vaginal anxieties in the fear of retribution by the mother for the girl's hostile fantasies.

While it was difficult to make systematic observations in Horney's day, more recently the work of Masters and Johnson (1966) has provided solid confirmation of her preliminary observations and speculations. Because Masters and Johnson studied the actual physiological responses of the genitals of women through direct observation by videotape, this material could be compared to the subjective responses of the subjects. It was clear immediately that the whole genital apparatus, including the clitoris, was involved in the sexual responses of these women. More recently yet (1966), Sherfey applied these observations to the psychoanalytic theories of female sexual function in an extensive review. Her main interest centered on the type and quality of orgasm in women. In the course of this review, she summarized in detail evidence both from embryology and from the work of Masters and Johnson, using this material for a reconsideration of aspects of Freud's theory of female sexual development. Interestingly enough, Horney does not appear in her bibliography.

It seems that Horney was ahead of her time in her work on female sexuality. How gratifying it is to see from the tone of many contemporary discussions how much of her thinking is appearing again and being validated. However, even now she does not seem to be accorded all the credit which her clear thinking and courage should merit; Sherfey's bibliography is not the only one which fails to cite Horney's papers.

For me, in particular, Horney's work was most important in adding strength to the view that female sexual development is neither a modified and inadequate version of male sexual development, nor centrally determined by reactions to male sexuality. My attention was originally drawn to the whole developmental theory because of the considerable number of women in my practice who were having problems in work or in academic life (Applegarth 1976). At that time the prevailing psychoanalytic climate supported the view that having ambitions and pursuing them outside the marriage and childbearing realm was to be understood as related to compensatory masculine striving originating in penis envy. Here was another important area where penis envy was unquestioningly considered to be a vital organizer of female psychology.

In any case, it had always seemed a doubtful proposition to me that all the many uses and enjoyments of the mind and its activities could be accounted for merely on the basis of vicissitudes of drive in either sex. It always seemed more plausible that these represent independent ego activities which are hugely added to or interfered with by drives and conflicts around them, and thus should be regarded as expectable ego activities of both sexes.

But Horney also pointed out, in passing, another important shortcoming of Freud's theory, namely, how inadequately it accounted for the intensity of the woman's wish for a child. This perception stimulated my own clinical and theoretical observations in this area (1988); it has seemed most plausible to me that this wish for a child has the force of a drive and should be regarded as an extension of psychosexual development in women.

Freud's theory of female development did offer an explanation of sexual object choice in terms of a response to penis envy, as Horney noted briefly, but, while disputing his version, she was not able to offer an explanation herself, other than to suggest an innate factor. We still do not understand what leads to sexual object choice, either hetero- or homosexual, and we are left with a central absorbing question.

Another area where Horney's thought has impinged upon my own work is with the topic of envy. While her work displaced penis envy as the central dynamic in women, it did not consider another potential observation, that is, whether envy generally is more commonly found in women. This question has stimulated my current observations and thinking about the topic of envy and its causes, especially the important question of whether it is something innate, as Klein has suggested.

As is apparent, I hope, all of Horney's writings on female development, not just the paper "Denial of the Vagina," have been important for my work. And I hope that my admiration of her courage, her clear observations, and her thinking are also equally clear.

REFERENCES

Applegarth, A. (1976). Some observations on work inhibitions in women. *Journal of the American Psychoanalytic Association* 24 (suppl.):251–269.

——— (1988). Origins of femininity and the wish for a child. *Psychoanalytic Inquiry* 8:160–176.

Fenichel, O. (1930). The pregenital antecedents of the Oedipus complex. In *The Collected Papers of Otto Fenichel*, first series, ed. H. Fenichel and D. Rapaport, pp. 181–203. New York: Norton, 1953.

——— (1934). Further light upon the preoedipal phase in girls. In *The Collected Papers of Otto Fenichel*, first series, ed. H. Fenichel and D. Rapaport, pp. 241–288. New York: Norton, 1953.

Fliegel, Z. O. (1973). Feminine psychosexual development in Freudian theory: a historical reconstruction. *Psychoanalytic Quarterly* 42:385–408.

Freud, S. (1931). Female sexuality. *Standard Edition* 21:225–243.

Hartmann, H. (1955). Notes on the theory of sublimation. *Psychoanalytic Study of the Child* 10:9–29. New York: International Universities Press.

Horney, K. (1924). On the genesis of the castration complex in women. *International Journal of Psycho-Analysis* 5:50–65.

——— (1926). The flight from womanhood: the masculinity-complex in women, as viewed by men and by women. *International Journal of Psycho-Analysis* 7:324–339.

——— (1932). The dread of women. Observation on a specific difference in the dread felt by men and by women respectively for the opposite sex. *International Journal of Psycho-Analysis* 13:348–360.

——— (1933). The denial of the vagina: a contribution to the problem of the genital anxieties specific to women. *International Journal of Psycho-Analysis* 14:57–70.

——— (1935). The problem of feminine masochism. *Psychoanalytic Review* 22:241–257.

Jones, E. (1927). The early development of female sexuality. In *Papers on Psychoanalysis*, pp. 438–451. Boston: Beacon, 1961.

——— (1933). The phallic phase. In *Papers on Psychoanalysis*, pp. 452–484. Boston: Beacon, 1961.

——— (1935). Early female sexuality. In *Papers on Psychoanalysis*, pp. 484–495. Boston: Beacon, 1961.

Lampl-de-Groot, A. (1927). The evolution of the Oedipus complex in women. *International Journal of Psycho-Analysis* 9:332–345.

Masters, W., and Johnson, V. (1966). *Human Sexual Response*. Boston: Little, Brown.

Sherfey, M. J. (1966). The evolution and nature of female sexuality in relation to psychoanalytic theory. *Journal of the American Psychoanalytic Association* 14:28–129.

The Denial of the Vagina: A Contribution to the Problem of the Genital Anxieties Specific to Women

KAREN HORNEY

The fundamental conclusions to which Freud's investigations of the specific character of feminine development have led him are as follows: first, that in little girls the early development of instinct takes the same course as in boys, both in respect of the erotogenic zones (in the two sexes only one genital organ, the penis, plays a part, the vagina remaining undiscovered) and also in respect of the first choice of object (for both the mother is the first love-object). Secondly, that the great differences which nevertheless exist between the two sexes arise from the fact that this similarity of libidinal trend does not go with similar anatomical and biological foundations. From this premise it follows logically and inevitably that girls feel themselves inadequately equipped for this phallic orientation of their libido and cannot but envy boys their superior endowment in that respect. Over and above the conflicts with the mother which the girl shares with the boy, she adds a crucial one of her own; she lays at her mother's door the blame for her lack of a penis. This conflict is crucial because it is just this reproach which is essential for her detachment from her mother and her turning to her father.

Hence Freud has chosen a happy phrase to designate the period of blossoming of childish sexuality, the period of infantile genital primacy in girls as well as boys, which he calls the *"phallic phase."*

I can imagine that a man of science who was not familiar with analysis would in reading this account pass over it as merely one of the many strange and peculiar notions which analysis expects the world to believe. Only those who accept the point of view of Freud's theories can gauge the importance of this particular thesis for the understanding of feminine psychology as a whole. Its full bearings emerge in the light of one of the most momentous discoveries of Freud's, one of those achievements which, we may suppose, will prove lasting. I refer to the realization of the crucial importance for the whole subsequent life of the individual of the impressions, experiences, and conflicts of early childhood. If we accept this proposition in its entirety, i.e., if we recognize the formative influence of early experience on the subject's capacity for dealing with his later experience and the way in which he does so, there ensue at least potentially, the following consequences as regards the specific psychic life of women:

1. With the onset of each fresh phase in the functioning of the female organs—menstruation, coitus, pregnancy, parturition, suckling and the menopause—even a normal woman (as Helene Deutsch[1] has in fact assumed) would have to overcome impulses of a masculine trend before she could adopt an attitude of wholehearted affirmation toward the processes taking place within her body.

2. Again, even in normal women, irrespective of race and of social and individual conditions, it would happen altogether more readily than in men that the libido adhered, or came to be turned, to persons of her own sex. In a word: *homosexuality* would be incomparably and unmistakably more common amongst women than amongst men. Confronted with difficulties in relation to the opposite sex, a woman would plainly fall back more readily than a man into a homosexual attitude. For, according to Freud, not only are the most important years of her childhood dominated by such an attachment to one of her own sex but, when she first turns to a man (the father), it is in the main only by way of the narrow bridge of resentment. "Since I cannot have a penis I want a child instead" and "for this purpose" I turn to my father. "Since I have a grudge against my mother because of the anatomical in-

---

[1]H. Deutsch: *Psychoanalyse der weiblichen Sexualfunktionen*.

feriority for which I hold her responsible, I give her up and turn
to my father." Just because we are convinced of the formative influence of the first years of life we should feel it a contradiction if
the relation of woman to man did not retain throughout life some
tinge of this enforced choice of a substitute for that which was
really desired.[2]

3. The same character of something remote from instinct, secondary and substitutive, would, even in normal women, adhere to the
   wish for motherhood, or at least would very easily manifest itself.

   Freud by no means fails to realize the strength of the desire
   for children: in his view it represents on the one hand the principal legacy of the little girl's strongest instinctual object-relation,
   i.e. to the mother, in the shape of a reversal of the original child–
   mother relationship. On the other hand, it is also the principal
   legacy of the early, elementary wish for the penis. The special point
   about Freud's conception is rather that it views the wish for motherhood not as an innate formation, but as something that can be
   reduced psychologically to its ontogenetic elements and [that]
   draws its energy originally from homosexual or phallic instinctual
   desires.

4. If we accept a second axiom of psycho-analysis, namely, that the
   individual's attitude in sexual matters is the prototype of his attitude toward the rest of life, it would follow, finally, that woman's
   whole reaction to life would be based on a strong, subterranean
   resentment. For, according to Freud, the little girl's penis-envy
   corresponds to a sense of being at a radical disadvantage in respect of the most vital and most elementary instinctual desires.
   Here we have the typical basis upon which a general resentment
   is wont to be built up. It is true that such an attitude would not
   follow inevitably; Freud says expressly that, *where development proceeds favourably*, the girl finds her own way to the man and to
   motherhood. But here, again, it would contradict all our analytical theory and experience if an attitude of resentment so early and
   so deeply rooted did not manifest itself extremely easily—by comparison much more easily than in men under similar conditions—

---

[2]In a later work I hope to discuss the question of early object-relations regarded as the basis of
the phallic attitude in little girls.

or at any rate were not readily set going as an undercurrent det-
rimental to the vital feeling-tone of women.

These are the very weighty conclusions with regard to the whole psychology of women which follow from Freud's account of early feminine
sexuality. When we consider them, we may well feel that it behooves us to
apply again and again the tests of observation and theoretical reflection to
the facts on which they are based and to their proper appraisal.

It seems to me that analytic experience alone does not sufficiently
enable us to judge the soundness of some of the fundamental ideas which
Freud has made the basis of his theory. I think that a final verdict about
them must be postponed until we have at our disposal systematic observations of *normal* children, carried out on a large scale by persons trained in
analysis. Amongst the views in question I include Freud's statement that
"it is well known that a clearly defined differentiation between the male
and the female character is first established after puberty." The few observations which I have made myself do not go to confirm this statement.
On the contrary I have always been struck by the marked way in which
little girls between their second and fifth years exhibit specifically feminine traits. For instance, they often behave with a certain spontaneous
feminine coquetry towards men, or display characteristic traits of maternal solicitude. From the beginning I have found it difficult to reconcile
these impressions with Freud's view of the initial masculine trend of the
little girl's sexuality.

We might suppose that Freud intended his thesis of the original similarity of the libidinal trend in the two sexes to be confined to the sphere of
sex. But then we should come into conflict with the maxim that the
individual's sexuality sets the pattern for the rest of his behaviour. To clear
up this point we should require a large number of exact observations of
the differences between the behaviour of normal boys and that of normal
girls during their first five or six years.

Now it is true that, in these first years, little girls who have not been
intimidated very often express themselves in ways which admit of interpretation as early penis-envy; they ask questions, they make comparisons
to their own disadvantage, they say they want one too, they express admiration of the penis or comfort themselves with the idea that they will have
one later on. Supposing for the moment that such manifestations occurred
very frequently or even regularly, it would still be an open question what
weight and place in our theoretical structure we should give them. Con-

sistently with his total view, Freud utilizes them to shew how much even the little girl's instinctual life is dominated already by the wish to possess a penis herself.

Against this view I would urge the following three considerations:

1. In boys of the same age, too, we meet with parallel expressions in the form of wishes to possess breasts or to have a child.
2. In neither sex have these manifestations *any influence on the child's behaviour as a whole*. A boy who wishes vehemently to have a breast like his mother's may at the same time behave in general with thorough-going boyish aggressiveness. A little girl who casts glances of admiration and envy at her brother's genital may simultaneously behave as a true little woman. Thus it seems to me still an open question whether such manifestations at this early age are to be deemed expressions of elementary instinctual demands or whether we should not perhaps place them in a different category.
3. Another possible category suggests itself if we accept the assumption that there is in every human being a bisexual disposition. The importance of this for our understanding of the mind has, indeed, always been stressed by Freud himself. We may suppose that though at birth the definitive sex of each individual is already fixed physically, the result of the bisexual disposition which is always present and merely inhibited in its development, is that *psychologically* the attitude of children to their own sexual role is at first uncertain and tentative. They have no consciousness of it and therefore naturally give naive expression to bisexual wishes. We might go further and conjecture that this uncertainty only disappears in proportion as stronger feelings of love, directed to objects, arise.

To elucidate what I have just said, I may point to the marked difference which exists between these diffuse bisexual manifestations of earliest childhood, with their playful, volatile character, and those of the so-called latency-period. If, at *this* age, a girl wishes to be a boy—but here again the frequency with which these wishes occur and the social factors by which they are conditioned should be investigated—the manner in which this determines her whole behaviour (preference for boyish games and ways, repudiation of feminine traits) reveals that such wishes emanate from quite another depth of the mind. This picture, so different from the earlier one, represents, however, already the outcome of mental conflicts[3] that she has been through and cannot therefore, without special theoretical assumptions, be claimed as a manifestation of masculinity wishes which had been laid down biologically.

Another of the premises on which Freud builds up his view relates to the erotogenic zones. He assumes that the girl's early genital sensations and activities function essentially in the clitoris. He regards it as very doubtful whether any early vaginal masturbation takes place and even holds that the vagina remains altogether "undiscovered."

To decide this very important question we should once more require extensive and exact observation of normal children. Josine Müller[4] and I myself, as long ago as 1925, expressed doubts on the subject. Moreover, most of the information we occasionally get from gynecologists and children's physicians interested in psychology suggests that, just in the early years of childhood, vaginal masturbation is at least as common as clitoral. The various data which give rise to this impression are: the frequent observation of signs of vaginal irritation, such as reddening and discharge, the relatively frequent occurrence of the introduction of foreign bodies into the vagina and, finally, the fairly common complaints by mothers that their children put their fingers into the vagina. The well-known gynecologist, Wilhelm Liepmann, has stated[5] that his experience as a whole has led him to believe that, in early childhood and even in the first years of infancy, vaginal masturbation is much more common than clitoral, and that only in the later years of childhood are the relations reversed in favour of clitoral masturbation.

These general impressions cannot take the place of systematic observations, nor therefore can they lead to a final conclusion. But they do show that the exceptions which Freud himself admits seem to be of frequent occurrence.

Our most natural course would be to try to throw light upon this question from our analyses, but this is difficult. At the very best the material of the patient's conscious recollections or the memories which emerge

---

[3]Horney: "On the Genesis of the Castration Complex in Women," *International Journal of Psycho-Analysis*, 1924, vol. 5.
[4]Josine Müller: "A Contribution to the Problem of Libidinal Development of the Genital Phase in Girls," *International Journal of Psycho-Analysis*, 1932, vol. 13.
[5]In a private conversation.

in analysis cannot be treated as unequivocal evidence, because, here as everywhere else, we must also take into account the work of repression. In
other words: the patient may have good reason for not remembering vaginal sensations or masturbation, just as conversely we must feel sceptical about
her ignorance of clitoral sensations.[6]

A further difficulty is that the women who come for analysis are just
those from whom one cannot expect even an average naturalness about
vaginal processes. For they are always women whose sexual development
has departed somehow from the normal and whose *vaginal* sensibility is
disturbed in a greater or lesser degree. At the same time it does seem as if
even accidental differences in the material play their part. In approximately
two-thirds of my cases I have found the following state of affairs:

1. Marked vaginal orgasm produced by manual vaginal masturbation prior to any coitus. Frigidity in the form of vaginismus and
   defective secretion in coitus. I have seen only two cases of this
   sort which were quite unmistakable. I think that, in general, preference is shown for the clitoris or the labia in manual genital
   masturbation.
2. Spontaneous vaginal sensations, for the most part with noticeable
   secretion, aroused by unconsciously stimulating situations, such
   as that of listening to music, motoring, swinging, having the hair
   combed, and certain transference-situations. No manual vaginal
   masturbation; frigidity in coitus.
3. Spontaneous vaginal sensations produced by extra-genital masturbation, e.g. by certain motions of the body, by tight-lacing, or by
   particular sadistic-masochistic phantasies. No coitus, because of
   the overpowering anxiety aroused whenever the vagina is about
   to be touched, whether by a man in coitus, by a physician in a
   gynecological examination, or by the subject herself in manual masturbation, or in any douching prescribed medically.

For the time being, then, my impressions may be summed up as follows: in manual genital masturbation the clitoris is more commonly se-

---

[6]In a discussion following the reading of my paper on the phallic phase, before the German
Psycho-Analytical Society, in 1931, Boehm cited several cases in which only vaginal sensations
and vaginal masturbation were recollected and the clitoris had apparently remained "undiscovered."

lected than the vagina, *but spontaneous genital sensations resulting from general sexual excitations are more frequently located in the vagina*.

From a theoretical standpoint I think that great importance should be attached to this relatively frequent occurrence of spontaneous vaginal excitations even in patients who were ignorant, or had only a very vague knowledge, of the existence of the vagina, and whose subsequent analysis did not bring to light memories or other evidence of any sort of vaginal seduction, nor any recollection of vaginal masturbation. For this phenomenon suggests the question *whether from the very beginning sexual excitations may not have expressed themselves perceptibly in vaginal sensations*.

In order to answer this question we should have to wait for very much more extensive material than any single analyst can obtain from his own observations. Meanwhile there are a number of considerations which seem to me to favour my view.

In the first place there are the phantasies of rape which occur before coitus has taken place at all, and indeed long before puberty, and are frequent enough to merit wider interest. I can see no possible way of accounting for the origin and content of these phantasies if we are to assume the non-existence of vaginal sexuality. For these phantasies do not in fact stop short at quite indefinite ideas of an act of violence, through which one gets a child. On the contrary, phantasies, dreams, and anxiety of this type usually betray quite unmistakably an instinctive "knowledge" of the actual sexual processes. The guises they assume are so numerous that I need only indicate a few of them: criminals who break in through windows or doors; men with guns who threaten to shoot; animals which creep, fly or run inside some place (e.g. snakes, mice, moths); animals or women stabbed with knives; or trains running into a station or tunnel.

I speak of an "instinctive" knowledge of the sexual processes because we meet typically with ideas of this sort, e.g. in the anxieties and dreams of early childhood, at a period when as yet there is no intellectual knowledge derived from observation or from explanations by others. It may be asked whether such instinctive knowledge of the processes of penetration into the female body necessarily presupposes an instinctive knowledge of the existence of the vagina as the organ of reception. I think that the answer is in the affirmative if we accept Freud's view that "the child's sexual theories are modelled on the child's own sexual constitution." For this can only mean that the path traversed by the sexual theories of children is marked out and determined by spontaneously experienced impulses and sensations in its organs. If we accept this origin for the sexual theories, which already embody an attempt at rational elaboration, we must all the more admit it in the case of that instinctive knowledge which finds symbolic expression in play, dreams, and various forms of anxiety, and which obviously has not reached the sphere of reasoning and the elaboration which takes place there. In other words, we must assume that both the dread of rape, characteristic of puberty, and the infantile anxieties of little girls are based on vaginal organ sensations (or the instinctual impulses issuing from these), which imply that something ought to penetrate into that part of the body.

I think we have here the answer to an objection which may be raised, namely, that many dreams indicate the idea that an opening was only created when first the penis brutally penetrated the body. For such phantasies would not arise at all but for the previous existence of instincts—and the organ sensations underlying them—having the passive aim of reception. Sometimes the connection in which dreams of this type occur indicates quite clearly the origin of this particular idea. For it occasionally happens that, when a general anxiety about the injurious consequences of masturbation makes its appearance, the patient has dreams with the following typical content: she is doing a piece of needlework and all at once a hole appears, of which she feels ashamed; or she is crossing a bridge which suddenly breaks off in the middle, above a river or a chasm; or she is walking along a slippery incline and all at once begins to slide and is in danger of falling over a precipice. From such dreams we may conjecture that when these patients were children and indulged in onanistic play, they were led by vaginal sensations to the discovery of the vagina itself, and that their anxiety took the very form of the dread that they had made a hole where no hole ought to be. I would here emphasize that I have never been wholly convinced by Freud's explanation why girls suppress direct genital masturbation more easily and frequently than boys. As we know, Freud supposes[7] that (clitoral) masturbation becomes odious to little girls because comparison with the penis strikes a blow at their narcissism. When we consider the strength of the drive behind the onanistic impulses, a narcissistic mortification does not seem altogether adequate in weight to produce suppression. On the other hand, the dread that she has done herself an irreparable

---

[7] Freud: "Some Psychological Consequences of the Anatomical Distinction between the Sexes," *International Journal of Psycho-Analysis*, 1927, vol. 8.

injury in that region might well be powerful enough to prevent vaginal masturbation, and either to compel the girl to restrict the practice to the clitoris, or else permanently to set her against all manual genital masturbation. I believe that we have further evidence of this early dread of vaginal injury in the envious comparison with the man which we frequently hear from patients of this type, who say that men are "so nicely closed up" underneath. Similarly, that deepest anxiety which springs out of masturbation for a woman, the dread that it has made her unable to have children, seems to relate to the inside of the body rather than to the clitoris.

This is another point in favour of the existence and the significance of early vaginal excitations. We know that observation of sexual acts has a tremendously exciting effect upon children. If we accept Freud's view we must assume that such excitation produces in little girls in the main the same phallic impulses to penetrate as are evoked in little boys. But then we must ask: Whence comes the anxiety met with almost universally in the analyses of female patients—the dread of the gigantic penis which might pierce her? The origin of the idea of an excessively large penis can surely not be sought anywhere but in childhood, when the father's penis must actually have appeared menacingly large and terrifying. Or again, whence comes that understanding of the female sexual role, evinced in the symbolism of sexual anxiety, in which those early excitations once more vibrate? And how can we account at all for the unbounded jealous fury with the mother, which commonly manifests itself in the analyses of women when memories of the "primal scene" are affectively revived? How does this come about if at that time the subject could only share in the excitations of the father?

Let me bring together the sum-total of the above data. We have: reports of powerful vaginal orgasm going with frigidity in subsequent coitus; spontaneous vaginal excitation without local stimulus, but frigidity in intercourse; reflections and questions arising out of the need to understand the whole content of early sexual games, dreams, and anxieties, and later phantasies of rape, as well as reactions to early sexual observations; and finally certain contents and consequences of the anxiety produced in women by masturbation. If I take all the foregoing data together, I can see only one hypothesis which gives a satisfactory answer to all the questions which present themselves, the hypothesis, namely, that *from the very beginning the vagina plays its own proper sexual part*.

Closely connected with this train of thought is the problem of frigidity, which to my mind lies *not* in the question how the quality of libidinal sensibility becomes transmitted to the vagina,[8] but rather, how it comes about that the vagina, in spite of the sensibility which it already possesses, either fails altogether to react or reacts in a disproportionately small degree to the very strong libidinal excitations furnished by all the emotional and local stimuli in coitus? Surely there could be only *one* factor stronger than the will for pleasure, and that factor is anxiety.

We are now immediately confronted by the problem of what is meant by this vaginal anxiety or rather by its infantile conditioning factors. Analysis reveals, first of all, castration-impulses against the man and, associated with these, an anxiety whose source is twofold: on the one hand, the subject dreads her own hostile impulses and, on the other, the retribution which she anticipates in accordance with the law of talion, namely, that the contents of her body will be destroyed, stolen, or sucked out. Now these impulses in themselves are, as we know, for the most part not of recent origin, but can be traced to old, infantile feelings of rage and impulses of revenge against the father, feelings called forth by the disappointments and frustrations which the little girl has suffered.

Very similar in content to these forms of anxiety is that described by Melanie Klein, which can be traced back to early destructive impulses directed against the body of the mother. Once more it is a question of the dread of retribution, which may take various forms, but the essence of which is broadly that everything which penetrates the body or is already there (food, feces, children) may become dangerous.

Although, at bottom, these forms of anxiety are so far analogous to the genital anxiety of boys, they take on a specific character from that proneness to anxiety which is part of the biological make-up of girls. In this and

---

[8]In reply to Freud's assumption that the libido may adhere so closely to the clitoral zone that it becomes difficult or impossible for sensibility to be transferred to the vagina, may I venture to enlist Freud against Freud? For it was he who showed convincingly how ready we are to snatch at fresh possibilities of pleasure and how even processes which have no sexual quality, e.g. movements of the body, speech, or thought, may be eroticized and that the same is actually true of tormenting or distressing experiences such as pain or anxiety. Are we then to suppose that in coitus, which furnishes the very fullest opportunities for pleasure, the woman recoils from availing herself of them! Since to my thinking this is a problem which really does not arise, I cannot, moreover, follow H. Deutsch and M. Klein in their conjectures about the transference of the libido from the oral to the genital zone. There can be no doubt that in many cases there is a close connection between the two. The only question is whether we are to regard the libido as being "transferred" or whether it is simply inevitable that when an oral attitude has been early established and persists, it should manifest itself in the genital sphere *also*.

earlier papers I have already indicated what are these sources of anxiety and here I need only complete and sum up what has been said before:

1. They proceed first of all from the tremendous difference in size between the father and the little girl, between the genitals of father and child. We need not trouble to decide whether the disparity between penis and vagina is inferred from observation or whether it is instinctively apprehended. The quite comprehensible and indeed inevitable result is that any phantasy of gratifying the tension produced by vaginal sensations (i.e. the craving to take into oneself, to receive) gives rise to anxiety on the part of the ego. As I showed in my paper "The Dread of Woman," I believe that in this biologically determined form of feminine anxiety we have something specifically different from the boy's original genital anxiety in relation to his mother. When he phantasies the fulfilment of genital impulses he is confronted with a fact very wounding to his self-esteem ("my penis is too small for my mother"); the little girl, on the other hand, is faced with destruction of part of her body. Hence, carried back to its ultimate biological foundations, the man's dread of the woman is genital-narcissistic, while the woman's dread of the man is physical.

2. A second specific source of anxiety, the universality and significance of which is emphasized by Daly,[9] is the little girl's observation of menstruation in adult relatives. Beyond all (secondary!) interpretations of castration she sees demonstrated for the first time the vulnerability of the female body. Similarly, her anxiety is appreciably increased by observations of a miscarriage or parturition by her mother. Since, in the minds of children and (when repression has been at work) in the unconscious of adults also, there is a close connection between coitus and parturition, this anxiety may take the form of a dread not only of parturition but also of coitus itself.

3. Finally, we have a third specific source of anxiety in the little girl's reactions (again due to the anatomical structure of her body) to her early attempts at vaginal masturbation. I think that the consequences of these reactions may be more lasting in girls than in boys, and this for the following reasons: In the first place she

---

[9]Daly: "Der Menstruationskomplex," *Imago*, bd. 14, 1928.

cannot actually ascertain the effect of masturbation. A boy, when experiencing anxiety about his genital, can always convince himself anew that it does exist and is intact:[10] a little girl has no means of proving to herself that her anxiety has no foundation in reality. On the contrary, her early attempts at vaginal masturbation bring home to her once more the fact of her greater physical vulnerability,[11] for I have found in analysis that it is by no means uncommon for little girls, when attempting masturbation or engaging in sexual play with other children, to incur pain or little injuries, obviously caused by infinitesimal ruptures of the hymen.[12]

Where the general development is favourable, i.e. above all where the object-relations of childhood have not become a fruitful source of conflict, this anxiety is satisfactorily mastered and the way is then open for the subject to assent to her feminine role. That in unfavourable cases the effect of the anxiety is more persistent with girls than with boys is, I think, indicated by the fact that, with the former, it is relatively more frequent for direct genital masturbation to be given up altogether, or at least it is confined to the more easily accessible clitoris with its lesser cathexis of anxiety. Not seldom everything connected with the vagina—the knowledge of its existence, vaginal sensations, and instinctual impulses—succumbs to a relentless repression: in short, the fiction is conceived and long maintained that the vagina does not exist, a fiction which at the same time determines the little girl's preference for the masculine sexual role.

All these considerations seem to me to be greatly in favour of the hypothesis that *behind the "failure to discover" the vagina is a denial of its existence*.

It remains to consider the question of what importance the existence of early vaginal sensations or the "discovery" of the vagina has for our whole conception of early feminine sexuality. Though Freud does not expressly

---

[10]These real circumstances must most certainly be taken into account as well as the strength of unconscious sources of anxiety. For instance, a man's castration-anxiety may be intensified as the result of phimosis.

[11]It is perhaps not without interest to recall that the gynecologist Wilhelm Liepmann (whose standpoint is not that of analysis), in his book, *Psychologie der Frau*, says that the "vulnerability" of women is one of the specific characteristics of their sex.

[12]Such experiences often come to light in analysis, firstly, in the form of screen-memories of injuries to the genital region, sustained in later life, possibly through a fall. To these recollections patients react with a terror and shame out of all proportion to the cause. Secondly, there may be an overwhelming dread lest such an injury should possibly occur.

state it, it is none the less clear that, if the vagina remains originally "un-discovered," this is one of the strongest arguments in favor of the assumption of a biologically determined, primary penis envy in little girls or of their original phallic organization. For, if no vaginal sensations or cravings existed, but the whole libido were concentrated on the clitoris, phallically conceived of, then and then only could we understand how little girls, for want of any specific source of pleasure of their own or of any specific feminine wishes, must be driven to concentrate their whole attention on the clitoris, to compare it with the boy's penis and then, since they are in fact at a disadvantage in this comparison, to feel themselves definitely slighted.[13] If on the other hand, as I conjecture, a little girl experiences from the very beginning vaginal sensations and the corresponding impulses, she must from the outset have a lively sense of this specific character of her own sexual role, and a primary penis-envy of the strength postulated by Freud would be hard to account for.

In this paper I have showed that the hypothesis of a primary phallic sexuality carries with it momentous consequences for our whole conception of feminine sexuality. If we assume that there is a specifically feminine, primary, vaginal sexuality the former hypothesis, if not altogether excluded, is at least so drastically restricted that those consequences become quite problematical.

---

[13]Helene Deutsch arrives at this basis for penis-envy by a process of logical argument. Cf. Deutsch: "The Significance of Masochism in the Mental Life of Women," *International Journal of Psycho-Analysis*, 1930, vol. 11.

8

ELSA FIRST
ON JOAN RIVIERE

Getting Worse for Their Sake

In June 1922, Freud wrote to Ernest Jones about the analysis of Joan
Riviere, whom Jones had sent on to Freud after his own efforts to work
with her had gone awry.

> Now I cannot give you the result of our analysis, it is not yet definite or
> complete. But one important point soon emerged. She cannot tolerate
> praise, triumph or success, not any better than failure, blame and repu-
> diation. She gets unhappy in both cases, in the second directly, in the
> first by reaction. So she has arranged for herself . . . *eine zwickmuhle* (a
> dilemma). . . . Whenever she has got a recognition, a favor or a present,
> she is sure to become unpleasant and aggressive and to lose respect for
> the analyst. You know what that means, it is an infallible sign of a deep
> sense of guilt, of a conflict between Ego and Ideal. . . . To be sure this
> conflict, which is the cause of her continuous dissatisfaction, is not known
> to her consciousness; whenever it is revived she projects her self-criti-
> cism to other people, turns her pangs of conscience into sadistic behav-
> ior, tries to render other people unhappy because she feels so herself.
> Our theory has not yet mastered the mechanism of these cases. It seems
> likely that the formulation of a high and severe ideal took place with her
> at a very early age. . . . [Kris 1994, p. 656]

A month later Freud had started on "The Ego and the Id" (1923), where he introduces the notion of a negative therapeutic reaction in similar words:

> There are certain people who behave in a quite peculiar fashion during the work of analysis. When one speaks hopefully to them or expresses satisfaction with the progress of the treatment, they show signs of discontent and their condition invariably becomes worse. One begins by regarding this as defiance and as an attempt to prove their superiority to the physician, but later one comes to take a deeper and juster view. One becomes convinced, not only that such people cannot endure any praise or appreciation, but that they react inversely to the progress of the treatment.

> There is no doubt that there is something in these people that sets itself against their recovery, and its approach is dreaded as though it were a danger.... [p. 49]

Joan Riviere's (1936a) paper on the negative therapeutic reaction is still astonishing in its intellectual freedom and the unmistakable authenticity of its voice. Riviere remarks by way of introduction that she is simply bringing Melanie Klein's (1935) new concept of the depressive position to bear on the "practical side" of working with the negative therapeutic reaction. Her modesty makes this sound like minor housekeeping. Considered Riviere's most original and generative paper, it brings theoretical domains that had hitherto not been connected into alignment. Riviere saw that the negative therapeutic reaction was the area of overlap between Freud's late work, concerned with aggression, masochism, and self-destructiveness, and Melanie Klein's pioneering interest in aggression and destructiveness in the early infant–mother relationship.

Freud (1923) attributed the negative therapeutic reaction (NTR) to unconscious guilt:

> In the end we come to see that we are dealing with what may be called a "moral" factor, a sense of guilt, which is finding its satisfaction in the illness and refuses to give up the punishment of suffering.... But as far as the patient is concerned this sense of guilt is dumb (*silent*); it does not tell him he is guilty; he does not feel guilty, he feels ill. This sense of guilt expresses itself only as a resistance to recovery which it is extremely difficult to overcome. [pp. 49–50]

Riviere, in her revision of Freud (in which current readers will look for what she felt to be lacking in Freud's work with her), found instead an unresolved unconscious loyalty to parental objects felt to be damaged and suffering. She links the NTR (as it is abbreviated in the literature) with the longing to repair these damaged "internal objects," and a sense of failure and despair at not being able to do so. Riviere says this "unconscious attitude of anxiety and concern is not the same as Freud's unconscious sense of guilt." Riviere's approach differs also in how profoundly she makes the internal object world (then a relatively new psychoanalytic concept) into the arena of psychological life. An important difference between internalized object relations and Freud's concept of unconscious guilt, Riviere makes clear, is that "Freud regards the love as past and over."[1]

Where Freud saw unconscious guilt, Riviere understood the negative therapeutic reaction as a form of self-sacrifice, in which the patient sacrifices her own treatment. The patient feels that she or he doesn't deserve to be cured until he or she has managed to cure all (internal) loved ones first. Riviere does not present this issue as gender based, but it has seemed to me especially applicable to work with women. I will return to this.

Rather than experience the full pain and grief at this failure, or the "desolation" of realizing the reality of earlier states of deprivation, the NTR patient keeps up a deceptive "status quo," getting neither better nor worse. In this state the patient holds on to the omnipotent belief that she or he should have been able and still might be able to cure the damaged loved ones. The patient is caught in a struggle to repair the original objects (parents and siblings), in despair over not being able to repair, and in anxiety over his or her continuing rage at the depriving and damaged objects. At the same time the patient tries by omnipotent defenses to ward off any awareness of this internal reality. Riviere points out that the sanction here is the dread that contacting internal reality would immediately make the patient suicidal. Riviere writes also of the dread that even embarking on the attempt to repair others would lead to suicide. It is a paradox that the patient is afraid to engage in any relationship that might involve some repair or rescue of the other for fear of being sucked in to utter self-sacrifice, while at the same time the patient is also desperate at the failure to repair. Riviere's account of the dilemmas and pathologies around unresolved reparative strivings makes the clinical phenomena recognizable and credible.

---

[1]This theme is more salient for Klein in the male/female dyad where men's sexual potency and fertility is seen as supporting and fulfilling wishes for reparations toward the woman as the attacked mother.

She explains the technical dilemmas of the analyst by relating them to the patient's subjectivity: "We cannot say, 'what you really want is to cure and help other people, those you love, and not yourself,' because that thought is precisely the most terrible thought in all the world to him; it brings up at once his despair and sense of failure—all his anxieties" (p. 316). Riviere suggests such an interpretation would have no traction until the patient could arrive at and tolerate an experience of how much she felt she had already failed with the original/internal objects. Meanwhile the patient, with masked contempt, tries to keep a magical control of the analysis, warding off spontaneity and making sure nothing really changes. But Riviere notably cautions against "only recognizing the patient's aggression" in the Kleinian style of that time because it would stimulate more unbearable guilt.

Meanwhile Riviere suggests the analyst will be helped to bear with the patient by recognizing the NTR as an overarching "organized system of defense" which monitors the patient's life as a whole and guards against any increase in autonomy or pleasure.

Riviere foresaw in this paper that to change a pervasive Negative Therapeutic Reaction would require a reworking in the transference of an early aggression-laden relationship.

It is not accidental that Riviere's exploration of the Negative Therapeutic Reaction is a pivotal paper in the history of psychoanalysis. It not only links Freud with Klein but drive theory with object relations theory. The study of the Negative Therapeutic Reaction is where drive theory makes a transition into object relations theory. As Loewald argued (1972), severe cases of NTR show that the drives themselves (for example destructiveness) are given form by the earliest object relationships.

CATASTROPHE AND
TRANSFERENCE

> To my mind it is the love for his internal objects . . . . that makes this resistance so stubborn. And we can counter this resistance only by unearthing this love and so the guilt with it. To these patients if not to all, the analyst represents an internal object. . . . [Riviere 1936a, p. 319]

In this quietly radical move Riviere extends both Klein's sense of internal objects and Strachey's (1934) idea of transference. Klein, from early on (1929), had seen that transference was the projection outwards of aspects of the internal self and object representations, but Riviere in this paper provides a richer sense of the emotionality of the inner world that gets re-found in the analytic relationship. When Strachey privileged interpretation of transference as the key mutative element in psychoanalysis he was imagining the moment when transference is seen through as unreal, because the analyst's act of interpretation reveals the contrast with the real analyst in the present.

In Riviere's sense of the analyst who represents an internal object, the analyst is at once an old object with whom the trauma or object relational "catastrophe" can be re-experienced, not merely seen through, and a new object with whom, as Riviere says, the buried capacity for love can be revived. Riviere seems to suggest that this capacity for love can then be made viable in a new form although she also describes the old love as greedy and insatiable in its wish for inseparability. An implied closed-system model and an open-system model seem to coexist in Riviere's stance.

A transmuting re-experiencing in the transference, rather than merely seeing through the transference, is suggested by Riviere's thought that trauma has to be relived in order to be owned and shed. The idea of a psychic catastrophe that has already happened is original in this paper: "The psychic truth behind his omnipotent denials is that the worst disasters have actually taken place; it is this truth that he will not allow the analysis to make real, will not allow to be 'realized' by him or us" (Riviere 1936a, p. 312). Patients mobilize defenses to ward off a traumatic collapse that has already happened; what is needed is to help the person realize that it *has* already happened: this idea is familiar from Winnicott's "Fear of Breakdown" (Winnicott 1974). We can suppose it came to Winnicott through his analysis with Riviere.

Winnicott's understanding of the importance of the mother's accepting the infant's spontaneous gesture also seems related to Riviere's particular understanding of the origins of reparative strivings in the infant's wish to share happiness with its love objects, not only to repair damage (Riviere 1936a,b).

Riviere's sense of the analyst as internal object is presciently close to our contemporary sense of the

> post-classical analyst as a new and an old object at once. . . . The analyst then becomes the new object with whom the trauma is experienced *in a new context*. The trauma has, after all, subjectively occurred, but has never been experienced. . . . It has happened but has at the same time not yet (emotionally) happened. [Treurniet 1993, p. 881]

ON NOT HAVING THE RIGHT TO A LIFE

Later analysts have continued intermittently to study the kind of pervasive and systematic self-erasure Riviere discovered in the negative therapeutic reaction. Modell evocatively identified the syndrome as "not having a right to a life" of one's own (Modell 1965). Referring to Riviere's work, Modell understood the abdication of a right to a life as based in intensely ambivalent and compromised early separation-individuation. He coined the phrase "separation guilt" for the resultant unconscious conviction that having a life and a self apart from the mother would in itself be harmful to the mother.

Riviere's NTR patients also resemble those Markson (1993) recently characterized who

> may experience no right to a pleasurable life of their own or even to a mind of their own. Instead they feel compelled to surrender themselves to the welfare of others in a painful reparative identification with the victimized parent. . . ." [p. 933] Not only does the patient fear damaging the object through ordinary usage, but has a persistent fear of being used, that is, of masochistic surrender to the object [analyst]. . . . [p. 937]

Markson stresses the need to maintain a bond with masochistic parents who offer intimacy only in states of shared misery, and who turned away from infantile exuberance. He also considers the child's guilt over the parents' misery, and how the child's own reparative strivings toward the parents come to seem futile. He gives a cogent account of developmental/relational factors that can create the despair over reparative capacity and agency which Riviere describes from the inside out.

Other work on the same or related psychic territory has been done by way of exploring the experience of a painful inner "emptiness," commonly reported in borderline conditions.

Borderline patients who experience themselves as "empty," have been understood to be emptying themselves out as a desperate defense "against painful object relations" (Lafarge 1989). In Lafarge's account, such patients are projecting all desire and agency onto others, and so know themselves only as spectators to other lives.

Self-erasure has thus been viewed from various perspectives. There is consensus, however, that an unbearably aggressivized early dyadic relationship is involved. Lafarge adds the helpful consideration that the patient's feeling internally destructive to the object is complicated by further rage at the object for allowing such a painful situation to occur.

MOTHERS, DAUGHTERS, AND REPARATIONS

The internal world, as Riviere renders it, is a present unconscious, strongly but only partly shaped by the past, malleable, in flux, and potentially open to being touched and changed by current relationships. It is a rich source of projective meaning which can add resonance to current engagements or, as in some of Riviere's clinical scenarios, keep the person self-enclosed.

A significant way Riviere's essay has worked on me is to focus clinical awareness on the strand of reparative striving in the lives of women patients. The various domains of the internal object world, current relationships and work, the transference, parenting and kinwork (Ruddick 1989) all interrelate in terms of reparative concerns. In contrast to reparative guilt, reparative accomplishment can facilitate autonomy.

Not all reparative strivings are defensive or compulsive. In my view, Riviere made the positive and wholesome side of reparative strivings more salient than Klein did. Klein sees the infant appreciating the goodness of the mother; Riviere portrays the infant wanting to share happiness with the mother, just as the NTR patient longs to make all the internal objects "well and happy." Klein stresses the wish to undo harm; Riviere gives room to wishes to nurture, to heal, and to enliven.

A woman's experience of successful reparations in relation to a child can lessen her reparative guilt toward her internal mother, while unrelenting reparative guilt toward the internal mother will interfere with her ability to help a child individuate.

I commonly notice how a current relationship with a daughter reflects how much the woman is able at that moment to work through reparative guilt toward her own evoked internal mother. An anecdotal example: a woman in her fifties is asked to explore her susceptibility to collude with an adult daughter's acting out. She associates to her own adolescent confusion in the face of her mother's delusional states. She then blames herself for not listening more respectfully, some years later, to those of her dying mother's complaints and suspicions that in fact were not mad. She herself connects this with how she feels when she surrenders to the daughter's demands and suppresses her own realization that the collusion feels "crazy."

Another married woman in her early fifties speaks of recently feeling less guilty at how difficult it was to elicit happiness in her dour, complaining, now-aged mother. At the same time she reports having been able to hold back from over-responding to an adolescent daughter's panic over academic work, which allowed both of them to discover the daughter could pull through on her own with less support. Feeling less reparative guilt toward her own mother goes along with this patient's being able to take more pleasure in her daughter's growing competence as the daughter becomes readier to leave for college.

IRREPARABLE OBJECTS AND SELF-SACRIFICE: INTERGENERATIONAL TRANSMISSION

Clinical experience suggests that guilt over failed reparations, or separation guilt (Modell 1963) is more commonly an issue for women than for men. It was Riviere's paper that directed my attention to how often women's self-sabotaging is linked not simply with "separation guilt" but with wrecked reparative strivings toward an internal object felt to be irreparable.[2]

What keeps embroilment going in the mother/daughter dyad? Women will tend to defend against painful object-relational situations by increasing the play of identification in the direction of merger (hysterical/borderline syndromes) while men will tend to defend against primitive anxieties by increased differentiation. Riviere's work suggests we look for the frustrated reparative striving in the woman patient's move toward a confusional closeness with a disturbed mother (which may be further defended against by emptiness).

For example, a 40-year-old woman realized she was kept in a state of frustrated anxious reparative concern by a mother who solicited her attention by revealing her financial risk-taking but not letting the daughter do anything about it. At the same moment she felt impelled to leave treat-

---

[2]Of course men also evidence NTR, and it would be a separate enquiry to specify differences, or to examine further whether, as Modell's material suggests, it occurs where the man's separation-individuation from mother is compromised and conflict dealt with by increased identification. One of Modell's examples was a male patient, "dominated by the urge to destroy all accomplishment," who could experience pleasure "only under conditions of self-debasement." Notably this male patient was extraordinarily "confused" with his mother, suffering in Modell's view a nearly "unmodified primary identification" with her.

ment. She could not yet realize how much she feared psychic submission and surrender of her own perceptions in the treatment also.

I suggest the time has come when we can reconsider the distortions of self-sacrifice in women from a perspective that is both psychoanalytic and feminist. It need not be assumed that masochistic self-sacrifice is a natural talent in women or that caretaking must be masochistic or reparative strivings compulsive. The early psychoanalytic assumption that masochism (including "moral masochism") was natural for women (Deutsch 1944–1946) has been adequately questioned. Women's capacities for imaginative empathy and skillful accommodation have also been revalued as strengths, not simply the skills of the powerless (Belensky et al. 1986, Gilligan 1982, Ruddick 1989). In a reconsideration of the idealization of painful self-sacrifice in women, Riviere's essay would be a good place to start.

NARCISSISM, RIVIERE, AND FREUD'S ERROR

In the first part of this essay Riviere manages, remarkably, to unify all psychoanalytic thought about narcissistic defenses up to that point—including a précis of Abraham's 1911 paper that reveals how astonishingly undated his observations are on narcissistic style in the analytic relationship. She connects Abraham's observations with Klein's ideas that omnipotence is a defense against experiencing dependency—or interdependency—in relationships (the "manic defense"). Clinical exploration of the topic of sadistic omnipotence was opened by this paper[3] (Rosenfeld 1987).

Freud's letters about the analysis of Riviere indicate (Hughes 1991, Kris 1994) that Freud was more aware of and thoughtful about the treatment of narcissistic problems than his published work up to that point reveals. Kris uses this to enhance his argument that the analytic concept of neutrality needs to be amended to include consideration of the patient's need for implicit affirmation of his intrinsic worth to counter the patient's pervasive unconscious self-criticism. Riviere's complaint, as later confided to Herbert Rosenfeld, whom she had supervised (Hughes 1991), was that Freud used her as a translator before her personal analytic relationship with him was consolidated. Anton Kris (1994), in his graceful reconstruction

---

[3]Riviere's contributions on omnipotence are not gender specific, and it would be beyond the scope of this introduction to consider gender differences in the use of omnipotent defenses.

of the events, which I am drawing on here, suggests Freud was well aware that Riviere, like other narcissistic patients, set up "a vicious cycle of punitive, unconscious self-criticism, self-deprivation and excessive demand" (p. 657). Kris thinks this is what Freud meant in referring to Riviere's "dilemma," and believes Freud "saw that Riviere turned against her wishes to be loved, especially when they might actually be satisfied, producing a state of self-deprivation that further strengthened her demands to be loved" (p. 657). Freud rationalized exploitation of her talents as a way to help Riviere with her self-devaluation. Freud wrote Jones, " 'A due recognition of her ability, while the treatment conquers her incapacity for her enjoying her success, is to her advantage as well as our own' " (Kris 1994, p. 656). In the NTR essay Riviere writes, " . . . recognition and encouragement by the analyst of the patient's attempts at reparation (in real life) allay them merely by the omnipotent method of glossing over and denying the internal depressive reality—his feeling of failure" (p. 320). The last section of this paper contains her implicit criticism of Freud as her analyst for co-opting her aggression and exploiting her gift for serving others rather than working through the anxieties she plainly later explored in order to arrive at this paper.

Riviere's understanding of the NTR as a pervasive systematic defense in which all progress will be attacked contributes to our being able to contain those attacks which are simultaneously attacks on the self and on the analyst's capacity: we will not be surprised when all of a woman's moves toward individuation, self-regulation, enhanced self-care, achievement, and thinking for herself are undermined, nor be inappropriately sidetracked into piecemeal consideration of particular conflicts, though at times that may be apt.

Riviere's graceful, clear, courageous, almost conversational style is also part of what is inspiring about her as a clinical thinker. Her world of psychic dilemmas, layered affective states, and "unconscious situations," sounds like what contemporary psychoanalysis has laboriously re-arrived at. Riviere is a foremother to go in search of, and as Hanna Segal (1991) has said, "many psychoanalysts working today have no idea of the debt they owe to her."

REFERENCES

Belenky, M. F., Clinchy, B. M., Goldberger, N. R., and Tarule, J. M., eds. (1986). *Women's Ways of Knowing*. New York: Basic Books.

Deutsch, H. (1944–1945). *The Psychology of Women*, vols. 1 and 2. New York: Grune & Stratton.

Freud, S. (1923). The ego and the id. *Standard Edition* 19:3–68.

Gilligan, C. (1982). *In A Different Voice*. Cambridge, MA: Harvard University Press.

Hughes, A. (1991). Joan Riviere: her life and work. In *The Inner World And Joan Riviere Collected Papers 1920–1958*, ed. A. Hughes, pp. 1–43. London: Karnac.

Klein, M. (1929). Personification in the play of children. In *Love, Guilt and Reparation*, pp. 199–209. London: Hogarth, 1975.

—— (1935). A contribution to the psychogenesis of manic depressive states. In *Love, Guilt and Reparation*, pp. 262–289. London: Hogarth, 1975.

Kris, A. (1994). Freud's treatment of a narcissistic patient. *International Journal of Psycho-Analysis* 75:649–664.

LaFarge, L. (1989). "Emptiness as a Defense in Severe Regressive States." *Journal of the American Psychoanalytic Association* 37(4):965–996.

Loewald, H. W. (1972). Freud's conception of the negative therapeutic reaction, with comments on instinct theory. In *Papers on Psychoanalysis*, pp. 315–325. New Haven, CT: Yale University Press, 1980.

Markson, E. (1993). Depression and moral masochism. *International Journal of Psycho-Analysis* 74(5):931–940.

Modell, A. H. (1965) On having the right to a life: an aspect of the superego's development. *International Journal of Psycho-Analysis* 46:323–331.

Paskauskas, R. A., ed. (1993). *The Complete Correspondence of Sigmund Freud and Ernest Jones: 1908–1939*. Cambridge, MA: Harvard University Press.

Riviere, J. (1936a). A contribution to the analysis of the negative therapeutic reaction. *International Journal of Psycho-Analysis* 17:304–320.

—— (1936b). On the genesis of psychical conflict in earliest infancy. *International Journal of Psycho-Analysis* 17:395–422.

Rosenfeld, H. (1987). Narcissistic patients with negative therapeutic reactions. In *Impasse and Interpretation*. London: Tavistock.

Ruddick, S. (1989). *Maternal Thinking*. Boston: Beacon.

Segal, H. (1991). Foreword. In *The Inner World And Joan Riviere, Collected Papers 1920–1958*, ed. A. Hughes. London: Karnac.

Strachey, J. (1934). The nature of the therapeutic action of psychoanalysis. *International Journal of Psycho-Analysis* 15:127.

Treurniet, N. (1993). What is psychoanalysis now? *International Journal of Psycho-Analysis* 74:873–891.

Winnicott, D. W. (1974). On the fear of breakdown. *International Review of Psycho-Analysis* 1:103–107.

A Contribution to the Analysis of the Negative Therapeutic Reaction [1]

JOAN RIVIERE

In this contribution my aim is to draw attention to the important bearing recent theoretical conclusions have on the practical side of the problem of the negative therapeutic reaction. I mean the latest work of Melanie Klein and in particular her Lucerne Congress paper on the depressive position. [2]

To start with, it is necessary to define what is meant by the negative therapeutic reaction. Freud gave this title to something that he regarded as a specific manifestation among the variety of our case-material, though he says that in a lesser measure this factor has to be reckoned with in very many cases. When I referred to Freud's remarks on this point, I was interested to find that actually they are not exactly what they are generally remembered and represented as being. The negative therapeutic reaction, I should say, is generally understood as a condition which ultimately precludes analysis and makes it impossible; the phrase is constantly used as meaning unanalysable. Freud's remarks on the point are almost all in *The Ego and the Id*, the last eighteen pages of which deal with the problem of

[1]Read before the British Psycho-Analytical Society, October 1, 1935.
[2]Klein, "A Contribution to the Psychogenesis of Manic-Depressive States," *International Journal of Psycho-Analysis*, vol. 16, pt. 2.

the unconscious sense of guilt. He says, "Certain people cannot endure any praise or appreciation of progress in the treatment. Every partial solution that ought to result, and with others does result, in an improvement or temporary suspension of symptoms produces in them for the time being an exacerbation; they get worse instead of better." This last sentence might imply that they are unanalysable; but he does not actually say so, and has just said the exacerbation is for *the time being*. He says the obstacle is "extremely difficult to overcome"; "often there is no counteracting force of similar intensity"; and that "it must be honestly confessed that here is another limitation to the efficacy of analysis"—but he does not say a preventive. Clearly the point is merely one of degree, and he might concur in the general attitude taken up. He is not, however, actually as pessimistic about it as people incline to suppose; and this interested me, because it is not intelligible why one reaction should be thought more unanalysable than another. The eighteen pages in *The Ego and the Id* are in fact part of his contribution towards analysing it; and our understanding of it has now been very greatly advanced by Melanie Klein.

Freud's title for this reaction, however, is not actually very specific; a negative therapeutic reaction would just as well describe the case of any patient who does not benefit by a treatment; and it would describe those psychotic or "narcissistic" patients whom Freud still regards as inaccessible to psycho-analysis. It seems to me that this specific reaction against a cure described by him may not differ so very greatly in character from those more general cases of therapeutic failures I mentioned, and that the difficulty may be due to some extent to the analyst's failure to understand the material and to interpret it fully enough to the patient. The common assumption is that even when the analyst has fully understood and interpreted the material, the super-ego of certain patients is strong enough to defeat the effects of analysis. I shall try to show that other factors are at work in this severity of the super-ego that until recently have not been fully understood and therefore cannot have been sufficiently or fully interpreted to our patients.

It will be clear now that what I propose to talk about is in fact the analysis of specially refractory cases. I do not think I can go much further in defining the type of case to which my remarks refer, partly because any one analyst's experience is necessarily limited, even of refractory cases; moreover, my expectation is that similar unconscious material may probably exist in other difficult cases of a kind I have not personally met with. I would say this, however, that the cases in which I have made the most use and had greatest advantage from the new understanding have been what we call difficult character-cases. The super-ego of the transference neurotic, it must be remembered, has always been placated by his sufferings from his sense of guilt, and by his symptoms, which are a real cause of inferiority and humiliation to him whatever episodic gain he has from them; the character-case has never placated his super-ego in these ways; he has always maintained the projection that "circumstances" have been against him. After some analysis he may guess that he has punished others all his life and feel that what he now deserves is not "cure," but illness or punishment himself; and he unconsciously fears that that is what analysis may bring him if he submits to it. Of course we find these motives for or against co-operation in all cases; I merely suggest that in character-cases they may have peculiar strength.

With reference to this matter of character-resistances I shall recall to your minds a paper of Abraham[3] in which he described and commented on a certain type of difficulty in analysis, that he virtually names the *narcissistic type* of character-resistance. He tells us that such analyses are very lengthy and that in no such case did he obtain complete cure of the neurosis, and we can see that the degree of negative therapeutic reaction in this type is what led him to distinguish it. The narcissistic features of this type are, shortly: that they show a chronic, not merely occasional, inability to associate freely, in that they keep up a steady flow of carefully selected and arranged material, calculated to deceive the analyst as to its "free" quality; they volunteer nothing but good of themselves; are highly sensitive and easily mortified; accept nothing new, nothing that they have not already said themselves; turn analysis into a pleasurable situation, develop no true positive transference, and oust the analyst from his position and claim to do his work better themselves. Under a mask of polite friendliness and rationalization they are very mean, self-satisfied, and defiant. Abraham shews the relation of all these features to anal omnipotence, and he especially emphasizes the *mask of compliance*, which distinguishes this type of resistance from an open negative transference and renders it more difficult to handle than the latter. And "These patients," he says, "*shut their eyes to the fact that the object of the treatment is to cure their neurosis.*" Incidentally, I do not suppose that Abraham was guilty of it, but I feel that

---

[3]Abraham, "A Particular Form of Neurotic Resistance against the Psycho-Analytic Method," *Selected Papers on Psycho-Analysis,* p. 303, 1919.

analysts themselves are not always incapable of shutting their eyes to a fact too, namely, that when a patient does not do what he ought, the onus still remains with the analyst: to discover the cause of his reaction. In my opinion the patient was entirely in the right who said, "Yes, doctor, when you have removed my inhibitions against telling you what is in my mind, I will then tell you what is in my mind," and the situation is similar in regard to getting well.

This paper of Abraham's suggests what I take to be a generally valid proposition, that in specially long and difficult analyses the core of the problem lies in the patient's narcissistic resistances. One surmises, further, that this narcissism may not be unconnected with the inaccessibility to treatment of the "narcissistic neuroses," as Freud has called certain psychoses. There is nothing very new, or immediately helpful, in the idea that narcissism is the root of the problem—for what is narcissism? I will mention only two general points in this connection. One—the old one—is that any marked degree of narcissism presupposes a withdrawal of libido from external objects into the ego, and secondly, the newer point, that ego-libido can now be recognized, especially in the light of Melanie Klein's more recent work, to be an extremely complex thing. Freud speaks of the secondary narcissism derived from the ego's "identifications," which most of us here now regard as including the ego's *internal objects*. And Melitta Schmideberg[4] suggests that love for the introjected objects is a part of narcissism. And now the significance of the ego's relations to its internalized objects shows clearly that this great field of object-relations within the ego, within the realm of narcissism itself, needs much further understanding; and it is my belief that more light in this direction will do much to explain such hitherto inexplicable analytic resistances as the narcissistic ones of Abraham and the super-ego one of Freud.

The concept of *objects* within the ego, as distinct from identifications, is hardly discussed in Freud's work; but it will be remembered that one important contribution of his to the psychology of insanity is built up almost entirely on this conception—I mean of course his essay on "Mourning and Melancholia," dealing with the problems of *depressive* states. His discussion in *"The Ego and the Id"* of the unconscious sense of guilt, too, is closely interwoven with aspects of the melancholic condition. This brings me to my second point. Observations have led me to conclude that where

---

narcissistic resistances are very pronounced, resulting in the characteristic lack of insight and absence of therapeutic results under discussion, these resistances are in fact part of a highly organized system of defence against a more or less unconscious depressive condition in the patient and are operating as a mask and disguise to conceal the latter.

My contribution to the understanding of especially refractory cases of a narcissistic type will therefore consist in the two proposals: (a) that we should pay more attention to the analysis of the patient's inner world of object-relations, which is an integral part of his narcissism, and (b) that we should not be deceived by the positive aspects of his narcissism but should look deeper, for the depression that will be found to underlie it. That these two recommendations are not unconnected might be guessed from Freud's paper, which links the two, and from Melanie Klein's view that the internal object-situation in this position is of supreme importance. The depressive position might be described as a miscarriage of introjection, she says; and *this* is the unconscious anxiety-situation that our narcissistic patients are defending themselves against and that should be the true objective of analysis in such cases.

Now this particular anxiety-situation, the depressive, has its own special defence-mechanism, the manic reaction, of which Melanie Klein also gives a general outline. The essential feature of the manic attitude is omnipotence and the *omnipotent denial of psychical reality*, which of course leads to a distorted and defective sense of external reality. (Helene Deutsch[5] has pointed out the inappropriate, impracticable, and fantastic character of the manic relation to external reality.) The *denial* relates especially to the ego's object-relations and its *dependence on its objects*, as a result of which *contempt* and depreciation of the value of its objects is a marked feature, together with attempts at inordinate and tyrannical *control and mastery of its objects*. Much could be written about the manic defence, and I hope will be, for in my opinion the future of psycho-analytic research, and therefore of all psychology, now depends on our belated appreciation of the immense importance of this factor in mental life. It is true that we have known of many of its manifestations and even had a name which would have represented it, if we had known how to apply it—the word omnipotence—but our knowledge and understanding of the factor of omnipotence has never yet been organized, formulated and correlated into a really useful theoreti-

---

[5] "Don Quichote und Donquichotismus," *Imago,* bd. 20, 1934.

cal unit. Omnipotence has been a vague concept, loosely and confusedly
bandied about, hazily interchanged with narcissism or with phantasy-life,
its meaning and especially its functions not clearly established and placed.
We ought now to study this omnipotence and particularly its special
development and application in the manic defence against depressive anxieties.

It will not be difficult to see how characteristic the most conspicuous
feature of the manic attitude, omnipotent denial and control by the ego
over all objects in all situations, is of our refractory patients with their
narcissistic resistances. Their inaccessibility is one form of their *denial;*
implicitly they deny the value of everything we say. They literally do not
allow us to do anything with them, and in the sense of co-operation they
do nothing with us. *They* control the analysis, whether or not they do it
openly. If we are not quick enough to be aware of it, too, such patients
often manage to exert quite a large measure of real control over the analyst—and can even do this when we are quite aware of it. So far, it seems
to me, we have not known, or not known enough, exactly where to place
this tendency or how to relate it to the rest of the analytic context and
so—we have not been able to analyse it. We have tended to see it as a
negative transference and as an expression of aggressive attitudes toward
the analyst. We have understood these as defences against anxiety, but we
have not realized that a *special* fear lay beneath this special way of attaining
security. I think Abraham's whole description, with every detail of the "narcissistic" resistances he describes, in fact presents an unmistakable picture of
various expressions of the manic defence—the omnipotent control of the
analyst and analytic situation by the patient—which yet, as he points out, is
often enough extremely cleverly masked. The conscious or unconscious
refusal of such patients to produce true "free associations," their selection
and arrangement of what they say, their implicit or explicit denials of
anything discreditable to themselves, their refusal to accept any alternative
point of view or any interpretation (except with lip-service), their defiance
and obstinacy, and their claim to supersede the analyst and improve on
his work all show their determination to keep the upper hand and their
anxiety of getting into the power of the analyst. Free association would
expose them to the analyst's "tender mercies"; love for the analyst, a positive transference, would do the same; and so would any admission of
failings in themselves. Along with their self-satisfaction and megalomanic
claims, their egotism is shown in pronounced meanness, and often in
an absence of the most everyday acknowledgements or generosity. Certain

patients of this type especially withhold from us all "evidence" of an indis-putable character in support of our interpretations. They leave us with dreams, symbols, voice, manner, gesture; no statements, no admissions from themselves. So we can say what we like, nothing is proved—yet of course they accept the help they get, but refuse us all help and all acknowledgements. Abraham interprets this trait as anal omnipotence. Beside this connection, it signifies especially their need to reserve and pre-serve everything of any value, all good things, to themselves, for various reasons, and especially for fear that others (the analyst) will gain in power by means of them. Above all, however, the trait of *deceptiveness,* the mask, which conceals this subtle reservation of all control under intellectual rationalizations, or under feigned compliance and superficial politeness, is characteristic of the manic defence. This mask owes its origin undoubtedly to the specialized dissimulation of the paranoiac; but it is exploited in the manic position not as a defence in itself but as a cover for the defence of securing exclusive control. To this description of this type of patient I would here add an important further detail: they show a quite special sensi-tiveness on the point of consciously feeling any anxiety; it is quite apparent that they have to keep control so as not to be taken unawares by, and not to be exposed to, a moment's anxiety. Abraham comments on their lack of affect, and this in my view is to be taken first as a dread of *anxiety*-affect. But their complete incapacity for any feeling of guilt is equally astonishing and is of course one of their most psychotic traits in its lack of the sense of reality: they deal with guilt-situations entirely by projection, denial, and rationalization.

Now it might be objected here that no analyst worth his salt has failed to interpret these manifestations in precisely this way time and again in his practice and this of course is true; but in my view there is all the difference in the world between what may be called single isolated inter-pretations, however correct and however frequent they may be, and the understanding and interpretation of such detailed instances as part of a general *organized system of defence* and resistance, with all its links and rami-fications spreading far and wide in the symptom-picture, in the formation of character and in the behavior-patterns of the patient. Analysis has to concern itself with daily details because only the immediate detail of the moment has affect and significance for the patient, but the analyst has to be careful not to become too affectively interested in working out detailed interpretations: he has to be careful not to lose sight of the wood for the trees. He must aim, not merely at understanding each detail in itself but at knowing where to place it in the general scheme of the patient's mental make-up and in the continuous context of the analytic work. Of course, what have been called "spot-analyses" or snapshot interpretations have long been condemned, and Ella Sharpe, for instance, once led a crusade against meaningless *ad hoc* symbol-interpretations which do not form part of a whole picture. What I am urging now is only a further application of this principle. I suggest that the common tendency we often see in patients to control the analysis and the analyst is even more widespread than we suppose, because it is largely masked and disguised by superficial compliance, and that it forms part of an extremely important general defensive attitude—the manic defence—which has to be understood as such.

Now what is the specific relation between this special line of defence and the negative therapeutic reaction; why does the need to control everything express itself so particularly in not getting well? There are certain obvious answers to this, all of which would show that not getting well is an unavoidable indirect result of these resistances. For instance, I have just suggested that hitherto these tendencies in patients to usurp all control have been regarded as expressions of a negative transference and hostility to the analyst. This interpretation, so far as it goes, is certainly correct; the patient is extremely hostile; but that is not all. Things are not so simple. The very great importance of analysing aggressive tendencies has perhaps carried some analysts off their feet, and in some quarters is defeating its own ends and becoming in itself a resistance to further analytic understanding. Nothing will lead more surely to a negative therapeutic reaction in the patient than failure to recognize anything but the aggression in his material.

The question why the defence by omnipotent control leads so characteristically to the negative therapeutic reaction cannot be answered fully until we consider the anxiety-situation underlying this defence; but I think there is one direct connection between the two which may be stated here. There actually is a kind of wish in the patient not to get well and this wish is itself partly in the nature of a defence. It comes from the desire to preserve a *status quo,* a condition of things which is proving bearable. It is built upon many compromises; the patient does not finish the analysis, but neither does he break it off. He has found a certain equilibrium and does not intend it to be disturbed. To my mind, this is an important general explanation of the phenomenon Freud comments on. He says,[6] "A few words

_____

[6]*New Introductory Lectures.*

of praise or hope or even an interpretation bring about an unmistakable aggravation of their condition." If the patient is changing, or is being changed, he is losing control; the equilibrium he has established in his present relation with the analyst will be upset; so he has to reinstate his former condition, and regain his control of things. Actually, this anxiety-reaction to the idea of making progress often disappears on being itself interpreted; and of course not interpreted only in this general way, but the detailed connection of the immediate resistance to the immediate anxiety made clear. Incidentally, there are many ways in which this aspect of the defence by control (namely that of prolonging and maintaining the *status quo*) verges on and merges into the obsessional technique of prolonging in time and preserving in space certain distances, always maintaining a relative, never an absolute or a final relation. But the connection between the manic and the obsessional forms of defense is not part of my subject here.

If the patient desires to preserve things as they are and even sacrifices his cure for that reason, it is not really because he does not wish to get well. The reason why he does not get well and tries to prevent any change is because, however he might wish for it, he has no faith in getting well. What he really expects unconsciously is not a change for the better but a change for the worse, and what is more, one that will not affect himself only, but the analyst as well. It is partly to save the analyst from the consequences of this that he refuses to move in any direction. Melitta Schmideberg said something of the same kind in the paper quoted already: "Inaccessibility in patients is due to a fear of something 'even worse' happening." Now what is the still worse situation which the patient is averting by maintaining the *status quo,* by keeping control, by his omnipotent defences? It is the danger of the *depressive position* that he is guarding himself and us against; what he dreads is that that situation and those anxieties may prove to be a reality, that that psychical reality in his mind may become real to him through the analysis. The psychic truth behind his omnipotent denials is that the worst disasters have actually taken place; it is this truth that he will not allow the analysis to make real, will not allow to be "realized" by him or us. He does not intend to get any "better," to change, or to end the analysis, because he does not believe it possible that any change or any lessening of control on his part can bring about anything but the realization of disaster for all concerned. I may say at once that what this type of patient ultimately fears most of all—the kernel, so to speak, of all his other fears—is his own suicide or madness, the inevitable outcome, as he feels it unconsciously, if his depressive anxieties come to life. He is keeping them still, if not dead, as it were, by his immobility. Patients I have analysed have felt this dread of losing the manic defence quite consciously during the analysis of it, have both threatened and implored me to leave it alone and not "take it away," and have foreseen that its removal would mean chaos, ruin to himself and me, impulses of murder and suicide: in other words, the depression that to some extent supervenes as the defence weakens. But I need hardly say the analyst has not this despair, for as the capacity to tolerate the depression and its anxieties gradually increases, very notable compensations accompany it and the capacity for love begins to be released as the manic stranglehold on the emotions relaxes.

The content of the depressive position (as Melanie Klein has shown) is the situation in which all one's loved ones *within* are dead and destroyed, all goodness is dispersed, lost, in fragments, wasted and scattered to the winds; nothing is left *within* but utter desolation. Love brings sorrow, and sorrow brings guilt; the intolerable tension mounts, there is no escape, one is utterly alone, there is no one to share or help. Love must die because love is dead. Besides, there would be no one to feed one, and no one whom one could feed, and no food in the world. And more, there would still be magic power in the undying persecutors who can never be exterminated—the ghosts. Death would instantaneously ensue—and one would choose to die by one's own hand before such a position could be realized.

As analysis proceeds and the persecutory projection defences, which are always interwoven with the omnipotent control position, weaken along with the latter, the analyst begins to see the phantasies approximating to this nightmare of desolation assuming shape. But the shape they assume is that of the patient, so to speak; the scene of the desolation is himself. External reality goes on its ordinary round: it is *within himself* that these horrors dwell. Nothing gives one such a clear picture of that inner world, in which every past or present relation either in thought or deed with any loved or hated person still exists and is still being carried on, as the state of a person in depression. His mind is completely and utterly preoccupied and turned inward; except insofar as he can project something of this horror and desolation, he has no concern with anything outside him. To save his own life and avert the death of despair that confronts him, such energy as he has is all bent on averting the last fatalities within, and on restoring and reviving where and what he can, of any life and life-giving objects that remain. It is these efforts, the frantic or feeble struggles to revive the oth-

ers within him and *so* to survive, that are manifested; the despair and hope-
lessness is never, of course, quite complete. The objects are never actually
felt to be dead, for that would mean death to the ego; the anxiety is so
great because life hangs by a hair and at any moment the situation of full
horror may be realized.

But struggle as he may and does under his unconscious guilt and
anxiety to repair and restore, the patient has only a slenderest belief unconsciously in achieving anything of the kind; the slightest failure in reality, the faintest breath of criticism and his belief sinks to zero again—death
or madness, his own and others', is ever before the eyes of his unconscious
mind. He cannot possibly regenerate and recreate all the losses and destruction he has caused and if he cannot pay this price his own death is
the only alternative.

I think the patient's fear of being forced to death himself by the analysis
is one of the major underlying factors in this type of case and that is why
I put it first. Unless it is appreciated many interpretations will miss their
mark. All his efforts to put things right never succeed *enough;* he can only
pacify his internal persecutors for a time, fob them off, feed them with
sops, "keep them going"; and so he "keeps things going," the *status quo,*
keeps some belief that "one day" he will have done it all, and *postpones* the
crash, the day of reckoning and judgement. One patient had woven this
into a lifelong defensive pattern: his death would be exacted, yes, but he
would see to it that this was postponed until his normal span had elapsed.
He had reached a position of success and recognition in his own department of the world's work, so in old age his obituary notices would eventually serve him still as last and final denials and defences against his
terrible anxieties and his own fundamental disbelief in any real capacity for
good within himself.

I said before that understanding of these refractory cases lay on the
one hand in our recognizing that the narcissistic and omnipotent resistances
were masking a depressive position in these patients. This has been my
own experience, but I might substantiate this theoretically in a simple way.
The patient does not get well. The analysis has no effect on him (or not
enough), because he resists it and its effect. Why? Now analysis means
unmasking and bringing to light what is in the depths of his mind; and
this is true in the sense both of external conscious reality and of internal
psychic reality. What he is resisting, then, is precisely this: becoming aware
consciously of what is in the depths of his mind. But this is a truism; all
of us and all patients do this, you will say. Of course that is true; only

these patients do it *more* than the others, for the simple reason that in them the underlying unconscious reality is more unbearable and more horrible than in other cases. Not that their phantasies are more sadistic; Glover has often reminded us that the same phantasies are found in everybody. The difference is that the *depressive position* is relatively stronger in them; the sense of failure, of inability to remedy matters is so great, the belief in better things is so weak; despair is so near. And analysis means unmasking, that is, to the patient, displaying in all its reality, making real, "realizing," this despair, disbelief, and *sense of failure,* which then in its turn simply means death to the patient. It becomes quite comprehensible why he will have none of it. Yet, with what grains of hope he has, he knows that no one but an analyst ventures to approach even to the fringes of these problems of his; and so he clings to analysis, as a forlorn hope, in which at the same time he really has no faith.

The patient's inaccessible attitude is the expression, then, of his denials of all that the analyst shows him of the unconscious contents of his mind. His megalomania, lack of adaptation to real life and to the analysis are only superficially denials of external reality. What he is in truth concerned to deny is his own *internal reality.* Here we come to my second point: the internal object-relations which are an integral part of his narcissism.

When we come to close quarters with the importance of the internalized objects in this connection, one general aspect of the situation will at once become clear in view of what has already been said about the depressive position. The patient's conscious aim in coming for analysis is to get well himself: unconsciously this point is relatively secondary, for other needs come first. Unconsciously his aim is: (1) on the paranoid basis, underlying his depressive position, his task is something far more urgent than getting well; it is simply to avert the impending death and disintegration which is constantly menacing him. But more even than this (for the paranoid aspect of things is not the most unbearable), unconsciously his chief aim must be (2) to cure and make well and happy all his loved and hated objects (all those he has ever loved and hated) before he thinks of himself. And these objects now to him are within himself. All the injuries he ever did them in thought or deed arose from his "selfishness," from being too greedy, and too envious of them, not generous and willing enough to allow them what they had, whether of oral, anal, or genital pleasure—from not loving *them* enough, in fact. In his mind every one of these acts and thoughts of selfishness and injury to others has to be reversed, to be made good, by sacrifices on his own part, before he can even be sure that his own life is secure—much less begin to think about being well and happy himself. Our offer of analysis to make him well and happy is unconsciously a direct seduction, as it were, a betrayal; it means to him an offer to help him to abandon his task of curing the others first, to conspire with him to put himself first again, to treat his loved objects as enemies, and neglect them, or even defeat and destroy them instead of helping them. On his paranoid level, this is all very well, and he wants nothing better; but there is always something more than the paranoid position; there is the only good thing he has, his buried core of love and his need to think of others before himself at last, to make things better for them and so to make himself better. And the analyst's offer to help him seems to him unconsciously a betrayal of them—of all those others who deserve help so much more than he. In addition, he does not for a moment believe that any good person really would be willing to help him before all the others who need it so greatly; so his suspicions of the analyst, and of his powers and intentions, are roused. One might suppose one could perhaps allay these suspicions by emphasizing how others will benefit by his cure; but on this point of technique I must here make an important digression. It will have struck you how incongruous and contradictory this picture of the patient's unconscious aim— one of them—(to make all his objects well and happy) is compared with his manifest egoistic behaviour. But its incongruity is of course no accident; the terrific contrast of extreme conscious egotism as against extreme unconscious altruism is one of the major features of the defence by denial. In order to disprove one underlying piece of reality, he parades its opposite extreme. So I have to remind you that his unconscious aims are really *unconscious* and that we cannot use them directly as a lever to help on the analysis. We cannot say "What you really want is to cure and help other people, those you love, and not yourself," because that thought is precisely the most terrible thought in all the world to him; it brings up at once all his despair and sense of failure—all his greatest anxieties. Any such imputation, if at all plainly and directly expressed, has the immediate effect of producing a paranoid resistance as a defence; because, when we see through his denials, the manic defence has failed him. We have to be as guarded about directly imputing any altruistic motives to such patients as about imputing sadism or aggression to a hysteric. Nevertheless, when we know the unconscious situation, we know how to watch our steps; and even if we cannot use this lever ourselves for a very long time at least, we know it is there and can bring into play any indications of it there are, in subtle, indirect, and gradual ways which do not rouse instant and unmanageable resistances.

This difficulty—that the patient unconsciously feels himself utterly unworthy of analytic help and, moreover, feels he is betraying the only good side of himself in accepting analysis, the side which would devote his life to making his loved ones happy—can only be got over in one way, namely, through the possibility that analysis, by making him better, will in the end make him at last capable of achieving his task for others—his loved ones. His *true* aim is the other way round—to make *them* better first and so to become well and good himself; but that is indeed impossible, both externally and internally, for his sadism is still unmanageable. The nearest hope is this reversal, again on the lines of a contradiction, or this compromise— to be cured himself in order then to cure others. It is only on this understanding, so to speak, unconsciously, and by placing all responsibility on the analyst, that such patients accept analysis at all; and I think this hope, and this only, is the ultimate source of the endless time, suffering, and expense that such patients will bring to continue analysis. We have to recognize that they do this much, even if they do not get well. Why they do it has not hitherto been fully understood. This single unconscious motive then, that he is to be cured in order at last to be capable of fulfilling his task to others, and not for his own ends, is the one slender positive thread on which the analysis hangs. But we can see at once how impotent this motive can remain, how it is weakened, obstructed, and undermined by innumerable counteracting forces. For one thing the patient does not for a moment believe in it; his fear of his own id and its uncontrollable desires and aggression is such that he feels no sort of security that he would eventually use any benefits obtained through analysis for the good of his objects; he knows very well, one might say, he will merely repeat his crimes and now use up the analyst for his own gratification and add him to the list of those he has despoiled and ruined. One of his greatest unconscious anxieties is that the analyst will be deceived on this very point and will allow himself to be so misused. He warns us in a disguised way continually of his own dangerousness.

Further, over and above this anxiety of accepting analysis on false pretences and deceiving and betraying his good objects again by it, there is an even greater fear, one which concerns the ego's fear for itself again, and links up with the fear of death unconsciously so strong in his mind. This is the dread that if he were cured by analysis, faithfully and truly, and made at last able to compass the reparation needed by all those he loved and injured, that the magnitude of the task would then absorb his whole self with every atom of all its resources, his whole physical and mental powers as long as he lives, every breath, every heartbeat, drop of blood, every thought, every moment of time, every possession, all money, every vestige of any capacity he has—an extremity of slavery and self-immolation which passes conscious imagination. This is what cure means to him from his unconscious depressive standpoint, and his uncured *status quo* in an unending analysis is clearly preferable to such a conception of cure—however grandiose and magnificent in one sense its appeal may be.

I hope that while I have spoken of the patient's unconscious aim of making others well and happy before himself, you will have borne in mind that the others I refer to always are the loved ones *in his inner world;* and these loved ones are also at the same moment the objects of all his hatred, vindictiveness, and murderous impulses! His egoistic self-seeking attitude corresponds accurately enough to one side of things in his unconscious mind—to the hatred, cruelty, and callousness there; and it represents his fears for his own ego if the love for his objects became too strong. We all fear the dependence of love to some extent.

I have spoken, too, of the contrast and incongruity of his love and need to save with his egoism, his tyranny, his lack of feeling for others. This egoism *is* his lack of a sense of reality. For his object-relations are not to real people, his object-relations are all within himself; his inner world is *all* the world to him. Whatever he does for his objects he does for himself as well; if only he could do it! he thinks; and in *mania* he thinks he *can*. So it is the overwhelming importance of the inner world of his emotional relations that makes him in real life so egocentric, asocial, self-seeking—so fantastic!

The unconscious attitude of love and anxiety for others in the patient is not identical with Freud's unconscious sense of guilt, though the feeling that the patient deserves no help till his loved ones have received full measure corresponds to it. This unworthiness finds atonement, as Freud says, in the illness, but only some atonement; the illness or the long analysis are compromises. To my mind it is *the love for his internal objects,* which lies behind and produces the unbearable guilt and pain, the need to sacrifice his life for theirs, and so the prospect of death, that makes this resistance so stubborn. And we can counter this resistance only by unearthing this love and so the guilt with it. To these patients if not to all, the analyst represents an internal object. So it is the positive transference in the patient that we must bring to realization; and this is what they resist beyond all, although they know well how to parade a substitute "friendliness," which they declare to be normal and appropriate and claim ought to satisfy us as "not neurotic." They claim that their transference is resolved before it has been broached. We shall be deluded if we accept that. What is underneath is a *love* (a craving for absolute bliss in complete union with a perfect object for ever and ever), and this love is bound up with an uncontrollable and insupportable fury of disappointment, together with anxiety for other love-relations as well.

In Freud's remarks on the difficulties of the negative therapeutic reaction he has a footnote which in this connection is extremely interesting. He says that this unconscious sense of guilt is sometimes a "borrowed" one, adopted from some other person who had been a love-object and is now one of the ego's identifications. And, "if one can unmask this former object-relation behind the unconscious sense of guilt, success is often brilliant." This is the view I have just stated; the love for the internal object must be found behind the guilt (only Freud regards the love as past and over). He adds a link, too, with the positive transference. "Success may depend, too," he says, "on whether the personality of the analyst admits of his being put in the place of the ego-ideal." But Freud's suggestion that the guilt is "adopted" from a now internal object shows us that the brilliant success rests on a *projection* (or localization) *of the guilt on to an object, though an internal one;* and this is an extremely common feature of the manic defence (which may of course have been built up on some facts in experience). And his suggestion that the personality of the analyst determines whether or not he plays the part of ego-ideal indicates that consciousness and external circumstances are being allowed to blur the issue—exactly as the manic patient employs them to do if he can. The analyst *is* unconsciously the ego-ideal, or prototype of it, already to these patients; if they can rationalize their overmastering love and idealize it, then they can to some extent realize it without analysis; and this is in part a reparation, of course. The true aggressive character of their love, and their unconscious guilt of that, is still denied. Freud admits that this is a "trick method" which the analyst cannot use. But the patient tries his utmost to trick us in this way. A great deal of our therapeutic success in former years in my opinion actually rested, and still may do, on this mechanism, without our having understood it. The patient exploits us in his own way instead of being fully analysed; and his improvement is based on a manic defensive system. Nowadays I regard this possibility as a danger, even if it was not so formerly; for the analysis of primitive aggression now rouses severe anxieties, while recognition and encouragement by the analyst of the patient's attempts at reparation (in real life) allay them merely by the omnipotent method of glossing over and denying the internal depressive reality—his feeling of failure. The result is that the patient may develop a manic defensive system—a denial of his illness and anxieties—instead of a cure, because the depressive situation of failure has never been opened up. In my experience the true analysis of the love and guilt of the depressive anxiety-situation, because they are so deeply buried, is far the hardest task we meet with; and the instances of success Freud quotes seem to be last-minute evasions of it by the patients' chosen methods of projection and denial.

The most important feature to be emphasized in these cases is the degree of unconscious falseness and deceit in them. It is what Abraham comments on; he, however, did not connect it with an unconscious sense of guilt. To us analysts both the full true positive and true negative transference are difficult to tolerate, but the *false* transference, when the patient's feelings for us are all insincere and are no feelings at all, when ego and id are allied in deceit against us, seems to be something the analyst can see through only with difficulty. A false and treacherous transference in our patients is such a blow to our narcissism, and so poisons and paralyses our instrument for good (our understanding of the patient's unconscious mind), that it tends to rouse strong depressive anxieties in ourselves. So the patient's falseness often enough meets with denial by us and remains unseen and unanalysed by us too.

9

NANCY J. CHODOROW
ON MELANIE KLEIN

From Subjectivity in General to Subjective Gender in Particular[1]

NANCY J. CHODOROW

When Donna Bassin invited me to select a paper for this volume, I knew instantly that it would have to be a paper by Melanie Klein. Klein is not an immediately obvious choice. She wrote few papers exclusively or primarily on female psychology. Differences between the sexes and anxieties and conflicts about being gendered and sexual do not seem especially central to the Kleinian project. Kleinians have not been major players in recent debates about the psychology of gender. Their developmental attention, as well as their attention to the clinical situation, have been elsewhere. Implicit attention to gender in contemporary Kleinian writing is found in an interpretive emphasis on the child's refusal to accept parental intercourse and the exclusivity of the parental couple. There is also a metaphoric extension of this interpretation into understandings of particular transference situations. A patient's inability to know, for example, may be an attempt to deny knowledge of the parents' exclusionary sexual relationship. A refusal to allow the analyst to think may be a way of warding off the envy or feelings of loss that come from recognizing that someone important can do things without

[1]I am grateful to the Guggenheim Foundation and the National Endowment for the Humanities for support while I was writing this commentary. Peter Goldberg and Elizabeth Bott Spillius gave helpful comments and criticism.

you. An inability to think together with the analyst may be engaged to prevent any unconscious associations to the primal scene of parental intercourse (see Britton et al. 1989, see also Bion 1959).

Yet, I knew that reading Klein and the contemporary Kleinians had deeply influenced my ability to think and work clinically, both substantively to understand my patients' unconscious fantasies, and to understand the analytic situation and process. Kleinians, it seemed to me, gave us an account of a psyche in process, continually active and changing. Klein brings conviction to a phenomenological-experiential sense of inner reality: you can talk to a patient in Kleinian terms, for example, pointing out how they put their own warded-off feelings or different aspects of themselves into you, or noting their refusal to think or make connections, or their attempts to deaden and make meaningless their interactions with you. Freud's writings before the consolidation of the structural theory—for example, the cases, the dream book, and his theoretical attempts to grasp what he found clinically—also give us very much a process psyche. But as a result of the ego psychological reliance on the structural theory, there has been in the Freudian legacy a tendency to conceptualize a fixed psyche enacting structural givens (see Chodorow 1996a). If you talk to a patient in the terms of ego psychology, you invite them to observe their inner workings as objective processes.

Perhaps my being drawn to Klein for the clinical understanding of women and psychoanalysis is peculiarly biographical. Previous to becoming a clinical psychoanalyst, I had thought long and hard about the psychology of women and had formulated many expectations, understandings, and insights. As I read the recent literature or reread the classics, then, I was looking less for further knowledge about the content of psychologies of gender (prevalent unconscious fantasies, self–other constructions, sexual senses of self, or body experiences and fantasies) and more for insight into how to help patients' unconscious senses of gender, body, and sexuality emerge, and into the ways that gender is related to other elements of the internal world and unconscious fantasy. According to my current understanding, gendered subjectivity—all elements of anyone's psychology of gender—is part of psychic functioning in general. In order to understand this psychology, we need the best possible general psychological theory and the best possible understanding of clinical process. We need to move beyond the old theories that base their psychologies of gender on a search for gender differences and a comparison of men and women, and that reduce gender psychology to one element (whether genital, relational, or anything else). We need a theory that can point us toward and help us to understand the clinical individuality of gender (see Chodorow 1994, 1995, 1996b). For this understanding, Kleinian theory—that theory which I had previously read least—was most helpful.

I also now recognized that the British Independent object-relations theorists who had so influenced me when I first became interested in psychoanalysis were in some sense neo-Kleinians. Klein's focus on the object provided the initial grounding for British object-relations theory, and many Independents were considerably influenced by Kleinian theory and technique even as they revised and expanded upon these and disagreed with some major Kleinian claims. Such recognition on my part may have been virtually impossible in the early 1970s, given the absolute proscription on Kleinian theory, not to mention the ignoring of British object-relations thinking, in American psychoanalysis.

Klein does give us several useful formulations directly concerning the psychology of women and men. In her paper "Early Stages of the Oedipus Conflict" (1928), she discusses a "femininity-phase" in both sexes. She describes a "femininity complex" in boys that includes male envy of female reproductive organs—"organs of receptivity and bounty" (1928, p. 190)— that is of equal virulence, but more obscured and displaced, than the castration complex in girls. She discusses the girl's dread of the mother (arising out of the girl's anxiety that the mother will attack and destroy her) as well as of the father, and shows how all these processes have consequences for the boy's and the girl's superego formation. *The Psycho-Analysis of Children* (1932) contains chapters on the effects of early anxiety situations on boys and girls (see Birksted-Breen, Chapter 10, this volume; see also Klein 1945, 1955, pp. 133, 135). In "Envy and Gratitude," Klein again takes as problematic women's envy or idealization of the penis and of men, tracing the roots of this envy and idealization not to something self-evidently superior in maleness or masculine genital equipment but to conflicts, envy, or anxiety in a girl's relation to her mother. In this paper, she also discusses male envy of the breast and other feminine attributes (1957, pp. 199–201). Unlike Freud, then, Klein provides an account of envy and idealization of the other gender that applies to both sexes and that has a dynamic and developmental explanation. In fact, the psychoanalytic feminist rethinking of the psychology of women would have been greatly advanced if we had taken Klein's few papers and comments as seriously as we took contemporaneous Freudian writings.

But the question of psychoanalysis and women is much broader than the psychology of women, including, importantly, men's theories and fantasies about women and about themselves as gendered. The psychology of women itself, moreover, includes every element that goes into how someone unconsciously and consciously fantasizes about and creates her senses of gender, well beyond the Freudian genital-centered understanding in which the psychology of women refers to normative woman in the development theory (on this see Chodorow 1994, Ch.1). In terms of this broader definition, the substantive content of Kleinian theory must be seen as completely gendered: all the important psychological processes of human life— projective and introjective processes, fantasies of goodness and badness, splitting, envy, and reparation—center around the maternal breast (of course, in Kleinian theory the breast is much more than a part of the maternal anatomy). An infant does not know that her or his mother's breast comes with female gendering, but learning about gender and unconscious gender fantasies eventually comes to include this knowledge.[2]

In this broader context, Klein's account of the consequences of a child's (girl's or boy's) fantasies about the terrors, fears, desires, or envy of the good and bad breast, described most powerfully in "Envy and Gratitude" (1957), must be seen also as indirectly gender-related, by tying unconscious fantasies about women to one of the most destructive intrapsychic and interpersonal emotions. As Klein and other writers note, these fantasies based on envy can also generate some of the deepest threats to clinical work and to the analyst's sense of well-being. If this is so, then patients of both sexes engender their analysis when they destroy either a woman or a man analyst's interpretations because their envy and projective fantasies make them unable to accept good from another: "The capacity to give and to preserve life is felt as the greatest gift and therefore creativeness becomes the deepest cause for envy" (1957, p. 202).

---

[2] It has always struck me that in discussing gender differences, psychoanalysts focus entirely on the genitals and virtually ignore the presence or absence of the anatomic breasts, which must also be so important to the young child and which are certainly important to women themselves (one wonders, even, if thinking about "the" breast, as if breasts don't come in plural pairs, is an extension of thinking about "the" penis). In contrast to the psychoanalytic literature, the anthropological literature makes clear that weaning, a new sibling, and the transition from babyhood have more widespread traumatic import for both sexes than learning about genital difference (see, e.g., Briggs 1971, Levy 1973, Whiting and Whiting 1975). Moreover, when ethnographers describe a sex that is preoccupied psychodynamically with envy, anxiety, and fear about its own gender, and with a need to repudiate cross-gender identifications, it is always the male, who is, like the generic baby, enmeshed in his early tie to his mother (see, e.g., Gregor 1985, Herdt 1981, Whiting et al. 1958).

It is not surprising, I think, that a breast-centered, or mother-centered, general theory written by a woman would be a promising approach to understanding psychoanalysis and women, whether or not Klein spends much time directly discussing female psychology. Nor is it surprising that you would need Klein (among others) to understand transferences toward a woman analyst (at least). Yet, for this volume, I have chosen to discuss a contribution that is not explicitly about the psychology of gender or sexuality, or even much about breasts, the mother's insides, or the primal scene. I have done so because it seems to me that although body configuration and gender-related fantasy of course play a part in gendered and sexual subjectivity, this part can only be understood in the context of other, perhaps more basic, Kleinian concepts. As Klein gives us an account of the creation of subjectivity in general, we are able to see exactly the processes that go to create subjective gender in particular.

Fundamental to the Kleinian contribution is Klein's account of the intertwining and mutual creation of inner and outer worlds. Klein's concept of projective identification describes how people endow the external world with unconscious meaning, animating or tinting this world with emotional and fantasy meaning (see Caper 1988). We need such a concept to understand how individuals experience and appropriate cultural gender, how they make personally meaningful cultural beliefs, stories, and fantasies. Unconscious fantasies help any individual to locate herself among these cultural beliefs and stories: I think of a patient whose unconscious masochistic fantasies, developed originally in relation to her father, help fuel an addiction to gothic romances and to images of herself as the mousy and finally triumphant woman. Gender for the individual also has a particular affective tonality, generated projectively by unconscious fantasies created through interaction with particular kinds of mothers and fathers. Experiencing a depressed mother, for example, may lead a woman to lend a diffuse depressive tonality to her unconscious sense of female self. Reciprocally, children understand the unconscious messages about gender transmitted by parents through introjective identification that filters these messages through unconscious fantasy, and that introjectively takes in fantasied aspects of the parent. Such unconscious messages include, for example, recognition and confirmation, or envy and disparagement, of the child's gender, body, and self, as well as the parents' own complex unconscious senses, feelings, and fantasies of self and gender.

Although they have not been developed with the psychology of gender in mind, then, Kleinian concepts of projection and introjection can be applied to help specify the psychic processes that create gendered subjectivity. Similarly, the Kleinian account of psychic positions seems to me relevant to understanding how anyone creates their gender. For some people, or during some periods of analysis, gender may be created more in paranoid-schizoid terms. Male and female will be radically split, the one good the other bad, one's own or the other gender repudiated and denied. Still in paranoid-schizoid fantasy, unconscious gender will become imbued with destructive envy, or one or the other sex becomes experienced in terrifyingly persecutory terms. Alternatively, gender may be created in more depressive terms, not dominated by persecutory anxiety and defensive splitting but with a rueful sense that something must be given up, something acknowledged, in the complex wholeness of one's gender. By extending Klein's theory to an understanding of gender in these ways, we begin to imagine how such shifts might occur throughout life and transferentially in relation to gender, creating the extensive complexity of any individual's unconscious sense of gender and gender fantasy. We can evaluate personal meanings of gender, sexuality, and body in terms of their dominant character as rigidly split or integrated, and their dominant associated affects and affective tone. We can explore the leading anxieties and defensive patterns and processes that create gender, as well as the creative and constructive elements that may animate, enliven, and enrich it.

The Kleinian concept of reparation (1937) provides another ostensibly nongendered concept of relevance to a gendered psychology. I am thinking here of the many developmental theories that consider separation from and rejection of the mother, along with turning toward or idealizing the father, as necessary development tasks for both sexes. As I and others have noted, a felt need for separation from and repudiation of the mother contributes to the installation of male-dominant heterosexuality and to psychological, social, and cultural male dominance (symbolized in psychoanalytic talk of the primacy of the phallus, the phallic world of difference, the name of the father, and so forth—almost as if theory here mirrors the child's supposed developmental task). In turn, this rejection and repudiation deeply affect how many women feel as mothers, and how we conceptualize (and blame) mothers clinically. The view that this transfer of idealization and attachment is a necessary developmental task contributes to the difficulty so many writers seem to find in holding evenhandedly in view the subjectivity of both mother and child. As I note earlier, Klein herself describes clearly and forcefully the repudiation of feminine identifications and maternal dependency in both boys and girls. She also describes the potent envy and fantasied destruction of the breast that lead to overvaluation of the penis and father. Yet in neither case does she suggest that such processes are necessary, and in both she describes them as defensive, growing out of anxiety.

In contrast to a development account that seems to require repudiation of the mother, Klein's (1935) work on manic-depressive states implies another goal. The main achievement of depressive-level functioning is the ability to create the mother as a whole person (to create a whole breast) with good and bad aspects, rather than fantasying mother, breast, and self as composed of split, fragmented, unintegrated good and bad bits. In the depressive position, as one recognizes that his or her destructiveness and rage have been directed against a whole object, there is guilt and a wish to make reparation. In this context, I believe that one could argue that the traditional rejection of the mother and turn to the father is a paranoid-schizoid solution to the felt need to separate. For both sexes, a non-misogynist, non-mother-repudiating psychological solution to fear, hatred, or rejection of the mother and envy of her breast may be not idealization of the father but depressive-level reparation toward the mother. Indeed, I believe that coming to terms with the internal and external mother is a major developmental project and a lifelong internal process for most women (for most men as well). My clinical experience only substantiates this claim, which I first articulated in 1978, although I have also become much more aware through clinical work of the great individual variation and complexity in such processes.

Fantasy reparation toward the whole object, whether it be through decreasing envy, direct recognition of one's own destructiveness, or a lessening of a protective idealization of one's mother that has covered genuine acknowledgement of her real limitations and one's own rage at these, all enable a sense of separate self based neither on the destruction of the mother nor on the severance of the connection to her. My point here is not that this reparative project describes women rather than men, but that it solves for both the developmental mother-rejection implicit in much psychoanalytic theory and practice. (I would make a similar point about coming to terms with the internal and external father. Insofar as this is done mainly through comparison of him with the mother and radical choice-making, this is a more paranoid-schizoid process. Insofar as his different aspects are engaged, appropriated, mourned, or rejected in relation to him himself, the achievement is more at the depressive level.)

I have chosen for this volume "Mourning and Its Relation to Manic-Depressive States." Klein developed the concepts I have been describing over many years and in many papers. Among these papers, "Mourning" to my mind covers many Kleinian clinical and theoretical themes succinctly and with moving eloquence. Cited infrequently in comparison to several of Klein's other papers and also in the psychoanalytic literature on mourning, "Mourning" gives us in detail an account of how inner worlds are built and rebuilt in development, in life, and in analysis. She describes with particular clarity, in her concept of "doubling," the relations of inner and outer worlds, and she documents how a sense of inner aliveness depends upon the aliveness of the outer world, as well as the reverse. She also provides an account (summarizing Klein 1935) of how the psyche can shift rapidly from paranoid-schizoid to depressive states and back again. Klein's topic is initially actual mourning for actual loss, but her account draws from and is extended to her understanding of internal loss. She begins from the understanding that from early infancy, all development and all change involve loss, in which the acknowledgement of the loss and the acknowledgement that one has survived it are both a threat. Loss of inner or outer objects must be endured without denial, a collapse into an internal sense of deadness, excessive guilt, complete destruction of the lost object and turning all its good aspects into bad, or hatred for abandonment. Any of these internal processes lead to paranoid splitting. On the other side is the danger of manic omnipotence, feelings of triumph over the other, and elation at surviving that also reflect splitting and denial.

These general processes have direct relevance as well to the psychology of women (not negligibly, the putatively aubiographical case of Mrs. A. also provides a powerful early psychoanalytic account of maternal subjectivity). I believe we can fruitfully apply Klein's account specifically to what happens for many women as they attempt to come to terms with their mother (see also Loewald 1979, on the developmental necessity of parricide, triumph, and atonement). They too find themselves in precarious balance between depressive sadness, reparation, and "progress in integration" (1957, p. 233) on the one hand, and on the other a pull toward paranoid-schizoid triumphant mania and elation at surviving her. But in this mania and elation, if the continued internal connection to the mother is denied, it eventually comes back to haunt. I have described elsewhere (Chodorow 1995) what I call "weeping for the mother," which I have found especially in my women patients whose active professional, personal, and sexual lives contrast sharply with the lives of their mothers, who are trapped in classically patriarchal marriages. Issues of mourning and conflicts about surviving and triumphing over the other also characterize a difficulty in the successful resolution of many guilt-laden or envious transferences, perhaps especially those characteristic of some woman analyst–woman patient pairs.

I have come to believe that we need to look at individuality in the psychology of gender and to move beyond generalizing and universalizing claims about "the" woman and "the" man (see Chodorow 1996b). Klein's substantive theory can be read as a universalizing developmental theory as well as a universalizing symbolic theory about the meaning of the breast. But I believe that her clinical guidance toward particularized introjective and projective fantasies and shifting transferences, and her understanding of the critical lifelong battle between paranoid-schizoid and depressive ways of functioning, both point us toward a clinical method that can uncover individuality in gender fantasies and transferences and varied levels of integrated or unintegrated gender. With such a theory, we are not always focused on the meaning of the genital, the meaning of a particular parent, or the comparison of males and females. Indeed, at this point in time, a psychology of gender that does not begin from overgeneralizations or reductionist claims about gender difference is consonant with both clinical observation and feminist theory.

REFERENCES

Bion, W. R. (1959). Attacks on linking. In *Melanie Klein Today*, vol 1., ed. E. B. Spillius, pp. 87–101. London and New York: Routledge, 1988.

Briggs, J. (1971). *Never in Anger*. Cambridge, MA: Harvard University Press.

Britton, R., Feldman, M., and O'Shaughnessy, E., eds. (1989). *The Oedipus Complex Today: Clinical Implications*. London: Karnac.

Caper, R. (1988). *Immaterial Facts: Freud's Discovery of Psychic Reality and Klein's Development of His Work*. Northvale, NJ: Jason Aronson.

Chodorow, N. J. (1978). *The Reproduction of Mothering*. Berkeley, CA: University of California Press.

——— (1994). *Femininities, Masculinities, Sexualities: Freud and Beyond*. Lexington, KY: University Press of Kentucky; London: Free Association Books.

——— (1995). Gender as a personal and cultural construction. *Signs* 20:516–544.

——— (1996a). Reflections on the authority of the past in psychoanalytic thinking. *Psychoanalytic Quarterly* 65:32–51.

——— (1996b). Theoretical gender and clinical gender: epistemological reflections on the psychology of women. *Journal of the American Psychoanalytic Association* 44 (suppl.):215–238.

Gregor, T. (1985). *Anxious Pleasures: the Sexual Lives of an Amazonian People*. Chicago: University of Chicago Press.

Herdt, G. (1981). *Guardians of the Flutes*. Chicago: University of Chicago Press.

Klein, M. (1928). Early stages of the Oedipus conflict. In *Love, Guilt and Reparation and Other Works 1921–1945*, pp. 186–198. New York: Delta, 1975.

―――― (1932). *The Psycho-Analysis of Children*. New York: Delta, 1975.

―――― (1935). A contribution to the psychogenesis of manic-depressive states. In *Love, Guilt and Reparation and Other Works 1921–1945*, pp. 262–289. New York: Delta, 1975.

―――― (1937). Love, Guilt and Reparation. In *Love, Guilt and Reparation and Other Works 1921–1945*, pp. 306–343. New York: Delta, 1975.

―――― (1940). Mourning and its relation to manic-depressive states. *International Journal of Psycho-Analysis* 21:125–153.

―――― (1945). The Oedipus complex in the light of early anxieties. In *Love, Guilt and Reparation and Other Works 1921–1945*, pp. 370–419. New York: Delta, 1975.

―――― (1955). The psycho-analytic play technique: its history and significance. In *Envy and Gratitude and Other Works 1946–1963*, pp. 122–140. New York: Delta, 1975.

―――― (1957). Envy and gratitude. In *Envy and Gratitude and Other Works 1946–1963*, pp. 176–235. New York: Delta, 1975.

―――― (1975a). *Love, Guilt and Reparation and Other Works 1921–1945*. New York: Delta.

―――― (1975b). *Envy and Gratitude and Other Works 1946–1963*. New York: Delta.

Levy, R. (1973). *Tahitians: Mind and Experience in the Society Islands*. Chicago: University of Chicago Press.

Loewald, H. (1979). The waning of the Oedipus complex. In *Papers on Psychoanalysis*, pp. 384–404. New Haven, CT: Yale University Press.

Whiting, B. B., and Whiting, J. M. W. (1975). *Children of Six Cultures: A Psychocultural Analysis*. Cambridge, MA: Harvard University Press.

Whiting, J. M. W., Kluckhohn, R., and Anthony, A. (1958). The function of male initiation ceremonies at puberty. In *Readings in Social Psychology*, ed. E. E. Maccoby, T. M. Newcomb, and E. L. Hartley, pp. 359–370. New York: Holt.

Mourning and Its Relation to Manic-Depressive States [1]

MELANIE KLEIN

An essential part of the work of mourning is, as Freud points out in "Mourning and Melancholia," the testing of reality. He says that "in grief this period of time is necessary for detailed carrying out of the behest imposed by the testing of reality, and . . . by accomplishing this labour the ego succeeds in freeing its libido from the lost object," [2] And again : "Each single one of the memories and hopes which bound the libido to the object is brought up and hyper-cathected, and the detachment of the libido from it accomplished. Why this process of carrying out the behest of reality bit by bit, which is in the nature of a compromise, should be so extraordinarily painful is not at all easy to explain in terms of mental economics. It is worth noting that this pain seems natural to us." [3] And, in another passage: "We do not even know by what economic measures the work of mourning is carried through; possibly, however, a conjecture may help us here. Reality passes

---

[1] This paper was read originally before the Fifteenth International Psycho-Analytical Congress, Paris, 1938. It was subsequently revised and enlarged with a view to its inclusion in the Ernest Jones Sixtieth Birthday Number of *International Journal of Psycho-Analysis*, vol. 20, parts 3 and 4, 1939.
[2] Freud: *Collected Papers*, vol. 4, p. 163.
[3] Freud: *Collected Papers*, ibid.

its verdict—that the object no longer exists—upon each single one of the memories and hopes through which the libido was attached to the lost object, and the ego, confronted as it were with the decision whether it will share this fate, is persuaded by the sum of its narcissistic satisfactions in being alive to sever its attachment to the non-existent object. We may imagine that, because of the slowness and the gradual way in which this severance is achieved, the expenditure of energy necessary for it becomes somehow dissipated by the time the task is carried through." [4]

In my view there is a close connection between the testing of reality in normal mourning and early processes of the mind. My contention is that the child goes through states of mind comparable to the mourning of the adult, or rather, that this early mourning is revived whenever grief is experienced in later life. The most important of the methods by which the child overcomes his states of mourning, is, in my view, the testing of reality; this process, however, as Freud stresses, is part of the work of mourning.

In my paper "A Contribution to the Psychogenesis of Manic-Depressive States," [5] I introduced the conception of the *infantile depressive position*, and showed the connection between that position and manic-depressive states. Now in order to make clear the relation between the infantile depressive position and normal mourning I must first briefly refer to some statements I made in that paper, and shall then enlarge on them. In the course of this exposition I also hope to make a contribution to the further understanding of the connection between normal mourning, on the one hand, and abnormal mourning and manic-depressive states, on the other.

I said there that the baby experiences depressive feelings which reach a climax just before, during, and after weaning. This is the state of mind in the baby which I termed the "depressive position," and I suggested that it is a melancholia in *statu nascendi*. The object which is being mourned is the mother's breast and all that the breast and the milk have come to stand for in the infant's mind: namely, love, goodness, and security. All these are felt by the baby to be lost, and lost as a result of his own uncontrollable greedy and destructive phantasies and impulses against his mother's breasts. Further distress about impending loss (this time of both parents) arises out of the Oedipus situation, which sets in so early and in such close connection

---

[4]Ibid., p. 166.
[5]*International Journal of Psycho-Analysis*, vol. 16, 1935. The present paper is a continuation of that paper, and much of what I have now to say will of necessity assume the conclusions I arrived at there.

with breast frustrations that in its beginnings it is dominated by oral impulses and fears. The circle of loved objects who are attacked in phantasy and whose loss is therefore feared widens owing to the child's ambivalent relations to his brothers and sisters. The aggression against phantasied brothers and sisters, who are attacked inside the mother's body, also gives rise to feelings of guilt and loss. The sorrow and concern about the feared loss of the "good" objects, that is to say, the depressive position, is, in my experience, the deepest source of the painful conflicts in the Oedipus situation, as well as in the child's relations to people in general. In normal development these feelings of grief and fears are overcome by various methods.

Along with the child's relation, first to his mother and soon to his father and other people, go those processes of internalization on which I have laid so much stress in my work. The baby, having incorporated his parents, feels them to be live people inside his body in the concrete way in which deep unconscious phantasies are experienced—they are, in his mind, "internal" or "inner" objects, as I have termed them. Thus an inner world is being built up in the child's unconscious mind, corresponding to his actual experiences and the impressions he gains from people and the external world, and yet altered by his own phantasies and impulses. If it is a world of people predominantly at peace with each other and with the ego, inner harmony, security, and integration ensue.

There is a constant interaction between anxieties relating to the "external" mother—as I will call her here in contrast to the "internal" one—and those relating to the "internal" mother, and the methods used by the ego for dealing with these two sets of anxieties are closely inter-related. In the baby's mind, the "internal" mother is bound up with the "external" one, of whom she is a "double," though one which at once undergoes alterations in his mind through the very process of internalization; that is to say, her image is influenced by his phantasies, and by internal stimuli and internal experiences of all kinds. When external situations which he lives through become internalized—and I hold that they do, from the earliest days onwards—they follow the same pattern: they also become "doubles" of real situations, and are again altered for the same reasons. The fact that by being internalized, people, things, situations, and happenings—the whole inner world which is being built up—become inaccessible to the child's accurate observation and judgement, and cannot be verified by the means of perception which are available in connection with the tangible and palpable object-world, has an important bearing on the phantastic nature of this inner world. The ensuing doubts, uncertainty, and anxieties act as a continuous incentive to the young child to observe and make sure about the external object-world,[6] from which this inner world springs, and by these means to understand the internal one better. The visible mother thus provides continuous proofs of what the "internal" mother is like, whether she is loving or angry, helpful or revengeful. The extent to which external reality is able to disprove anxieties and sorrow relating to the internal reality varies with each individual, but could be taken as one of the criteria for normality. In children who are so much dominated by their internal world that their anxieties cannot be sufficiently disproved and counteracted even by the pleasant aspects of their relationships with people, severe mental difficulties are unavoidable. On the other hand, a certain amount even of unpleasant experiences is of value in this testing of reality by the child if, through overcoming them, he feels that he can retain his objects as well as their love for him and his love for them, and thus preserve or re-establish internal life and harmony in face of dangers.

All the enjoyments which the baby lives through in relation to his mother are so many proofs to him that the love object *inside as well as outside* is not injured, is not turned into a vengeful person. The increase of love and trust, and the diminishing of fears through happy experiences, help the baby step by step to overcome his depression and feeling of loss (mourning). They enable him to test his inner reality by means of outer reality. Through being loved and through the enjoyment and comfort he has in relation to people his confidence in his own as well as in other people's goodness becomes strengthened, his hope that his "good" objects and his own ego can be saved and preserved increases, at the same time as his ambivalence and acute fears of internal destruction diminish.

Unpleasant experiences and the lack of enjoyable ones, in the young child, especially lack of happy and close contact with loved people, increase ambivalence, diminish trust and hope, and confirm anxieties about inner annihilation and external persecution; moreover they slow down and perhaps permanently check the beneficial processes through which in the long run inner security is achieved.

In the process of acquiring knowledge, every new piece of experience has to be fitted into the patterns provided by the psychic reality which

---

[6]Here I can only refer in passing to the great impetus which these anxieties afford to the development of interests and sublimations of all kinds. If these anxieties are over-strong, they may interfere with or even check intellectual development. (Cf. Klein, "A Contribution to the Theory of Intellectual Inhibition," *International Journal of Psycho-Analysis*, vol. 12, 1931.)

prevails at the time; while the psychic reality of the child is gradually influenced by every step in his progressive knowledge of external reality. Every such step goes along with his more and more firmly establishing his inner "good" objects, and is used by the ego as a means of overcoming the depressive position.

In other connections I have expressed the view that every infant experiences anxieties which are psychotic in content,[7] and that the infantile neurosis[8] is the normal means of dealing with and modifying these anxieties. This conclusion I can now state more precisely, as a result of my work on the infantile depressive position, which has led me to believe that it is the central position in the child's development. In the infantile neurosis the early depressive position finds expression, is worked through, and gradually overcome; and this is an important part of the process of organization and integration which, together with his sexual development,[9] characterize the first years of life. Normally the child passes through his infantile neurosis, and among other achievements arrives step by step at a good relation to people and to reality. I hold that this satisfactory relation to people depends upon his having succeeded in his struggles against the chaos inside him (the depressive position) and having securely established his "good" internal objects.

Let us now consider more closely the methods and mechanisms by which this development comes about.

In the baby, processes of introjection and projection, since they are dominated by aggression and anxieties which reinforce each other, lead to fears of persecution by terrifying objects. To such fears are added those of losing his loved objects; that is to say, the depressive position has arisen.

---

[7]*The Psycho-Analysis of Children*, 1932; in particular, Chapter 8.

[8]In the same book (p. 149), referring to my view that every child passes through a neurosis differing only in degree from one individual to another, I added: "This view, which I have maintained for a number of years now, has lately received valuable support. In his book, *Die Frage der Laienanalyse* (1926), Freud writes: 'Since we have learnt to see more clearly we are almost inclined to say that the occurrence of a neurosis in childhood is not the exception but the rule. It seems as though it is a thing that cannot be avoided in the course of development from the infantile disposition to the social life of the adult' (S. 61)."

[9]At every juncture the child's feelings, fears, and defences are linked up with his libidinal wishes and fixations, and the outcome of his sexual development in childhood is always interdependent with the processes I am describing in this paper. I think that new light will be thrown on the child's libidinal development if we consider it in connection with the depressive position and the defences used against that position. It is, however, a subject of such importance that is needs to be dealt with fully, and is therefore beyond the scope of this paper.

When I first introduced the conception of the depressive position I put forward the suggestion that the introjection of the whole loved object gives rise to concern and sorrow lest that object should be destroyed (by the "bad" objects and the id), and that these distressed feelings and fears, in addition to the paranoid set of fears and defences, constitute the depressive position. There are thus two sets of fears, feelings and defences, which, however varied in themselves and however intimately linked together, can in my view, for purposes of theoretical clearness, be isolated from each other. The first set of feelings and phantasies are the persecutory ones, characterized by fears relating to the destruction of the ego by internal persecutors. The defences against these fears are predominantly the destruction of the persecutors by violent or secretive and cunning methods. With these fears and defences I have dealt in detail in other contexts. The second set of feelings which go to make up the depressive position I formerly described without suggesting a term for them. I now propose to use for these feelings of sorrow and concern for the love objects, the fears of losing them, and the longing to regain them, a simple word derived from everyday language—namely the "pining" for the loved object. In short—persecution (by "bad" objects) and the characteristic defences against it, on the one hand, and pining for the loved ("good") object, on the other, constitute the depressive position.

When the depressive position arises, the ego is forced (in addition to earlier defenses) to develop methods of defence which are essentially directed against the "pining" for the loved object. These are fundamental to the whole ego-organization. I formerly termed some of these methods *manic defenses*, or the *manic position*, because of their relationship to the manic-depressive illness.[10]

The fluctuations between the depressive and the manic position are an essential part of normal development. The ego is driven by depressive anxieties (anxiety lest the loved objects as well as itself should be destroyed) to build up omnipotent and violent phantasies, partly for the purpose of controlling and mastering the "bad," dangerous objects, partly in order to save and restore the loved ones. From the very beginning, these omnipotent phantasies, both the destructive and the reparative ones, stimulate and enter into all the activities, interests, and sublimations of the child. In the infant, the extreme character both of his sadistic and of his constructive

---

[10] "A Contribution to the Psychogenesis of Manic-Depressive States," *International Journal of Psycho-Analysis*, vol. 16, 1935.

phantasies is in line with the extreme frightfulness of his persecutors—and, at the other end of the scale, the extreme perfection of his "good" objects.[11] Idealization is an essential part of the manic position and is bound up with another important element of that position, namely denial. Without partial and temporary denial of psychic reality the ego cannot bear the disaster by which it feels itself threatened when the depressive position is at its height. Omnipotence, denial, and idealization, closely bound up with ambivalence, enable the early ego to assert itself to a certain degree against its internal persecutors and against a slavish and perilous dependence upon its loved objects, and thus to make further advances in development. I will here quote a passage from my former paper:

> In the earliest phase the persecuting and the good objects (breasts) are kept wide apart in the child's mind. When, along with the introjection of the whole and real object, they come closer together, the ego has over and over again recourse to that mechanism—so important for the development of the relations to objects—namely, a splitting of its imagos into loved and hated, that is to say, into good and dangerous ones.
>
> One might think that it is actually at this point that ambivalence which, after all, refers to object-relations—that is to say, to whole and real objects—sets in. Ambivalence, carried out in a splitting of the imagos, enables the small child to gain more trust and belief in its real objects and thus in its internalized ones—to love them more and to carry out in an increasing degree its phantasies of restoration on the loved

---

[11]I have pointed out in various connections (first of all in "The Early Stages of the Oedipus Complex," *International Journal of Psycho-Analysis*, vol. 9, 1928) that the fear of phantastically "bad" persecutors and the belief in phantastically "good" objects are bound up with each other. Idealization is an essential process in the young child's mind, since the cannot yet cope in any other way with his fears of persecution (a result of his own hatred). Not until early anxieties have been sufficiently relieved owing to experiences which increase love and trust, is it possible to establish the all-important process of bringing together more closely the various aspects of objects (external, internal, "good" and "bad," loved and hated), and thus for hatred to become actually mitigated by love—which means a decrease of ambivalence. While the separation of these contrasting *aspects*—felt in the unconscious as contrasting *objects*—operates strongly, feelings of hatred and love are also so much divorced from each other that love cannot mitigate hatred.

The flight to the internalized "good" object, which Melitta Schmideberg (in "Psychotic Mechanism in Cultural Development," *International Journal of Psycho-Analysis*, vol. 11, 1930) has found to be a fundamental mechanism is schizophrenia, thus also enters into the process of idealization which the young child normally resorts to in his depressive anxieties. Melitta Schmideberg has also repeatedly drawn attention to the connection between idealization and distrust of the object.

object. At the same time the paranoid anxieties and defences are directed towards the "bad" objects. The support which the ego gets from a real "good" object is increased by a flight-mechanism, which alternates between its external and internal good objects. [Idealization.]

It seems that at this stage of development the unification of external and internal, loved and hated, real and imaginary objects is carried out in such a way that each step in the unification leads again to a renewed splitting of the imagos. But as the adaptation to the external world increases, this splitting is carried out on planes which gradually become increasingly nearer and nearer to reality. This goes on until love for the real and the internalized objects and trust in them are well established. Then ambivalence, which is partly a safeguard against one's own hate and against the hated and terrifying objects, will in normal development again diminish in varying degrees.[12]

As has already been stated, omnipotence prevails in the early phantasies, both the destructive and the reparative ones, and influences sublimations as well as object relations. Omnipotence, however, is so closely bound up in the unconscious with the sadistic impulses with which it was first associated that the child feels again and again that his attempts at reparation have not succeeded, or will not succeed. His sadistic impulses, he feels, may easily get the better of him. The young child, who cannot sufficiently trust his reparative and constructive feelings, as we have seen, resorts to manic omnipotence. For this reason, in an early stage of development the ego has not adequate means at its disposal to deal efficiently with guilt and anxiety. All this leads to the need in the child—and for that matter to some extent in the adult also—to repeat certain actions obsessionally (this, in my view, is part of the repetition compulsion);[13] or—the contrasting method—omnipotence and denial are resorted to. When the defences of a manic nature fail, defences in which dangers from various sources are in an omnipotent way denied or minimized, the ego is driven, alternately or simultaneously, to combat the fears of deterioration and disintegration by attempted reparations carried out in obsessional ways. I have described elsewhere[14] my conclusion that the obsessional mechanisms are a defence against paranoid anxieties as well as a means of modifying them, and here I will only show briefly

---

[12] "A Contribution to the Psychogenesis of Manic-Depressive States," op. cit., pp. 172–173.
[13] Klein, M. (1932). *The Psycho-Analysis of Children*, pp. 170 and 278.
[14] Ibid., Chapter 9.

the connection between obsessional mechanisms and manic defences in relation to the depressive position in normal development.

The very fact that manic defences are operating in such close connection with the obsessional ones contributes to the ego's fear that the reparation attempted by obsessional means has also failed. The desire to control the object, the sadistic gratification of overcoming and humiliating it, of getting the better of it, the *triumph* over it, may enter so strongly into the act of reparation (carried out by thoughts, activities, or sublimations) that the benign circle started by this act becomes broken. The objects which were to be restored change again into persecutors, and in turn paranoid fears are revived. These fears reinforce the paranoid defence mechanisms (of destroying the object) as well as the manic mechanisms (of controlling it or keeping it in suspended animation, and so on). The reparation which was in progress is thus disturbed or even nullified—according to the extent to which these mechanisms are activated. As a result of the failure of the act of reparation, the ego has to resort again and again to obsessional and manic defences.

When in the course of normal development a relative balance between love and hate is attained, and the various aspects of objects are more unified, then also a certain equilibrium between these contrasting and yet closely related methods is reached, and their intensity is diminished. In this connection I wish to stress the importance of *triumph*, closely bound up with contempt and omnipotence, as an element of the manic position. We know the part rivalry plays in the child's burning desire to equal the achievements of the grown-ups. In addition to rivalry, his wish, mingled with fears, to "grow out" of his deficiencies (ultimately to overcome his destructiveness and his bad inner objects and to be able to control them) is an incentive to achievements of all kinds. In my experience, the desire to reverse the child–parent relation, to get power over the parents and to triumph over them, is always to some extent associated with the impulse toward the attainment of success. A time will come, the child phantasies, when he will be strong, tall and grown up, powerful, rich, and potent, and father and mother will have changed into helpless children, or again, in other phantasies, will be very old, weak, poor, and rejected. The triumph over the parents in such phantasies, through the guilt to which it gives rise, often cripples endeavours of all kinds. Some people are obliged to remain unsuccessful, because success always implies to them the humiliation or even the damage of somebody else, in the first place the triumph over parents, brothers, and sisters. The efforts by which they seek to achieve something may be of a highly constructive nature, but the implicit triumph and the ensuing harm and injury done to the object may outweigh these purposes, in the subject's mind, and therefore prevent their fulfilment. The effect is that the reparation to the loved objects, which in the depths of the mind are the same as those over which he triumphs, is again thwarted, and therefore guilt remains unrelieved. The subject's triumph over his objects necessarily implies to him their wish to triumph over him, and therefore leads to distrust and feelings of persecution. Depression may follow, or an increase in manic defences and more violent control of his objects, since he has failed to reconcile, restore, or improve them, and therefore feelings of being persecuted by them again have the upper hand. All this has an important bearing on the infantile depressive position and the ego's success or failure in overcoming it. The triumph over his internal objects which the young child's ego controls, humiliates, and tortures is a part of the destructive aspect of the manic position which disturbs the reparation and recreating of his inner world and of internal peace and harmony; and thus triumph impedes the work of early mourning.

To illustrate these developmental processes let us consider some features which can be observed in hypomanic people. It is characteristic of the hypomanic person's attitude toward people, principles, and events that he is inclined to exaggerated valuations: over-admiration (idealization) or contempt (devaluation). With this goes his tendency to conceive of everything on a large scale, to think in *large numbers*, all this in accordance with the greatness of his omnipotence, by which he defends himself against his fear of losing the one irreplaceable object, his mother, whom he still mourns at bottom. His tendency to minimize the importance of details and small numbers, and a frequent casualness about details and contempt of conscientiousness contrast sharply with the very meticulous methods, the concentration on the smallest things (Freud), which are part of the obsessional mechanisms.

This contempt, however, is also based to some extent on denial. He must deny his impulse to make extensive and detailed reparation because he has to deny the cause for the reparation, namely the injury to the object and his consequent sorrow and guilt.

Returning to the course of early development, we may say that every step in emotional, intellectual, and physical growth is used by the ego as a means of overcoming the depressive position. The child's growing skills, gifts, and arts increase his belief in the psychical reality of his constructive tendencies, in his capacity to master and control his hostile impulses as well as his "bad" internal objects. Thus anxieties from various sources are relieved, and this results in a diminution of aggression and, in turn, of his suspicions of "bad" external and internal objects. The strengthened ego, with its greater trust in people, can then make still further steps toward unification of its imagos—external, internal, loved, and hated—and toward further mitigation of hatred by means of love, and thus to a general process of integration.

When the child's belief and trust in his capacity to love, in his reparative powers and in the integration and security of his good inner world increase as a result of the constant and manifold proofs and counter-proofs gained by the testing of external reality, manic omnipotence decreases and the obsessional nature of the impulses toward reparation diminishes, which means in general that the infantile neurosis has passed.

We have now to connect the infantile depressive position with normal mourning. The poignancy of the actual loss of a loved person is, in my view, greatly increased by the mourner's unconscious phantasies of having lost his *internal* "good" objects as well. He then feels that his internal "bad" objects predominate and his inner world is in danger of disruption. We know that the loss of a loved person leads to an impulse in the mourner to reinstate the lost loved object in the ego (Freud and Abraham). In my view, however, he not only takes into himself (re-incorporates) the person whom he has just lost, but also reinstates his internalized good objects (ultimately his loved parents), who became part of his inner world from the earliest stages of his development onwards. These too are felt to have gone under, to be destroyed, whenever the loss of a loved person is experienced. Thereupon the early depressive position, and with it anxieties, guilt, and feelings of loss and grief derived from the breast situation, the Oedipus situation and all other such sources, are reactivated. Among all these emotions, the fears of being robbed and punished by both dreaded parents—that is to say, feelings of persecution—have also been revived in deep layers of the mind.

If, for instance, a woman loses her child through death, along with sorrow and pain, her early dread of being robbed by a "bad" retaliating mother is reactivated and confirmed. Her own early aggressive phantasies of robbing her mother of babies gave rise to fears and feelings of being punished, which strengthened ambivalence and led to hatred and distrust of others. The reinforcing of feelings of persecution in the state of mourning is all the more painful because, as a result of an increase in ambivalence and distrust, friendly relations with people, which might at that time be so helpful, become impeded.

The pain experienced in the slow process of testing reality in the work of mourning thus seems to be partly due to the necessity, not only to renew the links to the external world and thus continuously to reexperience the loss, but at the same time and by means of this to rebuild with anguish the inner world, which is felt to be in danger of deteriorating and collapsing.[15] Just as the young child passing through the depressive position is struggling, in his unconscious mind, with the task of establishing and integrating his inner world, so the mourner goes through the pain of re-establishing and re-integrating it.

In normal mourning early psychotic anxieties are reactivated; the mourner is in fact ill, but, because this state of mind is so common and seems so natural to us, we do not call mourning an illness. (For similar reasons, until recent years, the infantile neurosis of the normal child was not recognized as such.) To put my conclusions more precisely: I should say that in mourning the subject goes through a modified and transitory manic-depressive state and overcomes it, thus repeating, though in different circumstances and with different manifestations, the processes which the child normally goes through in his early development.

The greatest danger for the mourner comes from the turning of his hatred against the lost loved person himself. One of the ways in which hatred expresses itself in the situation of mourning is in feelings of triumph over the dead person. I refer in an earlier part of this paper to triumph as part of the manic position in infantile development. Infantile death wishes against parents, brothers, and sisters are actually fulfilled whenever a loved person dies, because he is necessarily to some extent a representative of the earliest important figures, and therefore takes over some of the feelings pertaining to them. Thus his death, however shattering for other reasons, is to some extent also felt as a victory, and gives rise to triumph, and therefore all the more to guilt.

At this point I find that my view differs from that of Freud, who stated: "First, then: in normal grief too the loss of the object is undoubtedly surmounted, and this process too absorbs all the energies of the ego while it lasts. Why then does it not set up the economic condition for a phase

---

[15]These facts I think go some way toward answering Freud's question which I have quoted at the beginning of this paper: "Why this process of carrying out the behest of reality bit by bit, which is in the nature of a compromise, should be so extraordinarily painful is not all easy to explain in terms of mental economics. It is worth noting that this pain seems natural to us."

of triumph after it has run its course or at least produced some slight indication of such a state? I find it impossible to answer this objection off-
hand." [16] In my experience, feelings of triumph are inevitably bound up even
with normal mourning, and have the effect of retarding the work of mourning, or rather they contribute much to the difficulties and pain which the
mourner experiences. When hatred of the lost loved object in its various
manifestations gets the upper hand in the mourner, this not only turns the
loved lost person into a persecutor, but shakes the mourner's belief in his
good inner objects as well. The shaken belief in the good objects disturbs
most painfully the process of idealization, which is an essential intermediate step in mental development. With the young child, the idealized mother
is the safeguard against a retaliating or a dead mother and against all bad
objects, and therefore represents security and life itself. As we know, the
mourner obtains great relief from recalling the lost person's kindness and
good qualities, and this is partly due to the reassurance he experiences from
keeping his loved object for the time being as an idealized one.

The passing states of elation[17] which occur between sorrow and distress in normal mourning are manic in character and are due to the feeling
of possessing the perfect loved object (idealized) inside. At any time, however, when hatred against the lost loved person wells up in the mourner,
his belief in him breaks down and the process of idealization is disturbed.
(His hatred of the loved person is increased by the fear that by dying the
loved one was seeking to inflict punishment and deprivation upon him,
just as in the past he felt that his mother, whenever she was away from
him and he wanted her, had died in order to inflict punishment and deprivation upon him.) Only gradually, by regaining trust in external objects
and values of various kinds, is the normal mourner able once more to
strengthen his confidence in the lost loved person. Then he can again bear
to realize that this object was not perfect, and yet not lose trust and love
for him, nor fear his revenge. When this stage is reached, important steps
in the work of mourning and toward overcoming it have been made.

To illustrate the ways in which a normal mourner re-established connections with the external world I shall now give an instance. Mrs. A., in

---

[16] "Mourning and Melancholia," *Collected Papers* vol. 4, p. 166.

[17] Abraham writes of a situation of this kind: "We have only to reverse [Freud's] statement
that 'the shadow of the lost love-object falls upon the ego' and say that in this case it was not
the shadow but the bright radiance of his loved mother which was shed upon her son." (*Selected Papers*, p. 442.)

the first few days after the shattering loss of her young son, who had died suddenly while at school, took to sorting out letters, keeping his and throwing others away. She was thus unconsciously attempting to restore him and keep him safe inside herself, and throwing out what she felt to be indifferent, or rather hostile—that is to say, the "bad" objects, dangerous excreta and bad feelings.

Some people in mourning tidy the house and re-arrange furniture, actions which spring from an increase of the obsessional mechanisms which are a repetition of one of the defences used to combat the infantile depressive position.

In the first week after the death of her son she did not cry much, and tears did not bring her the relief which they did later on. She felt numbed and closed up, and physically broken. It gave her some relief, however, to see one or two intimate people. At this stage Mrs. A., who usually dreamed every night, had entirely stopped dreaming because of her deep unconscious denial of her actual loss. At the end of the week she had the following dream: *She saw two people, a mother and son. The mother was wearing a black dress. The dreamer knew that this boy had died, or was going to die. No sorrow entered into her feelings, but there was a trace of hostility toward the two people.*

The associations brought up an important memory. When Mrs. A. was a little girl, her brother, who had difficulties in his school work, was going to be tutored by a school-fellow of his own age (I will call him B.). B.'s mother had come to see Mrs. A.'s mother to arrange about the coaching, and Mrs. A. remembered this incident with very strong feelings. B.'s mother behaved in a patronizing way, and her own mother appeared to her to be rather dejected. She herself felt that a fearful disgrace had fallen upon her very much admired and beloved brother and the whole family. The brother, a few years old than herself, seemed to her full of knowledge, skill, and strength—a paragon of all the virtues, and her ideal was shattered when his deficiencies at school came to light. The strength of her feelings about this incident as being an irreparable misfortune, which persisted in her memory, was, however, due to her unconscious feelings of guilt. She felt it to be the fulfilment of her own harmful wishes. Her brother himself was very much chagrined by the situation, and expressed great dislike and hatred of the other boy. Mrs. A. at the time identified herself strongly with him in these resentful feelings. In the dream, the two people whom Mrs. A. saw were B. and his mother, and the fact that the boy was dead expressed Mrs. A.'s early death wishes against him. At the same time, however, the death wishes against her own brother and the wish to inflict punishment and deprivation upon her mother through the loss of her son—very deeply repressed wishes—were part of her dream thoughts. It now appeared that Mrs. A., with all her admiration and love for her brother, had been jealous of him on various grounds, envying his greater knowledge, his mental and physical superiority, and also his possession of a penis. Her jealousy of her much beloved mother for possessing such a son had contributed toward her death wishes against her brother. One dream thought, therefore, ran: "A mother's son has died, or will die. It is this unpleasant woman's son, who hurt my mother and brother, who should die." But in deeper layers, the death wish against her brother had also been reactivated, and this dream thought ran: "My mother's son died, and not my own." (Both her mother and her brother were in fact already dead.) Here a contrasting feeling came in—sympathy with her mother and sorrow for herself. She felt: "One death of the kind was enough. My mother lost her son; she should not lose her grandson also." When her brother died, besides great sorrow, she unconsciously felt triumph over him, derived from her early jealously and hatred, and corresponding feelings of guilt. She had carried over some of her feelings for her brother into her relation to her son. In her son, she also loved her brother; but at the same time, some of the ambivalence toward her brother, though modified through her strong motherly feelings, was also transferred on to her son. The mourning for her brothers, together with the sorrow, the triumph, and the guilt experienced in relation to him, entered into her present grief, and was shown in the dream.

Let us now consider the interplay of defences as they appeared in this material. When the loss occurred, the manic position became reinforced, and denial in particular came especially into play. Unconsciously, Mrs. A. strongly rejected the fact that her son had died. When she could no longer carry on this denial so strongly, but was not yet able to face the pain and sorrow, triumph, one of the other elements of the manic position, became reinforced. "It is not at all painful," the thought seemed to run, as the associations showed, "if *a* boy dies. It is even satisfactory. Now I get my revenge against this unpleasant boy who injured my brother." The fact that triumph over her brother had also been revived and strengthened became clear only after hard analytic work. But this triumph was associated with control of the *internalized* mother and brother, and triumph over them. At this stage the *control* over her internal objects was reinforced, the misfortune and grief were *displaced* from herself on to her internalized mother. Here denial again came into play—denial of the psychical reality that she and her internal mother were one and suffered together. Compassion and love for the internal mother were denied, feelings of revenge and triumph over the internalized objects and control of them were reinforced, partly because, through her own revengeful feelings, they had turned into persecuting figures.

In the dream there was only one slight hint of Mrs. A.'s growing unconscious knowledge (indicating that the denial was lessening) that it was she *herself* who lost her son. On the day preceding the dream she was wearing a black dress with a white collar. The woman in the dream had something white round her neck on her black dress.

Two nights after this dream she dreamt again: *She was flying with her son, and he disappeared. She felt that this meant his death—that he was drowned. She felt as if she, too, were to be drowned—but then she made an effort and drew away from the danger, back to life.*

The associations showed that in the dream she had decided that she would not die with her son, but would survive. It appeared that even in the dream she felt that it was good to be alive and bad to be dead. In this dream the unconscious knowledge of her loss is much more accepted than in the one of two days earlier. Sorrow and guilt had drawn closer. The feeling of triumph had apparently gone, but it became clear that it had only diminished. It was still present in her satisfaction about remaining alive—in contrast to her son's being dead. The feelings of guilt which already made themselves felt were partly due to this element of triumph.

I am reminded here of a passage in Freud's "Mourning and Melancholia":[18] "Reality passes its verdict—that the object no longer exists—upon each single one of the memories and hopes through which the libido was attached to the lost object, and the ego, confronted as it were with the decision whether it will share this fate, is persuaded by the sum of its narcissistic satisfactions in being alive to sever its attachment to the nonexistent object." In my view, this "narcissistic satisfaction" contains in a milder way the element of triumph which Freud seemed to think does not enter into normal mourning.

In the second week of her mourning Mrs. A. found some comfort in looking at nicely situated houses in the country, and in wishing to have such a house of her own. But this comfort was soon interrupted by bouts of despair and sorrow. She now cried abundantly, and found relief in tears.

---

[18]*Collected Papers*, vol. 4, p. 166.

The solace she found in looking at houses came from her rebuilding her inner world in her phantasy by means of this interest and also getting satisfaction from the knowledge that other people's houses and good objects existed. Ultimately this stood for re-creating her good parents, internally and externally, unifying them and making them happy and creative. In her mind she made reparation to her parents for having, in phantasy, killed their children, and by this she anticipated their wrath. Thus her fear that the death of her son was a punishment inflicted on her by retaliating parents lost in strength, and also the feeling that her son frustrated and punished her by his death was lessened. The diminution of hatred and fear all round allowed the sorrow itself to come out in full strength. Increase of distrust and fears had intensified her feeling of being persecuted and mastered by her internal objects and strengthened her need to master them. All this had expressed itself by a hardening in her internal relationships and feelings—that is to say, in an increase in manic defences. (This was shown in the first dream.) If these again diminish through the strengthening of the subject's belief in goodness—his own and others'—and fears decrease, the mourner is able to surrender to his own feelings, and to cry out his sorrow about the actual loss.

It seems that the processes of projecting and ejecting which are closely connected with giving vent to feelings, are held up in certain stages of grief by an extensive manic control, and can again operate more freely when that control relaxes. Through tears, which in the unconscious mind are equated to excrement, the mourner not only expresses his feelings and thus eases tension, but also expels his "bad" feelings and his "bad" objects, and this adds to the relief obtained through crying. This great freedom in the inner world implies that the internalized objects, being less controlled by the ego, are also allowed more freedom: that these objects themselves are allowed, in particular, greater freedom of feeling. In the mourner's situation, the feelings of his internalized objects are also sorrowful. In his mind, they share his grief, in the same way as actual kind parents would. The poet tells us that "Nature mourns with the mourner." I believe that "Nature" in this connection represents the internal good mother. This experience of mutual sorrow and sympathy in internal relationships, however, is again bound up with external ones. As I have already stated, Mrs. A.'s greater trust in actual people and things and help received from the external world contributed to a relaxing of the manic control over her inner world. Thus introjection (as well as projection) could operate still more freely, more goodness and love could be taken in from without, and goodness and love increasingly experienced within. Mrs. A., who at an earlier stage of her mourning had to some extent felt that her loss was inflicted on her by revengeful parents, could now in phantasy experience the sympathy of these parents (dead long since), their desire to support and to help her. She felt that they also suffered a severe loss and shared her grief, as they would have done had they lived. In her internal world harshness and suspicion had diminished, and sorrow had increased. The tears which she shed were also to some extent the tears which her internal parents shed, and she also wanted to comfort them as they—in her phantasy—comforted her.

If greater security in the inner world is gradually regained, and feelings and inner objects are therefore allowed to come more to life again, re-creative processes can set in and hope return.

As we have seen, this change is due to certain movements in the two sets of feelings which make up the depressive position: persecution decreases and the pining for the lost loved object is experienced in full force. To put it in other words: hatred has receded and love is freed. It is inherent in the feeling of persecution that it is fed by hatred and at the same time feed hatred. Furthermore, the feeling of being persecuted and watched by internal "bad" objects, with the consequent necessity for constantly watching them, leads to a kind of dependence which reinforces the manic defences. These defences, insofar as they are used predominantly against persecutory feelings (and not so much against the pining for the loved object), are of a very sadistic and forceful nature. When persecution diminishes, the hostile dependence on the object, together with hatred, also diminishes, and the manic defences relax. The pining for the lost loved object also implies dependence on it, but dependence of a kind which becomes an incentive to reparation and preservation of the object. It is creative because it is dominated by love, while the dependence based on persecution and hatred is sterile and destructive.

Thus, while grief is experienced to the full and despair at its height, the love for the object wells up and the mourner feels more strongly that life inside and outside will go on after all, and that the lost loved object can be preserved within. At this stage in mourning, suffering can become productive. We know that painful experiences of all kinds sometimes stimulate sublimations, or even bring out quite new gifts in some people, who may take to painting, writing, or other productive activities under the stress of frustrations and hardships. Others become more productive in a different way—more capable of appreciating people and things, more tolerant in their relation to other—they become wiser. Such enrichment is in my view gained through processes similar to those steps in mourning which we have just investigated. That is to say, any pain caused by unhappy experiences, whatever their nature, has something in common with mourning. It reactivates the infantile depressive position, and encountering and overcoming adversity of any kind entails mental work similar to mourning.

It seems that every advance in the process of mourning results in a deepening in the individual's relation to his inner objects, in the happiness of regaining them after they were felt to be lost ("Paradise Lost and Regained"), in an increased trust in them and love for them because they proved to be good and helpful after all. This is similar to the ways in which the young child step by step builds up his relations to external objects, for he gains trust not only from pleasant experiences, but also from the ways in which he overcomes frustrations and unpleasant experiences, nevertheless retaining his good objects (externally and internally). The phases in the work of mourning when manic defences relax and a renewal of life inside sets in, with a deepening in internal relationships, are comparable to the steps which in early development lead to greater independence from external as well as internal objects.

To return to Mrs. A. Her relief in looking at pleasant houses was due to the setting in of some hope that she could re-create her son as well as her parents; life started again inside herself and in the outer world. At this time she could dream again and unconsciously begin to face her loss. She now felt a stronger wish to see friends again, but only one at a time and only for a short while. These feelings of greater comfort, however, again alternated with distress. (In mourning as well as in infantile development, inner security comes about not by a straightforward movement but in waves.) After a few weeks of mourning, for instance, Mrs. A. went for a walk with a friend through the familiar streets, in an attempt to re-establish old bonds. She suddenly realized that the number of people in the street seemed overwhelming, the houses strange and the sunshine artificial and unreal. She had to retreat into a quiet restaurant. But there she felt as if the ceiling were coming down, and the people in the place became vague and blurred. Her own house suddenly seemed the only secure place in the world. In analysis it became clear that the frightening indifference of these people was reflected from her internal objects, who in her mind had turned into a multitude of "bad" persecuting objects. The external world was felt to be artificial and unreal, because real trust in inner goodness had gone.

Many mourners can only make slow steps in re-establishing the bonds with the external world because they are struggling against the chaos inside; for similar reasons the baby develops his trust in the object-world first in connection with a few loved people. No doubt other factors as well, e.g. his intellectual immaturity, are partly responsible for this gradual development in the baby's object relations, but I hold that this also is due to the chaotic state of his inner world.

One of the differences between the early depressive position and normal mourning is that when the baby loses the breast or bottle, which has come to represent to him a "good" helpful, protective object inside him, and experiences grief, he does this in spite of his mother being there. With the grown-up person however the grief is brought about by the actual loss of an actual person; yet help comes to him against this overwhelming loss through his having established in his early life his "good" mother inside himself. The young child, however, is at the height of his struggles with fears of losing her internally and externally, for he has not yet succeeded in establishing her securely inside himself. In this struggle, the child's relation to his mother, her actual presence, is of the greatest help. Similarly, if the mourner has people whom he loves and who share his grief, and if he can accept their sympathy, the restoration of the harmony in his inner world is promoted, and his fears and distress are more quickly reduced.

Having described some of the process which I have observed at work in mourning and in depressive states, I wish now to link up my contribution with the work of Freud and Abraham.

Following Freud's and his own discoveries about the nature of the archaic processes at work in melancholia, Abraham found that such processes also operate in the work of normal mourning. He concluded that in this work the individual succeeds in establishing the lost loved person in his ego, while the melancholic has failed to do so. Abraham also described some of the fundamental factors upon which that success or failure depends.

My experience leads me to conclude that, while it is true that the characteristic feature of normal mourning is the individual's setting up the lost loved object inside himself, he is not doing so for the first time but, through the work of mourning, is reinstating that object as well as all his loved *internal* objects which he feels he has lost. He is therefore *recovering* what he had already attained in childhood.

In the course of his early development, as we know, he establishes his parents within his ego. (It was the understanding of the processes of introjection in melancholia and in normal mourning which, as we know, led Freud to recognize the existence of the super-ego in normal development.) But, as regards the nature of the super-ego and the history of its individual development, my conclusions differ from those of Freud. As I have often pointed out, the processes of introjection and projection from the beginning of life lead to the institution inside ourselves of loved and hated objects, who are felt to be "good" and "bad," and who are interrelated with each other and with the self: that is to say, they constitute an inner world. This assembly of internalized objects becomes organized, together with the organization of the ego, and in the higher strata of the mind it becomes discernible as the super-ego. Thus, the phenomenon which was recognized by Freud, broadly speaking, as the voices and the influence of the actual parents established in the ego is, according to my findings, a complex object-world, which is felt by the individual, in deep layers of the unconscious, to be concretely inside himself, and for which I and some of my colleagues therefore use the term "internalized," or an internal (inner) world. This inner world consists of innumerable objects taken into the ego, corresponding partly to the multitude of varying aspects, good and bad, in which the parents (and other people) appeared to the child's unconscious mind throughout various stages of his development. Further, they also represent all the real people who are continually becoming internalized in a variety of situations provided by the multitude of ever-changing external experiences as well as phantasied ones. In addition, all these objects are in the inner world in an infinitely complex relation both with each other and with the self.

If I now apply this conception of the super-ego organization as compared with Freud's super-ego to the process of mourning, the nature of my contribution to the understanding of this process becomes clear. In normal mourning the individual re-introjects and reinstates, as well as the actual lost person, his loved parents—who are felt to be his "good" inner objects. His inner world, the one which he has built up from his earliest days onwards, in his phantasy was destroyed when the actual loss occurred. The rebuilding of this inner world characterizes the successful work of mourning.

An understanding of this complex inner world enables the analyst to find and resolve a variety of early anxiety-situations which were formerly unknown, and is therefore theoretically and therapeutically of an importance so great that it cannot yet be fully estimated. I believe that the problem of mourning also can only be more fully understood by taking account of these early anxiety situations.

I shall now illustrate in connection with mourning one of these anxiety-situations which I have found to be of crucial importance also in manic-depressive states. I refer to the anxiety about the internalized parents in destructive sexual intercourse; they as well as the self are felt to be in constant danger of violent destruction. In the following material I shall give extracts from a few dreams of a patient, D., a man in his early forties, with strong paranoid and depressive traits. I am not going into details about the case as a whole, but am here concerned only to show the ways in which these particular fears and phantasies were stirred in this patient by the death of his mother. She had been in failing health for some time, and was, at the time to which I refer, more or less unconscious.

One day in analysis, D. spoke of his mother with hatred and bitterness, accusing her of having made his father unhappy. He also referred to a case of suicide and one of madness which had occurred in his mother's family. His mother, he said, had been "muddled" for some time. Twice he applied the term "muddled" to himself and then said: "I know you are going to drive me mad and then lock me up." He spoke about an animal being locked up in a cage. I interpreted that his mad relative and his muddled mother were now felt to be inside himself, and that the fear of being locked up in a cage partly implied his deeper fear of containing these mad people inside himself and thus of going mad himself. He then told me a dream of the previous night: *He saw a bull lying in a farmyard. It was not quite dead, and looked very uncanny and dangerous. He was standing on one side of the bull, his mother on the other. He escaped into a house, feeling that he was leaving his mother behind in danger and that he should not do so; but he vaguely hoped that she would get away.*

To his own astonishment, my patient's first association to the dream was of the blackbirds which had disturbed him very much by waking him up that morning. He then spoke of buffaloes in America, the country where he was born. He had always been interested in them and attracted by them when he saw them. He now said that one could shoot them and use them for food, but that they are dying out and should be preserved. Then he mentioned the story of a man who had been kept lying on the ground, with a bull standing over him for hours, unable to move for fear of being crushed. There was also an association about an actual bull on a friend's farm; he had lately seen this bull, and he said it looked ghastly. This farm had associations for him by which it stood for his own home. He had spent most of his childhood on a large farm his father owned. In between, there were associations about flower seeds spreading from the country and taking root in town gardens. D. saw the owner of this farm again the same evening and urgently advised him to keep the bull under control. (D. had learnt that the bull had recently damaged some buildings on the farm.) Later that evening he received the news of his mother's death.

In the following hour, D. did not at first mention his mother's death, but expressed his hatred of me—my treatment was going to kill him. I then reminded him of the dream of the bull, interpreting that in his mind his mother had become mixed up with the attacking bull father—half dead himself—and had become uncanny and dangerous. I myself and the treatment were at the moment standing for this combined parent-figure. I pointed out that the recent increase of hatred against his mother was a defence against his sorrow and despair about her approaching death. I referred to his aggressive phantasies by which, in his mind, he had changed his father into a dangerous bull which would destroy his mother; hence his feeling of responsibility and guilt about this impending disaster. I also referred to the patient's remark about eating buffaloes, and explained that he had incorporated the combined parent-figure and so felt afraid of being crushed internally by the bull. Former materials had shown his fear of being controlled and attacked internally by dangerous beings, fears which had resulted among other things in his taking up at times a very rigid and immobile posture. His story of the man who was in danger of being crushed by the bull, and who was kept immobile and controlled by it, I interpreted as a representation of the dangers by which he felt threatened internally.[19]

I now showed the patient the sexual implications of the bull's attacking his mother, connecting this with his exasperation about the birds waking him that morning (this being his first association to the bull dream). I reminded him that in his associations birds often stood for people, and that the noise the birds made—a noise to which he was quite accustomed—represented to him the dangerous sexual intercourse of his parents, and was so unendurable on this particular morning because of the bull dream, and owing to his acute state of anxiety about his dying mother. Thus his mother's death meant to him her being destroyed by the bull inside him,

---

[19]I have often found that processes which the patient unconsciously feels are going on inside him are represented as something happening on top of or closely round him. By means of the well-known principle of representation by the contrary, an external happening can stand for an internal one. Whether the emphasis lies on the internal or the external situation becomes clear from the whole context—from the details of associations and the nature and intensity of affects. For instance, certain manifestations of very acute anxiety and the specific defence mechanisms against this anxiety (particularly an increase in denial of psychic reality) indicate that an internal situation predominates at the time.

since—the work of mourning having already started—he had internalized her in this most dangerous situation.

I also pointed out some hopeful aspects of the dream. His mother might save herself from the bull. Blackbirds and other birds he is actually fond of. I showed him also the tendencies to reparation and re-creation present in the material. His father (the buffaloes) should be preserved, i.e., protected against his—the patient's—own greed. I reminded him, among other things, of the seeds which he wanted to spread from the country he loved to the town, and which stood for new babies being created by him and by his father as a reparation to his mother—these live babies being also a means of keeping her alive.

It was only after this interpretation that he was actually able to tell me that his mother had died the night before. He then admitted, which was unusual with him, his full understanding of the internalization processes which I had interpreted to him. He said that after he had received the news of his mother's death he felt sick, and that he thought, even at the time, that there could be no physical reason for this. It now seemed to him to confirm my interpretation that he had internalized the whole imagined situation of his fighting and dying parents.

During this hour he had shown great hatred, anxiety, and tension, but scarcely any sorrow; toward the end, however, after my interpretation, his feelings softened, some sadness appeared, and he experienced some relief.

The night after his mother's funeral, D. dreamt that X. (a father figure) and another person (who stood for me) were trying to help him, but actually he had to fight for his life against us; as he put it: "Death was claiming me." In this hour he again spoke bitterly about his analysis, as disintegrating him. I interpreted that he felt the helpful external parents to be at the same time the fighting, disintegrating parents, who would attack and destroy him—the half-dead bull and the dying mother inside him— and that I myself and analysis had come to stand for the dangerous people and happenings inside himself. That his father was also internalized by him as dying or dead was confirmed when he told me that at his mother's funeral he had wondered for a moment whether his father also was not dead. (In reality the father was still alive.)

Toward the end of this hour, after a decrease of hatred and anxiety, he again became more cooperative. He mentioned that the day before, looking out of the window of his father's house into the garden and feeling lonely, he disliked a jay he saw on a bush. He thought that this nasty and destructive bird might possibly interfere with another bird's nest with eggs in it. Then he associated that he had seen, some time previously, bunches of wild flowers thrown on the ground—probably picked and thrown away by children. I again interpreted his hatred and bitterness as being in part a defence against sorrow, loneliness, and guilt. The destructive bird, the destructive children—as often before—stood for himself, who had, in his mind, destroyed his parents' home and happiness and killed his mother by destroying her babies inside her. In this connection his feelings of guilt related to his *direct* attacks in phantasy on his mother's body; whilst in connection with the bull dream the guilt was derived from his *indirect* attacks on her, when he changed his father into a dangerous bull who was thus carrying into effect his—the patient's—own sadistic wishes.

On the third night after his mother's funeral, D. had another dream: *He saw a bus coming toward him in an uncontrolled way—apparently driving itself. It went toward a shed. He could not see what happened to the shed, but knew definitely that the shed "was going to blazes." Then two people, coming from behind him, were opening the roof of the shed and looking into it. D. did not "see the point of their doing this," but they seemed to think it would help.*

Besides showing his fear of being castrated by his father through a homosexual act which he at the same time desired, this dream expressed the same internal situation as the bull dream—the death of his mother inside him and his own death. The shed stood for his mother's body, for himself, and also for his mother inside him. The dangerous sexual intercourse represented by the 'bus destroying the shed happened in his mind to his mother as well as to himself; but in addition, and that is where the predominant anxiety lay, to his mother inside him.

His not being able to see what happened in the dream indicated that in his mind the catastrophe was happening internally. He also knew, without seeing it, that the shed was "going to blazes." The 'bus "coming toward him," besides standing for sexual intercourse and castration by his father, also meant "happening inside him." [20]

The two people opening the roof from behind (he had pointed to my chair) were himself and myself, looking into his inside and into his mind (psycho-analysis). The two people also meant myself as the "bad" combined parent-figure, myself containing the dangerous father—hence his

---

[20]An attack on the outside of the body often stands for one which is felt to happen internally. I have already pointed out that something represented as being on top of or tightly round the body often covers the deeper meaning of being inside.

doubts whether looking into the shed (analysis) could help him. The un-controlled 'bus represented also himself in dangerous sexual intercourse with his mother, and expressed his fears and guilt about the badness of his own genitals. Before his mother's death, at a time when her fatal illness had already begun, he accidentally ran his car into a post—without serious consequences. It appeared that this was an unconscious suicidal attempt, meant to destroy the internal "bad" parents. This accident also represented his parents in dangerous sexual intercourse inside him, and was thus an acting out as well as an externalization of an internal disaster.

The phantasy of the parents combined in "bad" intercourse—or rather, the accumulation of emotions of various kinds, desires, fears, and guilt, which go with it—had very much disturbed his relation to both parents, and had played an important part not only in his illness but in his whole develop-ment. Through the analysis of these emotions referring to the actual parents in sexual intercourse, and particularly through the analysis of these internal-ized situations, the patient became able to experience real mourning for his mother. All his life, however, he had warded off the depression and sorrow about losing her, which were derived from his infantile depressive feelings, and had denied his very great love for her. In his mind he had reinforced his hatred and feelings of persecution, because he could not bear the fear of losing his loved mother. When his anxieties about his own destructiveness decreased and confidence in his power to restore and preserve her became strengthened, persecution lessened and love for her came gradually to the fore. But together with this he increasingly experienced the grief and long-ing for her which he had repressed and denied from his early days onward. While he was going through this mourning with sorrow and despair, his deeply buried love for his mother came more and more into the open, and his relation to both parents altered. On one occasion he spoke of them, in connection with a pleasant childhood memory, as "my dear old parents"— a new departure in him.

I have described here and in my former paper the deeper reasons for the individual's incapacity to overcome successfully the infantile depressive position. Failure to do so may result in depressive illness, mania, or para-noia. I pointed out [in the earlier paper] one or two other methods by which the ego attempts to escape from the sufferings connected with the depressive position, namely either the flight to internal good objects (which may lead to severe psychosis) or the flight to external good objects (with the possible outcome of neurosis). There are, however, many ways, based on obsessional, manic, and paranoid defences, varying from individual to individual in their relative proportion, which in my experience all serve the same purpose, that is, to enable the individual to escape from the sufferings connected with the depressive position. (All these methods, as I have pointed out, have a part in normal development also.) This can be clearly observed in the analyses of people who fail to experience mourning. Feeling incapable of saving and securely reinstating their loved objects inside themselves, they must turn away from them more than hitherto and therefore deny their love for them. This may mean that their emotions in general become more inhibited; in other cases it is mainly feelings of love which become stifled and hatred is increased. At the same time, the ego uses various ways of dealing with paranoid fears (which will be the stronger the more hatred is reinforced). For instance, the internal "bad" objects are manically subjugated, immobilized, and at the same time denied, as well as strongly projected into the external world. Some people who fail to experience mourning may escape from an outbreak of manic-depressive illness or paranoia only by a severe restriction of their emotional life which impoverishes their whole personality.

Whether some measure of mental balance can be maintained in people of this type often depends on the ways in which these various methods interact, and on their capacity to keep alive in other directions some of the love which they deny to their lost objects. Relations to people who do not in their minds come too close to the lost object, and interest in things and activities, may absorb some of this love which belonged to the lost object. Though these relations and sublimations will have some manic and paranoid qualities, they may nevertheless offer some reassurance and relief from guilt, for through them the lost loved object which has been rejected and thus again destroyed is to some extent restored and retained in the unconscious mind.

If, in our patients, analysis diminishes the anxieties of destructive and persecuting internal parents, it follows that hate and thus in turn anxieties decrease, and the patients are enabled to revise their relation to their parents—whether they be dead or alive—and to rehabilitate them to some extent even if they have grounds for actual grievance. This greater tolerance makes it possible for them to set up "good" parent figures more securely in their minds, alongside the "bad" internal objects, or rather to mitigate the fear of these "bad" objects by the trust in "good" objects. This means enabling them to experience emotions—sorrow, guilt, and grief, as well as love and trust—to go through mourning, but to overcome it, and ultimately to overcome the infantile depressive position, which they have failed to do in childhood.

To conclude. In normal mourning, as well as in abnormal mourning and in manic-depressive states, the infantile depressive position is reactivated. The complex feelings, phantasies, and anxieties included under this term are of a nature which justifies my contention that the child in his early development goes through a transitory manic-depressive state as well as a state of mourning, which become modified by the infantile neurosis. With the passing of the infantile neurosis, the infantile depressive position is overcome.

The fundamental difference between normal mourning, on the one hand, and abnormal mourning and manic-depressive states, on the other, is this. The manic-depressive and the person who fails in the work of mourning, though their defences may differ widely from each other, have this in common, that they have been unable in early childhood to establish their internal "good" objects and to feel secure in their inner world. They have never really overcome the infantile depressive position. In normal mourning, however, the early depressive position, which had become revived through the loss of the loved object, becomes modified again, and is overcome by methods similar to those used by the ego in childhood. The individual is reinstating his actually lost loved object; but he is also at the same time reestablishing inside himself his first loved objects—ultimately the "good" parents—whom, when the actual loss occurred, he felt in danger of losing as well. It is by reinstating inside himself the "good" parents as well as the recently lost person, and by rebuilding his inner world, which was disintegrated and in danger, that he overcomes his grief, regains security, and achieves true harmony and peace.

10

DANA BIRKSTED-BREEN
ON MELANIE KLEIN

Holding the Tension

DANA BIRKSTED-BREEN

Klein pursued with great strength her understanding of some of the most basic workings of the mind, in particular of the infant and child's intense and violent feelings and phantasies in relation to the mother's body and its contents, and of how these primitive fantasies give rise to anxieties which can greatly affect mental functioning. It has been said that Lacan called Melanie Klein *"une tripière de génie"*—a brilliant gut handler. In "The Effects of Early Anxiety Situations on the Sexual Development of the Girl," Klein describes how the fantasies of violent attacks on the mother's body lead to a specific *feminine* form of castration anxiety. This castration anxiety is the girl's fear that she will have her feminine organs destroyed by her mother as a consequence of her own fantasies of attacking the inside of her mother's body, and the babies and penis imagined to be inside the mother. She fears retaliation in kind for her wish to invade and rob her mother's body and its contents.

In my clinical work with women, I have found this configuration to be central, particularly in understanding women for whom femininity is conflictual and for whom making a relationship with a man and becoming a mother is problematic. These women often feel that having a feminine body involves stealing part of their mother's body or attributes, and a masculine stance protects them from the imagined retaliation of an angry mother. Often the mother and her fertility are thought to have been already damaged by the daughter's sadism, and she feels a need to placate the mother.

One patient of mine, a young anorexic woman in her twenties who had been amenorreic since her teens, started menstruating again a few years into her analysis. She immediately developed a lump in her breast which had to be removed; it proved to be benign but it emerged that in fantasy she believed her newfound fertility had been stolen from me in the maternal transference and now she was in turn being amputated in retaliation. It became clear that her anorexia had been in part an attempt to stop herself maturing because she believed that mother and daughter could only live at the expense of each other.

Another woman patient who had been a tomboy and, as an adult, liked to think of herself as having the body of a young man, developed a more feminine sense of herself during her analysis, but every time she made moves in a feminine direction she became frightened. "You will tear out my insides and my brains," she would complain. "Every time I'm successful," she would shout, "you scratch inside me with your long fingernails." It was possible to see how sessions in which she had been more receptive to my interpretations (the feminine position)—that is, able to listen, take in, and think about what I said rather than put up an instant barrier, would be followed by anxiety and a combative stance. This receptive feminine position was felt to be a threat in that it made her open to my forcing my way in and taking all the goodness and power (masculine and feminine) for myself (a projection of her wish in relation to me). She too had been anorexic but in her case the central fear was the invasion.

Klein also brought an important understanding to the phenomenon of penis envy. She believed that often it is not the expression of the masculine wish to be a boy, but the expression of the feminine wish to receive the penis in a feminine way. Therefore the hatred of the mother for not giving her a penis is in fact the girl's hatred toward the oedipal rival who keeps the father's penis for herself. It is this penis, imagined to be permanently contained inside the mother's body, that the girl wants to rob. It is relevant to note that, in German, *Penisneid* means both to envy (in the meaning of the English word) and also to desire. This double meaning is also there in the French language, while in English "penis envy" has only one meaning. The ambiguity of the word in German and French reflects an ambiguity which can be there in the analytic discourse and has led to differing interpretations of the material. For Klein it is the desire for the father's penis as a libidinal object which precedes the wish for a child, rather than the wish to possess a penis as an attribute as in Freud's account. The desire for a child can also be a means of overcoming anxiety and allaying a sense of guilt at having in fantasy made the mother sterile and becoming in turn sterile. The woman's longing to possess a beautiful child and her efforts to beautify the imaginary baby and her own body are connected with a fear of having produced in herself and put inside her mother bad, ugly children whom she likens to poisonous excrement. This helps to understand why one also often finds in the analysis of women who have had children similar anxieties around damaging the mother's body, though in this case the fear of retaliation is usually not as acute and the desire to repair is greater.

Klein writes that the central situation for the girl is of having to deal with the double frustration and resentment aroused in her by the mother "withdrawing the nourishing breast" and "not granting her her father's penis as an object of satisfaction." The foundation of the girl's sexual development is laid, Klein says, by the unconscious equation of the father's penis with the mother's breast and the vagina with the mouth. Destructive forces directed toward the breast can later impede sexual development.

For Klein—and, as we know, this was at the center of the so-named "Freud–Jones debate"—the vagina is always known unconsciously, but it is anxiety about the inside of the body which leads to the denial or repression of the knowledge. The vagina is the organ which "[women] regard as pre-eminently dangerous and endangered in their sadistic phantasies about copulation between their parents, [and this] is of fundamental importance in giving rise to sexual disturbances and frigidity in them and, in particular, in inhibiting vaginal excitability" (Klein 1952, pp. 288–289).

I find that Klein's description of a very early and primitive oedipal conflict and of a severe and primitive superego consequent to early unmitigated sadistic impulses, makes sense of my own clinical experience. In women for whom femininity is particularly conflictual I have been struck by evidence of a very strong and primitive oedipal conflict which has been split off and encapsulated. It is as if the archaic fantasy has remained unmodified over time, sometimes with a fairy-tale quality; it retains a powerful influence but is consciously unrecognized. One homosexual woman who claimed to be only interested in women described crying when she saw films of fairy tales in which the little girl gets her Prince, because *she* doesn't. While she claimed that her father was of no importance to her and simply a nuisance to be tolerated, she also recounted how her father had taken her to buy a beautiful long ball-gown that her mother had refused her, and this had made her feel like a woman although her mother had been angry. She had memories of her father chasing her around the garden like a bull and of his fury when she tickled him between the legs. As an adult she had had plastic surgery on different parts of her face on a number of occasions because she believed that the surgeon would turn her into a princess, as she told me, but her mother had disapproved and made her take the silicone out.

Many people have found Klein's views on femininity attractive because they speak more directly to women's experience than Freud's: the basic biological wish to have a baby, and femininity as primary rather than secondary to an early masculinity. Her approach appeals as counterbalance to what is felt to be a patriarchal theory.

Yet, while I find Klein's ideas invaluable, I have come to think that Freud's theory of femininity cannot simply be discarded as wrong or inappropriate to a post-Victorian era. I keep being struck by how, in the analysis of women for whom social equality is a reality, one still comes up time and again against an image of the feminine as lack. I do not think it is sufficient to think in terms of cultural phenomena. I also do not think it is sufficient to understand it as a denigration of the powerful maternal imago (although this is an important component well-described by Chasseguet-Smirgel 1964). I think there is something very basic involved at the level of a primal fantasy, something that Lacan refers to as the Phallus and which is connected with the place of the father as "third" and that has an organizing function. Lacan, in his rereading of Freud, brings out the meaning of the phallus in the unconscious, as that which represents a state of completion and which both sexes desire. The "something missing" is that which the girl believes would make her the object of her mother's desire. Neither sex has the phallus, but the boy can more easily believe that he has, owing to his penis.

In my view, the feminine is linked in the unconscious with the earliest two-person situation in which the infant experiences needs, frustrations, and dependency, and therefore with lack and anxiety, while the masculine ("the third") brings in a structuring element and comes to represent that which can remedy the situation. This structuring element is internalized by both boys and girls and becomes prized as permitting psychic distance from the maternal object. Its more manic representation is the phallus (the penis in never-ending erection), the possession of which is believed to remove all needs and frustrations. It is when the structuring function has not been sufficiently internalized that the individual (male and female) is driven compulsively to try and be or have the phallus. In that sense, I have suggested (Birksted-Breen 1996b) that penis envy is really phallus envy, the wish for a state without need or lack. The phallus is an unconscious primal fantasy, which may partly account for certain social phenomena which have given men greater status. The search for this phallus accounts for many pathological and, in particular, perverse clinical pictures. I distinguish this from what I have called the penis-as-link, which is the penis as representing in the unconscious the link between mother and father. Internalizing this penis-as-link is the backbone of mental health, of psychic bisexuality. It has a structuring function which underpins the process of thinking. Although it is the link of the parental relationship, and masculine and feminine are both implicated, I believe that the penis comes to represent that link. While, of course, in a sense it is (in reality) penis-in-vagina, I think that unconsciously the penis (and the masculine) represent the structuring element (because it brings in triangulation). When that structuring element is not securely established, it is sought for as the phallus. It is in this context that the experience of the feminine as lack can be understood.

The phallus and the penis-as-link exist as two psychic positions or structures. This is true for both men and women but seems to pose special problems for women, as the literature on female sexuality suggests, on two counts: because of the greater sense of lack due to the confusion of penis and phallus, and because of the special problems around the introjection of the penis due to the feminine anxieties described by Klein (fear of the mother, fear of damaging the penis, fear of being damaged by the penis).

When Freud discovered the importance of the girl's involvement with her mother he compared it to the discovery of a whole new civilization, the Minoan-Mycenean, hidden behind the Greek civilization. We can never cease to find hidden meanings behind other meanings, but nor should we therefore automatically discard the old meaning. We know from our work with patients that the trajectory is never a simple linear one and that we need to hold the tension of all the multiple facets. I believe that it is important to hold onto an inherent tension in women's unconscious between a femininity which is more bodily based and a femininity perceived as a lack. This tension accounts for women's unease. Freud and Klein each focused on one side of the duality at the heart of the feminine (Birksted-Breen 1996a, Breen 1993).

Freud's "What does a woman want?" can be taken as a symbol for the open-ended nature of the psychoanalytic quest.

REFERENCES

Birksted-Breen, D. (1996a). Unconscious representations of femininity. *Journal of the American Psychoanalytic Association* 44(suppl.):119–132.

——— (1996b). Phallus, penis and mental space. *International Journal of Psycho-Analysis* 77(4):649–657.

Breen, D. (1993). *The Gender Conundrum*. New York and London: Routledge.

Chasseguet-Smirgel, J. (1964). Feminine fruit and the Oedipus complex. In *Female Sexuality*. London: Virago, 1981.

Klein, M. (1952). The effects of early anxiety-situations on the sexual development of the girl. In *The Writings of Melanie Klein. Vol. 2: The Psycho-Analysis of Children*, pp. 268–325. London: Hogarth.

The Effects of Early Anxiety-Situations on the Sexual Development of the Girl

MELANIE KLEIN

Psychoanalytic investigation has thrown much less light on the psychology of women than on that of men. Since the fear of castration was the first thing that was discovered as an underlying motive force in the formation of neurosis in men, analysts naturally began by studying etiological factors of the same kind in women. The results obtained in this way held good in so far as the psychology of the two sexes was similar but not in so far as it differed. Freud has well expressed this point in a passage in which he says: ". . . and besides, is it quite certain that castration anxiety is the only cause of repression (or defence)? When we think of neuroses in women we must feel some doubts. True enough, a castration *complex* is always to be found in them; but we can hardly speak of a castration *anxiety* where castration is already an accomplished fact." [1]

When we consider how important every advance in our knowledge of castration anxiety has been both for understanding the psychology of the male individual and for effecting a cure of his neuroses, we shall expect that a knowledge of whatever anxiety is its equivalent in the female individual will enable us to perfect our therapeutic treatment of her and help us to get a clear idea of the lines along which her sexual development moves forward.

---

[1] *Hemmung, Symptom und Angst* (1926), s. 63.

THE ANXIETY-SITUATION OF THE GIRL

In my "Early Stages of the Oedipus Conflict" (1928) I have endeavoured
to throw some light on this still unsolved problem and have put forward
the view that the girl's deepest fear is of having the inside of her body
robbed and destroyed. As a result of the oral frustration she experiences
from her mother, the female child turns away from her and takes her father's
penis as her object of gratification. This new desire urges her to make
further important steps in her development. She evolves phantasies of her
mother introducing her father's penis into her body and giving him the
breast; and these phantasies form the nucleus of early sexual theories which
arouse feelings of envy and hatred in her at being frustrated by both parents. (Incidentally, at this stage of development children of both sexes
believe that it is the body of their mother which contains all that is desirable, especially their father's penis.) This sexual theory increases the small
girl's hatred of her mother on account of the frustration she has suffered
from her, and contributes to the production of sadistic phantasies of attacking and destroying her mother's inside and depriving it of its contents.
Owing to her fear of retaliation, such phantasies form the basis of her
deepest anxiety-situation.

In his paper on "The Early Development of Female Sexuality" (1927),
Ernest Jones gives the name *aphanisis* to the destruction of the capacity to
obtain libidinal gratification of which the girl stands in dread; and he considers that this dread constitutes an early and dominating anxiety-situation
for her. It seems to me that the destruction of the girl's capacity to obtain
libidinal gratification implies destruction of those organs which are necessary
for the purpose. And she expects to have those organs destroyed in the course
of the attacks that will be made, principally by her mother, upon her body
and its contents. Her fears concerning her genitals are especially intense, partly
because her own sadistic impulses against her mother are very strongly directed toward her genitals and the erotic pleasures she gets from them, and
partly because her fear of being incapable of enjoying sexual gratification
serves in its turn to increase her fear of having her genitals damaged.

EARLY STAGES OF THE OEDIPUS CONFLICT

According to my experience, the girl's Oedipus tendencies are ushered in
by her oral desires for her father's penis. These desires are already accompanied by genital impulses. Her wish to rob her mother of her father's

penis and incorporate it in herself is, I have found, a fundamental factor in the development of her sexual life. The resentment her mother has aroused in her by withdrawing the nourishing breast from her is intensified by the further wrong she has done her in not granting her her father's penis as an object of gratification; and this double grievance is the deepest source of the hatred the female child feels toward her mother as a result of her Oedipus tendencies.

These views differ in some respects from accepted psycho-analytical theory. Freud has come to the conclusion that it is the castration complex that introduces the girl's Oedipus complex, and that what makes her turn away from her mother is the grudge she bears her for not having given her a penis of her own.[2] The divergence between Freud's view and the one put forward here, however, becomes less great if we reflect that they agree on two important points—namely, that the girl wants to have a penis and that she hates her mother for not giving her one. But, according to my view, what she primarily wants is not to possess a penis of her own as an attribute of masculinity, but to incorporate her father's penis as an object of oral gratification. Furthermore, I think that this desire is not an outcome of her castration complex but the most fundamental expression of her Oedipus tendencies, and that consequently she is brought under the sway of her Oedipus impulses not indirectly, through her masculine tendencies and her penis-envy, but directly, as a result of her dominant feminine instinctual components.[3]

When the girl turns to her father's penis as the wished-for object, several factors concur to make her desire for it very intense. The demands of her oral-sucking impulses, heightened by the frustration she has suffered from her mother's breast, create in her an imaginary picture of her father's penis as an organ which, unlike the breast, can provide her with a tremendous and never-ending oral gratification.[4] To this phantasy her urethral-

---

[2] "Some Psychological Consequences of the Anatomical Distinction between the Sexes" (1927).
[3] In her paper, "On the Genesis of the Castration Complex" (1924), Karen Horney has supported the view that what gives rise to the girl's castration complex is the frustration she has suffered in the Oedipus situation, and that her desire to possess a penis springs primarily from her Oedipus wishes and not from her wish to be a man. She looks upon the desired penis as a part of her father and as a substitute for him.
[4] In her *Zur Psychologie der weiblichen Sexualfunktionen* (1925), Helene Deutsch has pointed out that already very early on in her life the small girl, in taking her father as the object of her affections next in order to her mother, directs towards him a great part of that true sexual

sadistic impulses add their contribution. For children of both sexes attribute far greater urethral capacities to the penis—where, indeed, they are more visible—than to the female organ of micturition. The girl's phantasies about the urethral capacity and power of the penis become allied to her oral phantasies, in virtue of the equation which small children make between all bodily substances; and in her imagination the penis is an object which possesses magical powers of providing oral gratification. But since the oral frustration she has suffered from her mother has stimulated all her other erotogenic zones as well and has aroused her genital tendencies and desires in regard to her father's penis, the latter becomes the object of her oral, urethral, anal, and genital impulses all at the same time. Another factor which serves to intensify her desires in this direction is her unconscious sexual theory that her mother has incorporated her father's penis, and her consequent envy of her mother.

It is the combination of all these factors, I think, which endows her father's penis with such enormous virtue in the eyes of the small girl and makes it the object of her most ardent admiration and desire.[5] If she retains a predominantly feminine position, this attitude toward her father's penis will often lead her to assume a humble and submissive attitude toward the male sex. But it can also cause her to have intense feelings of hatred for having been denied the thing which she has so passionately adored and longed for; and if she takes up a masculine position it can give rise to all the signs and symptoms of penis-envy in her.

------

libido, attached to the oral zone, with which she has cathected her mother's breast, since "in one phase of her development her unconscious equates her father's penis with her mother's breast as an organ for giving suck." I also agree with the writer in her view that in this equation of the penis with the breast the vagina takes on the passive role of the sucking mouth "in the process of displacement from above downwards," and that this oral, sucking activity of the vagina is implied by its anatomical structure as a whole (s. 54). But where according to Helene Deutsch these phantasies do not become operative until the girl has reached sexual maturity and has experienced the sexual act, in my opinion the early equation of the penis with the breast is ushered in by the frustration she has suffered from the breast in early childhood, and at once exerts a powerful influence on her and greatly affects the whole trend of her development. I also believe that this equation of penis and breast, accompanied as it is by a "displacement from above downwards," activates the oral, receptive qualities of the female genital at an early age, and prepares the vagina to receive the penis. It thus clears the way for the little girl's Oedipus tendencies—though these, it is true, do not unfold their full power until much later—and lays the foundation of her sexual development.

[5] She invests her mother with some of this glory and will in some cases only value her as the possessor of her father's penis.

But since the small girl's phantasies about the enormous powers and huge size and strength of her father's penis arise from her own oral-, urethral- and anal-sadistic impulses, she will also think of it as having extremely dangerous attributes. This aspect of its provides the substratum of her terror of the "bad" penis, which sets in as a reaction to the destructive impulses which, in combination with the libidinal ones, she has directed toward it. If her oral sadism is what is strongest in her she will regard her father's penis within her mother principally as a thing to be hated, envied, and destroyed;[6] and the hate-filled phantasies which she centres upon her father's penis as something that is giving her mother gratification will in some cases be so intense that they will cause her to displace her deepest and most powerful anxiety—her fear of her mother—on to her father's penis as a hated appendage of her mother. If this happens, she will suffer severe impairments in her development and will be led into a distorted attitude toward the male sex. She will also have a more or less defective relationship to her objects and be unable to overcome, or overcome completely, the stage of partial love.[7]

In virtue of the omnipotence of thoughts the girl's oral desire for her father's penis makes her believe that she has in fact incorporated it; and now her ambivalent feelings toward it become extended to this internalized penis. As we know, in the stage of partial incorporation the object is represented by a part of himself or herself and the father's penis stands for his whole person. That is why, I think, the child's earliest father-imagos—

---

[6]She will have the same attitude toward the children in her mother's body. We shall later on return to this subject and consider in what way her hostility to the children inside her mother affects her relations to her own brothers and sisters, to her own imaginary children, and, in after years, to her real ones.

[7]Cf. Abraham, "A Short Study of the Development of the Libido" (1924). My patient Erna, whose case-history has been related elsewhere, was a typical instance. Her father was in her eyes mainly the bearer of the penis which gratified her mother and not herself. It turned out that her penis-envy and her castration wishes, which were exceedingly strong, were ultimately based upon the frustration she had experienced in regard to his penis in her oral position. Since, in focusing her hatred on his penis, she imagined that her mother had possession of it, the feeling she entertained toward her mother, though filled with hatred, was a more personal one than what she felt for her father. It is true that another reason why she turned away from him was to protect him from her own sadism. And the concentration of her hatred on his penis also helped to make her spare him as an object (cf. Abraham in this connection). Analysis was able to bring out in her a more friendly and human attitude toward her father, and this advance was accompanied by favourable changes in her relations with her mother and her objects in general.—Concerning this relationship to the father's penis and the father himself, I should like to draw attention to the points of similarity that exist between my patient and two cases that Abraham has reported on p. 482 of his above-mentioned work.

the nucleus of the paternal super-ego—are represented by his penis. As I have tried to show, the terrifying and cruel character of the super-ego in children of both sexes is due to the fact that they have begun to introject their objects at a period of development when their sadism is at its maximum. Their earliest imagos assume the phantastic aspect which their own dominant pregenital impulses have imparted to them. But this impulsion to introject the father's penis, that is, the Oedipus object, and to keep it inside is much stronger in the girl than in the boy. For the genital tendencies which accompany her oral desires have a receptive character too, so that under normal circumstances her Oedipus tendencies are to a far greater extent under the influence of oral incorporative impulses than are those of the boy. It is a matter of decisive importance for the formation of the super-ego and the development of the sexual life of both boys and girls whether their prevailing phantasies are those of a "good" penis or of a "bad" one. But again the girl, being more subordinated to her introjected father, is more at the mercy of his powers for good or evil than is the boy in relation to his super-ego.[8] And her anxiety and sense of guilt in regard to her mother serve to complicate still further her divided feelings about her father's penis.

In order to simplify our survey of the whole situation we will first of all follow out the development of the girl's attitude to her father's penis and then try to discover how far her relations with her mother affect her relations with her father. In favourable circumstances the girl believes in the existence not only of a dangerous, introjected penis, but of a beneficent and helpful one. As a result of this ambivalent attitude she will strive to counteract her fear of the introjected "bad" penis by continually introjecting a "good" one in coitus,[9] and this will be a further incentive to her to undergo sexual experiences in early childhood and to indulge in sexual activities in later life, and will add to her libidinal desires for a penis.

Moreover, her sexual acts, whether in the form of *fellatio, coitus per anum,* or normal coitus, help her to ascertain whether the fears which play such a dominant and fundamental role in her mind in connection with copulation are well grounded or not. The reason why copulation has become fraught with so much peril in the imagination of children of both sexes is that their

---

[8] The girl's superego is consequently more potent than the boy's; and we shall later on discuss the effect this has upon her ego-development and object-relations.

[9] As we have already seen, the child's fear of the "bad" things inside itself, such as its internalized "bad" objects, dangerous excrements, and bodily substances, usually encourages it to try every kind of process of introjection and ejection and is thus a fundamental factor in its development.

sadistic wish-phantasies have transformed that act, as done between their father and mother, into a very threatening danger-situation.[10] We have already gone into the nature of these sadistic masturbation phantasies in some detail, and have found that they fall into two distinct, though interconnected, categories. In those of the first category the child employs various sadistic means to make a direct onslaught upon its parents either separately or joined in coitus; in those of the second, which are derived from a somewhat later period of the phase of maximal sadism, its belief in its sadistic omnipotence over its parents finds expression in a more indirect fashion. It endows them with instruments of mutual destruction, transforming their teeth, nails, genitals, excrements and so on, into dangerous weapons and animals, etc., and pictures them, according to its own desires, as tormenting and destroying each other in the act of copulation.

Both categories of sadistic phantasies give rise to anxiety from various sources. Turning once more to the girl, we see that in connection with the first category she is afraid of being counter-attacked by one or both parents, but more particularly by her mother as the more hated one of the two. She expects to be assailed from within as well as from without, since she has introjected her objects at the same time as she has attacked them. Her fears on this head are very closely connected with sexual intercourse, because her primary sadistic actions have to a very great extent been directed against her parents as she imagined them copulating together.[11] But it is more especially in phantasies belonging to the second category that copulation, in which, according to her sadistic desires, her mother is utterly destroyed, becomes an act fraught with immense danger to herself. On the other hand, the sexual act, which her sadistic phantasies and wishes have transformed into a situation of such extreme danger, is for this very reason also the superlative method of mastering anxiety—the more so because the libidinal gratification that accompanies it affords her the highest attainable pleasure and thus lessens her anxiety on its own score.

---

[10]The child's wish that its parents should copulate in a sadistic way is in my experience an important factor in the production and maintenance of its sexual theories, so that the latter not only owe their character to the influence which its pre-genital impulses have upon the formation of its phantasies but are the result of the destructive wishes it directs against its copulating parents. In analysing the child's sexual theories, therefore, I have found it important from a therapeutic point of view to pay attention to the fact that they spring from its sadistic desires and so give rise to a strong sense of guilt in its mind.

[11]These phantasies also give rise to danger-situations which are not in themselves attached to the sexual act.

These facts throw a new light, I think, on the motives which urge the individual to perform the sexual act and on the psychological sources from which the libidinal gratification he obtains from that act receive addition. As we know, the libidinal gratification of all his erotogenic zones implies a gratification of his destructive components as well, owing to the fusion of his libidinal and destructive impulses that has taken place in those stages of his development which are governed by his sadistic tendencies. Now, in my opinion, his destructive impulses have aroused anxiety in him as early as in the first months of his life. In consequence, his sadistic phantasies become bound up with anxiety, and this tie between the two gives rise to specific anxiety-situations. Since his genital impulses set in while he is still in the phase of maximal sadism—or so, at least, I have found—and copulation represents, in his sadistic phantasies, a vehicle of destruction for his parents, these anxiety-situations which are aroused in the early stages of his development become connected with his genital activities as well. The effect of such a connection is that, on the one hand, his anxiety intensifies his libidinal needs, and, on the other, the libidinal gratification of his various erotogenic zones helps him to master anxiety by diminishing his aggressive tendencies and with it his anxiety. In addition, the pleasure he gets from such gratification seems in itself to allay his fear of being destroyed by his own destructive impulses and by his objects, and to militate against his dread of *aphanisis* (Jones), i.e. his fear of losing his capacity to obtain sexual gratification. Libidinal gratification, as an expression of Eros, reinforces his belief in his helpful imagos and diminishes the dangers which emanate from his death-instinct and his super-ego.

The more anxiety the individual has and the more neurotic he is, the more the energies of his ego and his instinctual forces will be absorbed in the endeavour to overcome anxiety; and the more, too, will the libidinal gratification he obtains be employed for that purpose. In the normal person, who is further removed from his early anxiety-situations and has modified them more successfully, the effect of those situations upon his sexual activities is, of course, far less; but it is never entirely absent, I think. The impulsion he feels to put his specific anxiety-situations to the test in his relations to his partner in love strengthens and gives colour to his libidinal fixations also, and the sexual act always in part helps him to master anxiety. And the anxiety-situations which predominate in him and the quantities of anxiety present are specific determinants of the conditions under which he is able to love.

If, in making the sexual act a criterion of her anxiety-situations and thus submitting them to a test by reality, the girl is supported by feelings of a confident and optimistic kind, she will be led to take as her object a person who represents the "good" penis. In this case, the alleviation of anxiety which she obtains through having sexual intercourse will give her a strong enjoyment which considerably adds to the purely libidinal gratification she experiences and lays the foundations for lasting and satisfactory love relationships. But if the circumstances are unfavourable and her fear of the introjected "bad" penis predominates, the necessary condition for her ability to love will be that she shall make this reality-test by means of a "bad" penis—i.e. that her partner in love shall be a sadistic person. The test she makes in this case is meant to inform her of what kind of damage her partner will inflict on her through the sexual act. Even her anticipated injuries in this respect serve to allay her anxiety and are of importance in the economy of her mental life; for nothing she may suffer from any external agency can equal what she is already suffering under the strain of her constant and overwhelming fear of phantastic injuries and dangers from within.[12] Her choice of a sadistic partner is also based upon an impulsion once more to incorporate a sadistic "bad" penis (for that is how she views the sexual act) which shall destroy the dangerous objects within her. Thus the deepest root of feminine masochism would seem to be the woman's fear of the dangerous objects she has internalized, in especial her father's penis; and her masochism would ultimately be no other than her sadistic instincts turned inwards against those internalized objects.[13]

According to Freud,[14] sadism, although it first becomes apparent in relation to an object, was originally a destructive instinct directed against the organism itself (primal sadism) and was only later diverted from the

---

[12]The tendency the individual has to secure from the external world a tranquillization of his fears of imaginary dangers from within and from without is, I think, an important factor in the repetition-compulsion. The more neurotic he is, the more this tendency will be coloured by his need for punishment. The conditions to which the securing of such a tranquillization from external sources is attached will be increasingly unfavourable in proportion as the anxiety connected with his early danger-situations is powerful and his optimistic trend of feeling weak. In extreme cases only very severe punishments, or rather unhappy experiences which he feels as punishments, are able to fill the place of the imaginary punishments which he dreads.

[13]In her paper, "The Significance of Masochism in the Mental Life of Women" (1930), Helene Deutsch expresses views on the origins of masochism which differ widely from my own and which are based on the assumption, equally at variance with mine, that the Oedipus complex of the girl is introduced by her castration-wishes and castration-fears.

[14]Cf. his *Beyond the Pleasure-Principle* (1920), and "The Economic Problem in Masochism" (1924).

ego by the narcissistic libido; and erotogenic masochism is that portion of
the destructive instinct which has not been able to turned outward in this
way and has remained within the organism and been libidinally bound there.
He furthermore thinks that insofar as any part of the destructive instinct
which has been directed outward is once more turned inward and drawn
away from its objects, it gives rise to secondary or feminine masochism. As
far as I can see, however, when the destructive instinct has reverted in this
way it still adheres to its objects; but now they are internalized ones, and, in
threatening to destroy them, it also threatens to destroy the ego in which
they are situated. In this way in feminine masochism the destructive instinct
is once more directed against the organism itself. Freud says in his "Economic Problem in Masochism" (1924): ". . . in the manifest content of the
masochistic phantasies a feeling of guilt comes to expression, it being assumed that the subject has committed some crime (the nature of which is
left uncertain) which is to be expiated by his undergoing pain and torture"
(p. 259). There seem to me to be certain points in common between the
self-tormenting behaviour of the masochist and the self-reproaches of the
melancholiac, which, as we know, are in fact directed toward his introjected
object. It would seem, therefore, that feminine masochism is directed toward the ego as well as toward the introjected objects. Moreover, in destroying his internalized object the individual is acting in the interests of self-
preservation; and in extreme cases his ego will no longer be able to turn his
death-instinct outwards, for both life and death-instincts have united in a
common aim and the former has been withdrawn from its proper function
of protecting the ego.

We will now briefly consider one or two other typical forms which
may be assumed by the sexual life of women in whom fear of the introjected
penis is paramount.[15] Women who, besides having strong masochistic in-
clinations, are buoyed up by more hopeful currents of feeling, often tend
to entrust their affections to a sadistic partner and at the same time to make
endeavours of every kind—endeavours which often take up all the energies of their ego—to turn him into a friendly and "good" person. Women
of this kind, in whom fear of the "bad" penis and belief in the "good" one

---

[15]Of course, these various forms overlap in many cases. In dealing with such a wealth and
complication of material I can do no more than give a schematic account of one or two such
forms, my main object being to describe a few of the consequences that arise from this most
fundamental anxiety in the female individual.

are evenly balanced, often fluctuate between the choice of a "good" external object and a "bad" one.

Not seldom the woman's fear of the internalized penis urges her to be always renewing the process of testing her anxiety-situation, with the result that she will be under a constant compulsion to perform the sexual act with her object, or, as a variant to this, to exchange that object for another. In differently constituted cases, again, the same fear will have an opposite outcome and the woman will become frigid.[16] As a child, her hatred of her mother has made her view her father's penis no longer as a desirable and bountiful thing but as something evil and dangerous, and has made her transform the vagina into an instrument of death and her mother into a source of danger to her father in his sexual relations with her. Her fear of the sexual act is thus based both on the injuries she expects to receive from the penis and on the injuries she will herself inflict on her partner. Her fear that she will castrate him is due partly to her identification with her sadistic mother and partly to her own sadistic impulses.

As we have already seen, if the girl's sadistic tendencies are directed toward her internalized objects, she will adopt a masochistic attitude. But should her fear of the internalized penis impel her to defend herself against its threats from within by projection, she will direct her sadism toward the external object—toward the penis which is continually being introjected afresh in the act of coitus, and thus toward her sexual partner. In such cases, the ego has once more succeeded in turning the destructive instinct away from itself and from the internalized objects and in directing it toward an external object. If the girl's sadistic tendencies predominate, she will still regard copulation as a test by reality of her anxiety, but in an opposite way. Her phantasies that her vagina and body as a whole are destructive to her partner and that in *fellatio* she will bite off his penis and tear it to pieces are now the means of overcoming her fear of the penis she has incorporated and of her real object. In employing her sadism against

---

[16]Such an outcome depends greatly, it would seem, upon the extent to which the ego is able to overcome anxiety. [. . .] It sometimes happens that the individual can master his anxiety (or rather, transform it into pleasure) only on condition that the reality-situations which he has to surmount are of a particularly difficult or dangerous nature. We sometimes find similar conditions laid down for his love-relations, in which case copulation itself represents the danger-situation. Hence frigidity in women would in part be due to a phobic avoidance of an anxiety-situation. As far as can be seen, there is a close relation between specific conditions of mastering anxiety and of obtaining sexual gratification.

her external object she is in imagination also waging a war of extermination against her internalized objects.

THE OMNIPOTENCE OF EXCRETA

In connection with what has just been said we come to a factor which is of considerable importance for the development of the girl. In the sadistic phantasies of both boy and girl the excreta play a large part. The child's belief in the omnipotence of the function of the bladder and the bowels[17] is closely connected with paranoid mechanisms.[18] These mechanisms are in full swing in that phase in which, in its sadistic masturbation phantasies, the child destroys its copulating parents in secret ways by means of its urine, feces, and flatus; and they become reinforced and employed in a secondary way for defensive purposes on account of its fear of being counter-attacked.[19]

As far as I can judge, the girl's sexual life and ego are more strongly and permanently influenced in their development than are those of the boy by this sense of omnipotence of the function of the bladder and bowels. In children of both sexes the attacks they make with their excreta are leveled at their mother, in the first instance at her breast and then at the interior of her body. Since the girl's destructive impulses against her mother's body are more powerful and enduring than the boy's, she will evolve secret and

---

[17]Cf. Freud, *Totem und Tabu* (1912); also, Ferenczi, "Stages in the Development of a Sense of Reality" (1913), and Abraham, "The Narcissistic Evaluation of Excretory Processes in Dreams and Neurosis" (1917).

[18]For the connection between paranoia and anal functions, cf. Freud, Ferenczi, Von Ophuijsen, Stärcke, and others.

[19]Sadistic omnipotence of this kind, used primarily to destroy the parents or one of them by means of the excreta, becomes modified in the course of the child's development and is often employed to inflict moral pain on the object or to control and dominate it intellectually. Owing to this modification and because the child now makes its attacks in a secret and insidious fashion and has to display an equal watchfulness and mental ingenuity in guarding against counter-attacks of a corresponding character, its original sense of omnipotence becomes of fundamental importance for the growth of its ego. In his paper referred to above, Abraham takes the view that the omnipotence of the functions of the bladder and bowels is a precursor of the omnipotence of thoughts; and in his paper, "The Madonna's Conception through the Ear" (1923), Ernest Jones has shown that thoughts are equated to flatus. I too think that the child equates its feces, and more especially its invisible flatus, with that other secret and invisible substance, its thoughts, and furthermore that it imagines that in its covert attacks on its mother's body it has put them inside her by magic means.

cunning methods of attack, based upon the magic of excrements and other products of her body and upon the omnipotence of her thoughts, in conformity with the secret and hidden nature of that world within her mother's body and her own;[20] whereas the boy will concentrate his feelings of hatred not only on his father's penis, supposedly inside his mother, but on his real one, and thus directs them to a larger extent towards the external world and what is tangible and visible. He also makes greater use of the sadistic omnipotence of his penis, with the result that he has other modes of mastering anxiety as well,[21] while the woman's mode of mastering anxiety remains under the dominion of her relation to an inner world, to what is concealed, and therefore to the unconscious.[22]

As has already been said, when the girl's sadism is at its greatest height she believes that the sexual act is a means of destroying the object and that she is also carrying on a war to the knife against the internalized objects. She endeavours through the omnipotence of her excrements and thoughts to overcome the terrifying objects inside her own body and originally inside her mother's. If her belief in her father's "good" penis inside her is strong enough she will make it the vehicle of her sense of omnipotence.[23] If her belief in the magical power of her excreta and thoughts preponderates, it will be through their power that she will in imagination govern and control both her internalized and her real objects. Not only do these different sources of magical power operate at the same time and reinforce one another, but her ego makes use of them and plays them off against one another for the purpose of mastering anxiety.

---

[20]The fact that the woman attaches her narcissism to her body as a whole must be in part due to her connecting her sense of omnipotence with her various bodily functions and excretory processes, and thus distributing it to a greater extent over the whole of her body, whereas the man focuses it more upon his genitals. After all, in the last analysis it is through her body that she captures and controls her real objects by magic means.

[21]In this chapter [. . .] we shall consider how the anatomical differences between the sexes contribute to separate the lines along which the sense of omnipotence and consequently the modes of mastering anxiety develop in each sex.

[22]In my "Contribution to the Theory of Intellectual Inhibition" (1931), I have shown that in his unconscious the individual regards his penis as the representative of his ego and his conscious, and the interior of his body—what is invisible—as the representative of his super-ego and his unconscious.

[23]In her paper, "The Role of Psychotic Mechanisms in Cultural Development" (1930), Melitta Schmideberg has shown that the introjection of his father's penis (= his father) greatly enhances the individual's narcissism and sense of omnipotence.

EARLY RELATIONS TO THE MOTHER

The girl's attitude to the introjected penis is strongly influenced by her attitude to her mother's breast. The first objects that she introjects are her "good" mother and her "bad" one, as represented by the breast.[24] Her desire to suck or devour the penis is directly derived from her desire to do the same to her mother's breast, so that the frustration she suffers from the breast prepares the way for the feelings which her later frustration in regard to the penis arouse. Not only do the envy and hatred she feels toward her mother colour and intensify her sadistic phantasies against the penis, but her relations to the mother's breast affect her subsequent attitude toward men in other ways as well. As soon as she begins to be afraid of the "bad" introjected penis she also begins to run back to her mother, from whom, both as a real person and as an introjected figure, she hopes for assistance. If her primary attitude to her mother has been governed by the oral-sucking position, so that it contains strong currents of positive and optimistic feeling, she will be able to take shelter to some extent behind her good mother-imago against her bad mother-imago and against the "bad" penis; if not, her fear of her introjected mother will increase her fear of the internalized penis and of her terrifying parents united in copulation.

The importance which the girl's mother-imago has for her as a "helping" figure and the strength of her attachment to her mother are very great, since in her imagination her mother is the possessor of the nourishing breast and the father's penis and children and thus has the power to gratify all her needs. For when the small girl's early anxiety-situations set in, her ego makes use of her need for nourishment in the widest sense to assist her in overcoming anxiety. The more she is afraid that her body is poisoned and exposed to attack, the more she craves for the "good" milk, "good" penis, and children[25] over which she believes her mother has unlimited command. She needs these "good" things to protect her against the "bad" ones, and to establish a kind of equilibrium inside her. In her imagination her mother's

---

[24] [Elsewhere] we have seen how the "good" breast becomes turned into a "bad" one in consequence of the child's imaginary attacks upon it (for the child directs all the resources of its sadism in the first instance against the breast for not giving it enough gratification), so that a primary introjection of both a good and a bad mother-imago takes place before any other imagos are formed.

[25] We shall presently enquire in greater detail into the deeper significance attached to the possession of children. It suffices here to remark that the imaginary child inside the body represents a helpful object.

body is therefore a kind of storehouse which contains the gratification of all her desires and the appeasement of all her fears. It is these phantasies, leading back to her mother's breast as her earliest source of gratification and as the one most fraught with consequences, which are responsible for her immensely strong attachment to her mother. And the frustration she suffers from her mother in this connection causes her, under the rising pressure of her anxiety, to feel renewed resentment against her and to redouble her sadistic attacks upon her body.

At a somewhat later stage of her development, however, at a time when her sense of guilt is making itself felt in every quarter,[26] this very desire to get hold of the "good" contents of her mother's body, or rather her conviction that she has done so and thus exposed her mother, as it were, to its "bad" contents, arouses a most severe sense of guilt and anxiety in her. In having thus destroyed her mother she has, she believes, completely demolished that reservoir from which she draws the satisfaction of all her moral and physical needs. This fear, which is of such tremendous importance in the mental life of the small girl, goes to strengthen still further the ties that bind her to her mother. It gives rise to an impulsion to make restitution and give her mother back all that she has taken from her—an impulsion which finds expression in numerous sublimations of a specifically feminine kind.

But this impulsion runs counter to another impulsion, itself stimulated by the same fear, to take away everything her mother has got so as to save her own body. At this stage of her development, therefore, the girl is governed by a compulsion both to take away and to give back, and this compulsion, as has elsewhere been said, is important in the aetiology of obsessional neurosis in general. For instance, we see small children drawing little stars or crosses, which signify faeces and children, or older ones writing letters and numbers, on a sheet of paper that stands for their mother's body or their own, and taking great care to leave no empty spaces. Or else they will pile up pieces of paper neatly in a box until it is quite full. Very frequently they will draw a house to represent their mother, and then put a tree in front of it for their father's penis and some flowers beside it for children. Older girls will draw or sew or make dolls and dolls' dresses or books, etc.; and these things typify their mother's reconstituted body (either as a whole or

---

[26]It must be remembered that in her imagination, besides having attacked her parents, the girl has injured or killed her brothers and sisters inside her mother. Her fear of retaliation and her sense of guilt on account of this give rise to disturbances in her relation to her real brothers and sisters and consequently in her capacity for social adaptation in general.

each damaged part individually), their father's penis and the children inside her, or their father and brothers and sisters in person.

While they are engaged in these activities or after they have completed them, children will often show rage, depression, or disappointment, or even reactions of a destructive kind. Anxiety of this kind, which is an underlying obstacle to all constructive tendencies, arises from various sources.[27] The girl has in imagination taken possession of her father's penis and feces and children, and then, owing to the fear of penis, children, and excrements that sets in with her sadistic phantasies, she loses faith in their rightness. The questions in her mind now are: Will the things she gives back to her mother be "good," and can she give them back properly as regards quality and quantity and even as regards the order in which they should be arranged inside (for that, too, is a necessary part of the act of restitution)? Again, if she does believe that she has well and duly given her mother back the "good" contents of her body she becomes afraid of having endangered her own person by so doing.

These sources of anxiety give rise, furthermore, to a special attitude of distrust in the girl toward her mother. On entering my room many of my girl patients will look suspiciously at the stock of paper and pencils in the drawer reserved for them, in case they should not belong to them or be smaller in size or fewer in number than on the day before; or they will want to make sure that the contents of their drawer have not been disarranged, and that all is in good order and no article is missing or exchanged for something else.[28] From time to time they will wrap up their drawings or paper patterns, or whatever is symbolizing the penis or children for them at the time, tie them up and carefully deposit them in their drawer of toys, with every sign of the deepest suspicion towards me. On these occasions I am not allowed to come near the parcel or even the drawer and must more away or not look on while it is being done up. Analysis shows that the drawer and the parcels inside represent their own body and that they are afraid not only that their mother will attack and despoil it but will put "bad" things inside it in exchange for the "good" ones.

---

[27]If anxiety is so strong that it cannot be bound by obsessional mechanisms, the violent mechanisms belonging to earlier stages will be brought into play, together with the more primitive defensive mechanisms employed by the ego.

[28]I may mention that each child has a drawer of its own in which the toys, paper and pencils, etc., which I put out for it at the beginning of its hour and renew from time to time, are put away, together with the things it brings from home.

In addition to these many sources of anxiety the girl child is under certain further disabilities compared to the boy, owing to physiological reasons. Her feminine position gives her no support against her anxiety,[29] since her possession of children, which would be a complete confirmation and fulfillment of that position, is, after all, only a prospective one.[30] Nor does the structure of her body afford her any possibility of knowing what the actual state of affairs inside her is; whereas the boy finds support in his masculine position, for, thanks to his possession of a penis, he has the means of convincing himself by a reality-test that all is well within. It is this inability to know anything about her condition which aggravates what, in my opinion, is the girl's deepest fear—namely, that the inside of her body has been injured or destroyed and that she has got no children or only damaged ones.[31]

THE ROLE OF THE VAGINA IN INFANTILE SEXUALITY

The fact that the female child's anxiety concerns the inside of her body explains to a large extent, I think, why in her early sexual organization the part played by the vagina should be overshadowed by the activity of the clitoris. In her very earliest masturbation phantasies, in which she transforms her mother's vagina into an instrument of destruction, she shows an unconscious knowledge about the vagina. For although, owing to the predominance of her oral and anal tendencies, she likens it to the mouth and to the anus, she nevertheless thinks of it in her unconscious, as many details of her phantasies clearly demonstrate, as a cavity in the genitals which is meant to receive her father's penis.

But besides this general unconscious realization of the existence of the vagina the small girl often possesses a quite conscious knowledge of it. Analysis of a number of small girls has convinced me that, in addition to those quite special cases mentioned by Helene Deutsch in which the patient has undergone sexual assault and defloration and has in consequence obtained a knowledge of this sort and been led to indulge in vaginal masturbation, many small girls are consciously aware that they have an opening

---

[29]Cf. my "Early Stages of the Oedipus Conflict" (1928).

[30]In her papers, "The Significance of Masochism in the Mental Life of Women" (1930), Helene Deutsch points out this fact as an obstacle to the maintenance of the feminine position.

[31]This is partly the reason why female narcissism extends over the whole body. Male narcissism is focussed upon the penis because the boy's chief fear is of being castrated.

in their genitals. In some instances they have got this knowledge from mutual investigations made during sexual games with other children, whether boys or girls; in others, they have discovered the vagina for themselves. They undoubtedly have a specially strong inclination to deny or repress such knowledge—an inclination which springs from the anxiety they feel in regard to this organ and to the inside of their body. Analyses of women have shown that the fact that the vagina is a part of the interior of their body, to which so much of their deepest anxiety is attached, and that it is the organ which they regard as pre-eminently dangerous and endangered in their sadistic phantasies about copulation between their parents, is of fundamental importance in giving rise to sexual disturbances and frigidity in them and, in particular, in inhibiting vaginal excitability.

There is a good deal of evidence to show that the vagina does not enter upon its full functions until the sexual act has been performed.[32] And, as we know, it often happens that the woman's attitude to copulation is completely altered after she has experienced it and that her inhibition in regard to it— and, before the event, such an inhibition is so usual as to be practically normal—is often replaced by a strong desire for it. We may infer from this that her previous inhibition was in part maintained by anxiety and that the sexual act has removed that anxiety.[33] I should be inclined to attribute this reassuring effect of sexual intercourse to the fact that the libidinal gratification which she receives from copulation confirms her in the belief that the penis she has incorporated during the act is a "good" object and that her vagina does not have a destructive effect upon it. Her fear of the internalized and external penis—a fear which has been all the greater from being unverifiable—is thus removed by the real object. In my view, the girl's fears concerning the inside of her body contribute, in addition to the operation of biological factors, to prevent the emergence of a clearly discernible vaginal phase in her early childhood. Nevertheless I am convinced, on the strength of a number of analyses of small girls, that the psychological representatives of the vagina exert their full share of influence, no less than the psychological representatives of all the other libidinal phases, upon the infantile genital organization of the female child.

---

[32]Helene Deutsch supports this view in her book, *Zur Psychologie der weiblichen Sexualfunktionen* (1925).

[33]We have already considered the structure of those cases in which the sexual act fails to reduce anxiety and even increases it.

The same factors which tend to conceal the psychological function of the vagina in the girl go to intensify her fixation on the clitoris. For the latter is a visible organ and one which can be submitted to reality tests. I have found that clitoral masturbation is accompanied by phantasies of various descriptions. Their content changes extremely rapidly, in accordance with the violent fluctuations which take place between one position and another in the early stages of the girl's development. They are at first for the most part of a pre-genital kind; but as soon as the girl's desires to incorporate her father's penis in an oral and genital manner grow stronger they assume a genital and vaginal character (being often already accompanied, it would seem, by vaginal sensations) and thus, to begin with, take a feminine direction.[34]

Since the little girl begins to identify herself with her father very soon after she has identified herself with her mother, her clitoris rapidly takes on the significance of a penis in her masturbation phantasies. All her clitoral masturbation phantasies belonging to this early stage are governed by her sadistic tendencies, and that is why, I think, they, and her masturbatory activities in general, diminish or cease altogether when her phallic phase comes to an end, at a period when her sense of guilt emerges more strongly. Her realization of the fact that her clitoris is no substitute for the penis she desires is, in my opinion, only the last link in a chain of events which orders her future life and in many cases condemns her to frigidity for the rest of her days.

THE CASTRATION COMPLEX

The identification with her father which the girl displays so clearly in the phallic phase, and which bears every sign of penis-envy and castration complex,[35] is, as far as my own observations go, the outcome of a process comprising many steps.[36] In examining some of the more important of these steps

---

[34]In his paper, "One of the Motive Factors in the Formation of the Super-ego in Women" (1928), Hanns Sachs has suggested the possibility that, since a vaginal phase cannot establish itself at that age, the girl displaces her obscure sensations in the vagina on to the mouth.

[35]Cf. Abraham, "Manifestations of the Female Castration Complex" (1921).

[36]Karen Horney has been the first psychoanalyst to bring the castration complex of the woman into relation with her early feminine position as a small girl. In her paper, "On the Genesis of the Castration Complex in Women" (1923), this writer has pointed out certain factors which she believes are material in establishing in the girl an envy of the penis based on pre-genital

we shall see in what way her identification with her father is affected by
anxiety arising from her feminine position and how the masculine position
she adopts in each of her phases of development is superimposed upon a
masculine position belonging to an earlier phase.

When the female infant gives up her mother's breast and turns to her
father's penis as an object of gratification she identifies herself with her
mother. But as soon as she suffers frustration in this position too, she very
speedily identifies herself with her father, who, she imagines, obtains satisfaction from her mother's breast and entire body, that is, from those
primary sources of gratification which she herself has been so painfully forced
to relinquish. Feelings of hatred and envy towards her mother as well as libidinal desires for her go to create this earliest identification of the girl with
her father (whom she regards as a sadistic figure); and in this identification
enuresis plays an important role.

Children of both sexes regard urine in its positive aspect as equivalent
to their mother's milk, in accordance with the unconscious, which equates
all bodily substances with one another. My observations go to show that
enuresis, in its earliest signification both as a positive, giving act and as a
sadistic one, is an expression of a feminine position in boys as well as in
girls.[37] It would seem that the hatred children feel towards their mother's
breast for having frustrated their desires arouses in them, either at the same
time as their cannibalistic impulses or very soon after, phantasies of injuring and destroying her breast with their urine.[38]

---

cathexes. One of these is the gratification of scotophilic and exhibitionistic tendencies which
she notices that the boy obtains from urinating; another is her belief that possession of a penis
affords a greater amount of gratification of urethral erotism; while others are derived from
the difficulties that beset her in regard to her feminine position—such as envy of her mother
for having children—and increase her tendency to identify herself with her father as well as
intensifying her penis-envy. Dr. Horney believes, moreover, that the same factors which in-
duce the girl to take up a homosexual attitude lead, though in a minor degree, to the production of a castration complex in her.

[37] According to Helene Deutsch, enuresis is the expression of a feminine position in the boy
and a masculine one in the girl (*Psychoanalyse der Neurosen*, (1930), s. 51).

[38] In doing this they make use of a mechanism which is, I think, of general importance in the
formation of sadistic phantasies. They convert the pleasure they give their object into its opposite by adding destructive elements to it. As a revenge for not getting *enough* milk from
their mother they will produce in imagination an excessive quantity of urine and so destroy
her breast by flooding it or melting it away; and as a revenge for not getting *"good"* milk
from her they will produce a harmful fluid with which to burn up or poison her breast and
the milk it contains. This mechanism also gives rise to phantasies of tormenting and injuring
people by giving them too much good food. In this case the subject may suffer, as I have

As has already been said, in the sadistic phase the girl puts her greatest belief in the magical powers of her excreta, while the boy makes his penis the principal executant of his sadism. But in her, too, belief in the omnipotence of her urinary functions leads her to identify herself—though to a lesser extent than does the boy—with her sadistic father, to whom she attributes special urethral-sadistic powers in virtue of his possession of a penis.[39] Thus incontinence from having been primarily the expression of a feminine position very soon comes to represent a masculine one for children of both sexes; and in connection with the girl's earliest identification with her sadistic father it becomes a means of destroying her mother; while at the same time she gets hold of her father's penis in her imagination by castrating him.

The identification which the female child makes between herself and her father on the basis of his introjected penis[40] follows, in my experience, upon the primary sadistic identification she has made with him through her urinary incontinence. In her earliest masturbation phantasies she has identified herself alternately with each of her parents. When she occupies the feminine position she becomes afraid of her father's "bad" penis which she has internalized. In order to counter this fear she activates the defensive mechanism of identification with the anxiety-object and thus identifies herself more strongly with him. Her imaginary ownership of the penis she has stolen from

---

found in more than one instance, from the retaliatory anxiety of being suffocated or of being too full, etc., in connection with taking food. One patient of mine could hardly control his rage if he was offered, even in the friendliest way, food, drink, or cigarettes a second time. He would immediately feel "stuffed up" and would lose all desire to eat, drink, or smoke any more. Analysis showed that his behaviour was ultimately caused by phantasies of the early sadistic character described above.

[39]In her paper, "On the Genesis of the Castration Complex in Women" (1923), Karen Horney states that one of the factors which encourages the girl's primary penis-envy in connection with her urethral-erotic impulses is that her sadistic phantasies of omnipotence which are based on urinary functions are especially closely associated with the stream of urine which the boy is able to produce.

[40]In considering the origins of homosexuality in women, Ernest Jones, in his paper, "The Early Development of Female Sexuality" (1927), has come to certain very fundamental conclusions which my own findings fully endorse. Briefly, they are to the effect that the presence of very strong phantasies of *fellatio* in the female, allied to a powerful oral sadism, prepares the way for a belief that she has taken forcible possession of her father's penis and puts her into a special relation of identification with him. In her homosexual attitude, derived in this way, she will show a want of interest in her own sex and a strong interest in men. Her endeavor will be to win recognition and respect from men, and she will have strong feelings of rivalry, hatred, and resentment against them. As regards character-formation, she will exhibit in general marked oral-sadistic traits; and her identification with her father will be employed to a great degree in the service of her castration wishes.

him arouses a sense of omnipotence which increases her feeling that she wields destructive magic through her excreta. In this position her hatred and sadism against her mother become intensified and she has phantasies of destroying her by means of her father's penis; while at the same time she satisfies her feelings of revenge against the father who has frustrated her and finds in her sense of omnipotence and in her power over both parents a defence against anxiety. I have found this attitude especially strongly developed in one or two patients in whom paranoid traits predominated[41]; but it is also very powerful in women whose homosexuality is deeply coloured by feelings of rivalry and antagonism toward the male sex. It would thus apply to that group of female homosexuals, described by Ernest Jones, to which I have referred below in a footnote.

At this juncture the possession of an external penis helps to convince the girl in the first place that she has in reality got that sadistic power over both her parents without which she cannot master her anxiety,[42] and, in the second place, that by having this sadistic power over her objects she can overcome the dangerous penis and objects introjected within her; so that having a penis ultimately serves the purpose of protecting her body from destruction.

While her sadistic position, reinforced as it is by her anxiety, thus forms the basis of a masculinity complex in her, her sense of guilt also makes her want to have a penis. She wants a penis in order to make restitution toward her mother. As Joan Riviere has observed in the paper referred to below, the girl's wish to compensate her mother for having deprived her of her father's penis furnishes important additions to her castration complex and penis-envy. When the girl is obliged to give up her rivalry with her mother out of fear of her, her desire to placate her and make up for what she has done leads her to long intensely for a penis as a means of making restitution. In Joan Riviere's opinion the intensity of her sadism and the extent of her capacity to tolerate anxiety are factors which

---

[41]The reader may be referred in general to the case-history of Erna [see Note 7, this chapter]; but one characteristic point may be cited from it here. At the age of 6 Erna suffered from severe insomnia. She had a terror of burglars and thieves which she could only overcome by lying on her stomach and banging her head on the pillows. This meant having sadistic coitus with her mother, in which she played the part of her supposedly sadistic father.

[42]In her paper, "Womanliness as a Masquerade" (1929), p. 303, Joan Riviere has pointed out that in her anger and hatred against her parents for giving one another sexual gratification the girl has phantasies of castrating her father and taking possession of his penis and thus getting her father and mother into her power and killing them.

will help to determine whether she will take up a heterosexual line or a homosexual one.

We must now examine more closely why it is that in some cases the girl cannot make restitution to her mother unless she adopts a masculine position and is in possession of a penis. Early analysis[43] has demonstrated the existence in the unconscious of a fundamental principle governing all reactive and sublimatory processes, by which restitutive acts must adhere in every detail to the imaginary damage that has been done. Whatever wrongs the child has done in phantasy in the way of stealing, injuring, and destroying it must make good by giving back, putting to rights, and restoring, one by one. This principle also requires that the same instruments that have been used to commit the bad actions shall also be used to undo them. The child must transform its excretions, penis, etc., which in its sadistic phantasies are dangerous and destructive substances, into beneficent and remedial ones. Whatever harm the "bad" penis and "bad" urine have done, the "good" penis and "good" urine must put right again.[44]

Let us suppose that a girl has centred her sadistic phantasies more especially around the indirect destruction of her mother by her father's dangerous penis and that she has identified herself very strongly with her sadistic father. As soon as her reactive tendencies and her desires to make restitution set in in force, she will feel urged to restore her mother by means of a beneficent penis and thus her homosexual tendencies will become reinforced. An important factor in this connection is the extent to which she believes that her father has been incapacitated from making restitution, either because she has castrated him or has put him out of the way or has made his penis too "bad," and that she must therefore give up hope of restoring him.[45] If she believes this very strongly she will have to play his part herself, and this again will tend to make her adopt a homosexual position.

---

[43]On this, as on many other important points, my analytic observations are in full agreement with those of M. N. Searl.

[44]In her "Psychotic Mechanisms in Cultural Development" (1930), Melitta Schmideberg traces the part played in the history of medicine by a belief in the magical qualities of the "good" penis, as symbolized by medicine, and of the "bad" one, as symbolized by the demon of illness. She attributes the psychological effects of physical remedies to the following causes. The person's original attitude of aggression against his father's penis—an attitude which has turned that organ into an extremely dangerous one—is succeeded by an attitude of obedience and submission toward him. If he takes the medicines he is given in this latter spirit, they, as representing the "good" penis, will counteract the "bad" objects inside him.

[45]If her homosexuality emerges in sublimated ways only, she will, for instance, protect and take care of other women (i.e., her mother), adopting in these respects a husband's attitude

The disappointment and doubts and the sense of inferiority which overtake the girl when she realizes that she has not got a penis, and the fears and feelings of guilt which her masculine position gives rise to (in the first place toward her father because she has deprived him of his penis and of the possession of her mother, and in the second place toward her mother because she has taken her father away from her), combine to break down that position. Moreover, her original grievance against her mother for having prevented her from getting her father's penis as a libidinal object joins forces with her new grievance against her for having withheld from her the possession of a penis as an attribute of masculinity; and this double grievance leads her to turn away from her mother as an object of genital love. On the other hand, her feelings of hatred against her father and her envy of his penis, which arise from her masculine position, stand in the way of her once more adopting a feminine role.

According to my experience, the girl, after having left the phallic phase, passes through yet another phase, a post-phallic one, in which she makes her choice between retaining the feminine position and abandoning it. I should say that by the time she has entered upon the latency period her feminine position, which has attained the genital level and is passive[46] and maternal in character and which involves the functioning of her vagina, or at least of its psychological representatives, has been established in all its fundamentals. That this is so becomes still more probable when we consider how frequently small girls take up a genuinely feminine and maternal position. A position of this kind would be unthinkable unless the vagina was behaving as a receptive organ. Of course, as has already been pointed out, important alterations take place in the functions of the vagina as a result of the biological changes the girl undergoes at puberty and of her experience of the sexual act; and it is these alterations which bring the girl's development to its final stage from a psychological point of view as well and which make her a woman in the full sense of the word.

In this connection I find myself in agreement on many points with Karen Horney's paper, "The Flight from Womanhood" (1926), in which she comes to the conclusion that the vagina plays a part in the early life of

---

toward them, and will have but little interest in the male sex. Ernest Jones has shown that this attitude develops in female homosexuals in whom the oral-sucking fixation is very strong.
[46]Helene Deutsch also believes that the true passive feminine attitude of the vagina is to be found in its oral and sucking activity (*Zur Psychologie der weiblichen Sexualfunktionen* [1925]).

the female child as well as the clitoris. She points out that it would be reasonable to infer from the appearance of frigidity in women that the vaginal zone is more likely to be strongly cathected with anxiety and defensive affects than the clitoris. She believes that the girl's incestuous wishes and phantasies have been correctly referred by her unconscious to the vagina and that her frigidity in later life is the manifestation of a defensive measure undertaken against them by her ego on account of the great danger they involve for it. I also share Karen Horney's opinion that the girl's inability to obtain any certain knowledge about the conformation of her vagina or, unlike the boy who can inspect his genitals, to submit it to a reality test in order to find out whether it has been overtaken by the dreaded consequences of masturbation tends to increase her genital anxiety and makes her more likely to adopt a masculine position. Karen Horney furthermore distinguishes between the girl's secondary penis-envy, which emerges in the phallic phase, and her primary penis-envy, which rests upon certain pre-genital cathexes such as scotophilia and urethral erotism. She believes that the girl's secondary penis-envy is used to repress her feminine desires; and that when her Oedipus complex is given up she invariably—though not always to the same degree—relinquishes her father as a sexual object and moves away from the feminine role, regressing at the same time to her primary penis-envy.

The views I put forward a few years ago concerning the final stage of the girl's genital organization[47] agree in many essentials with those which Ernest Jones came to at about the same time. In his paper, "The Early Development of Female Sexuality" (1927), he suggests that the vaginal functions were originally identified with the anal, and that the differentiation of the two—a still obscure process—takes place in part at an earlier stage than is generally supposed. He assumes the existence of a mouth–anus–vagina stage which forms the basis of the girl's heterosexual attitude and represents an identification with her mother. According to his view, too, the normal girl's phallic phase is only a weakened form of the identification made by homosexual females with the father and his penis, and is, like it, pre-eminently of a secondary and defensive character.

Helene Deutsch is of a different opinion.[48] She assumes, it is true, the existence of a post-phallic phase which influences the final outcome of the girl's later genital organization. But she believes that the girl does not

---

[47]Cf. my "Early Stages of the Oedipus Conflict" (1928).
[48]Helene Deutsch, "The Significance of Masochism in the Mental Life of Women" (1930).

have any such thing as a vaginal phase at all, and that it is the exception for her to know anything about the existence of her vagina or to have any sensations there, and that therefore when she has finished her infantile sexual development she cannot take up a feminine position in the genital sense. In consequence, her libido, even though maintaining a feminine position, is obliged to retrogress and cathect earlier positions dominated by her castration complex (which in Helene Deutsch's view precedes her Oedipus complex); and a backward step of this kind would be a fundamental factor in the production of feminine masochism.

RESTITUTIVE TENDENCIES AND SEXUALITY

We have already examined the part played by the girl's restitutive tendencies in consolidating her homosexual position. The consolidation of her heterosexual position, too, depends upon that position being in conformity with the requirements of her super-ego.

As we saw in an earlier part of this chapter, even where the normal individual is concerned, the sexual act, in addition to its libidinal motivation, helps him to master anxiety. His genital activities have yet another motive force, which is his desire to make good by means of copulation the damage he has done through his sadistic phantasies.[49] When, as a result of the stronger emergence of genital impulses, his ego reacts to his super-ego with less anxiety and more guilt, he finds in the sexual act a pre-eminent means of making reparation to the object, because of its connection with his early sadistic phantasies. The nature and extent of his restitutive phantasies, which must correspond to the imaginary damage he has done, will not only be an important factor in his various activities and in the formation of his sublimations but will very greatly influence the course and outcome of his sexual development.[50]

Turning to the girl, we find that such considerations as the contents and composition of her sadistic phantasies, the magnitude of her reactive tendencies, and the structure and strength of her ego will affect her libidinal

---

[49]In her paper, "*Einige unbewusste Mechanismen im pathologischen Sexualleben*" (1932), Melitta Schmideberg has also come to the conclusion that restitutive tendencies are of great importance as an incentive to heterosexual and homosexual activities.

[50]If his sense of guilt is excessive, the fusion of his sexual activities and his reactive tendencies may give rise to severe disturbances of his sexual life.

fixations and help to decide whether the restitution she makes shall have a masculine or a feminine character or be a mixture of the two.[51]

Another thing which seems to me to be of importance for the final outcome of the girl's development is whether the restitutive phantasies which she builds up upon her specific sadistic ideas can impose themselves upon her ego as well as upon her sexual life. Ordinarily they work in both directions and reinforce one another, and thus help to establish a libido-position and an ego-position which are compatible with each other. If, for instance, the small girl's sadism has been strongly centred in phantasies of damaging her mother's body and stealing children and her father's penis from it, she may be able, when her reactive tendencies set in in force, to maintain her feminine position under certain conditions. In her sublimations she will give effect to her desire to restore her mother and give her back her father and children, by becoming a nurse or a masseuse, or by pursuing intellectual interests;[52] and if at the same time she has sufficient belief in the possibility of her own body being restored by having children or performing the sexual act with a "beneficent" penis, she will also employ her heterosexual position as an aid to mastering anxiety. Moreover, her heterosexual tendencies support her sublimatory ones which aim at the restoration of her mother's body, for they show her that copulation between her parents cannot have injured her mother, or at any rate that it can restore her; and this belief, in turn, helps to consolidate her in her heterosexual position.

What the girl's final position is going to be will also depend, given the same underlying conditions, upon whether her belief in her own constructive omnipotence comes up to the strength of her reactive tendencies. If it does, her ego can set up a further aim to be fulfilled by her restitutive tendencies. This is that both her parents should be restored and should once more be united in amity. It is now her father who, in her phantasies, makes

---

[51]Even where her sadism remains dominant, the means she employs to master her anxiety will influence her sexual life and may either lead her to maintain a homosexual attitude or adopt a heterosexual one, both positions being based upon her sadistic tendencies.

[52]In my "Infantile Anxiety-Situations Reflected in a Work of Art and in the Creative Impulse" (1929), I have analysed an account by Karen Michaelis of a young woman who suddenly developed a great talent for painting portraits of women without ever having handled a brush before. I have tried to show that what caused this sudden burst of artistic productivity was anxiety emanating from her most profound danger-situations, and that painting female portraits symbolized a sublimated restoration both of her mother's body, which she had attacked in phantasy, and of her own, whose destruction she awaited out of dread of retaliation; so that in this way she was able to allay fears arising from the deepest levels of her mind.

restitution to her mother and gratifies her by means of his health-giving penis;
while her mother's vagina, originally imagined as a dangerous thing, restores
and heals her father's penis which it has injured. In thus looking upon her
mother's vagina as a beneficent and pleasure-giving organ, the girl is not
only able to call up once more her earliest view of her mother as the "good"
mother who gave her suck, but can think of herself, in identification with
her, as a beneficent and giving person and can regard the penis of her partner in love as a "good" penis. Upon an attitude of this kind will rest the
successful development of her sexual life and her ability to become attached
to her object by ties of sex no less than of affection and love.

   As I have tried to show in these pages, the final outcome of the infantile sexual development of the individual is the result of a long-drawn-out
process of fluctuation between various positions and is built up upon a great
number of interconnected compromises between his ego and his super-ego
and between his ego and his id. These compromises, being the result of his
endeavours to master anxiety, are themselves to a great extent an achievement of his ego. Those of them which, in the girl, go to maintain her feminine role and which find typical expression in her later sexual life and general behaviour are, to mention only a few, that her father's penis shall gratify
herself and her mother alternately;[53] that a certain number of the children
shall be allocated to her mother, and the same number, or rather fewer, to
herself; that she shall incorporate her father's penis, while her mother shall
receive all the children,—and so on. Masculine components enter into such
compromises as well. The small girl will sometimes imagine that she appro-
priates her father's penis in order to carry out a masculine role towards her
mother, and then gives it back to him again.

   In the course of an analysis it becomes apparent that every change
for the better which takes place in the libido-position of the patient springs
from a diminution of his anxiety and sense of guilt and at once takes effect
in the production of fresh compromises. The more the anxiety and guilt
which the girl feels is decreased and the more her genital stage comes to
the fore, the more easily is she able to let her mother adopt, or rather,

---

[53]Phantasies with this content play a part in the homosexuality of women similar to that played
in the homosexuality of men by phantasies of meeting their father's penis, as an object of
gratification or of hatred, inside their mother's body. This may be because, where the girl's
attitude is predominantly sadistic, they represent the destruction, undertaken in common by
herself and her mother, of her father's penis; or, where it is predominantly positive, a libidinal gratification obtained in common with her from his penis.

resume, a feminine and maternal role and at the same time to take on a similar role herself and sublimate her male components.

EXTERNAL FACTORS

We know that the child's early phantasies and instinctual life on the one hand and the pressure of reality upon it on the other interact upon each other and that their combined action shapes the course of its mental development. In my judgment, reality and real objects affect its anxiety-situations from the very earliest stages of its existence, in the sense that it regards them as so many proofs or refutations of its anxiety-situations, which it has displaced into the outer world, and they thus help to guide the course of its instinctual life. And since, owing to the interaction of the mechanisms of projection and introjection, the external factors influence the formation of its super-ego and the growth of its object-relationship and its instincts, they will also assist in determining what the outcome of its sexual development will be.

If, for instance, the small girl looks in vain to her father for the love and kindness which shall confirm her belief in the "good" penis inside her and be a counter-weight to her belief in the "bad" penis there, she will often grow more firmly entrenched in her masochistic attitude and the "sadistic father" may even become an actual condition of love for her; or his behaviour to her may increase her feelings of hatred and anxiety against his penis and impel her to abandon the feminine role or to become frigid. Actually, whether the outcome of her development is to be favourable or unfavourable will depend upon the co-operation of a whole number of external factors.

For instance, her father's attitude to her is not the only thing which helps to decide what type of person she will fall in love with. It is not only a question, say, of whether he favours or neglects her too much in comparison with her mother or her sisters, but of his direct relations with those persons. How far she will be able to maintain her feminine position and in that position evolve a wish for a kindly father-imago also depends very greatly upon her sense of guilt towards her mother and thus upon the nature of the relations between her mother and father.[54] Furthermore, certain

---

[54]Since the way in which each child will receive the impressions of reality is already largely determined by his or her early anxiety-situations, the same events will have different effects

events, such as the illness or death of one of her parents or of a brother or sister, can assist in strengthening in her either the one sexual position or the other, according to the way in which they affect her sense of guilt.

Another thing which plays a very important part in the development of the child is the presence in its early life of a person, not its father or mother, whom it looks upon as a "helping" figure and who gives it support in the external world against its phantastic fears. In dividing its mother into a "good" mother and a "bad" one and its father into a "good" father and a "bad" one, it attaches the hatred it feels for its object to the "bad" one or turns away from it, while it directs its restorative tendencies to its "good" mother and "good" father and, in imagination, makes good toward them the damage it has done its parent-imagos in its sadistic phantasies. But if, because its anxiety is too great or for realistic reasons, its Oedipus objects have not become good imagos, other persons, such as a kindly nurse, brother or sister, a grandparent, or an aunt or uncle, can, in certain circumstances, take over the role of the "good" mother or the "good" father.[55] In this way its positive feelings, whose growth has been inhibited owing to its excessive fear of its Oedipus objects, can come to the fore and attach themselves to a love-object.

As has been pointed out more than once in these pages, the existence of sexual relations between children in early life, especially between brothers and sisters, is a very common occurrence. The libidinal craving of small children, intensified as it is by their Oedipus frustrations, together with the anxiety emanating from their deepest danger-situations, impels them to indulge in mutual sexual activities, since these, as I have more particularly tried to show in the present chapter, not only gratify their libido but enable them to obtain many refutations of their various fears in connection with the sexual act. I have repeatedly found that if such sexual objects have acted in addition as "helping" figures, early sexual relations of this kind exert a favourable influence upon the girl's relations to her objects and upon her later sexual

---

on different children. But there can be no doubt that the existence of happy and harmonious relations between their parents and between themselves and their parents is of underlying importance for their successful sexual development and mental health. Of course, a happy family life of this kind presupposes in general that the parents are not neurotic; so that a constitutional factor enters into the situation as well.

[55] A pet animal may also play the part of a "helping" object in the imagination of children and thus assist in diminishing their anxiety. And so may a doll or a toy animal, to which they often assign the function of protecting them while they are asleep.

development. Where an excessive fear of both parents, together with certain external factors, would have produced an Oedipus situation which would have prejudiced her attitude toward the opposite sex and greatly hampered her in the maintenance of her feminine position and in her ability to love, the fact that she has had sexual relations with a brother or brother-substitute in early childhood and that that brother has also shown real affection for her and been her protector, has provided the basis for a heterosexual position in her and developed her capacity for love. I have one or two cases in mind in which the girl had had two types of love-object, one representing the stern father and the other the kind brother.[56] In other cases, she had developed an imago which was a mixture of the two types; and here, too, her relations to her brother had lessened her masochism.

In serving as a proof grounded upon reality of the existence of the "good" penis, the girl's relations with her brother fortify her belief in the "good" introjected penis and moderate her fear of "bad" introjected objects. They also help her to master her anxiety in those respects, since in performing sexual acts with another child she gets a feeling of being in league with him against her parents. Their sexual relations have made the two children accomplices in crime, by reviving in them sadistic masturbation phantasies that were originally directed against their father and mother and causing them to indulge in them together. In thus sharing in that deepest guilt each child feels relieved of some of the weight of it and is also less frightened, because it believes that it has an ally against its dreaded objects. As far as I can see, the existence of a secret complicity of this sort, which, in my opinion, plays an essential part in every relationship of love, even between grown-up people, is of special importance in sexual attachments where the individual is of a paranoid type.

The girl also regards her sexual attachment to the other child, who represents the "good" object, as a disproof by means of reality of her fear of her own sexuality and that of her object as something destructive; so that an attachment of this sort may prevent her from becoming frigid or succumbing to other sexual disturbances in later life.

---

[56]Each type had become important at different periods of her life. Analysis showed that whenever her anxiety increased in amount and certain external factors became operative she was led to choose the more sadistic type of person or at least to be unable to resist his advances; while, as soon as she had succeeded in detaching herself from that sadistic object, the other, kindly type, representing her brother, emerged and she became less masochistic and was able to choose a satisfactory object.

Nevertheless, although, as we see, experiences of this kind can have a favourable effect upon the girl's sexual life and object-relationships, they can also lead to grave disorders in that field. If her sexual relations with another child serve to confirm her deepest fears—either because her partner is too sadistic or because performing the sexual act arouses yet more anxiety and guilt in her on account of her own excessive sadism—her belief in the harmfulness of her introjected objects and her own id will become still stronger, her super-ego will grow more severe than ever, and, as a result, her neurosis and all the defects of her sexual and characterological development will gain ground.[57]

DEVELOPMENT AT PUBERTY

The psychological upheavals which the child undergoes during the age of puberty are, as we know, to a large extent due to the intensification of its impulses which accompanies the physiological changes that are taking place in it. In the girl the onset of menstruation gives additional reinforcement to her anxiety. In her *Zur Psychologie der weiblichen Sexualfunktionen* (1926), Helene Deutsch has discussed at length the psychological significance of puberty for the girl and the trial it imposes on her, and she has come to the conclusion that the first flow of blood is equivalent in the unconscious to having actually been castrated and having forfeited the possibility of having a child, and is, therefore, a double disappointment. Helene Deutsch points out that menstruation also signifies a punishment for having indulged in clitoral masturbation and, in addition, that it regressively revives the girl's infantile view of copulation according to which it is nearly always a sadistic act involving cruelty and the flow of blood.

My own data fully bear out Helene Deutsch's view that the disappointments and shocks to her narcissism which the girl receives when she begins to menstruate are very great. But I think that their pathogenic effect is due to the circumstance that they reactivate past fears in her. They are only a few items in the inventory of her anxiety-situations which menstruation brings to the surface once more. These fears, as we have seen earlier in the present chapter, are, briefly, the following:

1. In virtue of the equation of all bodily substances with one another in the unconscious, she identifies her menstrual blood with her

---

[57]This is still more the case where the child has been seduced or raped by a grown-up person. Such an experience, as is well known, can have very serious effects upon the child's mind.

supposedly dangerous excreta.[58] Since she has early learned to associate bleeding with being cut, her fear that these dangerous excreta have damaged her own body seems to her to have been borne out by reality.

2. The menstrual flow increases her terror that her body will be attacked. In this connection various fears are at work: (a) Her fear of being attacked and destroyed by her mother partly out of revenge, partly so as to get back her father's penis and the children which she (the girl) has deprived her of. (b) Her fear of being attacked and damaged by her father through his copulating with her in a sadistic way,[59] either because she has had sadistic masturbation phantasies about her mother or because he wants to get back the penis she has taken from him. Her phantasy that in thus forcibly recovering his penis from her he will injure her genitals underlies, I think, the idea she has later on that her clitoris is a wound or scar where her penis once was. (c) Her fear that the interior of her body will be attacked and destroyed by her introjected objects either directly or indirectly as a consequence of their fight with one another inside her. Her phantasy that she has introjected her violent parents in the act of performing sadistic coitus and that they are endangering her own inside in destroying each other there calls out fears of a very acute kind in her. She regards the bodily sensations which menstruation often gives rise to in her, and which her anxiety augments, as a sign that all the injuries she has dreaded to receive and all her hypochondriacal fears have come true.

3. The flow of blood from the interior of her body convinces her that the children inside her have been injured and destroyed. In some analyses of women I have found that their fear of being childless

---

[58]Cf. Lewin, *"Kotschmieren, Menses und weibliches Über-Ich"* (1930).

[59]In her paper, *"Psychoanalytisches zur Menstruation"* (1931), Melitta Schmideberg has pointed out that the girl regards menstruation, among other things, as the result of having been copulated with sadistically by her father and that she is all the more terrified since she believes that this action on his part was done in retaliation for her aggression toward both him and her mother. Just as in her sadistic phantasies as a child he was the executive of her aggressive desire against her mother, so now he is the one to carry out the punishment her mother metes out to her. In addition, his sadistic coitus with her represents his own punishment of her for the castration-wishes she harbours against the male sex in connection with copulation.

(i.e., of having had the children inside them destroyed) had been intensified since the onset of menstruation and had not been removed until they actually did have a child. But in many cases menstruation, in adding to their fear of having damaged or abnormal children, causes them, consciously or unconsciously, to reject pregnancy altogether.

4. Menstruation, by confirming the girl in the knowledge that she has no penis and in the belief that her clitoris is the scar or wound left by her castrated penis,[60] makes it harder for her to maintain a masculine position.

5. In being a sign of sexual maturity, menstruation activates all those sources of anxiety, mentioned earlier on in this chapter, which are connected with her ideas that sexual behavior has a sadistic character.

Analyses of female patients at the age of puberty show that for the reasons given above the girl feels that her feminine position as well as her masculine one have become untenable. Menstruation has a much greater effect in activating sources of anxiety and conflicts in the girl than do the parallel developmental processes in the boy. This is partly why she is sexually more inhibited than he is at puberty.

The psychological effects of menstruation are in part responsible for the fact that at this age the girl's neurotic difficulties often increase very greatly. Even if she is normal menstruation resuscitates her old anxiety-situations, though, since her ego and her methods of mastering anxiety have been adequately developed, she is better able to modify her anxiety than she was in early childhood. Ordinarily, too, she obtains a strong satisfaction from the onset of menstruation. Provided that her feminine position has been well established during the first expansion of her sexual life, she will regard menstruation as a proof of being sexually mature and a woman, and as a sign that she may put still greater confidence in her expectation of receiving sexual gratification and having children. If this is so, she will look upon menstruation as evidence against various sources of anxiety.

---

[60]In my opinion, the girl's primary phantasy, mentioned under 2 (b), to the effect that her genitals (clitoris) have been damaged through her having had her introjected penis forcibly taken from her, or her fear that this will happen, forms the basis of her phantasy that her genitals have been damaged by castration.

RELATIONS TO HER CHILDREN

In describing the early sexual development of the female individual I did not go very fully into her desire to have children, since I wanted to deal with her infantile attitude to her imaginary children at the same time as I dealt with her attitude in later life, during pregnancy, to the real child inside her.

Freud has stated that the girl's desire to have a child takes the place of her wish to possess a penis;[61] but according to my observations, what it takes the place of is her desire for her father's penis in an object-libidinal sense. In some cases the principal equation she makes is between children and feces. Here her relation to the child seems to develop mainly on narcissistic lines. It is more independent of her attitude to the man and closely connected with her own body and with the omnipotence of her excrements. In other cases she mostly equates children with a penis; and here her attitude to her child rests more strongly upon her relations to her father or to his penis. There is a universal infantile sexual theory to the effect that the mother incorporates a new penis every time she copulates and that these penises, or a part of them, turn into children. In consequence of this theory the girl's relations to her father's penis influence her relations first of all to her imaginary children and later on to her real ones.

In the book which I have already quoted, *Zur Psychoanalyse der weiblichen Sexualfunktionen*, Helene Deutsch, in discussing the attitude of the pregnant woman to the child inside her puts forward the following view. The woman looks upon her child both as a part of her ego and as an object outside it "in regard to which she repeats all the positive and negative object-relationships which she has had toward her own mother." In her phantasies her father has been turned into her child in the act of copulation, "which, ultimately, represents to her unconscious the oral incorporation of her father," and he "retains this role in the real or imaginary pregnancy which ensues." After this process of introjection has taken place her child becomes "the incarnation of the ego-ideal which she has already developed earlier" and also represents "the embodiment of her own ideals which she has not been able to attain." The ambivalent attitude she has toward her child is partly due to this fact that it stands for her superego—often in strong opposition to her ego—and revives in her those ambivalent feelings

---

[61]Cf. Freud, "Some Psychological Consequences of the Anatomical Distinction between the Sexes" (1927).

toward her father which arose out of her Oedipus situation. But it is also partly due to her making a regressive cathexis of her earlier libidinal positions. Her identification of children with feces, of which she has a narcissistic valuation, becomes the basis of a similar narcissistic valuation of her child; and her reaction-formations against her original over-estimation of her excrements awakens feelings of disgust in her and makes her want to expel her child.

This view requires, I think, to be amplified in one or two directions. The equation which the female has made in the early stages of her development between her father's penis and a child leads her to give to the child inside her the significance of a paternal super-ego, since his internalized penis forms the nucleus of that super-ego. Thus her attitude to her imaginary or real child is not only an ambivalent one but is charged with a certain quantity of anxiety which exerts a decisive influence upon her relations to her child. The equation she has made between feces and children has also, I have found, affected her relation to her imaginary child when she is still quite small. And the anxiety which she feels on account of her phantasies about her poisonous and burning excreta, and which, in my opinion, reinforces her expelling tendencies belonging to the earlier anal stage, is one of the reasons why she has feelings of hatred and fear later on toward the real child inside her.

As I have already pointed out, the girl's fear of her "bad" introjected penis induces her to strengthen her introjection of a "good" penis, since it offers her protection and assistance against the "bad" penis inside her, her bad imagos, and her excreta, which she regards as dangerous substances. It is this friendly, "good" penis, often conceived of as a small one, which takes on the significance of a child. This imaginary child, which affords the small girl protection and help, primarily represents in her unconscious the "good" contents of her body. The support it gives her against her anxiety is, of course, purely phantastic, but then the objects she is afraid of are equally phantastic; or in this stage of her development she is mostly governed by internal and subjective reality.[62]

In my view it is because the possession of children is a means of overcoming her anxiety and allaying her sense of guilt that the little girl normally feels such an intense need to have children—a need which is greater

---

[62]Recognition of internal reality is the foundation of adaptation to external reality. The child's attitude to its imaginary objects, which, in this stage of its life, are phantastic imagos of its external, real objects, will determine its relations to those objects later on.

than any other desire. As we know, grown-up women often have a stronger desire to have a child than to have a sexual partner.

The small girl's attitude toward the child is also of great importance for the creation of her sublimations. The imaginary attacks she makes upon her mother's inside by means of her poisonous and destructive excreta bring on misgivings about the contents of her own body. Owing to her equation of feces with children her phantasies about the "bad" feces inside her lead her to have phantasies about having a "bad" child[63] in there, and that is equivalent to having a "horrible," malformed one. The girl's reaction-formations to her sadistic phantasies about dangerous feces give rise, it seems to me, to sublimations of a specifically feminine type. In analysing small girls we can see very clearly how closely their longing to possess a "beautiful" (i.e., "good" and healthy) child and their indefatigable efforts to beautify their imaginary baby and their own body are connected with their fear of having produced in themselves and put inside their mother "bad" and horrid children whom they liken to poisonous excrement.

Ferenczi has described the changes which the child's interest in feces undergoes in the various stages of its development, and has come to the conclusion that its coprophilic tendencies are early sublimated in part into a pleasure in shining things.[64] One element in this process of sublimation is, I think, the child's fear of "bad" and dangerous pieces of stool. From this there is a direct sublimatory path leading to the theme of "beauty." The very strong need which women feel to have a beautiful body and a lovely home and for beauty in general is based on their desire to possess a beautiful interior to their body in which "good" and lovely objects and innocuous excrements are lodged. Another line of sublimation from the girl's fear of "bad" and "dangerous" excrements leads to the idea of "good" products, in the sense of health-giving ones (though, incidentally, "good" and "beautiful" often mean the same thing to the small child), and in this way goes to strengthen in her those original maternal feelings and desires to give which spring from her feminine position.

If the small girl is sufficiently buoyed up by feelings of an optimistic kind she will believe not only that her internalized penis is a "good" one but that the children inside her are helpful beings. But if she is filled with fear of a "bad" internalized penis and of dangerous excrements, her relation

---

[63]The equation of a "bad" penis with a child has already been discussed. The two equations exist side by side and reinforce each other.
[64]Ferenczi, "The Origin in Interest in Money" (1914).

to her real child in later life will often be dominated by anxiety. Not seldom, however, where her relations to her sexual partner do not satisfy her, she will establish a relation to her child which will afford her gratification and moral support. In these cases, in which the sexual act itself has received too strongly the significance of an anxiety-situation and her sexual object has become an anxiety-object to her, it is her child which attracts to itself the quality of a "good" and helpful penis. Again, a woman who overcomes anxiety precisely by means of her sexual activities may have a fairly good relation to her husband and a bad one to her child. In this case she has displaced her anxiety concerning the enemy inside her for the most part on to her child; and it is her fears resulting from this which, I have found, are at the bottom of her fear of pregnancy and child-birth and which add to her physical sufferings while she is pregnant and may even render her psychological incapable of conceiving a child.

We have already seen in what way the woman's fear of the "bad" penis can increase her sadism. Women who have a strong sadistic attitude to their husband usually look upon their child as an enemy. Just as they regard the sexual act as a means of destroying their object, so do they want to have a child mainly in order to get it into their power as though it was something hostile to them. They can then employ the hatred which they feel for their internal, dreaded foe against external objects—against husband and child. There are also, of course, women who have a sadistic attitude to their husband and a relatively friendly one to their children, and *vice versa*. But in every case it is the woman's attitude to her introjected objects, especially her father's penis, which will determine her attitude to her husband and child.

The attitude of the mother to her children is based, as we know, upon her early relations to her objects. According as her child is a boy or a girl she will have toward it, to a greater or lesser degree, those emotional relationships which she had in early childhood toward her father and uncles and brothers, or toward her mother and aunts and sisters. If she has principally equated the idea of a child with that of a "good" penis, it will be the positive elements of those relationships which she will carry over to her child.[65] She will condense a number of friendly imagos in its per-

---

[65]The girl often identifies her imaginary child in her unconscious with a small and innocuous penis. It is partly in this connection that her relations with her brother or some other child help her to confirm her belief in the "good" penis. As a small child she ascribes an enormous amount of sadism to her father's penis and finds her brother's small penis, if less worthy of admiration, at any rate not so dangerous.

son,[66] and it will represent the "innocence" of infancy and will be in her eyes what she would like to picture herself as having been in early childhood. And one of the ultimate motives for the hopes she places upon its growing up well and happily is that she may be able, in retrospect, to turn her own unsatisfactory childhood into a time of happiness.

There are, I think, a whole number of factors which help to fortify the emotional relationship which the mother has toward her child. In bringing it into the world she has produced the strongest refutation in reality of all the fears that arise from her sadistic phantasies. The birth of her child not only signifies in her unconscious that the interior of her own body and the imaginary children there are unharmed or have been made well again but invalidates all sorts of fears associated with the idea of children. It shows that the children inside her mother—her brothers and sisters—and her father's penis (or her father) which she has attacked there, and also her mother, are all unharmed or made whole again. Having a baby thus represents restoring a number of objects—even, in some cases, re-creating a whole world.

Giving suck to her child is very important too, and forms a very close and special tie between her and it. In giving her child a product of her own body which is essential to its nourishment and growth she is enabled finally to disprove and put a happy end to that vicious circle which was started in her as an infant by her attacks upon her mother's breast as the first object of her destructive impulses and which contained phantasies of destroying the breast by biting it to pieces and dirtying, poisoning, and burning it by means of her excreta. For in her unconscious she regards the fact that she is giving her child nourishing and beneficial milk as a proof that her own early sadistic phantasies have not come true or that she has succeeded in restoring the objects of them.[67]

---

[66]In his "Civilization and Its Discontents" (1930), Freud says on p. 89: "It [aggression] is at the bottom of all the relations of affection and love between human beings—possibly with the single exception of that of a mother to her male child." Where the woman is strongly affected by the equation between the child and the "good" penis, she is especially liable to concentrate all the positive elements of her feeling upon her child, should it be a boy.

[67]She also takes this as a proof in reality that her urine, which she likens to milk, is not harmful; just as, on the other hand, she often looks upon her menstrual blood as a proof in reality that her urine and other excreta are dangerous substances. Moreover, the fact that her supply of milk does not give out is a refutation not only of her fear, arising from her sadistic phantasies, that her breast has been destroyed, but convinces her that her excrements are not harmful to her own body. These were the weapons she used to attack her mother's breast in her imagination, and she now sees that they have done no harm.

As has already been pointed out, the individual loves his "good" object the more because, by being something to which he can devote his restitutive tendencies, it affords him gratification and lessens his anxiety. No object possesses this qualification to such an eminent degree as does the helpless little child. Furthermore, in expending her maternal love and care upon her child she not only fulfills her earliest desires but, since she identifies herself with it, shares the pleasures she gives it. In thus reversing the relationship of mother and child she is able to experience a happy renewal of her earliest attachment to her own mother and to let her primal feelings of hatred for her recede into the background and her positive feelings come to the fore.

All these factors contribute to give children a tremendous importance in the emotional life of women. And we can readily see why it is that their mental balance should be so much upset if their child does not turn out well and, especially, if it is abnormal. Just as a healthy and thriving child is a refutation of a whole number of fears, so is an abnormal, sickly, or merely rather unsatisfactory one a confirmation of them, and may even come to be regarded as an enemy and a persecutor.

EGO-DEVELOPMENT

We shall now only consider briefly the relation between the formation of the girl's super-ego and the development of her ego. Freud has shown that some of the differences that exist between the super-ego formation of the girl and that of the boy are associated with anatomical sexual differences.[68] These anatomical differences affect, I think, both the development of the super-ego and the ego in various ways. In consequence of the structure of the female genitals, which marks their receptive function, the girl's Oedipus tendencies are more largely dominated by her oral impulses, and the introjection of her super-ego is more extensive than in the boy. In addition there is the absence of a penis as an active organ. The fact that she has no penis increases the greater dependence the girl already has upon her super-ego as a result of her stronger introjective tendencies.

I have already put forward the view [. . .] that the boy's primary sense of omnipotence is associated with his penis, which is also the representative in his unconscious of activities and sublimations proceeding from his mas-

---

[68] "Some Psychological Consequences of the Anatomical Distinction Between the Sexes" (1927).

culine components. In the girl, who does not possess a penis, the sense of omnipotence is more profoundly and extensively associated with her father's introjected penis than it is in the case of the boy. This is the more so because the picture which she has formed as a child of his penis inside her and which determines the standards she sets up for herself has been evolved out of extremely highly coloured phantasies and is thus more exaggerated than the boy's both in the direction of "goodness" and of "badness."

This view that the super-ego is more strongly operative in women than in men seems at first sight to be out of keeping with the fact that, compared to men, women are often more dependent upon their objects, more easily influenced by the outer world and more variable in their moral standards—that is, apparently less guided by the requirements of a super-ego. But I think that their greater dependence upon objects[69] is actually closely related to a greater efficacy of the super-ego. Both characteristics have a common origin in the greater propensity women have to introject their object and set it up in themselves, so that they erect a more powerful super-ego there. This propensity, moreover, is increased precisely by their greater dependence upon their super-ego and their greater fear of it. The girl's most profound anxiety, which is that some unascertainable damage has been done to her inside by her internalized objects, impels her, as we have already seen, to be continually testing her fears by means of her relations to real objects. It impels her, that is, to reinforce her introjective tendencies in a secondary

---

[69]Along with this greater dependence upon objects goes the greater degree to which they are affected by low of love. In his paper, "One of the Motive Factors in the Formation of the Super-Ego in Women" (1928), Hanns Sachs has pointed out the curious fact that although women are in general more narcissistic than men, they feel the loss of love more. He has sought to explain this apparent contradiction by supposing that when her Oedipus conflict comes to an end the girl tries to cling to her father either through her desire to have a child by him or by means of oral regression. His view agrees with mine in stressing the significance that her oral attachment to her father has for the formation of her super-ego. But according to him this attachment comes about through a regression after she has been disappointed in her hopes of having a penis and of obtaining genital satisfaction from her father; whereas in my view her oral attachment to her father, or, more correctly, her desire to incorporate his penis, is the foundation and starting-point of her sexual development and of the formation of her super-ego.

Ernest Jones attributes the greater effect which the loss of her object has upon the woman to her fear that her father will not give her sexual gratification (cf. his paper, "The Early Development of Female Sexuality" |1927|). According to him, the reason why the frustration of sexual gratification is so intolerable to her—and in this matter, of course, the woman is more dependent than the man on the other party—is because it stirs up her deepest anxiety, which is her fear of *aphanisis*, i.e., of having her capacity for experiencing sexual pleasure entirely abolished.

way. Again, it would seem that her mechanisms of projection are stronger than the man's, in conformity with her stronger sense of the omnipotence of her excrements and thoughts; and this is another factor which induces her to have stronger relations with the outer world and with objects in reality, partly for the purpose of controlling them by magical means.

This fact that the processes of introjection and projection are stronger in the woman than in the man not only affects, I think, the character of her object-relationships but is of importance for the development of her ego. Her dominating and deep-seated need to give herself up in complete trust and submission to the "good" internalized penis is one of the things that underlies the receptive quality of her sublimations and interests. But her feminine position also strongly impels her to obtain secret control of her internalized objects by means of the omnipotence of her excrements and of her thoughts; and this fosters in her a sharp power of observation and great psychological insight, together with a certain artfulness and inclination towards deceit and intrigue. This side of her ego-development is brought out in the main with reference to her maternal superego, but it also colours her relation to her paternal one.

In "The Ego and the Id" (1923), Freud writes:

> If they [the object-identifications] obtain the upper hand and become too numerous, unduly intense and incompatible with one another, a pathological outcome will not be far off. It may come to a disruption of the ego in consequence of the individual identification becoming cut off from one another by resistances; perhaps the secret of cases of so-called multiple personality is that the various identifications seize possession of consciousness in turn. Even when things do not go so far as this, there remains the question of conflicts between the different identifications into which the ego is split up, conflicts which cannot after all be described as purely pathological. [p. 38]

A study of the early stages of the formation of the superego and their relation to the development of the ego fully confirms this last statement. And, as far as can be seen, any further investigation of personality as a whole, whether normal or abnormal, will have to proceed along the lines Freud has indicated. It seems that the way to extend our knowledge of the ego is to learn more about the various identifications it makes and the relations it has to them. Only by pursuing this line of enquiry can we discover in what ways the ego regulates the relations that exist between those identifications, which, as we know, differ according to the stage of development in which they have

been made and according to whether they refer to subject's mother or father or a combination of the two.

The girl is more hampered in the formation of a super-ego in respect
of her mother than the boy is in respect of his father, since it is difficult for
her to identify herself with her mother on the basis of an anatomical resemblance, owing to the fact that the internal organs which subserve female sexual
functions and the question of possessing or not possessing children do not
admit of any investigation or test by reality. This obstacle increases, as we
have already learned, the power of her terrifying mother-imago—that product of her own imaginary sadistic attacks upon her mother—who endangers
the inside of her body and calls her to account for having deprived her of
her children, her feces, and the father's penis, and for possessing "bad" and
dangerous excrements.

The methods of attack, based on the omnipotence of her excrements
and of thoughts, which the girl employs against her mother influence the
development of her ego not only directly, as it seems, but indirectly too.
Her reaction-formations against her own sadistic omnipotence and the
transformation of the latter into constructive omnipotence enable her to
develop sublimations and qualities of mind which are the direct opposite
of those traits which we have just described and which are allied to the
primary omnipotence of her excrements. They incline her to be truthful, con-
fiding, and forgetful of self, ready to devote herself to the duties before her
and willing to undergo much for their sake and for the sake of other people.
These reaction-formations and sublimations tend once more to make her
sense of omnipotence, based upon her internalized "good" objects, and her
attitude of submission to her paternal super-ego, the dominating forces in
her feminine attitude.[70]

Moreover, an essential part in her ego-development is played by her
desire to employ her "good" urine and "good" feces in rectifying the effects of her "bad" and harmful excrements and in giving away good and beautiful things—a desire which is of overwhelming importance in her acts of
bearing a child and giving suck to it, for the "beautiful" child and the "good"

---

[70]As has already been seen, the different kinds of magic act in conjunction and are interchange-
able. They are also played off against one another by the ego. The girl's fear of having "bad"
children (feces) inside her as a result of the magical powers of her excrements acts as an incentive to her to over-emphasize her belief in the "good" penis. Her equation of the "good"
penis with a child makes it possible for her to hope that she has incorporated "good" children and these are an offset to the children inside her which she likens to "bad" feces.

milk which she produces represent sublimations of her harmful feces and dangerous urine. Indeed this desire forms a fruitful and creative basis for all those sublimations which arise out of the psychological representatives of parturition and giving suck.

The characteristic thing about the development of the woman's ego is that in the course of it her super-ego becomes raised to very great heights and much magnified and that her ego looks up to it and submits itself to it. And because her ego tries to live up to this exalted super-ego it is spurred on to all kinds of efforts which result in an expansion and enrichment of itself. Thus whereas in the man it is the ego and, with it, reality-relations which mostly take the lead, so that his whole nature is more objective and reasonable, in the woman it is the unconscious which is the dominating force. In her case, no less than in his, the quality of her achievements will depend upon the quality of her ego, but they receive their specifically feminine character of intuitiveness and subjectivity from the fact that her ego is submitted to a loved internal being. They represent the birth of a spiritual child, procreated by its father; and this spiritual father is her super-ego. It is true that even a markedly feminine line of development exhibits numerous features which spring from masculine components, but it seems as if it was woman's dominating belief in the omnipotence of her father's incorporated penis and of the growing child inside her which renders her capable of achievements of a specifically feminine kind.

At this point we cannot help comparing the mental disposition of women with that of children, who, as I maintain, are to such a much greater degree under the dominion of their super-ego and dependent upon their objects than is the adult. We all know that the woman is much more akin to the child than is the man; and yet in some respects she differs quite as much from it as he in her ego-development. The reason for this is, I think, that although she has introjected her Oedipus object much more strongly than he has, so that her super-ego and id occupy a larger share in her mental make-up and there is a certain analogy between her attitude and the child's, her ego attains a full development in virtue of the powerful super-ego within her whose example it follows and which it also in part endeavours to control and outdo.

If the girl clings in the main to the imaginary possession of a penis as a masculine attribute, her development will be radically different. In reviewing her sexual history we have already discussed the various causes which oblige her to adopt a masculine position. As regards her activities and sublimations—which she regards in her unconscious as a confirmation in reality of her possession of a penis or as substitutes for it—these are not only used to compete with her father's penis but invariably serve, in a secondary way, as a defense against her super-ego and in order to weaken it. In girls of this type, moreover, the ego takes a stronger lead and their pursuits are for the most part an expression of male potency.

As far as the girl's sexual development is concerned, we have already learned the significance which the existence of a good mother-imago has upon the formation of a good father-imago has upon the formation of a good father-imago in her. If she is in a position to entrust herself to the internal guidance of a paternal super-ego which she believes in and admires it always means that she has good mother-imagos as well; for it is only where she has sufficient trust in a "good" internalized mother that she is able to surrender herself completely to her paternal super-ego. But in order to make a surrender of this kind she must also believe strongly enough in her possession of "good" things inside her body—of friendly internalized objects. Only if the child which, in her imagination, she has had, or expects to have, by her father is a "good" and "beautiful" child—only, that is, if the inside of her body represents a place where harmony and beauty reign[71]—can she give herself without reserve, both sexually and mentally, to her paternal super-ego and to its representatives in the external world. The attainment of a state of harmony of this kind is founded on the existence of a good relationship between her ego and its identifications and between those identifications themselves, and especially between her father-imago and her mother-imago.

The girl-child's phantasies in which she tries to destroy both her parents out of envy and hatred of them are the fountain-head of her deepest sense of guilt and also form the basis of her most overpowering danger-situations. They give rise to a fear of harbouring in herself hostile objects which are engaged in deadly combat (i.e. in destructive copulation) with each other or which, because they have discovered her guilt, are allied in enmity against her ego. If her father and mother live a happy life together the immense gratification she obtains from this fact is to a great extent due to the relief which their good relations with each other afford the sense of guilt she feels on account of her sadistic phantasies. For in her unconscious the good understanding between them is a confirmation in reality of her hope of being able to make restitution in every possible way. And if her restitutive mechanisms have been successfully established she will not only be in har-

---

[71]This phantasy is also present in the boy.

mony with the external world, but—and this is, I think, a necessary condition for the attainment of such a state of harmony and of a satisfactory object-relationship and sexual development—she will be at one with her internal world and with herself. If her menacing imagos fade into the background and her kindly father-imago and mother-imago emerge to act in friendly cooperation and give her a guarantee of peace and security within her own body, she can work out her feminine and her masculine components under the auspices of her introjected parents, and she will have secured a basis in herself for the full development of a harmonious personality.

POSTSCRIPT

Since writing the above I note that a paper by Freud has appeared,[72] in which he more especially discusses the long period of time during which the girl remains attached to her mother, and endeavours to isolate that attachment from the operation of her super-ego and her sense of guilt. This, in my judgment, is not possible, for I think that the girl's anxiety and sense of guilt which arise from her aggressive impulses go to intensify her primary libidinal attachment to her mother at a very early age. Her multifarious fears of her phantastic imagos (her super-ego) and of her "bad," real mother force her, while she is still quite small, to find protection in her "good," real mother. And in order to do this she has to over-compensate for her primary aggression toward the latter.

Freud also points out that the girl feels hostility, too, toward her mother and is afraid of "being killed [eaten up?] by her." In my analysis of female patients of every age I have found that their fear of being devoured, cut to bits, or destroyed by their mother springs from the projection of impulses of their own of the same sadistic kind against her, and that those fears are at the bottom of their earliest anxiety-situations. Freud also states that female persons who are strongly attached to their mother have more especially reacted with rage and anxiety to enemas and anal irrigations which she has administered to them in their childhood. Expressions of affect of this sort are, as far as my experience goes, caused by their fear of sustaining anal attacks from her—a fear which represents the projection of their anal-sadistic phantasies on to her. I am in agreement with Freud's view that in

---

[72] "Female Sexuality" (1932).

females the projection in early childhood of hostile impulses against their mother is the nucleus of paranoia in later life. But, according to my observations,[73] it is the imaginary attacks they have made upon the interior of their mother's body by means of destructive excrements that poison, burn, and explode, which more particularly give rise to their fear of pieces of stool as persecutors and of their mother as a terrifying figure as a result of projection.

Freud believes that the girl's long attachment to her mother is an exclusive one and takes place before she has entered the Oedipus situation. But my experience of analysis of small girls has convinced me that their long-drawn-out and powerful attachment to their mother is never exclusive and is bound up with Oedipus impulses. Moreover, their anxiety and sense of guilt in relation to their mother also affects the course of those Oedipus impulses; for in my view, the girl's defense against her feminine attitude springs less from her masculine tendencies than from her fear of her mother. If the small girl is too frightened of her mother she will not be able to attach herself strongly enough to her father and her Oedipus complex will not come to light. In those cases, however, in which a strong attachment to the father has not been established until the post-phallic stage, I have found that the girl has nevertheless had positive Oedipus impulses at an early age, but that these often did not emerge to view. These early stages of her Oedipus conflict still bear a somewhat phantastic character, since they are in part centred round the penis of her father; but in part they are already concerned with her real father.

In some of my earlier papers I have adduced as primary factors in the withdrawal of the girl from her mother the grudge she feels against her for having subjected her to oral frustration (a factor which is also noticed by Freud in the paper under discussion) and her envy of the mutual oral gratification which, on the strength of her earliest sexual theories, she imagines that her parents obtain from copulation. These factors, assisted by the equation of breast with penis, incline her to turn toward her father's penis in the second half of her first year; so that her attachment to her father is fundamentally affected by her attachment to her mother. Freud, I may say, also points out that the one is built up upon the other, and that many women repeat their relation to their mother in their relation to men.

---

[73]Cf. my papers, "Early Stages of the Oedipus Conflict" (1928) and "The Importance of Symbol-Formation in the Development of the Ego" (1930).

CONTEMPORARY
CLASSICS

11

Gerald I. Fogel on William I. Grossman and Walter A. Stewart

A Postmodern Turn for Classical Metapsychology

GERALD I. FOGEL

Grossman and Stewart's classic 1976 paper, "Penis Envy: From Childhood Wish to Developmental Metaphor," accomplished several important things. Its manifest topic was a reexamination of the concept of penis envy from a classical psychoanalytic point of view. The paper was an important contribution to the emerging literature of the time that was soon to revolutionize contemporary views of the psychology of women.

The idea of a childhood fantasy as an organizing developmental metaphor was important as well—and also new in the classical literature. The authors may not have completely foreseen the full potential of this new theoretical tool for mainstream metapsychology. I have little doubt, however, that they knew how radical or strange such ideas might appear to the traditional analysts who were then their primary readers. Most of those analysts would have found the idea of a "metaphor" as a primary theoretical concept airy indeed, compared, say, to a "biological" instinctual drive or "objective" anatomical difference. In Grossman and Stewart's early use of what would become an important theoretical paradigm, anatomical metaphor, not merely anatomy, would be the new bedrock.

I see now that it was this new bridge between the past and future of classical psychoanalytic theory that accounted for much of my excitement when I first encountered the paper. The notion of ubiquitous childhood

sexual fantasies embedded in early bodily experience as inevitable core components of psychic life is as old as psychoanalysis. But suggesting that such
fantasies are psychological and social constructions, "organizers" that are
influenced and limited by, but never completely reducible to instinct or
anatomy, represents a postmodern, narrative turn for classical
metapsychology. In my introduction, I will therefore review not only the
paper's manifest topic, penis envy, but also this wider theoretical context,
one that takes us inevitably beyond the subject of a psychoanalytic psychology of women.

By the time Grossman and Stewart's paper appeared, the classical
Freudian concept of penis envy in women had already long been under siege,
for reasons that, in retrospect, seem obvious. The authors show how an
enlightened contemporary structural approach can make sense of the phenomena to which the concept of penis envy refers. Thus they make it possible not to throw out the baby (the apparent actual occurrence of fantasies
and wishes organized on the theme of envy of the penis in children and
adults) with the bathwater (the sexist and anatomically concrete or reduc-
tionistic ways that the concept had been understood and used in the past).
Their contemporary approach has both a theoretical and clinical aspect.

The theoretical aspect uses the concept of a fantasy based on the recognition of sexual differences as a developmental "organizer." There are
two childhood developmental stages where important (usually multiple)
issues can be "organized" (and condensed) around the theme of sexual difference. At an early stage, self–object differentiation, dependency issues,
preoedipal aggression, and narcissistic needs are central. Later comes a
stage where oedipal or triadic issues assume prominence. Such things as
inadequacy, shame, and low self-esteem, for example, or object hunger, disappointment in love relations, and regressive flight from sexuality or aggression can be organized and represented in a complexly layered,
overdetermined fantasy-metaphor, a defensive-adaptive compromise formation which "explains" the perceived lack or difficulty as a consequence of a
missing or inadequate penis. The point is, of course, that nothing is explained at all, since such an organizing metaphor can screen an infinite
variety of psychodynamic issues from varying developmental levels. Until
analyzed in a particular individual, one can say little at all analytically, not
even whether delusion and defense or individuation and adaptation are
mainly being served.

The clinical aspect demonstrates the grave dangers that exist for a
patient where there is an incorrect theory or clinical misapplication of an

(at least partially) correct one. Grossman and Stewart's case selection, as well as their implicit reproach of the former analysts of the two women whose analyses with the authors supplied their case material, demonstrates that penis envy is not inevitable in the psychology of women. For in both clinical cases, out of theoretical or countertransference limitations, the prior analysts had supplied their patients an "organizer" for what the authors refer to as "free floating envy," comprised of many individualized but as yet unanalyzed and unorganized components.

Thus, in these clinical examples, interpretations of penis envy had an "organizing effect, but not a therapeutic one" (Grossman and Stewart 1976, p. 194). These women had, in effect, been indoctrinated by the first analysts into the mistaken, dead-end belief, that their conflicts, problems, and bad feelings about themselves were rooted in concrete anatomical "bedrock," rather than family-induced and societally reinforced beliefs that were devaluing and self-defeating to themselves as persons and as women. In effect, their analysts had provided "proof" that their patients' feelings that they lacked something necessary for confidence, self-esteem, and psychic vitality were rooted in a reality that was "real"—anatomical, and therefore unchangeable.

Grossman and Stewart never take up the issue of whether or not penis envy is a common finding in the psychic life of girls or women, possibly a wise strategy at the time the paper was published. Ironically, severe preoedipal and narcissistic pathology may have partly accounted for the fact that neither of the women whose case material was presented in the paper brought to their analyses themselves any fantasies organized around the theme of penis envy. But clinical experience teaches us that such fantasies are not uncommon in normal and neurotic women—many of whom, of course, have high degrees of self integration, object constancy, and ego autonomy. In fact, these are the very patients who ordinarily are most likely to be engaged in successful analytic work. Such patients are more *organized*. They therefore are predisposed to organize the inevitable envy that arises developmentally in both sexes about perceived differences in relation to things that are actually different. Examples of such actual differences include differences between the generations and the sexes, and also the different *attitudes* regarding sexuality and sexual difference that are supplied by family and society as organizing structures. Unfortunately, these attitudes are often sexist and devaluing to women.

With the more damaged patients who are used as examples in this paper, the authors demonstrate how much early and permanent harm can be done by a parent or society that conveys devaluing sexist attitudes at an early or primitive stage of mental organization. Psychoanalysts can similarly take advantage of their power in the analytic situation to simply repeat that trauma. Analysts may still exist whose theories are so stereotypical, rigid, and sexist, but I would hope that few high-functioning women would tolerate these kinds of attitudes from such an analyst today. Unfortunately, there is always a danger that a more damaged and primitive patient in desperate need of organizing structure will be especially vulnerable to an authoritarian analyst who is willing to supply it.

It is plain to me that the general theoretical attitudes and clinical techniques based on them which Grossman and Stewart demonstrate in this landmark paper are widely applicable not only to all women, but also to all patients regardless of their actual sex—and not only to those who are primitive or whose psychodynamics contain penis envy. As I said earlier, it was this wider theoretical context that especially caught my attention when I first read the paper. So the personal significance of the paper to me—the excitement I felt reading it and its usefulness in my theoretical development—was determined by far more than its immediate subject. I was captivated by the concept of a fantasy as a developmental organizing metaphor. This concept was one that I had intuitively sensed as useful and interesting wherever I had found a psychoanalytically sophisticated application of it before. For example, an important stimulus of my initial interest in psychoanalysis was Erik Erikson's (1950) metaphorical expansion of Freudian psychosexuality into his eight developmental "ages of man." Erikson's imaginative synthesis of infantile drive and adult object relations, of personal and sociocultural, self and other, morality and aspiration, health and neurosis into such a stirring and rich vision of human nature was deeply grounded in classical Freudian metapsychology, and I found this vision profoundly inspiring, long before I considered myself a Freudian.

A similar spirit informs this paper, but in a way that focuses on analytic work with a single, unique individual. In such clinical work, recovery of early memories also blends bodily experience, bodily metaphor, a representational world comprised of self and other, a sociocultural milieu, and historical actuality to create the patient's own, living "developmental metaphors." Unlike Erikson's more broad generalizations, however, no two patient's developmental metaphors will ever be just alike. Though they might share certain formal characteristics, no two oedipal, castration, or mother complexes, separation-individuation crises, narcissistic vulnerabilities, or primal scenes will ever be exactly like someone else's. But, as Erikson does, these authors avoid both the danger of reduction to the concrete and material—anatomical and biological reduction—and the danger of fight into mere metaphor, which can sacrifice the unique historical actuality and bodily immediacy of the particular patient.

Take the following passage, for example:

> Her chronic panic was also illustrated by her fear of being close to or touched by her mother. One can say that she lived in a perpetual state of panic that she would be eaten, beaten, or penetrated. The fantasy of being radioactive, dangerous, and not to be touched was one defense. The other was to depersonalize. The alcoholism was a way of diminishing the panic, as was also the homosexuality, in which she took the male role, since men appeared to be less vulnerable. [Grossman and Stewart 1976, p. 203]

The psychic, bodily, and historical immediacy is obvious, yet a few sentences later, the authors explain that in this instance, "The interpretation of . . . penis envy exploited a metaphor, which seemed to represent both her fears and her defense against them. It created a type of delusional formation that brought order into her thoughts" (p. 203). Bodily metaphor is inevitable and ubiquitous where the inner life is truly brought alive, but can serve either fact or delusion, truth or defense.

The most important aspect of the paper for me was my recognition that in these authors' vision, metaphorical power and infantile sexuality combined in a way that transcended (although it did not deny) *anatomical* sexual difference. For a psychoanalyst, such factors play out in *psychic* reality, not material or so-called objective reality. For example, Grossman and Stewart (1976) state that penis envy, whether inferred or stated openly by the patient

> must be treated—like the manifest content of a dream or a screen memory—as a mental product. It is not to be regarded as an ultimate, irreducible, and even genetically necessary truth, impenetrable to further analysis. This is most obviously true in patients who come for analysis having interpreted their own dissatisfactions as "penis envy." It is particularly and more significantly true in patients such as ours, whose envy is conscious and where the narcissistic injury and fear of aggression are more central to the illness. In these cases, the 'wish for a penis' is but one highly condensed representation of these critical concerns. [p. 203]

The first time I read the paper, I had written in the margin next to that passage, "men too!"

In other words, this paper helped me see that the wish for a penis or "penis envy"—from a psychoanalyst's point of view—is always a wish for a *phallus*, which is itself a fantasy-metaphor, a symbolic fantasy-construction. Both men and women have longings for qualities in self and object that may be *represented* by an idealized "phallus." The longings and envy are directed not to a concrete, anatomical organ, but to what that organ comes to represent—whether to a patient, person, family of origin, or a whole culture. Therefore, whether in an individual or collective psyche, phallic aspirations, longings, and envy may sometimes include conscious or unconscious representations of the anatomical penis, sometimes not. Whether the anatomical penis is represented or not, the potential of such a fantasy to affirm or deny a patient's phallic aspirations cannot be known until it is fully analyzed. Naturally, phallic potentialities and vulnerabilities exist in both sexes, and models for identification or emulation in this regard may also be of either sex. Envy is ubiquitous in human development, and many other qualities and characteristics, and their anatomical or metaphorical correlates, are also objects for emulation or envy for both sexes.

In this paper, the authors speak of how an analyst sometimes does not know whether to take such fantasies and wishes in a concrete or a metaphorical sense. In a more recent paper, Grossman and Kaplan (1988) go further. They show that it is never psychoanalytic to think concretely or categorically about a patient's ideas about sexual anatomy or sexual difference, nor to reify childhood fantasies, however common their occurrence, into allegedly normal, fixed events or stages, confined to one sex or another.

What the authors could not see at the time they wrote of penis envy was that modern psychoanalysis would soon begin to regard such organizers of psychic experience as primary components of the human psyche—to conceive of "fantasy-metaphors" as elemental structures of the mind. Constructionist, representational theories of psychic structure and psychic reality introduce difficult problems for classical theory, but also free us from rigid, categorical, or sexist biological and anatomical conceptual constraints—they help us to enlarge our perspective and deepen our understanding of the sometimes quite ambiguous theoretical bonds that exist between anatomy and its psychic representations. No good Freudian wants to buy this welcome new freedom at the expense of our belief in the rootedness of psychic life in the realities of the body or material world;

these realms always provide contributing and limiting factors within which human meaning must operate in the construction of gender, self, and object world.

In my own work on male psychology (Fogel 1998) I have used ideas that build on these authors' seminal work in a similar attempt to integrate some of the findings of classical psychoanalytic ego psychology, object relations theory, and contemporary hermeneutic, linguistic, and feminist studies. I consider, for example, how recent advances in psychoanalytic understandings of women might be relevant to the psychology of men. Many recent studies demonstrate that the developmental evolution of women's experiences of their bodies and bodily integrity are linked to interiority—built upon organizing developmental metaphors which attach to early, psychosexually alive experiences of the inside of her body. Such experiences contribute to full psychosexual genitality, selfhood, and capacities for high-level object relating. In other words, strengths and vulnerabilities are observable in adult women that are "genital," postambivalent, triadic, yet conceptually separable from what we ordinarily call "phallic," as in phallic-oedipal. Since both men and women have an inside and an outside, if we give castration anxiety a postmodern twist, we have a new way to link higher level castration fears to full genitality in both sexes.

To do this, we need only demonstrate the obvious fact that men, like women, have an psychically and psychosexually alive inside as well as an outside. By analogy, their inner genital experience can be attacked and compromised ("castrated") just like a woman's. Further, as women do, men often have envy dynamics organized around regressive fantasy conceptions of an idealized phallus. Culture and anatomy predispose many of us, men and women, to take at face value the idea that "space" and "spaces" in either sex represent something missing or inferior. But, as with women, a fantasied, sexually alive inner space or opening need not mean that something "phallic" is missing or inadequate. The "space" may be something that is there, that contains power and potential of its own. The subject is human nature and higher mental organizations, not just the differences between the sexes. Just as a woman has a metaphorical "phallus," and therefore phallic powers and potentials that may evolve developmentally, a man has an analogous inner genital space with its correlative powers. Interiority and realization of full psychic potential require emancipation of such powers and their integration in higher mental organizations. The mature, embodied forms of such "feminine" powers include receptivity and openness, as well as groundedness, connectedness, and a tolerance of ambiguity.

Perhaps we can say that Grossman and Stewart's theoretical conception of an organizing fantasy as a developmental metaphor bridges and potentially integrates the best of the old theory and the most promising of the new. The venerated ancestor of the developmental metaphor concept in psychoanalysis is the compromise formation, substitutive structure, or screen memory. Like any screen or dream, such a mental structure may either reveal or conceal truth. Modern narrative and language theory posits pre- and protosymbolic language and gender templates that are hardwired into the human psyche—categories for the representation, construction, and reconstruction of gender, sex, and self. In this paradigm, even a universal fantasy or developmental metaphor—one that combines the actualities of the body and early object relations with what the human imagination is capable of making of it—can, like a screen or mask, both reveal and conceal a patient's own psychic truth. Thus, the authors' seminal contribution not only showed us a new way to look at penis envy, but also built a bridge that retained useful concepts from our psychoanalytic theoretical past and useful new conceptual tools to move us into our theoretical future—all without sacrificing either or reducing one to the terms of the other. No more can be asked of a classic.

REFERENCES

Erikson, E. (1950). *Childhood and Society*. New York: Norton.

Fogel, G. (1998). Interiority and inner genital space in men: what else can be lost in castration. *Psychoanalytic Quarterly*, October.

Grossman, W., and Kaplan, D. (1988). Three commentaries on gender in Freud's thought: a prologue to the psychoanalytic theory of sexuality. In *Fantasy, Myth, and Reality*, ed. H. Blum, Y. Kramer, A. K. Richards, and A. D. Richards, pp. 193–212. New York: International Universities Press.

Grossman, W. I., and Stewart, W. A. (1996). Penis envy: from childhood wish to developmental metaphor. *Journal of the American Psychoanalytic Association* 24:193–212.

Penis Envy: From Childhood Wish to Developmental Metaphor

WILLIAM I. GROSSMAN AND
WALTER A. STEWART

None of Freud's theories of female sexuality and psychology has been subject to more severe criticism than his concept of penis envy. The persisting controversy over this issue suggests that the basic theoretical questions have not yet been clarified. And because the theory lacks clarity, its clinical application does not always produce the results expected. Our presentation centers on two such instances, offering clinical vignettes wherein problems in the interpretation of penis envy are demonstrated.

Both patients were in second analyses. In both first analyses, because the patients expressed envy of men and an inability to accept femininity, both analysts interpreted the unconscious penis envy to their patients. Both patients accepted the interpretation with apparent conviction, yet the analyses became stalemated. Freud's (1937) famous dictum that, ". . . with the wish for a penis and the masculine protest we have penetrated through all the psychological strata and have reached bedrock, and thus our activities are at an end" (p. 252) seemed at first to have been vindicated.

Neither of the second analyses, however, confirmed this view. In the second analyses of both patients it became clear that the central conflicts involved a sense of identity, narcissistic sensitivity, and problems of aggression. These conflicts were expressed in terms of a general envy, a sense of worthlessness, inadequacy, damage, and deprivation. The patients apparently easily accepted the reductionism of the interpretation of penis envy in the first analyses primarily because it fitted into their own tendency toward this type of understanding. They regularly explained any unhappiness they experienced as due to some unfair deprivation. This led, of course, to a constant state of envy. The inexact interpretation (Glover 1931)—or at least the incomplete interpretation—of their penis envy reinforced their sense of being defective and deprived and increased their sense of injustice.

As we hope to show in our clinical examples, *the interpretation had an organizing effect, but not a therapeutic one*. The interpretation, in our view, functioned like a delusion: it brought order into what was otherwise a type of "free-floating envy" or a ready tendency to become envious. The idea of a wish for a missing and unobtainable organ provided a concrete and understandable explantation for dissatisfaction.

CASE PRESENTATIONS

The first patient, Mrs. A., diagnostically a narcissistic character, began her first analysis when she was 21 years old, shortly after she had graduated from college. In the last few months of her college career she had developed an obsessional concern with the meaning of words. This symptom, plus an intense shyness and depression, led to her treatment. She was the first child, four years older than her sister. She described her father as a shy man, successful in business and impatient with and critical of women. He was undemonstrative and objected to being touched. He patronized women and disliked what he considered their hyperemotionality. He was a chronic tease. The patient wanted to impress him and often entered into long, aimless arguments with him, which ended in her feeling defeated and running away in tears. Her mother was preoccupied with appearances and hid her anxiety under an aggressive, dominating façade. Insensitive to the feelings of others and often given to sudden enthusiasms for various lifestyles, she was self-indulgent and was indulged by her husband. Both drank considerably, and dinner often ended in angry recriminations.

The mother constantly criticized the patient for her shyness, her poor posture, and general awkwardness. The mother found these faults particularly irritating because she set such high value on popularity and social success. She liked to recall her social life abroad and recount the number of proposals she had had. Neither the father nor the mother felt there was any reason for a woman to acquire an education; they had no intellectual interests and never had any open discussions about ideas.

The avenue toward a successful feminine development was partly closed by the patient's feeling she couldn't compete with her mother. The mother's craving to be indulged and her self-indulgences meant she wanted to have and had all the advantages of being fed and catered to that belong to babyhood.

Little is known about the first analysis except that the analyst felt that the patient's penis envy was the central issue. In fact, it became so central an obsessional preoccupation that the patient seriously considered going to Denmark for a transsexual operation in which she expected the transplant of a penis could be accomplished. This bizarre response notwithstanding, the patient appeared to have benefited from the first analysis. For the first time in her life she was seeing a man her parents found acceptable. Partly to gain their further approval, she impulsively decided to marry him. Because of this decision and with some satisfaction with the apparent improvement, the analyst decided to terminate the analysis—a decision the patient accepted. The analyst later mentioned to one of us that he felt pleased that the analysis had led the patient to give up her bohemian ways and to marry a respectable man of her own class.

After the marriage, the patient adopted the role of the upper-middle-class "devoted wife and mother with healthy outside interests." This role-playing did not prevent her from becoming progressively more depressed and dissatisfied. She returned to analysis for short periods of time over the next ten years. Her dissatisfaction finally reached such a pitch, she wanted to separate from her husband. She felt he was totally self-absorbed and that their sexual life was an empty ritual. She decided to re-enter analysis, and, because her first analyst was not available, he referred her to one of us.

In the first few sessions she complained that her husband dominated all social gatherings so that by comparison she felt totally unimportant and neglected. He became an overnight expert on a wide variety of subjects, particularly any in which she showed an interest.

In retrospect, she felt the marriage had been a mistake, that she had married because her analyst seemed to approve. She recalled that soon after the termination she felt a sense of surprise and anger that the relationship with the analyst had ended. It seemed that in her mind the marriage was meant to make her more acceptable to the analyst; that he would continue to see her, protect her, and recognize her true but hidden values. Later she came to feel that she had too readily and indiscriminately accepted the interpretation that she wanted a penis.

Mrs. A. was a shy woman who spoke in clichés. She tended to see all issues in black or white, and as having cosmic implications which were not clear to her. Similarity implied an identity, and difference of tastes, opinions, or interests implied a total misfit. Because she disliked a picture in the analyst's waiting room, she felt she and her analyst were so different and incompatible that he would never understand her or be able to analyze her. She saw herself as a radical and a feminist and felt her difficulties stemmed primarily from the social discrimination against women. She saw the analyst as an uncritical disciple of Freud's who would only see her social protests as penis envy and would attempt to influence her to return to the kitchen and find fulfillment in submission to a man. She felt that, if she agreed to anything the analyst said, she would have to agree to everything.

It became apparent that she had taken the interpretation of her "penis envy" in the first analysis simply as the "proof" of her worthlessness. She had not seen it as an interpretation, but rather as an accusation and a confirmation of her worst fears that she was in fact hopeless and worthless. To the extent that she admired any quality in a man, she became depressed and felt despair. The only solution she could envisage was that she should admit and accept her degraded state.

Her emotional responses were positive and negative extremes. Her affection became infatuation, her admiration, idealization. In the analysis, her sense of worthlessness and her need for love and admiration were central issues. She was rivalrous with and envied both men and women.

The admiration–rivalry conflict reminded her of her feelings for a male cousin who lived with the family when she was in her early teens. She loved and admired him and was impressed by the fact that he could go to the village and date girls there. She looked up to him, but felt he could never be interested in her. She felt awkward, shy, and inarticulate in his presence. This awe of men was still present when she entered the second analysis. She admired men "who could travel to Chicago on business." The patient's awe of men and her sense of relative worthlessness led to the analysis of her masochistic trends, which took the form of spanking fantasies and fantasies of anal rape. The focus of her complaints about being a woman dealt more with the fear of humiliation and ridicule than with the sense of castration—that is, anal and masochistic features were the most prominent. Since admiration always led to rivalry and envy, and sexual interest to aggression, the only permanent tie to the object was of a sadomasochistic nature. She chose the masochistic role and the defense of a mild paranoid attitude. Indeed, the "helpless acceptance" of the penis envy interpretation in the first analysis seemed masochistically gratifying.

Even to interpret her masochism posed the threat that the interpretation would be experienced as a "put-down" and gratify her masochistic impulse; all interpretations, if not narcissistically gratifying, gratified masochistic wishes. They were felt as attacks in which her worthlessness, her defectiveness, and her aggression were unmasked. The analysis threatened to become interminable, one in which the relationship to the analyst was maintained, but only at the price of an analytic stalemate.

Over many years the patient was able to recognize her need to be a mistreated little girl, rather than to face her disappointments as a grown woman. The emphasis on the male–female dichotomy gradually lessened and focused more on the problem of her status. As she increasingly experienced the positive values in being a woman rather than a victimized child, she became less clinging, more outgoing, and her sense of humor increased. The sadistic impulses behind the masochistic submission have become clear to the patient. Finally, interpretations were experienced as illuminating and helpful. The case is now in a terminable phase.

In summary, the issue of wanting a penis never came up in that form. Rather, the conflict appeared more widely narcissistic in terms involving the patient's importance and value, although it was expressed chiefly in terms of the disadvantages of being a woman. When, in the first analysis, an interpretation of her penis envy was offered, she took the interpretation quite literally and concretistically, as shown by her plan to go to Denmark for a transsexual operation. Her envy of men was only one aspect of an envy that dominated her life. Her complaints were that in all situations she had been cheated. Her sister got her mother's breast. Her mother had the baby, was loved and indulged by the father, and had everyone's love and admiration, even the patient's. Mrs. A. felt doomed to be the one who has nothing, and has no claim to love or fame.

She could not do what many of our patients can do: see the emotions and experiences that lie behind this way of expressing their conflicts. *As analysts we may also on occasion have similar difficulties in knowing how concretely the metaphors of development are to be understood.*

Our second case, Mrs. B., a 28-year-old married secretary, had begun her analysis with a woman analyst. She stated, with seeming unconcern, that she was homosexual and alcoholic. She subsequently reported a doll phobia. She had been married for one and a half years when she confessed her homosexual interests and activities to her husband. He insisted she see the family physician, who referred her for analysis.

The patient was the oldest of three children and the only girl. Her brothers were two and half and five years younger. The father was an angry, anxious man. The patient said that if he looked at a lovely view, the only thing that caught his attention would be the garbage dump. The mother was a flirtatious woman, the life of the party. She paid little attention to the patient except when the father was away, when she would take the patient into bed with her. The patient recalled lying in "spoon position" next to her, stiff with fear. Mrs. B. had had almost no direct contact with the father, all communications being routed through the mother. The father's father had been an improvident man with many get-rich-quick schemes. She recalled with a great sense of loss and guilt that he had taken her sledding, caught pneumonia, and died. She had felt she would be accused of murder. This grandfather had three children, the patient's father being the youngest. There were two older sisters, both of whom had been promiscuous, possibly prostitutes, and certainly alcoholic. The father held up his sisters as bad examples of what would happen to the patient if she ever did anything of which he disapproved.

During adolescence, she recalled "playing dead," for a long period of time and frightening her playmates. She also remembered cutting her wrists, which she claimed was in order to get attention, thinking it was the equivalent of the injuries boys got when they played football. She had always had the wish and expectation of becoming a priest, ignoring the fact that, at that time, this was not possible. She had consciously wished to be a boy because boys had greater freedom and companionship. Her dreams had a bizarre quality and were full of injuries and bleeding. In one dream she became radioactive and was therefore a threat to all who came near her. In another dream a young man had his tongue cut out.

The first analyst felt the patient was identified with men and that she was pretending to be a man. When asked if she really wanted to be a man, the patient replied, yes, she did, but then added, "Of course, not consciously." She felt her brothers were better off, being stronger, able to win medals and admiration. A dream stating that "All people should have medals that no one was stupid!," along with other material, convinced the first analyst that the patient resented being the "only one in the family who did not get a penis."

The first analyst interpreted the patient's penis envy to her. The patient quickly agreed that this was the issue and, in fact, the only reason for her coming into analysis. Since her wish could not be fulfilled, there was no point in her continuing the analysis. A sadomasochistic impasse developed in which the patient felt the analyst treated her as if she were a criminal. In response, the patient refused to listen to anything the analyst said or to tell her anything meaningful about herself. This was the situation after one year; in the face of this impasse, she was referred to one of us.

Mrs. B. was a short, stocky woman who looked younger than her stated age. She was obviously under great tension, which she handled by acting in a pseudo-tough manner. When asked about her feelings at suddenly being transferred to a new analyst, she said she felt it was "just in time," and that she was "lucky to get out alive." She "interpreted" this to mean that in her "unconscious she must be murderously angry," and then added, "but this is only one interpretation . . . there may be others."

It was apparent that in the first analysis Mrs. B. had experienced all interpretations, including the one of penis envy, as accusations and as an assault. During her second analysis she recalled that her younger brother by two and a half years had had severe colic as a baby and had cried constantly. On one particular occasion, he was left to "cry it out" in the patient's room. She recalled being afraid of her wish to strangle him. When he finally stopped crying and fell asleep, she was afraid he was dead or, even more frightening, that he had crawled out of his crib and was snaking across the floor, creeping toward her with the intention of eating her up.

Her dreams and associations suggested that she was the illegitimate daughter of one of the father's sisters. This suspicion was confirmed, and then the fact of her extraordinary early neglect emerged. Her biological mother, the more delinquent of the two sisters, had been totally incapable of taking care of her. The patient had been so severely neglected, she had to be hospitalized in a starved condition. She remained in a Catholic home between the ages of 14 and 18 months. In an eerie manner she recalled a number of experiences from this time, and one particularly traumatic event. She recalled an evening when a child in the crib next to her was crying inconsolably. She refused to stay down in the crib and had to be tied down. When the patient woke next morning, she saw that the girl in the crib had died, having suffocated in her own vomitus. This was the incident screened by the memory of the brother's crying and was the major contributing experience to her doll phobia.

The diagnostic category of borderline seemed quite clear when she reported that she bathed each evening because she might meet the analyst in her dreams. This type of thinking also illustrated the patient's inability to distinguish between the reality of an experience and its possible symbolic meaning. On one occasion, when at the beach with her nieces, she wanted to keep them warm by wrapping the terry cloth robe she was wearing around them. She felt she could not do this because it would signal her wish to be pregnant and she couldn't afford to let anyone know of this.

In the analysis, the central issue was the patient's fear of aggression. The pseudo-tough demeanor and the conscious wish to be a man were her defenses against her fear of the man's aggression. This in turn was based, of course, on the projection of her own aggressive and destructive impulses which she quite correctly felt she couldn't control. As a consequence she was constantly tense, frightened, and on guard. When her mother once asked about her analysis and if her analyst was handsome, the patient had a fantasy that the mother would storm into the analyst's office, break up the furniture, and either kill or seduce the analyst.

The patient's "wish to be a man" was in part a response to her father's feeling that most women were dirty and unable to exert any self-control. It was also an effort to overcome some envy of her brothers. Of much more significance was the role of the "penis envy" as a defense against castration. In regard to the man's phallic aggression, penis envy represented an identification with the aggressor. But the patient was afraid of impulses from all stages of psychosexual development. She was perhaps most afraid of being devoured and of her own cannibalistic impulses. These fears were based, of course, on the early neglect and frequent abandonment. The early neglect contributed to poor ego boundaries and poor self–object differentiation. The consequent projective identification is clear—in her fear of her brother's cannibalistic impulse, the aggressive sexuality of all men, and the firm belief that she was lucky to have "gotten away alive" from her first analyst. Her chronic panic was also illustrated by her fear of being close to or touched by her mother. One can say that she lived in a perpetual state of panic that she would be eaten, beaten, or penetrated. The fantasy of being radioactive, dangerous, and not to be touched was one defense. The other was to depersonalize. The alcoholism was a way of diminishing the panic, as was also the homosexuality, in which she took the male role, since men appeared to be less vulnerable.

The interpretation of the penis envy exploited a metaphor, which seemed to represent both her fears and her defense against them. It created a type of delusional formation that brought order into her thoughts. It is reminiscent of Schreber's (Freud 1911) delusional system, which also involved homosexuality and self-transformation, and which was intended to act as a defense against aggression.

These two cases help to explain why a woman's "wish for a penis" or "envy of the penis," whether inferred and interpreted as an unconscious wish during analysis or stated openly by the patient, must be treated—like the manifest content of a dream or a screen memory—as a mental product. It is not to be regarded as an ultimate, irreducible, and even genetically necessary truth, impenetrable to further analysis. This is most obviously true in patients who come for analysis having interpreted their own dissatisfactions as "penis envy." It is particularly and more significantly true in patients such as ours, whose envy is conscious and where the narcissistic injury and fear of aggression are more central to the illness. In these cases, the "wish for a penis" is but one highly condensed representation of these critical concerns. We have been told of other cases in which the interpretation was made that what the patient "really wanted was a penis, a penis of her own," in which the envy of men hid a sense of deprivation, worthlessness, and fear of abandonment. These feelings and the experiences that led to them were the critical issue. The interpretation of penis envy, even when it referred to real experiences, reduced the multiple sources of dissatisfaction to a single cause. Whether intentionally or unintentionally, a clinical metaphor was thus created.

DISCUSSION

For over fifty years the role of penis envy in feminine psychosexual development and in pathology has been questioned. For Freud, the discovery of the anatomical distinction between the sexes marked the real beginning, or more accurately, the nodal point, in the differences between male and female psychosexual development. He regarded libidinal development prior to this moment as essentially similar in boys and in girls and did not concern himself with other factors—for example, the effect on development of the different ways in which parents treat their sons and daughters. Freud may not have recognized the importance of these particular environmental determinants in psychosexual development or, more likely, he may have been primarily interested in reconstructing the *typical* ways in which the child's distorted understanding of reality influenced his development. In any event, he seems to have focused on the route by which object relations developed out of narcissism and how the succession of libidinal goals resulted from the transformation of instincts. He saw the little girl's observation of a penis as marking a turning point in her psychosexual development, observing that girls react to this discovery with a feeling of damage, deprivation, and envy. Their response is a narcissistic injury and an envy that is concerned with genital differences and often focuses on the penis. Freud felt the wish for a penis had to be transformed into a wish for a baby if normal feminine development was to be accomplished. More precisely, he stated that the wish for a penis added to the wish for a child, which originated in other sources (1917, 1933). The optimal solution to the penis–baby transformation, in Freud's view, was one of the *forces* that led to the change from the girl's preoedipal attachment to the mother to the oedipal attachment to the father.

Freud's formulation of the girl's development was based on a comparative approach to the development of both boys and girls. It seemed to highlight the ubiquitous factors common to both sexes (Freud 1931), while sharply contrasting the differences entailed in the development of masculinity and femininity. Freud's examination of early female sexuality led him to emphasize certain aspects of the preoedipal period. He stressed the role of early disappointment, narcissistic injury, fixation, and penis envy in the development of women's psychosexual pathology. He thought that the failure to resolve in an optimal way the developmental challenges posed by penis envy would of necessity impair the change of object and the change of leading genital zone. Character disorders, neurosis, genital inhibition, and the rejection of femininity would almost inevitably be the result.

In contrast to these views was a series of papers by Horney which led to an apparently irreconcilable difference between the two. She (1967) acknowledged an early "narcissistic" penis envy, but discounted its importance in pathology. In her view, penis envy did not promote development, but was the result of the girl's disappointment in her naturally developing attachment to her father. Penis envy could help to repress the little girl's fears of penetration of the vagina by the large penis of the father. Horney's approach thus had the value of pointing to the need to clarify the origins of penis envy, its defensive function, and its role in early object relations.

We shall not pursue here the ramifications of this interesting controversy. The important point for clinical and theoretical understanding of penis envy is that we need to resolve the false antithesis generated by the apparent disagreement. "Penis envy" and the "denial of the vagina," "early narcissistic injury" and "disappointment in object relations," are different facets of the same issues of normal and pathological development. The overemphasis of one facet or the other promotes the tendency to reductionism in clinical interpretation, as occurred in the first analysis of each of the patients we presented.

Freud and Horney agreed that penis envy could occur during development on a narcissistic basis and as a result of oedipal disappointment. They differed with regard to which type was more important for pathology. The differing views can be reconciled with an epigenetic approach, an approach that enables us to recognize that the child's awareness of the genital differences is an important organizer of experiences at many levels of psychic differentiation and integration (Grossman 1976).

We suggest that, of the two distinctly recognizable phases (see Greenacre 1953), in the earlier phase, the awareness of the genital differences becomes meaningful in terms of the child's sense of her worth and in terms of her attempt to differentiate herself from her mother. Narcissistic needs and self–object differentiation are then the critical developmental issues (Galenson and Roiphe 1976, Mahler 1975, Mahler et al. 1975). In the later phase, the relationships to both parents as a function of the sexual difference is the important issue and leads to the familiar fantasies of the phallic stage and the oedipal period; conflicts having to do with object relations and drive impulses are central, along with the formation of the ego ideal and superego. Once the genital differences are discovered, and once penis envy appears, the latter becomes enmeshed in those relations that give it meaning. The working out of the oedipal relations will have an important influence in determining to what extent both conscious and unconscious penis envy come to stand as the representation of earlier and later conflicts.

Thus, to the child, the meaning of the discovery of the "anatomical distinction" will depend on a complex variety of preparatory experiences. The timing of this discovery will be important, since the child's cognitive and libidinal levels will naturally play a part in his interpretation of this new information. Narcissistic conflicts and the child's relations to both parents will determine the final result. Parental attitudes toward the sex of the child, toward their own genitals and sexual relationships, will aid or disrupt the child's integration of the awareness of the genital differences.

We think the awareness of the importance of these factors, which is forced upon us by the clinical examples we have presented, helps to resolve some current criticisms of the penis-envy concept.

Finally, it follows from our discussion that, in the clinical setting, the emergence of "penis envy" must be treated as a manifest content, the significance of which will only emerge in the analysis. Narcissistically fixated patients, for example, when they confront the fact of the genital differences, will experience this awareness as a further narcissistic injury. To narcissistically oriented patients, "penislessness" can at any time in the psychosexual development become a prime example of deprivation, and they experience this in the same way as when they were 18 months old. A severe disturbance in the narcissistic development will create a traumatic vulnerability to the discovery of the genital differences and to all experiences of deprivation. Thus, the primal scene, too, will be traumatic because, as another instance of stimulation without gratification or resolution, it is experienced as a narcissistic affront.

Clinically, the problem is to distinguish penis envy as it represents an attempted regressive solution to oedipal conflicts from penis envy as part of a general narcissistic character disorder. As in the cases we have presented, the penis envy is apt to be merely one means of representing the narcissistic injuries of all levels of development.

Whether penis envy is, in a particular instance, a contributing factor in the development of narcissistic character pathology, or whether it is a consequence of this pathology or otherwise implicated in it, the attendant ego disturbances present technical problems. We have observed other patients similar to those presented and have recognized certain factors making the analysis of "penis envy" difficult. Commonly found factors include global identifications and the associated fears of merging and abandonment, domination–submission conflicts, fear of overwhelming aggression, masochistic fantasies, primitive defenses, and extreme sensitivity to narcissistic injury. Patients with narcissistic character disorders also responded in a remarkably similar way to any interpretation of "penis envy" or their "wish for a penis" in particular. They seemed unable to distinguish fantasy, metaphor, or symbolic representation from reality. This is very clear in Mrs. B.'s fear of warming her nieces by wrapping them in the terry cloth bathrobe she was wearing—not permissable because it meant a wish to be pregnant. The original wish to warm the children was totally ignored because the symbolic meaning of the act became the only "reality."

The patients clearly did not respond to the interpretation of their "penis envy" in a way that was useful to them. They heard it as a final immutable truth. Although they readily agreed to the interpretation, it was with a feeling of despair—for it confirmed their worst fears of being worthless.

Is the problem of interpretation one of technique, in the sense that the interpretation was, for example, incorrect or poorly timed? Or is the stalemate that occurred in these cases due to a lack of clarity in our clinical theory?

We believe that the interpretation of the penis envy was correct in the sense that it described the patient's defensive effort toward the resolution of an inner conflict, and, yet, in some sense it must be incorrect, since it was not helpful (mutative) to the patient.

Perhaps the issue can be more clearly seen from another perspective. We wish to focus on the way theoretical constructs and developmental models are sometimes applied to clinical situations. Certainly, examples such as ours can serve only as illustrations. Furthermore, our understanding of these cases can be enriched if countertransference and other technical problems are considered as well. Still, there is a problem of the application to interpretation and reconstruction of theory and developmental understanding. The analyst's understanding of his patient is informed by psychoanalytic theory, especially conceptions of drive and defense and their role in development. We have a shorthand for describing patients' conflicts that we use in presenting cases, and penis envy is part of that shorthand. When we speak of penis envy we may be referring to a number of things simultaneously, including experiences, fantasies, wishes, derivatives, and so on. In this sense, then, the concept of penis envy may be said to be a metaphor belonging to the theory, since the concept derives its name from a specific experience. To classify clinical material under the heading of penis envy is to "interpret" the case, according to one way we use the word interpretation.

What about the patient's "wish for a penis"? It may be conscious from the start of treatment as an intellectualization. It may, as in the cases presented, be a conscious wish as the result of a prior analysis. In that instance, it needs to be analyzed, for it is a conscious mental content whose unconscious meaning must be understood.

We are suggesting that in these cases, the analysts lent the patients their theoretical metaphor and the patients accepted it. In these cases, too much that was important in the patient's conflicts was condensed under this heading. For them, the metaphor was an apt one in that it represented one of their desires and sources of dissatisfaction. However, the wish for a penis was not their own developmentally derived metaphor, their own unconscious shorthand for representing their childhood disappointments. Nor was the disappointment over the discovery of the genital difference the starting point of the derivatives later to be interpreted as penis envy. The misapplication of the theoretical metaphor to the clinical situation was a confusion of theory and clinical situation which reduced the patient's conflicts to the "bedrock" of a concretely apprehended metaphor. We believe that, in development as well, the wish for a penis may also become the unconscious, concretely apprehended metaphor for childhood disappointments that are associated with the recognition of the genital difference.

The tendency to use theoretical formulations directly in clinical interpretations, in a sense, like a theoretical cliché, undoubtedly arises with the failure of clinical understanding. It is a misuse of theory that is common and to which theory easily lends itself. The analyst may then explain his lack of success as due to the fact that the interpretation involves the "bedrock" wish, or that there is faulty reality testing, a thought disorder, or other defect. Thus he explains the "immutability" of the wish.

The interpretation of the patient's wish for a penis is correct in that it makes conscious the metaphoric representation of the conflict. It offers a frame of reference from which the patient can look at the experience. It is incorrect as a clinical interpretation because it forces a theoretical impersonal form onto the material. It has only an organizing function; nor a therapeutic one. This miscarriage of the purpose of an interpretation seems to have characterized the analytic approach in the first analyses of the patients presented.

Some patients, primarily those with neurotic conflicts, are not misled by the metaphor and will make the interpretation meaningful and therapeutic. These patients, quite unlike the category of patients our examples illustrate, generally resist the interpretation at first. Indeed, it takes hard and time-consuming analytic work to convince the neurotic patient that the unconscious fantasy of possessing a penis is derived from childhood, but is active as a determinant of her current life activities and the nature of her object relations. We think these clinical differences can be accounted for if the early narcissistic syndromes of penis envy are distinguished from the later object-related forms.

We believe this distinction rests on and also supports the theoretical formulations presented earlier in the paper. Finally, we hope the theoretical distinction helps in understanding why the early controversy concerning penis envy and the current criticisms of the concept have not been resolved.

SUMMARY

Two phases of penis envy are considered. The first regularly occurs early in development and is registered as a narcissistic injury which can be resolved under optimal conditions and can contribute to female psychosexual development. If, however, it is not favorably resolved or, even more significantly, if the basic character disorder is of a narcissistic type, the awareness of the genital difference becomes one of the many narcissistic traumas.

A later phase of penis envy usually represents a regressive effort to resolve oedipal conflicts. In the past, these two phase-oriented forms of penis envy have not been adequately distinguished.

Two clinical examples are presented in which the envy of men was only part of a tendency to envy in a narcissistic character disorder. In the analysis, the interpretation of the penis envy offered a metaphor around which all of the "free-floating" envy could coalesce. The cases illustrate the necessity to consider penis envy as the manifest content of a symptom that needs analysis, rather than as "bedrock" or ultimate conflict.

REFERENCES

Freud, S. (1911). Psychoanalytic notes upon an autobiographical account of a case of paranoia. *Standard Edition* 12:3–82.

———— (1917). On transformations of instinct as exemplified in anal eroticism. *Standard Edition* 17:126–133.

———— (1931). Female sexuality. *Standard Edition* 21:225–243.

———— (1933). Femininity. *Standard Edition* 22:112–135.

———— (1937). Analysis terminable and interminable. *Standard Edition* 23:216–253.

Galenson, E., and Roiphe, H. (1976). Some suggested revisions concerning early female development. *Journal of the American Psychoanalytic Association* 24(5):29–57.

Glover, E. (1931). The therapeutic effect of inexact interpretation: a contribution to the theory of suggestion. *International Journal of Psycho-Analysis* 12:397–411.

Greenacre, P. (1953). Penis awe and its relation to penis envy. In: *Drives, Affects, Behavior*, ed. R. M. Loewenstein, pp. 176–190. New York: International Universities Press.

Grossman, W. I. (1976). Discussion on "Freud and Female Sexuality." *International Journal of Psycho-Analysis* 57:301–311.

Horney, K. (1967). *Feminine Psychology*, ed. H. Kelman. New York: Norton.

Mahler, M. S. (1975). *Discussion of "Some suggested revisions concerning early female development" by E. Galenson and H. Roiphe.* Presented at the New York Psychoanalytic Society, February 11.

Mahler, M. S., Pine, F., and Bergman, A. (1975). *The Psychological Birth of the Human Infant.* New York: Basic Books.

12

Owen Renik on
Elizabeth Lloyd Mayer

Empiricism and Clinically Relevant Theory Building

OWEN RENIK

The term *classic*, as applied to psychoanalytic papers, has been cheapened by overuse. It should refer only to truly original contributions whose utility remain undiminished over time. Mayer's article is an example par excellence of a classic on the subject of the psychology of women. We are presented with a striking, previously unreported observation concerning girls' psychological development. Mayer reflects upon the data she has collected and comes up with an important theoretical innovation. She goes on to use the new theory she has developed to illuminate a ubiquitous clinical phenomenon in a way that is directly helpful in creating avenues for therapeutically beneficial analytic work with women patients.

There is special satisfaction in the fact that the bit of child observation with which Mayer begins is not fundamentally gender-specific. It reflects the narcissism of all children, male and female, who at first believe that "Everybody must be just like me."

> Emily, a bright little girl of 20 months, for the first time commented on the matter of sexual differences to her mother with the following series of remarks. "Mummy," she began, "*Mummy* has a bottom . . . and Mummy, *Daddy* has a bottom . . . and Mummy, *Emily* has a bottom." Emily's mother assented to each of these observations and Emily thoughtfully continued, "And *Mummy* has a vulva . . . and *Emily* has a

vulva . . . but Mummy, Daddy has something *funny* in his vulva!" [Mayer 1985, p. 331]

From this charming vignette Mayer draws conclusions that permit us to identify specific, concrete, and clinically consequential manifestations of the important concept of *primary femininity*. Mayer points to the overlooked importance of a young girl's *external genitalia* as a much-valued aspect of her developing body image. It follows from the fact that girls can know and value their external genitalia that they can experience *female castration anxiety*, that is, a fear that these visible, important sexual parts might be lost or damaged.

Mayer's conception of female castration anxiety is a crucial psychoanalytic theoretical breakthrough. Psychoanalysts have long been familiar with women's concerns about damage to their internal genitalia, but those anxieties pertain to body parts which remain ill-defined—indeed, often unknown—until relatively late in development. Because they can only be known and represented ambiguously, a girl's internal genitalia alone cannot possibly function as the clear and definite, cherished foundation of her body image and gender identity (as do penis and testicles for a boy). Common psychoanalytic wisdom, even in the era of feminist revision, has been that girls are different than boys in that girls' sexual self-images depend entirely upon a sense of inner space—wonderful and mysterious but necessarily vague—whereas boys' sexual self-images are based more clearly and definitively upon images of external body parts.

Mayer exposes this assumption as a sexist misunderstanding. She reminds us that the female genitalia include external and visible, as well as internal and invisible, components, and reminds us that this complete genital representation becomes incorporated into a developing girl's body image. In so doing Mayer helps us understand that female castration anxiety is not an imitation of male castration anxiety (fear of loss of an illusory penis) but a fear in the girl that her primary femininity will be harmed. In other words, Mayer suggests that girls value themselves and worry about loss of what they value exactly as boys do. The implications of Mayer's point affect long-standing psychoanalytic notions about women's susceptibility to depression, so-called normal masochism in women, and related issues.

The next step that Mayer takes relates to defenses against female castration anxiety:

A number of female patients have reiterated to me a view of men in which certain stereotypic features recur: men, these women assert, are *emotionally closed, unable to be receptive or empathic, and without access to inner feelings or inner sensations.* [emphasis added] The absolutism of these characterizations, their repetitiveness, their frequency, and the stubborn determination with which they are retained, have struck me as requiring explanation. As I have investigated such women's characterizations of men, I have been impressed that certain themes recur. *In brief: these women are determined to believe that men are lacking something crucial; they associate the missing something with what are explicitly described as "feminine" capacities*; [emphasis added] these women are at some level deeply anxious about their own capacities to be feminine; and they ultimately report versions of a fantasy that the capacity to be *genitally open* is a capacity that can be endangered, can be lost, and indeed *has* been quite literally lost by the male sex. Their characterizations of men as emotionally closed appear to represent derivatives of an unconscious conviction that men have actually been closed over genitally, and that men therefore represent the frightening possibility that such a thing could really happen to a woman. [Mayer 1985, pp. 331–332]

Here Mayer gives us new insight into a kind of contempt that certain women have for men, a female chauvinism that corresponds exactly to the well-known male version. Any psychoanalytic clinician is familiar with this costly and destructive symptomatic attitude, harbored by some women patients. Mayer helps us understand that the need to see men as closed off and unreceptive functions defensively to bolster a woman's desperate need to allay her female castration anxiety by saying, "Something's wrong with *him*, not *me*; *he's* the one who's missing something!" Mayer illustrates the therapeutic applications of this insight by cogent case examples (it should be mandatory that a copy of Mayer's paper accompany every volume of *Men Are from Mars, Women Are from Venus*! [Gray 1991]).

In my own work (Renik 1992), I have found Mayer's emphasis on female castration anxiety invaluable in understanding the vicissitudes of primary feminism as a clinical concept. For example, awareness of the importance of female castration anxiety and defenses against it—as well as the defensive functions female castration anxiety itself can serve—was crucial in helping me successfully analyze a case of premenstrual distress.

A young woman physician sought analysis because she was having trouble deciding how she wanted to arrange her professional life. After completing a residency in internal medicine, she had established a very successful general practice that was in some ways quite satisfying to her. She was particularly proud of the kind of care she gave: besides doing thorough physical examinations, she took the time to really listen to patients, to answer their questions, and to provide reassurance when needed. She thought of her talent for empathy and sensitive attention as a particularly feminine trait, something she noted to be conspicuously absent in the majority of male doctors.

Unfortunately being a primary care physician meant long office hours and a demanding call schedule. That would make it hard to care for the children she was planning to have in a year or two. Also, she was aware of wishing for more intellectual challenge than she received from the management of routine medical problems in her general practice. A convenient solution to these practical difficulties existed. There was a prestigious department chairman who knew the patient and thought highly of her. He had made it known to her that whenever she liked she could do a specialty fellowship with him, to be followed by a guaranteed place in his group practice. If she took up this offer she could become a consultant, tackling complex medical questions during a predictable and circumscribed working day, even part-time if she liked.

However, she felt that the medicine she would then be practicing, though more intellectually stimulating to her, would be less helpful to other people. The nature of the specialty was such that it consisted essentially of establishing accurate diagnoses of ailments that were, by and large, untreatable. Contact with patients would be of a much more limited and impersonal kind. She would be a guest expert who made brief appearances within an academic hospital setting. Furthermore, the physicians, mostly male, who would be her colleagues, the sort of people who were drawn to this kind of work, she was sure were uptight, closed-off, unreceptive, and uncaring. She had a horror of spending her days in their company. Not only would she find them alien and distasteful, but she was afraid that in order to assimilate herself into their milieu she might become just like them. Such was her dilemma.

Here was a woman whose frankly expressed, conscious attitudes suggested the strong influence of female castration anxiety. She idealized and highly valued what she thought of as her uniquely feminine abilities. She was contemptuous of men, whom she saw as defective because they lack what women have; and she was afraid that contact with have-not males might somehow cause damage to her cherished female parts. Her view of her history was consistent with this set of ideas. She admired her mother greatly. A traditional woman of her time, the patient's mother had not followed a professional career; but she was a much sought-after figure, a person regarded as wise and thoughtful, to whom friends came for comfort and advice. The patient's father was a professor of medicine whose intelligence and competence she certainly respected. However, both the patient and her mother had always known that he had no tolerance for feelings, in himself or in anyone else. In this respect he was to be pitied, to be treated with special care lest he be overwhelmed by the demands of intimate family life, and sometimes to be resented for the way he failed to carry out his emotional tasks.

For example, as a little girl, the patient had never been comfortable coming to her parents if her feelings had been hurt at school, because she felt her father would be disappointed and annoyed with her. Clearly, her father was missing some important emotional equipment and wanted her to be just like himself. Also, the patient worried that perhaps she had married a man too much like her father. Her husband was an attorney, and definitely a high achiever. She found her husband interesting but exasperating because of his disregard for feelings and his tendency toward self-absorption. Would he be able to relate properly to a child?

Expectably, this young woman had a similar view of me. I could not be a very humanely concerned sort of doctor, since I was willing to work with such a limited number of patients. If my remarks or questions suggested that I thought there might be anything at all to look into about the emphatic altruism that complicated her thinking about her career choice, it was because I could not empathize with her deep concern for others. Lacking the capacity for such feelings myself, I had no way of sharing her experience. As her father had been dismissive of her mother's sensitivity, so I could not regard the patient's caring attitude as valid. Her impression was that, all in all, I was responsible and skillful, but basically distant from the people around me, shut up within myself, like so many men. In fact, at a certain point she revealed to me her conviction that I was completely without any empathetic ability. It was true that she often felt understood by me in important and helpful ways, but this was because by virtue of being extremely smart I was able to figure things out about her, not because I had any capacity for emotional receptivity.

As an entrée into elucidation of the patient's manifest anxiety about damage to her special female assets I raised the obvious question of why, if she felt as she did about men, she wanted to see a male analyst. At first she talked about knowing she had problems in her relations with men and therefore needing to work them out with a man, but she soon realized that this did not entirely explain her choice. It was an important achievement during this phase of our work together when she came to recognize her disdain for me—and ultimately, her disdain for men in general. She had customarily criticized men for being contemptuous of her and looking down on all that she held valuable. When she had to acknowledge that her criticisms of men involved a measure of presumption and disdain on her own part, she was quite ashamed.

She could not avoid recognizing that her contempt for men formed a good offense, adopted for defensive reasons. As long as the crucial issue in the forefront of her mind had been whether unreceptive, insensitive men were worth working with, there was no need to ask herself whether she felt adequate to do the work men did; but now that she saw how contemptuous of men she was, her complaints lost their power to keep self-doubt at bay. It emerged that she worried she didn't really have the kind of finely tuned intelligence required for medical specialty practice. Though it was true that she valued her ability to empathize with patients, secretly she felt that it compensated for limits in her ability to see complex medical problems through to a careful and complete solution. In her thoughts about her father, the accent now was less on his impoverished emotional life and more on her admiration for his powerful and disciplined intellect. She began to feel admiration for and envy of me.

It was in this context that she first described how she invariably became irritable, easily upset, and had great difficulty concentrating during the week or ten days before she would menstruate each month. Because she had considered her premenstrual distress a neuroendocrine phenomenon, she had thought it of no relevance to her analysis, and therefore had never mentioned it. Now it came into view as an aspect of her anxiety about her intellectual inferiority, and it made clear that the intellectual limitations about which she was concerned were connected in her mind with the fact that she was a woman. Obscured by her indictments of her father's arrogance had been her conviction that neither she nor her mother could think as clearly as he, and a deep sense of inferiority connected with this invidious comparison. Menstruation meant messiness and injury to her. Mental and physical sloppiness were linked, and thoughts about both preoccupied her during the premenstruum.

Worries about damage to her valued female parts had been compensating for and warding off the patient's awareness of her idealization of what men have and her belief that she was inferior to men because she was different from them. As she pursued her thoughts about menstruation and we gained a fuller picture of her confusions between mind and body, we found evidence of a concrete, anatomical aspect to the warded-off sense of defect. She explored her admiration for men's penises, as well as their minds, and discovered a sentiment of envy in herself that accompanied her admiration. She had large and shapely breasts, and was gratified by men's attraction to them. She especially enjoyed it when her husband kissed her breasts and sucked her nipples, making them erect. Somewhat alarmed, she realized that sometimes her pleasure involved imagining him having the same sorts of feelings she did when she performed fellatio. She recalled how during college she had taken to wearing a large, long pendant that dangled between her breasts, and how she experienced a strange kind of excitement when her boyfriend would kiss and suck it as well as her breasts. She recovered an image of her father's glimpsed-at, semi-erect penis—actually seen or retrospectively imagined, it was impossible to know—which fascinated her. Having a man's penis in her mouth gave her a sense of possession of it; the fact that she could cause it to go up and down made her feel like it was hers.

The exaggerated feminism that involved the patient's feeling she had something special and valuable that was in danger of being destroyed was a derivative of her female castration anxiety. It was also a disguised expression of her phallic rivalry, and protected her against feeling penis envy. One thing special and valuable that she wanted to believe she possessed was an illusory penis. She enacted this fantasy in her sex life. Her belief that specialty training was dangerous arose from her phallic castration anxiety, her fear that her magical fantasy of being phallic would be exposed and discredited. The patient's sense of herself as a *have* imperiled by *have-not* males reversed underlying feelings of inferiority to men, and her protests against men's lack of humanitarian concern denied her own envious hostility and competitiveness. Her phallic castration complex, a shameful image of herself as physically and mentally defective in comparison with men, was now unveiled.

Once this dispiriting self-image became available to the patient for conscious examination, she could recognize its irrationality. It occurred to her that in reality there is nothing wrong with the female genital and that, similarly, there is nothing wrong with the female intellect. Just as the patient's sexual parts had always functioned quite well, so had her mind. In fact she had always been an excellent medical thinker. There was every reason to believe that the department chairman's confidence in her was well-founded. She realized that although she was not a man, sexually and intellectually she was on a par with her admired father. She made plans to pursue specialty training.

Later the patient began to experience loyalty conflicts. She felt excited by our collaboration and the results it produced. Her relationship with her husband seemed rather lackluster when compared with her analysis, and this caused her to feel quite guilty. A bit further on, when she began specialty training and found that she was enjoying it, she reluctantly admitted to me that she looked down on psychiatry. She worried I would feel left out and demeaned because her flirtatious relationship with her mentor had begun to eclipse her interest in me.

Transferred into these triangular concerns was her long-suppressed childhood conviction that her mother was deeply hurt by the fact that father really preferred his daughter to his wife. The patient's loud protests against her father's lack of emotional responsivity had been covering over a secret belief that his reserve was a way of holding himself in check. She recalled how much her father used to enjoy teaching her things, the obvious pleasure he took in her interest and brightness, and his proud excitement when she decided to pursue a career in medicine. She sensed in him a kind of affectionate contempt for her mother, and a frustration at her mother's inability to share in his rich intellectual life. It seemed to the patient that her father must have been threatened by the sexual aspect of his love for her, because when she matured into womanhood he withdrew from her. At the same time, during her adolescence if she stayed out too late on a date, he would fly into an inappropriate rage. He must have been disturbed by his jealousy and attraction. Hurt and frightened, she too retreated, developing an alliance with her mother based on shared complaints about her father's lack of emotional availability.

As we clarified this fantasy of oedipal triumph we learned more about the phenomenology of the patient's premenstrual distress. Our previous work had acquainted her with some of the derogatory meanings she had attached to menstruation itself, but her premenstrual symptoms—the irritability, difficulty concentrating, and tendency to upset—she had still regarded simply as the manifestation of hormonal shifts toward the end of her cycle. Now she noticed that certain hypochondriacal preoccupations were a feature of her premenstrual moods. This came to light because in exploring her guilt about betraying me with her professor, as she felt she had betrayed her mother with her father, she became aware of a feeling of anxiety and vague ideas about being punished. I commented to her that it sounded as if she believed she would not be allowed to get away with it, and my remark brought to mind her long-standing conviction that she would become seriously and incurably ill early in her life.

Her medical knowledge helped elaborate her fear of illness. She imagined various awful eventualities; but as we looked into them, it became apparent that she dwelled especially on the possibility that she would suffer from a lingering disease that would cause her to deteriorate and become disgusting. She knew that these thoughts were always particularly on her mind premenstrually, but she had assumed that her morbid concerns were produced by her mood, which was physiologically determined. She was therefore taken a bit aback when I suggested that it might also be the other way around: her morbid thoughts could be causing her mood. If for some reason the approach of menstruation led her each month to think about punishment and dire illness, one could easily imagine how these concerns in themselves would be enough to make her irritable and to interfere with her ability to concentrate during the premenstrual phase of her cycle.

She then remembered how it was when she was 12 years old and brownish fluid began to leak from her vagina. Although she had discussed menstruation quite explicitly with her mother, it never occurred to the pubertal girl that this might be the beginning of her periods. Instead, she thought she was sick. It had been her custom to masturbate in the bath by letting the tap run full force over her genitals, and she was sure that because of this some water had gotten trapped up inside her and was now making things rotten there. For six months she hoped the leaking would stop, and said nothing about it to anyone. Only when it became worse and her fears for her life overcame her shame did she talk to her parents and realize the truth.

Obviously, the anxiety that had accompanied my patient's menarche had never been completely banished. It recurred anew each month as once again she faced the onset of menstruation. The anxiety produced hypochondriacal worries, which were at the core of her premenstrual distress. Our investigation of the patient's premenstrual fantasy of genital damage had brought us back to the female castration anxiety that had come up earlier in her analysis. However, this time it was not the defensive function of her female castration anxiety, but rather the conflicts generating it that received our attention. She worried that she was becoming less feminine, "one of those women who pushes herself forward too much." This idea of losing her feminine receptivity and becoming phallic was a punishment fantasy. Succeeding like her father made her feel close to him, a forbidden gratification for which she would suffer the Dantesque fate of becoming more like her father than she wanted.

The patient's romance with her analyst, which excluded her husband, then her romance with her medical professor, which excluded her analyst, invoked feelings that she had experienced in childhood when she believed she had captured her father's affection to the exclusion of her mother. Those feelings had included an anxiety of conscientious origin: because she had been an unfaithful daughter and had superseded her mother as a woman, she would have to suffer damage to her own womanhood—hence her misinterpretation of menarche. In fact *she had been looking forward to beginning her periods as a sign of sexual maturity* and had been talking about it with her friends. But her disapproval of her own ambitions was so strong that it won out in shaping her perception, and the much-desired gratification was incorrectly identified as the dread penalty.

What she had specifically imagined at menarche was that the walls of her vagina were rotting away. This meant a dreadful loss because it would deprive her of the capacity to receive and hold a penis inside her. Whereas earlier in the analysis we had explored the importance of vaginal receptivity as a means to the end of feeling in possession of an envied and admired phallus, now primary feminine pleasures were in the forefront. Having a penis in her vagina was stimulating, like sucking on something delicious. Also, the mucosal rubbing felt wonderful. (During another phase in her analysis when she was exploring her homosexuality, she had a dream in which she and another woman were sliding their open labia together in a kind of ecstatic genital kiss.) A sense of prowess accompanied the knowledge that her vagina was an instrument with which she could please men. She was proud of the strength of her vaginal muscles and her ability to squeeze her husband's penis with them, which he loved. Looking toward the future, she worried about her vaginal musculature becoming too stretched and losing tone as a consequence of childbirth.

Now clarification of her female castration anxiety and the oedipal conflicts that set it in motion was added to our previous work on her phallic castration anxiety and phallic castration complex. With this expansion of the patient's awareness of the multiple determinants of her fantasy of genital damage, her premenstrual distress syndrome faded away. A few memories recovered in the process suggested some of the preoedipal, narcissistic roots of her female castration anxiety. Associations to a feeling she had always had that her father was in some way physically clumsy led her to recall a childhood view that little girls' bodies were clean and neat, made for running, jumping, and the like. When she had first seen a penis it had seemed to her a gratuitous and awkward addition. This was an aspect of her reaction to the memory image of her father's penis that she had not brought forward earlier. As a girl she used to squat over a mirror and watch herself urinate, so she knew she did not need a penis to perform that function. On the other hand, she had always wondered what her vagina was for, just as she had wondered what men's penises were for. It was not until she learned the facts of life that she really understood the function of the anatomical difference between the sexes, and her understanding had soon become embroiled in conflict.

This clinical experience is only one of many I could present that would illustrate the utility of Mayer's original work on female castration anxiety. By completing a symmetry between male and female narcissistic vulnerability, sexual body image, anxiety, and defense, Mayer permits us to think beyond the specific matter of gender, and to consider universals concerning the relation between self and other. By dispelling long-standing misconceptions about illusory differences between men and women, and by placing the real differences between men and women in perspective, Mayer opens the way for us to find new commonalities between men and women. Her contribution invites us to ask: In what ways is gender a kind of pseudospeciation and in what ways not? Like any true classic, Mayer's paper puts some questions behind us and opens new ones for us to consider.

REFERENCES

Gray, J. (1991). *Men Are from Mars, Women Are from Venus*. New York: Harper Collins.

Mayer, E. L. (1985). "Everybody must be just like me": observations on female castration anxiety. *International Journal of Psycho-Analysis* 66:331–347.

Renik, O. (1992). A case of premenstrual stress: bisexual determinants of a woman's fantasy of damage to her genitals. *Journal of the American Psychoanalytic Association* 40:195–210.

"Everybody Must Be Just Like Me": Observations on Female Castration Anxiety

ELIZABETH LLOYD MAYER

The concept of primary femininity has been invoked with increasing frequency as an important basis on which Freud's views of female development require challenge. According to this concept, a sense of femininity develops not only or even primarily in response to feelings of disappointment, deprivation, or fantasies of having been castrated. In support of the concept, numerous authors have described that little girls appear in some way feminine from a very early age (Parens et al. 1976, Stoller 1976, Tyson 1982). But a number of questions remain. What kinds of early mental representations define a sense of femaleness for the girl? What are the phase-specific evolutions of such mental representations? How are they affected by recognition of the anatomic differences between the sexes? How does an early awareness of femininity become caught up in the intrapsychic conflicts of each developmental stage? In what forms are the attendant anxieties expressed?

The following is an attempt to suggest one way in which an early sense of femaleness may be mentally represented by the girl and to suggest a particular form of female castration anxiety which may develop in consequence. I will offer some clinical vignettes in the hope both of elaborating some of the ways in which such a mental representation and its derivatives may be observed in clinical work, and also in the hope of stimulating further consideration of the frankly preliminary ideas presented here.

> Emily, a bright little girl of 20 months, for the first time commented on the matter of sexual differences to her mother with the following series of remarks. "Mummy," she began, "*Mummy* has a bottom . . . and Mummy, *Daddy* has a bottom . . . and Mummy, *Emily* has a bottom." Emily's mother assented to each of these observations and Emily thoughtfully continued, "and *Mummy* has a vulva . . . and *Emily* has a vulva . . . but Mummy, Daddy has something *funny* in his vulva!"

Emily, like Freud's prototypical little Hans, has made a simple assumption about the nature of genitals: "everyone is and must be like me." But unlike Freud's little Hans, this assumption has led her to believe that everyone has and must have a vulva. (Emily is a child of the 1980s; she has been taught a word which explicitly denotes her external genitalia.) Emily's new observation is that Daddy has something funny *besides*—and, she imagines, *inside*, although more of that later.

A number of female patients have reiterated to me a view of men in which certain stereotypic features recur: men, these women assert, are emotionally closed, unable to be receptive or empathic, and without access to inner feelings or inner sensations. The absolutism of these characterizations, their repetitiveness, their frequency, and the stubborn determination with which they are retained, have struck me as requiring explanation. As I have investigated such women's characterizations of men, I have been impressed that certain themes recur. In brief: these women are determined to believe that men are lacking something crucial; they associate the missing something with what are explicitly described as "feminine" capacities; these women are at some level deeply anxious about their own capacities to be feminine; and they ultimately report versions of a fantasy that the capacity to be *genitally open* is a capacity that can be endangered, can be lost, and indeed *has* been quite literally lost by the male sex. Their characterizations of men as emotionally closed appear to represent derivatives of an unconscious conviction that men have actually been closed over genitally, and that men therefore represent the frightening possibility that such a thing could really happen *to a woman*. While the defensive functions of such material have been frequently pointed out in the psychoanalytic literature (i.e., "something's wrong with *him*, not with *me; he's* the one who's missing something!"), I believe that there may be additional ways of understanding such material that could contribute to our comprehension of female psychology.

The remarks of little Emily may prove illuminating in pursuing this line of thought. I believe that we can observe in her reflections a phase of female psychosexual development that invites further investigation, particularly in its clinical implications.[1] I would like to suggest that, given the egocentric nature of small children, the vicissitudes of the girl's later development will rest on her early conviction that boys as well as girls have female genitals, much as we are accustomed to assuming the importance to the boy of his early conviction that everyone has a penis. Thus, according to Emily, Daddy *must* have a vulva for his penis to be *in*. Certainly it has been widely demonstrated that the little girl's first perception of a penis leads her to wonder at her lack. Relatively unemphasized has been her response to noting that the boy does *not* have what she has, a vulva, a parting between the labia with the potential for an opening and for something inside. But, I suggest, this first awareness of the possibility of being without a vulva may contribute to the development of a true female castration anxiety. As such, it would have decisive influence on the course of female development and would affect as well the ways in which girls perceive boys (and women perceive men). It would constitute an observation that must be worked over repeatedly as solutions to each phase of psychosexual conflict are attained by the girl.

It is my impression that such a female castration anxiety may be observed clinically, and that it is distinct from the female castration complex as that complex has been widely described in the psychoanalytic literature. I suggest that *castration anxiety* in men or in women, is anxiety over losing that genital which is actually possessed. It bears a particular relationship to oedipal conflicts and is given great force by perception of the opposite sex as lacking one's valued genital. The *castration complex*, on the other hand, has traditionally referred to the girl's fantasy of having had a penis that was lost. Such a definition of the castration complex implies an essentially

---

[1] I present Emily's remarks as frankly suggestive, and far from "data" in the rigorous sense. However, there exists little observational research that systematically examines how young girls mentally represent the genitals that they actually have as opposed to their responses at observing what they *don't have*. Roiphe and Galenson (1981), for example, while apparently agreeing in theory with those authors who postulate an early awareness of genital femaleness, present very few observations related to such an awareness; their observations emphasize how young girls react to discovering that they have no penis (cf. Mayer 1983). In the relative absence of research that examines how little girls imagine their actual female organs, Emily's remarks may at least encourage speculation.

phallocentric experience and resolution of female castration concerns. Though important, I believe it describes only one dimension of how girls may experience and cope with those concerns. So, for purposes of clarity in this paper, I will refer to that set of fantasies as the *phallic* castration complex. I will use the term female castration anxiety to refer to anxiety, in girls or in women, over the fantasied loss of *female* genitals. Clinical manifestations of female castration anxiety and the phallic castration complex may merge, but I believe that the phenomena themselves have distinct origins, follow distinguishable developmental lines, bear a complicated relationship to each other, and are certainly not exclusive of each other.

Historically, the phallic castration complex has been elaborated to the exclusion of the identification of a true female castration anxiety. Female oedipal conflict and resolution, female superego development, and numerous clinical phenomena in women have been understood in conjunction with the phallic castration complex but not in conjunction with female castration anxiety. The ramifications of that emphasis have been significant in the psychoanalytic exposition of female psychology. In this paper I will delineate what I take to be one expression—undoubtedly not the only one—of female castration anxiety. I will only briefly address the very important question of the relationship between that female castration anxiety and the phallic castration complex.

From the beginning, Freud declared the significance of the child's early assumption that all genitals are the same. However, he explicitly understood "same" to mean "male," and his portrayal of female sexuality was dominated by what he described as the girl's shock at discovering that she was without male genitals. In 1905 he wrote, "The assumption that all human beings have the same (male) form of genital is the first of the many remarkable and momentous sexual theories of children" (p. 195). Or again, in 1914, "Children have, to begin with, no idea of the significance of the distinction between the sexes; on the contrary, they start out with the assumption that the same genital organ (the male one) is possessed by both sexes . . . " (p. 55). And in 1923, "The main characteristic of this 'infantile genital organization' . . . consists in the fact that, for both sexes, only one genital, namely the male one, comes into account" (p. 142).

The psychoanalytic literature concerning women has been debating these assertions and their derivatives for decades (and, of course, Freud frequently declared his own views on female sexuality to be tentative). The arguments have devolved upon Freud's use of the modifier "male"; is the only genital really a male one in the mind of the little *girl*? While the mental representation of genital femaleness may, as Freud portrayed, be impossible until late in the *boy's* development, is it likely that the *girl's* ability mentally to represent some form of femaleness is equally delayed? A number of authors have argued that Freud's description seems apt from the standpoint of the little boy but has questionable implications from the little girl's point of view (Chiland 1980, Fast 1979, Greenacre 1950, Horney 1924, 1926, Jones 1927, 1933, 1935, Stoller 1968, 1976). It suggests that the girl has formed little positive image of her own genitals during the phases of her development that precede her first appreciation of the anatomical difference between the sexes.

But, as parents, pediatricians, and observers of infant development readily inform us, little girls, beginning in the first year of life, demonstrate significant pleasurable interest in and curiosity about their genitals (Kleeman 1975, 1976, Spitz 1962). In the second year of life this interest consolidates into a set of genital experiences which Roiphe and Galenson (1981) deem sufficiently organized and organizing to constitute a specific phase of psychosexual development—what they have termed the early genital phase. Given psychoanalytic understanding of the young child's mental organization, we must consider that the little girl's genital interest is experienced by her as interest in a "something," not in a lack of a something. As Freud repeatedly pointed out, the earliest mental representations of the genitals are built out of sensory experience, out of the bodily experience of what one *is* and *has*, not yet the experience of what one isn't and hasn't.

Psychoanalysts have long suggested that the girl's earliest sense of what she has entails a clitoris cathected in some kind of isolation from the rest of her genitals, a clitoris which is perceived and experienced as essentially phallic in nature. In part, this emphasis has resulted from a view that distinguishes between the clitoris as the *external* female genital and the vagina as the *internal* female genital. This distinction between internal and external has seemed necessary, since the extent of infantile awareness of an internal organ, the vagina, is quite unclear. Certainly the vagina is not easily seen or explored by the young girl, and this has significant implications for the extent to which she can mentally represent such an organ at an early age.

But the little girl's *external* genitals include a vulva as well as a clitoris. While the concentration of the girl's genital excitement may be focused in her clitoris, those clitoral sensations are embedded in a vulva that has definite and readily discerned perceptual and sensory attributes.[2] While the extent of infantile vaginal awareness and sensation remains controversial, the girl's genitals have several externally observable and touchable aspects in which reside pleasurable sensation: the mons, the labia, the parting between the labia, and the introitus. Particularly relevant to this paper is the fact that mental representation of these external aspects may constitute early precursors to conceptualization of the vagina in so far as they lead the little girl to experience her genitals *as having an opening and potential inside space.* Specifically, the parting between the labia can be recognized as an opening and associated with genital pleasure long before the vagina *per se* is likely to be imagined. A further step in the eventual mental representation of "vagina" is probably awareness of the introitus which, as Barnett (1966) described, suggests a space existing beyond a recognized opening in advance of the capacity for conceptualization of the vagina. In brief, the association of an opening and potential inside space with the girl's genitals need not require, in the girl's own mind, a capacity for representation of the vagina. (I would like to emphasize that I am speaking of what goes on in the girl's mind, not what goes on in the mind of the boy, to whom *any* aspect of the girl's external genitals must largely signify lack of *his* kind of genital.)

If the girl's early sense of her vulva incorporates, however vaguely, the notion of an opening and potential inside space, it seems plausible that a mental image of genital femaleness is in the making at an earlier age than the psychoanalytic literature has generally suggested.[3] If the girl's earliest

---

[2]In this context, it is interesting that, according to Masters and Johnson (1966), direct and localized clitoral stimulation that excludes other aspects of the female external genitals is *rarely* a preferred form of female masturbation or alloerotic stimulation. Child observers have frequently noted that masturbation in young girls includes the labia, mons, and so on. These kinds of observations are at least suggestive against the notion that the genital mental representations which are built on earliest genital sensation and masturbatory experience would isolate the clitoris from other aspects of the vulva.

[3]At what precise age such a mental representation ordinarily begins to become possible is an important but exceedingly complex question that I do not find answerable on the basis of the clinical and observational data with which I am familiar. My point is that such a representation may occur earlier than analysts have generally considered, is a logical outcome of experiencing genital sensations throughout the vulva, and is likely to precede the attachment of meaning to the perception of sexual differences. However, it is relevant to the *capacity* for such a mental representation that, according to a number of recent findings, the ability to perceive three-dimensionality (a necessary precursor to the notion of "opening" or "inside") is well-established in the normal infant during the first few days of life (Bower 1977). The capacity to reach into a cup for the purpose of fingering an object inside is normally obtained by 40 weeks, and the

genital sensations and genital explorations lead her mentally to represent her vulva as something which is not only or even essentially phallic, I think we must consider that there will be implications for the impact which the perception of sexual differences will have on her. We are familiar with how, when faced with the boy's genital difference, the girl develops some version of a wish to possess the phallic something which she perceives the boy to have. If she has mentally represented her vulva in the ways I have suggested, it seems likely that the girl's first perceptions of genital differences will also lead her, for at least some moment of her development, to the anxious thought that everyone *isn't* the same, and if he could be without the vulva that she has valued, perhaps something could happen to hers. It seems especially likely that, as the girl recognizes the forbidden nature of her oedipal wishes (wishes that are intimately associated with genital cathexis and genital pleasure) she imagines that retribution might entail loss of those very genitals that play such a part in her oedipal fantasies.

In sum, if we recognize that the girl, like the boy, is engaged in a process of gradual discovery, cathexis, and mental representation of her own genitals, I think that we have to question whether the standard description of the female castration complex, the *phallic* castration complex, represents a complete portrayal of the girl's castration concerns. According to that description, the girl's response to the anatomical difference between the sexes is to be preoccupied with her fantasy of what she imagines she had and has lost, that is, the penis. Significance is not ascribed to her fantasies of how the absence of a vulva in the boy leads her to imagine that she could lose what she *has*, that is, her vulva, in its external aspects *and with its opening and potential for an inside organ*, however imprecisely that inside organ may be mentally represented.

---

capacity to place an object inside a cup, spontaneously or in response to the request "put it in there," is normally achieved by 52 weeks (Gesell and Amatruda 1974). Even this highly abbreviated overview suggests that, in rudimentary form, some capacity for understanding "in" and for manipulating the mental representation of "inside" is present by the end of the first year. Erikson's work (1968, 1974), while not addressing cognitive aspects of the capacity for conceptualizing inner spaces, speaks to the emphasis accorded such mental representations by the girl precisely because of their relation to her experience of her own body. Roiphe and Galenson (1981) have confirmed Erikson's ideas. They report that, with the emergence of genital awareness between 15 and 19 months of age, girls (unlike boys) start to build largely enclosed structures, reflecting the girl's mental representation of her genitals as an enclosed space, as having an inside.

Here I would like to return to little Emily's remarks. She appears not yet to be in possession of the realization that Daddy, the prototype of maleness, is without a vulva. She has noted, with interest and (for the moment, at least) apparent contentment, the funny something that Daddy has. But she has located it firmly in what she imagines to be his vulva. Now what will happen when Emily—who clearly expresses her notion that a vulva is something with an inside, and who has engaged in focused genital play in and around her vulva since the age of 8 months—discovers that Daddy has no vulva for his penis to be *in*?

To guess at how Emily will solve this problem is, of course, sheer speculation. But it does not seem farfetched to imagine that at some point Emily will have to pose it to herself *as* a problem. I believe that the female patients whom I described above are attempting to solve precisely this problem, in their insistence that men are emotionally closed, unable to be receptive, without access to inner feelings, and so on. These women, I suggest, have suffered from the obverse of what Freud identified as the boy's castration reaction upon his discovery that the girl doesn't have a penis. The boy thinks, "if *she* doesn't have a penis, then *I* could lose mine, so her lack of a penis scares me." These women appear to have experienced a kind of equivalent: "if *he* doesn't have a vulva with its opening and potential inside, then *I* could lose mine, so his lack of a vulva scares me." They have developed the unconscious conviction that men have been sealed over, have lost access to their inner genital, their inner sensation and receptivity. They have to believe that men had it and lost it or are hiding it. They cannot accept men as truly different from themselves but able, that difference notwithstanding, to love and be receptive. They partake of an unconscious belief much like a man's unconscious belief that women are incomplete without penises: a man is incomplete without a vulva, an introitus, and, ultimately, a vagina. The motivation for this belief can be traced, I think, to a kind of castration anxiety, to a woman's pathogenic fear that to accept the possibility of a vulva-less, vagina-less man is to accept the possibility of herself losing her own genitals, her own capacity for genital pleasure, and her own experience of herself as a woman.

Several case examples may be illuminating. I will present only isolated aspects of each case in the attempt to highlight how the women described shared a particular self-punitive fantasy of genital loss in which they imagined that they could become genitally closed over as they supposed men to be. I will first attempt simply to document the fantasy as one that seems to me to occur more commonly than the psychoanalytic literature has generally suggested. I will further point out how certain conscious and stereotypic views of men, shared by these women, appeared to have the function of warding off anxieties about their own genital intactness. Finally, I will point to ways in which the particular image of losing a genital opening appeared at least suggestively associated with early perceptions of sexual differences and fantasies of punishment for oedipal wishes. Inevitably, the question will arise of whether this material could be best understood as a defensive elaboration of the phallic castration complex. Certainly penis envy was present in each case, to varying degrees. I believe, however, that the material allows for an alternative set of interpretations that are not exclusive of the phallic castration complex but may complement it. In that interest, I will focus on describing what I have called the female castration anxiety that emerged in each case. There is a great deal that I will not take up, including the complex ways in which observation of the mother's body, identifications with her, etc. contributed to a sense of femininity in these women.

CASE 1

Juliet O. was a 35-year-old doctoral student in elementary education when she began analysis. Her sense of femininity was intimately bound up with feeling herself to be open and receptive. She described men as emotionally closed, impossible to get through to, and so on. She felt compelled to assert her openness and receptivity in one situation after another. She frequently presented herself as a caricature of femininity, desperate to reassure herself that she was truly feminine. Meanwhile she sought out men who were caricatures of masculinity because, by contrast to them, her feminine capacities were not in doubt.

Ms. O. entered analysis complaining of a series of repetitively unsatisfying relationships with men. She was a buxom, extroverted woman whose life was packed with activity and women friends. She rapidly settled into the analytic situation, spilling over with feelings and stories about her life. She organized the waiting room magazines prior to our sessions, chatted freely with other waiting patients, and supplied an admittedly sickly foyer plant with plant food. By her own account, she was inordinately altruistic, always putting others' needs ahead of her own and feeling unrecompensed for her trouble, especially by men.

Ms. O. began her analysis with a deliberate and characteristic appearance of openness about herself. She flooded the hours with feelings, dreams, memories, and details concerning her day-to-day life. She systematically exposed herself, soon remarking upon how reassuring it felt, in her own words, to be *open* with a woman analyst.

One of the things about Ms. O. that initially caught my interest was how stereotyped and repetitive her use of the words "open" and "closed" seemed. It was a dichotomy with which she seemed preoccupied, especially in describing herself and other women, as opposed to men.[4] Ms. O. explained that she felt with me the way she felt with her mother and her women friends; we were the same, we could understand each other, we could be "open" with each other. As Ms. O. described her relationships with women, it became apparent that she ascribed an almost magical significance to this reassuring sameness that women revealed when they were open with each other. Over and over again she would tell me how simply amazing and enormously gratifying it was that she and Jane or Mary or Liz had felt *exactly* the same way over the weekend, had experienced *exactly* the same response to a movie, and so on. Women were the same and their sameness, in Ms. O.'s mind, was repeatedly associated with the capacity to be "open."

This was in marked contrast to Ms. O.'s descriptions of her relationships with her father and with men. Men were not "open"; men never understood, never really cared, and men were endlessly insensitive to her needs. The image of a porcupine occurred to her in describing her feelings about men: "You know, men are *prickly*, like porcupines, things sticking out all over that suddenly come flying at you; they can't be open, they can't be empathic." She insisted that men were always wanting to invade her and trample her insides—and she laid herself open to them.

Her own problem, she suggested, came down to that: she was just too open. Ms. O.'s declared openness soon became a central focus of our work. It gradually developed that she had been keeping some significant secrets from me as well as from her current and past boyfriends. With distress, she began to experience the subterfuge in her openness and the anxiety that her openness was somehow a fraud. She mused:

---

[4]In fact, it was as I noticed a similar preoccupation in certain other women patients that I began to think that the very stereotypy and repetitiveness with which the words were used must highlight some symptomatic function. While the distinction between 'open' versus 'closed' certainly had numerous psychological meanings to Ms. O. and the other women whom I will describe, I will focus on a single train of associations from each of these patients which appeared central to their preoccupations with 'openness', and which seemed to bear a particular relationship to their sense of themselves as female.

I used to feel I had never learned how *not* to be open all the time. I always felt open and couldn't ever shut myself off. But actually what I do is *look like* I'm open on the outside so I take people in, they think I'm really open. But sometimes I am frightened I can't really let them in at all, in fact I don't even want to. I stay shut off inside so people can't invade my space. If people can't see where my space is, they can't invade it. I can hide it. Like having a hole in a wall and I scurry around patching the whole wall so no one knows where it is and they can't get in.[5]

Shortly thereafter, Ms. O. began to fear that, during her analytic hours, she would become unable to talk or let her feelings out. She would panic and choke; she would "close up." In conjunction with this fantasy of closing up verbally and emotionally, she developed what she described as an intense genital sensation of "closing up inside" on the couch, which left her momentarily shaken and dissociated. For months she had insisted that my capacities for receptivity and empathy could not be questioned: we were women, we were the same, so I must understand her. As she began to experience this sensation of closing up on the couch, she developed a suspicious conviction that I had been taking her in all along. I was not really listening to her, in fact maybe I was unable to listen at all: maybe *I* was the one who was closed up, unable to take anything in. Maybe I wanted *her* to close up, maybe I was contemptuous of what she had to say and, it came to mind, maybe I was contemptuous of her ability to be a real woman. The genital sensation of closing up inside felt to her as if she were losing some sexual part of her that was closely connected to feeling sexually desirable and womanly. Maybe I *wanted* her to lose that part of her.

She recalled a childhood compulsion to look at boys genitals. With embarrassment and apology she revealed that her fascination had been less with the boy's penis than with the skin behind his testicles. Repeatedly she had been disbelieving and horrified by how there were no folds, no opening, no mucous membranes, nothing that revealed "an inside kind of skin between the folds." Ms. O. was convinced that genital excitement was a function of having "an inside kind of skin on the outside" (i.e., exposed mucous membranes). Since childhood she had strongly associated her own genital excitement with these mucous membranes, and she was disbelieving that boys could be without that locus of sensation. Each time she would

---

[5]The excerpts of clinical material cited are quoted verbatim.

inspect a boy's genitals she recalled feeling anxious and incredulous at how his skin was "ordinary" between his anus and his testicles, "like an arm or a leg or a finger kind of *outside* skin." He was "closed up." In adolescence, Ms. O. had developed a masturbatory fantasy of a man with an awesomely large penis (her admiration of penises was outspoken) behind which was "a crack, wet folds, that inside kind of skin, and an opening way into his body." The huge penis of this fantasy she associated with the way her father's penis must have looked to her as a child. She realized that the frightening feeling of closing up inside that she had experienced seemed related to her anxious fascination with how closed up she had thought boys were behind their testicles; also, there was something exciting and reassuring about her adolescent fantasy of a man who was *not* closed up. She remembered that she had refused to see a male analyst because she was sure that men could not be receptive or empathic. She began to see this assertion as a derivative of her declaration that men were genitally closed up, and her refusal to see a male analyst as a way of avoiding intimacy with someone whom she perceived as closed up, someone who might remind her of her own fear that *she* could be closed up.

As she began to understand the defensive nature of her criticisms of men she became increasingly questioning of her idealization of our closeness, and aware of a fantasy that I could only tolerate her femininity if she deluded me into thinking that her recent successes with men were not really hers but a tribute to me, a result of my analytic work, not hers. She complained that I didn't really want her to be a sexually active woman, except under my auspices. Her perfect alliances with her mother and other women started to come under question, and she experienced her wishes to be with a man and for a man's penis inside her in less guarded fashion. She recalled previously disavowed yearnings to be close to her father, and feelings that her mother had been jealous of Ms. O.'s happy times with her father. Repeatedly she returned to analysis of a sequence of feelings that I would call her openness a fraud, that *she* would call her openness a fraud, that her femininity was a fraud compared to mine, and so on. We gained the most in analyzing these feelings when we focused on how tenuous and conflicted was her sense of femininity, and how intimately she associated femininity with the openness and receptivity that she expressed such fear of losing.

Ms. O. began to understand at least one aspect of her characterization of herself as open and of men as invading; if men were always invading her openness she could avoid the feeling of being closed up that so frightened her. Her fears of being raped and invaded functioned to prove that she was not and could not be closed up. There *was* an opening to be invaded. Meanwhile, her openness was a trick; she literally took men in but they never really "got into her space," they never found out her secrets. Ms. O. realized that she had always imagined men as wanting to take away her space and her secrets. They wanted to possess her so that they could possess the secrets that made her feel like a woman, the secrets that she shared only with other women. One of the secrets that she felt men wanted to take from her was her ability to keep her sexual excitement inside, not showing. It gave her power over men whose excitement (their erections) showed; men's excitement was on the *outside*, not hidden inside an opening.

In conjunction with these realizations, her caricatured view of men started to soften and the caricatured nature of her own femininity became more evident. She realized that her choice of boyfriends had been dominated by two paradigms: "If he's a real man he can't be caring and receptive." Alternatively, "If he's caring and receptive, he's not a real man." Time after time she had sought out a real man according to these criteria, and time after time she had incurred the inevitable consequence of some variety of abuse. But at least those men made her feel like a real woman; *she* was the open one, the one with the nurturing, caring, receptive capacities. Those capacities of hers, by contrast with the man's, were reassuringly evident and unquestioned.

Ms. O. gradually realized that her professional life had been significantly inhibited by her phobic avoidance of "acting masculine." She came to see her extreme altruism (or, more accurately, pseudo-altruism) as a way of proving that she was a true woman, always receptive and sensitive to the needs of others. She began to see how her assertiveness had been inhibited out of the anxiety that she would feel like a man. *She had a frightening dream, after a date that had been unusually happy and mutually satisfying, in which she grew a penis and dropped a basket of eggs that smashed.* She woke up in a panic and associated the panic with her dreaded feelings of being closed up and with some kind of punishment for having had a wonderful time with a man. She thought of a friend who had recently had a hysterectomy and anxiously wondered whether her friend could still feel like a woman at all. She described a dream in which she was sewn up between her legs; she analyzed this image as a loss of her femininity and as a punishment for wishes to be happier with men than she felt her mother had been.

As we began to elucidate Ms. O.'s neurosis, her fear that she could lose her capacity to be a woman became increasingly evident. The images in which she couched this fear had largely to do with being closed up and sealed over in the ways she imagined that she had repeatedly observed boys to be. These images merged with fears that she could lose her inside space (even her basket of eggs). Ultimately, drawing an analogy from her work, she observed:

> You know, in teaching little kids with learning difficulties, you *don't deny their differences*, you capitalize on the strengths that they innately have as individuals. That seems like something which sort of applies to how I see men. Unless I believe men have something to give, I won't ask for what I need. But the thing is, if I believe men have something to give, then I'll have to be able to be receptive. It seems like each time I feel a little stronger I can tolerate seeing what's *not* there in a man, what he *can't* give me, without doubting myself or losing interest in him.

A central feature of Ms. O.'s neurosis appeared to entail a fantasy of castration that robbed her of her female organs and left her sealed over as she imagined men to be. Several versions of this fantasy emerged in the transference; each time, such an emergence provided an opportunity to elucidate some important aspect of Ms. O.'s relationship with me as well as of her symptomatology. As the functions and dynamics of this fantasy were clarified. Ms. O. became significantly more able to engage in satisfying heterosexual relationships.

CASE 2

Marian T. was an engaging and self-possessed young woman who sought treatment in response to dissatisfaction with her marriage. She had been married for three years when she presented herself for treatment. She felt that her relationship with her husband Sam had always been companionable but lacking in passion. Despite her complaint of a passionless marriage, it soon emerged that Ms. T. harbored a real scepticism about the possibility of passion between men and women. She matter-of-factly observed that she habitually disbelieved scenes of passion in movies, books, or even as she encountered them in daily life. She was surprised at my apparent interest in this disbelief since she felt that no serious-minded person could really be taken in by *Gone with the Wind, Brigadoon,* the great love stories, or young lovers embracing on the street. Didn't everyone see and secretly doubt that such a thing was really what it seemed? Gradually Ms. T.'s impressively syntonic disbelief in portrayals of passion assumed a symptomatic aspect in her own eyes and she began to question the origin of her resolve to disbelieve in passion between the sexes.

After several months of treatment, Ms. T. developed a characteristic monologue that ran as follows and was remarkably similar upon each rendition:

> Sam is just incomprehensible to me. He has no insides! He can't ever talk about his feelings, he doesn't even want to, how can he *be* the way he is? It's always on the outside with him, outside activities, that's where he lives. I just can't believe he really *is* like that. Maybe he is that different from me. But I don't believe it, I think he just chooses not to think about anything he has inside. He tells me he loves me but not so I feel he's telling me about anything deep inside him. He's just different, he just isn't like me, he doesn't *feel* inside like I do, he doesn't care about feelings. But when I bring it up he says he may be different but he can still love me. How can I want to make love when he never really *talks* to me. He says he does but I know he isn't telling me what he really feels about things. Maybe he really doesn't *have* feelings, can that be true? Not all men are like that. I *know* not all men are like that, especially my father wasn't. I can't feel receptive to Sam. I *want* to but I can't, I can't be responsive to him, I can't control it. Maybe there's something really wrong with me; I just can't have those feelings, maybe I'm fated not to. I used to have them though. Then I wasn't thinking about wanting to get pregnant. I just can't feel receptive to him, I've almost lost a sexual part of me, he's just too different from me.

It seems to me that this monologue starts off with a structure parallel to the ruminations familiar in psychoanalytic material from certain male patients, that is, "She *can't* be without a penis—she *must* have a penis—she doesn't—she does—she can't—she must—*can* she really be that different from me?" Ms. T. is saying in effect: "He *must* have what I have inside—he doesn't—he does—he does but he won't admit it—he must—*can* he really be that different from me?" She then continues in a way that suggests something about the worry that motivates her doubts about how her husband is made: "Maybe it's *me* who has something wrong inside—*I'm* the one who can't feel receptive—maybe I'm fated never to feel sexual again—maybe I've lost or will lose or could lose what *I* have inside, *my* sexual parts."

I was especially struck by the form of Ms. T.'s anxious internal debate over the differences between herself and her husband. She is clearly and specifically focused on her view that her husband seems to have "no insides," or is hiding the fact that he does and is secretly just like her inside. Her anxiety seems palpably to be anxiety over her female organs, her own receptive and feminine capacities, and (not coincidentally) her anxiety over feeling sexual in conjunction with having babies. If only, she reiterates, she could feel satisfied that her husband *does* have insides just like hers, maybe then she could feel less inhibited in her sexual feelings.

As Ms. T. and I began to become familiar with this monologue, we addressed the obvious, that she seemed to find it hard to believe that her husband really might be different than she was. She agreed that this seemed true and associated for the first time to memories of her early observations of sexual differences. She remembered seeing her father urinate; she reiterated firmly that nothing had surprised her about the way her father had looked. Then she remembered that it had been her father who had explained sex to her. Actually, she remarked, it made sense that it would have been her father who did the explaining because he had been able to explain about men *and* women. I questioned her about this and she observed that he could and did explain about what boys had as well as what she herself had and what girls had; her mother, on the other hand, couldn't have explained as easily about penises, not being possessed of one herself. We were both struck by the obvious implication: did her father, then, have what girls had? Ms. T. found this idea startling, amusing, but peculiarly descriptive. "It *is* peculiar," she remarked later, "I have thought of my father as a different species, as a man but like a woman, too."

She went on to detail how she had just never encountered a man who was as much of everything as her father had been. A fantasy of her father that endowed him with female as well as male sex organs was barely concealed in her various descriptions of him. Other men were stimulating *or* receptive, sexual *or* caring, intellectual *or* emotional, exciting *or* gentle. But her father had been both along every conceivable dimension; he was everything a man was, but everything a woman was as well. She guessed maybe she could never be happy with any other man, because other men just couldn't "be both" the way her father had been. Because other men couldn't be open the way her father was, she couldn't be open with them; with her father and her father alone, she could feel truly feminine. But, she would remind herself, maybe other men could "be both" too, and were simply withholding from her, hiding their capacities for caring and receptivity. Maybe men wanted her simply in order to appropriate *her* capacities for caring and receptivity:

> It's not, anymore, my virginity that a man wants but he wants me to make him feel taken care of and he can't do it himself. I feel used; *he needs to take something sexual away from me* so he can feel happy and cared for because men just can't do it themselves.

I will not detail the ways in which, as Ms. T. became aware of aspects of ambivalence in her feelings toward me and toward women, she became increasingly able to recognize the anxiety in her highly romanticized tie to her father and the conflicted nature of the femininity that such fantasies revealed. It is worth mentioning, however, that it was in this context that she for the first time elaborated a history of vaginal tightness during intercourse and of significant dyspareunia. She analyzed this tightness as a symptom related to her wish to placate her mother by closing herself off to men, meanwhile experiencing men as closed off to her. She realized that the condition for her becoming lubricated and experiencing orgasm during intercourse was that her husband would have somehow proved himself to be "open" to her, "with feelings inside," before or during their lovemaking. The rigid quality of this condition and the nature of the transitory reassurance which it offered had an almost fetishistic quality that became evident as Ms. T. described how intimately she associated "openness" with being able to feel sexual, and feeling like a woman. Gradually, she found herself less threatened by seeing her husband as male and as different from her in a number of ways. Particularly, her insistence that *he* be open so that *she* could be open became less driven. Like the man who depreciates women out of anxiety about his own masculinity, Ms. T. had felt compelled to depreciate men, specifically their capacities for receptivity, and for feeling or loving. Instead of "girls can't do math," Ms. T. declared, "men can't be open; men can't feel." How, she protested, *could* men really feel or love without the organs that women feel and love with; after all, *she* certainly couldn't. The resolution of her sexual inhibitions centrally entailed her growing ability to reassess the import of the fact that men are indeed different from women, and a growing conviction that her own genitalia and femininity were not at risk if she accepted men as being without her kind of insides and without her kind of openness.

CASE 3

Jenifer L., a highly competent lawyer, was 29 years old when she began analysis. Despite a generally happy social life with men, she had her own version of the complaints which I have enumerated. Men weren't emotionally available, they couldn't be receptive, and so on. At the age of 22, she had become pregnant and had had an abortion (D&C). She had been businesslike and calm throughout the procedure and its aftermath. When she first mentioned the abortion to me, she noted that it had not been traumatic and that she had been only briefly upset afterward. Some months later her thoughts turned to the abortion again and she revealed that the oddest thing about the experience had been that she had been peculiarly unable to envision how the abortion would take place. She had imagined the doctor making an abdominal incision, while in full possession of the knowledge that there would be no incision. But, as she put it, she "couldn't imagine how he would get *in* there." As she pondered this denial of her vagina, her thoughts ran to her father and their very close relationship. He was a judge and she thought of how, as a child, she had missed him when he was, in her words, "closed in his chambers." She went on: she had become a lawyer like her father out of a wish to be like him and perpetuate their closeness. But, she said, being a woman lawyer was different. She couldn't close herself off to distractions and personal relationships the way her father had been able to do and the way men could do. On the one hand she envied men for being able to do that; on the other she felt lucky to have other things in her life that she felt men missed out on. She worried that to be a successful lawyer she would have to deny her femininity and close herself off to things that gave her pleasure as a woman.

At one point I mentioned to Ms. L. that I was struck by how often she was using the words "closed off" and "closed," that she seemed to have a view of men as literally closed in their chambers, but that this was not so far from the view of herself she had described in imagining the abortion. She was surprised at the parallel and described feeling embarrassed in response. She described a sensation in her vagina, of feeling threatened, of wanting to cover her genitals with her hand and of wanting to hold on to her vulva. She felt that this would be somehow reassuring and she felt an urge to protest, "I want to keep my vagina to myself!" She analyzed this feeling as a response to the frightening fantasy of having no vagina, the fantasy of being genitally "closed in her chambers"—the fantasy of being closed off like a man.

In the elaboration of this very rich material, many themes arose, including Ms. L.'s phallic idealizations and envy of men. But also present was an explicit fantasy of herself as genitally closed, without a vagina. This fantasy was experienced by her as frightening, and it appeared linked to making herself unfeminine and like her view of men. It appeared linked as well to her anxiety and self-punishment over her still somewhat sexualized tie to her father. We were able to piece together how she had experienced her abortion as a punishment for her wishes to be sexual with men, and part of that punishment appeared to entail the fantasied loss of her female opening. As her analysis proceeded, Ms. L.'s fantasy that she could accomplish feeling feminine only by borrowing a sense of femininity from me became increasingly clear. This fantasy had many functions, but, in coming to understand them, we repeatedly found ourselves observing how subject to anxiety and loss Ms. L. felt her capacity to be feminine was.

In each of the women described, I suggest that we can see evidence of a castration fantasy in which the women have imagined their specifically female genitalia to be at risk in conjunction with forbidden sexual wishes. For each of these women, the form of such a fantasy appeared significantly determined by early perceptions of the male as being without her kind of genitalia. As the fantasy was elaborated, men came to be viewed as sealed-over women, and the man's lack of female genitalia was perceived as a threat to the woman's own. The dynamics of the fantasy, in each of the cases cited, appeared associated with imagined punishment for oedipal wishes. While fantasies related to the phallic castration complex were present in each of these women, fantasies that their *female* genitalia could be endangered were present as well.

I believe that the term "castration" is appropriate to describe this imagined danger, even though castration has typically been employed to refer to the loss of male genitalia, specifically the penis. According to Webster, while the first meaning of "castrate" begins "to deprive of the testicles; to emasculate, to geld," it continues "by extension, to deprive of the ovaries, to spay."[6] So on strictly etymological grounds, traditional psy-

---

[6]Additional meanings of "castrate" offered by Webster and *The Oxford English Dictionary* may add connotation to psychoanalytic usage: "to remove the anthers (or the pistil) of (a flower) before fecundation," "to remove a part of (a writing) so as to render it innocuous," "to deprive of vigour, force, or vitality (obs.)," and finally, under "castration," "the act of taking away a portion of the honey from the hive (obs.)" (*Webster's New International Dictionary*, Second Edition, 1948; *The Oxford English Dictionary*, 1933).

choanalytic usage is already imprecise: according to Freud (1923), the boy's castration anxiety concerns his *penis,* "[that] part of the body, which is easily excitable, prone to changes and so rich in sensations" (p. 142), not the testicles.

Freud was explicit that castration anxiety develops concerning that portion of the body which is so richly invested with sensation, that it is heavily influenced by the perception of humans who are anatomically lacking that portion of the body, that it is closely linked with the Oedipus complex, and that it becomes the motive for the giving up and transformation of oedipal wishes. It is precisely that elaboration of castration anxiety which has proved so central to psychoanalytic understanding of psychological development. If, then, the girl experiences a parallel anxiety that is heavily influenced by her perception of humans who are anatomically lacking the portion of her body that is so richly invested with sensation, an anxiety that is closely linked with her Oedipus complex and becomes a motive for the giving up and transformation of her oedipal wishes—what are we to call that anxiety? It seems eminently sensible to rely on the time-honored term "castration anxiety," bearing in mind that this castration anxiety in women is not the equivalent of the phallic castration complex as it has been described since Freud's early expositions of female psychology. Similarly, the mutilation fears that have frequently been described in women are not the equivalent of a castration anxiety which is based in perception of the opposite sex as lacking one's valued genital and which bears the particular relation to oedipal wishes that Freud outlined. (This is not to say that such mutilation fantasies are unrelated to the specific female castration fantasies that I have been describing; I will not, however, take up the issue of more general mutilation fantasies in this paper.)

Of course, we are only justified in speaking of castration anxiety in women if the oedipal girl feels that she has something to lose. This gets us back to the central question: How *are* the little girl's genitalia mentally represented by her?

It seems to me that we are warranted in making at least one generalization concerning such a mental representation on the basis of the preceding clinical material. The patients whom I have described suggest that a crucial and basic sense of their own genitalia has something to do with *not* feeling closed over, with having a vulva that parts, that permits the possibility of an opening. As I described above, I believe that such a mental representation may be an early precursor to mental representation of the vagina and may make possible an early sense of genital femaleness—

an early sense, therefore, of having something genital to lose. A number of authors have pointed to an apparent vaginal awareness in young female patients based on references to holes, openings, and so on. Some have also described the difficulty of distinguishing these references from references to the vulva (Fraiberg 1972, Kestenberg 1968, Roiphe and Galenson 1981). If the young girl's mental representation of her vulva focuses centrally upon its quality of having an opening, this difficulty may be at least partially explained. Ultimately, an image of the vulva as having an opening and potential inside space is likely to merge with an image of the vagina, since external and internal genital sensations are rarely entirely separable for the girl or for the adult woman (Fraiberg 1972, Masters and Johnson 1966).

If the girl does feel that she has something genital to lose, she must, when faced with her first perceptions of genital differences, come to terms with observing not only something which she does *not* have but also, eventually, with observing a lack of something which she *does* have. When she reaches that point her egocentricity is truly shattered and she sees that everyone is not made in her image. She is indeed likely to develop a wish for the penis which she discovers herself to be without, particularly as she observes its visual accessibility, urinary prowess, exhibitionistic advantages, and so on. (Her feelings about the penis will inevitably have a multitude of aspects that I will not take up here.) But that reaction will, I suggest, proceed in some kind of tandem with her realization that the boy appears sealed over where she has her vulva. The wish for a penis does not necessarily eradicate or replace the girl's cathexis of her very different genital, though it may seem to do so in various expressions of the phallic castration complex. Little Emily, for example, some months following her announcement regarding the location of Daddy's penis in his vulva, declared her wish for a penis. At around the same time she remarked to her father, "Daddy, *you* don't have a surprise drawer like Mummy; men can't have surprise drawers, just ladies and girls can." At the age of 2, Emily has started to appreciate the impact of who has what, and she has realized that she is without something that other people have. She wants a penis for herself, but she is also asserting the fact that she and her mother have something men are without. Indeed, given the bisexual nature of human beings, it seems quite likely that Emily wants to be possessed of everything (Fast 1979, Kubie 1974). Her wish for a penis coexists with her developing awareness of what she values about her female genitalia. It is worth noting that what she values about herself is not dependent upon the capacity for delayed gratification that imagining breasts and babies entail; she values what she *has*.

In fact, wishing for something which one hasn't may become a convenient defense against worrying about losing what one *has*, particularly if that loss is imagined as the threatened outcome of one's own impulses. To view the penis as the only genital that really counts can function as a proclamation of innocence on the girl's part; if she denies the value of her own genitalia, can the impulses associated with those genitalia really be that dangerous? Imagining the clitoris as a phallus (and an inadequate one at that) may have the same function: denial of those aspects of the female genitals that are perceived as most explicitly feminine.

Horney's description of this defensive function of penis envy, published in 1926, still stands as one of the most concise:

> What is the economic gain of this flight [from femininity and towards masculinity]? Here I would refer to an experience that all analysts have probably had: they find that the desire to be a man is generally admitted comparatively willingly and that, when once it is accepted, it is clung to tenaciously, the reason being the desire to avoid the realization of libidinal wishes and fantasies in connection with the father. Thus the wish to be a man subserves the repression of these feminine wishes . . . It is true that this attempt to deviate from her own line to that of the male inevitably brings about a sense of inferiority . . . Although this sense of inferiority is very tormenting, analytical experience emphatically shows us that the ego can tolerate it more easily than the sense of guilt . . . hence it is undoubtedly a gain for the ego when the girl flees from the Scylla of the sense of guilt to the Charybdis of the sense of inferiority. [pp. 335–336]

Horney speaks here of the threat posed to the girl by her feminine wishes, and of the girl's defensive need to abandon pleasure in her specifically female genitalia. Indeed, Horney refers to the presence of a *"female genital anxiety, like the castration-dread of boys,* [which] invariably bears the impress of feelings of guilt" (p. 335, my italics). She is not explicit concerning the nature of this female genital anxiety, except to observe women's dread of vaginal injury and fear of penetration.

In brief, penis envy and castration anxiety in women are far from mutually exclusive explanatory concepts. The dynamic function of penis envy becomes, however, quite different when it is understood in conjunction with a woman's fear that she could lose what she *has*, not only as the inevitable outcome of feeling that her female genitalia are already castrated ones. This distinction is of dynamic importance no matter how mingled may appear clinical manifestations of unconscious fantasies that one has been castrated, is presently castrated, or is about to be castrated.

In each of the cases described, female castration fantasies appeared to be associated with guilt over oedipal impulses. Now if the oedipal girl does indeed mentally represent her own genitalia such that she feels she has something specifically female to lose, and if that loss is imagined as a punishment for oedipal wishes, there are meaningful implications for our view of female superego development. It has long been the prevailing psychoanalytic position that, while the girl's phallic castration complex ushers in her positive oedipal phase, castration *anxiety* does not motivate her oedipal resolution and superego development as it does for the boy. Freud's view of superego development in women was a logical consequence of his view that, since the girl feels already castrated, fantasied genital loss cannot constitute the potent threat for the girl that it does for the boy. But the fantasied genital loss to which Freud referred was loss of a *penis*, not loss of a female genital that the girl cathects and begins mentally to represent to some extent independently of her feelings about the penis.

While, as Applegarth (1976) has pointed out, superego content is undoubtedly different for the girl and for the boy, the motives for superego development may not be so very different. There has been much debate over the supposed inferiority of the woman's superego and there have been attempts to postulate motives for female superego development which are functional equivalents of the boy's castration anxiety. I do not believe that these attempts have proven particularly clarifying, and it may be that they are unnecessary. If the presence of castration anxiety in women is demonstrated, we may find that castration anxiety concerning the genital which is actually possessed motivates the girl's superego development much as it motivates the boy's.[7]

---

[7] Dr. Maurice Marcus has pointed out to me (personal communication) that the frequent development of mutism in girls who have engaged in father–daughter incest may be usefully understood in this light. He writes: "Such mutism is usually incompletely interpreted on an interpersonal level: that is, "not spilling the beans." In two cases I worked with, I found that the childhood symptom of mutism, which immediately followed the incestuous activity, served not only as a declaration of innocence, but also as a guilty self-punishment and as a statement of castration. The mutism (an oral "closing up") was later replaced by complete repression of memories of the incest, repression that was lifted in the course of treatment. I believe that the oral closing up did indeed serve as an equivalent of a genital closing up which represented the loss of a feminine sexuality–in short, a castration."

Finally, it is not my intention to suggest that, if women experience castration anxiety, male and female development are isomorphic to each other. They clearly are not. Rather, I am suggesting that *certain aspects* of female development may be motivated by female castration anxiety in ways that parallel the impact of male castration anxiety on male development. Because males and females mentally represent their respective genitals differently, the form of the fantasies that describe the phenomenon of castration anxiety will be different for each sex.

I have described the essentially similar form of the castration fantasies portrayed by each of the cases presented. I would like in addition briefly to address certain distinctive aspects of each case that may be relevant to the elucidation of castration anxiety in women and which may offer opportunity for speculation concerning various clinical phenomena as they appear in women.

Both Juliet O. and Marian T. shed, I believe, particular light on how a split in the ego (that same split which Freud ascribed to fetishists) develops in women. Marian T.'s disbelief in sexual differences led to impressive disavowals of reality when she was confronted with portrayals of passion. These disavowals, like the disavowals of the fetishist, were not experienced as symptomatic by her. She could maintain contradictory ideas concerning male anatomy simultaneously in consciousness: men were without a vulva-vagina but they also had it and were hiding it. They were sealed over but they weren't. Her father was a man but not without female genitalia. Indeed, Marian T.'s view of her father was reminiscent of Freud's (1923) description of the little boy who, while "reconciled" to penis-less little girls, continues to endow his mother with a penis: "Women whom he respects, like his mother, retain a penis for a long time" (p. 145). Marian T.'s father retained both male and female genitalia for a very long time. This view of her father facilitated her disavowal of the perception that males have no opening behind their testicles.

Juliet O.'s incredulous and anxious fascination with what boys looked like behind their testicles, and her adolescent fantasy of a man with female genitals behind his penis are also relevant here. In fact, consideration of both cases led me to wonder whether the comparative ease with which girls can continue to imagine a vulva and potential vagina behind the testicles (as opposed to the boy's more direct confrontation with the lack of a penis in the girl) may partially explain the more blatant fetishistic manifestations in men than in women. My interest in this question led me to ask some women acquaintances who had intimate contact with baby boys about their first responses to diapering a boy. They replied first concerning their feelings about the penis: their anxiety at how to clean it, surprise at how big it could be, and surprise at how the urine could spray. When I asked if they had noticed anything else in their reactions, several described (with, it seemed to me, more hesitancy and self-consciousness), their surprise and peculiar feelings at how closed up and sealed over the babies were behind their testicles.

Perhaps this fantasy of a vulva behind the testicles is a more common one than is generally reported, and is an idea that, like the fetishist's idea of a phallic woman, mentally coexists with the recognition of the opposite sex as it actually is. Perhaps we can see a fetishistic equivalent in at least the more strident aspects of the insistence which is so frequently heard from women, that they cannot enjoy sex unless the man continually proves himself to be emotionally *open, receptive*, that is, proves himself to be *not* sealed over. Marian T., for example, was able to realize that her persistent need to get her husband to be "open" often proceeded in the face of his being (by her own account) quite available and emotionally open to her. It was only as she became aware of her wish to endow men with female capacities and female genitalia that she could relax this insistence and recognize moments of genuine intimacy between herself and her husband.

In the case of Juliet O., a motive for masochistic object choice is suggested that appears to have its source in female castration anxiety. Her "real men" were men who abused her in a variety of ways. But with them she could feel like a "real woman" insofar as her own capacities for receptivity and emotional openness were, by comparison to the men, plainly evident and unquestioned. At a heavy price, she extracted the repeated reassurance that the *men* were closed up, not she herself. Similarly, her preoccupation with fears of being raped and invaded functioned to prove that she was not and could not be closed up; there unequivocally was an opening to be invaded. Her stringent avoidance of behavior that she viewed as "masculine" was, as well, an outcome of her anxiety over her ability to feel like a woman, and led to significant masochistic submission in her professional life. Her definition of what constituted masculine behavior was counterphobically determined by her anxiety that she was in danger of losing her femininity.

Both Juliet O. and Marian T. had the tenacious fantasy that men wanted to appropriate their female organs. This fantasy was certainly multiply determined, reflecting in part a reversal of the wish to appropriate the man's penis, and reflecting in part a response to a culture in which women are indeed expected to give over certain aspects of their identities to men (names, for example). But in both of these women, the most dynamically powerful source of their conviction seemed to be their view that men must feel castrated without female genitalia. They found it inconceivable that men could feel complete in their sealed-over state, thus men *must* want to appropriate the woman's specifically female capacities.

Finally, it is worth making some mention of the time and the culture in which the preceding considerations are raised. While I do not believe that the phenomenon of female castration anxiety is in any sense new, it may be increasingly accessible to observation in conjunction with recent cultural developments. For example, as noted earlier, little Emily is a highly contemporary child: she has learned a word that explicitly denotes her external genitalia. This will not in itself alter the course of her psychosexual development, but it may facilitate her expression of certain ideas that have remained unarticulated by little girls who have had no such word.

Similarly, the preceding clinical material bears the stamp of recent cultural shifts in how women view themselves and their expectations for relationships with men. The women discussed are struggling to establish their womanhood at a time when traditional distinctions between masculinity and femininity are under some fire in the culture at large. Women are adopting roles and attitudes traditionally reserved for men, and, equally relevant to the ideas presented here, women (young women in particular) are demanding that men be more emotionally available, receptive, and nurturing—more of what has traditionally been called feminine. It is in this context that the patients discussed protest that men are closed, unable to be open or loving, and so on. Their protest undoubtedly draws some of its force from the wider culture and the times. But precisely because of the current cultural syntonicity of that protest, it is important to tease out the intrapsychic forces that motivate such protests. Ultimately, these women are asking what it is to be a woman and what sexual differences are really all about. The questions are as old as civilization, but the vocabulary in which such questions are currently being addressed by patients may highlight aspects of female development such that psychoanalytic understanding is enriched, and such that the concept of primary femininity may be refined.

SUMMARY

The concept of primary femininity entails an assumption that the girl develops some mental representation of genital femaleness at an early age. I have suggested one form that such a mental representation may take and a particular expression of female castration anxiety that may develop in consequence. I have suggested that the young girl begins by assuming that everyone has a vulva like hers, with the possibility of an opening and the possibility of an inside space. Among the consequences of such an assumption may, in certain girls, be the development of a castration fantasy in which males represent the frightening possibility that such an opening *in a female* could be endangered, lost, or closed up as that opening is imagined to be in males. I have suggested that certain sterotypic features of the ways in which some women characterize men (i.e., men are emotionally closed, unable to be receptive, without access to inner feelings or sensitivities, etc.) may be understood at least in part as derivatives of this fantasy.

REFERENCES

Applegarth, A. (1976). Some observations on work inhibitions in women. *Journal of the American Psychoanalytic Association* 24(Suppl.):251–268.

Barnett, M. (1966). Vaginal awareness in the infancy and childhood of girls. *Journal of the American Psychoanalytic Association* 14:129–141.

Bower, T. G. R. (1977). *A Primer of Infant Development.* San Francisco: Freeman.

Chiland, C. (1980). Clinical practice, theory and their relationship in regard to female sexuality. *International Journal of Psycho-Analysis* 61:359–365.

Erikson, E. (1968). Womanhood and the inner space. In *Women and Analysis,* ed. J. Strouse, pp. 291–319. New York: Viking, 1974.

——— (1974). Once more the inner space. In *Women and Analysis,* ed. J. Strouse, pp. 320–340. New York: Viking.

Fast, I. (1979). Developments in gender identity: gender differentiation in girls. *International Journal of Psycho-Analysis* 60:443–453.

Fraiberg, S. (1972). Some characteristics of genital arousal and discharge in latency girls. *Psychoanalytic Study of the Child* 27:439–475. New Haven, CT: International Universities Press.

Freud, S. (1905). Three essays on the theory of sexuality. *Standard Edition* 7:125–248.

——— (1914). On the history of the psychoanalytic movement. *Standard Edition* 14:3–66.

——— (1923). The infantile genital organization (an interpolation into the theory of sexuality). *Standard Edition* 19:41–148.

Gesell, A., and Amatruda, C. (1974). *Developmental Diagnosis,* 3rd ed. Hagerstown, MD.: Harper & Row.

Greenacre, P. (1950). Special problems of early female sexual development. *Psychoanalytic Study of the Child* 5:122–138. New York: International Universities Press.

Horney, K. (1924). On the genesis of the castration complex in women. *International Journal of Psycho-Analysis* 5:50–65.

——— (1926). The flight from womanhood: the masculinity complex in women, as viewed by men and by women. *International Journal of Psycho-Analysis* 7:324–339.

Jones, E. (1927). The early development of female sexuality. In *Papers on Psychoanalysis*, pp. 438–451. Boston: Beacon, 1961.

——— (1933). The phallic phase. In *Papers on Psychoanalysis*, pp. 452–484. Boston: Beacon.

——— (1935). Early female sexuality. In *Papers on Psychoanalysis*, pp. 485–495. Boston: Beacon.

Kestenberg, J. S. (1968). Outside and inside, male and female. *Journal of the American Psychoanalytic Association* 16:457–520.

Kleeman, J. (1975). Genital self-stimulation in infant and toddler girls. In *Masturbation: From Infancy to Senescence*, ed. I. Marcus and J. Francis. New York: International Universities Press.

——— (1976). Freud's views on early female sexuality in the light of direct child observation. *Journal of the American Psychoanalytic Association* 24(Suppl.):3–27.

Kubie, L. (1974). The drive to become both sexes. *Psychoanalytic Quarterly* 43:349–426.

Masters, W., and Johnson, V. (1966). *Human Sexual Response.* Boston: Little, Brown.

Mayer, E. L. (1983). Review of *Infantile Origins of Sexual Identity* by H. Roiphe and E. Galenson. *International Journal of Psycho-Analysis* 64:365–369.

Oxford English Dictionary (1933). London: Oxford University Press, 1961.

Parens, H., Pollack, L., Stern, J., and Kramer, S. (1976). On the girl's entry into the Oedipus complex. *Journal of the American Psychoanalytic Association* 24(Suppl.):79–101.

Roiphe, H., and Galenson, E. (1981). *Infantile Origins of Sexual Identity.* New York: International Universities Press.

Spitz, R. (1962). Autoerotism re-examined. *Psychoanalytic Study of the Child* 17:283–315. New York: International Universities Press.

Stoller, R. (1968). The sense of femaleness. *Psychoanalytic Quarterly* 37:42–55.

——— (1976). Primary femininity. *Journal of the American Psychoanalytic Association* 24(Suppl.):59–78.

Tyson, P. (1982). A developmental line of gender identity, gender role, and choice of love object. *Journal of the American Psychoanalytic Association* 30:61–86.

Webster's New International Dictionary of the English Language, 2nd ed. (1938). Springfield, MA: G. & C. Merriam Co.

13

MURIEL DIMEN ON
MARGO RIVERA

From Breakdown to Breakthrough[1]

MURIEL DIMEN

Now let me ask you this, Professor: is it easy or is it hard to reconcile life and theory, the things we learn from books and life as we live it?
Jorge Amado, *Tent of Miracles*

A SENSIBILITY OF THE MARGINS

According to Pierre Bourdieu (1977), each culture generates two sorts of question. On the one hand, there are the questions that may be asked, those within the "doxa," or orthodox systems of knowledge. On the other, there are the questions that are commonly thought to be unaskable (and therefore not usually asked), those pertaining to "paradoxic" regions of knowledge. In any discipline, work can proceed within the received paradigm (to switch to Thomas Kuhn's instantly classic, but also unfortunately instantly clichéd characterization of Western science [1970]). Or, struggling to make the paradoxic intelligible, thought can break through to the "heterodox" frontier, posing unconventional questions about the paradigm's odds and ends, which themselves furnish the raw material for new knowl-

[1]I wish to thank Michelle Price, C.S.W., and Sue Shapiro, Ph.D., for their careful readings of this chapter.

edge and new paradigms. Owen Lattimore (1951), an American anthropologist, held that cultural change tends to occur at the frontiers or outposts of culture, the regions of diversity where different ways of being, doing, and thinking meet, clash, and mix.

Margo Rivera's unconventional, paradigm-shifting "Linking the Psychological and the Social: Feminism, Poststructuralism, and Multiple Personality" (1989), is situated at just such a heterodox frontier, which is one reason it felt like home to me. At the time of its publication, other theorists—notably Jane Flax (1990) and Judith Butler (1990)—were also busy linking psychoanalysis, feminism, and postmodernism. Rivera's essay, however, is remarkable for its splicing of practices, its negotiation of not only different theoretical traditions, but also the psychopolitics of the clinic. It demonstrates the interimplicatedness of postmodernism and "the woman question," psychoanalytic and social theory, the suffering of individuals, the dilemmas of the therapist, and the problem of social inequity.

Most deeply, Rivera's theme is dualism, which, the reader will perhaps not be surprised to learn, is also the heart of my own work. For almost twenty years, my essays and books have, in both form and content, overtly or implicitly taken as their concern the problem of dualism. Whether thinking about the relation between individual and society, or the oppositions of gender, or the varieties of sexual desire, or the disciplinary divisions of biology, psychology, and culture, I have been searching for ways to think that do not commit us to reductions or determinisms. For example, my 1979 "Seventeen Sexual Propositions, or Variety Is the Spice of Life," whose thesis was the variability of sexual desire in, among, and between individuals, and across time and place as well, broke with scholarly convention, consisting of a series of notes (think Susan Sontag's "Notes on Camp" [1966] or Roland Barthes' *The Pleasure of the Text* [1975], which were not my immediate inspiration but do constitute models for all of us). The effort to publish that essay (1981, 1982) is a story in itself, which I shall reserve for another time. My last "proto-postmodernist" work of that decade saw light of day only in 1989, but had been written already in 1982. Called "Power, Sexuality, and Intimacy," it used form to demonstrate content; spicing theoretical sections with personal anecdotes, it argued that to understand sexuality and gender, one had to think on two tracks at once, social and psychological. It was, indeed, the working paper for my last book, *Surviving Sexual Contradictions* (1986), which juxtaposed fiction and theory as one way of making its synthesizing point about dualism. The high-theoretical synopsis of ideas that were to be spun out for a more general audience, that paper ironically received publication three years after the book itself had been published, partly because of academics' resistance to its novel(istic) form.

Indeed, it is not going too far to say that transcending dualism is the intellectual project of feminism altogether. Arguably the legatee of the "Marx-Freud synthesis," feminist theory mediates social theory and psychoanalysis, challenging both to exceed their premises. This triangulation completes a historical process begun and then suspended in the 1920s and 1930s. As Jacqueline Rose (1986) puts it, the project uses psychoanalytic insights into interior life to understand, in order to alter, "the internalisation, effectivity and persistence of some of the most oppressive social norms" (pp. 6, 8). The debate over psychoanalysis and politics (recall here Freud's quarrel with psychoanalyst and communist Wilhelm Reich, as well as the interests of other "political Freudians," such as Otto Fenichel and Edith Jacobson [Jacoby 1983]) coincided with that over women, but the two controversies were not to engage until a half-century later: "It is rather as if the theoretical/clinical debate about female sexuality and the more explicitly Marxist debate about ideology and its forms were historically severed from each other—at least until [second-wave] feminism itself forged, or rather, demonstrated, the links" (Rose 1986, p. 8).

Marx and Freud stand here as signifiers for the body/mind binary, itself posing the classic Western paradigm of dualism. At the same time, their literatures critique dichotomy. Both social theory and psychoanalysis, to put it more broadly, address what feminist philosopher Naomi Scheman (1993) terms the core modern epistemological problem of identifying and then bridging gaps, such as those between mind and body, masculine and feminine, psyche and society, and so on (p. 3). How psychoanalytic feminism takes up this problem depends on the use it makes of bridging theories, notably those inhabiting the postmodernist turn in philosophy, linguistics, and psychoanalysis. The danger it courts as it does so, as we shall see, is that of remembering the psyche while forgetting politics.

FROM BREAKDOWN TO BREAKTHROUGH

Rivera's essay makes one such bridge. Herself trained unconventionally, first as a psychoanalytically oriented therapist in Therafield, a therapeutic community in Toronto modeled on R. D. Laing's Kingsley Hall, and only later as a clinical psychologist at the University of Toronto, Rivera records in this essay the progress of her thought. We follow her step by step as she moves back and forth between theoretical and clinical practice, starting with feminist social theory and then incorporating the multiple personality literature, allowing each to be transformed by encounters with her patients, until, overloaded, she finds a sort of mediator in postmodernism, a discovery that constitutes a genuine breakthrough.

Out of a disciplinary breakdown—the failure of any one discipline either to cure her patients or to secure a resting place for her own thought—there emerged a different way of thinking that positioned itself at, and as, the juncture of practices. Working on the border of clinic and theory, engaged simultaneously with the twin problems of psychological and social suffering, Rivera found herself at a crossroads, the junction of feminism, psychoanalysis, and postmodernism. There she produced what for many psychoanalysts might serve as a sampler of the particular interdisciplinarity that is so helpful in the study of gender.

About ten years into contemporary feminism, it began to be clear to feminist theorists that gender, as simultaneously psychic and social, demands—equally—social and psychological perspectives. Recently, this dual perspectivism has come under the deconstructive microscope, a turn of events of which Rivera takes advantage. Poststructuralism—by which general term she denotes postmodernist thinking altogether as well as the specific literary practice of deconstruction—appeals to her because it dissolves an impasse, the disciplinary wall between the psychological and the social. This dissolution is accomplished through theories of what Foucault called discourse, or "a system of possibilities for knowledge" (Flax 1990, p. 205) that transcends conventional disciplinary boundaries. Cultural and psychic representations share a set of terms, occupy the same symbolic space, a space of heterogeneity and difference. Rivera explains further: "Semiotics is a metaphysics of symbols that is based on the premise that reality is not knowable except through its representations in language, its signs" (p. 26). The knowing of reality is the process of making meaning, tantamount to producing that reality itself. "This [linguistic] structure, far from reflecting some sort of natural world outside its domain, itself constitutes social reality for human beings" (p. 26).

A parallel, or recursion, between the postmodernist juxtaposition of disciplines and its utility for thinking about multiple personality affords, as well, new light on the contested terrain between fragmentation and multiplicity. Cultural and personal ways of being are, in the postmodernist view, neither fixed, universal, nor homogeneous. They are made, not given, hence internally diverse, changing through different points of stability. For a clinician like Rivera, who works with people experiencing multiple personalities, the poststructuralist interpretation of psychological and social systems as internally nonidentical is greatly illuminating. It yields a compassionate way to understand, give voice to, and make use of the heterogeneity and instability that, to presumptions of unitary identity, seem so alien and so ill. Rivera's experience prompts a new thought: if psychic multiplicity is instead normative, then the clinician has a route both into and out of psychic fragmentation.

The attractions of Rivera's essay are, likewise, multiple. For clinicians, it is a pragmatically grounded account of the journey of gender theory into psychoanalysis, a passage that might briefly be recounted as follows. "Man" is traditionally the universal human being in both social theory and psychoanalysis. But as long as "Man" stands for "men" and "women," gender remains an invisible category and "woman" a special one. Only when "the woman question" is raised does gender, and hence masculinity, become a problematic of general interest to both social and psychoanalytic theory. The problem for psychoanalysis, as well as for the psyche, is to recognize difference (Benjamin 1988, McDougall 1995). In effect, the very notion of "gender," insofar as it stands for "difference" altogether (at least in psychoanalysis), constitutes such a recognition. Once "Man" is no longer the universal human being, once it is accepted in principle that women and men are equally (if not equal) human beings, then a given, undifferentiated human nature becomes chimerical.

How thick the plot next becomes. First, gender complicates the nature of human nature. Next, a satisfyingly knowable gender-nature itself dissolves under the lens of difference. If the concept of gender arose in feminist theory to de-naturalize "sex" as the conventional representation of sexual difference (Haraway 1991), postmodernist approaches within psychoanalysis have evolved to counter the re-naturalizing of gender that takes place when gender-identity is lashed to selfhood. Perhaps, as I and other psychoanalytic postmoderns have been thinking, what is healthy is not the subordination of all identity to one model—a rule following Freud's dictum (1905) in the "Three Essays on the Theory of Sexuality" that all sexual desire come under the sway of genitality, that is, reproductive heterosexuality—but the flexible ability to negotiate heterogeneous aspects of gender, varied representations of self in diverse gendered and sexual mixes (Bassin 1996, Benjamin 1996, Dimen 1991, Goldner 1991, Harris 1991, Price 1995, Shapiro 1993).

There has been an echo, or perhaps call and response, between the psychoanalytic study of gender and the illuminations of postmodernism. New doctrine has emerged quite quickly from radical critique. Tolerance of "gender ambiguity" (Benjamin 1996) or, in more traditional terms, of bisexual psychic structure (Bach 1995, Kernberg 1995, McDougall 1995), has become a new norm. This up-to-date psychoanalytic gender convention (Harris 1996) finds early articulation in one of Rivera's three instantly classic pronouncements on multiple personality. She argues with those clinicians who regard psychic integration as the sole therapeutic goal for people experiencing multiple personality. Integration and fragmentation, she says, are constituted in a dialectical flow (Layton 1995). Integration does not require choosing one alter—one of the multiple selves fragmenting and cohering—as the dominant personality. Instead, it "prescribes . . . . the growing ability to call all those voices 'I,' to disidentify with any one of them as the whole story, and to recognize that the construction of personal identity is a complex continuing affair in which we are inscribed in culture in a myriad of contradictory ways" (p. 28). She goes on to say, in the second of her classic statements: "It is not the multiplicity which the individual with multiple personality experiences that is problematic but the defensive dissociation and the consequent limited awareness and ability to act on that awareness" (p. 29). Enlightened by this phrasing, we can then see the problem: it is not that gender identity shifts but that its instability is refused (Aron 1995, Butler 1990, Dimen 1991, Flax 1990, Goldner 1991, Harris 1991).

As disturbing as clinical psychoanalysts might find Rivera's valorization of multiplicity, they will appreciate her critique of the principal drawback of the postmodernist contribution. She corrects an inclination to glorify the very instability whose recognition she posits as central to psychic well-being. Citing Flax, she argues that "poststructuralist writers . . . are naive and unaware of their own privileged cohesion when they call for a decentered self" (p. 29). She chides poststructuralists for the implicit sexism in their interpretation of self: they seem to confuse selfhood with a Marlboro-man stereotype, "the unitary, mentalist, de-erotized, masterful, and oppositional" ideal called masculinity. She emphasizes the therapeusis of helping patients to hold in one central consciousness those varying and often contradictory states of mind otherwise "encapsulated" in alter personality states.

If the suffering, fragmented subject inhabits the margins of postmodernism, power is at the psychoanalytic frontier. Many awkward attempts at bridging social theory and psychoanalysis later, postmodernist approaches seem like the light at the end of the tunnel. Poststructuralism, Rivera reminds her readers, "insists that forms of subjectivity are produced historically in a field of power relations" (p. 26). Working clinically, she renders the power relation of sex a constituent of psychic fragmentation. Read her illustration, where contradictions of femininity reproduce the political inequities of gender in the psychodynamics of multiple personality: "Within one woman, for example, a particular alter often identifies with the position of woman as sexual object for the use of men, another identifies with the position of woman as emotionally vulnerable and invested in creating and nurturing personal relationships with others, and yet another with the position of woman as self-sacrificing and masochistic" (p. 27). Here are splits indeed painful to bridge: sexual instrument, maternal nurturer, martyr. Not only do these gendered fissures, adaptations to sexual abuse that are incorporated into the psyche as separate identities, develop idiosyncratically. They also stand for "the extremes of stereotypical self-identification which are central to the constitution of femininity as it is lived by all women in a patriarchal society" (p. 27).

From which school of thought, however, do these representations of gender domination come? While Rivera credits poststructuralism, the credit is in fact due elsewhere. If psychoanalysis can tell postmodernism about psychic pain and postmodernism can tell psychoanalysis about power, neither can tell the other anything much about gender hierarchy, one of the most important political structures of suffering and fragmentation in "the contemporary West" (in Flax's phrase [1990]). When it comes to the subordination of women, in fact, they have complementary amnesias—and even Rivera participates in an odd way with what in fact amounts to an occlusion of feminist thought.

Postmodernism remembers power and splits off gender, while psychoanalysis, as we shall shortly see, does just the opposite. Foucault's thesis, for example, revolutionizes our understanding of sexual politics altogether but keeps mum about gender (1975). While, in some lights, postmodernism is a version of late capitalist ideology (Jameson 1991), deconstruction in general, and Foucault's contribution in particular, nevertheless can be seen to have been founded on a politics. Foucault's theory of sex as produced, not repressed, answers not only Sigmund Freud but also Karl Marx, who contended that power resides in social and economic, that is, "material," forces. Foucault wants to reclaim the mental: How is it that people collude in their own oppression? Like the Frankfurt School of

Critical Theorists (Jay 1973), he was trying to explain how it is that people can remain subordinate, how it is that, even without a policeman at every door, people become their own jailers. Through linguistic practices operating at once in culture and in psyche, power/pleasure/knowledge systems of representation interdigitate identity, desire, and power. His brilliant exegesis of how "biopower" both materializes and regulates sexuality assumes, however, a universally masculine subject (Hunt 1992). His unmarked erasure of women thus manages, unobtrusively, to eclipse a central power dynamic and structure of domination. Gender hierarchy has no place on Foucault's map of the world.

For its part, psychoanalysis, even in its more socially aware relational variant, is happy to omit the troubles of the political (you say "political," it says "not psychoanalytical") (see Kovel 1983, Price 1996). It has come, however, to like gender quite a bit. It prefers, especially, gender-identity and its development (or "socialization," as Flax chides [1996, p. 585]). Psychoanalysis has also, as I have already noted, developed a taste for gender multiplicity, instability, and indeterminacy. It finds much less palatable, however, gender's borders with power. For example, the omnipotentiality which psychoanalysis has recently attributed to gender pays insufficient attention to the hierarchy that defines gender as we know it. The presence of power in gender relations should create a skepticism about that version of gender-multiplicity, "psychic bisexuality," in which one joyously recoups a sexual and gender totality (e.g., Aron 1995, Elise 1996). It does not. The temptation to diagnose is irresistible: the recent and sudden psychoanalytic appropriation of postmodern insights about heterogeneity, provisionality, and polyphony (not only in psychoanalytic gender studies but across the field altogether [see, e.g., Barratt 1993, Grey 1996, Hoffman 1991, S. Mitchell 1993, Stern 1990]) begins to look like a manic rush—a defensive impulse against some of the more critical, political dimensions of deconstruction.

Rivera, in her eagerness to enlighten the clinical world about the value of postmodernism, seems to have forgotten the source of her own insights. If there is one school of thought that recalls both gender and power, surely it is feminism. Put it another way: the power structure postmodernism forgets is the one feminism remembers—the subordination of women. Perhaps Rivera's momentary amnesia has to do with the pervasiveness of splitting in contemporary intellectual and professional life. It is easy, in pondering postmodernism and psychoanalysis, to slip into the binary thinking that, once excitedly deemed the truth by the structuralists (Eagleton

1983), has a psychodynamic counterpart in processes of splitting, in idealization, and in repudiation. Does Rivera, in repudiating the traditional
clinical approaches to multiple personality, idealize postmodernism? In
asking those clinicians concerned with the suffering ensuing from multiple
personality to attend to matters of power, she offers poststructuralism as
the answer. She thereby blocks out feminism's contribution to twentieth-
century thought: gender as multidimensional and interdisciplinary, at once
political, cultural, psychological, and representational. That sexism or patri-
archy, call it what you will, constitutes gender as we know it is feminism's
core insight; the basis of the new psychoanalytic gender theory, it also—I
would hazard—is in some way responsible for Foucaultian thought.

HAVING IT ALL: THE CONDITION OF CHANGE

Three's company. It is only in the triangle created by psychoanalysis, feminism, and postmodernism that we have a shot at understanding the dynamics of gender, psyche, and power. Having it all, that is to say
gender-multiplicity, means moving beyond the splitting tendencies implicit
in theories of psychic bisexuality. It means embracing that which Lacan
(1953) calls the Symbolic, the representations of culture contextualizing
the analytic pair. It means taking account of internal representations of both
power and weakness. We know a lot, to be sure, about the psychic
manifestations, not to mention consequences, of masochism—or victim-
ization. What, however, about internal traffickings in power? What about
sadism, the delight that ramifies internally as well as externally, psychically
and politically (which was surely the psychoanalytic point of Foucault's
power/knowledge/pleasure nexus)? How do sadism and masochism, sexed
and gendered, make themselves felt in the projective identifications of transference and countertransference?

   How shall we address such acutely painful conflicts as are daily reproduced in the prosaic politics of gender (the contradictions of gender, in
fact; see my notion, the "subject-as-object," the paradigmatic condition of
Woman, a projective identification of Mankind, in which femininity means
taking oneself as the object one is taken to be, thus willy-nilly participating in the erasure of one's subjectivity [Dimen 1986]; see also Dimen 1992,
Harris 1991, Benjamin 1988)? We may imagine, for example, yet another
turn of the screw in the happy psychoanalytic espousal of gender-multiplicity. Consider the affective relationships among one's multiple gender
identities. What would happen if (just to keep it simple) we were to add,

to the several femininities Rivera notes—sex object, mother, and victim—a heterosexual and patriarchal masculinity? Suppose instead we started with such a masculinity—in a man or a woman—and coupled it with a sense of submissive femininity? A dominant femininity (the so-called "phallic mother," perhaps)?

While Rivera tends to think of these senses as "roles," we can, following her lead, continue in psychoanalytic mode. Provisionally relying on Otto Kernberg's (1995) view of identity as built by identifications "with a relationship to an object rather than with the object itself" (p. 11), a relationship made of affect, we would want to think about how those two gender positions unconsciously engage to create an internal world. The relation that most immediately comes to mind is, of course, heterosexual, for whatever the relations of heterosexuality are, they also entail the affects and states of mind that accompany power. What about the intra-psychic dynamics of being/identifying with being the one in power, a (male or female) patriarch? When sex and gender meet sadism and masochism, is heterosexuality implicated in psychic suffering?

The psychopolitics of gender-multiplicity, the next plot-twist in the postmodernist and feminist intervention in the psychoanalysis of gender, leads us (back) to clinical and cultural frontiers: How shall we retain at the heart of psychic process a place for the dis/eases of the life we know, that is to say, for the social contradictions that, as encountered through the dilemmas of psychic life, are the substance of which character is made and, as Rivera contends, continually being remade? In Rivera's interpretation, identity is necessarily troubled; she critiques not so much unitary identity but the positing of "a non-problematic individual identity" (p. 28). Her essay reminds us of what we dislike remembering in life and in the consulting room: the lifetime presence of pain and contradiction. "Men and women," she says, "must struggle to fit themselves into the proper gender positionings that the laws of society demand, and the outcome of this struggle is never secure" (p. 29). At the border of the psychic and the social, her work challenges psychoanalytic dualisms—especially ideals of health and normality versus pathology and deviance—to make room for the consequences of that continuing struggle, so powerfully and poignantly rendered in the third of her classic pronouncements, which will lead us toward concluding this introduction to a paper every psychoanalyst should read: "The failure to slip easily into cultural roles and relationships lies at the heart of a rich psychic life" (p. 29).

Rivera's work makes us remember not only paradox, but its difficulty.

Analysts speak easily these days about paradox, nor are they all followers of Winnicott who introduced the topic to us (Winnicott 1972). I worry that, as paradox becomes palatable even to classical thinkers (e.g., Bach 1995), the contradictions of social and economic life to which paradox corresponds may become normalized into psychic paradox. I have drawn a distinction between contradiction and paradox in regard to money matters in psychoanalysis: "In the psychoanalytic contact, the contradiction between money and love, a relation between contraries that can be transformed, finds a temporary, reparative resolution in the paradox between love and hate, a relation between contraries that never changes" (Dimen 1994, p. 98). Both concepts denote opposition, but give it different meaning. Contradiction indicates contraries, the tension between which may achieve resolution (as in the Hegelian thesis, antithesis, synthesis). Paradox, in contrast, marks those contraries between which lies an eternal tension requiring habitation, exploration, toleration. Contradiction is a relation between contraries that are historical and therefore mutable but only by a political change that resolves their opposition. The resolution of paradox, Ghent has argued (1992), is always another paradox—or, in Kleinian terms, the achievement of ambivalence and the depressive position (Elliott 1996).

Thinking and living at the margins, in a place of breakdown, in discomfort, is the condition of insight. It is also the condition of personal and political change. One cannot feel resolution about unresolved social injustice and the psychic suffering it incites and rests on. If resolving dualism means not splitting, thinking marginally means bearing the pain of such necessary irresolution. To transcend dualism is to maintain possibility: the mobile, dynamic space between binaries yields resolutions that in turn give on to new complexity. Psychoanalysis needs to embrace the complexity of the social, to complicate, not simplify, its understandings.

Here then, a final thought, on the complexity of psychoanalytic feminism. Feminism, like psychoanalysis, has at its heart a critical tension between two main goals, one of which is ameliorative, the other, revolutionary. On the one hand, feminism aims to better the lives women lead, hence, the Women's Liberation Movement. On the other, feminism aims to radically reconfigure what we *mean* by Woman, hence feminist postmodernism. On the face of it, these goals are no news to anyone. However, if you look into them, you find that they contradict one another. Feminism tries to empower women so that they can create the lives they want, but it also, and simultaneously, puts their very desires into question, for it asks whether there are wants women have not yet begun, or dared, to imagine. Like any progressive social movement, feminism tries to improve what already exists, while at the same time it undermines the status quo. In so doing, it generates a tension, a paradox between the desire and need to better women's lives, and the wish and necessity to redefine them.

The heart of psychoanalysis is equally strange. Indeed, it is this strangeness, the initial, revolutionary shock of psychoanalytic theory, that Lacan's impossible language is meant to memorialize. Lacan wants to combat the ameliorating pull of clinical practice toward rationalizing the weirdness, "undecidability," and difficulty of the psychic interior (Bowie 1990, Rose 1986). The theory of the unconscious, so at odds with daily life and ordinary speech, remains the most radical of Freud's contributions (even though the idea of it had long preceded him [Ellenberger 1970]). For it's here, in the once-known and then repressed, or, as some analysts are thinking these days, in the never-known and dissociated (Bromberg 1994, Davies and Frawley 1992) that lives what cannot be thought. In the tension of conscious and unconscious lies the potential for psychic integration, which is to say, paradoxically, for personal change and meaning. The psychoanalytic session is a chance to say the unspeakable and think the unthinkable, to imagine what does not yet exist. It's not much fun: psychoanalysis offers individuals what feminism and other varieties of political action offer collectivities, the subversive opportunity of digging up the ground beneath your feet. But, like feminism, it's got possibilities.

REFERENCES

Aron, L. (1995). The internalized primal scene. *Psychoanalytic Dialogues* 5(2):195–238.

Bach, S. (1995). *The Language of Perversion and the Language of Love*. Northvale, NJ: Jason Aronson.

Barratt, B. (1993). *The Postmodern Impulse in Psychoanalysis*. Baltimore, MD: Johns Hopkins University Press.

Barthes, R. (1975). *The Pleasure of the Text*, trans. R. Miller. New York: Hill and Wang.

Bassin, D. (1996). Beyond the he and the she: toward the reconciliation of masculinity and femininity in the post-oedipal female mind. *Journal of the American Psychoanalytic Association* 44 (Suppl.): 157–190.

Benjamin, J. (1988). *The Bonds of Love*. New York: Pantheon.

—————— (1996). In defense of gender ambiguity. *Gender and Psychoanalysis* 1:27–44.

Bourdieu, P. (1977). *Outline of a Theory of Practice*. Cambridge: Cambridge University Press.

Bowie, M. (1990). *Lacan*. Cambridge, MA: Harvard University Press.

Bromberg, P. (1994). "Speak! That I May See You": some reflections on dissociation, reality, and psychoanalytic listening. *Psychoanalytic Dialogues* 4:517–548.

Butler, J. (1990). *Gender Trouble*. New York and London: Routledge.

Davies, J. M. and Frawley, M. G. (1992). Dissociative processes and transference–countertransference paradigms in the psychoanalytically oriented treatment of adult survivors of childhood sexual abuse. *Psychoanalytic Dialogues* 2:5–36.

Dimen, M. (1979). *Seventeen sexual propositions, or variety is the spice of life*. Forum on Sex in History, Mid-Atlantic Radical Historians Organization, New York, February 9.

—— (1981). Variety is the spice of life. *Heresies, # 12: The Sex Issue*: 3(4):66–70.

—— (1982). Notes for the reconstruction of sexuality. *Social Text* 6:22–30.

—— (1986). *Surviving sexual contradictions*. New York: Macmillan.

—— (1989). Power, sexuality, and intimacy. In *Gender/Body/Knowledge: Feminist Reconstructions of Being and Knowing*, ed. A. M. Jaggar and S. Bordo, pp. 34–51. New Brunswick, NJ: Rutgers University Press.

—— (1991). Deconstructing difference: gender, splitting, and transitional space. *Psychoanalytic Dialogues* 1(3):335–352.

—— (1992). Theorizing social reproduction: on the origins of decentered subjectivity. *Genders* 14(Fall):98–125.

—— (1994). Money, love and hate: contradiction and paradox in psychoanalysis. *Psychoanalytic Dialogues* 4(1):69–100.

Eagleton, T. (1983). *Literary Theory*. Minneapolis, MN: University of Minnesota Press.

Elise, D. (1996). *Primary femininity, bisexuality, and the female ego ideal*. Paper presented at the meeting of Division 39, American Psychological Association, New York, April.

Ellenberger, H. (1970). *The Discovery of the Unconscious*. New York: Harper.

Elliott, A. (1996). *Subject to Ourselves: Social Theory, Psychoanalysis, and Postmodernity*. Cambridge: Polity.

Flax, J. (1987). Remembering the selves: Is the repressed gendered? *Michigan Quarterly Review* 16:92–110.

—— (1990). *Thinking Fragments*. Berkeley, CA: University of California Press.

——— (1996). Taking multiplicity seriously. *Contemporary Psychoanalysis* 32(4):577–594.

Foucault, M. (1975). *The History of Sexuality*, vol. 1. New York: Vintage.

Freud, S. (1905). Three essays on the theory of sexuality. *Standard Edition* 7:125–245.

Ghent, E. (1992). Process and paradox. *Psychoanalytic Dialogues* 2(4):135–160.

Goldner, V. (1991). Toward a critical relational theory of gender. *Psychoanalytic Dialogues* 1(3):249–272.

Grey, C. (1996). *Culture, postmodernism, and psychoanalysis*. Paper presented at the meeting of Division 39, American Psychological Association, New York, April.

Haraway, D. (1991). *Simians, Cyborgs, and Women*. London: Free Association Books.

Harris, A. (1991). Gender as contradiction. *Psychoanalytic Dialogues* 1(2):197–224.

———— (1996). The conceptual power of multiplicity. *Contemporary Psychoanalysis* 32(4):537–552.

Hoffman, I. (1991). Some practical implications of a social constructivist view of the psychoanalytic situation. *Psychoanalytic Dialogues* 2:287–304.

Hunt, L. (1992). Foucault's subject in *The History of Sexuality*. In *Discourses of Sexuality*, ed. D. C. Stanton, pp. 79–83. Ann Arbor, MI: University of Michigan Press.

Jacoby, R. (1983). *The Repression of Psychoanalysis: Otto Fenichel and the Political Freudians*. Chicago: University of Chicago Press.

Jameson, F. (1991). *Postmodernism, or the Cultural Logic of Late Capitalism*. Durham, NC: Duke University Press; Boston: Little, Brown.

Jay, M. (1973). *The Dialectical Imagination*. Boston: Little, Brown.

Kernberg, O. (1995). *Love Relations: Normality and Pathology*. New Haven, CT: Yale University Press.

Kovel, J. (1981). *The Age of Desire*. New York: Pantheon.

Kuhn, T. (1970). *The Structure of Scientific Revolutions*. Chicago: University of Chicago Press.

Lacan, J. (1953). The function and field of speech and language in psychoanalysis. In *Écrits: A Selection*, trans. A. Sheridan, pp. 30–113. New York: Norton, 1977.

Lattimore, O. (1951). *Inner Asian Frontiers of China*, 2nd ed. Irvington-on-Hudson, NY: Capitol.

Layton, L. (1995). Trauma, gender identity, and sexuality: discourses of fragmentation. *American Imago* 52(1):107–125.

McDougall, J. (1995). *The Many Faces of Eros*. New York: Norton.

Mitchell, S. (1993). *Hope and Dread in Psychoanalysis*. New York: Basic Books.

Price, M. (1995). Gender talk: discussion of Muriel Dimen's "Third Step." *American Journal of Psychoanalysis* 55:321–330.

———— (1996). The power of enactment and the enactment of power. Paper presented at the meeting of Division 39, American Psychological Association, New York, April.

Rivera, M. (1989). Linking the psychological and the social: feminism, poststructuralism, and multiple personality. *Dissociation* 2:24–31.

Rose, J. (1986). *Sexuality in the Field of Vision*. London: Verso.

Scheman, N. (1993). *Engenderings*. New York and London: Routledge.

Shapiro, S. (1993). Gender-role stereotypes and clinical process: commentary on papers by Gruenthal and Hirsch. *Psychoanalytic Dialogues* 3(3):371–388.

Sontag, S. (1966). Notes on camp. In *Against Interpretation and Other Essays*, pp. 275–292. New York: Anchor.

Stern, D. B. (1990). Courting surprise. *Contemporary Psychoanalysis* 26:452–478.

Winnicott, D. W. (1971). *Playing and Reality*. London: Tavistock.

Linking the Psychological and the Social: Feminism, Poststructuralism, and Multiple Personality

MARGO RIVERA

The issue of multiple personality is embedded in the issue of child abuse, particularly the sexual abuse of little girls. Two independent studies drawing their cohorts from individuals in treatment with a wide variety of mental health practitioners found that nine out of ten of the people with multiple personality seen in clinical settings are women (Putnam et al. 1986, Ross et al. 1989). Ninety-seven percent of individuals with multiple personality have a documented history of child abuse, usually severe and prolonged, and in the majority of the cases this included childhood sexual abuse, usually incest (Putnam et al. 1986).

There is a growing literature that explores various aspects of the etiology, phenomenology, and treatment of multiple personality. Two landmark contributions have been edited volumes of essays by innovators in this field (Braun 1986, Kluft 1985). This literature addresses such questions as: How does multiple personality develop within an individual? In what ways is this internal organization different from and similar to psychological and physiological processes in individuals who are not divided in the same way? What methods are effective in treating individuals with multiple personality? This work has opened up an understanding of a phenomenon that had previously been ignored, distorted, or sensationalized by clinicians and the general public alike. There is a growing awareness among the helping professions that multiple personality is not rare at all (Braun 1984, Coons 1986) and that it can be treated effectively (Kluft 1984, 1986). Many individuals who are suffering from the effects of severe dissociation are now, for the first time, able to get help.

However, though there has been a significant increase in knowledge and understanding about the phenomenon of multiple personality, it has thus far been seen almost entirely in a psychological light. Multiple personality has been framed as a mental health issue, and its investigation remains largely the purview of the professions focused on the treatment of individual pathology, mainly psychiatry and psychology. Though multiple personality is intimately connected with the issue of incest, it has not been raised as a social and political issue in the way that the sexual abuse of children has been in the past ten years.

This paper explores the issue of multiple personality from a feminist perspective, using some basic concepts of poststructuralism to elucidate this viewpoint. A social as well as a cognitive and psychodynamic understanding of multiple personality is necessary in order to place it in its historical context (Rivera 1988a). This broader conceptualization of the problem is important if we are to succeed, not only in helping suffering individuals deal with the consequences of their childhood abuse, but in pointing to the roots of the oppression these individuals experience, and therefore address the issue of prevention.

CHILD SEXUAL ABUSE AS A FEMINIST ISSUE

The issues of incest and child sexual abuse were brought into public awareness by the women's movement of the 1970s and early '80s (Armstrong 1979, 1983, Butler 1978, Herman 1981, Herman and Hirschman 1977, Rush 1974, 1977, 1980). Social action programs responding to the needs of rape victims uncovered childhood histories of sexual abuse in large numbers of victims (Butler 1978). Some of the silence about the widespread sexual exploitation of children in our society began to be lifted, and some of the cultural myths that surrounded the issue—for example, that incest is rare (one case in a million in the general population according to the 1975 edition of the *Comprehensive Textbook of Psychiatry* [Freedman et al. 1974]) and that children frequently lie about being sexually abused by adults—began to be challenged.

Feminist theorists and clinicians who address the issue view violence against women and children not simply as a manifestation of the sickness of individual abusers or pathological family systems, but as an inevitable consequence of the inferior social and economic status of women and children, and social structures in which male power over women and children is institutionally integrated (Rush 1980). In response to the findings of her large, random-sample, retrospective study of adult women in the general population, Russell (1986) found that 38 percent of them had experienced sexual abuse before they were 18 years old, and 16 percent of them were victims of incestuous abuse. Ninety-five percent of the perpetrators were male, and only 5 percent of the incidents were ever reported to the police. As a result of her data, Russell concluded that two of the major—and most neglected—causal factors in the occurrence of extrafamilial and intrafamilial child sexual abuse are the way males are socialized to behave sexually and the power structure within which they act out this sexuality.

It was in 1980, when I began to work almost exclusively with children who were victims of sexual abuse and their families, that I had my first solid realization about sexual politics. The families I worked with had many differences, differences in racial, ethnic, and cultural backgrounds, different levels of education, different economic status. What they had in common was that the physical and sexual abuse of children by adults and of women and children by men were central issues in almost all of these families, in their past and in their present. As part of trying to understand what I was seeing, I began to read everything I could find about sexual abuse and violence against women and children. The feminist literature in this area made the most sense to me, and I started to frame the suffering I was seeing in broader terms than individual and psychological circumstances. It was also in this context that I met the first woman I had recognized as having developed multiple personality as a result of long-term, sadistic abuse in childhood.

The multiple personality literature (though there was not very much to read on this subject as of yet) helped me put a clinical framework around what I was experiencing with this woman and others whom I began to work with. Consequently, after a volatile beginning, I was able to work more deliberately and planfully.

My experiences with the women I was seeing who had multiple and highly dissociated personality states were also giving new meaning to the feminist literature I was reading, and to my growing feminist perspective. It became increasingly clear to me that multiple personality and the abuse that precipitates it is not only a personal problem for the women who suffer from it, but is also a manifestation of the oppressive power relations be-

tween adults/children and men/women, and that are endemic in a patriarchal culture. I began to see multiple personality, one of the most severe
personal consequences of child sexual abuse, as a feminist issue as well as
a psychiatric concern.

Much of both the multiple personality and the feminist literature made
sense to me, reflected accurately my own perceptions and, what is more,
it was pragmatically helpful in my encounters with my clients. The only
trouble was that everything I was learning from one type of literature
seemed to contradict everything else I was learning from other literatures.
The multiple personality literature, mostly written up to this point by a
few doctors, with one notable exception all men, never addressed politics
or social oppression at all, and the feminist literature about violence against
women declaimed the medical model of understanding women's abuse as
one of the foremost ongoing oppressors of women. I learned a great deal
from both of these sources that helped me offer the individuals with multiple personality compassionate and informed help. But they did not fit with
each other at all.

I found that the struggle that the women with multiple personality
were going through in therapy, I was encountering in trying to put my
thoughts together about multiple personality. A plethora of voices—inside
my head and outside—were talking to me about this issue. Both feminist
theory and the scientific literature about multiple personality seemed to
illuminate certain aspects of the condition, and each seemed to me to be
crucial to a full understanding of multiple personality as it is lived out in
a western patriarchal culture. But the medical profession talked in the language of disorder and pathology; popular literature labeled the experience
exotic, weird, and wonderful; and feminists would sometimes discount the
specificity of the experience, protesting, "But aren't we all multiples after
all?"

Because such a large percentage of individuals with multiple personality are women and because the issues I address in this paper relate most
obviously to the experience of women in our society, I shall use the female generic (she/her) in this paper. This does not indicate any denial on
my part of the experience of the many men who suffer from multiple personality. A social analysis of multiple personality as it is manifested in men
in a patriarchal society would be likely to have many similarities and some
significant differences from one that relates largely to women. But that is
a project for the future.

POSTSTRUCTURALISM AND MULTIPLICITY

In order to make some links between these two perspectives, the social emphasis of feminist theory and the psychological perspective of the scientific literature, it is useful to look at a third perspective about multiplicity, that of poststructuralism. The literature of poststructuralism does not directly address the issue of multiple personality. Rather, it questions the very existence of non-multiple unitary identity.

Many influences have helped constitute current poststructuralist theory. One of the most fundamental, though often unacknowledged, of these was the development of quantum theory by physicists in the first three decades of the twentieth century. Quantum theory (Bohr 1958, Heisenberg 1971) replaced the determinism of classical Newtonian physics (with its basic principle that material creation moves in a way that can be predicted with absolute accuracy and is independent of human will and purpose) with the notion of randomness at the foundation of natural processes. This does not mean that knowledge is impossible but that it is relative, a matter of probability distributions, the correlating of random sequences. The symbol of the universe evolved from that of Newton's clock to one of a game of dice or a pinball machine (Pagels 1982). From the point of view of quantum theory, Bohr (1958) declares that the task of physics is not to find out how Nature is, but rather to discover what we can say about Nature.

At the same time that these revolutions in physics were taking place, the science of structural linguistics was evolving, and poststructuralist theory in derived more immediately and consciously from this new field, that came to be called semiotics. Semiotics is a metaphysics of symbols that is based on the premise that reality is not knowable except through its representations in language, its signs. The basic insight of poststructuralism was first taken from the structural linguistics of Ferdinand de Saussure (1974) in which he challenged the modernist assumption that knowledge (which is always framed in language) reflects a reality that is outside itself, that is, that we can study objects. Saussurean structural linguistics posits a pregiven fixed structuring of language, prior to its actualization in speech or writing. Language, for Saussure, is a chain of signs, an abstract system. This structure, far from reflecting some sort of natural world outside its domain, itself constitutes social reality for human beings (Weedon 1987).

This notion of universal structures that construct our social reality was taken up in a number of different areas. The psychoanalyst Lacan (1975) applied the principles of structuralist semiotics to the work of Freud, pointing to universal social structures that guarantee psycho-sexual development along certain lines. The anthropologist Levi-Strauss (1963) developed a structuralist theory of human society in which the incest taboo and the exchange (as property) of women by men are the universal principles that underlie the functioning of all societies. These notions of fixed and universal meanings were central to the structuralism that poststructuralism grew out of and transformed.

The term poststructuralism is applied to a range of philosophical positions, some very different from others. Foucault's (1972, 1981, 1982) theory of discourse and power, Derrida's (1976) critique of the notion that language is a tool for expressing something beyond itself, and the French feminist challenge to white male definitions of identity and self (Cixous 1986, Irigaray 1985a,b, Kristeva 1986) all represent streams of poststructuralism. What they all have in common is a radical critique of the humanist notion of the coherent, essentially rational individual who is the author of her own meanings and the agent of her own productions. They also profess an abandonment of the belief in an essential unique individual identity. Poststructuralism deconstructs the object that psychology takes as pre-given, the human subject. It insists that forms of subjectivity are produced historically in a field of power relations. The notion of the individual has no meaning outside the socially and historically specific practices which constitute her (Henriques et al. 1984).

A modernist philosophy of science views the human being as the center and agent of all social production, including knowledge. This humanist perspective defines the self as essentially coherent and rational. Mistakes in socialization, conflicting and confusing stimuli, sometimes cause glitches in the smooth and predictable running of the machinery, and these need to be set right through appropriate intervention. We are all imbued to a large extent with this view of the world and ourselves as orderly and knowable entities.

However, though this is a comforting view, we live in a time when the modernist faith in a science that claims to study objects and claims the knowledge derived as an object is under attack and indeed has been effectively undermined. A poststructuralist philosophy, rather than attempting to map the contours of nature and to grasp the object of study, attempts to study constructions of knowledge, using a language of verbs rather than nouns. Within the field of psychology this contemporary movement to challenge the nature of knowledge has been called the social constructionist movement. Social constructionism views the role of psychology as exploring the processes by which people come to account for their lives in the world, rather than describing and explaining those people and that world (Gergen 1985).

Poststructuralism posits language as the place where our identities and our social organizations are constructed, defined, and contested. The basic insight that poststructuralism draws from semiotics is that language, far from reflecting the "natural" world or social reality, constitutes these realities for us. Different discourses are competing ways of giving meaning to the world and of organizing social institutions and practices, offering the individual a range of modes of subjectivity (Weedon 1987).

Poststructuralist theory offers an explanation of why changing conceptualizations in psychiatry and psychology often have more to do with shifting relations of power than they do with scientific advance. The decline of interest in the concept of dissociation and in hypnosis as a treatment technique in the early twentieth century, for example, reflects patterns of social history that kept multiple personality almost entirely unacknowledged and untreated for the better part of a century after Pierre Janet (1889) and Morton Prince (1906) both offered ground-breaking explanations and treatment paradigms for dealing with the phenomenon. Freud discounted this important work, and with the growing ascendance of psychoanalysis as the theory and technique of prestige, both the concept of dissociation and the diagnosis of multiple personality fell into disrepute. There were two significant contributions to the decline in professional interest in hypnosis and multiple personality (Ellenberger 1970): Freud's positing of *repression* rather than Janet's notion of dissociation as identifying the mechanism by which information becomes inaccessible to conscious recollection, and Bleuler's introduction of the term schizophrenia (and stating that multiple personality is a form of schizophrenia).

In the Middle Ages and the Renaissance, when the discourse of religion was the most powerful force in Western culture, women who displayed multiple personality would have been considered under the power of the devil, and they would have been punished, usually burned, for their sinfulness. Twentieth-century ideology frames that practice as ignorant and barbaric. We call *multiple personality disorder* a *mental health problem*. Within the contemporary western discourse of psychiatry, the notion of multiple personality disorder refers to a mental abnormality that demands psychiatric intervention. It contains, therefore, all the conceptualizations and social practices that relate to the framing of the phenomenon in this way. In other cultures and at other times, *speaking in tongues* was interpreted as a

sign of spiritual insight and giftedness. The individual who can take on
different voices and personae at different times was considered an adept,
and she experienced herself and played a particular role in society concomi-
tant with that definition. Isadore (1986) explores some of the varying discourses that exist around dissociation in different cultures and the roles
and functions they play in the maintenance of societal norms and functions
within those cultures.

Poststructuralist theory addresses an individual's experience by showing where it comes from and how it relates to material social practices and
the power relations that structure them. It addresses issues such as desire,
meaning, and the relationship of socially and historically constructed desires and meanings to the development of identity and social practices
(Henriques et al. 1984). Poststructuralists do not deny the complexity of
the often unconscious forces that contribute to the construction of the individual—indeed, one important stream of the poststructuralist movement
emerged from within psychoanalysis in France (Irigaray 1985a,b, Kristeva
1986, Lacan 1975)—but they emphasize the reconstruction of our culture
in the life history of every new member of the human race (Mitchell
1974).

POSTSTRUCTURALISM AND MULTIPLE PERSONALITY

The phenomenon of multiple personality is a vivid illustration of
poststructuralism in action. Following the poststructuralist emphasis on the
production of forms of subjectivity through social apparatus, we can look
at the construction of the alter personalities of an individual with multiple
personality as an example of the continual production and reproduction of
specific social positionings and practices. Each personality state identifies
with a particular position according to the role that that personality state
learned to play as part of the individual's overall survival strategy. We can
learn a great deal about both the individual and the culture by watching
the interplay among personalities.

In my experience working with women who experience multiple personality, it is very common for their vulnerable child personalities and their
seductive and/or compliant personalities to be female and their aggressive
protector personalities to be male, and other therapists have also found this
to be the case, though there has been no research so far on the subject
(Kluft, personal communication 1987). The experience of these alter personalities as they fight with each other for status, power, and influence over

the individual and her behavior is powerfully illustrative of the social construction of masculinity and femininity in our society.

Also, the range of positions offered to the states in which the individual perceives herself as female are illuminative. Within one woman, for example, a particular alter often identifies with the position of woman as sexual object for the use of men, another identifies with the position of woman as emotionally vulnerable and invested in creating and nurturing personal relationships with others, and yet another with the position of woman as self-sacrificing and masochistic. Each of these roles enables her to respond adaptively as a child in a situation of threat and sexual assault. These roles, as they are incorporated into the increasingly consolidated identities of the alter personalities as the little girl grows into womanhood, are developed in an idiosyncratic way in response to her particular circumstances. They also represent the extremes of stereotypical self-identification which are central to the constitution of femininity as it is lived by all women in a patriarchal society.

The interactions of these personalities are a play in which social processes can be viewed with more clarity than is usually possible. For every personality who identifies with one position (the compliant little girl, for example) there is often another personality who ferociously resists that position (the antisocial boy). Thus, both social control and resistance to that control can be clearly seen in the life of the individual with multiple personality. The dynamic of power and powerlessness inheres in the differences between personalities and in the shifts from one to another depending on the circumstances and their responses to those circumstances at any given moment. Each alter personality also illustrates within itself aspects of both social regulation and resistance to that regulation (for example, the woman who sees her duty as servicing men sexually may keep a razor blade handy, and she may occasionally use it on an unsuspecting customer), and they all influence each other. Thus, in the life of a woman with multiple personality at the florid stage of her condition, we have an unusual opportunity to watch personal identity as it continues to be constructed and reconstructed with the social context of the individual and within the larger social order.

In witnessing and participating in the therapeutic journey of a woman with multiple personalty, the notion of identity undergoes a shift. The search for identity does not appear to be a digging for an essential self, the *true self* of the object relations psychoanalysts (Winnicott 1965) that is hidden beneath protective layers of socialization. What emerges is a multiple, shifting, and often self-contradictory identity made up of heterogeneous and heteronomous representations of personal experiences of gender, race, class, religion, and culture (deLauretis 1986).

I have found many powerful and telling insights in this work on the deconstruction of identity that are useful for understanding the phenomenon of multiple personality. It opens up for study the complex relations of power and domination—such as the widespread devaluation and oppression of children and women—that structure our world as an area of exploration when looking for the causes of multiple personality, rather than simply focusing on the immediate casual factors of child abuse, seen as a consequence of individual or family pathology. It emphasizes the reality that individuals construct their identities in relation to their social positionings that are intimately related to variables such as race, class, gender, and religion, rather than responding to oppression by developing symptoms that can be seen and addressed in an ahistorical and universal way. It points to the important similarities between the contradictory personalities and positionings within the individual who uses her dissociative capacities to create an array of clearly distinguishable personalities and the rest of us who are capable of pretending to a unified, noncontradictory identity and denying our complex locations amid different positions of power and desire. It challenges simple notions of *fusion* and *integration* as a togetherness that dissolves all contradictions, and it problematizes our psychological and cultural construction of categories such as gender, sexual identity, and sexual orientation. Each of these areas merits exploration, but, for the purposes of this paper, let me address just one of the issues in a little more detail: notions of fusion and integration.

COMING TOGETHER: FUSION AND INTEGRATION

Notions of *fusion* and *integration* are pivotal in the literature about multiple personality. They are often juxtaposed to concepts such as identity problems and fragmentation, the latter being the problems and the former the solution, the goal of the therapeutic process. Multiple personality is, above all, a severe and chronic phenomenon of dissociation, of dividedness. There has been a great deal of discussion about the relative merits of integration as a goal of the clinical treatment of multiple personality, with some practitioners and some individuals with multiple personality opting for functional dividedness with negotiated cooperation among alters. However, most experienced therapists have found, empirically, that those individuals who did not move toward integration and continued, throughout treatment, to guard their separations jealously were much more likely to lapse into their earlier state of dysfunctional dividedness and acute suffering (Kluft 1986). Consequently, moving in the direction of replacing dividedness with unity, and learning other ways of coping with stress than dissociating, are usually among the long-term goals of therapy.

In the lexicon of poststructuralism, concepts such as a unified self and a well-defined individual identity are not only not viewed as ideals but are considered to be dangerous ideological fictions used to erase the awareness of differences within and between human beings. The notion of a self constructed throughout a lifetime of multiple positionings and practices elaborated by poststructuralism is used to undermine the concept of nonproblematic individual identity. It poses a challenge to both the epistemological basis of mainstream psychology and psychiatry and the practices of social control that often emerge from them (Henriques et al. 1984).

Is there any way to combine clinical notions of integration as a therapeutic goal with the poststructuralist challenge? At first glance, these perspectives, as they relate to the notion of integration, appear polarized, perhaps even irreconcilable. Placing them side by side raises important questions for therapists working with people who have multiple personality. What are we suggesting when we talk about integration as the goal of therapy? Are we fostering the creation of someone who will fit in better, who will not always be torn by conflicting voices and desires? Someone who is complacent in the knowledge that she has constructed about who she is and her place in the world? Someone who can suppress the awareness of the terrible contradictions we live with every day in a racist, sexist, classist society? Whether these notions are inherently contradictory depends on what it is that we mean when we use terms like integration. Given the challenge to the notion of a unified, noncontradictory individual identity or self that conforms with social expectations that poststructuralism properly raises, is there any way of talking about integration, fusion, or unification as regards the phenomenon of multiple personality without falling into a trap of creating the illusion of a stable, nonproblematic notion of identity that lends itself to manipulation and social control? Is the concept of integration a useful one at all?

I think so. Effective therapy demands that the person with multiple personality attempt to hold different and sometimes contradictory emotional states and points of view that have been encapsulated in the alter personality states in one central consciousness. We can talk about the erosion of dissociative barriers to a central consciousness that can handle the contradictions of the different voices and different desires within one person in a way that offers a functional and useful definition of integration, and I think we need this kind of vocabulary when we are talking about the therapeutic process. This definition of integration prescribes—not the silencing of different voices with different points of view—but the growing ability to call all those voices "I," to disidentify with any one of them as the whole story, and to recognize that the construction of personal identity is a complex, continuing affair in which we are inscribed in culture in a myriad of contradictory ways.

Within this framework, the goal of treatment is not to stop this continuous process of the construction of identity but to open it up to examination, so that, in eroding the dissociative barriers between the personality states with their often contradictory positions, the individual who has had relatively little control over her personalities can reflect upon the power relations which constitute her and the society in which she must live and work. This opening up of previously hidden, disguised, or inaccessible areas offers her—not unlimited freedom—but an opportunity to choose from a wider range of options and to produce new meanings for herself that are less rigidly constrained by the power relations of her past. It offers her more maneuverability among the power structures that frame all our lives.

For example, a woman who develops an array of personality states some of whom she subjectively experiences as male and others of whom she experiences as female does not necessarily, through the process of integration, relax into a comfortably and stereotypically feminine sense of her identity as a woman as our society defines woman. The claims of the different personalities to be different genders offers us a unique opportunity to explore an area that is often taken for granted, the social construction of the notion of gender in our society and the way in which it shapes our lives (Rivera 1988b).

A poststructuralist perspective expands the notion of gender beyond its concrete manifestation in the different physical reproductive organs of women and men and points to the reality that the notion of "natural" sexual difference functions in our culture to mask, on the grounds of incontrovertible facts of nature, the social opposition of men and women (Wittig 1982). By examining the various ways different cultures, subcultural groups, and individuals in different contexts within the same culture understand gender, the referents for the terms *women* and *man* are obscured (Gergen

1985). Possibilities are opened up that destabilize and reframe the question of gender differences.

The polarization of man and woman that is a result of differential socialization in a patriarchal culture is not a natural process. The relationship of human beings to their sexed bodies is not a simple instinctual one, as it is in most mammals. Men and women must struggle to fit themselves into the proper gender positionings that the laws of society demand, and the outcome of this struggle is never secure. The notion of a preexistent sexual difference that secures sexual identity for both sexes is a myth (Mitchell and Rose 1982), and the position that there is a natural, essential sexuality that predates the child's insertion into the process of her or his socialization blinds us to the more complex and problematic nature of sexuality and gender difference that is central to the individual's difficult insertion into culture.

Opening up an awareness of the social construction of categories such as male and female, as they are applied to human beings, offers a wider scope for the integrated individual with multiple personality so that integration need not involve a simple solution to her conflicts regarding gender identity. The failure to slip easily into cultural roles and relationships lies at the heart of a rich psychic life, and a woman who has integrated dissociated personality states into one central consciousness need not pretend that this is not so. Her state of struggling consciously with what it means to be a woman in our society can be an example of what Freud declared to be the situation of all women—they do not assume their femininity without a struggle and only at great cost (Freud 1931). The range of healthy and happy outcomes of this struggle is wider for a woman who has acknowledged a variety of contradictory impulses and desires in terms of her gender identity than Freud might have dreamed possible.

It is not the multiplicity which the individual with multiple personality experiences that is problematic but the defensive dissociation and the consequent limited awareness and ability to act on that awareness. Jane Flax (1987), a feminist psychoanalytic psychotherapist, notes that—though she recognizes the contribution poststructuralist writers have made in deconstructing the artifacts of white male concepts of self—they are naive and unaware of their own privileged cohesion when they call for a decentered self. They tend to confuse all possible forms of self with the unitary mentalist, de-eroticized, masterful, and oppositional selves they rightfully criticize. In "Remembering the Selves: Is the Repressed Gendered?" she argues that it is important for women to retrieve repressed aspects of the self, and to hold them in our consciousness together, rather than abandoning any claim to agential identity and cohesiveness. She suggests that, though it is important to be skeptical toward the humanist myth of the rational unitary individual, it behooves us to be suspicious as well about voices that may be urging us to submit to our limitations as the essence of our nature. Flax (1987) asks the question, "Is our only choice a masculine, overly differentiated, unitary self or no self at all?" (p. 106). She answers the question with another question—"Without remembered selves, how can we act?" (pp. 106–107).

So, the vocabulary of *integration, fusion*, and *personality unification* proves necessary. However, it is also important to recognize the dangers involved in any such discourse and to be aware of the pitfalls of taking for granted that we know just what integration is or to assume that it is more than it is. Integration—or consciousness-raising—does not accomplish itself by replacing old discourses with new unproblematic ones. It is accomplished as a result of the contradictions in our old positions, desires, and practices mingling and dialoguing with the contradictions in our new ones (Hollway 1984) with more flexible tools for constructing consciousness.

SUMMARY

Poststructuralist philosophy points to the similarities between individuals who elaborate multiple personality as an outcome of child abuse and others who, although they do not use the radical dissociative defenses individuals with multiple personality do, also construct their identities in a field of power relations, both personal and political, in multiple and contradictory ways. This perspective can aid us in seeing multiple personality more clearly and consistently, not as a strange and exotic phenomenon, a clinical oddity, but as one of the many manifestations of alternative forms of consciousness that are on the continuum of the personal human responses both to our immediate, intimate environment that effects our growth and development, and also to the wider social and historical context which has a no less powerful, although often less obvious, impact on determining who we become as persons.

Integrating psychological understandings of multiple personality with social and political ones is helpful in a number of ways, philosophically, clinically, and practically. That maxim of feminist praxis, *the personal is political*, can be an effective principle in the therapy of individuals with multiple personality. Much of the rage and fear and confusion in the woman with multiple personality is a direct result of social oppression, both in her childhood and in her present-day life. One of the consequences of placing her experiences within a larger framework is that an individual can begin to take her history less personally at the same time as she is personally reclaiming that history. This can be a liberating answer to the perennial question of the abused child—Why me? What is there about me that causes the people who are supposed to care for me to hate me and hurt me? In combination with recovering her own past, a woman can come to understand that it was *not* just her, that she shares her oppression with other women, and to some extent, with all women. This then usually eases considerably the shame that pervades her sense of herself (Rivera 1987).

Framing multiple personality as a social and political issue as well as a psychological problem for the individuals who suffer from it not only enhances the healing process for traumatized individuals, but also opens up a wider field for investigation and intervention beyond the treatment of those who have already suffered from severe abuse. The critical issue of prevention of the abuse of children must be linked to an accurate and full understanding of the multileveled causes of this crime. In order to effect change in the high prevalence rates, prevention strategies must be directed to as many levels of the problem as possible. So far, much of the emphasis in prevention programs has been on the individual child and family, and little work has been done on the relationship between social norms, structures, and practices (such as child pornography and the sexualization of children in the media) and the prevalence of child abuse (Finkelhor 1984). The cultural configuration of societies that have high levels of child abuse and sequellae such as multiple personality is an area that deserves further scholarly exploration similar to some of the research that has been carried out regarding rape (Sanday 1981).

Multiple personality is a rich clinical phenomenon. It offers valuable potential for studying the psychophysiologic makeup of the human being (Putnam 1984). Its exploration provides a unique learning experience for both researchers and clinicians. The depth, complexity, and volatility of its treatment present a challenge to even the most experienced practitioner. But it is essential to remember that multiple personality is, above all, a vulnerable child's response to abuse and terrorization and the adult's ongoing incorporation of these defensive adaptations into her life in ways that often result in a great deal of suffering. Ultimately, taking into consideration the social and political aspects of the issue of multiple personality is important because it expands in our capacity to address this suffering on many levels, in the broadest and most effective way.

REFERENCES

Armstrong, L. (1979). *Kiss Daddy Goodnight*. New York: Hawthorn.

────── (1983). *The Home Front: Notes from the Family War Zone*. New York: McGraw-Hill.

Badgley, R. (1984). *Sexual Offences against Children*. Ottawa, ON: Canadian Government Publishing Centre.

Bohr, N. (1958). *Atomic Physics and Human Knowledge*. New York: Wiley.

Braun, B. (1984). Foreword: symposium on multiple personality. *Psychiatric Clinics of North America* 7:1–2.

──────, ed. (1986). *Treatment of Multiple Personality Disorder*. Washington, DC: American Psychiatric Press.

Brownmiller, S. (1975). *Against Our Will: Men, Women and Rape*. New York: Simon & Schuster.

Butler, S. (1978). *Conspiracy of Silence: The Trauma of Incest*. San Francisco: New Glide Publications.

Cixous, H. (1986). Sorties. In *The Newly Born Woman*, ed. H. Cixous and C. Clément. Minneapolis, MN: University of Minnesota Press.

Coons, P. (1986). The prevalence of multiple personality disorder. *Newsletter of the International Society for the Study of Multiple Personality and Dissociation* 4:6–7.

deLauretis, T. (1986). Feminist studies/critical studies: issues, terms and contexts. In *Feminist Studies/Critical Studies*, ed. T. de Lauretis. Bloomington, IN: University of Indiana Press.

Derrida, J. (1976). *Of Grammatology*. Baltimore, MD: Johns Hopkins University Press.

Ellenberger, H. (1970). *The Discovery of the Unconscious*. New York: Basic Books.

Finkelhor, D. (1984). *Child Sexual Abuse: New Theory and Research*. New York: Free Press.

Flax, J. (1987). Remembering the selves: Is the repressed gendered? *Michigan Quarterly Review* 16:92–110.

Foucault, M. (1972). *Madness and Civilization: A History of Insanity in the Age of Reason*. New York: Vintage.

────── (1981). *The History of Sexuality* vol. 1, *An Introduction*. Harmondsworth, England: Pelican Books.

────── (1982). The subject and power. *Critical Inquiry* 8:777–789.

Freedman, A., Kaplan, H., and Sadock, B., eds. (1974). *Comprehensive Textbook of Psychiatry*, 2nd ed. Baltimore, MD: Williams and Wilkins, 1975.

Freud, S. (1931). Female sexuality. *Standard Edition* 21:223–246. Original version published in 1924.

Gergen, K. (1985). The social constructionist movement in modern psychology. *American Psychologist* 40:266–275.

Heisenberg, W. (1971). *Physics and Beyond*. New York: Harper & Row.

Henriques, J., Hollway, W., Urwin, C., et al. (1984). *Changing the Subject: Psychology, Social Regulation and Subjectivity*. London: Methuen.

Herman, J. (1981). *Father–Daughter Incest*. Cambridge, MA: Harvard University Press.

Herman, J., and Hirschman, L. (1977). Father-daughter incest. *Signs* 2:1–22.

Hollway, W. (1984). Gender differences and the production of subjectivity. In *Changing the Subject: Psychology, Social Regulation and Subjectivity*, ed. J. Henriques, W. Hollway, C. Urwin, et al. London: Methuen.

Irigaray, L. (1985a). *Speculum of the Other Woman*. Ithaca, NY: Cornell University Press.

——— (1985b). *This Sex Which Is Not One*. Ithaca, NY: Cornell University Press.

Isadore, S. (1986). *The Role and Function of Dissociative Reactions in Society*. Paper presented at the Third International Conference on Multiple Personality/Dissociative States. Abstract published in *Dissociative Disorders, 1986*. Chicago: Rush-Presbyterian St. Luke's Medical Center, September.

Janet, P. (1889). *L'Automatisme Psychologique*. Paris: Alcan.

Kluft, R. (1984). Treatment of multiple personality disorder: a study of 33 cases. *Psychiatric Clinics of North America* 7:9–29.

——— (1986). Personality unification in multiple personality disorder: a follow-up study. In *Treatment of Multiple Personality Disorder*, ed. B. Braun. Washington, DC: American Psychiatric Press.

———, ed. (1985). *Childhood Antecedents of Multiple Personality*. Washington, DC: American Psychiatric Press.

Kristeva, J. (1986). *The Kristeva Reader*. Oxford, England: Blackwell.

Lacan, J. (1975). *Le seminaire Livre XX: Encore*. Paris: Editions du Seuil.

Levi-Strauss, C. (1963). *Structural Anthropology*. New York: Basic Books.

Mitchell, J. (1974). *Psychoanalysis and Feminism: Freud, Reich, Laing and Women*. New York: Norton.

Mitchell, J., and Rose, J., ed. (1982). *Feminine Sexuality: Jacques Lacan and the École Freudienne*. New York: Norton.

Morgan, R. (1980). Theory and practice: pornography and rape. In *Take Back the Night*, ed. L. Lederer. New York: Bantam.

Pagels, H. (1982). *The Cosmic Code: Quantum Physics as the Language of Nature*. New York: Simon & Schuster.

Prince, M. (1906). *The Dissociation of a Personality*. New York: Longmans, Green.

Putnam, F. W. (1984). The psychophysiology investigation of multiple personality disorder. *Psychiatric Clinics of North America* 7:31–39.

Putnam, F., Guroff, J., Silberman, E., et al. (1986). The clinical phenomenon of multiple personality disorder: 100 recent cases. *Journal of Clinical Psychiatry* 47:285–293.

Putnam F., Loewenstein, R., and Silberman, E. (1984). Multiple personality disorder in a hospital setting. *Journal of Clinical Psychiatry* 45:172–175.

Rivera, M. (1987). Multiple personality: an outcome of child abuse. *Canadian Women Studies/Les Cahiers de la Femme* 8(4):18–22.

——— (1988a). *All of Them to Speak: Feminism, Poststructuralism and Multiple Personality*. Ph. D. dissertation, University of Toronto, Toronto, ON, Canada.

———— (1988b). Am I a boy or a girl? Multiple personality as a window on gender differences. *Resources for Feminist Research/Documentation sur la Recherche Feministe* 17(2):41–46.

Ross, C., Norton, G., and Wozney, K. (1989). Multiple personality disorder: an analysis of 236 cases. *Canadian Journal of Psychiatry.*

Rush, F. (1974). The sexual abuse of children: a feminist point of view. In *Rape: The First Sourcebook for Women*, ed. N. Connell and C. Wilson. New York: New American Library.

———— (1977). The Freudian cover-up. *Chrysalis* 1:31–45.

———— (1980). *The Best Kept Secret: Sexual Abuse of Children*. New York: McGraw-Hill.

Russell, D. (1986). *The Secret Trauma: Incest in the Lives of Girls and Women*. New York: Basic Books.

Sanday, P. (1981). The socio-cultural of rape: a cross-cultural study. *Journal of Social Issues* 37:5–27.

Saussure, F. de (1974). *A Course in General Linguistics*. London: Fontana.

Weedon, C. (1987). *Feminist Practice and Poststructuralist Theory*. Oxford, England: Basil Blackwell.

Winnicott, D. (1965). *The Maturational Processes and the Facilitating Environment*. New York: International Universities Press.

Wittig, M. (1982). The category of sex. *Feminist Issues* 2:103–111.

14

ADAM PHILLIPS ON
CHRISTIANE OLIVIER

Having It Both Ways

ADAM PHILLIPS

I prefer to start from the assumption that psychoanalytic theory has nothing to do with practice and then work backwards, as it were. That is to say, I only read the psychoanalytic theory—or rather psychoanalytic authors, not merely topics—that interest or intrigue me; and then occasionally notice when and if (not how) it fits into my clinical practice. Theories, like novels or poems, are more food for dream-work, not a way of adding to some putative repertoire of clinical skills, or a rather elusive store of knowledge. I don't equip myself; I usually forget what I read—I usually want to forget it—and then I see what returns to make me think, which I prefer not to do, but can't avoid.

And yet, of course, this is partly a wish, merely an attempt to both resolve and sustain a fundamental conflict. On the one hand there is the pragmatics of use, of theories as tools or performances. On the other hand there is the instrumentalizing of knowledge, of knowing too precisely what something is for, of wanting the means to insure the ends rather than to put them into question. And this is echoed in the ways we might describe our sexuality as either dream or function. Indeed these questions about the use and point of theory seem particularly pertinent in choosing a paper for this book. Partly because it is not clear, from a psychoanalytic point of view, what it means to use a theory. Is theory, for example, used like children use their infantile sexual theories, or like day-residues are used by the dream-work? For me, psychoanalysis is, as much as possible, the antithesis of—the radical alternative to—instrumental reason. It is not a how-to book. So the pragmatist has to have an unconscious, one that uses him or her, one in which it is never clear who is using who, or what is using who. All this is by way of a necessary prelude to the puzzle of psychoanalytic papers on female sexuality; of what these papers are for, and what they want.

Faced with the insistence of the question of sexual difference we should wonder, Why would someone want to make generalizations about the difference between the sexes, or want to join a club called male or female sexuality? And if they did make them, for how long would they be true, and in which contexts? Why the difference between the sexes rather than the difference between individuals, something far more difficult to theorise about? But then, of course, one's irritation, one's inevitable anxiety about all this is arrested every so often by something said, or by something one reads. One finds oneself assenting, recognizing something rather than merely agreeing with it. There seem to be affinities at work; or at least—in the disillusioned language of psychoanalysis—a transference has taken. In other words, at first I found Christiane Olivier's writing evocative, and only, much later and more obscurely, do I find it useful: somewhere, in William James's words "to go from."

When it comes to theory—as with sex—our preferences, fortunately, do not always accord with our standards. There are things in this paper I find disagreeable—the author's assumptions, for example that women are in some sense essentially heterosexual, or that homosexuals are merely frightened of women, are obviously over-simple—and yet in her writing, unlike a lot of modern theory about gender, she is not phobic about her essentialisms. She asserts them, we can take them or leave them; or, perhaps in Olivier's case, be tempted to do both (we can't prove our first principles, Isaiah Berlin once remarked, we can only love them. He didn't mention that we can hate them too). But to like a paper on sexual difference—given this is something about which we cannot be indifferent—we must like some of its prejudices, those fraught wishes, those beliefs we need to be true. Because Olivier is quite explicit in this paper about the ways in which femininity is socially constructed, she promotes, implicitly, not only analytic understanding but political action. As long as infants and young children are exclusively cared for by mothers, she suggests, rather than both sexes, then certain patterns of disillusionment will be sustained. The little girl will be disillusioned about her sexuality as something she is forever made to wait for; the boy will be disillusioned about his freedom as something he has to endlessly, forlornly assert. The woman has to wait—to get from the mother to the father; the man has to dominate—to keep the mother at bay. The risk, Olivier intimates, is that psychoanalytic theory and practice covertly reinforce this arrangement—that they encourage women to accommodate to a frustrated sexuality, and that they mock men's wishes for independence. As though both sexes, in the light of a certain version of the Oedipus complex, are prone to to be too hopeful.

As a psychoanalyst, Olivier does not see the problem as simply one of social arrangements. It is the conflict in this paper between its practical suggestions—its political idealism—and its sense of psychic resistance that makes it so compelling. Olivier's psychoanalytic sense of how costly and divisive development is keeps her paper torn between a sexual utopianism and an ironic dismay. "There are no genuine little girls," she writes in her rather more affectionate version of femininity as a masquerade, "there are only make-believe little women" (1989, p. 45). And yet if mothers desired their daughters, if they could allow, or believe in their homosexual passion; if mothers could affirm the existence and value of the little girl's clitoris rather than the deferred hope of the vagina; if fathers didn't abandon mothers to be responsible for—and so blamed about—the children; if fathers could bear to be more practically and emotionally present for their daughters right from the beginning; . . . —and so on. Olivier's canny description of the double-binds of oedipal development are always persuasive, and there to contest. She describes a knot—an impasse—between the sexes we cannot help seeing again and again in our clinical work, and not only there. And like any trauma it stubbornly resists the mobility of perspectives. It presents itself as something to be endured or reenacted rather than interpreted. But we need a good description to make what we call an interpretation possible. This, above all, is what Olivier's paper offers us.

"Here then," she writes, with a nod at Dante, "we see the infernal circle taking shape in which the woman, undesired in childhood, goes begging as an adult for the desire and approval of the man, while he, given the master's role, will take advantage of the fact to get his own back on the woman (in memory of his failure to get his own back on his mother)" (p. 50). Relations between the sexes always drift toward sadomasochism, a mixture of abjection and revenge—a division of unpromising labor—this is Olivier's stark picture.

Olivier presents in this paper a dispiritingly vivid account of women's (it is always the plural, the generalization that is the problem) dissatisfied lack of conviction about their bodies. For Olivier this is the oedipal complicity par excellence; not a given, but a coercion from outside. This corrosive cycle of misogyny, this unconscious contract between the sexes, makes one wonder how often in analysis we reconstruct not merely the history of the patient's gender identity as a man or a woman, but as a man and a woman. The reconstruction—the history of our bisexual development—seems to be one of the messages of Olivier's paper. It is as though we don't know how to take our bisexuality seriously enough.

We are spellbound by the fantasy of being able to be a satisfying object—an ultimately satisfying object—for someone. In Olivier's view the girl can never be one for the mother—and the boy can't avoid being one. The problem for the boy is getting *it*; the problem for the girl is getting *in*. This is the conundrum, the cross-current, recreated in the transference. Olivier's eloquent description of the trap is not exactly news, not exactly information, not a how-to story, but something better: a good story about an essential perplexity.

REFERENCE

Olivier, C. (1989). Oedipal difference: where the trouble starts. In *Jocasta's Children*, pp. 32–51. Andover, UK: Routledge.

Oedipal Difference: Where the Trouble Starts

CHRISTIANE OLIVIER

The Oedipus complex, however, is such an important thing that the manner in which one enters and leaves it cannot be without its effects.

Sigmund Freud
Standard Edition 19:257

Symmetry/asymmetry in the development of boy and girl: this is the problem that Freud has left behind him for us to argue over. His own final conclusion was: "We have, after all, long given up any expectation of a neat parallelism between male and female sexual development." [1]

If we take the trouble to reread his last writings on female sexuality, we shall have little difficulty, with hindsight, in seeing that there, in those writings, are the canvas, the sketch of that famous difference between the sexes which Freud always sought to trace back to a hypothetical comparing of bodies among children, whereas oddly enough he had, ready to hand, all he needed to explain it differently. If we simply put into the appropriate order what appears in Freud in no particular order, we arrive at something like the following argument:

I will tell you, then, that the most remarkable thing about the sexual life of children seems to me that it passes through the whole of its very

---

[1] Freud, S., *Standard Edition* 21:226.

far-reaching development in the first five years of life.[2]

Later, but still in the first years of infancy, the relation known as the *Oedipus complex* becomes established: boys concentrate their sexual wishes upon their mother.[3]

We see, then, that a child's first object-choice is an *incestuous* one.[4]

In the case of a boy there is no difficulty in explaining this. His first love-object was his mother. She remains so.[5]

With the small girl it is different. Her first object, too, was her mother. How does she find her way to her father? How, when and why does she detach herself from her mother?[6]

In little girls the Oedipus complex raises one problem more than in boys.[7]

It is only in the male child that we find the fearful combination of love for the one parent and simultaneous hatred for the other as a rival.[8]

The Oedipus complex, then, is the story of unconscious sexual desire: a very beautiful or a very sad story according as it is viewed as preliminary to any and every "love-story" or as responsible for all the difficulties of love.

But, "I will tell you," this Oedipus complex, this "incestuous" cross-sex activity—the boy's desire for his mother and her desire for him—is a one-sided business. In our society, this incest which Freud himself pronounced "a regular and very important factor in a child's mental life"[9] only gets into the air breathed by the boy-child brought up by his mother or another woman.

What happens to the girl during this period—the girl who, brought up by her mother and kept away from her "incestuous object," the father, does not experience this cross-sex activity? Is it only empty air that she breathes, this girl who so often in later years will display phobias about emptiness, fearsome bulimias, shattering anorexias? There is far too much

---

[2]Freud, S., *Ibid.,* 20:210.

[3]Freud, S., *Ibid.,* 20:36.

[4]Freud, S., *Ibid.,* 20:37.

[5]Freud, S., *Ibid.,* 21:225.

[6]Freud, S., *Ibid.,* 21:225

[7]Freud, S., *Ibid.,* 19:251.

[8]Freud, S., *Ibid.,* 21.

[9]Freud, S., *Ibid.,* 15:207.

going on in that area, as far as women are concerned, for us not to pose the question: What does the girl herself want, in psychic terms, when she is given the bottle by a woman who does not desire her, since they are both of the same sex? Can the girl "get enough" from her mother? Apparently not, since, once past this first adventure with another woman, we shall find the majority of women bound to the desire of men.

How do they get there? The history of their relation with desire must be strange indeed if it can bring them to a point where they will pay any price not to have to leave, ever again, the orbit of male desire. This clinging to the position of "desired object" will give the woman a hard time in many ways, especially in that it will turn her into an ideal target for all the ideologies that men find convenient.

This morning a woman said to me: "If I'm wanted, it means I'm not just nothing." What "nothing" can she remember, is she remembering? And who is it that is doing the wanting, if not a man? If we search about in her life as a little girl, we shall not come across any men, for there is no father hovering by the crib or the pram; and in any case it is not his job to look after her.

Is it possible not to see that, for years on end, the "fatal" Oedipal relation simply does not exist for the girl? Where is it that she can come up against the man who desires her and her sex? Certainly not where her nappies get changed. Nor in her kindergarten or nursery school, where women hold sway.

Where are the new novels, where are the way-out cartoons (apart maybe from those of Claire Bretécher) that show us a father "mothering" his child? Giving it its bottle, changing it when it's dirty? We haven't really got there yet, outside exceptional cases, outside deliberate opposition to local norms. For in general the man doesn't want it that way. And then, supposing he did, would the woman put up with it? The man and the woman are at one in accepting a sharing out of roles in which the man, having excluded the woman from any social responsibility, allocates to her alone the responsibility for the family. Sexism within the family, it seems, is just as intransigent as it is outside.

The woman is taken up with the child, the man is taken up with money. Who will deny that this is so, in a country where, for years now, there has been pressure for a proper salary for mothers, but where any proposal for extended paternity leave is turned down flat?

In "Latin" countries like France, the father has not been brought up to look after the baby—his own or anybody else's. He has no part in the upbringing of the young child, and, in order to get even a small part, he has to be exceptionally obstinate, whether with his male colleagues or with his wife, who will delegate to him only part of the responsibilities that she sees as hers by vocation—by birth and by nature, as she is so often told.

Meanwhile, the man's main function, it seems, is bringing in money to feed the protagonists in the drama that is being staged under his roof without his being, for the most part, involved in it. It is always the mother who tells the story of "the child and its neurosis," seldom the father, who leaves all that to the mother (indeed it's the only thing he does leave her). He has charge of everything else, and when he comes home in the evening what he wants is to be relieved of responsibility. It is peace that he longs for, as if he felt war unbearable, yet found it his lot to face it every day; as if all he ever came across was war, whether outside the family or inside it.

What is it about the relationship of man to war, about the war he fought long ago with his mother or the one he sees going on now between his wife and his son? Is what he remembers of the mother–child relation so awful that he won't hear of getting involved in it? Has the "incestuous choice" he once made so marked him that he couldn't even think of standing between his wife and his son?

Is he still somehow afraid of the all-powerful mother, this man who dares not stand out against her in the control she has acquired over their son? Is it not his memories of war which now set off his longing for peace?

So it comes about that, all because of his own oedipal struggles, he will fail to attend to his son's, and will make his daughter's impossible.

Most often he will prefer to read—to read about wars and conflicts taking place outside the family. He will bury himself in his newspaper, demand silence round the television, forcing the others to play down their personal conflicts in favor of national and international disputes. What a strange sort of father this is, who has longed for children yet will not look after them! What a strange sort of mother we are seeing, who can exult in having sole charge of the children! And yet this system can't be holding up all that well, since apparently fewer and fewer parents want children.

This rigidity in family roles, this single-sex upbringing: who better to speak of them than the psychoanalyst, who keeps seeing women ending up in her consulting room with their children, almost always on their own—and glad of it? The child's neurosis is no business of the father's, unless the analyst really insists.

This child, wanted by both parents, becomes, because it is born into a patriarchal family, the mother's exclusive "object." And it is a rare woman

who doesn't believe that in the upbringing of the child, she is irreplaceable and the man useless!

But where did these ideas come from in the first place, if not from
the man who, desperate to keep away from the woman, has divided up
responsibilities into "family" and "outside"? Keeping the outside for himself, he has left family care to his wife, so that never again, as he sees it,
will they meet on common ground.

No doubt. But surely this area that has been handed over to women
is huge, gigantic, out of all proportion to the man's area? For if the man's
work never moves very far from questions of status and purchasing power,
is it not the woman's task to awaken the appetite—and the appetites—of
the future consumer?

And did any of this cause Freud even a moment's hesitation? For
whether she likes it or not, whether she knows it or not, it is the mother
who sets off all the baby's sensations and intense pleasures. She it is from
whom it will learn them all, even masturbation, frequently observed in children, but in fact merely carrying on from the stroking that the mother did
in all innocence.

> A child's intercourse with anyone responsible for his care affords him
> an unending source of sexual excitation and satisfaction from his ero-
> togenic zones. This is especially so since the person in charge of him,
> who, after all, is as a rule his mother, herself regards him with feelings
> that are derived from her own sexual life . . . A mother would probably
> be horrified if she were made aware that all the marks of affection were
> rousing the children's sexual instinct and preparing for its future inten-
> sity . . . Moreover, if the mother understood more of the high impor-
> tance of the part played by instincts in mental life as a whole . . . she
> would spare herself any self-reproaches even after her enlightenment.
> She is only fulfilling her task in teaching the child to love. After all, he
> is meant to grow up into a strong and capable person with vigorous
> sexual needs.[10]

Could there be any clearer way of making the point that, in anything
to do with the erotic, the mother is the child's first teacher, its "older
woman"; and that the child's pleasure is a response to its mother's? In this
phase, it is her genital desire which will appear as determinant of the baby's

---

[10]Freud, S., *Ibid.*, 7:223.

sexual awakening. Freud, it seems, after touching briefly on the question, was not interested enough in the mother's sexual life and the typical orientation of her desire toward the male sex. Faced with similar patterns of desire in children of both sexes, he hypothesized similar patterns of adult response. This put the boy and girl on the same footing in sexual terms, and Freud had to bring difference back in by way of a relatively late, and in any case hypothetical comparing of anatomies.

Whereas if one keeps one's eye on the fact that the child's mothering figure is, in the majority of cases, a woman, for whom there is no complementarity but with the male sex, it is at once clear that, for her, the son is a "sexual object" whereas the daughter is not; which in its turn results in the boy's finding his mother a "satisfactory sexual object," whereas only the father could be that for the girl.

This is something pointed up by Béla Grunberger, who observes, in her study of feminine sexuality:

> As Freud emphasized, the only really satisfactory relationship is that which connects the mother to her male child, and we have every reason to suppose that even the most loving of mothers will be *ambivalent* toward her daughter. A real sexual object can only be of the opposite sex, and, unless in cases where there is some sort of congenital homosexuality, the mother cannot be a *satisfactory* object for the girl in the way that she can for the boy. . . .
>
> Thus Freud says that the girl child has to struggle with the difficulty of "changing her sexual object," moving on from the mother to the father, but we are entitled to think that the girl needs no change of object because, in the first place she has none.[11]

I am not alone in thinking that there is no moment at which the baby's sex is a matter of indifference in respect of the desire of the adult responsible for bringing the child up; or that what comes out of this confrontation between an infantile libido, intent on ensuring the baby's autoerotic satisfaction, and a parental libido which is powerfully genital, is the establishing of the individual's male or female constitution.

The fact that the same mother, feminine in gender, looks after both boy and girl is all that is needed to bring about a fundamental asymmetry between the sexes; with one sex, the male, having an adequate object from

---

[11]Grunberger, B. (1976). In *La Sexualité féminin,* ed. J. Chasseguet-Smirgel, Paris.

the moment of birth, and the other, the female, having none and being forced to wait until eventually the man appears before she can find satisfaction. There can be no doubt that this unsatisfiedness has a profound effect on the woman's character.

In relation to the mother, any symmetry between the sexes is ruled out from the start, and this difference, this differentness which first appears in the cradle will become a divergence which adult men and women will find it hard indeed to accept.

By the same token, if Freud had taken his reasoning further, or simply brought together his different pronouncements—one bearing on the awakening by the mother of the child's sexuality, the other saying that the child's first "object" is an "incestuous" one—he would have seen that, right from the earliest moments, there is a problem facing the girl, and that if, later, she turns toward her father (a matter never fully worked out by Freud), it is because for her there is no sexual awakening possible with the mother.

In terms of the Freudian theory of the Oedipus complex as that which structures personality, the girl cannot experience this structuring, or can only experience it by a different route, without recourse to fixation on the opposite sex. There is a first stage in which no one desires the girl's body, her sex.

Did Freud take fright at his own discoveries? For it is when we carry on his own arguments, when we follow his logic through that we come up against the stark fact that the girl has no primary love-object (rare indeed are the fathers who stay at home and look after their daughters). Let me put it this way: of all the hypothetical oedipal women who have had their father as primary love-object, I have not, or not yet, come across a single one. What I know is daughters who have come through a relationship with their mother that had no desire in it, and then, more or less belatedly, switched to their father.

No doubt the "new man" that the feminists are demanding, the man who will not refuse to mother his child, will father a "new son"; but above all he will father a "new daughter" who, right from the moment of birth, will have an adequate "sexual object" and will no longer be driven by the devils of unsatisfiedness to the point where only perfectionism can bring her reassurance.

All this lies ahead. Meanwhile let us take a closer look at what makes up the character of the man and the woman in their relation with their mothers and within the present nuclear, patriarchal family.

THE DEVELOPMENT OF THE BOY

We start with him since it was his development that Freud called "more logical" and easier to interpret than the girl's.

And what in fact do we see? An extremely simple infantile situation: from the moment of birth the boy finds himself exposed to the opposite sex, since his love-object is his mother, and therefore already in an elementary oedipal position, since the famous "incestuous" object is right there by the cradle. For the male child there will be no problem about setting up the oedipal relation or getting into it since he is in it from the outset as a result of his birth—at the hands of a woman. Rather, it might be said, he falls into it head first, and the really hard thing for him is coming out again, getting out of this "fatal" conjunction of the sexes while managing to keep his integrity.

For it is in her son that the mother has her only chance of seeing herself in male form. This child that has come out of her belongs to the other sex, and so the woman gets the chance of believing in that ancient dream that all humans have: bisexuality, so often represented in Greek statuary in the guise of the androgyne.

Just watch how proudly she carries this son who has come along to complete her in a way that no one else can. Just look at the utter satisfiedness painted on the faces of all those "virgins with child." Surely all those Italian Madonnas are giving praise to the woman-and-mother who achieves happiness and wholeness without involving herself with the father, here banished to a myth. God the Father—a religion of men, laid down by men who recognize nothing in women but the womb that bore them. An oedipal religion, if ever there was one, since the father is pushed out to make more room for the mother—just as he is in our own day.

Motherhood: for the man, paradise lost, haunting him so much that he wants to be master of it, be the one who decides on it. If he can't carry the child, let him at least be able to compel "the other" to do the carrying. The woman "gets" pregnant, in the phrase everyone knows. As if with brutal suddenness she had contracted something by accident, something unexpected that would lay her low. Men whom we have seen angrily buzzing round the problem of motherhood and abortion in a display of extraordinary violence; men who will build up the mother in order the better to put down the woman, who, it appears, has no right even to the "desire" for a child—that is something that can be settled on her behalf. No question of her being in command. What have we not had to suffer, all because of the farrago of myths and envious feelings that the man always carries along with him on the subject of our reproductive organs!

It's a lucky woman that has a son! Is that perhaps why Lacan vengefully reminds her that "woman is not everything"? Let her not imagine that she might occupy that position that causes so much envy in the man, who sees himself condemned to the solitary experience of single-sexedness.

No, no, don't worry: this mother is not "everything"—even if she is strongly tempted to think that she is—for this little boy is neither her nor hers and if, briefly, she may have thought that she had the other sex in her possession, her son as he grows will not fail to take away her illusions. The longer the mother believes in her oneness with her son, the more violent and perdurable will be the opposition he puts up.

And if the first months of dependence and of mother–child symbiosis seem to hold fewer problems for boys than for girls, it is a different story as far as the next period is concerned, the period of anal opposition and self-assertion. For then the difficulties will fall on the boy who, in this phase, will have to defend himself against the maternal fantasy of completeness so as to win his independence: an independence which his mother is less than wholehearted about wanting.

The woman has unconscious difficulties about giving up the only male she has ever been able to keep by her; she whose father let her down and whose husband is more often away than at home.

There is a further difficulty (not described by Freud) which the little boy has to overcome, for he has to make his escape from the oedipal stage *against* his mother, who does not want him to go away and leave her. This is the start of the longest but least obvious of wars against female desire; the place where the boy joins battle in the oedipal war of the sexes. Against his own mother.

When his mother says to him: "You'll be grown up soon enough," is she not giving expression to her desire? Is this not a way of holding on to him? Have I not known mothers who urged their sons to pull out their first facial hairs, that token of the onset of male adulthood?

Is it not on account of this desire of the mother's that the boy stays "little" so much longer than the girl of the same age? Do we not learn from tests that there is a considerable gap in maturity between the sexes up to puberty and even beyond?

Here surely we are seeing the outward sign of the difficulty in growing up that is experienced by the boy pinioned in the maternal love-trap. Is it not the boy who wets the bed, who soils himself, who, in a word, refuses to grow up? The bad time that the male child goes through here leaves its mark on him forever, in the form of a deep fear of female domination.

It looks as if the famous "trap" so often alluded to by men must be the trap of a symbiosis with the mother that is seen as "imprisoning." Symbiosis, psychosis? At all events, a "prison" that sets off panic in the man at the thought of any symbiosis with any other woman. Never again to be caught up in the same place, in the same desire as the woman: this is the main driving force of the man's misogyny. Holding the woman away from him, keeping her confined to areas designed for her alone (family, schooling, home) is the primary objective of the masculine campaign.

Setting up at all points a barrier, whether physical or social, between him and her, standing out against her desire in any and every way, keeping his distance by any and every means will be the man's greatest obsession. Even his sexual behavior will be affected: he will be that much more sparing of the gestures and words that might recall something of his symbiotic lovingness with the mother.

So: no painless escape from the Oedipal stage; it will never be irreversibly achieved, and it will leave the man forever suspicious of women. Sometimes, no escape at all, which will bring mother and child to the psychotherapist's door. At this stage in the life of the human being we see three times more boys that girls (their turn will come later). That fact alone is proof of the order of difficulty that this battle with the mother faces the boy with. Where there is neurosis, it will be because the battle has made the boy into:

either a child who has been so keen to resist the mother than he has forgotten to exist for his own sake: a child dead to all desire. Such a one will be spoken of as featureless; he will speak neither at home nor at school, for the shutdown is total. In order to find out how to get rid of "her" and her permanent desire, he has had to jettison all desire.

or a child who has turned aggressive: first with his mother, and later, by extension, with all and sundry; defying the teacher, picking fights with the boys, being mean to the girls. Wherever he is, battle is never very far away; wherever he goes, his arrival rings the alarm bell, for he is set on proving that he is the tough one. Tougher than "her," and then tougher than anyone. What he really wants is to get the better of his mother and her control. Unstable sometimes, his increasing fidgetiness is a sign of his urge to get away from her at every moment.

And what about the father? What is he doing all this time? Where is he? Can he not see, does he not know, from having gone through it all himself, what is happening? Of course he knows. Of course he remembers. But he does not dare pull his son free of female power: the only power his wife can enjoy undisturbed, since all other forms of power fall to him. The son has little hope of being able to count on his father to get him out of the bad time he is having with his mother, for the father deliberately keeps out of this conflict. More often than not, the first the boy will know of homosexuality will be in adolescence, with other boys of his age who are just emerging from the dangerous labyrinth. And in that context homosexuality in males acts as a defense against mothers, women, girls. Homosexuality in boys is above all a way of defending themselves against the opposite sex. We shall see later that homosexuality in girls is wholly unrelated to this way of being.

Here then, in summary form, are the general nature and effects of the problem of the male Oedipus complex; the story of the man's coming into being, as fruit of the fateful congress of the sexes, at the hands of a woman. For the man, what is born here is the tenderest of all loves, followed by the most long-drawn-out of wars. From this the man emerges showing signs of distrust, silence, misogyny; in a word, all the things women reproach men with.

It costs the man no small effort to get to the point where he can shake free of the woman he has loved best (no mother will contradict me if I say that boys are far more loving than girls) and who has loved him best. And all this is the result of cross-sex dealings within the family, where only the mother has the child-rearing role, only the mother has to live close up against her son.

In the old days there would have been grandfathers and great-grandfathers, uncles, cousins—any number of male images to break up this dangerous one-to-one. Nowadays the all-powerful mother lives with her son who satisfies all the longings she had long ago, makes up for the father who was never there and the husband who has gone away. The little boy *is* there, so he must pay for them. After all, a woman has to get a man wherever she finds him: too bad if it's in the cradle!

After the terrible struggle with this all-powerful mother, how could men possibly avoid opting for wariness in anything to do with women and their power, that power which must be held in check? How could they possibly not spend their time setting limits to our world, shutting us away with our duties and responsibilities? How could a man's love for a woman be anything but ambivalent?

Is there a man, is there a son anywhere who can say that he really has got rid of his mother? Oh, he'll have left her, all right, but how far did he get? At what age? Left her for whom? Is there a mother anywhere who could say that she has given up her son, even when she's 80? He is still "the one," even where no word is said, even if respect for others requires that nothing be said, even if there really are brave men and mothers above reproach.

The bond that is woven in the darkness of infancy between mother and son binds them forever. When a woman marries, she can only ever marry another woman's son. Hence the clashes that go on between mothers-in-law and daughters-in-law over the same man, until such time as the younger one has a son of her own. Until she abandons the battle for the past in favor of the battle for the future with her son; this for want of the chance to hold on to the adult male, who is unavailable because invariably, mysteriously, tied up with his mother; because he is still ambivalent as between his past and his future.

Which is how the story carries on from one generation to the next: a son, secretly bound to his mother, takes a wife so that he can really get going, so that he can reproduce; but keeps his distance from her and allows her no rights beyond love-bed or child-bed. A woman without a husband, without a male equal, will foot the bill for the war in which she finds herself involved for no other reason than that she has taken over from the mother; a woman who will find in her son the only male that is really close to her. The circle has been closed, the loop looped: because the woman has been kept at a distance by her husband, she will invest in her son and prepare in him the ground of "distance" for the other woman, the one who is yet to come. Misogyny is a crop sown by one woman and reaped by another.

THE DEVELOPMENT OF THE GIRL

Now let us take a look at what is happening on the other side: While the boy is desperately struggling to break free of his mother's fondness for him, what is the girl going through—this little girl whom the same mother is conspicuously not binding to herself with hoops of steel, since in the mother–daughter relationship there is no sexual desire?

One question may be put straightaway: Might the girl not be better off, since she avoids the "fateful" combination of the sexes? Alas, not at all. But the risks are not the same, and neither are the results: if the boy finds it hard to get rid of a love-object which is "too adequate," the terrible thing for the girl is failing to find any adequate object along her way, and so having to stay outside oedipal relations until well into her life. The boy may start out from fusion/complementarity; the girl's early experience is of the body/mind split: she will be loved as a child but not desired as a girl's body. She is not a satisfactory object for her mother in sexual terms; only for her father could she be one.

Only the father could give his daughter an easy (because fully sexed) position, since he sees the female sex as complementary to his own and therefore indispensable to sexual pleasure (something that the mother only rarely feels about her daughter's sex, for, outside exceptional cases, the mother does not desire her own sex as object of pleasure, but rather the sex that is complementary to her own, that is, the man's).

The girl, as a non-oedipal object for her mother, will feel that she is unsatisfactory, incapable of satisfying. This is the first of the consequences of her mother's non-desire: the girl—and later the woman—is never satisfied with what she has or what she is. She is always yearning for a body other than her own: she would like a different face, different breasts, different legs. Every woman, by her own account, has something about her body which does not look right.

For the first thing that did not look right was indeed something about the body, since it was about her sex not triggering desire in her mother. The little girl, in her mother's eyes, will be sweet, lovable, graceful, good—anything but sexually alive, tinged with desire. The color of desire will not be found in the little girl that has been handled by a woman.

And yet, even at that time, her sex is a fact, and the vulvo-clitoral area is hypersensitive to the mother's touch when she cleans the child; but that sex is not an object of desire for the mother who, in line with the culture, does not see this part of herself as "typically female," rather reserving that distinction for her vagina, which the man has pronounced "fit for orgasm." It is the mother, then, who first bars the way to her daughter's clitoral orgasm and institutes silence on the subject of that orgasm.

The "thou art a clitoral child" is replaced by the "thou shalt be a vaginal woman who will come to climax with a man—later on." A present tense which is forbidden for the sake of a future which must be waited for: that, alas, is how it will be for a great many women, still caught up in the wait for the orgasm of the adult woman who, like the little girl, knows that there is a climax lying ahead but is never aware of one at the time. So the girl is denied in her own sexuality and told to wait for her future sexuality as a woman; she must keep to herself what she is (a clitoral child) and believe in what she is not (a vaginal woman).

Grasping the dialectic that is being imposed on her, guessing that only the woman in regarded as a sexual being, she plays at being a woman: she borrows the tricks of her trade: the lipstick, the high heels, the handbag. The little girl gets herself up as a woman, just as later on the woman will disguise herself to look like another woman, different from the one she is.

That is the origin of the permanent "displacement" of the woman with respect to her own body: there's never any harm, in her view, in the odd bit of cheating if it means being accepted as a woman. Her real sex is not enough; she is always having to make more of it. And what do women's magazines go on about, if not the "really natural woman," the "womanly woman," the "woman that *is* a woman," and so on? As if there always had to be something added to the woman's own sex, as if the woman were not woman by nature, as if her sex were not the signifier of her femininity. Surely all this is—once more, once again—the story of the little girl who has to show herself as sexed differently from how she actually is? And was it not right back in childhood that the woman first started to tell lies about her actual sex? There are no genuine little girls; there are only make-believe little women.

Everyone knows that to get yourself recognized as a girl, it is not enough just to be one: you have to be continually adding on proofs of femininity which, often, have nothing to do with sex.

> The boy is desired for his own sake. . . . The girl is desired—if and when she is so—according to a scale of values. . . :
> –girls are more loving. . .
> –they are more grateful. . .
> –they are sweet and charming. . .
> –they help about the house. . . .[12]

All in all, the girl is pronounced "girl" for a thousand reasons which never have anything to do with her actual sex; she is given conditional recognition as "girl," while the boy is recognized as boy entirely because of his sex. The girl always has to bring forward proofs of her femininity. Following on from that, how could women not be haunted by the need to put the signs of that femininity on public display? What a life it is for the

---

[12]Belotti, E. G. (1976). *Du Côté des petites filles,* Paris.

woman who thinks she has to go on proving all her life long that she really is a woman! A woman—something even she is never wholly certain of being, since her social identity seems never to have stemmed from the sex of her body.

A painful dialogue in which *identification* (being like) matters more than *identity* (being oneself), in which *make-believe* replaces *genuine*. Identity blocked by lack of desire from the other sex, identification imperiled by the difficulty she has in seeing her own body as being like her mother's: these are the twin hazards that lie along the girl's road.

The little girl's trouble is that her body is not like anyone's. She possesses neither a sex like her father's nor the distinguishing features of her mother (who has breasts, comes in at the waist and out at the hips, has public hair). The little girl sees herself as naked, flat, and with a slit—something like the sexless dolls on sale in shops.

She does have something which really is "like," but it is something she can't see, something hidden away inside her slit. And no one ever tells her about this clitoris, the only sexual point of comparison with her mother.

For anyone who really wants to see some lightening of the darkness that surrounds women's sexuality, the clitoris—so much built up by feminists, so much played down by male chauvinists—may well be one of the earliest links that must not be bypassed in the developmental chain. For when the girl is not told about this part of her sexuality, what happens is that she is denied mention of what she has, and told instead, in general terms, about her as yet nonfunctioning genital endowment. She is told about what she does not have (periods, reproductive processes) and her mother does have.

And because of all this, the mother cannot be a locus of identification for the girl. Homosexual feelings between them are ruled out: only in adolescence will the girl discover that there are bodies like hers—hence the importance of friendship between girls in that period, setting up the femininity which could not be set up with the mother.

On the other hand, faced with this mother who is unlike her, who is better endowed than she is, the girl does discover envy and jealousy which do not—as Freud thought—stem from the relationship with the male body, but from the overwhelming comparison with that of the woman-and-mother.

It is not uncommon to see a little girl touching first her mother's breasts and then her own chest and saying "Katie no boobs." Long before the man's penis, is it not rather, in view of the mother's predominant presence, the sexual attributes of the mother that are felt as missing from the child's body? Creating in the boy the irreversible lack and enduring fantasy of the comforts of the maternal breast, and, in the girl, the endless comparing with and jealousy of any other breast (any other body) better shaped than her own?

In any case, if that is where women are stuck, and if jealousy has taken the place of homosexuality, it is because the mother, first and foremost of the women to be encountered, was unable to bring herself to recognize or name that part of her daughter's body which in fact is like part of hers. Out of shame? Out of fear? No woman ever talks to her daughter about the clitoris.

And so, in despair at having no sex (the clitoris unrecognized), and no sexual object (the father absent), the little girl will go on, not, as Freud thought, to repress her sexuality, but to displace a sexuality which, as such, is impossible.

If there is nothing sexual in her sex, there will be enough and to spare everywhere else. The girl sexualizes everything: her body, which has to be feminine, her acts, which have to be in line with those of her kind, her language, which becomes seductive. The woman will sexualize whatever can be seen by the other. Since her sex got no recognition when she was a little girl, the woman will contrive to get it for the other, unsexed parts of her body. With the result that sometimes she will take her whole body as a sexual signal and then will be afraid to display it; like the woman who said to me one day: "When I have to get up and speak, and everyone can see me, I get confused about what I want to say, my mind goes blank. I'm overcome with shame, all I can think of is my body, and then I just don't know where to put myself."

The woman learns in childhood to use her external features to signify her internal sex. The little girl spends her time giving external proofs of her femininity, which the adults round her keep a closely guarded secret, and, following on from that, she will stop being able to tell what is sexual about her and what is not.

It will be said of her that she becomes hysterical because she appeals continually to the gaze of the other to guarantee her sexual identity. What difference is there between her and the man, other than that the man is given this desiring gaze from the outset, by his mother? The absence of any paternal gaze in earliest childhood seems to register in the girl as sexual anxiety, as an identificatory doubt that has forever to be allayed, forever made good by the gaze of another in adulthood.

What woman can claim to be indifferent to the gaze that is directed at her? Whether it is perceived as conferring or as demolishing structure, the fact is that the woman finds great difficulty in moving outside the orbit of the gaze, and in especial the gaze of the man. This is the explanation of the difficulty, the ambivalence, that women feel over leaving the phallocratic world of the man for the world of the feminist woman who reckons as valueless the judgement of the man, and derives no prestige from his consideration.

Women are afraid that, if they do, they will lose something like the ability to "attract" the man. Women do not trust other women in anything that has to do with recognition: they are afraid, when in the company of women, of finding themselves once again facing the rivalry they knew with the first woman of all, their mother. The war with the mother, with Jocasta, has ushered in the reign of mistrust rather than homosexuality. And women find it very hard to get through their mistrust of one another. The "sisterhood" is not an obvious next step: it requires them to give up the pattern of existence they learn from outside and to take up instead the existence that comes from inside. And that is a very unfamiliar direction for a woman to move in.

In honor of women we shall have to alter Descartes' "I think therefore I am" to read "I attract therefore I am." Which sets up between the physical and the moral a fundamental antinomy which is exclusive to women, as witness the dreaded anorexia in girls that comes about in adolescence when the signs of femininity become outward and visible and there is no getting away from attracting. Some girls experience the change as the surrender of their own identity to the identity conferred on them by the gaze of the "other," any they are the ones who will do everything to elude this gaze, to hide these new features, which they see as their downfall.

The anorexic is "her own woman," she refuses to be a woman "for others," and so she will have nothing to do with the usual canons of beauty and femininity. She lives by norms of her own which allow her to elude desire. These girls reveal, through their frequently suicidal outlook, that the adolescent girl faces a basic choice between body and mind, for, oddly enough, these girls who so obviously refuse the body as site of alienation for the gaze of others present a much higher level of intellectual development than most of their classmates, who have gone over to the other side, the desirable women.

There can be many obstacles on the road to "femininity" and psychoanalysts, while they may see very few little girls (for they are not yet caught in the body–mind dilemma and can live among the dreams and sublimations vouchsafed to them by the neutrality of their bodies), see a great many adolescents and women whose development has been stopped by the refusal to attract. They generally put the blame on their mother, finally identified as the source of their troubles, since she gave them only a place without a sex and they refuse the place of woman that is being pushed at them, too late, and even then conditional. The girl's oedipal opposition (to desire from the opposite sex) cannot come out into the open until the actual encounter with masculine desire, until adolescence, therefore; but it can last a lifetime. The status of "desired woman," because always acquired too late, will always be a locus of ambivalence among women, unless indeed it sets off open revolt, as recently with the emergence of feminism and the systematic refusal to submit to the desire of the "desiring" male. Who, it seems, is totally taken aback: such violence from his partner amazes him, scandalizes him, for up till now he has never really grasped that the business of being a woman means giving up other kinds of success elsewhere, and that "womanly women" are, intellectually speaking, so many "underdeveloped areas."

So it seems as if it might be because they have deliberately given up "attracting" that women now are starting to talk, to write, to draw, to sing. How odd! Might there be, after all, an inverse relationship between "attracting" and "knowing," between woman-as-object and woman-as-mind? The social ideal might lie in the woman who can keep the delicate balance between these two.

THE OEDIPAL TRACE

From this oedipal relation, in which the father is so overshadowed by the mother, we all of us emerge bruised and battered, bearing the mark of our mother and dreaming of our father.

In the man, this takes the form of a resentment of women which no man ever gets over entirely or for good. Male identity is stamped with the refusal of the woman as equal. In the woman, it is more like a frantic chase after male desire, a chase which will make her bow to the law of the man and mistrust other women. Female identity is stamped with the desire to encounter the man who has so long been missing from her life.

Here then we can see the infernal circle taking shape in which the woman, undesired in childhood, goes begging as an adult for the desire and approval of the man, while he, given the master's role, will take advantage of the fact to get his own back on the woman (in memory of his failure to get his own back on his mother). And so the woman searching for the reparative love of a man will stumble into the castrating love of the man who has made up his mind that never again would "she" be in command. It seems that what has been lived through with Jocasta will trigger both jealousy in women (over the conquest of the man), and misogyny in men. With the result that the woman finds herself viewed with distrust by both sexes; it will be hard indeed for her to avoid war.

And to think that what women are suffering under is something they brought on themselves by insisting on having sole charge of the child's upbringing! To think that it is mothers who train up the future misogynists who will make their daughters' lives a misery!

Are we, men and women alike, forewarned of all this? Apparently not, since women still seem to go in both for claiming the child as theirs and for needing to be "recognized" by the adult male. Women cannot get out of the place men assign them to. This is what they are complaining of at present, without any idea that, for the man, this is the only way he can win the battle with his mother, first and foremost of the women in his life.

Whatever appearance the couple may take on, it is still the place where the woman wants to be "recognized" by someone who cannot grant her "recognition" without feeling endangered; which is why men are deaf to feminist grumbles, for all that these are often justified.

But it is not by mistaking conclusions for premises that women are going to be able to put right the wrongs that have been done to them; it is by changing the premises. Then they will produce men who, having been much less subject during childhood to the power of women, will feel far less need to defend themselves against that power when grown up.

It is the women who do the grumbling, because under the present system it is they who are the more oppressed. But they must realize that the more they ask to be given the care of the child (and not a day passes but the state suggests they should), the more they will perpetuate the phallocratic system that confines them. One sex must step back so that the other can take its place in the child's oedipal configuration. Can women face giving away so much? Can men face taking on their share of oedipal power?

15

BETSY DISTLER ON DORIS BERNSTEIN

A Bold Return
to the Body

BETSY DISTLER

The climate in which one receives one's initial training and clinical experience has a decisive impact on the particular sensitivities and understanding
that one brings to psychoanalysis. Having been trained in the seventies, a
time of radical feminism, I experienced a striking disparity between the
awakening feminist awarenesses and certain parts of analytic theory, for
example, the oedipal sequence laid out for girls, and the focus on castration anxiety. Feminist voices were articulating difference, self-definition.
Both the female oedipal sequence and the idea of castration seemed to limit
to one possibility the more complex, multiple strands and levels of thought
about women's experience. It was not only bewildering to try to live in
and embrace both of these worlds simultaneously: in clinical practice, I
felt that some kind of reworking, synthesis, and integration were urgently
necessary.

Doris Bernstein had been trained in the same traditional ("classical")
psychoanalysis a bit earlier. While impacted and informed by the women's
movement, as an analyst she also had an abiding belief in the unconscious,
and therefore in the complexity and conflictual nature of the problems and
responses that were being articulated by feminists. Her first written attempt
to address some of these issues was published as a chapter in a book entitled *Career and Motherhood: Struggles for a New Identity*, which appeared

in 1979. The book was addressed to an informed general public, and Bernstein's paper is somewhat sociological in its scope. Yet, writing from an analytic perspective, she explores some implications of the women's movement in terms of their impact on psychic structure. For example, while in the traditional view (and supported by a stable culture), "femininity" depended on the repression of the girl's masculinity, of her aggressive strivings, and her projection of these parts of herself onto her husband, developing her own potential in the changing culture demanded autonomy and assertiveness, and therefore a new integration of her aggressive drives. Thus, Bernstein is suggesting that the breaking down of role expectations demands an internal reorganization, a new "identity synthesis," in both men and women. She goes on to discuss three aspects of female development that contribute to women's difficulties in the face of this societal change: problems in separation-individuation, the nature and contents of the female superego, and problems in forming identifications as they influence the adult identity synthesis. In fact, one can see in this paper the seeds of what would occupy her in her further psychoanalytic writings.

At this time she was teaching and supervising at the Institute for Psychoanalytic Training and Research (IPTAR), where I was training, and she was articulating what she was hearing from her female analysands. I recall how radical it seemed to hear a classical psychoanalyst address issues that were also surfacing in the discourse of the culture. And how utterly reassuring it felt to hear her using the psychoanalytic theory and method itself to forge a deeper understanding of female sexuality and development which was beginning to sound theoretically different from what had been offered in training. The very notion of challenging "basic" Freud—of allowing a spirit of inquiry to guide one's reading—carried with it more a stigma of rebelliousness than a potential for deepening one's understanding. I recall that even Doris moved cautiously and not without anxiety over challenging accepted theory. And when I responded to her ideas with my own affirmation, she seemed horrified that she might have touched off a revolution in my mind! My comment had been simply about a case I was trying to write up and my finding that Freud's notion of the girl's turning from the mother out of rage and disappointment omitted an important part of my patient's experience, which had to do with her strong pull toward her mother, her longing to hold onto the mother. There was no denying that the spirit of open analytic inquiry that guided Bernstein's thinking was providing powerful support for similar ventures among many of us; it lent a sense of conviction to my own analytic listening as well.

At this time, there were new ideas about female development, most notably the papers in the 1976 *Journal of the American Psychoanalytic Association* Supplement, *Female Psychology*, edited by Harold Blum. But there was not as yet a clinical/theoretical scaffolding that might provide a cohesive context for clinically based observations. A female analysand whose treatment had gone well for some five years seemed on the verge of a breakthrough in her creative work. Her father had been ill at the time, and both of them used the opportunity of spending time together to work toward a more loving and communicative relationship. During this same period, the analysand also ended a long term dead-end relationship with an older married man. In our analytic work, the transference had gradually shifted from a collegial working alliance in which she was often emotionally withdrawn, toward a stronger maternal one in which early loving feelings and an enlivened maternal introject were able to emerge. In this context, she complained that her mind felt "fuzzy" during our sessions; it frightened her not to be clear-headed and able to think. Then she became disturbed by dreams with flaming floral images that felt strange and overwhelming. I struggled to help her understand the personal meaning of those images, and her anxiety as it was manifested in the transference. However, within weeks she fled treatment. The case remained in my mind, and I continued to try to put together the various pieces of what I understood. I knew that her anxiety came from her beginning to experience the positive early maternal transference and her own inner life and feminine sexuality. Early and persistent experiences of a strongly disappointing mother had been carried around in a dead maternal introject and schizoid withdrawal. Now the reawakening (or awakening) of her own inner experience was finding expression in a series of personal images in a particular transference context, and I needed to be able to address and decipher enough to be able to help my analysand transform her images into verbal symbolization. Without as yet an adequate conceptual frame myself, I was then unable to offer something that I think in retrospect might have enabled her to remain in treatment. I will return to this case later.

The issue of language, of symbolization, seemed to be at the heart of the matter—the difficulty in symbolizing the complex feelings in the female analysand. Freud's writings had suggested a female sexuality constituted by his own viewpoint, which involved comparison. From that place, external to the female patient, her fantasies and experiences appeared to be based solely upon a comparative point of view, derived in relation to the male at the moment of the discovery of genital difference. Absent was the voice of the woman as subject of her own inner bodily experience, in and of itself. To articulate that voice required naming her experiences. In the "Genital Anxieties" paper that follows, Bernstein (1990) forges such a language. She addresses the question of whether it is helpful or appropriate to speak of the girl's genital anxieties solely as "castration anxiety." She states, quite simply: "Having recognized and included the body's role in psychic development, it is ironic that it should be just one, the male, whose experience has become the model for human psychology, and only the boy's anxieties and developmental crises the model for all human developmental crises" (p. 151). And a bit further on: "If we do agree that the body is centrally involved in children's psychic development, it seems appropriate that the girl's body, her experiences with it and conflicts about it are as central to her development as the boy's body is to his" (p. 152). With this simple idea, she stands "truth" on its head: where is the *female* body experience in this male-based context? (Perhaps we are to believe it is defined by its absence.) Certainly a fantasy sequence of castration may appear in response to any number of traumatic notions in the course of trying to make sense of one's complex early world. But one also has to be shaped by the body world in which one actually lives, and the impact of that reality must play out at every moment. Bernstein proposes three terms to describe the complex constellation of female genital anxieties: access, penetration, and diffusivity. These particular experiences impact the developmental tasks faced by the girl, and Bernstein discusses their effects on psychic structuring and on the formation of mental representations. She lays out the various pathways by which the specifically female bodily experience shapes the female body ego and the female identity configuration.

For those familiar with Bernstein's work, it had by now become impossible to listen to female patients without hearing the deeper substrate of bodily experience and bodily fantasy. Further, and most importantly for clinical work, Bernstein demonstrated how the little girl uses specific modes of mastery to achieve the integration of her genitals into her body ego at each successive phase of development. These efforts to deal with new levels of genital anxiety tend to follow the pattern of using temporary regressions to earlier stages where a sense of mastery has already been achieved. Similarly, in the clinical setting, the adult female analysand works through each deeper level of genital anxiety by regressively using previously mastered modes. Bernstein offers as a clinical example the oft-encountered women's dream of open windows and her anxious effort to secure the entries. Penetration anxiety is reflected in this dream imagery of bodily vulnerability, and the dreamer attempts to control her anxiety by controlling the points of entry. How such a dream can be addressed in the clinical situation, in the context of a maternal transference, is a matter that raises further issues. Here, Bernstein reminds us, the analyst is in a delicate transference position. She or he has the opportunity to offer the analysand a chance to rework what Bernstein considered to be the most difficult area of the mother–daughter relationship: the daughter is dependent on her mother for help at the same moment that she is struggling to achieve individuation and autonomy. Specifically here, the daughter is dependent upon her mother's help with her unseen and vulnerable genital, in her task of integrating the experience of her genital, at the very same and critical moment that she is experiencing the thrust toward separation and individuation. Bernstein insists that the analyst must recognize this dual aspect of the transference and address interpretations to both the (regressive) dependency needs and the (progressive) autonomy needs. Thus—to return to the adult female analysand's dream of open windows—interpreting along the lines of the analysand's fear and helplessness about the fantasy of someone entering has the potential to be heard as a suggestion that she should just make her peace with her sorry lot, leaving both analyst and analysand bound in helplessness in the face of their shared biological reality. But interpreting the dreamer's efforts to secure the entries as regressive moves back to the anal defenses that gave her a sense of mastery via sphincter control addresses the active struggle for mastery. This opens the way toward mastery of the genital anxiety and thus toward the integration of the genital into her identity. Such an approach involves recognizing that the anxiety has served as a signal to move into a mode that has permitted a sense of mastery, and this allows the anxiety then to be analyzed. (This is consistent with Freud's second theory of anxiety, specifically with the importance of signal anxiety.) Understanding this most crucial set of conflicts offers the analyst a way out of a potential transference dilemma that threatens to bog down many analyses. And interpreting along these suggested lines allows the analyst to maintain neutrality and thereby to help the analysand work through the deepest, stickiest levels of the maternal transference and reach the core of her feminine identifications.

Bernstein's delineation and naming of the female genital anxieties, as well as her insight into the transference dilemma of the separation-individuation struggles, provide a theoretical scaffolding for clinical observations that are based within the female analysand's perspective. This important contribution now provides me with the means of thinking further about my analysand who fled treatment (discussed above). Of course these are only speculations, lacking the verification of actual analytic work. You will recall that she fled treatment just after feeling overwhelmed with anxiety which she could only express as feelings of mental "fuzziness" and via dream images of flaming flowers. One could hypothesize, using Bernstein's work, that my analysand's mental fuzziness referred to feeling overwhelmed by genital sensations that felt diffuse within her and that escaped the bounds of language; and that the flaming flowers are images for the genital, in which there are dangerous (hot) sensations. This can be supported in the clinical material. She had been able to experience with her terminally ill father a lively and loving connection. This represented a retrieval of an early, loving, reliable, and helpful dyadic father, and this in turn was making it feel safer, gradually, to shift (deepen) the level of emotional connection with the analyst, in the maternal transference. For a number of years, a schizoid deadness had characterized the maternal transference, reflecting a defensive struggle against feeling the devastating impact of her early longings for mother being interrupted by her mother's episodes of depression, withdrawal, and suicide attempts; she would have needed her father's help, but he apparently withdrew emotionally as well. Oedipal wishes now emerged in relation to father, and the patient gave up a long-term "dead" (her description) relationship with an unavailable man to open the way toward finding a deeper, more loving relationship. Her father then died. Her feelings of grief were palpable; however, she was also grateful for the time with father—time to prepare herself for his death, within a loving context. This experience reawakened her very different experience with her mother, who killed herself when my analysand was in early adolescence and had been angrily asserting her autonomy from her mother. The earlier separation-individuation struggles, with the unusable "dead" maternal introject experienced as inadequate to help her with her excited, autonomous strivings and enlivening genital sensations and fantasies, cast a shadow over the adolescent reworking of similar issues in the form of an actual dead mother; aggressive feelings, so important in both phases and interwoven in the relationship with the internal maternal object, add to the confusion. All of this becomes focused in the maternal transference and needed to be addressed to help her stay in analysis. I would add also that she was left with nowhere else to turn—that is, she had lost both men in her life (boyfriend and father), forcing her into greater dependency on mother and probably reawakening the separation-individuation dilemma of old. For me, issues with the dyadic and oedipal father emerge here as crucially important.

Throughout her papers, Bernstein alluded to the importance of the father's role in his support of his daughter's individuation and femininity. It was something she was giving further thought to when her work was interrupted by her untimely death in January 1990. When she asked me (and my colleague Norbert Freedman) to edit her papers for publication, she also requested that I write and develop a paper (Bernstein and Distler 1993) from some notes she had used for a 1985 American Psychological Association workshop on the theme of Cinderella. It was to offer me an opportunity to develop the father theme—to pursue some thinking (hers and mine) on the girl's oedipal phase. After writing about the impeded Electra of the unavailable father, Bernstein had turned to fairy tales in a search for a successful oedipal. She had discussed at her Cinderella workshop that the current conception of Cinderella as a masochist was based in but one tradition of the tale, culminating in the Disney vision. In another version, Cinderella was a more active and determined heroine who moved from a downtrodden "Cinderella type" to a princess. She noted in passing that the father was a presence in the latter tales. I returned to this point, reading various versions of the tale and ultimately writing about the very different heroines in two versions, one by Perrault (the pretty and sweet drudge), the other by the Brothers Grimm. Analysis of both revealed that in Grimm, full use was made of the father, as both an important external object and for internalization and identification. The various functions of the father are looked at as symbolized in the tale, and it is understood how they effect Cinderella's eventual resolution of the oedipal.

This experience further expanded my interest in the father's role— and the impact of the father when lost early in the girl's life or when otherwise unavailable. Numerous cases have opened windows on the rich, complex, and ongoingly difficult relationship that ensues between the little girl and her mother when there has been a loss of the paternal other. The complex transferences that develop in analyzing such cases bring to the fore the importance of recognizing and analyzing the early, dyadic paternal transferences, for they provide a crucial psychic sense of otherness that enables the early maternal connections to be tolerated in the transference regression and feminine identifications to be built safely, without fear of regressive merger into de-differentiation. This work builds on Bernstein's early recognition of the enormous difficulty and developmental importance for the girl of resolving issues of separation-individuation—certainly a crucial developmental moment in the facilitation of full oedipal resolution. It also fleshes out the difficulties she raised and addressed in her work on difficulties in the female analyst–female analysand dyad.

Much remains to be understood, of course. Our theoretical literature has grown. Doris Bernstein has left us a body of work that seems to provide an ever-renewing generativity, thinking that sends us back to the clinical situation to listen more closely. I have drawn stimulation and inspiration from her writings, perhaps because, most importantly, Bernstein has given me a language for symbolizing female bodily-based fantasies and experience.

REFERENCES

Bernstein, D. (1979). Female identity synthesis. In *Career and Motherhood: Struggles for a New Identity*, ed. A. Roland and B. Harris, pp. 104–123. New York: Human Sciences Press.

———— (1990). Female genital anxieties, conflicts, and typical mastery modes. *International Journal of Psycho-Analysis* 71:151–165. Also in *Female Identity Conflict in Clinical Practice*, ed. N. Freedman and B. Distler, pp. 39–68. Northvale, NJ: Jason Aronson, 1993.

Bernstein, D., and Distler, B. (1993). On Cinderella. In *Female Identity Conflict in Clinical Practice*, ed. N. Freedman and B. Distler, pp. 159–180. Northvale, NJ: Jason Aronson.

Blum, H., ed. (1976). Female psychology. *Journal of the American Psychoanalytic Association*, suppl. 24.

Female Genital Anxieties, Conflicts, and Typical Mastery Modes

DORIS BERNSTEIN

In "Inhibitions, Symptoms and Anxiety" (1926), an essay that informs all contemporary psychoanalytic thinking, Freud outlined two ways of viewing anxiety. First, he introduced a new theory, signal anxiety; second, he introduced a developmentally based hierarchical conception of anxiety which has the concept of genital anxiety at its apex. Genitality has become a watershed on the path to psychic maturity; the recognition of the differentiation between maleness and femaleness, the attainment of one's own relative wholeness vis-à-vis the object and the tolerance for conflict are the rewards of this achievement.

Freud outlined age/phase specific dangers, with separation anxiety from the maternal object or figure as the paradigm for subsequent anxieties; he conceptualized phallic-phase anxieties differently for boys and girls. For boys, anxiety lay in the threat to their body integrity, specifically in castration anxiety (derived from separation from the penis); for girls the danger lay in loss of love of the object (derived from separation from the object). There was no recognition of the role that the girl's own genitals may play in her development or in generating anxiety. Nor does Freud give any recognition to the differences that would follow from such dramatically different formulations; his formulations define the boys' anxieties as much more narcissistically oriented and define the girls' anxieties as much more object embedded.

One of Freud's most brilliant achievements, and that which differentiates psychoanalysis from other perspectives, is that it unifies psyche and soma. Body and soul, mind and body had in previous psychologies and philosophies been perceived as separated, if not outright antagonistic. Freud achieved a conceptual unity, a comprehensive, complementary interdependence between the body and the psyche; they function as one. Indeed, he elaborated the profound and ongoing impact of the body on the development and functioning of the psyche, on character formation, on critical superego differences (Bernstein 1983), and on relationships with others. Having recognized and included the body's role in psychic development, it is ironic that it should be just one, the male, whose experience has become the model for human psychology, and only the boy's anxieties and developmental crises the model for all human developmental crises.

At no time did Freud consider the impact of the girl's own body on her psychic development. He considered her genital awareness to be limited to her preoccupation with the penis and her body image based on its absence. In describing genital anxiety in "Inhibitions, Symptoms and Anxiety," genital is equated with phallus, and the girl's genital is dismissed. "Where castration has already taken place" (1926, p. 125), anxiety occurs in relation to the object. It is as if she had no genital of her own. Indeed, Freud considered early childhood to be identical for boys and girls until the phallic phase, when the girl's discovery that she lacked the valued penis became the central organizer of her psychic life. He considered her own genitals inert, inactive, unknown, not to be discovered until their maturation in puberty. This position was challenged quite early by analysts. Horney (1924) considered the undiscovered vagina to be a repressed vagina; Müller (1932), originally a pediatrician, reported girls' early genital interest. Reports of childhood masturbation abound in the literature (see Clower 1976). Kestenberg (1956) has described the ebb and flow of infant girls' genital excitement; Erikson discussed the girl's "inner space" (1964) as her preoccupation with her inner genital. More recently Stoller (1968) and Money and Ehrhardt (1972) have demonstrated that gender identity is established long before the phallic phase and that there is no evidence to sustain Freud's position that the little girl considers herself "*un homme manqué.*" Despite these observations about little girls' genital awareness and interest, their genital anxiety has always been described as "castration" anxiety, a legacy of Freud's earlier formulations.

If we do agree that the body is centrally involved in children's psychic development, it seems appropriate that the girl's body, her experiences

with it and conflicts about it are as central to her development as the boy's
body is to his. As the bodies are different, the nature of the resulting anxieties, the developmental conflicts, the means of resolution, and many of the
modes of mastery must of necessity be different as well.[1]

These anxieties, conflicts, and modes of mastery have a pervasive
impact on the resolutions of all childhood developmental tasks, the achievement of separation-individuation, the development of autonomy, the formation of the superego, and the critical identification and resolution of the
"Oedipal crisis" (Bernstein 1983, 1989). A full discussion of these issues
is beyond the scope of this paper.

The issues surrounding girls' and women's reactions to the penis, that
is, penis envy and castration anxiety, are described, documented, and elaborated in the psychoanalytic literature. Full discussions abound. Here I will
try to separate out the two issues deriving from the role of anatomy in the
girl's development. I will attempt to define and explore the impact of her
own genitals, assessing their centrality. I will discuss her reactions to the
penis only in so far as these reactions affect her integration of her own
body image and experience. While several authors (Barnett 1966, Keiser
1953, 1958, Montgrain 1983, Müller 1932) have addressed female genital
anxieties, I am attempting to understand their role in her psychic development, thus viewing her genitals to be as important to her as the boy's genitals are to him. While Roiphe and Galenson (1976) have recently studied
toddlers' reactions to the sight of opposite-sex genitals, they have viewed
their material from the standpoint of a "genital equals phallic" perspective
and have not addressed the issue of integrating the girl's own genitals into
her body ego. Their conclusions reaffirm Freud's phallic orientation, although placing the recognition of the differences between the sexes at an
earlier age. The timetable is significant since the children studied were
between 18 and 24 months old, the same age that Stoller (1968) places
for the establishment of core gender identity. Thus, this discovery of geni-

---

[1]I am using the phrase "modes of mastery" to describe the engagement and integration of developmental tasks. Like crawling, drinking from the cup, walking, and acquiring language, integrating the body image, including the genitals, into the psyche is a necessary developmental
achievement. Defense is the more usual psychoanalytic term, but always implies danger and
conflict. While any developmental task, particularly the integration of the genitals into the self-
image, can become conflictual, thereby motivating defense. I do believe there are aspects of
each task which are conflict free (Hartmann 1939), simply requiring integration into the ongoing developmental process. "Mastery" seems to me a more appropriate word to describe
aspects of developmental integration than "defense."

tal differences takes place in the traditional anal phase or in the phase of separation-individuation. It is my thesis that the task of integrating one's own genital into one's body image interacts with these other developmental tasks and that some of the anxieties the girl experiences at this time are the result of her struggles with her own body experience. Generally speaking, the female has been described as an open system and the male as a closed system (Kestenberg 1956). In this paper I attempt to explore some of the implications of this formulation.

ACCESS, PENETRATION, AND DIFFUSIVITY ANXIETIES

The genital anxieties of girls are not nearly as focused and tidy as boys' anxieties. The boy's penis, with its clearly defined presence, contours, visibility, sensations, and vulnerability, is quite clear. The girl's genitals differ in every respect. It is my impression, also noted by other observers (Keiser 1953, 1958, Montgrain 1983), that these differences have multiple effects on psychic structuring and forming mental representations that have pervasive influences on female mental functioning.

I do not mean to suggest that "castration-like" anxieties do not appear in women; these refer to a host of fears and fantasies about lost, damaged, or missing parts of the body. I have found these ubiquitous in the analyses of women. However, I have not found that they serve exclusively or even dominantly to describe women's genital anxieties. I am proposing three terms, each of which contains several components and references, a far more complex constellation than "castration." Access, penetration, and diffusivity seem to describe several clusters of female genital anxieties.

"*Access*" refers to several different experiences. The girl herself does not have ready access to her genitals; this touches on many levels of experience. She cannot see them as she and the boy can see the boy's genitals. This creates immense difficulty in forming a mental representation of parts of her body in which there are most intense physical sensations. The role of sight in forming mental representation is critical; for example, it has been found that blind children show marked developmental delay in forming body ego/self-images (Fraiberg 1968, Kestenberg 1968).

In addition to the visual difficulty, she does not have complete tactile access to her own genitals; she cannot touch and manipulate them in a desexualized way as can the boy. Hence, she does not acquire tactile, familiar, and sensual knowledge of her body that is not forbidden or tied to forbidden fantasies. Moreover, when she does touch her genitals, there is a spread of sensation to other areas; wherever she touches, yet another area is stimulated. Location shifts not only within the genital, from clitoris to vagina, but to pelvis and to urethral and anal sensations as well. This stimulation spread for the girl contrasts with that of the boy, in whom stimulation focuses.

This spread of sensation leads to a second anxiety, that of *diffusivity*. Development requires the child to define and articulate its body and its world. Touching, seeing, controlling, manipulating, and naming (Kleeman 1976) are the equipment with which children build up mental representations of their own bodies, the outer world, and their power and control over themselves, people, and things. If, indeed, ego is at core a body ego, and body ego is an essential reference to the outer world, the diffuse nature of the girl's genital has a significant impact on the nature of her development. Montgrain (1983) discussed this diffusivity in adult women; he noted a "general understatement of the overflowing capacity of women's sensuality that escapes the bind of language." Further, "the insufficient anchorage is an anatomical reality and has a correlative effect on the symbolic level" (p. 170). Language and imagery are essential for women to build a symbolic world which can be controlled and managed. Under stimulation, the entire apparatus of mind and body is mobilized so that a mind–body interaction that underlies thinking can be reactivated under any stress. It is extraordinary how frequently one hears, in women's analyses, complaints that when they are under stress, particularly intellectual, they cannot "think straight," their minds blur, they get "fuzzy," or they experience an incapacity to articulate. One hears equally often that, after an initial "blank," they are surprised to find how much they really "know" about a given topic, and how much knowledge they had "tucked away." The ordinary senses, sight and touch, are insufficient for girls at this stage of their development. They must rely on additional means, which I will describe fully later as modes of mastery, to articulate and integrate their genitals into their body image.

The third and central cluster of anxieties centers around issues of *penetration*. The vagina is a body opening over which there is no control over opening or closing as there is with the mouth and anus; girls feel they cannot control access by others or by themselves. The fantasy of the genital as "hole" is based on the child's experiences with holes in the external world. They are, indeed, passive and inert. Little girls cannot imagine their genitals' functions and cooperation in coital and childbirth experiences; the lubrication and elasticity of her organ is unknown. This contrasts with the boy's awareness of changes in his organ as part of his daily experiences. The penis and testes respond visibly to temperature, tactile, and erotic stimulation. Girls experience genital excitement as heat, or an itch, or a discomfort, often without awareness of the genesis and often without visible or tactile cause. It is frightening to have an open hole into which things can come and go, and which there is no way to close or open, and no control over access. A derivative appears in a woman, who, angry at her lover, demands the return of her key, so that "he has no access to me." Other openings, the mouth and anus, may be drawn into efforts to master the genital.

One implication of the girl's lack of control over access to her genital is awareness that the access can put her into "penetration" danger. Not only can things go in and come out, but she fears harm from these things. Girls fear damage to their little bodies from the exciting paternal penis. And, very early, they fear damage to their bodies from the babies they long to create.

Girls struggle with definition and boundaries. Boundaries provide definition and mediate access. The imagined penetration carries not only fear of harm but also arouses anxiety about the crossing of the body boundary. Intercourse requires entry to the inside of the body, which can threaten newly established or confirmed body integrity.

Two additional anxieties arise during adolescence when the girl is confronted with "wetness" for which she knows no source (indeed many adult women do not), and menstruation. "Wetness" necessarily invokes a regressive potential to all the anxieties and conflicts surrounding early bladder and sphincter control, a full discussion of which is beyond the scope of this paper.

It is important to consider the changed timetable for the discovery of anatomical differences and the establishment of gender identity in order fully to appreciate the impact that these anxieties about access, penetration, and diffusivity have on girls' development and the role that they play in women's psyches.

Stoller has demonstrated rather convincingly that gender identity is established by 15 to 18 months of age. Roiphe and Galenson (1976) have noted the recognition and reaction to genital differences at approximately the same time. Hence the discovery and integration of genital differences falls into an already established, though perhaps rudimentary sense of gender identity. These developments take place during the period of development classically considered the anal phase, from Mahler and colleagues' standpoint (1975), the phase dominated by strivings toward separation-individuation. In the realm of cognition, the rapid development of language gives articulated, symbolic form to the developing sense of self and world. In the families of many women with whom I have worked, there is no specific name given to the female genitals (see Lerner 1976, Silverman 1981). Phrases like "down there," "boopee," "hokee" describe the entire genitourinary anatomy. One woman assures me that in her language (a sophisticated Indian dialect), no word for the female genital exists, whereas there is a word for the penis.

The integration of genital differences has an impact on all the developmental tasks, and particularly complicates the process of separation-individuation for girls. All the genital anxieties I have just described bring unique problems to phase-specific struggles. The separation-individuation struggle is played out in two directions—in relation to the girl's own body and in relationship to her mother. This interplay affects the girl's efforts at mastery. It is my impression that the achievement and maintenance of separation-individuation is the central developmental issue for girls.

FEMALE MASTERY EFFORTS

This variety of specific female anxieties focusing on issues of access, control, and definition is central to the developmental task of achieving individuation. There seem to be specific developmental efforts at mastery that are typical in female development. These are different from the mastery efforts in boys and not aberrations of them. Roiphe and Galenson (1976) have noted differences in boys' and girls' reactions to their observations of genital differences. "The boys reflected the effect of the genital emergence in their choice of those toys and play activities which are usually considered typically masculine, and in the onset of a mild degree of hyperactivity. Furthermore, their masturbation was continued and fairly vigorous from then on." They describe this as "low incidence of overt reaction." By contrast, "all thirty-five girls in our research sample showed a definite and important reaction to the discovery . . . and eight . . . developed extensive castration reactions" (pp. 46–47). First, I think it is incorrect to describe these boys as having a "low incidence of overt reaction"; it is more correctly characterized as a more uniform and specific reaction. Their concern is clearly with the penis; their reaction is active, stimulating, in control, self-reassuring, and perhaps even counterphobic. This *is* their attempt at mastery over anxieties aroused by genital differences. The activity observed was paralleled by an increase in identification with their fathers. Rather than characterize the girls as having important reactions while the boys had none, it would seem more accurate to describe these reactions as quite different.

The girl is confronted with a different task—she must comprehend, integrate, and locate what is beyond sight, touch, focus, and control. I am suggesting that she mobilizes specific mechanisms to perform this task.

The internal, spreading quality of her sensation quickly and automatically arouses anal and urethral confusion. Roiphe and Galenson (1976) report observing oral-regressive behavior, anal-zone exploration, and masturbation. I view these turns to these zones not only as regressive but also as a potential turn to modes of mastery. Manipulation, opening and closing, control of access, and holding in are all possible in these body areas.

The following material illustrates the ways in which our usual ways of organizing material can distract us from other essential aspects. The "phallic equals genital" formulation informs both Parens and colleagues' (1976) and Roiphe and Galenson's (1976) work, masking the girl's own genital anxiety about being open and her need to feel in control. Parens and colleagues described this in their report of 2½-year-old Candy (pp. 88–89), who, after exposure to sex differences, became markedly preoccupied with a hole in her sock, troubled, distressed, tried to make the hole go away. When her mother sewed up the hole, Parens described her as seeming relieved and able to leave her preoccupation and join other children in play.

Following this incident, Candy, although previously toilet trained, began having accidents, in which she wetted and then suffered much distress and shame. She then reached for and clung to a large doll, and then showed concern about broken things and wanted only whole crackers. She then "sought the help of her mother and staff to effect a return of her toileting controls" (pp. 88–89). This description was considered by Parens and colleagues to be "ample" evidence that Candy was in the phallic phase. What this seems to describe more accurately is that Candy was preoccupied with a hole that she could not close, that this led to regressive wetting that she could not control, and anxiety about things being intact. There is not reported in this material a particular fear of loss of something or damage to her body that would warrant the interpretation of phallic anxiety nor does there seem to be any justification for describing this as her genito-urinary concerns, that is, her *castration complex. They are not the same.* After her turn to her mother for help in regaining control, "ample genital masturbation emerged" (pp. 88–89). Anxiety aroused an array of reactions in Candy; mastery had to precede the pleasure—here a much more complicated route than for the boy, involving *confusion, regression, loss of control, panic, a turn to others* before a resynthesis, including the genitals, permitted the emergence of genital pleasure that was so readily, directly available to boys. Parens and colleagues' description seems to support the complexity of the girl's task; "castration" does not do justice to the richness of the girl's experience.

Similar issues are illustrated in the dream of an adult woman during analysis. This woman has particular difficulty in articulating her genital experiences. Raised in a very strict Catholic boarding school, she was trained to dress and undress without looking at or touching her own or other girls' bodies. The prepubescent and adolescent activities of self and mutual exploration, mirror looking, and so on, were all suppressed, as were the infantile sexual explorations in her repressive home.

She dreamt that

> there was a snake in her apartment; she was scared and didn't know where it was, feared that it would touch her. There was a woman psychologist in a wheelchair but the patient was not sure she could help since she had some kind of illness or disability.

I interpreted as follows: she was frightened of having her husband "touch her" sexually and she was worried whether I, a woman whom she saw as a weak, disabled creature, would be able to help her with her fear, which focused on the fact that she didn't know where "it" was. The patient, who had been quite depressed and listless, came to the next session with the first smile seen in two years of work, and with a twinkle told me of a sudden renewed interest in the stock market, of some trades she had made in the intervening day, of her contemplating buying a seat on a new exchange that was opening that she would *control*, but not necessarily use herself, and earn money by renting the seat to others who wanted to trade. Her movement was clearly to a position in which she did not feel helpless, but could control, manipulate, and enjoy; clearly she resurrected an anal position. To have focused on her perception of me as castrated and disabled would have put the two of us together in a helpless heap. She was afraid not only of her husband's penis, but of sex in her own body. Would I be able to help her with the scary sex that she couldn't see and that could dart out from anywhere?

Like Candy, frightened by the invisible sexuality, she regressed to a mode in which she had already established control (her old interest in the stock market) and turned to an object (the analyst) to help her in establishing not only control but pleasure. For Candy, for my patient, for all little girls, this threatening temporary disorganization must be tolerated by the mother, and the subsequent forward movement toward erotic investment must be welcomed both by mother and father.

Debby, a 24-year-old woman in psychoanalytic therapy, demonstrates a confluence of several of these issues. Unable to have sexual intercourse for five years, following a half-dozen experiences in college that were relatively successful but accompanied by some bleeding, she broke dates, stayed at home, and had eating binges. She described her genitals as a "mystery" and felt that they were damaged, concretized in the memory of a bicycle accident before menarche at the age of 12. She had fallen off her bike into a split with vaginal bleeding. The accident and subsequent medical examination were painful, but there was no medical damage. Nevertheless the memory came up repeatedly as proof of a damaged state. She became sexually aroused on dates, but then tightened her genitals and felt "no one can enter me, I am too tight." Attempts at intercourse were indeed unsuccessful. Her mother had warned Debby against sexual activity until marriage so that she could have control over the man. Her mother also told her not to buy the fur coat she wanted, to wait and let a man buy her one. The therapist began to focus her interventions on Debby's being in control of her pleasures rather than things being done to her or for her. A visit to a gynecologist for a diaphragm brought associations to worries that her hole is not big enough to have anything go in and a disbelief that her vagina could stretch to accommodate either penis or baby. She watched in the mirror as she practised with her diaphragm, but still was anxious about not seeing her "insides." The therapist empathized with her longing to see but encouraged her to define her sensations by feel and touch. Throughout this period (about three months) there was a weight loss of about eight pounds and a sense of stabilization about food, although neither had come up for manifest work.[2] The therapist interpreted her weight loss in terms of her efforts to control her other opening, her vagina. The therapist worked

---

[2]A colleague with whom I have discussed this material has found it useful clinically to interpret the oral disturbance in terms of vaginal control issues.

simultaneously on issues of separation from her mother; Debby recognized her own difficulties in feeling separate from her mother when there was disagreement between them. The confluence occurred when she had successful, pleasurable intercourse, she in a new position, on top (more in control). She longed to run and tell mother but did not act. The focus on her control of her own body, her genital, led her to integrate both sex and food with a sense of mastery and separateness from her mother.

The material I have just described focuses on the efficacy of regression and identification in achieving mastery over the elusive genital and the contribution this can make in developing a sense of mastery. There are other mechanisms girls use for dealing with the internal confusion, some potentially considerably less adaptive. While all the mechanisms I am describing here are also found in boys, it is because they carry an extra burden for the girl in her development that I am emphasizing them in this context.

Renunciation of sexuality (Jacobson 1964) is another mechanism utilized by girls when confronted with sexuality and unsatisfactory pregenital development to support the new demand. The girl who renounces sexuality often turns into a character type we often meet, who is her boss's right arm, her father's nurse, a woman who has an intense but desexualized relationship to (usually) an older man (Chasseguet-Smirgel 1970).

Another of the mechanisms for mastery of this internal body confusion is *externalization*, elaborated by Kestenberg (1956). Onto the doll, which is already a beloved baby and self, is projected erotic investment. Kestenberg finds that play changes to genital-urethral preoccupation; there is more bathing, wiping, examining in contrast to earlier feeding and cuddling. Girls externalize onto other objects. They develop preoccupation with manipulating and collecting crayons and pens (sometimes father's). While this preoccupation is considered to be a manifestation of a penis envy response to genital differences (Kestenberg 1956, 1968, Roiphe and Galenson 1976), I would emphasize a different interpretation of the search for manipulable objects. I see this behavior as an extension of the need for concretization, control, and mastery of the undefined, as demonstrated by the fantasy frequently found clinically: "I have a penis, one will grow, it is hidden inside."

Penis envy and fantasy penises can be conceptualized as extremely adaptive fantasies in the girl *at this time*. Confronted with intense sensations in the genital area, to see the boy's penis and think, "ah, that's what causes these sensations" is a sensible and imaginative fantasy that can bring order to chaos. As with other childhood fantasies, it should be reworked and absorbed in the process of normal development. The presence and use of the fantasy varies. For example, an adult female patient had a dream: "I am riding in a car with a man and am growing more and more sexually aroused. I look down at my crotch and see an erect penis. I think to myself, 'How else will he know that I am sexy?' " A pregnant woman, who had just associated to penises, said: "It's just so nice to think something solid that you can imagine is in there. It's always so vague to think about my vagina." The penis may become an object of covetousness because its fantasied possession is a coherent, cognitive, adaptive explanation for multiple sensations. In fact, there are times when it seems that "having a penis" means having sexuality itself—as a concrete, visible, boundaried word concept. Having a concrete image and a word, that is, language, is an essential part of the ego development that children undergo at this time, and the acquisition of language is inherent and intrinsically linked to the child's ability to manipulate images and ideas. The fantasies that should be transient during the early genital and phallic phases can become central and the girl can be unable to absorb them. What should be transient becomes fixed, leading to either manifest or covert phallic feminine organization and to a girl who lacks access to her femininity.

A., an accomplished professional woman, always felt a fraud. Analysis revealed the common unconscious equation of "brains equals penis." Intense envy colored relationships with male colleagues who seemed to her to be able to think and work easily and without conflict, and with great conviction of the value of all their utterances. During a session she described all that she admired and envied in a male colleague—his height, his agility, his strength, his clear thinking, his clear lectures. She was complaining bitterly how much she envied all these attributes. I pointed out one significant omission that really differentiated them, namely his penis, the lack of which in her experience gave her thoughts and lectures a feeling of inauthenticity. She responded by saying she could never relinquish her "phallic" brain and her competitiveness; without them, what would motivate her in her work? After a few minutes silence, she reported an image of a baby sitting in a corner of a playpen; I asked her what the baby was doing. Her response was that the baby was biting the wooden bars; her mother often told her she had done that. I responded by saying that I thought she was answering her own question; she didn't need a fantasy penis, she could "sink her teeth" into a problem, she was not lacking instruments for mastery.

An illustration of a woman's concerns appears in the dreams of a 40-year-old woman in analysis who had been commenting upon her recent and unusual lack of interest in sex, and complaining about her lover's frequent interest.

> I have a wound on my hand. I have been bitten—several bites—but it's not bleeding. It becomes like a slash—I can see inside—the tissue, the tendon—there is a skin graft done—two pieces in front, one in back of it—one from me—one brown skin—it all fits beautifully—very clean and tidy—but the two men helping are not being careful to be antiseptic. If they are not careful, there will be infection. The next scene is funny. There is this machine examining the inside of a toilet bowl—I think "hey, this thing is an x-ray machine"—I can hold up my hand [she holds up the same one she used to illustrate the bite/slash] and you can see the inside—then I put my head in front of it and you can see the inside but what is clear are the lips, which seem very bright red.

This is a complex dream; I present it because of the many elements of anxiety expressed. The bite, the dirt, the slash, the men who are not careful, the machine which "sees" but can be dangerous. As we can gather from "it's not bleeding," the patient comments that she is menstruating at this time. In addition, in both dream scenes, *one can see inside*; this element repeats in relation to the hand wound, the inside of the toilet bowl, again with the x-ray, the hand, and the head. An analysis of all elements is of course necessary. It would be an error to focus only upon the obvious—the patient herself commented "I know that the slash is equated with the vagina—that's so classic" with little concern, affect, or conviction. My noting how frequently in the dream she was *looking* and could see inside, brought forth more intense feelings. It is of note that this woman, a physician, had recently been expressing worry about not identifying organs correctly during surgery, an anxiety for which there had been no reality base as her familiarity with anatomy is in no way deficient. The patient had begun a menstrual period the prior day, was casual about birth control, and somewhat concerned about her fertility. Her dream responds, "There is no blood, the bites are easily repaired, how clean, how tidy! All is well." The dream illustrates the confluence of material drawn into genital anxiety and the varied mechanisms attempted to master it; prominent is her wish to see, which must be given equal attention with the more familiar interpretation that she feels her genitals are wounded. This (not incorrect but incomplete) interpretation leaves the female in the helpless condition so often attacked by critics of castration anxiety as central for women. That the very *looking* may be dangerous (the x-ray machine) demonstrates that looking has taken on the familiar dangers of infantile sexuality, to be sure, but again to focus only on the dangers of looking does injustice to her attempt to master her anxiety. Her need to see and know what is inside must be dealt with as positive and adaptive; this woman suffers from feeling insufficiently in control. She often complains (in this session too) that her brain melts and she cannot keep ideas straight. Being able to see and identify is an important element of mastery.

The following week, this same patient presented another dream, this one illustrating the need for control over access:

> I had one of my house dreams [these were varied]. There is a big old-fashioned kind of Victorian house with windows all around—like a porch—not like Joe's father's—modern and sleek. I am worried about getting locks, it's so open all around. Then I get the locks and somehow you have to put the locks in a fruit, it turns into a puddle, a muddy dirty puddle.

Here the beautiful house is in danger as a result of its lovely, gracious openness. Anxiety over being able to secure entry (the lock) appears (the house is not like the man's). The genital reference is made clear by the fruit, which she describes as very soft and juicy. The fruit turns into the dirty, muddy hole, that is, the genital is experienced in anal imagery, *but that is where the lock is* in this patient's dream, that is, where the sphincter has control.

The confusion of anal and genital has long been noted in analytic literature; the vagina is often experienced as dirty, because of the internal location which easily leads to equating the vagina with the rectum. The confusion is reinforced by the diffusion of sensation, amply demonstrated by cloacal theories of childbirth. While all of this is familiar to us, what I wish to introduce as an additional and important factor for the female is that the anal sphere is one in which the female has been able to demonstrate "control." It therefore carries meaning of power which, in boys, is distributed between the anal component and the phallic ones.

While girls have long been described as neater, cleaner, and more easily toilet trained, I am proposing that an independent source of this development derives spontaneously from the girl's need to master and integrate genital anxieties, that the internal nature of the genital connects with anality, and genital excitement redoubles her need to exercise control. This occurs independently from influences of the relationship with her mother.

INHERENT CONFLICTS

In the preceding discussion of what I consider to be typically female efforts at mastery of genital anxieties, I did not elaborate the inherent conflicts involved in each attempt at mastery. It is essential to realize that these efforts are not simple, harmonious experiences. One predominant element, the reliance on the mother, is occurring within a relationship fraught with difficulties inherent in the age. A relationship of trust is essential; the girl must rely on her mother's reassurance that her genital is, indeed, inside (Keiser 1953). "Seeing is believing" gives concrete reality to boys' definition whereas girls must integrate their genital on a sense of faith; she must "know" it without evidence and must trust her mother's explanation.[3]

The girl's need for her mother to help her master her genital anxieties occurs during the same period in which the natural thrust of development calls for a turn away from her in the service of the task of separation-individuation. Viewed from a libidinal perspective, this is the period in which children are struggling for "control" over their own bodies and often are engaged in a power struggle with their mothers. Two of the specific genital anxieties repeat and intensify anxieties already inherent in developmental conflicts. The turn to mother threatens re-engulfment, requires a "yes" (I am like you) when autonomous strivings require a "no." Hence, the ambivalence and intensity of battles between mother and daughter, the clinging and fighting, are fueled from multiple sources long before rivalry for father is an issue.

Not only must the little girl turn to her mother in her mastery efforts, she also must, like the little boy with his father, form an identification with her as a female. Kleeman (1976) has pointed out the importance role labeling plays in organizing the child's gender identity, and language begins to play a major role in organizing the world during this same period. This very organizing function, that of being female like mother, important for the integration of genital and gender experiences, threatens the task of individuation, which requires being different from mother. Moreover,

---

[3]Proprioceptive and vascular sensations occur spontaneously but can be either repressed or integrated; parental support is critical for integration to occur.

every identification is built upon older experiences (Reich 1954), so that the resurrection of the earliest, symbiotic primary identification and diffusivity threatens the ego's struggle for definition. This reverberation between genital anxieties and symbiotic anxieties contributes to the girl's difficulty in articulating boundaries; diffusivity and control issues are pervasive.

The interaction between control of her body and differentiation from her mother is demonstrated by a woman who dreamt *of a building in which she was anxiously trying to secure the doors and window, barring entry*.[4] The associations merited the interpretation that the invasion (her dream word) she feared was genital and that she was trying to secure control over genital entry. Associations to a rape during adolescence confirmed the interpretation and the patient felt relieved of a sullen recalcitrance that had characterized her mood during several sessions. She said she really felt "understood" and left feeling lightened. She opened the following session with "I can't give you any credit for my feeling better, you'll make it all yours," a theme often demonstrated in this treatment by chronic complaints that mother always took over her feeling.[5] She again described her inability to have anything good because mother takes it, feeling it more than the patient herself. Associations to the recent illness of her boyfriend reiterated her blurring of boundaries in that his pain became her pain. The whole issue of psychic boundaries flowed from the anxiety about body boundaries.

While there has been a current trend, primarily in academic psychology, sociology, and among some psychoanalysts to idealize the mother–daughter tie, it does not reflect accurately the struggles that emerge in the analytic situation, where intense ambivalence seems to predominate. The longing and fear of being one with mother parallel the wish to be like her and both parallel the wish to be different. Whichever way the girl turns at this point, anxiety is generated.

Derivatives of this position seem to present themselves in adult women during pregnancy. A new genital anxiety confronts pregnant women and

---

[4]In my experience, female patients of all ages dream quite frequently of anxiety about entry through doors and windows. Standard interpretation would be about sexual anxiety. I have found that interpretation of the anxiety being over control of the opening to be efficacious in mastery of that anxiety. It makes a big difference whether the patient's fear that she is invadable is confirmed or if her wish for control is confirmed.

[5]Such problems are more acute when mothers over-identify with their children, as did A.'s mother, or are generally intrusive. Mothers seem to be in this position more frequently with their daughters than with their sons. I think the reflection from the genital to psychic is inherent in girls although it can be made more difficult by particular kinds of mothering.

one hears all the infantile anxieties; women fear damage to their bodies from the forthcoming childbirth, they cannot imagine their body's participation, and they fear the pain. They feel an urgency about being close to their mothers but simultaneously push them away. They wish to merge with their forthcoming infants but often structure their lives so as to ensure not becoming immersed in the maternal experiences, as one woman put it, "being lost in the swamp" of motherhood. As in early childhood, in pregnancy one witnesses all the inner confusion, the regression to other modes of control (sometimes in work, sometimes controlling husband or others by making demands), before some balance of identifications and differentiation from their own mothers is integrated with the physical experience. During pregnancy, fantasies of an internal penis are resurrected as a concretization of the unknown experience. In recent years, several women who have had ultrasound scans during their pregnancies have been delighted about the concretization given by the visual experience of "seeing" their fetuses. Despite all the explicit educational material available to women, the mysteriousness of what is going on inside their bodies seems to me to reflect that early, undefined mysteriousness. One woman enacted the search for concretization by looking closely into the mirror and finding that, if she looked closely, she could "see" something of her genital. Another revealed the use of a pen for masturbation, describing the need and pleasure in defining her genital experience.

In a case presented to illustrate some of the developing girl's difficulties, Silverman (1981) illustrates the confluence of anxieties. Faith demonstrates the symbolic use of the penis as an instrument of control over what can come out of her body. If she had one of those, she could see, touch, and, although not manifestly stated, show her "overalls." The little girl, Faith, had a boot fetish (worn whenever she left home) and, when excited, wet herself. At 6½ she was insufficiently differentiated from her mother so that she was unable to attend nursery school. Analysis of the fetish revealed two components: Boots was the name of a cat "whom mother continually threatened to send away because periodically it went round the house spraying the furniture . . . living in terror that she herself would be sent away for her own wetting, Faith had contrived to keep Boots with her in one form or other at all times" (p. 591).

Recalling her wetting led to the second insight.

She had watched her mother watering the garden and had seen that she *controlled* (italics mine) the stream with something, a nozzle, that

very much resembled her brother's penis. If only she had had one of
those, she told me, she would have been able to *control* (italics mine)
her urinary stream and would have been able to avoid all her con-
sternation and misery. [p. 591]

Silverman interprets this material as an example of penis envy and
genital confusion. After considerable work in this direction, Silverman made
the interpretation to Faith that she wanted what her brother Frank had.
Again I quote: " 'That's right!' she shouted, and she pounded the table with
her fist. 'I want my overalls *outside* like he has. He can *see* his overalls. He
can *touch* his overall. I can't see mine, I can't touch mine. I don't *know myself*.' After this the fetish was given up" (Silverman 1981, p. 591).

I find this case an extraordinary example of the girl's preoccupations.
Her needs to have access, to concretize, to control, and to retain her object are all expressed in the boots. Here penis envy is clearly metaphor
(Grossman and Stewart 1976) for her own concerns over mastery through
sensory modes and demonstrates the interaction between body integrity
and the developmental task of individuation. While Silverman does not
elaborate, we can assume that the relinquishing of the fetish was accompanied by an increment in psychic individuation and that she became more
capable of leaving her own mother as a result. Some resolution of conflicts over mastering her own body diminished anxiety and enabled her to
relinquish dependency on an object (Boots/mother/penis), that is, to effect separation. Her anxiety over genitals that were beyond voluntary sensory control kept her dependently clinging to her mother.

Mastery over the body is a central issue as toddlers attempt individuation and autonomy. The issues I have been describing seem to be central
for little girls. While the separation-individuation struggle is predominantly
an issue between the girl and her mother, fathers play a significant role
that has been underestimated. Fathers have not been seen as significant in
the first two years of life; they seem to appear as "knights in shining ar-
mor" in the toddler phase and become fully important only during the
oedipal phase.

Recent research finds infants particularly like the father's low voice
at 28 weeks; Mohaczy (1968) found a mild stranger reaction only where
the fathers were not actively interacting with their infants. Abelin (1971)
found precursors of attachments to fathers very early; all but one of the
infants studied recognized the father with a happy smile before 6 months
and all were firmly attached to their fathers by 9 months. The girls he
observed attached themselves earlier and more intensely than boys did.

In Abelin's studies, during the toddler phase, most relevant to this discussion, toddlers' relationships with their fathers were markedly different from those with their mothers. The relationship with fathers were filled with "wild exuberance"; fathers appeared a "stable island"; while mothers were ambivalently cathected. Fathers were not experienced as rivals at a time when other children were experienced as rivals for mother's attention. A few weeks following the rapprochement crisis, father images were evoked in play, stories, and pictures when children were distressed with their mothers. Abelin suggests the resolution of the separation-individuation struggle might be impossible for both mother and child without having father to turn to. Brooks and Lewis's (1979) findings that 15-month-olds were able to identify their fathers from a picture, but none was able to identify the mother, stresses the importance of difference in the forming of articulated images.

Chasseguet-Smirgel (1970) has recognized the importance of fathers to girls in their attempts to separate from mothers. Viewing the struggle as saturated with aggression, fathers emerge as those with power over mother. In fantasy, the girl seizes the father's penis to find power against her image of the angry, controlling mother (created by the projection of her own rage), and subsequently the tie to her father is colored by her guilt toward him for having castrated him. The research on early development I described above suggests the existence of a more benign relationship with her father (the stable island). The father as a reliable resource is as important, if not more so, to girls as he is to boys, since girls must rely more than boys do on others to effect separation. Since her own anatomy cannot help her, the girl's mastery requires a turn to objects for both support and identifications. I will not here elaborate the conflicts inherent in this relationship (see Bernstein 1989); at this early stage it seems to be relatively nonconflictual for children of both genders; I wish to stress the ongoing object embeddedness in the girl's development.

Vignettes from a two-year period of an analysis illustrate the interaction between mastering female genital anxieties and individuation, and the reliance on others to achieve this. Miss C. dreamt *she was in her bedroom and there were two heavy doors to give her safety; but high above was a small open transom window she could not lock, leaving her vulnerable.* This imagery, which I discussed earlier, is always expressive of multiple anxieties, including genital ones. In this case the genital anxieties of access and penetration, and relationship issues involving an intrusive mother and domineering powerful men converge in the attempt to achieve individuation. The patient's associations at this time led her to never having privacy or being able to make her own decisions, and to her cultural world in which men indeed had all the power and women were expected peaceably to submit to all their wishes, including sexuality. To interpret solely along the lines of her fear and helplessness about someone entering would not be helpful because the issues involved individuation and autonomy as well. Note that in this dream the patient is quite alone, the only condition in which she has any measure of safety. During the subsequent two years of analytic work, several themes were developed. One of the prominent ones was what I (Bernstein 1979) have called a forbidden identification with the powerful grandfather who lived in and dominated her childhood home. This forbidden identification deprived her of a satisfactory route out of the immersion with her mother and the preparatory familiarity (Glover and Mendell 1982) that would help her into a comfortable relationship with men. Some work on her fear of this unconscious identification led to the transference dream that *she was driving her doctor's car around, having a wonderful time, although somewhat anxious that she did not have permission to take it.* This anxiety reflects both what I have called a forbidden identification and Chasseguet-Smirgel's description of a guilt-ridden sign of the father's power. The next dream that took place in that same room illustrated her fear of being overwhelmed not only by a man but by her own powerful sexual impulses; she dreamt that *the ceiling was wide open and everything could come pouring in.* The door, as image, reappeared following some interest in an appropriate man during the analyst's vacation: "*A man is trying to get in the door, it is not locked, I turn to this woman in a rage, screaming 'Why are you not helping me?*' " A proper rage at her own mother, whose passivity in all things left my patient unaided in her feminine development, was now alive in the transference. As work progressed along these lines of interpretation, the patient dreamt that *she was trying to get from one floor to another on an elevator, but there was no control panel. She finally found a cleaning woman who helped her.* Association led to a maid who in childhood had washed the patient's hair, and, with further exploration, to memories that she bathed her, including her genitals. My interpretation that she felt she had no control panel but had to rely on others to master her body experiences finally led to the concretization of these anxieties in a dream in which *a bicycle or motorcycle went from between her legs straight at her mother*, with all the overdetermination of that image. These themes in this patient's analysis illustrate several of the issues under discussion: the need to feel in control of her own body sexually as well as in relation to others, her need for a

paternal identification to precede sexual involvement, and the need for her
mother to support her in her sexuality. The wish to control her own body
(space) carries both referents of psychic autonomy and body integrity.

There are implications for psychoanalytic and psychotherapeutic technique that have been implicitly suggested in the material that I have presented; here I would like to make them explicit. Viewing female anxieties
as unique leads to a variety of issues central to the developing self. The
girl's genital anxieties parallel other anxieties characteristic of the early stages
of development. One of the most important mechanisms available to her
is that of identification, itself a natural mode for both girls and boys in
mastering the developmental conflicts of the age. Turning to her mother
to help her master anxiety, she is faced with anxiety emanating from the
very identification she needs to consolidate. Anxiety rises from conflicts
over regression versus progression; identification versus differentiation;
dependency versus autonomy; control versus helplessness. Unlike identifications with father, for both boys and girls, the identifications with mother
are dangerous because of the early relationship which is resurrected when
the more advanced identifications are being made.

If one interprets the conflicts in these terms, the women will find
sources for mastering their anxiety and resolving their conflicts, a far different aim from that of helping them "accept" a castrated state and settle
for substitutes. Female resolution may lead to a wider range of solutions
than we are accustomed to seeing in the male; A. reached control over
anality (money and entry, she will decide who can sit in the seat *she* owns);
B. will "sink her teeth" gleefully into many of life's problems and intellectual pursuits without feeling a fraud; D. has taken control of her own pleasures, sexual as well as others. All girls must find a way of resolving the
anxiety aroused by the necessary identifications with their mother on whom
they must rely far more than is necessary for boys. This object
embeddedness has long been considered the hallmark of feminine character (Gilligan 1983).

CONCLUSION

I have tried to illustrate that girls' genital anxieties derive from the characteristics of the female genitalia and to identify some of these anxieties. Her
fears, anxieties, and psychic fantasies must be explored in relation to her
own body in the same way that castration anxiety, phallic preoccupation,
and fantasy must be elaborated for boys. As the nature of the genitals and

genital anxieties are different, of necessity, the mechanisms for mastering them differ also.

Here, I have identified three interrelated anxieties: access, penetration, and diffusivity. I am suggesting that the girl's experience with the unfocused, open, penetrable nature of her genital creates difficulties in forming mental representations of her body that have clear boundaries and sharp definition. Further, I suggest that this unfocused representation of the genitals complicates the formation of ego boundaries and a firm sense of self, and contributes to both the mental and body issues of which women complain; they describe mental "fuzziness" in trying to think and complain of fluid body images (see Lerner 1976).

Attempts at mastery include externalization, concretization, regression, and, most unique to the girl, a greater reliance on others than for boys. She must rely on trust, dependency, and identification, quite different from the boy's directly sensory modes: visual, tactile, manipulable. This, in turn, contributes to the object embeddedness of the girl's existence, so long an observed female characteristic.

The timetable for integrating gender and the body into the emerging self is complicated because she must turn to her mother at the time that development of autonomy requires a turn away from her. Critical identifications with her father are as important to the girl at this stage as they have always been considered to be for boys. Fathers have a dual role at this point; the girl requires both his affirmation of her femininity and his welcoming identifications with him.

It is not possible here to discuss the girl's oedipal phase (see Bernstein 1989), only to suggest that the fantasies at this time are an overlay of the earlier ones and the preferred modes of mastery again appear. If the girl has been able to integrate her early genital anxieties, identify with her mother, be at one with her in her femaleness *and*, simultaneously, identify with a father who sees her as female but facilitates identification with him securing her difference from her mother, and she is developmentally in a position to enter the fraught rivalrous nature of the oedipal, bear the fears and disappointments of that phase, and arrive at true genitality.

SUMMARY

This paper focuses on the female experience of her own body, the unique anxieties that arise from the nature of the female genitals, and the role of the female body in female development. Following Freud's theories of the importance of integrating body experiences in the development of psychic structures, the girl's body and her efforts to integrate it are seen as uniquely feminine.

Three anxieties are described—access, penetration, and diffusivity. These represent dangers to body integrity comparable to, but different from, boys' experience of castration anxiety. Not only do different genitals give rise to different anxieties, the different body experiences give rise to different modes of mastery (defense) shaping different character structures.

While males can readily form discrete, concrete, mental representations of their genitals, females cannot. While the boy can rely on direct sensory experience, the developing girl must rely on proprioceptive experiences, symbolization, and other people to aid her in defining her elusive genital experience. This interpretation of the female genital experience provides a psychoanalytic framework for the object embeddedness long observed as part of the feminine character.

REFERENCES

Abelin, E. L. (1971). The role of the father. In *The Separation-Individuation Process*, ed. J. B. McDevitt and C. G. Settlage, pp. 229–252. New York: International Universities Press.

Barnett, M. C. (1966). Vaginal awareness in the infancy and childhood of girls. *Journal of the American Psychoanalytic Association* 14:129–141.

Bernstein, D. (1979). Female identity synthesis. In *Career and Motherhood*, ed. A. Roland and B. Harris, pp. 104–123. New York: Human Sciences Press.

——— (1983). The female superego: a different perspective. *International Journal of Psycho-Analysis* 64:187–201.

——— (1989). The female Oedipus complex. In *Personal Myth and Theoretical Streaming*, ed. I. Graham. New York: International Universities Press.

Brooks, G., and Lewis, M. (1979). *Social Cognition and the Acquisition of Self.* New York: Plenum.

Chasseguet-Smirgel, J. (1970). Feminine guilt and the Oedipus complex. In *Female Sexuality*, ed. J. Chasseguet-Smirgel. Ann Arbor, MI: University of Michigan Press.

Clower, V. L. (1976). Theoretical implications in current views on masturbation in latency girls. *Journal of the American Psychoanalytic Association* 24(Suppl.):109–125.

Erikson, E. (1964). Reflections on womanhood. *Daedalus* 2:582–606.

Fraiberg. S. (1968). Parallel and divergent patterns in blind and sighted infants. *Psychoanalytic Study of the Child* 23:264–300. New York: International Universities Press.

Freud, S. (1924). Dissolution of the Oedipus complex. *Standard Edition* 19:173–182.

———— (1926). Inhibitions, symptoms and anxiety. *Standard Edition* 20:77–178.

Gilligan, C. (1983). *In a Different Voice*. Cambridge, MA: Harvard University Press.

Glover, L., and Mendell, D. (1982). A suggested developmental sequence for a preoedipal genital phase. In *Early Female Development: Current Psychoanalytic Views*, ed. D. Mendell. New York: Spectrum.

Grossman, W. I., and Stewart, W. A. (1976). Penis envy: from childhood wish to developmental metaphor. *Journal of the American Psychoanalytic Association* 24:193–212.

Harley, M. (1971). Some reflections on identity problems in prepuberty. In *The Separation-Individuation Process*, ed. J. B. McDevitt and C. G. Settlage. New York: International Universities Press.

Hartmann, H. (1939). *Ego Psychology and the Problem of Adaptation*. New York: International Universities Press, 1958.

Horney, K. (1924). On the genesis of the castration-complex in women. *International Journal of Psycho-Analysis* 5:50–65.

Jacobson, E. (1964). *The Self and the Object World*. New York: International Universities Press.

Keiser, S. (1953). Body ego during orgasm. *Yearbook of Psychoanalysis* 9:146–157.

———— (1958). Disturbances in abstract thinking and body image formation. *Yearbook of Psychoanalysis* 6:628–652.

Kestenberg, J. (1956). Vicissitudes of female sexuality. *Journal of the American Psychoanalytic Association* 4:453–476.

———— (1968). Outside and inside, male and female. *Journal of the American Psychoanalytic Association* 16:457–520.

———— (1976). Regression and reintegration in pregnancy. *Journal of the American Psychoanalytic Association* 24:213–250.

Kleeman, J. A. (1976). Freud's early views. *Journal of the American Psychoanalytic Association* 24:3–27.

Lerner, H. (1976). Parental mislabeling of female genitals as a determinant of penis envy and learning inhibitions in women. *Journal of the American Psychoanalytic Association* 24:269–283.

Mahler, M. S., Pine, F., and Bergman, A. (1975). *The Psychological Birth of the Human Infant*. New York: International Universities Press.

Mohaczy, I. (1968). Cited by Abelin, E. L., in *The Separation-Individuation Process*, ed. J. B. McDevitt and C. G. Settlage. New York: International Universities Press.

Money, J., and Ehrhardt, A. (1972). *Man and Woman; Boy and Girl*. Baltimore, MD: Johns Hopkins University Press.

Montgrain, N. (1983). On the vicissitudes of female sexuality, the difficult path from "anatomical destiny" to psychic representation. *International Journal of Psycho-Analysis* 64:169–187.

Müller, J. (1932). A contribution to the problem of libidinal development of the genital phase in girls. *International Journal of Psycho-Analysis* 13:361–368.

Parens, H., et al. (1976). On the girl's entry into the Oedipus complex. *Journal of the American Psychoanalytic Association* 24:79–107.

Reich, A. (1954). Early identifications as archaic elements in the superego. *Journal of the American Psychoanalytic Association* 2:218–238.

Roiphe, H., and Galenson, E. (1976). Some suggested revisions concerning early female development. *Journal of the American Psychoanalytic Association* 24(Suppl.):29–57.

Silverman, M. A. (1981). Cognitive development in female psychology. *Journal of the American Psychoanalytic Association* 29:581–605.

Stoller, R. J. (1968). *Sex and Gender: On the Development of Masculinity and Femininity*. New York: Science House.

———— (1976). Primary femininity. *Journal of the American Psychoanalytic Association* 24:59–78.

Credits

The editor gratefully acknowledges permission to reprint the following:

Chapter 1: "Unpacking My Library: A Talk about Book Collecting" (1931) by Walter Benjamin, in *Illuminations*. Copyright © 1955 by Suhrkamp Verlag, Frankfurt a.M., English translation by Harry Zohn, copyright © 1968 and renewed 1996 by Harcourt Brace & Co., reprinted by permission of Harcourt Brace & Co. This essay, published by Jonathan Cape in 1970, will be included in the collected works of Walter Benjamin to be published by Harvard University Press.

Chapter 2: "Observations on Transference-Love (Further Recommendations on the Technique of Psycho-Analysis III)" (1915) by Sigmund Freud, in *The Collected Papers, Vol. 2*, authorized translation under the supervision of Joan Riviere. Published by Basic Books Inc. by arrangement with The Hogarth Press, Ltd. and The Institute of Psycho-Analysis, London, and reprinted by permission of Basic Books, a division of HarperCollins Publishers, Inc. Also in the *Standard Edition of the Complete Psychological Works of Sigmund Freud*, vol. 12, pp. 159–171, and reprinted by permission of Sigmund Freud Copyrights, The Institute of Psycho-Analysis, and The Hogarth Press.

Chapter 3: "The Relation of Beating-Phastasies to a Day-Dream" (1922) by Anna Freud, in the *International Journal of Psycho-Analysis*, vol. 4, pp. 89–102, copyright © 1923. Also in *The Writings of Anna Freud, Vol. 1*, pp. 137–157, copyright © 1974 by International Universities Press.

Chapter 4: "The Flight from Womanhood: The Masculinity-Complex in Women, as Viewed by Men and by Women" (1926) by Karen Horney, in the *International*

Index

Abelin, E. L., 492, 493
Abraham, K., 15, 97, 137, 217, 223, 224
Adler, A., 66, 161
Amado, J., 407
Anna O. case (Breuer and Freud), 35
Anxiety-situations sexual development and, Klein, M., 287–333
Applegarth, A., 10, 191, 399
Arden, M., 13
Arendt, H., 7
Armstrong, L., 422
Aron, L., 93, 122, 412, 414

Bach, S., 412
Bachelard, G., xiv
Barnett, M. C., 382, 477
Barratt, B., 414
Barthes, R., 408
Bassin, D., 11, 12, 13, 93, 121, 122, 123, 241, 411
Beating fantasy
  Freud, A. on, 71–83
  Novick and Novick on, 63–70

Beebe, B., 41
Belensky, M. F., 217
Benjamin, J., 12, 13, 15, 37, 92, 115, 118, 121, 122, 411, 412, 415
Benjamin, W., xii
  Bassin on, 5–20
  essay of, 21–28
Bernfeld, S., 65, 83
Bernstein, D., 89, 149
  Distler, B. on, 467–474
  genital anxieties, conflicts, and mastery modes, 475–499
Bion, W. R., 6, 242
Birksted-Breen, D., 285
Bloom, H., 9, 10
Blum, H., 469
Bohr, N., 425
Bollas, C., 6, 117
Bourdieu, P., 407
Bowie, M., 418
Braun, B., 421, 422
Breen, D., 285
Breuer, J., 35
Brierley, M., 13

Britton, R., 242
Bromberg, P., 418
Brooks, G., 493
Butler, J., 117, 121, 408, 412
Butler, S., 422

Caper, R., 245
Castration anxiety
  female, Mayer, E. L., 377–404
  Horney on, 88, 90, 92
  Klein on, 305–312
  masculinity-complex in women,
    Horney on, 97–111
Catastrophe, transference and, negative
  therapeutic reaction, 212–213
Chasseguet-Smirgel, J., 89, 90, 91, 144,
  284, 485, 493, 494
Chiland, C., 381
Child sexual abuse, Rivera, M., 421–438
Chodorow, N. J., 90, 242, 243, 244,
  248, 249
Cixous, H., 426
Clower, V. L., 476
Coen, S., xiv, 6, 9, 10
Comfort, A., 65
Conflicts, Bernstein, D., 475–499
Coons, P., 422

Daly, 204
Daumer, E., 119
Davies, J. M., 418
deLauretis, T., 430
Denial of vagina, Horney, K., 193–206
Derrida, J., 426
Descartes, R., 461
Deutsch, H., 9, 87, 98, 103, 175, 176,
  178, 217, 225, 311, 312, 318, 321
Dickes, R., 40
Dimen, M., 121, 149, 411, 412, 415
Dinnerstein, D., 90
Distler, B., 149, 473
Domenici, T., 115

Eagleton, T., 8, 414
Ehrhardt, A., 476
Elise, D., 12, 414
Ellenberger, H., 418, 427

Elliott, A., 417
Erikson, E. H., 15–16, 342, 476

Fantasy, beating fantasy
  Freud, A. on, 71–83
  Novick and Novick on, 63–70
Fast, I., 88, 92, 381, 397
Feldman, S., 14
Female castration anxiety, Mayer, E. L.,
  377–404
Femininity, Riviere, J. on, 127–137
Feminism, Rivera, M., 421–438
Fenichel, O., 188, 409
Ferenczi, S., 35, 101, 102, 128
Finch, A., xi
Flax, J., 408, 410, 412, 413, 414, 433,
  434
Fliegel, Z. O., 8, 87, 88, 89, 142, 88
Fogel, G., 345
Foucault, M., 121, 410, 413, 415, 426
Fraiberg, S., 6, 397, 478
Frawley, M. G., 418
Freedman, A., 422
Freedman, N., 149, 473
Freud, A., 9, 147
  on beating phantasy, 71–83
  Novick and Novick on, 63–70
Freud, S., xiii, 9, 14, 16, 64, 65, 67,
  68, 71, 80, 81, 87, 88, 91, 92, 93,
  97, 98, 104, 116, 119, 122, 142,
  143, 144, 145, 147, 154, 156, 158,
  159, 160, 163, 164, 170, 171, 172,
  173, 175, 176, 177, 181, 182, 188,
  191, 193, 194, 195, 196, 197, 198,
  200, 202, 205, 209, 210, 211, 218,
  221, 222, 228, 236, 251, 252, 260,
  262, 266, 270, 271, 283, 284, 286,
  287, 295, 296, 321, 328, 332, 333,
  347, 354, 356, 357, 378, 380, 381,
  396, 400, 409, 411, 413, 418, 427,
  433, 445, 449, 451, 453, 468, 471,
  475, 476, 477, 496
  Tessman on, 33–48
  transference love observations,
    49–60
Fuller, M., 12

Gabbard, G. O., 41, 42
Gaddini, R., 67
Galenson, E., 357, 397, 477, 480, 481, 482, 485
Gallop, J., 8
Gates, H. L., Jr., xiii
Genital anxieties, Bernstein, D., 475–499
Gergen, K., 427, 432
Ghent, E., 417
Gilbert, S. M., 8, 9, 10, 12
Gill, M., 38
Gilligan, C., 217, 495
Glover, E., 232, 348
Glover, L., 494
Goethe, 16
Goldner, V., 115, 117, 121, 411, 412
Gray, J., 367
Green, A., 6
Greenacre, P., 381
Grey, C., 414
Grimm, A. L., 24
Groddeck, G., 105
Grossman, W. I., 11, 148, 492
    Fogel, G. I. on, 339–346
    penis envy, 347–361
Grunberger, B., 450
Gubar, S., 8, 9, 10, 12

Haraway, D., 411
Harris, A., 12, 115, 117, 121, 411, 412, 415
Harrison, B., xiv
Hartmann, H., 190
Haviland, J. M., 40
Heath, S., 117
Heilbrun, C., 9
Heisenberg, W., 425
Henriques, J., 426, 428, 431
Herman, J., 422
Hirschman, L., 422
Hittleman, J. H., 40
Hoffman, I., 414
Hoffman, L., 141, 142, 143, 145, 146, 148, 149
Hoffman, M. L., 40

Holland, N., 6
Hollway, W., 433, 434
Horney, K., 9, 116, 133, 141, 142, 145, 146, 154, 157, 159, 160, 161, 170, 171, 172, 174, 178, 310, 311, 357, 381, 398, 476
    Applegarth on, 187–192
    Benjamin, J. on, 87–95
    denial of vagina, 193–206
    on masculinity-complex in women, 97–111
Hughes, A., 217
Hunt, L., 414

Irigaray, L., 426, 428
Isadore, S., 428

Jacobs, T., 39
Jacobson, E., 409, 485
James, W., 442
Jameson, F., 413
Janet, P., 427
Jay, M., 414
Johnson, V. E., 149, 189, 190, 397
Jones, E., 87, 116, 117, 118, 123, 127, 136, 188, 218, 288, 294, 308, 311, 381
    Hoffman on, 141–152
    phallic phase, 153–184
Jung, C. G., 35, 66, 143

Kaplan, D., 11, 17, 344
Kaplan, L., 91
Keiser, S., 477, 478
Kernberg, O., 16, 412, 416
Kestenberg, J. S., 397, 476, 478, 485
Kleeman, J. A., 381, 479, 489
Klein, M., 15, 87, 91, 116, 133, 144, 145, 146, 147, 156, 159, 160, 171, 174, 175, 176, 178, 180, 181, 191, 203, 210, 212, 215, 221, 222, 224, 225, 230
    anxiety-situations and sexual development, 287–333
    Birksted-Breen, D. on, 281–286
    Chodorow, N. J. on, 241–250

mourning and manic-depressive
    states, 251–278
Kluft, R., 421, 422, 428, 431
Kovel, J., 414
Kris, A., 217, 218
Kristeva, J., 426, 428
Kubie, L., 397
Kuhn, T., 407
Kulish, N., 141, 149

Lacan, J., 8, 93, 281, 415, 418, 425,
    428, 453
Lachmann, F., 41
Lafarge, L., 214
Laing, R. D., 409
Lampl-de-Groot, J., 87, 175, 188
Lattimore, O., 408
Layton, L., 412
Lerner, H., 149, 481, 496
Lesser, R., 115
Levinson, N., 141, 142
Levi-Strauss, C., 426
Lewis, M., 493
Liepmann, W., 198
Loewald, H. W., 14, 15, 39, 42, 45,
    212, 248
Lorde, A., 14

Mahler, M. S., 357, 479
Maletesta, C. Z., 40
Manic-depressive states, mourning and,
    Klein, 251–278
Markson, E., 214
Marx, K., 409, 413
Masculinity-complex, in women, Horney
    on, 97–111
Masters, W. H., 149, 189, 190, 397
Mastery modes, Bernstein, D., 475–499
Masturbation
    beating fantasy, 66–67
    clitoral, 107
Mayer, E. L.
    female castration anxiety, 377–404
    Renik, O. on, 365–375
McDougall, J., 12, 145, 411, 412
Meissner, W. W., 10

Mendell, D., 494
Miller, N., 10, 15
Missac, P., 5, 6
Mitchell, J., 93, 428, 433
Mitchell, S., 149, 414
Modell, A. H., 38, 214, 216
Mohaczy, I., 492
Money, J., 476
Montgrain, N., 477, 478, 479
Moskowitz, M., 17
Mourning, manic-depressive states and,
    Klein, 251–278
Müller, J., 171, 176, 198, 476, 477
Multiple personality, Rivera, M.,
    421–438

Narcissism, negative therapeutic
    reaction, 217–218
Negative therapeutic reaction
    Riviere, J. on, 221–237
    statement of, 209–219
Newton, I., 425
Novick, J., 64, 65, 66
Novick, K. K., 63, 64, 65, 66

Oates, J. C., 6
Oedipal differences, Oliver, C. on,
    445–463
Oliver, C.
    oedipal differences, 445–463
    Phillips, A. on, 441–444

Pagels, H., 425
Palos, E., 35
Parens, H., 377, 482, 483
Paskauskas, R. A., 143
Payne, S., 13
Penis envy
    Grossman and Stewart on, 347–361
    masculinity-complex in women,
        Horney on, 97–111
Person, E. S., 39, 40
Pfeffer, A. Z., 42
Phallic phase, Jones on, 153–184
Phillips, A., 9
Poststructuralism, Rivera, M., 421–438

Price, M., 411, 414
Prince, M., 427
Putnam, F., 421, 435

Rabinbach, A., 7
Rado, S., 137
Reich, A., 490
Reich, W., 409
Reik, T., 17
Renik, O., 39, 43, 367
Rich, A., 10
Richards, A. K., 149
Rivera, M.
    Dimen, M. on, 407–420
    multiple personality, 421–438
Riviere, J., 145, 180, 308
    First, E. on, 209–219
    negative therapeutic reaction, 221–237
    Schwartz, A. E. on, 115–125
    womanliness as masquerade, 127–137
Robbe-Gillet, 15
Roiphe, H., 357, 397, 477, 480, 481,
    482, 485
Rose, J., 89, 119, 409, 433
Rosenfeld, H., 217
Ross, C., 421
Rubinstein, L., 63
Ruddick, S., 215, 217
Rush, F., 422, 423
Russell, D., 423

Sagi, A., 40
Sanday, P., 435
Saussure, F. de, 425
Scheman, N., 409
Schmideberg, M., 224, 229
Schwartz, A., 115, 120, 122
Segal, H., 218
Sexton, A., 11
Sexual development, anxiety-situations
    and, Klein, M., 287–333
Shakespeare, W., 10
Shalom, G., 7
Shapiro, S., 411
Shaw, R., 149
Sherfey, M. J., 189, 190
Showalter, E., 9, 11

Silverman, D., 40
Silverman, M. A., 481, 491, 492
Simmel, G., 89, 98, 101, 110
Simner, M. L., 40
Sontag, S., 408
Spielrein, S., 35
Spinoza, 22
Spitz, R., 381
Stern, D., 122
Stern, D. B., 414
Stewart, W. A., 148, 492
    Fogel, G. on, 339–346
    penis envy, 347–361
Stimmel, B., 12
Stoller, R., 377, 381, 476, 477
Strachey, J., 38, 212, 213
Strouse, J., xi–xii

Tessman, L. H., 37, 44, 45
Thoreau, H., xiii
Transference, catastrophe and, negative
    therapeutic reaction, 212–213
Transference love
    Freud's observations on, 49–60
    Tessman on, 33–48
Treurniet, N., 213
Turner, V., 15
Tyson, P., 377

Vagina, denial of, Horney, K., 193–206
van Ophuijsen, 97
Vendler, H., 46

Walker, A., xiii
Wallerstein, R., xiii
Weedon, C., 425, 427
Weinberg, K., 40
Wharton, E., 12
Whitford, M., 14
Wilkinson, S. M., 42
Winnicott, D. W., 41, 42, 63, 213, 417,
    429
Wittig, M., 432
Womanliness, as masquerade, Riviere, J.,
    127–137

Young-Bruehl, E., 64, 68, 141